Groundwater for the 21st Century

For
William B. Hall

Groundwater
for the 21st Century

A Primer for Citizens of Planet Earth

by

John A. Conners, Ph.D.

The McDonald & Woodward Publishing Company
Granville, Ohio

The McDonald & Woodward Publishing Company
Granville, Ohio

GROUNDWATER FOR THE 21ST CENTURY
A PRIMER FOR CITIZENS OF PLANET EARTH

Text copyright © 2013 by John A. Conners

Photographs, unless otherwise credited,
copyright © 2013 by John A. Conners

Diagrams, unless otherwise credited,
copyright © 2013 by The McDonald & Woodward Publishing Company

All rights reserved; first (1C) printing September 2013
Printed in the United States of America by
McNaughton & Gunn, Inc., Saline, Michigan

10 9 8 7 6 5 4 3 2 1
20 19 18 17 16 15 14 13

Library of Congress Cataloging-in-Publication Data

Conners, John A., 1941–
    Groundwater for the 21st century : a primer for citizens of planet earth /
    by John A. Conners.
        p. cm.
    Includes bibliographical references and index.
    ISBN 978-1-935778-10-3 (pbk. : alk. paper) — ISBN 978-1-935778-11-0
    (casebound : alk. paper)
    1. Groundwater. I. Title. II. Title: Groundwater for the twenty-first century.
    GB1003.2.C66 2012
    551.49 — dc23

2012032955

Contents

Preface vii

Chapter 1: Introduction 1

Chapter 2: Geology.. 45

Chapter 3: The Hydrologic Cycle 81

Chapter 4: Surface Water................................... 109

Chapter 5: Vadose Water 143

Chapter 6: Phreatic Water 155

Chapter 7: Wells 205

Chapter 8: Aquifers and Hydrogeologic Regions 245

Chapter 9: Groundwater Chemistry 331

Chapter 10: Groundwater Pollution.................... 351

Chapter 11: Applied Hydrogeology 405

Chapter 12: Contemporary Groundwater Supply
Issues 445

Chapter 13: Facing the Challenge 501

Chapter 14: Perspectives on Tomorrow.............. 543

Appendixes

    A. Abbreviations, Acronyms, Prefixes, and Symbols
Used in This Book 567

    B. Conversion Table for Units Used in This Book 571

    C. US Environmental Protection Agency Maximum
Contaminant Levels for Drinking Water 573

References 582

Index 617

Tables

Table 1.1 Selected Water-Related Scientific Disciplines and Their Principal Focus of Study 12

Table 1.2 Periodic Table of the Elements 16

Table 1.3 The Common Crustal Elements 18

Table 1.4 pH Values of Common Substances 32

Table 1.5 Some Physical Properties for Water 39

Table 1.6 The Distribution of Water on Earth 44

Table 2.1 The Geologic Time Scale 48

Table 2.2 Table of Common Rocks 50

Table 2.3 Common Types of Regolith 62

Table 2.4 Porosity Ranges for Some Common Earth Materials 68

Table 3.1 Quantity of Water Moving through the Global Hydrologic Cycle 83

Table 3.2 Average Residence Times for Selected Water Reservoirs 84

Table 6.1 Representative Specific Yield Values for Some Common Earth Materials 172

Table 8.1 Major Aquifers of the World 246

Table 8.2 Groundwater Depletion and Related Information on Five Aquifer Basins in the United States 254

Table 8.3 Surface Drainage Regions of the Conterminous United States 264

Table 8.4 Hydrogeologic Provinces of the United States 266

Table 9.1 Selected Water Impurity Categories and Impacts ... 333

Table 10.1 Priority Pollutants 356

Table 11.1 Groundwater Pollution Mitigation Methods 423

Table 12.1 Global Renewable Freshwater Resources and Use . 452

Table 12.2 Examples of Average Estimated Water Footprints .. 454

Table 12.3 Water Use in the United States, 2005 458

Table 13.1 Geophysical Techniques Useful in Groundwater Studies 534

Table 14.1 Global Water Supply and the Human Population ... 545

Table 14.2 Groundwater Resources and Withdrawals 545

Preface

Why Water?

Why learn about water? For one thing, water is fascinating. What child doesn't enjoy playing in puddles and streams? Water is many things: beautiful and comforting, strange and mysterious, terrifying and destructive. Above all, it is necessary. Water is our most important natural resource. Too much water can be disastrous; too little will mean the end of life. Without water, no life as we know it can exist — on Earth or anywhere else. Despite this, water resources have been abused, ignored, wasted, taken for granted, contaminated, and depleted to such an extent that billions of people are presently threatened with water scarcity, water-borne diseases, floods, and other water-associated problems.

The water upon which our survival depends is fresh liquid water, and some 99% of that water exists beneath the land's surface. It is groundwater! The main reason for learning about groundwater, then, is its vital importance as an essential resource for humankind — indeed, for all life on Earth — and the rapidly encroaching necessity to manage and conserve fresh water far more effectively than we have ever done before.

On this small, isolated, and overpopulated planet, the greener pastures of yesteryear no longer exist to support a continuation of humanity's material growth and greed. At this moment, millions are suffering, and many thousands will die within the next 24 hours simply because they lack clean, fresh water. Over the span of a year, water-related human deaths number in the millions. Most are children, over 4,000 of them every day, and their afflictions and deaths are unnecessary. Enough water, food, and other resources still exist to sustain our current population. It is not water *per se* which is lacking. It is the knowledge, priorities, actions, and morality of humans which require improvement. If solutions are to be found, unprecedented suffering averted, and the prospect for a healthy, hopeful future preserved, humankind needs to understand and utilize this resource far better than it has done in the past.

All too often, we tend to deny that which we find unpleasant or threatening, especially if it produces feelings of discomfort or guilt, may require extra effort from us, or yields an economic disadvantage — that is, if it costs money, reduces profits, or requires a redistribution of wealth and resources. Our nature is to grasp at simplified, poorly conceived quick fixes which rarely succeed. Lasting solutions will require dramatic changes in the standard economic and political approaches, not to mention a rarely achieved degree of honesty and humility.

And time is not on our side. Even for those living in wealthy nations, the time to act intelligently is growing frighteningly short.

Why This Book?

Groundwater for the 21st Century is a broad, flexible resource that will be of value to a wide audience of readers. This is not a textbook, it does not have pages filled with differential equations or other expressions demanding expertise in more advanced sciences or engineering. Neither is it a "popular science" book, filled with human interest stories and local investigations. Rather, it is a volume that aims to provide a basic understanding of groundwater science and resources, and the use of those resources by humans, in a manner which is accessible to all — and particularly those who are not specialists.

When teaching my first course focusing on water some 30 years ago, I had a difficult time finding publications suitable for use in such a class. Hydrogeology and groundwater textbooks required an understanding of higher level math and assumed considerable knowledge of engineering or geology, none of which my students possessed. More popular books about water focused on environmental and resource concerns, including many detailed stories about specific places and their water issues. People can relate to these stories and how water problems have affected individuals, their families, and communities. Well-told stories often make a much stronger impression upon an audience than does cold, hard science. Many excellent books and other publications about water resources are available, and several of these are listed in our References.

Nothing is wrong with either the hard-core science books or the more accessible popular publications dealing with water. Both are necessary. The technical science books, however, are often beyond the reach of most readers while the more popular books tend to skim over or completely avoid the basic science of water, especially groundwater. In addition, most students — and the general public — today are less well prepared in science and math than they were 30 years ago, this at a time when pressure on maintaining and managing water resources has never been greater and continues to increase. Hopefully, this book will help to fill the yawning gap between the advanced texts and the popular science publications that are now available. Increasingly, people need to know the basic science of groundwater, how that resource is being used, and the implications of that use — and to have the confidence in their knowledge to use it. In so many cases, past and present, untold cost and suffering could have been avoided, if only more knowledge of the critical groundwater resource had been available and utilized.

As water issues become ever more acute, large numbers of people of diverse backgrounds find themselves needing to understand, and make decisions involving, complex water issues. The values of water knowledge are apparent to those in scientific and engineering fields which involve water. But just as important is the fact that countless others whose education and experience may not have included a strong science component also need to cope with water issues. Attorneys, businessmen, agricultural experts, ecologists, urban planners, politicians, economists, geographers, conservationists, foresters, engineers, and many others, including millions of average citizens and vast segments of global society as a whole, can benefit from a basic understanding of water. Virtually every government in the world is or soon will be facing serious water problems. The major limiting factor in agriculture's ability to feed the world's growing population is water supply. Many plans to address the growing energy crisis will be limited by the large amounts of water needed to retrieve and process basic fuels and raw materials and/or the high cost of obtaining water. Not surprisingly, water-related litigation is growing by leaps and bounds.

Groundwater for the 21st Century is intended for use by citizens who have diverse interests in and concerns about fresh water and its fundamental influence on their lives. In it, I have attempted to cover basic scientific and hydrogeologic principles in a way that will be understandable to individuals who may lack a strong background in geology, engineering, math, chemistry, or science in general. Introductions to some very basic science are included to provide a context within which the genuine understanding of concepts, interrelationships, applications, and implications relevant to groundwater might be realized. Expanded coverage of the science, use, and abuse of groundwater follows. Numerous diagrams provide clear graphic illustrations of basic groundwater patterns and behavior.

Regarding terminology, the groundwater field, like all sciences, is awash with both a vocabulary of precision and jargon. If one wishes to learn about, and communicate in, this vitally important field, s/he will need to have some familiarity with the terminology. While I have attempted to limit use of highly technical terms in this book, many terms are so widely used and important that I felt it necessary to introduce them. It is also beneficial to point out widely used equivalent terms along with inconsistencies in terminology use. When a term is first encountered and defined, or is a key-word for the topic being presented, the word will be **boldfaced**.

Content

Focus on Subsurface Water

The primary purpose of this book is to provide an introduction to subsurface waters: their nature and distribution, their behavior, their interactions with the surface environment, their value as a resource, and the major issues associated with groundwater resources today.

Qualitative and Quantitative Aspects

Although the emphasis here is on attaining a qualitative understanding of the subject matter, the nature of water science requires some quantitative treatment at times. For these sections, math through elementary algebra will be needed. Where appropriate, sample problems are provided in the text to illustrate the use of various simple but important formulae or equations.

Units and Measures

Scientists prefer the **metric** or **SI** (*Système International d'Unités*; *System Internationalle*) **system** of units due to its ease of use and worldwide usage. Unfortunately the United States clings to the more cumbersome **English system**. Familiarity with both systems is a valuable asset and both systems are employed in this book. Both units are not used in every case because an abundance of parentheses tends to impair readability. To improve readability and save space, common abbreviations are frequently used in the text. A key to the abbreviations, acronyms, prefixes, and symbols used in this book is provided in Appendix A. Units and conversion factors important in water studies are given in Appendix B.

Current Water Resource Issues

For perspective, examples of groundwater resource issues are noted throughout the text and overviews of important water topics and problems are provided in chapters 12, 13, and 14.

Thumbnail Sketches of Each Chapter

Chapter 1: Introduction. The stage is set with a brief perspective on vital water-related issues, and a review of water itself and its importance. Following a brief review of very basic chemistry and physics, the characteristics, origin, types, and distribution of water are examined in some detail.

Chapter 2: Geology. It is impossible to understand the nature and behavior of subsurface water without some knowledge of geology. This chapter provides a minimalist introduction to the geologic features and principles most important to the water sciences.

Chapter 3: The Hydrologic Cycle. This chapter reviews the major steps and processes involved in the constant recycling of water throughout Earth's environment. The hydrologic aspects of the atmosphere, vegetation, terrain, soils, climate, and related factors are discussed.

Chapter 4: Surface Water. Water which reaches Earth's land surface from the atmosphere is the source of nearly all subsurface water. This chapter focuses upon the intimate relationship between water running off or sitting upon the land and water seeping into or out of the outer part of the solid Earth.

Chapter 5: Vadose Water. This chapter describes subsurface water in the unsaturated zone — that is, the types and behavior of water occurring between Earth's surface and "true groundwater."

Chapter 6: Phreatic Water. Here we describe the behavior of subsurface water in the saturated zone: types of water, how it moves, fluctuations in the water table, natural and human influences, various types of groundwater flow regimes, and the basic methods of determining groundwater movement, flow direction, and magnitude.

Chapter 7: Wells. Wells are critical components in the study of groundwater. Wells provide water for our use and enable us to determine groundwater behavior and quality. Many types and uses of wells are reviewed.

Chapter 8: Aquifers and Hydrogeologic Regions. Aquifers are the primary sources of usable groundwater supplies. Basic aquifer types, properties, and examples are examined, followed by a review of the major hydrogeologic environments of Earth.

Chapter 9: Groundwater Chemistry. What's in water besides water? The natural chemicals found in groundwater and the chemical reactions which influence them are examined.

Chapter 10: Groundwater Pollution. This chapter describes the major groundwater pollutants and their sources, impacts, transport, and fate.

Chapter 11: Applied Hydrogeology. This chapter discusses the practical skills and activities required of a hydrogeologist, including water sampling, site characterizations, groundwater remediation, modeling, ethics, and related topics.

Chapters 12: Contemporary Groundwater Supply Issues. Water use and supply, the impacts of groundwater depletion, legal and ethical considerations, conflicts over water, and climate change and its impacts are addressed in this chapter.

Chapter 13: Facing the Challenge. The focus here is on corrective actions, including conservation and management of groundwater resources and locating alternate sources of water.

Chapter 14: Perspectives on Tomorrow. This concluding chapter provides an overview of the global and regional impacts of diminishing water resources as well as the implications of, and possible solutions to, current megascale problems.

Appendixes. Three appendixes provide definitions of abbreviations, acronyms, prefixes, and symbols used throughout the book; conversion tables for numerous quantitative values and systems useful in the science and use of groundwater; and an annotated list of maximum contaminant levels for drinking water in the United States.

References. The references listed at the back of this book include those cited in the text and other relevant publications. A separate list of periodicals, organizations, and other important sources of information is also provided. All references cited in the text have been assigned a unique number and are identified in the text by their corresponding number placed within brackets, as, for example, [132].

Acknowledgments

I would like to thank the following individuals for their help in the preparation of this book: Jodi Melfi of Jodi Melfi Design for producing final drafts of the many drawings; Trish Newcomb of McDonald & Woodward for her many efforts in preparing this manuscript, including the acquisition and preparation of numerous maps, photos, and tables; Jerry McDonald of McDonald & Woodward for his faith in this endeavor and protracted encouragement as it progressed toward completion, not to mention his role in the primary editing and ultimate production of this book; and William B. (Bill) Hall, fellow geomorphologist, mentor, and friend, without whose patronage this work would not have been possible.

I also greatly appreciate the generosity of the following individuals and other entities who provided many of the photographic images used in this work. William B. Hall: Plates 2 Top and Bottom, 8 Top, 13 Top; Figures 2.2C, 2.2J, 2.6B, 2.7A, 2.7B, 2.8B, 2.8C, 2.8D, 2.8E, 2.8G, 2.12B, 2.14, 4.16C, 4.19, 8.4, 8.7, 8.16, 8.36. Jerry N. McDonald: Plates 1 Bottom, 9 Top, 10 Bottom, 15 Bottom, 16 Top; Figures 8.31, 12.4. Rajeev Nair / Wikimedia: Figure 1.1. Sta-Rite Industries: Figure 7.2. US Agency for International Development (USAID): 7.1A, 7.1B (Samia Mehdi), 12.2A, 12.2B (Fred LeGregam), 13.3 (Jal Bhagirathi Foundation). US Bureau of Reclamation: Plate 12 Bottom. US Geological Survey (USGS): Plate 15 Top right; Figures 8.21, 8.24, 12.6A, 12.6B, 12.6C. US National Air and Space Administration (NASA): Figure 14.2. US National Oceanic and Atmospheric Administration (NOAA): Figure 8.14D. Susan L. Woodward: Plate 10 Top; 7.21A, 7.21B, 8.32, 12.3. (All photographs not credited here were taken by the author.)

1

Introduction

When the Earth, its products, its creatures become his
concern, man is caught up in a cause greater than his own life
and more meaningful. Only when man loses himself in an en-
deavor of that magnitude does he walk and live with humility
and reverence.

— William O. Douglas

1.1 Opening Perspectives

1.1.1 Reliability and Truth

In the purest sense, science is the search for truth, and surely one of humankind's greatest and most meaningful endeavors. In an age saturated with "spin," commercialism, outright mendacity, and other manipulative, self-serving tactics, many people are justifiably skeptical of everything. Truth can be difficult to ascertain and it may not be what we would like it to be. But we must strive for truth and do our best to deal responsibly with reality, be it hopeful or grim. If documented realities are ignored, the outcomes will often be disastrous.

When applied to the natural world, this search for truth is often described as the "**scientific method**." This method can be characterized by four major steps: (1) a phenomenon is observed and a working idea, or **hypothesis,** is formed to explain what is observed; (2) the phenomenon or problem is researched to determine what is known about the subject matter; (3) experiments, additional observations, and tests are undertaken and repeated, often by many individuals over a considerable period of time; (4) if the hypothesis stands up to repeated applications, examinations, and tests and appears to be valid, it may become a widely accepted **theory,** such as evolution or plate tectonics. If no exceptions to a widely experienced phenomenon have ever been observed, it may be called a **law,** such as the laws of universal gravitation or thermodynamics.

1

In preparing a book such as this, many ideas, prognoses, estimates, and statistics are encountered, and not all are in agreement. I have attempted to use the most reliable data and identify the major sources. However, it is not feasible to discover and provide the original source for each and every idea and statistic. Statistics and ideas are constantly evolving, being repeated, updated, and revised. The data in any book is always somewhat suspect, somewhat out of date, and subject to the biases of the author(s).

Economics, available data, political influences, research goals, ideologies, and prejudices of all sorts can exert considerable influence over the quantity and quality of information. Many sources of water data exist and their quality varies greatly in dependability. Most water data are estimates. Some states within the United States (US) have good data, some poor. The same applies to nations. The United States Geologic Survey (USGS) is one of the world's most reliable sources of water data [519]. The USGS produces a National Water Use Information Program report every five years, yet even it must rely to a great extent upon incomplete information provided by states, industries, and other organizations. Groundwater data are especially sketchy, since many withdrawals are not reported. This means that, for many rural and agricultural areas in particular, groundwater usage is likely to be understated by 40% or more. Among the sources of global groundwater statistics are the Food and Agriculture Organization [471], the World-wide Hydrological Mapping and Assessment Program [541], the International Groundwater Resource Assessment Center [485], and I. A. Shiklomanov's *World Water Resources: A New Appraisal for the 21st Century* [362]. The References section located at the end of this book includes a special "Miscellaneous" section of water-related organizations and information sources.

Water may be a natural resource, but its use and misuse are guided more by self-serving contrivances than by science. If water is to be wisely used, solid scientific contributions to the dialogue are essential. Most scientists are loathe to become involved in legal, social, political, religious, and related controversies. This is unfortunate. All too often, political decisions are made based upon short-term electability concerns or financial pressures from vested interests while good science is neither sought nor acted upon. We might note that bad science (or BS if you prefer!) is not infrequently invoked to justify bad decisions. All the more reason for responsible scientists to get involved and promote intelligent policies and actions.

1.1.2 Importance of Water

When the well is dry, they know the worth of water.

— Benjamin Franklin

We call our little planet "Earth." But it has often been said that "Water World," "Aqua," or "Hydro" would be more appropriate names than Earth. Three-quarters of our planet's surface is completely immersed in liquid water, nearly all of its land area is covered by, or underlain by, frozen or liquid water, and water is a critical component of our atmosphere. At any one time, about 60% of Earth's surface is shrouded by clouds made of small particles of liquid or solid water.

Far more important, liquid water is the primary, indispensable ingredient of protoplasm, of living matter itself. Water is essential to all life, more basic and vital even than air or soil. For the human species, clean drinkable water is THE most vital of all natural resources. To meet the vast and growing needs of humanity, an adequate supply of unpolluted liquid fresh water is essential. Ironically, on this water world of ours, the type we need the most, liquid fresh water, represents considerably less than 1% of the total, and much of that is not available for human consumption. Of that liquid fresh water, about 99% is subsurface water, and perhaps half of all potable water supplies now comes from underground water.

1.1.3 Historical Perspectives

Man becomes pure by the touch of the water, or by consuming it, or by expressing its name.

— Lord Vishnu, referring to the Ganges (Ganga) River

It has often been said that the story of water is the story of mankind, or even of life itself. Throughout history, water has been intimately associated with human development. Even without the direct human needs of water for drinking, sanitation, food production, and the like, huge amounts of additional water are required for such ubiquitous human undertakings as energy production, industrial processes, mining, and business operations. Travel routes, cities, cultural behavior, agriculture, and so much more are often determined in large part by the presence of, and the nature of, nearby waters [115, 370].

Water plays a significant role in all major religions. Thousands of springs, rivers, and other hydrologic features are regarded as sacred or having great power. To take just one example, the Ganges River of India is sacred to the Hindus. Gangotri, a village near the river's source, is overwhelmed by nearly a million pilgrims a year. Ironically, recent increases in visitors to holy places in the Himalayas have resulted in heavy commercial development yielding deforestation, erosion, and extensive pollution by silt, human wastes, and garbage, all fouling that same sacred river in which millions of Hindus living downstream will bathe. Evidence of water's importance abounds in ancient writings, including the Bible, which includes many references to water. Jesus even described himself as "living water" when speaking to the woman at Jacob's well, as presented in John 4, verses 5-26.

Ancient civilizations were built, and lost, by virtue of their access to potable water and the food supplies that water made possible. When water supplies diminished or were degraded by drought or misuse, these civilizations were greatly weakened, or disappeared completely. Many of the most amazing engineering feats of ancient peoples resulted from their search for and use of water. The world's first major engineering works were probably the canals and associated irrigation works constructed over 6,000 years ago by the Egyptians in the Nile Valley and the Sumerians in Mesopotamia — the Tigris-Euphrates Valley of present-day Iraq. The Mesopotamians developed sophisticated systems of wells, canals, dams, and subsurface infiltration galleries (Figure 7.21, Section 7.5.6.2) to provide irrigation water. The earliest records available indicate that water and water rights were always major concerns.

Later civilizations, including those of the Greeks and the Romans, developed remarkable water control structures, including the famous Roman aqueducts [256]. Ancient civilizations in India constructed complex series of cisterns connected by ever descending steps and platforms to access groundwater. These impressive engineering marvels are often called stepped ponds or step wells (Figure 1.1).

Despite such impressive accomplishments, superstitions and bizarre misconceptions about water have always been popular, even being enshrined in numerous laws. That is especially true of the unseen oceans of water which lie below the land surface. Groundwater has been viewed from time immemorial with a sense of wonder. It lies hidden below, unseen except when it bursts forth miraculously from the earth in springs, or seeps slowly and mysteriously onto the surface or into a pit from its unknown depths. Not surprisingly, many believed that groundwater possessed supernatural powers, either for good or evil. In 1856, the Ohio Supreme Court said groundwater was "secret" and "occult," a declaration not changed until 1984.

4

Figure 1.1. This step well is located in northern India and represents a very old engineering solution to providing long-term access to water from dug wells. The large diameter and steps allow people access to groundwater as the water table fluctuates. Due to overpumping of groundwater, many such wells are now dry.

Even today, many continue to attribute fantastical properties to water, a fact not lost on the promoters of various water-related enterprises from beer to books to bottled water to tourist resorts. One can purchase — at premium prices, of course — water claimed to make you holy, sexy, healthy, smart, or energetic. "Liquid OM" water, for example, purports to emanate an energy field generated by using gongs and Tibetan bowls which can be felt just by holding the bottle [272]! Books continue to be written about the magical properties of water.

Some groundwater does indeed possess odd characteristics. It may exude strange odors and possess even stranger tastes, be clear or cloudy, have odd colors, be boiling hot or numbingly cold. Some tastes so bad as to be undrinkable, yet may do no harm or even be beneficial to health. Some waters look and taste marvelous but contains invisible poisons and can kill.

Groundwater behavior can be highly erratic. In rare instances, gushing springs can appear overnight, and disappear just as quickly. Some lakes and ponds are known to drain away in a few hours, then reappear suddenly. Such behavior is often found where groundwater flows through large subterranean caves or fissures. Changes in pressure from the rapid draining of a subsurface chamber or the lowering of water levels in local lakes and streams can cause strange and sudden changes in water bodies many miles away. Many the bewildered well owner who has experienced rapid changes in water level or water quality, including complete loss of water, geysers of water gushing forth from the well, or mud and pollution where clean water should be. The causes of such disruptions may be many miles distant, be natural or, more commonly, man-made. Operations which may produce serious impacts on groundwater include construction, mining, waste disposal, water storage, water diversion, well construction, and agricultural activities.

1.1.4 The Advance of Groundwater Science

> *This book records the birth and describes the development of a new science — coordinated scientific data regarding the occurrence, motions, and activities of subsurface water, and the hydrologic properties of water-bearing materials — christened by O. E. Meinzer "Ground-water Hydrology."*
>
> — C. F. Tolman, 1937 (opening paragraph of the Preface of the first hydrogeology textbook in English) [391]

Groundwater is mostly invisible and difficult to access. No surprise then that it remained shrouded in mystery through most of human history and that hydrogeology is among the latest of the natural sciences to develop.

An ancient and widely accepted idea was that springs and streams obtained their water directly from the seas. This hypothesis was laid to rest in the sixteenth century when Bernard Palissy of France convincingly refuted the concept. Most major advances in our understanding of subsurface water had to wait until the eighteenth century when many important hydraulic principles were advanced by scientists like Bernoulli, Chezy, Henri de Pitot, and Leonard Euler. By using basic knowledge of geology and confined pressure, Francois Arayo of the French Academy of Science predicted that water could be obtained from the subsurface Albian sands. In 1840, at Grenelle, 90 kilometers (km) west of Paris,

France, French engineers proved that Arayo was correct when groundwater from a depth of some 600 meters (m), or 2,000 feet (ft), rose through a primitive drill hole from the Albian sands to the surface [277]. The nineteenth century saw the introduction of numerous basic hydrology concepts by Darcy, Mulvaney, Manning, and many others, as well as important advances in water sanitation. Efficient drilling techniques emerged in the late nineteenth and early twentieth centuries following the development of new turbine pumps and convenient energy from petroleum and electricity [330]. This led to a huge increase in drilling for water around much of the world. Soon extraction of groundwater at rates far above natural recharge rates, and the environmental impacts accompanying such depletion, were common.

New developments in water sciences took off in the twentieth century and great strides were made in gathering and analyzing data on groundwater behavior. "Classic" reports by Meinzer, Theis, Jacob, and others helped to establish hydrogeology as a distinct, albeit highly interdisciplinary, field of science [199, 264, 265, 266, 385, 386]. From 1950 on, awareness of the importance of water resources has been growing at an ever-increasing rate. Knowledge of groundwater chemistry experienced major progress beginning in the 1950s. Other important advances have focused on understanding the behavior of ground and surface water over large areas, and over long periods of time. Until the 1960s, most hydrogeological work focused upon exploration and development of the groundwater resource. At that time, growing concern for the many environmental consequences of resource exploitation and modern technologies led to a strong focus on groundwater quality and depletion, and their associated impacts.

Unfortunately the pace of growth in human population, resource demands, and other conflicting needs have also grown exponentially. Beginning with the International Hydrologic Decade (1965-1974) sponsored by the United Nations (UN), many conferences, programs, and assorted events and agreements have been used to build awareness and encourage progress toward better management of water resources. The emphasis was usually on the use and abuse of surface waters. Only recently has groundwater begun to receive some serious attention, albeit not what it merits. Hundreds of events occur each year focusing on water resource issues. The great challenge for hydrogeology involves assessing groundwater response to the ever-increasing demands and threats which humanity is placing upon it. This will require major improvements in our ability to monitor and understand the response of groundwater and ecosystems to ongoing withdrawals, contamination, and climate change. The scientific knowledge obtained then needs to guide the enactment and implementation of intelligent policies regarding the use of this essential resource. Needless to say, this will not be easy.

1.1.5 Inequalities in Time and Space

The temporal and spatial distribution of both water and people is a huge part of any water problem. Water itself exhibits high variability in both space and time. Large parts of Earth's terrain are almost always dry, others perpetually wet (Plate 1). Still other areas experience far too much water at one time and far too little at other times.

People have not always settled where fresh water is abundant, but once settled, they are loath to move. In many locations, water was once adequate, but now, due to increasing human population and water consumption, or other trends such as changing climate, the water supply is insufficient. At the other extreme, hundreds of millions live in areas frequently threatened by too much water, such as floodplains and low-elevation coastal areas. But even here, the water may be heavily contaminated.

The average amount of water present at a locality is usually not as important as how that water supply varies through time and the rate at which it is being recycled (Chapter 3). Some parts of the world are swamped with water part of the year and suffer from water deficits at other times. For example, at Cherrapunji, in eastern India, the monsoons bring some 250 centimeters (cm), or 100 inches (in), of drenching rains during July. But Cherrapunji gets only about 0.2 centimeters (0.1 inch) of rain during January. The amount of water stored in the world's rivers at any one time is only about 2,000 cubic kilometers (km³) — about half the annual withdrawal by humans; but over the span of a year, those rivers discharge about 45,500 km³ of water to the seas.

An average person requires a minimum of about 24 liters (L), or 6.3 gallons (gal), a day for basic household needs such as drinking, cooking, washing, and cleaning. In developed nations, most people can simply turn a faucet on to get an abundance of clean water at low cost right in their home. In developing nations, hundreds of millions must devote a large part of their time and income just to obtain enough water to live on. Some must walk many miles, and the water they find is little and frequently contaminated. Others must wait in long lines and pay an exorbitant price. Increasingly, the needy fail to find safe water at all. Where developing nations do have delivery systems for water, it typically costs much more than in developed nations.

Huge inequities exist in human uses also. Water consumption in the US averages around 380 liters per capita per day (L/cap/day) compared to only 20-30 L/cap/day in many developing countries.

1.1.6 A Crisis of Quantity and Quality

I fear for the future of water – and humanity.

— Senator Paul Simon

Water is rapidly emerging as the primary limiting factor in determining how many people our planet can support and the phrase "water crisis" is increasingly heard in reference to both local and the global water situations. A "food crisis" of unprecedented proportions is also in the offing. Without water, of course, there can be no food from any source or at any price. Over the past century, water use has increased six-fold, roughly twice the rate of population growth. Adequate supplies of safe, fresh water are in jeopardy over large parts of Earth, and over half the world's people live and depend upon water in those areas. As noted previously, most of that water is underground where it is invisible, and its depletion easily ignored. If this vital resource is not used more efficiently and managed more intelligently, massive environmental losses and human suffering will be unavoidable.

Water quantity and quality are vital concerns to people and nations everywhere on Earth, and the concerns are growing as human demands on this limited resource continue to accelerate. Surface and ground waters are being overexploited at an increasing rate even as contamination continues to impair those same water supplies. By the mid-1990s, one species, *Homo sapiens*, was believed to have been claiming over half of all accessible freshwater supplies on Earth [140]. River discharge to the seas has decreased by some 60% due to human interventions. Human population has topped seven billion and continues to grow by perhaps 80 million annually. The needs of these people, combined with ever soaring expectations (per capita consumption), urbanization, industrialization, agricultural production, land degradation, and pollution, are placing enormous pressure on water resources. Water resource planning and investment are not keeping pace with the ever-growing demand by humans.

1.2 The Water Sciences

If there is magic on this planet, it is contained in water.

— Loren Eiseley

1.2.1 Terminology

Sloppy use of basic terminology is a thorn in the flesh of many fields of study. It has been especially thorny in the field of hydrogeology, where some still can't agree on what to call that which they are studying. Without burdening the reader with lengthy discussions of the pros and cons — of which there are many — here are a few definitions and comments regarding some oft-encountered "water" terms. First, two common prefixes, *aqui-* (Latin) and *hydro-* (Greek), both mean water.

Hydrology (literally "water science," or **hydroscience**) is the study of water. The term generally implies the study of water on Earth wherever and however it occurs — in streams, lakes, and oceans; beneath the surface; and in solid, liquid, and gaseous forms. The physical behavior and chemical characteristics of water as well as its relations to environmental, cultural, and economic concerns may all be included in this vast field of study.

Geology ("earth science") is the study of planet Earth. Most geology emphasizes the solid parts of Earth — or, in the case of astrogeology, of other celestial bodies — but it also includes the surface of the planet and the processes which shape and otherwise influence that surface. The study of surficial processes and landforms is **geomorphology**.

Hydrogeology ("water earth science") is defined herein as the study of water below the planet's surface and its interactions with surface water. Many consider the terms **groundwater hydrology**, **groundwater geology**, and **geohydrology** to be synonymous with hydrogeology; others use geohydrology only when there is more emphasis on hydrology. Stone prefers to use hydrogeology for the application of geologic methods to water studies and geohydrology for the application of hydrologic methods to geologic phenomena [378]. Some authors restrict hydrogeology and even hydrology to the study of subsurface water with little if any consideration of surface water. "Ground water" can be written as "groundwater." "Ground-water" is used by some as a modifier (adjective). The term sometimes refers to all water below the ground surface. Hydrogeologists prefer to use **groundwater** for that water which completely saturates the material in which it occurs — that is, no air spaces are present — and which moves in response to hydrostatic forces or pressure, and that is how it will be used in this book.

This is but the tip of the terminology iceberg. An additional problem is the widespread misuse of many terms by individuals with limited knowledge of groundwater science and its literature. Usage of many water terms is inconsistent even among qualified professionals. Perhaps this is an unavoidable consequence of the fact that hydrogeology is a very young science with terms and principles borrowed from many other long-established fields of study. The people who work in hydrogeology, or who frequently must use hydrogeologic knowledge, come from many different backgrounds: engineers, geologists, natural resource specialists, planners, geographers, meteorologists, ecologists, and many others. To top it off, most laws and regulations, which tend to determine what will or won't be done in the "real world," have been written by lawyers or politicians and their assistants, most of whom have little or no solid scientific expertise in hydrogeology. The results can be confusing, to say the least. In this book, we will use, when possible, the most widely accepted, useful, and/or clear-cut definitions of terms.

Some fields of study involving water are provided in Table 1.1. Numerous modifiers (applied, practical, arid, coastal, fresh water, introductory, advanced, for engineers, for idiots, and so forth) can be used with these sciences, not to mention compound and esoteric terms (hydrobiogeochemistry, for example).

1.2.2 Hydrogeology Careers

Presumably, most users of this book are not, and will not become, professional hydrogeologists. However, as noted in the Preface, individuals in dozens of fields are finding themselves increasingly involved with water supply and water quality issues and their knowledge of groundwater and water resources can be invaluable.

Professional hydrogeologists, those who undergo advanced training in hydrogeology or closely related fields, are in great demand. The largest sources of employment are private consulting and engineering firms. A hydrogeologist's work may consist simply of finding water, but more commonly, it will involve assessing and cleaning up localities where soil and groundwater have been contaminated. These activities are usually referred to by the terms **site characterization** (investigating and assessing a site) and **site remediation** (cleaning up a site). Specific tasks which the consulting hydrogeologist performs or oversees include planning and directing the installation of boreholes and monitoring wells, collecting and describing soil and water samples, interpreting the results of chemical analyses of those samples, obtaining water data from wells and other sources to determine subsurface conditions, conducting various water and pumping tests, analyzing data, and writing reports. Chapter 11 provides more detailed information on these aspects of hydrogeological work.

Table 1.1. Selected Water-Related Scientific Disciplines and Their Principal Focus of Study

DISCIPLINE	FOCUS[1]
Archaeohydrology	Water management practices of early cultures
Climatology	Long-term meteorological conditions
Engineering	Application of science to practical ends (design, construction, operation of project, structure, etc.)
Fluvial Geomorphology	Streams and stream processes
Geohydrology	The role of water in geologic processes
Geology	Solid Earth and the processes affecting it
Geomorphology	Surficial processes and landforms
Ground-Water Geology	Geologic aspects of groundwater
Ground-Water Hydrology	Subterranean waters
Hydraulics	Fluids in motion
Hydrogeochemistry	Chemistry of groundwater
Hydrogeology	Subsurface waters and related geologic aspects of surface waters
Hydrography	Distribution of water; often restricted to surface waters only
Hydrology	Water
Hydrometeorology	Application of meteorology to hydrology
Hydrostratigraphy	Classification of rock units based on their hydrologic properties
Limnology	Standing freshwater bodies (lakes, ponds)
Meteorology	Weather and atmosphere
Oceanography/Oceanology	Oceans and their connected seas
Pedology	Soil science, specifically its morphology, origin, and classification
Speleology	Caves
Surface-Water Hydrology	Lakes and streams

[1] These brief definitions reflect the author's preferences; be aware that alternate definitions of principal focus exist for many of the disciplines listed in this table.

Other hydrogeologists work in local, state, or national regulatory agencies where they help enforce environmental laws and manage water data. Their tasks often include writing their own reports and reviewing reports required of others who use, pollute, or otherwise impact water resources. They also keep tabs on reporting deadlines, visit sites to determine if regulations are being followed, testify in court cases, do research, and participate in educational programs for businesses and the general public.

Many industries work with and/or generate hazardous wastes, or must find and use large quantities of fresh water. Such businesses hire hydrogeologists to help devise and manage water and hazardous waste programs, comply with regulations, or locate water supplies.

Still other hydrogeologists will teach and do research in colleges or universities, or undertake research with government or private organizations and agencies that deal with water resources and environmental concerns. The US Bureau of Labor Statistics estimates that demand for hydrogeologists will continue to grow at a much higher rate than most professions.

1.3 Some Elementary Science

Knowledge of some very basic science, mainly physics and chemistry, is essential if one is to understand water and its behavior. Let us begin therefore by making sure we understand and properly use certain fundamental terms. Much of this material can be skipped over by those with adequate backgrounds in basic science.

1.3.1 Matter

Water is matter. **Matter** is anything that has mass and takes up space. **Mass** is basically substance, or more specifically the amount of matter present. Matter exerts an attractive force called **gravity** on all other matter. The greater the mass, the greater the attractive force. All matter is made up of minute units called **atoms**. Atoms are the basic building blocks of matter.

1.3.2 Subatomic Particles

Atoms consist of three major types of subatomic particles: electrons, protons, and neutrons. Very low-mass negative charges called **electrons** rapidly orbit a tiny dense **nucleus** which contains two heavy particles: positively charged **protons** and uncharged **neutrons**.

A. Electrons

Electrons have very little mass, are negatively charged, and are highly mobile. They can be gained, lost, or shared with other atoms and in so doing they determine the chemical behavior of the atom. Negatively charged electrons are attracted to the positively charged nucleus; they circle around the nucleus, enshrouding it in a "cloud" of rapidly moving charges. The diameter of this electron cloud is a hundred thousand times greater than that of the nucleus (imagine a pea in a huge outdoor stadium), yet each proton in that minute nucleus is about two thousand times heavier than an electron. Only two electrons are able to fit in the limited space close to the nucleus. This area or zone of two electrons is often referred to as the inner "**electron shell**" or "energy level." Farther from the nucleus, eight electrons are needed to fill an electron shell. Atoms are more chemically stable when they have a complete outer "shell" of either two (if in the innermost zone only) or eight electrons and thus have a strong propensity to fill this outer shell with electrons. It is this tendency to attain a complete outer shell that causes most atoms to join up with other atoms. The mutual attraction, or links, holding atoms together are called **bonds**. When bonds are formed or broken, existing substances change into new substances in a process called a **chemical reaction**.

Normal atoms are electrostatically neutral. That is, they contain an equal number of electrons (negative charges) and protons (positive charges). An atom or group of atoms with a charge is an **ion**. If a neutral atom gains one or more electrons, it becomes a negatively charged atom, an **anion**; if it loses electrons, it becomes a positively charged atom, a **cation**. For example, a sodium atom, represented by the chemical symbol: Na, has just one electron in its outermost shell which makes it very unstable. Hence, it will readily lose this electron to produce a sodium ion (or cation) with a charge of plus one (+1: often indicated as Na^+, Na^{1+}, or Na^{+1}). Calcium (Ca) has two outer electrons and often loses both, thereby forming the calcium ion (Ca^{2+}). The chlorine (Cl) atom has 7 outer electrons and thus tends to gain one electron, producing a chlorine ion with a -1 charge (Cl^{1-}), and so on (Figure 1.2). Oppositely charged ions will attract each other to form an **ionic bond**, also called an electrovalent bond.

Ionization potential is the voltage — the force or push — needed to remove an electron from its atom. The higher the ionization potential, the harder it is to remove an electron. The ionization potential for a sodium atom is very low. Hence, sodium is always found combined with

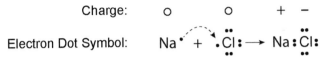

Figure 1.2. "Electron dot symbols" are often used to illustrate the electrons in the outer electron "shell" or the energy level of an atom. Here a neutral sodium atom readily loses its lone outer electron to a neutral chlorine atom resulting in a positively charged sodium ion and a negatively charged chlorine ion. The oppositely charged ions then form an ionic bond producing common salt, sodium chloride (NaCl).

other elements in nature. For an element like mercury, the ionization potential is quite high. Therefore, the mercury atom is quite stable and elementary (pure) mercury is sometimes found in nature.

B. Protons

The number of protons gives each atom its **atomic number** and determines the basic nature, the physical properties, of the atom. For example, hydrogen (H) is atomic number one and each of its atoms will always contain just one proton, and helium (He) is atomic number two and will always have two protons. Change the number of protons, and you change the type of atom and the basic properties of the substance.

Substances made of only one type of atom are **elements**. Each element has a specific atomic number, a name, and a chemical symbol. This, and other information, is provided on the **Periodic Table of Elements** (Table 1.2). The organization of the table reflects the fact that certain important properties keep repeating — that is, they are periodic. For example, the elements in the far left column (Group 1A) all have just one electron in their outermost shell. They all tend to lose this electron very readily and thus are very reactive (unstable) in the elemental state. Group 2A elements tend to lose two electrons. Group 7A elements, the **halogens**, have 7 electrons in their outer shell and thus tend to gain electrons readily. The elements in the far right column are the noble gases or **inert** (inactive) elements. When in the elemental (uncharged) state, they have filled outer electron shells and hence are very stable and do not react with other elements.

If we ignore the inert gases, as one goes from the upper right corner (F) to the lower left corner (Fr) of the periodic table, the tendency of the atoms to pick up an electron, a property often called **electronegativity**, diminishes. Electronegativity, or the power to attract electrons, is

15

Table 1.2. Periodic Table of the Elements

1A	2A	3B	4B	5B	6B	7B	8B	8B
1 **H** 1.00794 Hydrogen								
3 **Li** 6.941 Lithium	4 **Be** 9.012182 Beryllium							
11 **Na** 22.989769 Sodium	12 **Mg** 24.3050 Magnesium							
19 **K** 39.0983 Potassium	20 **Ca** 40.078 Calcium	21 **Sc** 44.955912 Scandium	22 **Ti** 47.867 Titanium	23 **V** 50.9415 Vanadium	24 **Cr** 51.9961 Chromium	25 **Mn** 54.938045 Manganese	26 **Fe** 55.845 Iron	27 **Co** 58.933195 Cobalt
37 **Rb** 85.4678 Rubidium	38 **Sr** 87.62 Strontium	39 **Y** 88.90585 Yttrium	40 **Zr** 91.224 Zirconium	41 **Nb** 92.90638 Niobium	42 **Mo** 95.96 Molybdenum	43 **Tc** [98] Technetium	44 **Ru** 101.07 Ruthenium	45 **Rh** 102.90550 Rhodium
55 **Cs** 132.9054519 Cesium	56 **Ba** 137.327 Barium	57-71 Lanthanides	72 **Hf** 178.49 Hafnium	73 **Ta** 180.94788 Tantalum	74 **W** 183.84 Tungsten	75 **Re** 186.207 Rhenium	76 **Os** 190.23 Osmium	77 **Ir** 192.217 Iridium
87 **Fr** [223] Francium	88 **Ra** [226] Radium	89-103 Actinides	104 **Rf** [267] Rutherfordium	105 **Db** [268] Dubnium	106 **Sg** [271] Seaborgium	107 **Bh** [272] Bohrium	108 **Hs** [270] Hassium	109 **Mt** [276] Meitnerium

57 **La** 138.90547 Lanthanum	58 **Ce** 140.116 Cerium	59 **Pr** 140.90765 Praseodymium	60 **Nd** 144.242 Neodymium	61 **Pm** [145] Promethium	62 **Sm** 150.36 Samarium
89 **Ac** [227] Actinium	90 **Th** 232.03806 Actinium	91 **Pa** 231.03588 Protactinium	92 **U** 238.02891 Uranium	93 **Np** [237] Neptunium	94 **Pu** [244] Plutonium

not constant; it varies depending upon the chemical environment of the element — for example, with what other elements it is bonded.

Only about 90 elements occur naturally on Earth, and many of those are quite rare. Roughly 98% (by weight) of the common crustal rocks of Earth consist of only 9 elements (Table 1.3). Most of the materials around us are **compounds**, which are pure substances composed of two or more different atoms chemically bonded together. For example, the sodium and the chlorine ions noted above are strongly attracted to each other because they have opposite charges. Hence they tend to

8B	1B	2B	3A	4A	5A	6A	7A	Inert gases
								2 **He** 4.002602 Helium
			5 **B** 10.811 Boron	6 **C** 12.0107 Carbon	7 **N** 14.0067 Nitrogen	8 **O** 15.9994 Oxygen	9 **F** 18.9984032 Flourine	10 **Ne** 20.1797 Neon
			13 **Al** 26.9815386 Aluminum	14 **Si** 28.0855 Silicon	15 **P** 30.973762 Phosphorus	16 **S** 32.065 Sulfur	17 **Cl** 35.453 Chlorine	18 **Ar** 39.948 Argon
28 **Ni** 58.6934 Nickel	29 **Cu** 63.546 Copper	30 **Zn** 65.38 Zinc	31 **Ga** 69.723 Gallium	32 **Ge** 72.64 Germanium	33 **As** 74.92160 Arsenic	34 **Se** 78.96 Selenium	35 **Br** 79.904 Bromine	36 **Kr** 83.798 Krypton
46 **Pd** 106.42 Palladium	47 **Ag** 107.8682 Silver	48 **Cd** 112.411 Cadmium	49 **In** 114.818 Indium	50 **Sn** 118.710 Tin	51 **Sb** 121.760 Antimony	52 **Te** 127.60 Tellunium	53 **I** 126.90447 Iodine	54 **Xe** 131.293 Xenon
78 **Pt** 195.084 Platinum	79 **Au** 196.966569 Gold	80 **Hg** 200.59 Mercury	81 **Ti** 204.3833 Thallium	82 **Tn** 207.2 Lead	83 **Bi** 208.98040 Bismuth	84 **Po** [209] Polonium	85 **At** [210] Astatine	86 **Rn** [222] Radon
110 **Ds** [281] Darmstadtium	111 **Rg** [280] Roentgenium	112 **Cn** [285] Copernicium	113 **Uut** [284] Ununtrium	114 **Fl** [289] Flerovium	115 **Uup** [288] Ununpentium	116 **Lv** [293] Livermorium	117 **Uus** [294] Ununseptium	118 **Uuo** [294] Ununoctium

63 **Eu** 151.964 Europium	64 **Gd** 157.25 Gadolinium	65 **Tb** 158.92535 Terbium	66 **Dy** 162.500 Dysprosium	67 **Ho** 164.93032 Holmium	68 **Er** 167.259 Erbium	69 **Tm** 168.93421 Thulium	70 **Yb** 173.054 Ytterbium	71 **Lu** 174.9668 Lutetium
95 **Am** [243] Americium	96 **Cm** [247] Curium	97 **Bk** [247] Burkelium	98 **Cf** [251] Californium	99 **Es** [252] Einsteinium	100 **Fm** [257] Fermium	101 **Md** [258] Mendelevium	102 **No** [259] Nobelium	103 **Lr** [262] Lawrencium

develop an ionic bond to form the compound sodium chloride (Figure 1.2), also known as halite (its mineral name), rock salt, and table salt. The chemical formula for sodium chloride is NaCl.

The **chemical formula** gives the symbols for the elements present and uses subscripts to show the relative number of atoms, if more than one, of each element present. In the case of sodium chloride, one atom of sodium and one atom of chlorine are present. The formula for calcium carbonate, whose mineral name is calcite, is $CaCO_3$, indicating that one calcium atom, one carbon atom, and three oxygen atoms are present.

Table 1.3. The Common Crustal Elements

ELEMENT	PERCENT BY WEIGHT
Oxygen	46.6
Silicon	27.7
Aluminum	8.1
Iron	5.0
Calcium	3.6
Sodium	2.8
Potassium	2.6
Magnesium	2.1

C. Neutrons

The neutrons in atoms strongly influence the stability of the atom as well as add to its mass. The **atomic mass,** or atomic weight, of an element is defined as the number of protons plus neutrons in its nucleus. Atoms can have differing numbers of neutrons in their nucleus. Atoms of a given type — that is, atoms with the same number of protons — but with different weights due to different numbers of neutrons are called **isotopes** of that atom. If the isotope is unstable, its nucleus tends to break down and it is called a **radioisotope**, radioactive isotope, or radio-nuclide. For example, hydrogen (H) has three isotopes: H-1 (ordinary hydrogen with one proton in its nucleus); H-2 (heavy hydrogen or deuterium, with one proton and one neutron in its nucleus); and H-3 (tritium, with one proton and two neutrons in its nucleus). Notations such as H-1 or ^{1}H and H-2 or ^{2}H indicate the element and its atomic mass.

Deuterium and tritium are radioisotopes and change or "decay" over time to other isotopes of the same or different atoms. The time required for half of a given amount of a specific radioisotope to break down into another form — into a different nuclear configuration — is the **half-life** of that radioisotope. Half-lives range from fractions of a second to billions of years.

1.3.3 Molecules and Compounds

The two major subdivisions of chemical compounds are organic and inorganic. **Organic compounds** contain one or more carbon atoms and were once thought to owe their existence to living organisms, although we now know that this is not always true. Carbon atoms have four electrons in their outer shell and do not completely lose or gain electrons like sodium or chlorine. Instead, they readily join with other atoms by sharing electrons, forming a **covalent bond**. Carbon atoms can form a virtually infinite variety of chemical structures ranging simple isolated molecules to chains, rings, and complex three-dimensional structures (Figure 1.3). The connecting bars in Figure 1.3 represent shared electrons or covalent bonds. **Inorganic compounds** lack carbon, form various chemical bonds (including covalent and ionic), and are sometimes simply called mineral substances.

The smallest part of any pure substance, element or compound, that can exist and still be that substance is a **molecule**. A molecule may be made of only one atom, or of many thousands of chemically linked atoms. The size and behavior of different molecules likewise vary enormously. Most molecules are inconceivably small; one molecule of

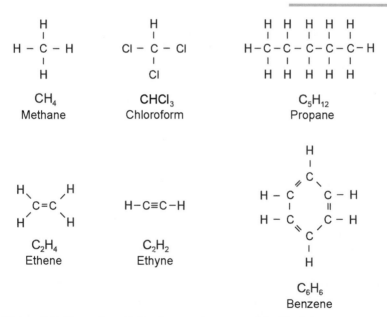

Figure 1.3. Examples of simple organic compounds. Each bar represents a shared electron pair, a covalent bond, and the arrangement of the atoms provides a simplified view of the atoms' structure. Note that more than one electron pair may be shared as indicatged by the double bonds in ethene and benzene and the triple bond in ethyne. Hydrogen is often replaced by other atoms, or groups of atoms, as in chloroform.

water, H_2O, contains three atoms, and one drop of water contains some 1,700,000,000,000,000,000 (1.7 quintillion) molecules.

Water is an inorganic chemical compound made of two atoms of the element hydrogen covalently bonded to one atom of the element oxygen. Expressed in chemical shorthand, it is **H_2O** (dihydrogen oxide). Oxygen needs two electrons to complete its outer shell, and each hydrogen atom has just one electron which it can share with the oxygen. Hence it takes two hydrogen atoms to satisfy one oxygen atom, resulting in H_2O. The combining ability of an atom is called **valence**, or valency. The valence of hydrogen is +1 because it tends to lose or share one electron with other chemicals. The valence of oxygen is –2 because it tends to gain or share two electrons with other chemicals. The chemical reaction of hydrogen and oxygen to form water is indicated in chemical shorthand as:

$$2H_2 + O_2 \rightarrow 2H_2O$$

This is called a **chemical equation**. The hydrogen and oxygen are the **reactants** and water is the **product** of this reaction. The "yield" arrow indicates the direction in which the reaction proceeds. In this case, two molecules of hydrogen combine with one molecule of oxygen to yield two molecules of water. Both hydrogen and oxygen occur as diatomic molecules — meaning each molecule is composed of two atoms of these elements — and must be written as H_2 and O_2. All equations must be balanced so that the total number of reactant atoms equals the total number of product atoms. After balancing the above equation, we can see that it takes two molecules of hydrogen and one molecule of oxygen to yield two molecules of water.

Another expression commonly used in chemistry is the mole. A **mole** is a quantity whose mass, or weight, is numerically equal to its molecular mass. Most texts consider a mole to be a gram (g) molecular mass, or the mass of a molecule expressed in grams. For example, a mole of hydrogen (H_2) would be 2 grams of hydrogen (the molecule contains two atoms of hydrogen, each with an atomic mass of 1, therefore $2 \times 1 = 2$). A mole of oxygen is 32 grams (two times oxygen's atomic mass of $16 \times 2 = 32$ grams). For the water molecule, H_2O, a mole is 18 grams ($2 \times 1 + 16 = 18$ grams).

Additional basic science is covered in the following section on water characteristics. Chemical processes are discussed in more detail in Chapter 9.

1.4 Important Characteristics of Water

Be Praised, My Lord, through Sister Water; she is very useful, and humble, and precious, and pure.

— Saint Francis of Assisi, Canticle of the Sun (c. 1225)

In spite of its familiarity, abundance, and importance, water is far from ordinary; it is in fact one of the oddest substances known. Water exhibits several vitally important characteristics, many of which are unusual, or even unique.

1.4.1 Occurs in All Three Phases

A. The States of Matter

Water is the only compound occurring naturally in all three common phases, or **states of matter**, in Earth's surface environment. The three common states of matter are:

- **solid**, in which the molecules are close together and held tightly in place by an attractive force that exists between like molecules;
- **liquid**, in which the molecules are farther apart and can slip past each other but not completely escape each others' pull; and
- **gas**, in which the molecules are far enough apart to escape binding forces and float freely.

Water can exist in all three states simultaneously in a given area — as a solid, ice; a liquid, water; and a gas, water vapor.

B. Phase Changes

When matter changes its physical state, energy must be exchanged — absorbed or released. **Energy** is the ability to do work. To do **work**, one must apply a **force** (a push or a pull) and move something. The two most basic forms of energy are **kinetic** (energy by virtue of movement) and **potential** (energy by virtue of position). Energy causes molecules to vibrate; an increase in energy causes a molecule to vibrate more rapidly and a decrease in energy causes a molecule to vibrate more slowly. An increase in molecular motion is accompanied by an increase in temperature, while a decrease in motion is accompanied by a decrease in temperature.

For ice to melt, energy must be added to the ice. This increased energy causes the molecules of water to vibrate more rapidly and is indicated by an increase in **temperature**, and this in turn tells us that energy, as heat, has been added. When a critical or threshold temperature is reached, the molecules break free from their fixed positions in the ice, move farther apart, and begin to slide past each other. We observe this as **melting** of the ice and the temperature at which it occurs is the **melting point**. If temperatures drop, the liquid water loses heat, the molecular movements slow and the water refreezes.

Similarly, when liquid water absorbs enough energy for the molecules to escape completely from attractive forces, the molecules can move independently and the water undergoes another phase change, this time to the gaseous state, a process called **evaporation**. The temperature at which this change occurs is the **boiling point**.

Water's constant phase changes in the atmosphere are a vital means of transferring heat energy around Earth, thus regulating our climate. The same amount of energy that went into melting or evaporating a quantity of water will be released when the liquid water freezes or when water vapor **condenses** — that is, when it changes from a gas to a liquid.

C. Systems of Measurement

Past scientists recognized the importance of water and often made it the standard by which numerous properties of all other substances were to be measured and compared. The **metric system** of measurement uses water in this way. For temperature, for example, the melting point of ice (solid water) was used to determine 0 degree (0°) Celsius or Centigrade (C) and its boiling (vaporization) point was used to determine 100°C. Note that the melting point is also the freezing point and the boiling point is the condensation point. What you call it depends upon whether your temperature is rising or falling.

For the most part, the US continues to use the awkward **English system** of measurement which uses units such as feet, pounds, and degrees Fahrenheit (°F). Scientists prefer the modern SI, or metric, system of measurement because it employs a simple decimal system based on the number ten, making it much easier to use.

D. Additional Influences

Changes in the states of matter, including boiling or melting temperatures, will vary with changes in environment. Two conditions which can alter the temperatures at which changes of state occur are pressure and impurities. For example, lower pressure allows water to boil or vaporize at considerably lower temperature. Lower pressure favors the more voluminous or expansive form of matter. Because the mass of air that lies overhead is less at high elevations, air pressure decreases as elevation increases. Thus, at an elevation of 14,000 feet, water boils at 186°F but at –1,000 feet it boils at 214°F. Tibetans like to drink their tea at the boiling point, which is a quite tolerable temperature at 20,000 feet in Tibet. But when they go to a low elevation and try this, they often scald themselves.

The presence of impurities causes water to melt at a lower temperature. Hence we add salt to icy roads, which can lower the melting point sufficiently to make the adjacent ice turn back into water in spite of subfreezing temperatures. Chemists consider "standard" temperature and pressure to be 0°C and 1 atmosphere.

1.4.2 High Specific Heat

Water has very high specific heat. Only lithium and ammonia are higher. **Specific heat** is the quantity of heat needed to raise the temperature of a given amount of a pure substance by 1 degree. In the metric system, the standard unit of mass is 1 gram, which is rather small. It requires 28.35 grams to equal one ounce. Again, the metric system uses water as the standard and defined the calorie, its basic unit of heat, as the amount of heat that would raise the temperature of 1 gram of water by 1 degree C. Hence the specific heat of water is 1 calorie per gram per degree Centigrade (1 cal/g/°C). Thus it requires 100 calories of heat to raise the temperature of 1 gram of water from 0° to 100°C. In the English system, heat is measured in British thermal units (btu) and the specific heat of water is 1 btu per pound per degree Fahrenheit (1 btu/lb/°F).

The high specific heat of water gives the fluid remarkably high **heat capacity**, the capacity to retain heat. Water heats up slowly, cools down slowly, and is very effective at storing heat. Hence the local climate is more moderate and experiences fewer extremes of temperature near large bodies of water than would be characteristic of the climate of places located far from large water bodies. The water retains heat during cold spells, releasing it slowly and warming the air of the surrounding area. When air temperatures are high, the water absorbs heat slowly and remains relatively cool, generating breezes and keeping the temperature of adjacent land areas lower than it otherwise would be. Due to the insulating effects of rock and soil, the temperature of shallow groundwater approximates the average annual air temperature. In the human body, water performs a similar and vitally important function by helping to maintain a relatively uniform body temperature.

1.4.3 Highest Heat of Vaporization

Water has the highest heat of vaporization of all liquids. **Heat of vaporization**, or latent heat of vaporization, refers to the amount of heat required to vaporize a given quantity of any substance at the boiling point. To evaporate one gram of water at the boiling point requires 540 calories of heat. This is 5.4 times more heat than was needed to raise the temperature of that gram of water 100°C from the melting point to the boiling point. Water evaporates at lower temperatures also, but it will require a bit more energy due to the lower energy state of the molecules — for example, at 0°C, the heat of vaporization is 597 cal/g. This heat energy does not go toward increasing the temperature of the water as specific heat does — no temperature change occurs, hence the frequent use of the term *latent*. Temperature is a result of the vibrational motion of the molecules, a form of kinetic energy. Once the boiling temperature is reached, the added heat goes instead into overcoming the attractive forces between molecules, increasing the distance between them, thus increasing the potential energy between molecules. The attractive forces diminish as the distance apart increases. When the molecules are far enough apart, evaporation occurs and the water becomes a gas — water vapor. When water vapor condenses back to a liquid, as when water droplets form in clouds, its latent heat energy is released to the surrounding environment. Hence we say that evaporation is a cooling process and condensation a warming process. The chill we feel when stepping out of a shower or a swimming pool results from the heat being absorbed from our bodies by the small amount of evaporation taking place next to our skin. Imagine the quantity of heat being absorbed by water during evaporation over the world's tropical oceans. This heat energy is stored in the water vapor and carried great distances by wind systems. When cooling and condensation take place, that energy is released into the atmosphere where it can power huge storms and hurricanes. The amount of energy released by one typical hurricane is on the order of 600 trillion watts, or about 200 times greater than worldwide electric generating capacity.

The capacity of water to absorb, transport, and release vast amounts of heat without becoming too hot itself is the most important factor enabling the distribution of heat around Earth, and hence in moderating global climate.

Water's heat of vaporization is vital in many other processes also, including the regulation of bodily temperatures in organisms.

1.4.4 High Heat of Fusion

Water has an exceptionally high heat of fusion. Of all liquids, only ammonia is higher. Latent **heat of fusion** refers to the heat absorbed when a solid melts or the heat released when the liquid refreezes. Hence, it is also referred to as heat of melting or heat of freezing. The heat of fusion for water is 80 cal/g.

Ice can also change directly into a gas without entering into the liquid state. **Sublimation** refers to the change of state of a solid into a gas or a gas into a solid. During sublimation, both heat of vaporization and heat of fusion are released, or absorbed, during the phase change. A considerable amount of sublimation occurs from snow and ice when the weather is cold, dry, and sunny. It also occurs in the atmosphere and in home freezers. You may have noticed how snow banks, or ice cubes in the freezer, get smaller after sitting for a few days or weeks even though no melting has occurred. Sublimation from water vapor directly to ice is responsible for the formation of many clouds and of frost.

1.4.5 Expansion During Freezing

Water expands 9% upon freezing. Nearly all other materials contract when they turn from the liquid to the solid state. They also expand whenever heated and contract whenever cooled. But not water. Water achieves maximum density at 4°C (39.2°F), then begins to expand if temperature continues to decrease. This strange property is important for many reasons. For one, it makes ice less dense than liquid water, thus allowing a protective, insulating layer of ice to form over water during subfreezing weather. If water did the usual thing and contracted upon freezing, ice would sink to the bottom. Ponds and rivers would then freeze from the bottom up and become solid ice, which would make survival of most aquatic plants and animals impossible.

The pressure exerted by freezing water at –22°C (–7.6°F) when confined is about 216 million pascals (55 tons per square foot), about a tenth of that when unconfined. Expansion upon freezing makes water an especially effective agent in breaking down and moving rock and surficial materials in cold climates, via a process called **frost action**. Frost action is an important example of weathering, the in-place breakdown of solid earth materials by chemical or mechanical means (Chapter 3).

1.4.6 Wetting Ability

Water has exceptional **wetting ability**. This property is due in large part to the attraction between water molecules and other types of molecules. The attraction of unlike substances is **adhesion**. If water molecules did not adhere to other molecules, it would be a very different, and very less livable, world. Most plants depend on soil moisture, the water which adheres to soil particles, for their survival. It would be very difficult to clean ourselves or our clothes were it not for water's wetting ability.

Adhesive capacities of water molecules enable them to surround certain other molecules as well as small solid particles, isolating them and, in effect, suspending them within a semi-solid medium. A suspension of very small (0.001 μm to 1 μm diameter) particles is called a **colloid**. Colloids have a very high surface-to-volume ratio allowing maximum exposure to the water. Thousands of common substances, including many gels, emulsions, protoplasm, plastics, and rubber, are colloidal; think of mayonnaise, mustard, or jello. Colloids exert a strong influence upon aquatic chemistry since they provide a relatively large surface area upon which chemical reactions and other processes can occur.

1.4.7 Surface Tension

Water has the highest surface tension of any material except mercury. **Surface tension** is a force which tends to limit the spreading out of a fluid. The effect is much like that of a thin membrane stretched out across the surface. Surface tension results from the attraction between water molecules. Attraction between like substances is **cohesion**. Surface tension is produced because molecules near the surface of water experience attraction from underlying water molecules, but not from above. These unequal cohesive forces cause small masses of liquid water to draw together, minimizing surface area and forming curved surfaces or droplets such as those decorating the spider web in Figure 1.4.

These cohesive and adhesive properties give water strong capillary action. **Capillary action** (capillarity) refers to the migration of a liquid through other matter due to the liquid's attraction for like and unlike molecules. This permits water to seep through cloth, up a wick, and up the stems of plants to the leaves where it is essential for the metabolic processes upon which nearly all life is dependent.

Figure 1.4. Here a spider web is bejeweled by spherical droplets of water held together by surface tension, cohesive forces between water molecules.

1.4.8 The Universal Solvent

A. Terminology

Water is the best **solvent** there is and is often referred to as "the universal solvent." Water is capable of dissolving, to varying degrees, thousands of different solids, liquids, and gases. During the act of dissolving, one or more materials are combined and form a homogeneous mixture. The resulting material is a **solution**, and the process is called solution or **dissolution**. The materials a solvent dissolves are called **solutes**. The opposite of dissolution is **exsolution**. Like most changes that occur in nature, the solutional process is reversible and a substance which has been dissolved under one set of conditions may be released from the soluble state when different conditions are encountered. For example, if salty water is evaporated, the salt, which cannot be evaporated under normal conditions, will be left behind as a **precipitate**, a solid.

B. Electrical Conductance

In water, the dissolved material may exist as charged ions or as uncharged (nonionic) molecules. Many common inorganic substances, including most salts, acids, and bases, form ionic solutions by rapidly dissolving in water. In general, the more ions — dissolved mineral matter — present in water, the more readily it can conduct an electric current. A liquid which will conduct an electric current is called an **electrolyte**. The ability of water to conduct electricity is specific electrical conductance, or just **conductivity**. Simple instruments for measuring conductivity of water in the field are readily available and are often used to estimate how much dissolved inorganic solute is present in the water. In general, the conductivity of seawater will be about a thousand times greater than relatively pure mountain stream water.

Some substances, including most organic compounds and common rocks, form solutions with water only very slowly. But even so, water dissolves billions of tons of rock from the world's land masses each year. The many elements present in seawater and the vast quantities of sediment precipitated from seawater over the eons are a direct consequence of this.

C. Saturation

When a solvent such as water contains all the solute it can hold, the solution is said to be **saturated**. The amount or concentration of a solute in a saturated solution under standard conditions is the **solubility** of that solute. Excess dissolved material tends to return to a solid state in which it is often precipitated out of the solution. In oceans and lakes, precipitated matter heavier than water will settle to the bottom of the water body where it may be buried and eventually harden into common rock types such as limestone, dolomite, and gypsum. Under certain conditions, a solution can become **supersaturated** with a solute. For example, by increasing the pressure, water can be supersaturated with carbon dioxide; when the pressure is released, for example, by opening a bottle of soda, the excess carbon dioxide will effervesce — form bubbles — and escape. The solubility of most gases decreases with increasing temperature and the solubility of most solids will increase with increasing temperature.

Many of the solutes carried by water are vital to the functioning of life forms and Earth's basic biogeochemical or nutrient cycles, such as the carbon, sulfur, nitrogen, and phosphorous cycles. Water is the primary medium in which most essential biochemical reactions are carried out. It would also be a strange and less interesting world without water's solutional capacity: we cannot taste or smell substances which are not soluble — if your tongue were not moist, you would taste nothing and if your nose were completely dry, fragrances and odors would go unnoticed.

Not all materials dissolve well in water. In particular, oils, greases, and numerous other organic substances are insoluble. Most gases have limited solubility in water but their presence in water can still be of critical importance. Only about 8 parts per million (ppm) of elemental oxygen (O_2) can exist in water that is saturated with air at 25°C, yet the presence of that oxygen is critical to many aquatic life forms. For example, most fish require 6 to 7 ppm oxygen to survive.

D. Concentrations

The **concentration** of a solute is often indicated as mass, or weight, of solute per unit mass of the water, the solvent. If a million grams of water contained 5 grams of a solute, it could be expressed as 5 g/1,000,000 g, or 5 ppm. More commonly, it is indicated as mass per unit volume, for example, milligrams/liter (mg/L). Concentrations are also often expressed as mass per unit mass in relation to the kilogram (kg), in which case our 5 ppm can become 5 milligram per kilogram (5 mg/kg). Because 1 kilogram of water equals 1 liter of water, 5 mg/kg is equal to 5 mg/L. The units ppm, mg/kg, and mg/L, can be considered equal when dealing with low concentrations or dilute solutions such as fresh water, which has a density close to 1.00 g/cm³. In very salty or mineralized water, however, water's density is higher and the units will differ. For example, if the water density is 1.2 g/cm³, the mg/L value for solute concentration will be 0.20 (20%) higher than the ppm value. Various other ways of expressing concentration also exist.

E. Impurities

Many of the impurities found in water are present in such small quantities that it is difficult to believe they might represent a threat. Yet many pollutants can be a threat in minute quantities. Some molecules present in only parts per trillion, analogous to a few pennies out of 10 billion dollars, can have important impacts, as in triggering cancers or abnormal development of a fetus.

Identifying impurities in water has become a great challenge due to the vast and growing array of pollutants, especially complex organic molecules. Much detection and measurement is now done by computer-linked **spectrochemical analyses**. These techniques are based upon the fact that chemicals will emit or absorb specific wavelengths of light which are characteristic of elements present, much like a fingerprint, thus enabling precise identification of the chemicals present.

Not all substances present in water will be dissolved in the water. In addition to solutes, water can transport materials as separate liquid, solid, or gaseous phases. During transport, these materials often undergo transformations, including various chemical reactions, attachment to particles, and changes of phase, which greatly complicate the study of groundwater chemistry and contamination.

The term **leaching** is widely used to refer to the dissolving-out of impurities by subsurface waters from a source, such as a landfill or rock formation. The contaminant-containing water, or **leachate**, will form a **plume** of contamination, the shape of which reflects the movement of the groundwater.

1.4.9 Most Abundant Substance

Water is the most plentiful substance in the outer 5 kilometers of Earth, six times more abundant than the next most abundant substance, the feldspar minerals. If the solid surface of Earth formed a perfectly smooth sphere, a layer of water 2.7 kilometers (1.6 miles) deep would cover everything.

1.4.10 Stability and Neutrality

A. Water Ions

Water is stable and neutral. If water were not a stable compound, it would not be so plentiful. However, in the very active universe of atoms and molecules, stable does not mean static. Under normal conditions, a small percentage of the molecules in pure liquid water will separate, or **dissociate**, into **hydrogen ions (H$^+$)**, which are hydrogen atoms with a charge of +1, and **hydroxide** (or hydroxyl) **ions (OH$^-$)**, which consist of an oxygen and a hydrogen atom bonded together and having a charge of -1. Note that a hydrogen ion is also just a proton, and the terms are often used interchangeably! Most of the hydrogen ions will attach to a water molecule and produce a **hydronium ion** (H$_3$O$^+$), which functions much the same as a hydrogen ion. The dissociation of H$_2$O into H$^+$, H$_3$O$^+$, and OH$^-$ ions, and their recombining back into H$_2$O, is an ongoing process in water. The charges (+1 and -1) balance, so, in spite of the ionization, pure water remains neutral. The ions are important, however, because they can react readily with other chemicals thus increasing water's remarkable solvent ability.

B. Acids and Bases

To most people, an "acid" is a liquid which has a sour taste and is good at dissolving many substances. A "base," on the other hand, tastes bitter, often feels smooth or slippery, and can be used to neutralize, or to **buffer**, acids. To a chemist, however, an **acid** is a substance which easily loses protons — that is, it yields many hydrogen ions. A **base** is a chemical which readily gains protons, or has an abundance of hydroxide ions. As noted above, hydroxide ions readily unite with hydrogen ions to form water. The capacity of water to yield hydrogen ions, and hence neutralize hydroxide ions, is called **acidity** and its capacity to accept hydrogen ions is called **alkalinity** or basicity.

If a substance such as dry hydrogen chloride (HCl) is added to water, it dissolves, producing many hydrogen ions (H^+), or protons, and chloride (Cl^-) ions. The abundance of hydrogen ions yields an acidic solution or acid, and the solution is now called hydrochloric acid. Hydrochloric acid is a strong acid, meaning it completely dissociates into ions in water yielding a large number of hydrogen ions. When a chemical, such as sodium hydroxide (NaOH), completely dissociates and produces many hydroxide ions, it is called a strong base. The less completely an acid or base dissociates, the weaker the acid or base will be (fewer H^+ or OH^- ions are produced). Most natural waters will be somewhat alkaline (basic). Highly alkaline water often contains high levels of dissolved solids. Acidic waters often indicate pollution.

The presence of ions allows water to readily conduct an electric current, which is why you should never turn an electrical appliance on or off with wet hands. The ions also greatly increase corrosion as anyone who drives where roads are heavily salted during winter can tell you.

C. The pH Scale

The degree of acidity or alkalinity of a solution is indicated by the **pH scale**, which generally extends from 1 (very strong acid) to 14 (very strong base) with 7 being neutral. Pure water is neutral because each H_2O molecule forms just one hydrogen and one hydroxide ion so that an equal number of H+ and OH− ions will always be present. The numerical pH value represents the negative logarithm of the hydrogen ion concentration. The value for hydrogen ions in pure water is 1×10^{-7} mole per liter (0.0000001 mole/L) at a temperature of 25°C and a pressure of 1 atmosphere. The negative of the negative exponent ($^{-7}$), and hence the pH, is 7; the corresponding value for OH^- ions in this water will also be 1×10^{-7}. Additional factors such as temperature and other ions present in the water can influence the number of hydrogen ions present, which is why we specified "pure" water and 25°C.

Table 1.4. pH Values of Common Substances

Substance	pH
Lye	13.0
Ammonia	12.0
Baking Soda	8.2
Distilled Water	7.0
Milk	6.5
Carrot	5.0
Tomato	4.2
Carbonated Drinks	3.0
Stomach Acid	1.1

D. pH of Natural Waters

Table 1.4 provides the pH, the "potential of hydrogen," of some familiar substances. Most natural waters have a pH range of 6-8, but can vary considerably depending on circumstances. Pure natural rainwater is slightly acidic (pH 5.3±) due to the solution of carbon dioxide in water, producing a mild acid — carbonic acid. Due to various impurities, actual pH of rainwater can vary from about 4 to slightly above 6. If lower than 5, it is considered to be **acid rain**. Lakes tend to be alkaline. The allowable range of pH for drinking water established by the World Health Organization (WHO) and US Safe Drinking Water Act is 6.5 to 8.5. Drinking water treatment facilities generally try to avoid distributing even mildly acidic water because it will tend to react with metals causing corrosion and can release harmful metals such as lead to the water. Extreme pH values can occur in certain environments, such as on alkali flats in arid regions and where sulfur-bearing deposits are exposed to air. In the latter cases, sulfur combines with oxygen in air to yield sulfur dioxide which yields sulfuric acid in water. The pH of water can be easily measured using a variety of convenient papers, meters, and pens.

E. Salts

In chemistry, a **salt** is a compound made of a positively charged cation (other than H^+) and a negatively charged anion (other than OH^-). Because opposite charges attract, the cation and anion are held together by an ionic bond. When an acid and a base react together, the result will be water (from the combining of the H⁺ and OH⁻) along with positive and negative ions, which constitute the salt. For example, in water, hydrochloric acid (HCl) and sodium hydroxide (NaOH) will both dissolve (dissociate) into ions. The H^+ and OH^- ions then combine to produce water containing dissolved sodium chloride (NaCl, common table salt):

$$H^+ + Cl^- + Na^+ + OH^- \rightarrow Na^+ + Cl^- + H_2O$$

1.4.11 Transparency

Water is **transparent**. That is, it allows light, visible electromagnetic radiation, to pass through it. Some visible light and longer-wave ultraviolet radiation are able to penetrate water to depths of over 100 meters (330 feet) in clear liquid water, but most light will be gone within the upper 10 meters of a water column. Life began and evolved in water, but this would not have been possible without the presence of an energy source such as light within the water. The majority of ocean-, lake-, and river-dwelling organisms depend upon water's transparency for survival.

1.4.12 Viscosity and Mass

Liquid water has very low viscosity. **Viscosity** is a measure of a substance's internal resistance to flow. Highly viscous materials, such as cold molasses, flow very slowly. The low viscosity of water gives it exceptional mobility allowing it to generate powerful currents. Water also possesses considerable mass and when mass is multiplied by velocity (v), momentum results. Large coastal waves and rapidly flowing floodwaters are capable of tossing about freight cars and large boulders as though they were toys. Stream water is the most significant of all agents in shaping the landscapes of Earth. Viscosity and mass also contribute mightily to water's buoyancy and the ability of fish, ships, sediment, and other objects to move upon or through water. Buoyancy is the upward force exerted by displaced water, thus enabling many objects to float in or on water. Water's mass and weight are important considerations in water supply. Reliance upon groundwater is growing, but large quantities are required, and a cubic meter (35.3 ft³) of water weighs about a ton. As near-surface water supplies are exhausted, the cost and energy requirements of accessing deeper subsurface supplies become major obstacles in the increasingly critical search for fresh water.

1.5 The Water Molecule

1.5.1 Bonding in Water

Why does water possess such remarkable and unusual properties? Many properties are closely related to the geometry of the water molecule. Hydrogen is the lightest and simplest of atoms, consisting of just one proton and one electron. Oxygen has eight protons and eight electrons. Two electrons fill oxygen's inner electron shell and six occupy the outer shell. As noted in Section 1.3.3, atoms want to achieve the more stable configuration of eight electrons in the outer shell or two for the innermost shell. Hence, oxygen will tend to attract two additional electrons to complete its outer electron shell. Electrons tend to form pairs, a result of a magnetic attraction caused by the spinning of electrons. Two electrons with opposite spin directions will attract and form a pair. When atoms of hydrogen and oxygen are brought together under suitable conditions, one oxygen will link up with two hydrogens. Each of the hydrogen atoms shares its one electron with oxygen and the oxygen shares each of its two unpaired electrons with hydrogen, yielding the H_2O molecule. The two empty electron positions in the outer shell of oxygen are located off to one side and this is where the hydrogens will attach to the oxygen, producing an asymmetric molecule (Figure 1.5). Oxygen, with eight positive protons in its nucleus, has a stronger affinity for electrons than the hydrogen with its single proton. Thus, the electrons spend more time circling around the oxygen nucleus than around the hydrogen nucleus (Figure 1.5C). This leaves the molecule with a net negative charge at the oxygen side and a positive charge on the other side where the hydrogen nuclei are located. If we take a closer look, we can see that the water molecule actually has two areas of positive charge on one end and two areas of negative charge on the other as shown in Figure 1.5, parts B and C.

1.5.2 The Hydrogen Bond

Molecules with oppositely charged ends, such as water, are called **dipolar** — they have two opposing "poles." Because unlike charges attract, the negative side of a water molecule will attract the positive side of another water molecule, much like opposite poles of magnets. This special link between water molecules is called a **hydrogen bond** (Figure 1.6). Although a relatively weak force, this attraction between water molecules gives water many of its special properties, including its

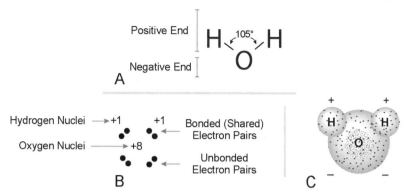

Figure 1.5. Three simple representations of the water molecule. (A) Bars, separated by an angle of 105°, represent the covalent bonds binding each hydrogen atom and the shared oxygen atom. (B) Here, dots represent electrons in the outer shell of the molecule and show the four areas of excess charge on the molecule. (C) As rapidly moving electrons zip along their orbits around the oxygen and hydrogen nuclei, they may be imagined to create a cloud. Atomic nuclei are actually very tiny — the volume occupied by an atom is overwhelmingly just orbital space.

life-giving abilities and its cohesive/adhesive properties. Indeed, without hydrogen bonds, water molecules would rapidly fly off into space as a gas, even at very low temperatures.

The significance of hydrogen bonding can be hinted at by comparing water to a similar molecule, carbon dioxide (CO_2), which is not dipolar and lacks hydrogen bonding. Carbon dioxide boils at –79°C but water must be heated to 100°C. Most of that 179-degrees-worth of extra energy is needed for just one task: to break apart the hydrogen bonds between water molecules. When ice melts or liquid water evaporates, even more additional energy is needed to separate the molecules sufficiently to produce the phase change. Hence water's abnormally high heats of fusion and vaporization.

The dipolar character and the small size of the water molecule are largely responsible for water's remarkable capacity to dissolve materials and produce colloids. The molecules of many materials, and of many particles themselves, have electrostatic charges due to the constant mobility and leapfrogging of electrons. Table salt (NaCl) consists of positively charged sodium ions and negatively charged chlorine ions. Little water molecules are able to infiltrate between the ions of solid salt where it can interfere with the attraction between the sodium and chlorine, causing

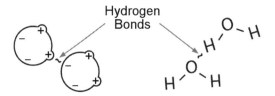

Figure 1.6. Two illustrations of hydrogen bonding between water molecules.

the sodium and chlorine ions to break free from each other and go into solution.

Within an aqueous medium, water molecules can surround and cling to many different ions and particles, thus keeping them isolated, that is, in a dissolved (solutional) or suspended (colloidal) state (Figure 1.7). Due to their dipolar nature and orientation, the water molecules directly adjacent to a charged ion or particle in turn attract other water molecules, in effect enclosing the central ion in a water sphere (sometimes called a hydration sheath). Within the water medium, electrostatic attraction may cause many molecules and ions to clump together, often forming larger colloidal aggregates.

Only 100 grams of water can dissolve 82 grams of hydrogen chloride gas to yield a strong solution of hydrochloric acid (HCl). The hydrogen ions in this solution do not exist only as isolated H+ ions, they often attach to water molecules to form hydronium ions (H_3O^+) or larger ion aggregates such as $H_5O_2^+$ or $H_7O_3^+$. The same is true for most solutions and other water mixtures. Any ion — for example, a metal such as sodium or iron — in a water solution can exist in various forms or "species" depending upon the number of, and structural organization of, the water molecules associated with the ion. A detailed discussion of this topic is beyond the scope of this book, but we should realize that the many different water-associated species are important because they can strongly influence biological processes, solubilities, transport properties, and other important characteristics of aqueous solutions.

As temperatures drop, water molecules move more slowly — their kinetic energy decreases. When the molecular energy is sufficiently low, at about 4°C, electrostatic attraction takes over allowing the molecules to begin restructuring themselves even before the freezing point is reached. Water reaches its maximum density at a temperature of 4°C (39.2°F) rather than 0°C (32°F). Below 4°C, hydrogen bonds cause the water molecules to clump together, most often as tetrahedrons — pyramids

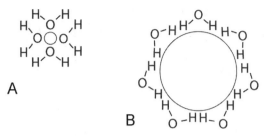

Figure 1.7. Here dipolar water molecules surround (A) a small ion and (B) a much larger charged particle.

with triangular bases. The tetrahedral form is encouraged by the fact that the water molecule actually has two areas with a stronger positive charge (due to the two hydrogen nuclei) and two with a stronger negative charge (due to oxygen's two paired electrons) as shown in Figure 1.8. Tetrahedral forms take up more space than the loose but more closely packed molecules of liquid water. As the temperature decreases from 4° to 0°C, more tetrahedra form and water expands — therefore its density decreases, an important factor in the circulation and turnover of water in lakes and other bodies. At the freezing point, water molecules position themselves into a more widely spaced, low-density pattern and additional expansion occurs.

A **supercooled fluid** is a fluid which has been cooled to below its normal freezing point. This is a common condition in clouds where the temperature may be well below freezing but liquid water still exists. This condition often occurs when water is unable to find a particle to freeze upon. It is supercooled water that produces ice buildup (rime) on airplanes, trees, and other objects when subfreezing clouds are encountered. When supercooled, water, unlike most liquids, experiences a

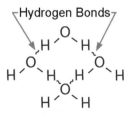

Figure 1.8. Hydrogen bonds resulting from the four areas of charge on the water molecule allows water to form open tetrahedral structures at low temperatures.

Figure 1.9. Ice can take many forms. Above the dark water of Upper Spearfish Creek in South Dakota, shelf ice is visible on the water surface and fragile ice spicules and plates (hoarfrost) adorn the nearby vegetation. A slender blade of grass extends across the stream to form an icy garland.

marked increase in both its ability to absorb heat and in its compressibility. Hydrogen bonding is still at work.

Local variations in the bonding configurations and clumping of water molecules are probably responsible for the multi-phase character of liquid and solid water. Liquid water is unusual in that it appears to consist of two distinct forms or molecular configurations. As ice, water may exist in at least 13 different crystalline arrangements, and an almost infinite number of noncrystalline forms are possible. At least two distinct forms of ice have crystallized above the stream shown in Figure 1.9.

Water possesses many other odd and complex properties, the nature and significance of which are poorly understood. It is truly one of the most mysterious substances known.

Table 1.5 summarizes some of the basic physical properties of water.

1.6 The Origin of Water

Water has been an abundant substance in the Universe since the earliest times. Vast quantities have been detected in distant stars and

Table 1.5. Some Physical Properties for Water

Property	Expression
Color	Colorless
Taste	Tasteless
Odor	Odorless
Density (maximum)	1 g/cm^3 at 4°C (39.2°F)
Specific Gravity	1 at 4°C (39.2°F)
Weight/Mass (all at 0°C, 32°F)	1 gal = 8.33 lb;
	1 imperial gallon = 10.0 lb;
	1 ft^3 = 62.4 lb;
	1 m^3 = 1000 kg = 1 tonne
Boiling Point	212°F at sea level (1 atmosphere pressure); 193.7°F at 10,000 ft
Freezing Point	0°C; 32°F
Specific Heat	1 cal/g/°C; 1 btu/lb/°F
Heat of Vaporization	2,260 joules/g at 100°C and 1 atmosphere
Heat of Fusion	330 joules/g at 0°C
Latent Heat of Vaporization	540 cal/g at 100°C; 600 cal/g at 0°C
Latent Heat of Fusion	80 cal/g at 0°C

galaxies. In July, 2011, astronomers announced the discovery of a distant quasar, probably powered by a supermassive black hole. Quasars are remote "quasi-stellar" objects which may emit more light than ten trillion average stars. It is located about 12 billion light years from Earth, which means the light took 12 billion years to reach us, so we are seeing something that existed when the Universe was very young — a mere 1.6 billion years old. This quasar is surrounded by an enormous cloud of water vapor. This one cloud is believed to contain about 140 trillion times more water than all of Earth's oceans. Today, water exists in various states in our Solar System's gaseous planets and many of their moons.

The origin of Earth's water continues to generate controversy. Earth formed a solid outer crust some 4.55 billion years ago. For several hundred million years before that, a mostly molten proto-Earth was present, its matter gathered together, or accreted, by gravitational attraction of heavy matter orbiting a youthful sun. The heavy matter consisted of innumerable small particles along with larger meteors, asteroids, and comets. Initially, light-weight matter — including hydrogen and water — was largely expelled from the inner part of the solar system by the strong solar wind, which consists of subatomic particles and energy being blasted outward by the sun. As the young Earth took shape, less-dense matter was concentrated near the surface as heavier matter gravitated toward the center of the accumulating mass. Trapped within the molten rock generated as Earth formed were relatively small quantities of light-weight elements which can combine to form volatiles. **Volatiles** are materials which exist as gases under normal atmospheric conditions. One theory is that these volatiles, including water, carbon dioxide, and nitrogen were emitted when molten rock (lava) reached the surface during the fierce volcanic activity of the young Earth. The emissions gradually built up Earth's atmosphere, including water vapor. As temperatures cooled, the water formed clouds, fell from the sky, and gathered in vast pools which covered much of the surface. The process is sometimes called **outgassing**. Volatiles continue to be emitted during volcanic episodes today.

While many scientists favor outgassing from molten rock as the primary source of Earth's water, another set of theories suggests that substantial water may have come from the abundant asteroids, meteoroids, comets, and related bodies which collided with Earth during our solar system's youth. This "heavy bombardment period" lasted from roughly 4.5 to 3.8 billion years ago. These plentiful bodies contain vast quantities of water. For example, the cores of comets are likened to "dirty snowballs." The water contained in these minor members of our solar system may have generated most of Earth's surface waters, although which bodies contributed water, when, and how much remains shrouded in mystery [171, 210].

Water is also present deep inside Earth, but it is not clear how much of this water is derived from downward migrating seawater and how much has been trapped in the interior since the planet's formation.

Earth is the only well-known celestial body capable of sustaining liquid water and higher life forms. Why don't the moon, Mars, or other nearby bodies possess a life-giving atmosphere and hydrosphere? The primary answers appear to be that only Earth (1) has sufficient mass, hence gravity, to hold onto the light-weight gases and (2) is located at an appropriate distance from the sun, thus providing it with a suitable range of temperatures for liquid water to exist. The moon lacked the gravity to prevent loss of atmospheric gases to space; Mars also has far less gravity than Earth and is a bit too far from the sun; Venus is too hot with a crushing and poisonous atmosphere. As a receptacle for water, life, and the sustainability of both, Earth is unique, irreplaceable — at least within that minute part of the Universe which is accessible to us. When viewed from space, Earth appears as an incredibly beautiful, yet lonely and isolated, blue ball, decorated with attractive patterns and filigrees of white clouds. Both blue and white colorations are courtesy of water.

1.7 Basic Types of Water

Water is composed of two gins. Oxygin and hydrogin.
Oxygin is pure gin. Hydrogin is gin and water.

— anonymous (a student's answer to the question,
"What is water composed of?")

1.7.1 Some Common Terms

A bewildering array of terms are applied to water: sweet water, sour water, hard water, soft water, mineral water, grey water, raw, influent, inland, storm, acid, tidal, and on and on. The terms "blue water" and "green water" are often encountered. Blue water usually refers to water withdrawn from surface or subsurface supplies; the water vaporized from surface waters and plants is green water.

In general usage, the term "**salt water**" is synonymous with seawater or **saline** water and it constitutes over 97% of all water on Earth. By far the most abundant salt dissolved in seawater is sodium chloride. Seawater contains approximately 34,500 mg/L (34,500 ppm) of dissolved solids. On average, a cubic mile of seawater will contain over 150 million tons of minerals. Water which is "salty" but contains appreciably less salt than sea water (specifically, 1,000-10,000 mg/L) is often called **brackish water**. Water containing 3,000-10,000 mg/L is considered moderately saline; from 10,000 to 35,000 is very saline. Water containing more than 35,000 mg/L is a **brine**.

Fresh water is often defined as any water containing less than 1,000 mg/L of dissolved solids or, more generally, as any water suitable for drinking — that is, **potable** water. But be careful. Whether water containing, say, 500 mg/L of solids is acceptable for drinking depends upon exactly what dissolved minerals are present. In general, water suitable for drinking and for many industrial purposes should contain 500 mg/L or less of dissolved solids. Stream waters average around 120 mg/

L in dissolved solids but vary greatly from less than 50 mg/L in pure mountain streams to over 50,000 mg/L in streams which flow over saline materials.

Polluted water generally refers to any water containing impurities which make it unfit or undesirable for a certain use. Most commonly, polluted water indicates water capable of causing disease or death due to the presence of toxic substances or organisms. The term, **contaminated water**, is often used as synonymous with polluted water, but technically, contaminated refers merely to the presence of impurities, which may or may not be harmful. Dozens of other water terms are in common use and many will be introduced later in this book.

1.7.2 Atmospheric Water

Atmospheric water consists of water vapor, ice crystals, and liquid droplets — the last two, in sufficient quantity, make up clouds. The amount of water in Earth's atmosphere varies, ranging from less than 0.02% (by volume) in arid areas to as much as 4% or 5% in warm, humid areas. If all the atmospheric water were to precipitate out at once, it would equal a layer one inch (2.5 centimeters) deep over Earth's surface. When this water falls to the earth as precipitation, it may become either surface water which collects upon or runs off the land, or it may seep into the earth. Atmospheric water helps shield us from hazardous ultraviolet radiation and also acts as a greenhouse gas by intercepting outgoing infrared radiation, or heat, from Earth. A **greenhouse gas** is any gas that intercepts outgoing heat from Earth, thus warming the atmosphere. Water vapor results in more warming of the lower atmosphere than any other greenhouse gas.

1.7.3 Surface and Subsurface Water

Surface water refers to all waters — salt water, fresh water, ice, snow — which exist on Earth's surface. **Subsurface water** is water that resides below the land surface. Most of this water is the **groundwater** which saturates the rock material it occurs in and which moves in response to the forces acting upon it. The upper surface of groundwater is called the **water table** and is designated in diagrams in this book by a broken line and an inverted triangle, ∇ (Figure 1.10). Above the water table, most water shares open spaces in the earth material with air, hence this unsaturated area is called the **zone of aeration** and the area below the water table is the **zone of saturation**. Water in the zone of saturation is often called **phreatic water**; water in the zone of aeration is **vadose**

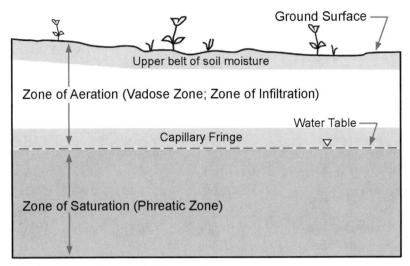

Figure 1.10. Major zones of subsurface water.

water (think of the "va" as implying many "*va*cant" pore spaces). As shown on Figure 1.10, the vadose zone also includes an upper belt of soil moisture vital to plant growth and a saturated bottom zone of water held in place by capillary forces. Section 5.5 examines these features in detail. The vadose/unsaturated and phreatic/saturated zones are not static. Their extent and properties vary through time in response to numerous seasonal, climatic, and human influences.

1.8 Distribution of Water

Table 1.6 provides a basic list of the occurrence and quantity of water present on and near Earth's surface.

Earth has three, four, or five oceans, depending upon who is defining them, covering about 71% of Earth's surface area. The Pacific Ocean alone accounts for half the surface area of Earth's oceans and over half of the water volume. If we add lakes, inland seas, and ice cover, the water-covered part of Earth increases to 74.4% of the planet's surface area, representing a total area of 146 million mi^2 (380 M km^2).

About 70% of the world's fresh water is in the solid state, and 90% of that is on Antarctica and most of the remainder is on Greenland. Nearly all of this is in the form of **glaciers** — dense, plastically deforming (moving) masses of ice that form wherever subfreezing temperatures and precipitation allow snow to accumulate over time faster than it can melt.

Table 1.6. The Distribution of Water on Earth

Category of Water	Volume[1] (km³)	Volume[1] (mi³)	Percent of: Fresh Water	Percent of: Total Water
Sea water	1,338,000,000	321,000,000		96.54
Glaciers/snow	24,064,000	5,773,000	68.6	1.74
Groundwater	23,400,000	5,614,000		1.69
Saline groundwater	12,870,000	3,088,000		0.93
Fresh groundwater	10,530,000	2,526,000	30.1	0.76
Permafrost	300,000	71,970	0.86	0.022
Lakes	176,400	42,320		0.013
Freshwater lakes	91,000	21,830	0.26	0.007
Salt-water lakes	85,400	20,490		0.007
Wetlands	17,000	4,080	0.05	0.001
Soil moisture	16,500	3,959	0.05	0.001
Atmosphere	12,900	3,095	0.04	0.001
Rivers	2,120	509	0.002	0.0002
Biological water	1,120	269	0.003	0.0001
Total fresh water	34,700,000	8,300,000		2.5
Total water	1,386,000,000	332,500,000		

[1] A cubic kilometer (km³) of water is about one trillion liters, or 264 billion gallons. A cubic mile (mi³) is about 4.2 trillion liters, or 1.1 trillion gallons. Sources: [283, 295, 360, 513, 535].

Sandwiched between the Antarctic ice sheet and its bedrock base lies a complex network of freshwater lakes, marshes, and transient streams containing at least 10,000 km³ of fresh water [196].

The remaining 30% of Earth's fresh water is liquid water and roughly 99% of that is groundwater, based upon the figures in Table 1.6. Other evaluations of world water distribution may vary slightly from these figures, depending upon the assumptions and data employed.

Water locked up in rocks and minerals deep within the crust and mantle is not a usable water resource and is not included in the statistics given in Table 1.6.

Geology

Geology is the music of the Earth.

— Hans Cloos

2.1 Introduction

We are concerned with water on or in the outer part of the solid Earth. The study of planet Earth is geology, and some knowledge of geology is essential if one is to understand the distribution and behavior of water on our planet.

The planet Earth, with which humans interact, is often considered to comprise four "spheres," including:

- the **atmosphere,** the gaseous envelope surrounding the planet;
- the **hydrosphere,** the waters of Earth;
- the **biosphere,** the life forms of Earth; and
- the **geosphere,** the solid, inorganic part of Earth.

This chapter offers a brief overview of the geosphere, especially its outer shell, and the major patterns and processes that make it up, all of which is necessary to a basic understanding of hydrogeology. Figure 2.1 illustrates the major subdivisions of the geosphere.

The **lithosphere** (rock sphere) is the brittle outer part of the geosphere. The lithosphere has an average thickness of about 100 kilometers (60 miles). Below the lithosphere, high temperatures and pressure cause the rock to lose rigidity and behave like a plastic material. **Brittle** materials tend to fracture or rupture under strong forces; **plastic** materials, even though solids, tend to bend or flow rather than break. This is **plastic deformation** — think of the flowing of cold molasses, or perhaps a glacier, or the bending of an iron rod.

The upper part of Earth's brittle lithosphere is the **crust** and the lower part consists of the uppermost zone of the mantle (Figure 2.1). The crust is made of the common rocks and extends to an average depth of about 40 kilometers (24 miles) under continents and 7 kilometers (4.3 miles)

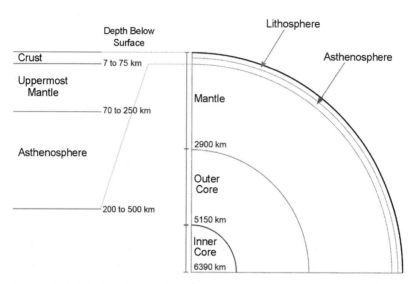

Figure 2.1. The interior structure of Earth. The distances are depth below the surface to the major boundaries between Earth's interior zones. Note that the mantle extends upward into the lithosphere and includes an uppermost brittle zone underlain by a very plastic "weak" zone, the asthenosphere, which facilitates the movements of the overlying lithospheric plates — the uppermost mantle and crust. The boundaries between the upper zones at the left are highly variable, generally being very thick below high elevation areas of continents and thin below ocean basins.

under oceans. It is the least dense zone of Earth's geosphere. The **mantle** consists of heavier rock rich in iron and magnesium and extends inward some 2,900 kilometers (1,740 miles) to a core rich in iron and nickel. The **outer core** is liquid and the source of Earth's magnetic field. The **inner core** is solid.

2.2 Tectonic and Volcanic Processes

Earth is a very active planet. Two major types of geologic activity — tectonic and volcanic — affect the lithosphere. **Tectonic** activity involves the deformation of solid rock by forces generated within the geosphere. Examples include **faulting** which occurs when masses of rock slip or grind past each other along zones of displacement called **faults** (Plate 2: Top), **folding** which develops when plastic deformation causes layers of rock to bend, and simple fracturing. The results of tectonic activity are seen in the basic architecture of Earth's crust with its vast array of structural forms and arrangements. When rock masses slip rapidly past each other, **earthquakes** are generated. When huge amounts of sediment accumulate in one area, that part of the lithosphere slowly sinks under the weight, much like adding cargo to a ship. This vertical downsinking, or **subsidence**, is possible because of the plastic nature of the rock below the lithosphere. These and many other forms of earth movements are tectonic in origin.

Volcanic activity, or volcanism, occurs when hot material from the interior impacts Earth's solid surface. **Volcanoes** are hills or mountains built up by the accumulation of rock matter around a conduit or vent (Plate 2: Bottom). Other types of volcanism include massive outpourings of molten rock (**lava flows**) and violent explosions.

2.3 Geologic History

When considering geological processes, our normal, human time perspective needs to shift gears. Many geological activities, such as the formation of rock or the uplift and shaping of mountain ranges, require many millions of years to produce readily perceivable results. Even geologically rapid processes such as the formation of canyons, caves, glaciers, or large river deltas and floodplains are painfully slow compared to human time perspectives, which tend to be shaped by our life span of decades and our recorded human history of a few thousand years. The evidence strongly indicates that the age of Earth's oldest rocks are on the order of 4.55 billion years, meaning that nature has had a virtually unfathomable stretch of time in which to generate and modify the landscapes and lifeforms that characterize our planet.

Table 2.1 offers a simplified version of geologic time. The major subdivisions of geologic time are **eras** which in turn are broken down into **periods**. Periods are further subdivided into **epochs**. In this book, we will be mainly concerned with the current period, the Quaternary, which can be loosely thought of as the most recent "ice age." The **Quaternary Period** of geologic time represents the last 2.6 million years of Earth history and is characterized by colder than normal conditions during which much of Earth's fresh water has existed as ice. The Quaternary is broken down into lengthy time intervals called **glacials** and shorter intervals called **interglacials.** Glaciers covered some 30% of Earth's land area during glacial intervals, compared to about 10% during interglacials. Due to the substantial changes in the amount of water locked up in ice, sea level fluctuated during the Quaternary, rising during interglacials and falling during glacials, by a maximum of about 140 meters

Table 2.1. The Geologic Time Scale

Duration[1]	Era	Period	Epoch
2.6-0	Cenozoic	Quaternary	Holocene/Recent
65-2.6		Tertiary	Pleistocene
145-65		Cretaceous	Pliocene
200-145	Mesozoic	Jurassic	Miocene
251-200		Triassic	Oligocene
			Eocene
300-251		Permian	Paleocene
311-300		Pennsylvanian[a]	
355-311		Mississippian[a]	
418-355	Paleozoic	Devonian	
441-418		Silurian	
490-441		Ordovician	
544-490		Cambrian	
4,550-544	Precambrian		

[1] Duration is shown in approximate millions of years before present.

[a] Outside of North America the Pennsylvanian and Mississippian periods are combined into what is called the Carboniferous Period.

(460 feet). This produced major impacts on coastal regions around the world. For the last 12,000 years, Earth has been experiencing an interglacial episode, often called the Holocene, or Recent, Epoch. During glacials, many regions of Earth which were not covered by glacial ice had environments different than they do today. Some places that are currently arid or semiarid, for example, were much wetter than they are today and abundant groundwater reserves accumulated. Today, these regions no longer receive enough precipitation to recharge those groundwater reserves.

2.4 Rocks and Minerals

2.4.1 Rock Classification

Rocks are aggregates of minerals. **Minerals** are naturally occurring, inorganically formed crystalline solids with a definite chemical composition. A **crystalline** solid is one possessing a periodic, or repeated,

48

internal arrangement of atoms, much like a three-dimensional wallpaper motif. Their crystalline nature and chemical makeup give minerals the characteristic properties by which they can be identified.

Rocks are classified into three main groups — igneous, sedimentary, and metamorphic. **Igneous** rocks are those which formed from molten rock material. The two types of igneous rock are intrusive, or plutonic, rocks and extrusive, or volcanic, rocks. **Intrusive** rocks are formed from **magma**, molten rock located below the surface of Earth. Important igneous rocks include granite, pegmatite, diorite, and gabbro. **Extrusive** rocks include (a) those formed from **lava,** molten rock discharged onto the surface of Earth, examples of which are basalt, andesite, rhyolite, and obsidian, and (b) those formed from fragmental debris associated with volcanic activities, examples of which are tuff and volcanic breccia.

Sedimentary rocks are formed by lithification, or the hardening of sediment. **Clastic**, or fragmental, sedimentary rocks are formed by the lithification of solid particles (clasts or fragments); examples include conglomerate, sandstone, and shale. **Chemical sedimentary rocks** are precipitated from solution; examples include limestone, dolomite, and gypsum.

Metamorphic rocks are formed in the solid state by the alteration of preexisting rock by heat, pressure, or hot circulating (hydrothermal) fluids; examples include slate, schist, gneiss, and marble.

Table 2.2 provides a simple, condensed classification scheme for some basic rock types. The classification is based primarily upon the rock's mode of origin. Extensive schemes exist for more detailed naming and classifying of specific rock types such as "granitic" rocks or carbonate rocks (those such as limestone and dolomite that contain the CO_3 radical). Most rocks contain only one to five different minerals. About 60% of the minerals that make up Earth's crustal rock belong to a group of aluminosilicate minerals — minerals that contain aluminum, silicon, and oxygen — called the **feldspars**. Feldspars tend to weather chemically into clay. The second most abundant mineral is quartz, SiO_2, or silica. **Quartz** is hard, difficult to break, and chemically quite stable, and thus quite resistant. Hence, rocks with abundant quartz tend to be well represented in peaks, ridges, and other high-elevation landforms. The term **felsic** is often applied to rocks rich in white or reddish-colored feldspars and quartz. These rocks tend to be light in both color and weight. For rocks at the opposite end of the compositional spectrum, the term *mafic* is used. **Mafic** rocks lack quartz and the light-colored feldspars but are rich in magnesium and iron. Mafic rocks tend to be dark in color and heavy.

Table 2.2. Table of Common Rocks

DESCRIPTION	ROCK NAME
Igneous	
Extrusive (formed on Earth's surface)	
Glassy	
- light, frothy	Pumice
- many vesicles (air holes)	Scoria
Pyroclastic (composed of fragments)	
- fine-grained	Tuff
- coarse-grained	Volcanic Breccia
Intrusive (formed below Earth's surface)	
Felsic composition (minerals light in color and mass)	
- fine-grained	Rhyolite
- coarse-grained	Granite
Intermediate composition	
- fine-grained	Andesite
- coarse-grained	Diorite
Mafic composition (minerals dark in color, heavy)	
- fine-grained	Basalt
- coarse-grained	Gabbro
Sedimentary	
Clastic (composed of fragments)	
Coarse-grained (fragments >2 mm)	
- angular	Breccia
- rounded	Conglomerate
Medium-grained (1/16 - 2 mm)	Sandstone
Fine-grained (1/256 - 1/16 mm)	Siltstone
Very fine-grained (<1/256 mm)	Shale
Chemical Precipitates	
Composed of $CaCO_3$ (calcite)	Limestone
Composed of $CaMg(CO_3)_2$ (dolomite)	Dolomite
Composed of SiO_2 (silica)	Chert, Agate, etc.
Composed of $NaCl$ (halite)	Rock Salt
Composed of $CaSO_4 \cdot 2H_2O$ (gypsum)	Gypsum

Table 2.2, continued

DESCRIPTION	ROCK NAME

Sedimentary (continued)

Organic

Composed of carbon and impurities	Coal

Metamorphic

Foliated (contains elongated, parallel mineral grains)

Very fine-grained	Slate
Fine-grained	Phyllite
Coarse-grained, platy minerals common	Schist
Coarse-grained, layered appearance	Gneiss

Non-Foliated

Composed of quartz	Quartzite
Composed of calcite or dolomite	Marble

2.4.2 Rock Origins and Properties

A. Igneous Rocks

When molten rock hardens or freezes below Earth's surface, its chemical constituents form mineral crystals which slowly grow and eventually produce a three-dimensional mosaic of interlocking grains — the result is known as a **crystalline texture**. The most common intrusive rocks tend to form fairly homogeneous masses of coarse-grained (visible to the naked eye) rock. The most common intrusive rock is **granite**, a massive felsic rock (Figure 2.2A). Granite-like rock constitutes most of the crust underlying Earth's continents.

Volcanic rock is produced either by the flowing of molten rock onto Earth's surface or by fragments ejected into the air (Figure 2.2B). When magma is extruded onto the surface, it is called **lava** (Figure 2.2B). Lava rocks are fine-grained (most mineral grains are not visible to the naked eye) and typically result from repeated outpourings of molten rock. Each outpouring produces an extensive puddle or sheet of molten rock which soon hardens (Figure 2.2C). Hence large exposures will exhibit a crude layered appearance formed by the various flows (Figure 2.2D). The most

Figure 2.2. Examples of various rock types. **A.** Granite in the Laramie Range, Wyoming. Granite is a massive, felsic, intrusive rock that crystallized deep below the surface. **B.** Large cinder cone volcano in southwest Utah, built up from fragments ejected during eruption. In the foreground is the edge of a young mafic lava flow which was extruded from the base of the volcano. **C.** Aerial view to northeast along US Route 20/26/93 at the Snake River Plain in southern Idaho. The dark area to the right of the highway consists primarily of young basaltic lava flows near the entrance to the Craters of the Moon National Monument. The area to the left is older volcanic terrain and thus has some soil and grass cover. At the lower left is Grassy Cone, one of numerous cinder cones in the area. At the upper left is the black lobe of a

young lava flow. **D.** Flood basalts exposed at Dry Falls in the Columbia Plateau of central Washington. **E.** Camel Rock in the Sand Creek area along the Colorado-Wyoming border shows stratification in horizontal sedimentary rock. **F.** Shear cliffs of resistant sandstone in Canyon de Chelly National Monument, Arizona. **G.** Soft, nonresistant sedimentary rock strata in badlands near the Little Missouri River in western North Dakota. **H.** Poorly sorted clastic bedrock exposed at Chimney Rock along the south side of the Shoshone River Valley in western Wyoming. **I.** Pig Hole, Giles County, Virginia, is a deep karst shaft in limestone. **J.** Foliation in a granitic gneiss. Circular masses are comprised of the mineral garnet. From a roadcut along the Pend Oreille River in northern Idaho.

common volcanic rock is **basalt**, a mafic lava rock which makes up most of the crust underlying the oceans, although some extensive areas of basalt, often called flood basalts, occur also on continents (Figure 2.2C and D).

Pyroclastic, or fragmental, volcanic rock is generated when eruptions send rock debris, blobs of molten rock, and fine ash into the air. The coarse debris will be deposited nearby, where it may form a volcano (Figure 2.2B) or be carried downslope by streams or mudflows. The fine ash can be carried many miles by wind. During violent eruptions, heavy superheated masses of ash may be ejected and deposited nearby to form rocks known as ashflow tuffs or welded tuffs.

B. Sedimentary Rocks

A **sediment** is a solid material made of mineral fragments. Most sediment is deposited by settling out of a fluid, usually water or air. Sediment may consist of detritus (fragments of preexisting rock), chemical precipitates, or organic matter. The **detrital**, or **clastic**, sediments range in size from large boulders to microscopic platelets of clay. **Chemical precipitates** are made of crystals which form directly from an aqueous solution. Chemical precipitates may be inorganic or biologic in origin. Biochemical sediments are precipitated through the action of organisms such as corals and shell-making plants and animals. The category of **organic sedimentary rock** is generally limited to accumulations of plant matter which may eventually form coal. Sediments are laid down in successive episodes of deposition, one blanket of sediment upon another, producing a distinctive horizontal layering (Figure 2.2E, F, and G). The individual layers are called **strata** and the layered structure which results is called **stratification**. Upon burial, the sediments are subjected to compaction from increasing pressure, cementation by binding agents deposited by circulating groundwater, or other processes which **lithify** the sediments, turning them into stone. Organic material may be trapped in sedimentary rock where it forms deposits of natural gas, crude oil, or solid petroleum matter.

Sedimentary rocks vary greatly in their properties. The coarse-grained conglomerates and sandstones tend to be rich in quartz and quite resistant to weathering and erosion (Figure 2.2E and F). Fine-grained shales, formed from tiny clay fragments, tend to be soft and easily eroded. **Sorting** refers to the degree of uniformity in a certain characteristic, such as grain size. Some sediments will have a wide range of particle sizes and are described as poorly sorted (Figure 2.3). Other sediments and rocks will be composed almost entirely of one particle size, such as a well-sorted

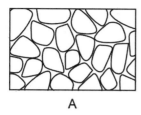 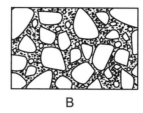

A   B

Figure 2.3. Sorting and grading. These terms are opposites. A well-sorted sediment is poorly graded and vice versa. **A** shows a well-sorted (uniformly sized) sediment and **B** shows a poorly sorted sediment containing a wide variety of grain sizes. More water can be present and water will flow more easily through **A** because of the unfilled spaces between the grains.

sandstone. Another commonly used term to describe uniformity in clastic sediment is **grading**. A well-graded sediment has a wide variety of sediment or clast sizes — that is, it is poorly sorted (Figure 2.2H).

Limestone and dolomite vary greatly in texture, though most are made of fine interlocking crystals of the minerals calcite ($CaCO_3$) and dolomite ($CaMg[CO_3]_2$). These rocks dissolve much more readily than most rocks, resulting in subsurface conduits and caves formed by circulating groundwater (Figure 2.2I). This produces a unique type of topography called **karst**, a landscape characterized by a lack of surface streams and numerous depressions called **sinkholes** which result from the dissolving away of underlying rock.

C. Metamorphic Rocks

Metamorphic rocks form when preexisting rock develops distinctive new textures or minerals in response to changes in the physical and chemical environment. Heat, pressure, and chemicals brought in by circulating groundwater can cause new minerals to grow, existing grains to become deformed, new fractures to develop, and other significant changes. Many metamorphic rocks — such as slate, schist, and gneiss — have a distinctive alignment of mineral grains called **foliation** (Figure 2.2J). In others, a general fusing together and recrystallization of minerals occurs, creating a more homogeneous rock. Hence a limestone can be metamorphosed to a marble, or a quartz sandstone, to a quartzite.

2.5 Plate Tectonics

The common rocks described above constitute Earth's outermost solid zone, the crust. The crust envelopes the entire sphere of the planet and is divided into two major types. The **continental crust**, the part that underlies the continents, is thick and dominated by low-density granites and similar rocks of a dominantly felsic composition. The **oceanic crust** is thin and formed mostly of basalt. Below the crust is a heavier, more mafic rock matter belonging to the mantle. The uppermost part of the mantle is brittle like the crust, but below this the heat and pressure causes rock to behave plastically. The crust and uppermost mantle make up the **lithosphere** which can be envisioned as floating upon this denser underlying plastic material.

The lithosphere is broken up into a mosaic of irregular pieces, called **tectonic plates**. Most tectonic and volcanic activity tends to occur along the edges of the plates where the lithospheric segments jostle each other for position. The root source of these activities appears to be heat generated by pressure and the decay of radioactive isotopes in Earth's interior. Unequal distribution of the heat, combined with the plastic nature of the rock material below the lithosphere, causes currents to develop within the mantle. These movements produce considerable **stress** (force or pressure) and **strain** (deformation) in the overlying lithosphere.

Hot material deep in the mantle will slowly rise until it reaches the lithosphere. There, it will split into laterally moving currents which drag the overlying plates of the lithosphere along with them. This produces extensive linear zones of great tension where the brittle lithosphere is literally being torn apart. This constitutes a **divergent boundary**, one of the three major types of plate boundaries, as shown in the central part of Figure 2.4. Many divergent boundaries are characterized at the surface by large **mid-ocean ridges** generated by the upward motion of the subcrustal currents. Most divergent boundaries contain **rift zones** along their crests produced by the down-dropping of blocks of lithosphere along the central axis of extension. Examples include the rift along the Mid-Atlantic Ridge and the African Rift zone.

When a laterally flowing mantle current encounters another, opposing mantle current, an area of massive compression is generated where two lithospheric plates are colliding. As the underlying plastic material slowly flows along just below the lithosphere, it loses heat to the overlying plate and then to the atmosphere. The cooling causes the lithospheric slab to become denser and thicker as more brittle rock is added at the base of the lithosphere. By the time a slowly creeping plate encounters another plate and its associated mantle current, the slab and its underlying plastic mantle matter are typically cool enough and heavy enough to begin sinking back into Earth's interior, as shown on the left and right

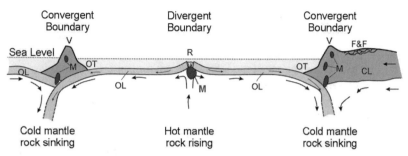

Figure 2.4. Simplified cross-section of the upper part of the solid Earth showing the relationships between the brittle lithosphere and the underlying plastic mantle at three important plate boundaries. The vertical scale is greatly exaggerated. Arrows represent direction of movement of mantle currents and the lithospheric plates. Key: CL = continental lithosphere (continental crust and uppermost mantle); F & F = folding and faulting of the continental crust; M = magma bodies; OL = oceanic lithosphere (oceanic crust and uppermost mantle); OT = ocean trench; R = rift valley; V = volcanoes.

sides of Figure 2.4. The resultant zone of compression in the lithosphere constitutes a **convergent boundary.**

At convergent boundaries, a deep **oceanic trench** often develops at the surface. The trench results when a downward-plunging mantle current drags its overriding lithospheric plate along with it, a process called **subduction.** If low-density continental crust is present on the converging edge of one of the lithospheric plates, the denser oceanic plate will be subducted into the mantle and the lighter continental plate will be forced upward. The enormous horizontal forces generated by this contact produces huge linear mountain ranges containing intensely folded, faulted, and metamorphosed masses of rock on the adjoining parts of the continental plate. If both of the colliding plates are continental, the abundance of low-density continental crust can generate exceptionally massive mountain ranges such as the Himalayan Mountains.

Large quantities of sediment, great chunks of crustal rock, water, and other low-density surface materials can be dragged down into a subduction zone where they can mix with other rock material. Under the great heat and pressure generated by this huge lithospheric vice, the rock material which originated in cooler, near-surface environments will be unstable and often melts, yielding magmas. Some magma hardens underground to form large intrusions and other magma migrates to the surface to generate volcanic activity. Intrusions, volcanism, earthquakes, and other characteristics of today's young, active mountain ranges are all nicely explained by plate tectonics. On Figure 2.4, the convergent boundary between ocean plates at the left would develop a long chain of volcanoes, an **island arc**, adjacent to the trench. The convergent boundary at the right would produce a major mountain-building episode, an **orogeny**, on the adjacent continent.

A third major contact between lithospheric plates is a **transform boundary**. Here, the plates tend to slip past each other along large zones of displacement called **transform faults**. The notorious San Andreas Fault of California is such a boundary. Figure 2.5 identifies the major tectonic plates and boundaries of Earth.

It is worth noting that water is a vitally important participant in most deep-seated geologic processes and in the formation of many minerals and rocks at depths well below those in which normal groundwater occurs. Water has profound influences upon nearly all geologic processes including metamorphism, plutonic and volcanic activity, and plate tectonics.

2.6 Surficial Processes

Nothing is static for long in or on Earth. Once formed, rocks continue to be altered by changes in temperature, pressure, chemical environment, and other forces or agents acting within the planet or at its surface.

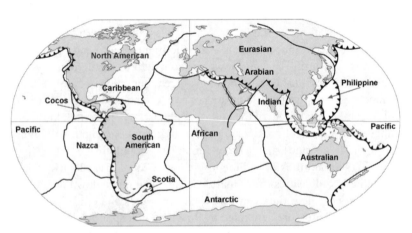

Figure 2.5. Major tectonic plates of Earth. Simple lines represent divergent boundaries; toothed lines represent convergent boundaries with the teeth pointing in the direction the downward-sinking plates are moving.

2.6.1 Weathering

Most rocks are formed below the surface where pressure, temperature, and the chemical environment are much different than at the surface. When exposed to conditions at Earth's surface, rocks are unstable and slowly, by human standards, become **weathered** — broken down in place. Two major types of weathering operate synergistically to alter exposed bedrock. **Mechanical weathering** breaks solid masses of rock down into smaller fragments, a process also known as **disintegration** (Figure 2.6A). **Chemical weathering** alters the basic chemistry of the rock material, such as when a feldspar mineral is changed to a clay mineral. The upper part of exposed bedrock often becomes extensively weathered to form a zone of unconsolidated rock debris called **saprolite** (Figure 2.6B). This in-place weathered bedrock is most extensive in moist environments because water greatly accelerates most weathering processes. Saprolite can range from a few inches to hundreds of feet in depth.

2.6.2 Mass Wasting

Landscapes consist largely of slopes and the weathered material underlying these slopes will migrate downslope under the influence of gravity. The downward movement of surficial rock material due to gravity — that is, without the help of another medium such as running water — is called **mass wasting**, or mass gravity movement. Mass wasting encompasses movements ranging from imperceptibly slow (creep) through moderate (earthflows, rotational slides, soil slips) to catastrophic (rockslides, avalanches) events. Some examples of mass wasting are provided in Figure 2.7 and Plate 3. The deposits left by mass wasting are called **colluvium** (Table 2.3).

Water is a primary cause or expeditor of nearly all weathering and mass wasting processes, both chemical and mechanical. For example, water undergoing numerous episodes of freezing and thawing in rock fractures and interstices generates considerable pressure and greatly aids the physical disintegration of bedrock. The constant agitation of regolith by repeated freeze-thaw cycles accelerates the downslope movement of everything from huge blocks of rock to minute soil particles. Frequent freeze-thaw episodes over many years create a unique suite of surface features characteristic of cold climates. The field of **periglacial geology** focuses on these cold-climate processes.

Figure 2.6. A. Coarse weathered rock fragments litter the ground around this knob of granitic bedrock in northern Idaho. **B.** Roadcut of granitic saprolite near Sasheen Lake in northern Idaho. The round boulder at the top, called a corestone, has survived the weathering; the boulder is about five feet in diameter.

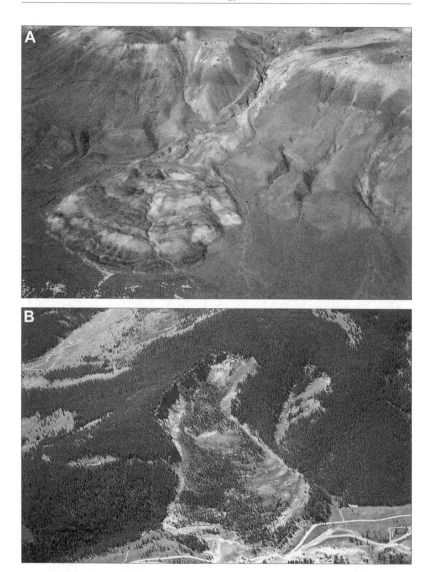

Figure 2.7. Examples of mass wasting. **A.** Aerial view of large earthflow along the north side of the Columbia River valley in Washington state. At this site, earth debris flows slowly but perceptibly from higher elevations down a side valley and forms a large spatulate toe at the base of the slope. **B.** Aerial view of Taylor Fork rockslide, Madison Range, Montana. Rockslides are rapid, often catastrophic events that occur when masses of bedrock become unstable due to such factors as weathering, erosion, or saturation with water.

Table 2.3. Common Types of Regolith

ORIGIN	NAMES
Residual (Sedentary) Deposits	
In-place weathering of bedrock; original rock structures preserved	Saprolite
In-place weathering of parent material; original structures not preserved	Residuum (residual material)
Weathering and related influences of near-surface regolith or rock	Soil
Very old soils, usually buried	Paleosols
Surface accumulations of organic material	Peat, Swampy Deposits, etc.
Transported Deposits	
Mass wasting along slopes	Colluvium
Stream deposition	Alluvium
Wind deposition of silt	Loess
Wind deposition of sand	Aeolian Sand, Dune Sand, etc.
Wave deposition	Beach Sand, Pebbles
Glacial deposition (all)	Drift
Deposited directly by glacial ice	Till
Deposited by glacial meltwater	Outwash
Exposed lake deposits	Lacustrine Sediments
Chemical precipitation (common in arid regions, along coasts, from mineral-laden waters, etc.)	Salt, Limestone, Marl, Tufa, Travertine, Coral, etc.
Air-borne volcanic fragments	Volcanic Ash, Cinders, Bombs, Ejecta, etc.

Note: Numerous gradations and subdivisions of these terms have often been employed.

2.6.3 Erosion and Deposition

Erosion is the entrainment (picking up) and transport of mineral matter by an external agent such as running water, wind, glaciers, groundwater, or waves. These same erosional agents also deposit mineral matter as sediment, a process called **deposition** or **sedimentation**. The most influential agent of erosion and deposition at Earth's surface is running water. Water which flows over Earth's surface is **runoff**. **Overland flow** is runoff which is spread over the land surface, usually as thin sheets of flowing water or in small ephemeral rills. **Streamflow** or natural channel flow — rivers, creeks, brooks, and other "streams" — is runoff which is confined to a channel. Additional information on surface water is provided in Chapter 4.

The mineral matter carried by streams, be it in solution or as particles, is called **load**. Stream, or **fluvial**, deposits are **alluvium**. Alluvium may consist of thin deposits which cover only small areas or may accumulate over thousands of square miles and to depths of several miles. Streams constantly pick up and carry off rock particles. This fluvial erosion gradually deepens the channel. At the same time, weathering and mass wasting along the sides of the valley deliver sediment to the stream. Eventually, the downcutting will reach an elevation, or a **base level**, below which vertical stream erosion cannot continue. When this occurs, the stream will expend its energy meandering from side to side, thus widening the valley floor, a process called **lateral planation**. The nearly level landform which is eventually formed along the valley bottom is a **floodplain**. Runoff erosion also produces gently sloping, planar landforms called **pediments** at the base of many highland areas. If the base level remains the same and planation by running water continues for a long period of time, an extensive, nearly level plain — called a pediplain or peneplain — may form. In some areas, usually semiarid regions with relatively soft, poorly consolidated rock, very rapid stream erosion will occur, forming densely gullied landscapes called **badlands**.

Wind can also pick up and carry loose particles. Wind, or **aeolian**, deposits include sand and **loess** — aeolian silt or dust-sized deposits. **Glaciers** are moving masses of ice and, where present, they dominate the erosional and depositional processes. Sediment deposited directly by glaciers is **till**; if the sediment is washed out of the glaciers by meltwater and then deposited, it is called **outwash**. Figure 2.8 illustrates several common erosional and depositional landforms.

Figure 2.8. A few common erosional and depositional landforms. **A.** The most important erosional agent affecting Earth's surface is running water. Streams in upland areas, as in this view of Elk Creek Falls in Idaho, are actively eroding bedrock as they deepen their valleys. **B.** When streams encounter flat or gently sloping areas, they tend to drop their solid load forming extensive deposits of alluvium. This air photo shows a large alluvial apron at the base of the White Knob Mountains in Idaho. **C.** When streams enter standing water, they will deposit their sediment to form a delta. This small delta is being deposited in Sherburne Lake, Canada. **D.** Mountain landscapes shaped mainly by glacial erosion are characterized by rugged peaks and U-shaped valleys as seen in this view in the Teton Range of Wyoming. **E.** Glaciers erode and deposit large quantities of rock debris. Some of the debris is deposited along the margin of the glacier as moraines. In this

aerial view, Wallowa Lake, near Joseph, Oregon, occupies the position of a former tongue of ice that flowed out of the Wallowa Mountains. The lake is bordered by two large lateral moraines which were deposited along the edge of the glacier. **F.** View of a large deflation hollow south of Laramie, Wyoming. This depression was formed primarily by wind carrying away fine sand and silt loosened by weathering of the local bedrock. **G.** The sand and silt carried by wind is eventually deposited, often in fields of sand dunes as in this air view in southern Idaho. **H.** Along coasts, waves constantly attack the land and/or redistribute sediment. Shorelines are among the most active and rapidly changing environments. This view along the Oregon coast north of Newport shows a fairly level surface (a wave-cut platform) and sea cliffs produced by wave erosion as well as some wave-deposited sand.

2.6.4 Regolith and Soil

A general term for all terrestrial (land-based) unconsolidated material overlying solid rock (bedrock) is **regolith**. Regolith is important in groundwater studies because most of the world's fresh liquid water is in the subsurface and the best, most accessible, and most utilized subsurface water often occurs in some type of regolith. Also, over most of Earth's surface, water must penetrate these surficial materials to reach the water table and become groundwater. Common types of regolith are identified in Table 2.3.

The upper part of the regolith, the material immediately underlying most of Earth's land surface, is generally called "soil." Good healthy soil is one of the three most vital resources on Earth; clean liquid fresh water and breathable air being the other two. It is also a notoriously difficult term to define, and means different things to different people. To engineers, for example, "soil" is a general term for any near-surface material which can be removed by a shovel or backhoe. If the material is hard and must undergo blasting or other disruption before removal, it is termed "rock." To an agronomist or farmer, soil is the medium which supports plant growth. To many average folks, soil is, God forbid, just "dirt." Geologists and soil scientists (pedologists) need to be more precise when describing the vast variety of materials which provide the foundation upon which we live, build, and grow our food. Herein, **soil** is defined as a naturally occurring earth material, usually exhibiting horizons, which has developed over time in response to the surface environment. Soil **horizons** are zones within the soil, roughly parallel to the surface, which exhibit distinct characteristics developed in response to weathering processes and water migration, usually downward infiltration. The six major factors which influence soil formation are climate, the material the soil forms from, slope of the terrain, organic activity, time, and local geological processes influencing the site.

2.6.5 Denudation

The result of the three surficial processes of weathering, mass wasting, and erosion is a ceaseless lowering of the overall elevation of the terrain. This reduction in elevation is called **denudation**. During denudation, the terrain is sculpted into a vast array of hills, valleys, plains, and other landforms that characterize and beautify our planet's surface. If ongoing tectonic and volcanic processes did not create new mountain ranges and generate uplift, the entire land surface would be reduced to a nearly level erosional surface, a peneplain, in some 300 million years. Earth's geological landscapes are, then, a product of two great forces: internal forces, powered by internal heat, which tend to build up and external forces, powered by the sun, which tend to wear down.

2.7 Porosity and Permeability

The characteristics which were part of an original rock are often called **primary** properties and those which formed later are **secondary** properties. Hence the spaces between the grains or the strata of a sedimentary rock are primary features; fractures or other openings which developed later are secondary features.

Especially important in determining the hydrologic characteristics of any earth material are the two properties of porosity and permeability. **Porosity** is the percent of open space — pores or interstices — in a material. In equation form, porosity (P) equals pore volume (V_p) divided by total volume (V_t) of the material:

$$P = \frac{V_p}{V_t}$$

Example: Using the Equation

If a container of sediment occupies 50 cm³ (V_t) and 6 cm³ of that volume is void space (V_p), the porosity (P) is 6/50 = 0.12, or 12%. A rock with 12% porosity is 88% solid rock and 12% open space.

The pores are not empty, of course; they will contain gases or liquids. Pore spaces come in many guises bearing many names. Pore space may be represented by the spaces between grains of sediment, solutional cavities, trapped air bubbles, or fractures.

Primary porosity refers to the initial porosity of a mineral material such as a sediment or rock when it first formed. The term "intergranular porosity" is sometimes used as a synonym for primary porosity. Additional void space which may form later, such as from fracturing or dissolution, is called **secondary porosity**. Total porosities can vary from near zero to 60% or more (Table 2.4). For sediments in general, the smaller the particle sizes, the higher the porosity. Well sorted materials have higher porosity than poorly sorted. For rocks made of interlocking crystal grains — such as granite, basalt, and many

Table 2.4. Porosity Ranges for Some Common Earth Materials

Material	Total Porosity (%)
Clay	34 – 60
Silt	34 – 61
Soil	30 – 50
Sand	25 – 46
Gravel	24 – 38
Glacial Till	10 – 25
Sandstone	5 – 30
Basalt	3 – 35
Saprolite	1 – 50
Limestone and Dolomite	0 – 40
Shale	0 – 10
Fractured Solid Crystalline Rock	0 – 10
Solid Crystalline Rock (e.g., granite, gabbro)	0 – 5

limestones — primary porosities tend to be very low and total porosity will depend upon development of secondary porosity, usually from fracturing, solution, or weathering. Some factors influencing porosity are illustrated in Figure 2.9.

Permeability is the ability of a material to transmit a fluid. Rock and regolith will have high permeability and allow water to seep through them when the pore spaces are relatively large and interconnected (Figure 2.9A, F, and G). A subsurface area which is characterized by moderate to high permeability and enough porosity to provide a usable supply of water to a well is an **aquifer**.

When rock is solid and unbroken, initial or **primary permeability** is often low. This is because most rock forms at depth under high pressure and large interconnected openings are rare. Important exceptions are coarse clastic sedimentary rocks such as conglomerate and sandstone, which often have good permeability, a result of incompletely filled spaces between the grains of resistant minerals, usually quartz, which resist compaction (Figure 2.9A and C). In addition, a variety of sedimentary structures formed during or shortly after deposition may contribute to primary permeability in sediments. These include bedding

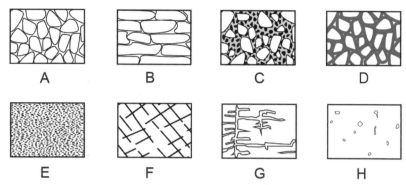

Figure 2.9. Some factors influencing porosities of rock [264]. **A.** Well rounded, roughly spherical and coarse-grained particles such as sand have large interconnected openings (high intergranular porosity), allowing water to move quite easily through the material. **B.** Irregularly shaped particles such as the flattened clasts shown here fit more closely together and tend to reduce porosity and permeability. **C.** In poorly sorted materials, smaller particles fill in the openings between large particles, significantly reducing porosity and permeability. **D.** Cementation reduces pore space and impedes water movement. **E.** Very fine particles such as clay will have many very small openings. Considerable water may be present but due to the small openings and capillary forces, little movement of the water will occur. **F.** Fractures tend to increase both porosity and permeability. **G.** Solutional openings increase porosity and permeability. **H.** Isolated openings and cavities increase porosity but, without interconnections, they will have little influence on permeability.

planes, mud cracks, fossils, aligned grains, and contorted strata. Most coarse-grained sediments, like sand and gravel, will have high primary permeability and make excellent aquifers.

Secondary permeability is produced after the rock has formed. Most secondary permeability is caused by either chemical activities such as solution or by stresses acting upon rock which generate a variety of fractures (Figure 2.9F and G).

2.8 The Influence of Geologic Structures on Groundwater

In the broadest sense, a geologic structure is any feature which constitutes an element of, or part of, a rock formation. Structures

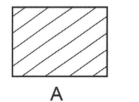 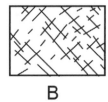

A   B

Figure 2.10. Directional permeability. **A.** Bedding planes shown here provide increased permeability toward the lower left. **B.** Connections between the joints shown here permit increased water movement toward the lower right. Foliation, parallelism of fragments, and other factors can also influence the direction of groundwater flow.

include huge uplifted crustal masses, faults and folds, and microscopic fractures. The layers, cracks, miscellaneous openings, and their orientations are of great importance in determining the behavior of groundwater. Tectonic forces generate compressive and tensional stresses which produce fractures and distortions both great and small in the rocks of Earth's crust. Additional structures are created during chemical reactions, the deposition of sediments, and the cooling of once-molten rock. Some of the more important structural features are noted below.

2.8.1 Bedding Planes

The surfaces or contacts between sedimentary strata are **bedding planes**. Deposition of sediment is not steady and continuous. Fluctuations in depositional rates and sediment types along with short episodes of erosion or nondeposition produce bedding planes. Bedding planes separate depositional events and often form planar zones of greater permeability within sedimentary rock (Figure 2.10A). In general, the more bedding planes and the more pronounced they are, the greater the permeability.

2.8.2 Unconformities

Lengthy periods of nondeposition or major episodes of erosion often occur, leaving behind buried surfaces which often are associated with high permeability. A major buried surface of erosion is an **unconformity** (Plate 4: Top). Unconformities often separate rocks which differ in age by millions of years and are totally different in character. Erosional surfaces often possess high permeability due to weathering and exploitation of the rock while exposed to the surface environment.

In addition, the first rock unit deposited upon an erosional surface is often a permeable conglomerate or sandstone which further increases the significance of many unconformities on the distribution and movement of groundwater

2.8.3 Joints

Rocks, especially near the surface, typically contain a wide variety of cracks or fractures. **Joints** are regularly spaced, parallel, smooth sets of cracks (Figure 2.11). Joints may be caused by any processes which generate

Figure 2.11. Examples of jointing. **A.** Devils Post Pile National Monument on the east side of the Sierra Nevada, California. The Devils Post Pile is a 60-foot-high exposure of exceptionally well-displayed columnar jointing in a basaltic lava flow. **B.** The polygonal shape of the columnar joints is clearly seen in this view at the top of the "post pile." The rock also shows polish and grooves produced by glaciers grinding across the surface.

force and cause strain in solid earth materials. For example, in fine-grained soils, wetting causes expansion and drying causes shrinkage. The shrinkage will produce cracks allowing water penetration and increased permeability. Freeze-thaw cycles may yield a similar effect due to the expansion and contraction of water. After lava or near-surface magma hardens, shrinkage occurs as the rock continues to cool. This produces tension and results in cooling cracks oriented perpendicular to the cooling surfaces. The distinctive columnar jointing seen in many lava flows and some intrusive bodies is the result.

Rocks may be stressed over huge areas by lithospheric plate movements resulting in regional joint patterns. Both compression and tension can cause joints to form in rock. Rocks are especially vulnerable to even small amounts of extension and joints typically form as a means of accommodating the tension. For example, when lithospheric plates are pushed together, a large part of the crust is under compression. Extension of the crust, and thus the formation of joints, will occur perpendicular to the compressive forces, much like stepping on a hard snowball will cause it to flatten out — it expands at right angles to the applied force of your weight. When compressive forces are released, crustal rock will again expand slightly producing another set of joints, often at right angles to first set (Plate 4, Bottom).

Another example of joint formation occurs when erosion removes overlying rock, thus reducing the weight on the underlying rock. The underlying rock will expand upward in response to the reduced pressure and develop tension cracks parallel to the ground surface. This "**unloading**" will form joints, especially in tight, massive bedrock such as granite, thick sandstone strata, or gneiss. When convex-upward joints result, a distinctive landform called an **exfoliation dome** may be produced (Plate 5, Top). These joints may also be called sheet fractures, or **sheeting**, especially when flat-lying, and the process may be referred to as exfoliation or sheeting. Other types of cracks in rock include rock cleavage or shear fractures, formed when planes of minute slippage occur within the rock, usually due to compressional forces.

Planar features such as joints and bedding planes, even though they are often subtle and almost unnoticeable at depth, are readily penetrated by water and then exploited by weathering and erosion at and near the surface. These processes widen and deepen fractures and other openings in rock, allowing still more water access which in turn increases permeability and exposure to weathering processes. This, and the unloading effects noted above, are important reasons why permeability of a given rock type almost always decreases with depth.

In general, the more pronounced, abundant, longer, and more closely spaced any fracture sets or similar openings are, the greater the porosity. On the other hand, permeability in any given direction will depend largely upon the connections between openings. In Figure 2.10B, groundwater movement will be facilitated along the upper left-lower right trend. Flow perpendicular to this trend will be restricted due to the lack of connectivity. In the three-dimensional subsurface, networks of fractures and other openings in the material can be very complex, which can make prediction of groundwater movements very difficult and imprecise.

The presence of joints, bedding planes, and other zones of higher permeability serve to concentrate groundwater flow along sheet-like surfaces and along the lines of intersection between surfaces. In soluble rock such as limestone, concentrated flow leads to the development of open conduits and caves. As a result, groundwater can move very rapidly in these karst areas.

2.8.4 Tilted and Folded Rock Layers

When a part of Earth's crust experiences compression, uplift, subsidence, and other forces, once-horizontal rock layers end up tilted. The inclination, or dip, of the rock units can have significant influences upon groundwater flow. Where lithospheric plates converge, the horizontally directed forces cause layered rock to be slowly crumpled into elongate and often complex upfolds (**anticlines**) and downfolds (**synclines**), as illustrated in Plate 5 (Bottom) and Figure 2.12. If an upwarped area has a circular or elliptical outline, it is a **dome**. A similarly shaped downfold is a structural **basin**.

The folding of stratified rock sets up stresses in the rock producing more joints and fractures, often with distinct trends. For example, along the crest (top) of anticlines, the upward bending of brittle rock will generate tensional joints which make the rocks more susceptible to weathering and erosion. This can result in erosional valleys along the crests of anticlines and erosional basins atop domes. The broad central valley seen in Figure 2.12A was eroded along the crest of an anticline. This breaching of these structural features produces a phenomenon called topographic inversion in which a structurally higher area such as an anticlinal crest may form a low elevation area in the terrain and vice versa (Figure 2.13). Such structurally controlled trends also influence groundwater flow directions and may produce distinct localized zones of higher or lower permeability.

Figure 2.12. Examples of folding. **A.** Aerial view of ridge and valley terrain in the folded Appalachian Mountains in southwest Virginia. The central valley has been eroded along less resistant rock (limestones, shales); the ridges are held up by resistant rock (sandstones, conglomerates). See also Figure 2.13. **B.** Aerial view of the Lemhi Range in Idaho showing complex folding and faulting in sedimentary rock.

2.8.5 Faults

Tectonic forces often cause rock to become heavily fractured. When movement occurs along a zone of rupture, the surface or zone of displacement is called a **fault** (Plate 2, Top; Figure 2.14). Whereas joints tend to be ubiquitous, faults are localized. Both tension and compression can produce faults and the amount of displacement can range from inches to hundreds of miles. Movements along the fault may be fast or slow and can occur intermittently over many millions of years. Faults may be active and capable of current movement, inactive, or may be reactivated by changes in forces influencing the subsurface environment. Movement of the rock masses on either side of a fault may be mostly vertical (up and down), mostly horizontal, or oblique. Large vertical movements have profound influences on terrain and can create abrupt changes in surface elevation called **scarps**, if small, or **escarpments**, if large. Plate 6, Top shows the Teton Range in Wyoming where, over the past 10 million years or less, faulting has uplifted the rock of the mountains some 24,000 feet relative to the corresponding rock buried beneath the sediment of the adjacent valley [556]. Note the terraces of the Snake River in the foreground. This lowland is called Jackson Hole, "hole" being a pioneers' term for a broad open valley surrounded by mountains.

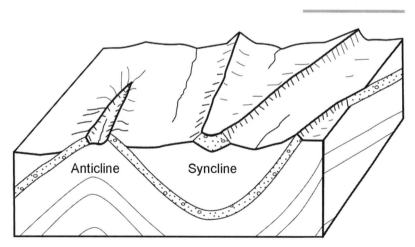

Figure 2.13. Block diagram showing anticline (left) and syncline (right). More resistant rock, such as sandstones and conglomerates, will support high areas, and less resistant rock, such as shales and limestones in humid regions, will form valleys and lowlands.

Figure 2.14. Young fault scarp along Kirkland Creek, Madison Canyon area, Montana. On August 17, 1959, an earthquake occurred in this area west of Yellowstone National Park. The displacement, to a maximum of about 30 feet, produced the light-colored scarp seen across the central part of this photo, taken by William B. Hall five days after the earthquake.

Violent earthquakes remain a real threat in areas such as this. Scarps may also be purely erosional in origin.

Large-scale faulting can severely disrupt nearby rock, especially by fracturing, producing important zones of high permeability which may serve as major conduits for groundwater transport, even deep in the crust. In some situations, the rock along the fault becomes pulverized into a very fine-grained material called **fault gouge** which can be highly impermeable. The presence of faults often has a major impact on groundwater occurrence and behavior. For example, in addition to causing increased permeability along a fault, the displacement may bring totally different rock types into contact producing abrupt changes in hydrologic properties (Figure 2.15). Faults may also permit surface waters to circulate deep within the crust, or allow deep waters access to the surface environment.

2.8.6 Topographic and Hydrologic Evidence of Geologic Structures

Structural features can be used to better understand and anticipate both surface and subsurface water movements. Faults, fracture traces, and other trends can often be recognized on aerial photographs or topographic maps. They can be especially useful in finding good locations for water supply wells.

Many surface features formed or influenced by water can be used to determine geologic structures. Bedrock exposures are closely related to the structures present. Streams often reflect the underlying structure because their channels tend to form along zones of least resistance in the underlying rock material. For example, a rectangular channel pattern probably indicates rectangular jointing in the local bedrock. The "trellis" pattern of long subparallel streams with short stubby tributaries usually reflects a series of anticlines and synclines. Linear patterns of springs, or unusually straight, isolated stream segments often reflect the intersection of an underlying fault with the ground surface. Long linear trends thousands of feet in length are often called lineaments. Figure 2.15 provides three examples of fault-controlled linear trends.

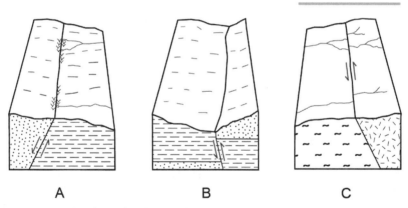

| A | B | C |

Figure 2.15. Linear landscape features often associated with faults. **A.** Alignments of vegetation and springs often indicate an underlying fault. In this case, water moving to the right through the sandstone (dotted pattern) abruptly encounters impermeable shale at the fault. The water tends to migrate toward the surface where it produces springs and supports water-seeking vegetation. **B.** Extended linear streams or stream segments often suggest fault control. Slopes are steeper on the right because sandstone is a more resistant rock than shale. **C.** The movement along this fault is lateral rather than vertical, but it will still produce linear landscape features such as the offsets in the streams shown here.

2.9 Summary: Earth Materials and Groundwater Availability

So many factors influence groundwater movement and behavior that it becomes risky to generalize. Most common earth materials exhibit a wide range of groundwater flow rates, even within a given type of material (Section 6.6). Nevertheless, some general observations regarding rock and groundwater availability may be made.

2.9.1 Intrusive and Metamorphic Rock Materials

Intrusive and metamorphic rocks are generally poor aquifers with low permeability and porosity. The average porosity for these bedrock types ranges from about 1% to 3%. Fracturing can increase porosity by a few percent but can yield huge increases in permeability (100-1,000×). The water is usually of excellent quality, but rapid migration through fractures make it vulnerable to pollution. Most fractures are closed by pressure at depths below about 30 meters (100 feet) and many wells will thus be less than 100 feet deep. To find water, one must often seek zones where rocks have undergone considerable fracturing and/or weathering. Zones of extensive fracturing can often be located by noting linear trends, especially of topographic lows, on maps and aerial photographs. In some areas saprolite may exceed a hundred meters (several hundred feet) in thickness, especially along major fracture zones. Saprolite often forms the main aquifers in metamorphic and intrusive rock terrain.

2.9.2 Sedimentary Materials

Both clastic sedimentary rocks and the sediment they formed from tend to possess medium to high porosity with coarse-grained types having high permeability and fine-grained types having low permeability. Sand and gravel deposits in glaciated terrains and along floodplains and coasts make excellent aquifers but can be contaminated easily by surface spillage, leaking tanks and pipelines, and pesticide use, among others. The hydrogeologic properties of sedimentary rock units depend upon two major influences: (1) their origin, especially the initial depositional environment which determines, or at least strongly influences, the composition, texture, continuity, extent, and geometry of the rock units; and (2) postdepositional processes, including cementation, compaction, chemical changes, and structural impacts such as fracturing, faulting, or folding. The coarse-grained varieties, mainly sandstone, are the best water producers. Important sandstone aquifers underlie large parts of North

America and other continents. Fine grained rock like shales and claystones make up more than 65% of all sedimentary rock by volume. They are usually impermeable at depth due to compaction but, if heavily fractured, shales can provide groundwater near the surface.

Chemically precipitated sedimentary rocks often consist of interlocking crystals with very low porosity and permeability. However, due to the solutioning of these rocks, secondary permeability and porosity can be very high.

2.9.3 Volcanic Materials

Many volcanic rocks, because of their layered nature, are similar to clastic sedimentary rocks. Rocks formed from lava flows tend to have heavily fractured zones of high permeability and porosity, especially at the top and bottom of the flows. In addition, sediments deposited on lava flows may be buried by later lavas to form interbeds. Alluvial interbeds can form excellent aquifers within lava sequences.

Predicting groundwater behavior in any location requires a good knowledge of geology in the immediate vicinity. It is also useful to categorize large areas based upon the anticipated behavior of groundwater. This leads to the concept of hydrologic regions or terrains which will be discussed in Chapter 8 along with more detailed information on the impact of geology on groundwater.

The Hydrologic Cycle

The hydrologic system of precipitation, streamflow, sediment, dissolved salts, ground water and evaporation is typical of a system that can be deranged.

— Luna B. Leopold

3.1 Earth's Dynamic Water Realm

The **hydrologic cycle**, or water cycle, refers to the solar-powered transfer of water between various surface and near-surface reservoirs. The water involved in the cycle moves through three critical environments:

- the atmosphere, where it exists primarily as water vapor, water droplets, and ice crystals;
- the land surface, where it resides in glaciers, streams, wetlands, lakes, and, of course, the oceans; and
- the upper part of Earth's subsurface where it moves through, or is stored in, regolith and rock.

Figure 3.1 provides a simple overview of the hydrologic cycle. Water enters the atmosphere, where it is called atmospheric or **meteoric water**, largely by evaporation from surface water bodies, mainly the oceans. Winds in the lower atmosphere transport the water far and wide over Earth's solid and liquid surface. Eventually meteoric water falls back to Earth as precipitation in a liquid or solid state. There it can again accumulate in oceanic or terrestrial basins, be added to an ice mass, re-evaporate, be used by plants, flow across the surface as runoff, collect in the soil, or percolate downward to become subsurface water.

For Earth as a whole, evaporation and precipitation will be equal over time. Estimates of the actual volume of water making its way through the worldwide water cycle in a year range from roughly 400,000 to 500,000 km³/yr (96,000-120,000 mi³/yr) [185]. Eventually, most surface and groundwater will return to the oceans.

81

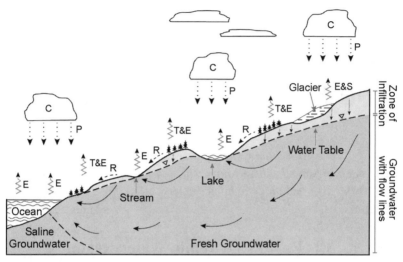

Figure 3.1. The major features of the hydrologic cycle. Many processes take place concurrently. Evaporation can occur wherever liquid water is present, such as from the oceans, lakes, runoff, cloud and rain droplets, leaves, or soil. Sublimation may occur wherever ice is present, such as in glaciers, soils, frost, or fallen snow, and in the atmosphere. Groundwater may return to the ground surface via water bodies (oceans, lakes, streams), soil, or plant transpiration. The dominant processes indicated on the drawing are: C = condensation; E = evaporation; P = precipitation; R = runoff; S = sublimation; T = transpiration.

The volume of water involved in some parts of the hydrologic cycle at any given time may be small, but due to ongoing renewal, the importance of that water may be huge. For example, only about 2,000 km^3 of water is present, or "stored," at any one time in all the world's rivers, but the total volume passing through those rivers in a year, their annual discharge, is about 45,500 km^3 [295]. Hence the amount being recycled through a river provides the most meaningful measure of the river as a water resource. Table 1.6 indicates the storage capacities of Earth's major water reservoirs. Table 3.1 provides estimates of the quantity of water that moves through parts of the hydrologic cycle each year.

The liquid fresh water on or under Earth's land surface at any one time is roughly 2 million mi^3. This, along with the 7 mi^3 stored in glaciers, all arrived from the atmosphere. Of course, gravity is needed to cause water to flow downward and generate the force which enables it to

Table 3.1. Quantity of Water Moving through the Global Hydrologic Cycle

Annual precipitation over ocean	391,000 km^3
Annual precipitation over land	111,000 km^3
Land precipitation as rain	98,500 km^3
Land precipitation as snow	12,500 km^3
Annual evaporation from ocean	436,500 km^3
Annual evapotranspiration from land	65,500 km^3
Total annual runoff to ocean	45,500 km^3
Subsurface "runoff"	30,200 km^3
Surface runoff	15,300 km^3

Source: [295].

do work, such as the erosion, transportation, and deposition of mineral matter. But it is solar energy that keeps the hydrologic cycle operating. Without the sun to power evaporation and winds, all water would seek the lowest level and remain there leaving land masses dead and dry.

As these waters have made their way over and through Earth over time, they have repeatedly eroded away entire mountain ranges and deposited the eroded sediment at lower elevations on, and near the margins of, the continents. They have created great chasms such as Grand Canyon, and deposited billions of tons of sediment, most of it now sedimentary rock, over much of Earth, often in thicknesses of many miles. Even on a much smaller scale, water's work is impressive. A 1-inch rainfall over 1 mi^2 of land produces some 72,000 tons of water and the heat released during the condensation of that water equals the amount of heat generated by the combustion of 65,000 tons of high-grade coal.

The water cycle is a closed cycle. Except for very minor amounts of "new" water added from volcanism or meteors, or water molecules escaping into space from the upper atmosphere, the quantity of water involved remains quite constant as does the recycling rate of that water for the world as a whole. Many processes involved in the hydrologic cycle act to effectively purify water. For example, evaporation and freezing exclude most impurities, streams add oxygen, and movement of water through the ground filters impurities. A state of **dynamic equilibrium**, a constantly shifting state of balance, is maintained as water interacts with atmospheric, surface, and subsurface environments.

Table 3.2. Average Residence Times for Selected Water Reservoirs

Antarctic ice sheet	20,000 years
Deep groundwater	10,000 years
Oceans	3,200 years
Shallow groundwater	100-200 years
Lakes	50-100 years
Glaciers	20-100 years
Rivers	2-6 months
Seasonal snow cover	2-6 months
Soil moisture	1-2 months
Atmosphere	9 days

Notes: These are broad estimates; actual residence times will vary greatly depending upon local conditions. For example, some ice in Antarctica today approaches a million years in age and some deep groundwater is many millions of years in age. Source: [560].

Rates of water transfer vary greatly in different parts of the water cycle. The average time a given quantity of water remains in one part of the system is the **residence time**. Table 3.2 gives approximate residence times and storage quantities for the major components of the hydrologic cycle. The volume of groundwater is very large, but because it enters and leaves the ground very slowly, it can require large periods of time to be replenished, or to be cleansed should it become polluted. Most actual groundwater residence times will vary from weeks to many tens of thousands of years, depending upon how far and how rapidly it moves. The time needed to replenish all groundwater within 750 meters of the surface is roughly 2,000 years compared to perhaps 20 days to replace all the water in the world's rivers. Figure 3.2 provides a more detailed model of the water cycle, including important statistics on the volume of water stored in and transferred among the various parts of the water cycle during the course of a year.

3.2 Evaporation

Evaporation occurs when molecules of a liquid absorb enough energy to enter into the gaseous state. As noted above, sublimation refers to the change from a solid directly to a vapor or a vapor directly to a

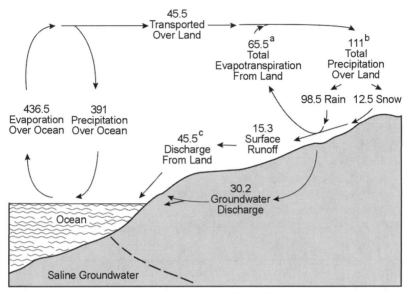

Figure 3.2. Water transfers in the hydrologic cycle. The numbers represent estimated thousands of cubic kilometers per year (1000 km³/yr) of water moving through the global hydrologic cycle, exclusive of Antarctica [295]. [a] The value for terrestrial evapotranspiration may be subdivided as follows: forests, 29; grasslands, 21; croplands 7.6; lakes 1.3; wetlands, 0.2; and others, 6.4. [b] The value for terrestrial precipitation may be subdivided as follows: forests, 54; grasslands, 31; croplands, 11.6; lakes, 2.4; wetlands, 0.3; and others,11.7. [c] All but about 10% (4,550 km³/yr) of the discharge from land enters the oceans via rivers. Most of that remaining 10% is discharged directly into the oceans from groundwater.

solid without entering a liquid phase. Most evaporation will occur at the surface of water bodies, especially where the temperatures are high and sunshine is abundant. The amount and rate of evaporation vary greatly from place to place, and even at the same location. For example, about 400 millimeters per year (mm/yr), or 15.7 in/yr, of water will vaporize annually in cloudy parts of the Pacific Northwest compared to over 2,500 mm/yr (98.4 in/yr) in the dry southwestern rangelands of the US. Annual precipitation in the latter area is only 10-20 in/yr. Such data are essential for proper management of crops, reservoirs, irrigation, and water supply requirements. The map in Figure 3.3 provides an overview of mean evaporation rates over the US. Evaporation is measured in several ways. Perhaps the easiest is to use a standard **evaporation pan**, which

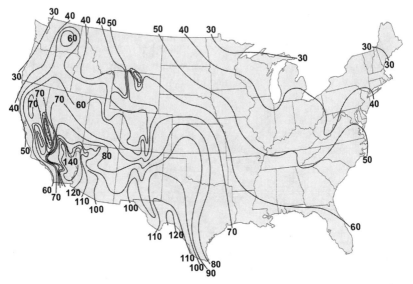

Figure 3.3. Contour map of average annual pan evaporation rates in the conterminous United States. Rates are given in inches per year. Note the higher rates in the southwestern part of the country [554].

measures 48 inches in diameter and 10 inches deep, along with various correction factors [423].

The rate of evaporation depends primarily on three factors: humidity, wind, and temperature. **Humidity** is a measure of the amount of water vapor in air. It is usually indicated as **relative humidity**, or the percent of water vapor present compared to the maximum the air could hold at that temperature. Hence 50% humidity means the air contains half the water it is capable of holding and 100% means the air is saturated. **Absolute humidity** refers to the actual quantity of water vapor in air. For example, a kilogram of saturated air at 20°C (68°F) will contain 14 grams of water at sea level pressure (1.4% water). The actual amount of water in air varies from near zero in dry climates to about 5% by weight in very warm humid climates.

Another means of measuring humidity is vapor pressure. All matter has mass and exerts a downward force due to the pull of gravity. That part of the atmospheric pressure attributable to water vapor is often called the **vapor pressure** of water. If water is placed in a closed container of completely dry air, water will evaporate and the vapor pressure will increase. When the air reaches saturation (100% humidity), no more water vapor can be added at that temperature. This does not mean that evaporation completely ceases; both evaporation and condensation continually take place at the water surface. When net evaporation is occurring, many more molecules are leaving the liquid than are entering it. As vapor pressure increases, the number of water molecules forced back into the liquid increases. When 100% saturation, or saturation vapor pressure, is achieved, as many water molecules enter the liquid as are leaving it. An increase in temperature would impart increasing kinetic energy to the molecules and cause more evaporation and an increase in humidity or vapor pressure. In general, every 10°C (18°F) increase in temperature will nearly double the amount of water the air can hold. Hence warm air can hold much more water than cold air.

As winds increase in velocity, so does evaporation. Wind removes air containing recently evaporated water molecules from near the water surface and replaces it with drier air, keeping the air over the water surface undersaturated. Friction with moving air produces waves and mist, exposing more water surface. Both effects yield increases in evaporation. As previously noted, increases in temperature also favor vaporization. These three factors will vary significantly with such factors as time of day, depth and shape of the water body, local weather, and climate patterns. Latitude, the angular distance north or south of the Equator, also is an important influence on evaporation because of differences in the hours of daylight and the directness of the incoming rays of sunlight.

Evaporation can remove large amounts of surface water resulting in huge losses of needed surface water, especially in arid regions where human constructs such as reservoirs, canals, and irrigation systems have greatly increased the amount of water surface exposed to air. The Colorado, Nile, and many other rivers have severely depleted flows due to evaporation. For example, Lake Mead behind Hoover Dam on the Colorado River loses approximately a million acre-feet (326 billion gallons) of precious water every year — about ten times more water than the city of Phoenix uses in a year. Evaporation also increases the concentration of impurities, such as salts and other pollutants, in the water left behind.

3.3 Transpiration

Most plants absorb water primarily through their roots. The water rises to the leaves where water is lost through **stomata** (pores) on the underside of leaves in a process known as **transpiration**. Over 99% of the water utilized in a plant's leaves is transpired; the remainder goes into plant matter. The quantity of water transpired varies greatly depending upon the type of vegetative cover. For example, a thirsty Douglas fir forest of the northwestern US annually transpires water equal to a layer of water 4 feet deep. A single crop of corn (maize) will require around 10 inches of water.

Because it is difficult to distinguish transpiration from evaporation, the two processes are often combined as **evapotranspiration**. This term generally refers to all water lost to the atmosphere that does not come from an open water surface, such as a lake or stream. To obtain a good estimate of evapotranspiration, a field instrument called a **lysimeter** is often employed. A lysimeter consists of a tank or basin with closed sides and an underlying drain to catch water which percolates through the overlying earth material. The tank contains representative soil and vegetation for the area being studied. Water present in the tank can be periodically weighed and compared to precipitation measurements. The precipitation may be natural or artificial. Water seeping through the tank is captured and measured separately. The difference between liquid water entering and leaving the lysimeter indicates evapotranspiration. Using instruments such as lysimeters which measure actual field conditions can be difficult, long-term, and costly. But such tests are often necessary for the intelligent management of all activities which depend upon water, from crop production to ecosystem requirements.

Evapotranspiration represents the major water use in nearly all environments, except some very humid and cool locations. As such, it exerts a huge influence upon soil moisture, groundwater recharge, and streamflow. In the arid to semiarid parts of the western US, studies in a representative location (Douglas County, Colorado) found that, in an average year, 97% of the precipitation is lost to the atmosphere by evapotranspiration and sublimation, leaving only 3% for runoff and groundwater. In a dry year, 100% is lost; in a wet year, 85% [240]. The rate of evapotranspiration depends mainly on six factors: temperature, humidity, wind, time of year, type of vegetation, and density of vegetation. The influence of the first three were noted above under evaporation. The time of year is significant because of greatly increased transpiration during the growing season and seasonal variations in precipitation and other meteorological conditions.

Vegetation type and density can yield large variations in water demand. In undisturbed natural environments, a dynamic balance between available water and vegetation usually exists. When native vegetation is converted to cropland or certain plants are reduced in abundance or eliminated, as by overgrazing or overharvesting, regional evapotranspiration patterns are altered and this can have important repercussions on the local hydrologic cycle.

Example: Phreatophytes

One group of plants of special importance to water supply are the **phreatophytes**. These are plants possessing deep roots which access underground water. Common phreatophytes in the southwestern US include mesquite, creosote, Chinese tallow, juniper, and tamarisk. The tamarisk (salt cedar) was imported as a windbreak and an ornamental in the mid-1800s. By 2010, it had blanketed some 1.6 million acres across the western US, mostly along streams (Plate 6, Bottom). In addition to displacing more valuable native vegetation, an acre of tamarisk can lower the underlying water table by as much as 4 feet per year, greatly reducing groundwater input to streams. Most phreatophyte roots extend a few meters into the earth, but some may penetrate far deeper in their quest for water — 30 meters (100 feet) or more for mesquite. In the western US, phreatophytes cover millions of acres and transpire over 30 billion cubic meters of water per year. Millions of dollars have been spent to eradicate them, but such efforts often have been ill-advised and have actually worsened the water supply situation in many areas. For example, eradication efforts have destroyed good wildlife habitat, increased flooding and erosion, caused aesthetic blight, and decreased shade, thereby raising the temperature of water and increasing evaporation losses. Reduction of phreatophytes can be beneficial, but it should be part of a well-balanced effort to restore the entire natural ecosystem, not just a bulldozing exercise.

Many phreatophytes have proliferated in arid and semiarid regions around the world due at least in part to unwise land use practices. Many such areas originally supported diverse natural grasslands and savannahs, grasslands with scattered trees in semiarid lower-latitude environments. Such factors as overgrazing, fire suppression, and vagaries of weather eliminated many of the native grasses and favored the invasion of woody shrubs and trees. Loss of grass reduced infiltration rates while increasing storm runoff and erosion rates,

---

resulting in lowered water tables and depletion of surface waters. With their deep tap roots, phreatophytes have a competitive advantage and often form dense thickets of only one or two types of vegetation. As a result, entire ecosystems can be dramatically altered and degraded. Data from Africa, Europe, Australia, and elsewhere indicate that tree and shrub expansion in these environments often results in a 30-75% loss of local stream flow, or even a complete loss of runoff [382].

The term **potential evapotranspiration** is often used to indicate the amount of water that would be evaporated or transpired from a surface if water were at all times present on that surface. Actual evapotranspiration in a hot desert may be very low simply because almost no water is present on the surface, but if water were to be made available, the evapotranspiration rate would be very high. Potential evapotranspiration is useful in determining the moisture demands of a region. For example, if an area is being considered for irrigated cropland, knowledge of potential water demand will help determine: (1) how much water will be required to maintain the crop at various times of the year; (2) if local precipitation can provide adequate water; and (3) if not, how much water would need to be imported or extracted from beneath the surface.

The importance of evapotranspiration in the water cycle is shown by the values in Figure 3.2. These data take on added significance when compared to the precipitation values as shown on figures 3.3 and 3.4 and help to delineate areas of water surplus or scarcity. For example, they show that the southwestern US receives much less precipitation but has much higher evaporation rates than the eastern US. Overall, the US receives an average of 30 inches of precipitation annually, equivalent to some 4,400 billion gallons per day (gpd) (4 mi^3), of which 70% is returned to the atmosphere via evapotranspiration. The remaining 30% will become groundwater or surface water.

3.4 Precipitation

As air is cooled, its capacity to hold water vapor decreases. All air contains some water. Extremely warm, humid air may be 5% water by weight. Because air can hold progressively less water as temperature decreases, the relative humidity of air increases as it cools. Cooling air

Figure 3.4. Mean annual precipitation in the United States. ▶

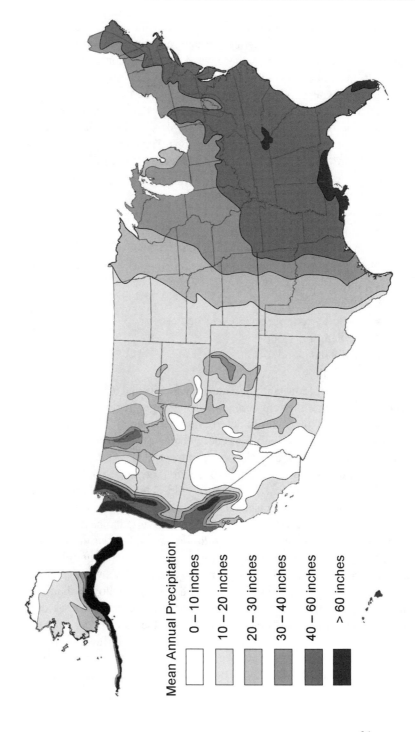

Mean Annual Precipitation

0 – 10 inches

10 – 20 inches

20 – 30 inches

30 – 40 inches

40 – 60 inches

> 60 inches

eventually reaches a saturation point, or 100% humidity. The temperature at which this occurs is called the **dew point**. If cooling continues, excess moisture builds up in the air and the air becomes "supersaturated." In this condition, the water molecules attach readily onto available surfaces where they are often manifested as dew or frost. In the atmosphere, sublimation or condensation occurs upon minute nuclei of salt, dust, or other particles, forming tiny droplets which eventually merge and become heavy enough to form raindrops. The end result of this process is **precipitation**, which can be thought of as any form of water — rain, snow, sleet, hail, and others — falling from the sky. The three major factors required for precipitation are:

- sufficiently humid air;
- cooling of air to its dew point; and
- formation of water droplets or ice crystals.

The major influences on precipitation are:

- latitude;
- altitude;
- proximity to large open water bodies;
- temperature;
- local winds; and
- topography.

These factors constantly interact both locally and regionally to yield conditions which either encourage or discourage precipitation. For example, latitude is important in determining the amount of incoming solar energy with progressively less energy being received as the poles are neared. Hence the stark contrast between tropical (low latitude) and polar (high latitude) regions which helps set up large-scale circulation patterns in the atmosphere which in turn help determine where deserts, rainforests, or temperate grasslands will exist. Air is heated mainly from Earth's surface where solar energy has been converted to heat. Hence air temperature becomes cooler as altitude increases; but warm air is less dense than cool air which causes warm air to rise, generating turbulence and carrying moist air into the higher, cooler atmosphere where condensation will occur. Water bodies warm and cool more slowly than land and thus moderate local climatic conditions and generate local winds in addition to providing a source of moisture for the atmosphere.

A fine example of the interaction of the above influences on precipitation, and one relevant to the hydrologic cycle and local water resources, is the **orographic effect**. The orographic effect (Figure 3.5) refers to the influence of elevated terrain on precipitation, and hence on local weather and climate. In the US, due to prevailing westerly winds, the stoss (windward) slopes of mountainous areas receive considerably more rain and snow than the lee (downwind) slopes.

When moist air approaches a high elevation area, it must rise. Temperatures in the lower atmosphere decrease at a rate of 9.8°C/1,000 meters (5.4°F/1,000 feet) of elevation, largely due to decreasing atmospheric pressure — the air expands, density decreases, and fewer heat-generating molecular collisions occur within the air mass. The cooling often causes the air to reach the dew point. Condensation occurs, water droplets and ice crystals form clouds, and rain or snow falls on the stoss slopes. Condensation and sublimation release heat during cloud formation. Much of that heat remains in the air as it passes over the mountains. Additional heating occurs as the air descends the lee slopes and air density increases. Thus, the air downwind from the mountains is both drier and warmer than it was on the upwind side. Although mountains have the same effect worldwide, the Cascade Range of the northwestern US is one of the world's finest examples of the orographic effect. On the western slopes, cloudy, moist, cool conditions with some 200-300 inches

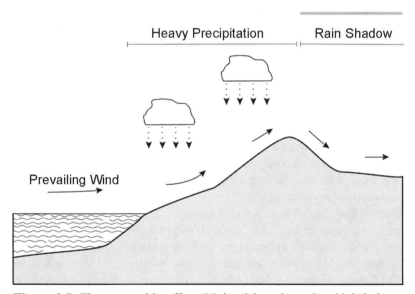

Figure 3.5. The orographic effect. Moist rising air cools which induces condensation, releases heat, and leads to precipitation. As a result, air tends to be both warmer and drier in the rain shadow, the downwind side of a mountain range, than on the upwind side.

of precipitation annually is normal. On the east side of the Cascades we have more arid regions, including deserts which in places receive less than 10 inches of precipitation per year.

3.5 Interception

Interception refers to the water caught by vegetation and other surface cover, then evaporated back to the atmosphere. As shown on Figure 3.6, the process of intercepting water above the ground level by the leaves of trees is called **canopy interception**. If low-lying vegetation and ground litter do the intercepting it is **litter interception**. Water which falls from the canopy is **throughfall** and water which flows along trunks and stems to the ground below is **stemflow**. Canopy interception can be calculated by the equation:

$$C = P - (S + T)$$

where C is canopy interception, P is precipitation, S is stemflow, and T is throughfall.

Assuming no runoff, the net amount of rainfall entering the underlying soil — that is, the infiltration — can be approximated by:

$$I = P - (C + L)$$

where I is infiltration, P is precipitation, C is canopy interception, and L is litter interception [108].

The volume and destination of water involved in interception can vary greatly depending on the type of precipitation and the physical characteristics of the vegetation and associated ground cover — this includes the rate and form of precipitation, leaf size and density, bark roughness, and litter thickness, among other variables. The hydrologic impact is especially significant in forests where runoff may be almost entirely through the litter. The layer of decaying litter, roots, and other debris may be a meter or more thick in dense virgin forests as in some present-day Pacific coastal forests and the high-elevation ancestral forests of the eastern US. In the temperate forests of the interior US, litter tends to be 1 to 5 centimeters thick. Virtually all of the water captured by vegetation and litter during light intermittent showers may be evaporated back to the atmosphere. In some well vegetated areas, the intercepted evaporation may yield four times more water than transpiration. On the other hand, during extended or heavy rain events, vegetation will be drenched,

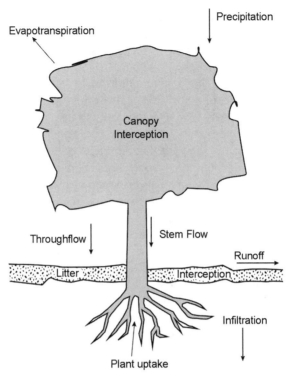

Figure 3.6. Examples of interception.

excess water will flow over the land surface, and the quantity of water intercepted as a percent of the total precipitation will often be relatively insignificant.

Closely related to interception is **fog precipitation**. This process typically involves heavy condensation on leaves at night. Excess water then drips or flows along stems to the ground. In some areas, as along the northern California coast where coastal redwoods abound, fog and fog precipitation can be the major sources of moisture.

3.6 Snow Hydrology

The percent of precipitation falling as snow is a very important aspect of the water cycle. This aspect of hydrometeorology is often called **snow hydrology**. About 13% of the total US precipitation is snow. On average, 10 inches of fresh cold snow is equivalent to 1 inch of rain. Ten inches of cold fluffy snow will equal about 0.5 inches of water; if wet snow, 10 inches will equal about 2 inches of water [422]. When snow accumulates during the winter melts, it produces high stream discharges and frequent flooding for a few weeks in spring. In Vermont, where snow equals 30% of total precipitation, 50% of the annual surface run-off is generated in less than one month in early spring. The disproportionately high amount of runoff from snow results because, compared to liquid water, much less snow is lost via evapotranspiration and infiltration to the ground.

Another aspect of the hydrologic cycle very important to agricultural and municipal planning, hydroelectric generation, navigation, fisheries, and even coastal environments is the snowpack, the depth to which snow accumulates during winter in mountains. In areas such as the western US, where snow may constitute 70% of the annual precipitation, water supplies for the entire year must often be planned based on available **snowmelt**. Global warming poses a severe threat to water resources in such regions.

Snow is an excellent insulator which protects the underlying earth and provides important soil moisture for the start of the growing season. In moderately cold, dry areas such as the Great Plains of the US, winter snow cover protects underlying soil from wind erosion during blizzards and provides a measure of insulation that prevents deep freezing of soil which can kill crops and seeds. When soil lacks snow cover, ice forms in the cold soil, expands, and fills pore spaces. This prevents effective infiltration which can deplete groundwater and produce rapid runoff and flooding during rain events and rapid thaws.

3.7 Infiltration

Infiltration, or percolation, is the movement of a fluid into a solid substance. In hydrogeology, the term refers to the seepage of water into soil, rock, or other materials at the surface of Earth. The infiltrated water then becomes **subsurface water**.

The terms **infiltration capacity** and **infiltration rate** refer to the maximum rate at which soils or other materials can absorb the water that reaches their surface. As long as rainfall does not exceed the infiltration rate of the local surface material, no runoff will be produced [108]. If the rainfall exceeds the infiltration rate, runoff will be produced (see example in Figure 3.7). In equation format:

Runoff = Rainfall Intensity minus Infiltration Rate

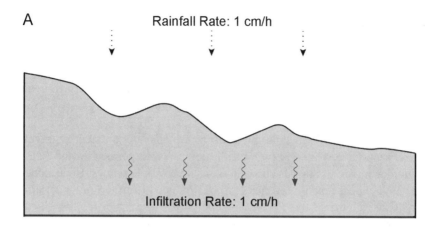

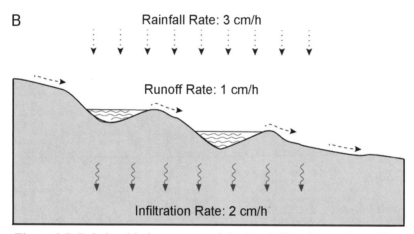

Figure 3.7. Relationship between precipitation, infiltration, and runoff. In example A, no runoff will be produced because the infiltration rate is equal to the rainfall rate. In B, precipitation exceeds the infiltration capacity by 1 cm/hour, which yields runoff as shown [100].

If surface depressions are present, they will begin to accumulate water once runoff begins.

The two methods of infiltration are gravity flow and capillary action. **Gravity flow** occurs when gravity pulls water downward through larger openings in soil, such as cracks, spaces between particles, root openings, or wormholes. **Capillary action** occurs when water is drawn, in any direction, into very small or narrow openings by adhesive and cohesive forces as shown in the enlarged view of a small crack on Figure 3.8.

Capillary action is usually not significant except in fine textured materials where infiltration is very slow. The finer the cracks or interstices between or within particles, the greater the capillary forces. The larger the interconnected openings, the greater the gravity flow will be.

In general, permeable and coarser-grained materials such as gravel and sand have relatively high infiltration rates. Impermeable and fine-grained materials such as clay and shale have very low rates. Hence, one should expect much more runoff to be produced from terrain underlain by clay-rich materials than by sand and gravel. The major factors which control infiltration rates are soil properties, rainfall characteristics, vegetation, topography, and land use. These factors will be discussed in Chapter 5.

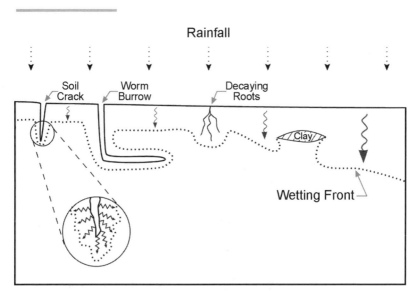

Figure 3.8. Advance of a wetting front into a soil. Larger openings allow more rapid penetration of water. The enlarged circle shows water seeping from the crack into the surrounding soil by both capillary action and gravity flow. The small clay lens inhibits the downward water seepage. The deeper penetration of the wetting front at right suggests that the soil in that area is more permeable than the soil to the left.

3.8 Subsurface Water

3.8.1 Downward Percolation

The water that infiltrates beneath the land surface becomes subsurface water. Some will cling to rock and soil particles in the zone of aeration where it will provide essential moisture for plants. Excess water continues to percolate downward as gravity water. The **wetting front** is the boundary between the downward seeping water and the drier soil or rock below it. The wetting front will remain quite constant as it advances downward in uniform soils. Figure 3.8 shows how such factors as soil cracks, worm burrows, decaying roots, and a lens of impermeable clay may impact the advance of the front. If water percolating through the vadose zone (Figure 1.10) reaches the water table atop the zone of saturation it becomes true groundwater. It is estimated that, on average, about 5 to 6% of the annual precipitation will become groundwater. Not infrequently, the infiltrating water will encounter an impermeable zone of rock or regolith while still well above the main water table. The impermeable material acts like a dam and results in a water-saturated zone immediately above it. A **perched water table** occurs whenever a zone of saturation (and its water table) is separated from another, underlying water table by a zone of aeration (Figure 3.9).

Closer to the surface, infiltrating water may encounter shallow zones of reduced permeability, often at the base of the litter or in the soil, such as a clay-rich B horizon. This causes water to migrate laterally through

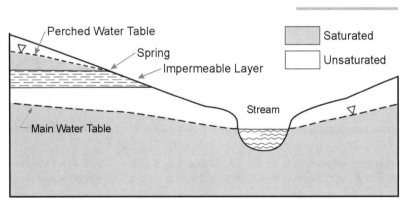

Figure 3.9. Perched groundwater lies in a zone of saturation separated from underlying groundwater by a zone of aeration.

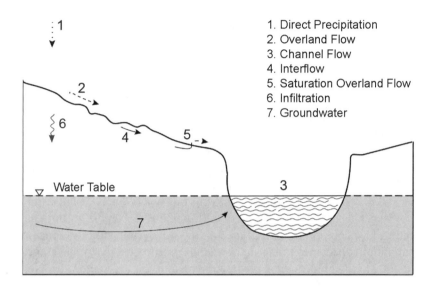

1. Direct Precipitation
2. Overland Flow
3. Channel Flow
4. Interflow
5. Saturation Overland Flow
6. Infiltration
7. Groundwater

Figure 3.10. Water pathways near a stream.

the litter or upper part of the unsaturated zone. The term **interflow** is often applied to this subsurface flow. It is usually considered to be a type of runoff. Some of the pathways which water may follow are illustrated in Figure 3.10, along with corresponding terminology.

3.8.2 Subsurface Water Pressure

In the unsaturated zone, the force exerted by water — the water pressure — is negative, or less than atmospheric pressure. Hence, water in the unsaturated zone will cling to soil and rock particles and cannot enter a well. At the water table itself, the water pressure is equal to atmospheric pressure. In the saturated zone below the water table, water is under positive pressure — the pressure in that water exceeds the atmospheric pressure. This is because, in addition to the atmospheric pressure, the weight of water at higher elevations in the saturated zone is also exerting force on the water below it. Thus, if we drill, or bore, a hole — that is, a well — into this zone, the water will be forced out and will seep into the borehole. If the pressure within the groundwater were not greater than the pressure exerted by the weight of the atmosphere, water could not enter the borehole and water could not be retrieved from a well.

The behavior of this great subsurface body of groundwater is largely determined by confining forces generated by the weight of the water itself. This force within the groundwater reservoir is called **hydrostatic pressure**. As water is added from above, its weight pushes down on underlying water and forces it to slowly migrate through the rock and soil. Groundwater flows from areas of higher pressure to areas of lower pressure. The lowest pressure within the groundwater occurs where the water exits the zone of saturation. The pressure here is simply atmospheric pressure, the weight of the atmosphere. These are **discharge** areas, and the major discharge areas often contain streams, springs, or permanent water bodies such as lakes and oceans.

Topographic relief refers to local differences in elevation — the ups and downs of the terrain. Relief is an essential ingredient in producing groundwater flow. The surface of the groundwater roughly mimics the overlying topography. Water entering the zone of saturation at higher elevations, **recharge** areas, generates the force which causes the groundwater to move. The greater the elevation difference between areas of recharge and discharge, the greater the pressure difference, and the faster the groundwater tends to flow. To maintain this pressure difference, water from the atmosphere must be added periodically to the recharge areas. Without this replenishment, elevation differences within the groundwater mass would diminish, and we would be left with a level water table and stagnant conditions — no flow — in the groundwater reservoir.

Figure 3.11A features a cross-sectional view of a simple idealized groundwater flow system in homogeneous material. The long arrows indicate the general flow path of groundwater from areas of recharge to the more localized discharge areas, which are along streams in this example — the streams are receiving water from the groundwater. Note that the groundwater movement is downward relative to the surface in recharge areas and upward toward the surface in discharge areas. The groundwater follows a curvilinear flow path, diverging downward from the recharge area and converging upward toward the discharge area. Figure 3.11B shows the same area from a map perspective. This map, and others in the book, uses contour lines — lines that connect points of equal elevation or other values, such as pressure or precipitation. The contours in this figure represent elevations at the top of the groundwater — that is, it represents the top of the water table, not the ground surface. The water surface in the stream represents the intersection of the water table and the terrain. The actual discharge area for the groundwater may

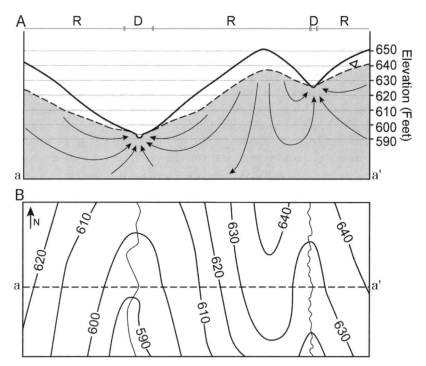

Figure 3.11. Idealized groundwater flow system in homogeneous material. **A.** Cross-sectional view across two stream valleys. Both streams are receiving water from the ground. The inverted triangle indicates the water table. Groundwater flow paths are indicated by arrows. R represents a groundwater recharge area and D represents a discharge area. **B.** Map showing elevation contours on the water table. Line a-a' is the location of cross-section A. The contour interval is 10 feet and both streams flow to the south.

extend beyond the stream banks. This is because the groundwater may be discharged by evaporation through the soil and by direct removal via vegetation.

3.9 Hydrologic Budgets

3.9.1 Determining a Hydrologic Budget

At our current state of knowledge, the quantity of water moving through a given part of the water cycle can only be approximated, but even crude approximations provide a valuable perspective. Worldwide,

Shiklomanov estimated that approximately 61 to 66% of the annual precipitation returns to the atmosphere as evapotranspiration [361]. Of the remaining 34 to 39%, about two-thirds will become surface or near-surface runoff and the remaining one-third, roughly 10% of the annual precipitation, will enter the subsurface and become groundwater. This 10% represents the average annual renewable groundwater resource for Earth. This part of the groundwater responds quite rapidly to seasonal precipitation changes and interacts frequently with the surface environment through such processes as direct inflow to surface waters, transpiration, and evaporation. As such, it is sometimes referred to as **transient groundwater**. The remaining groundwater can be regarded as having been accumulated over a long period of time and, for all practical purposes, is a nonrenewable resource. The actual figures for specific locations on Earth will often vary greatly from these overall estimates.

Sufficient data have accumulated to provide some perspective on water supply in the US. One inch of water over the US — 1 inch of rainfall over the entire country — amounts to some 161 million acre-feet (53 trillion gallons) of water. The atmosphere carries approximately 150 inches worth of water over the US each year, of which about 30 inches descends to the surface as rain and snow. Of that 30 inches, roughly 21 inches is returned to the atmosphere as evapotranspiration. Of the remaining 9 inches, about 8 inches becomes runoff and 1 inch becomes groundwater. Nearly all the groundwater will eventually find its way into streams; a relatively insignificant amount of fresh groundwater, less than 0.1 in/yr, discharges directly into the oceans. The average annual discharge of US rivers into the oceans amounts to 9 inches of precipitation, balancing our water budget.

Engineers, hydrologists, agronomists, planners, and many others often need to quantify the part of the hydrologic cycle operative in their study area. This entails measuring, calculating, and estimating the amount of water entering and leaving their study area, and may involve lakes, drainage basins, the local groundwater, part of a stream, snowpacks, or any other domain involved in the hydrologic cycle. Quantifying these water transfers over time requires establishing a **hydrologic budget**.

Accurate determination of a hydrologic, or water, budget can require a complex, long-term effort. If, for example, the water budget for a lake were to be evaluated, one might start with data on precipitation for the desired time period, preferably gathered from several rain gages situated about and on the lake. The surface area of the lake can be measured and amount of precipitation falling directly on the water calculated. Stream measurements along with estimates of overland flow and subsurface inflow around the lake perimeter can then be added to the inputs. Water outputs that can be measured include the water evaporated from the lake and flowing out of the lake as runoff. Any changes in the lake level itself would need to be carefully measured. Other factors such as water added or removed by humans and transpiration from water or swampy vegetation may also need to be considered. When all these data are collected for the required time period, discrepancies between the determined water inputs and outputs can probably be attributed to additions or losses via groundwater.

Direct measurement of groundwater inflow or outflow from a lake bed, stream bed, or wetland is also possible, most often with a seepage meter or seepage bucket. A **seepage meter** is a pail-like device whose open end is forced into the sediment beneath the stream or lake. A tube leads from the side of the pail to a plastic bag which contains a given quantity of water. All else being equal, if a stream or other water body is gaining water from the ground, water will flow into the bag; vice versa if the body is losing water. After a period of time, hours or days, the change in the amount of water in the bag can be measured and used to calculate the groundwater seepage into or out of the water body. For lakes, wetlands, and large stream segments, measurements may need to be taken at numerous locations to obtain an accurate estimate of seepage gains or losses.

Groundwater gains from or losses to a stream can also be determined directly by measuring stream discharge at two or more locations along a given stream. This procedure is called a **seepage run**. Water temperature may also provide clues as to where water enters or leaves the stream; for example, in summer, significant groundwater input will usually produce a drop in the temperature of stream water.

3.9.2 The Groundwater Budget

The **groundwater budget** refers to the balance between water entering (input, or recharge) and leaving (output, or discharge) the groundwater. The water in the zone of aeration may need to be considered in some water budget studies, such as those relating to the water content of soil in agricultural areas. The basic equation is:

Change in Storage = Input minus Output   or $\Delta S = I - O$

3.9.3 Groundwater Recharge

Groundwater recharge occurs in three major ways: (1) infiltration of rainwater or snowmelt; (2) seepage from surface water bodies, such as streams, lakes, or reservoirs; and (3) artificial recharge — for example, leaking water lines and septic tanks, infiltration of irrigation water, pumping water into the ground, or channeling runoff into constructed basins where it is allowed to seep into the ground.

Recharge is encouraged by several conditions, including:

1. **High permeability.** In general, the more permeable the rock or regolith at the ground surface, the more infiltration and recharge will occur.

2. **Lengthy wetting periods.** The longer the duration of rainfall or snowmelt events, the more water can infiltrate the ground. High intensity rains and rapid snowmelt lead to higher runoff rates and lower subsurface recharge rates.

3. **Thin unsaturated zones.** All else being equal, the closer the water table is to the surface, the more rapidly groundwater recharge will occur.

4. **High antecedent moisture.** Water already present in the near-surface materials is called **antecedent moisture**. The more moisture present in soils or rock material, the more readily saturated conditions and infiltration can develop [107].

In humid and temperate climates, the water table tends to be fairly close to the surface and reflects the surface topography. Most recharge takes place on the higher elevations.

In arid and semiarid regions of the world, most groundwater experiences little or no significant recharge at present. The water table may be well below the surface and what little recharge there is often occurs by infiltration from surface water, whenever and wherever it is present. Groundwater resources in dry regions are often an inheritance from previous climates and are often referred to as **"fossil water."** When we withdraw and use this fossil water, we are **mining** the groundwater. As with the extraction of petroleum or metals, this precious resource cannot, for all practical purposes, be replaced. Most fossil water accumulated during the glacial episodes of the Quaternary Period in areas which were considerably wetter than they are today. Any groundwater withdrawal in excess of that which can be replenished can be considered mining of a nonrenewable resource.

3.9.4 Groundwater Discharge

Discharge of groundwater occurs primarily by:

- evapotranspiration from phreatophytes;
- seepage to the surface, such as into lakes, streams, marshes, or oceans; and
- pumpage, the direct withdrawal of groundwater by humans.

Discharge tends to occur at the lower elevations of a terrain. Groundwater movement in discharge areas is directed toward the land surface (Figure 3.11A). As noted above, the discharge site itself may be marked by a spring, seepage area, lake, stream, or other water feature. Or it may exhibit none of these; virtually all of the discharge may be taken up by vegetation or by evaporation from porous soils before reaching the ground surface. Localized ecosystems, or "econiches," often owe their existence to the amount of water available. For example, groundwater-seeking plants (phreatophytes) may be locally abundant as may salt-tolerant plants (halophytes), especially in more arid regions. Salts are often left behind in soils or on the ground surface due to the evaporation of groundwater, especially in regions with arid and semi-arid climates.

Where groundwater discharges, the upwelling water exerts a force, sometimes called **seepage pressure**, which can reduce the weight and frictional forces holding earth materials together. This can result in less stable materials and may lead to slope failures, formation of noncohesive sediments which may produce phenomena such as quicksand and mud volcanoes, geysers, and other troublesome occurrences.

3.9.5 Human Influences

It is obvious that human activities can significantly affect the groundwater budget. We inject large quantities of water into the earth and pump far larger amounts of water out of the earth. Every roadway, building, and livestock pond will have some impact, however small, on the groundwater. For example, on heavily suburbanized Long Island east of New York City, the groundwater was basically stable prior to the mid-1950s, and also polluted due mainly to recharge from septic tanks. Following the installation of sanitary sewers in the mid-1950s, recharge decreased and the water table began declining — 3 meters in the first 10 years. This in turn led to a decrease in groundwater discharge into streams.

3.9.6 Groundwater Dating

The longer that groundwater has resided in one place, the slower its movement and the more stagnant its budget. This **residence time** is often loosely referred to as the "age" of the water, though, as noted previously, most of the water itself has been lurking about our Earth since its inception 4.5 billion years ago. Determining how long groundwater has remained in a particular area is difficult and inexact due to the many reactions and changes in environment that may affect the water. One dating approach uses the concentration of suitable radioisotopes in water. Tritium, whose groundwater levels experienced a hike following atmospheric testing of nuclear weapons in the 1950s, is useful for dating very young water, water up to about 40 years of age. Carbon-14 can be used to date groundwater up to around 40,000 years, and chlorine-36 can obtain dates up to about 2 million years. In addition, the age of groundwater can often be estimated by interpreting the changes in the composition of certain chemicals such as oxygen-18 and chlorofluorocarbons as they migrate along with the groundwater [108]. The groundwater underlying many of Earth's arid regions appears to have been residing in those locations for 25,000 years or more.

3.10 Weather and Climate

Although substantial quantities of water are constantly moving through the hydrologic cycle, the total amount of water and the rate of recycling vary greatly from place to place and from time to time. This uneven and often erratic distribution of water over Earth's surface both results from, and strongly influences, the vast differences in local weather conditions and climates. **Weather** refers to the atmospheric conditions at any given moment and includes such factors as temperature, wind, cloud cover, precipitation, and barometric pressure. **Climate** refers to the long-term weather conditions, primarily temperature and precipitation, that endure on land areas for several decades or more. According to the widely used Koeppen system, there are five major climate groupings, each identified by a letter, as follow:

A. **Tropical.** Hot and rainy, found in low-latitude areas, sufficient warmth (18°C or more every month) and precipitation to support forests year round;

B. **Dry.** Found in mid- to low-latitude areas, insufficient precipitation to support forests (precipitation is less than potential evapotranspiration), broken into **arid** climates (deserts with less than 25 cm precipitation/yr) and **semi-arid** climates (grasslands with 25-50 cm precipitation/yr);

C. **Subtropical.** Moist with mild winters, found in low- to mid-latitudes, no persistent snow cover, enough precipitation to support forests;

D. **Continental.** Moist with cold winters, found in mid-latitude areas, adequate precipitation to support forests, strong seasonal variations in temperature; and

E. **Polar**: Found at high latitudes or high elevations, cold year round (warmest month less than 10°C), treeless, very short growing season.

4 Surface Water

The interaction between surface water and ground water is complex and site-specific.

— National Ground Water Association

4.1 Water on the Land

Surface waters constitute only about 0.5% of the liquid fresh water on Earth (Table 1.6), yet the importance of surface waters to humankind is difficult to overestimate. Humans, and vast multitudes of other life forms, rely upon these water bodies for survival. Understanding the links between surface waters and groundwater is of vital, yet underappreciated, importance. Very small changes in the volume of groundwater can have very large impacts on surface water bodies. As much as 32% of the most critically important terrestrial ecosystems depend directly upon shallow groundwater. Worldwide, some 17% of Earth's land surface is covered by watery land-based ecosystems such as small lakes, rivers, and wetlands which are maintained by shallow groundwater. An additional 5 to 15% of the land is covered by plants which depend on a shallow water table — that is, their roots tap into groundwater or the capillary fringe [117].

Water enters the subsurface from the surface. The behavior of water on and near the ground surface is a critical factor in determining how much water will ultimately become subsurface water. Surface and subsurface water are constantly interacting. To a large extent, the characteristics and condition of the land surface will control the rates of runoff and infiltration. Human activities, especially devegetation and soil disturbance, can drastically alter the local hydrologic cycle and yield harmful impacts such as accelerated erosion, increased flooding, and decreased groundwater recharge. Large-scale modern land-use practices, especially agriculture, have seriously disrupted large areas of Earth's land surface, reducing or even destroying the capacity of ecosystems to survive. This often means that such areas can no longer produce even the water and food needed to sustain human communities.

4.2 Runoff

Runoff refers to the water which flows along the land surface, either atop the surface or slightly below it. In addition to the influences noted in the previous two chapters, a factor called **depression storage** is often important in determining the relative amounts of runoff, infiltration, and evapotranspiration resulting from a given precipitation event. Depressions occur on all land areas throughout the world and range in size from large basins in which lakes accumulate to tiny pockets in soil and rock surfaces. Some of the water attempting to flow downslope will be trapped in these depressions where it will either infiltrate or evaporate. In the formerly glaciated interior of North America — in Minnesota, North Dakota, and Saskatchewan, for example — numerous basins, large and small, were left by melting ice from the former continental ice sheet. In this area, most of the runoff will be directed into such depressions. If the depressions are drained to make more crop or pasture land available, as has often occurred, one result can be dramatic increases in the volume of water running into local streams which, in turn, can lead to unprecedented flooding. The increased runoff leads to decreased infiltration, which can lead to equally serious decreases in available groundwater.

Runoff includes two basic types of surface flow: overland flow and channel flow. Water which moves over the general ground surface is called **overland flow**, or Horton overland flow, after Robert E. Horton (1875-1945), a well-known US hydraulic engineer. Surface flow constricted to a trough or channel is **channel flow**.

4.2.1 Overland Flow

Overland flow is that part of the precipitation which remains after infiltration and evapotranspiration (including interception) have taken their share. In equation form:

$$R_o = P - I - E$$

where R_o = overland flow, P = precipitation, I = infiltration, and E = evapotranspiration.

The two types of overland flow are sheetwash and rill wash. **Sheetwash** refers to water moving over the ground surface in a thin, fairly uniform sheet up to about 1 centimeter in depth at speeds of 10-500 meters per hour (m/hr). Sheetwash is often hidden from view beneath grass and litter, but often can be clearly seen on paved surfaces, roof tops, and unvegetated ground (Figure 4.1).

The volume of water which a slope can store at any one time is called **surface detention**. The amount of surface detention increases with decreasing slope. The depth and velocity of overland flow increases downslope as more and more water is added to the volume which must be transported along the ground surface.

Rill wash is very similar to sheetwash except that the water flows as rivulets along short-lived gullies (rills) as shown in Figure 4.2.

The rate of overland flow tends to be very high and can dominate runoff during heavy rainfall events in arid, semiarid, and disturbed areas such as city centers, recently plowed fields, construction sites, or devegetated areas where infiltration rates are low. This makes such areas prone to **flash flooding** events in which water levels along local streams rise and fall very rapidly in response to high-rainfall events.

In terrain consisting of moderate to steep slopes located in humid regions, much of the water entering streams following rain events comes from the shallow subsurface. Due to the permeable nature of the upper soil, a result of abundant humus and many large interconnected pores,

Figure 4.1. Scene in Alpine, Texas, following a heavy downpour. Sheetwash from receding waters covers most of the pavement.

111

Figure 4.2. Rills (small ephemeral gullies) in a roadcut along the Alamosa River in New Mexico.

most newly fallen precipitation will seep into the soil and proceed to lower elevations through the subsurface. This ephemeral subsurface water moves parallel to the ground surface through saturated near-surface soil and litter, generally flowing much slower than overland flow. Hence flooding along small local streams in more humid regions is not as "flashy" as in more arid regions. However, flooding in these humid environments tends to last longer than in arid regions.

Numerous terms have been loosely applied to this short-term shallow subsurface flow, including **interflow**, storm seepage, stormflow, subsurface runoff, and throughflow. It is usually considered to be part of the runoff. Indeed, it appears to be the major runoff process in many areas. Interflow helps to maintain high stream flows for some time following a rainstorm. Interflow near streams often merges with the underlying capillary fringe and groundwater to form a soggy area of saturated surface soils. The interflow, along with infiltration from a major rainfall event, can contribute to a significant rise in the water table, an expansion of wetlands in low-lying areas, and a large increase in streamflow, as illustrated in Figure 4.3. Step B shows several processes proceeding simultaneously as ongoing precipitation yields overland flow, an advancing wetting front, interflow, and saturation overland flow. These processes are occurring upstream also, causing a rise in the stream water level. If rain continues long enough, the merging of advancing gravity water, capillary fringe, and groundwater can yield the conditions shown in Step C of Figure 4.3 and in Figure 4.4. If sufficient rainfall occurs upstream, water may fill the downstream channel and flood surrounding lowlands, where infiltration of surface water and a rise in the underlying water table can occur.

Overall, approximately one-eighth (12.5%) of annual runoff is thought to flow directly overland to streams or surface water bodies; most of the remainder enters the subsurface at least briefly.

4.2.2 Channel Flow

Runoff confined to a channel constitutes a **stream**. **Fluvial** processes are those which pertain directly to streams and stream activity. The stream channel is a long narrow trough which confines the flowing water. The stream attempts to shape the channel so as to make it as efficient as possible for transporting water and sediment. The stream and its channel represent a system in dynamic equilibrium which is constantly changing in response to variations in water flow, topography, the type and size of sediment being delivered to the stream, and other environmental factors. Two major forces influence streamflow: gravity and friction. Gravity becomes more effective as the stream gradient — the slope of the water surface — increases. **Friction** is simply resistance to motion. In a stream, friction arises (1) between the water and the sides and floor of the channel and (2) within the water itself due to turbulence, which consists of irregularities in the water's flow rate and direction.

Types of Streams: Numerous classification schemes have been devised for streams. One very useful way to categorize streams and their valleys is based on water flow or discharge characteristics.

Perennial (permanent) streams maintain flow nearly all the time (Plate 7, Top left). They typically receive input from groundwater year-round. Of course, even these may dry up during extended droughts.

Intermittent streams contain no flow most of the year, though they may flow continuously for periods of a month or more. The stream shown on Plate 7, Top right, probably receives little or no groundwater input at this location and contains water only following significant rain or meltwater events. The two top photographs of Plate 7 were chosen to illustrate perennial and intermittent streams because both show valleys of similar size and character — a precipitous gorge eroded from sandstone. Of course, most stream valleys do not exhibit impressive gorges such as these.

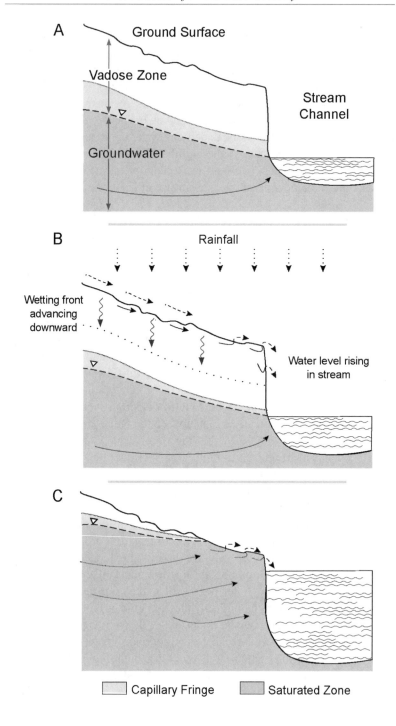

Ephemeral streams contain water only during heavy runoff events (Plate 7, Bottom). These usually occupy small gullies and ravines in humid areas. In arid regions, ephemeral streams may form large gullies in easily eroded rock or regolith.

Effluent streams, sometimes called gaining or receiving streams, are those which are gaining water from the subsurface. In general, about 35 to 40% of river runoff is from groundwater. As long as groundwater is contributing to the streamflow, the stream will be permanent and its discharge will tend to increase downstream (Figure 4.5A).

Influent streams, sometimes called losing streams, are those which are losing water to the ground. Intermittent and ephemeral streams tend to be influent most of the time. Figure 4.5B and C show two examples of

Figure 4.4. Heavy rainfall in the heavily farmed Palouse region of Washington and northern Idaho has produced runoff erosion and mass movements on hills in the background. Saturated conditions in the foreground probably result from both saturation overland flow and sheetwash.

Figure 4.3. Three sketches showing rise in the water table near a stream during a significant, and usually lengthy, rain event. The wetting front advances downward to merge with the capillary fringe and the underlying groundwater, often causing the water table to rise to the surface.

influent streams. In B, water infiltrating into the subsurface will produce a "mound" or ridge in the underlying water table. In C, the water table actually rises to meet the stream, but unlike Figure 4.5A, the stream is at a higher elevation than the surrounding groundwater and thus loses water to the ground.

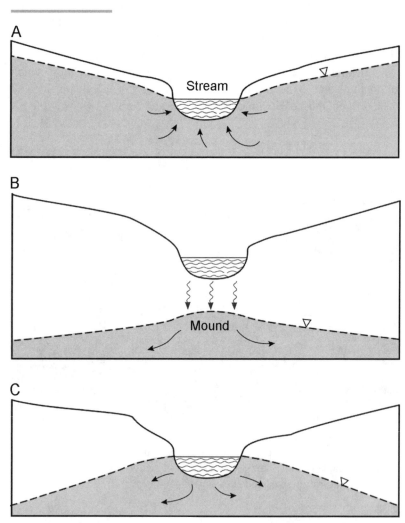

Figure 4.5. Relationships between groundwater and streams. **A.** A typical effluent (gaining) stream. **B.** An influent (losing) stream and an underlying water table showing a mound or ridge. **C.** An influent stream connected to the water table.

These stream terms are often more applicable to stream segments than to entire source-to-mouth rivers. The same river may be influent in some areas or at certain times — for example, during droughts — and effluent at others. Even the mightiest rivers typically begin in small upland swales containing only ephemeral streams perched above the underlying water table. Where the stream channel intersects the water table, a permanent stream containing water will form. If the water table drops below the stream bed, the stream will lose water and become influent, and possibly intermittent. The term **exotic stream** applies to stream segments which flow through an extensive dry (water-poor) area where water is lost by infiltration and evapotranspiration. Important exotic streams include the Nile, Colorado, and Rio Grande. During, and for a short time following, floods, some influent streams may become effluent due to the rise of the water table adjacent to the stream.

Note the importance of groundwater to the various stream types. Groundwater input keeps streams flowing when runoff ceases — which is most of the time. The contribution of groundwater to total streamflow may vary from 0 to 100%. Over the course of a year, the world's major rivers probably receive an average of nearly 40% of their flow from groundwater [423].

4.3 Drainage Basins

The area which contributes runoff to a stream constitutes the **drainage basin**, or catchment area. In the US, the term **watershed** is widely used as synonymous with drainage basin, but this usage is confusing and ambiguous. "Watershed" originally referred to a high-elevation feature which causes water to shed, or flow off, in different directions, such as a ridge top or a mountain peak. Unfortunately, the misuse of watershed as drainage basin may be too firmly entrenched in the US to be undone.

Drainage basins are often measured from the mouth or lower end of a stream; examples include from where a tributary stream enters another stream or from where a river enters the ocean or other standing water body. However, any location along a stream can be used as the place from which to measure the upstream area which supplies the water that passes through that particular cross-section of the stream.

The line connecting the high points such as hills and ridges which surround, and thus outline, drainage basins is the **drainage divide** (Figure 4.6). The drainage divide may also be defined as the boundary between adjacent drainage basins. In Great Britain, the drainage divide is commonly called the watershed. All stream systems and individual tributaries, no matter how small, will have their own basins. The world's largest drainage basin is the Amazon River basin. The concept of drainage basins and divides is also applied to groundwater flow systems.

4.4 Discharge

The volume of water flowing through a given stream channel per unit time is discharge. It can be calculated by the following relationship:

$$Q = Av$$

where Q is the quantity of water or discharge, A is the cross-sectional area of the channel, and v is the average velocity of water flowing through the channel. Water discharge is given as water volume (Q) per unit time (T). Common examples and abbreviations include gallons per minute (gpm), cubic meters per second (m^3/s), and cubic feet per second (cfs; also called "cu-secs" or "second-feet" by many US engineers).

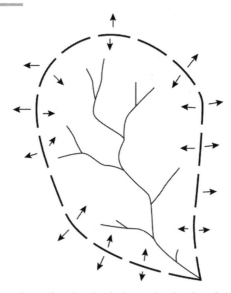

Figure 4.6. Map view of a simple drainage basin showing a trunk stream with tributaries. The drainage divide (dashed line) outlines the basin and separates surface runoff flowing downslope into this set of streams from runoff flowing into adjacent areas (indicated by the small arrows along the divide).

If the cross-sectional area of a stream or any other water-carrying conduit becomes smaller, then the velocity of the water must increase if the same discharge is to be maintained. Hence, flow velocity will tend to increase when a pathway is constricted and decrease when the pathway enlarges. If velocity cannot increase enough to accommodate the discharge, water will pile up just above the constriction, a phenomenon known as **hydraulic damming**.

If all conditions influencing the conduit and its environment — climate, rock type, and so forth — remain the same, a 1:1 ratio will exist between the mean annual discharge of any stream and the area it drains. Thus, if the size of a basin were doubled, one would anticipate a doubling of the average runoff volume. For the US, the average discharge typically varies from about 40-100 cfs/mi^2. Area-discharge relationships are less reliable for basins in arid or snowy regions due to the irregular nature of much of the runoff.

Stream gaging is the procedure of measuring the channel cross-section and stream velocity at a given point along a stream for the purpose of determining stream discharge. The US Geological Survey [519] has over 6,000 stream flow measurement stations, or **gaging stations**, around the US. The streamflow data from these stations are critical water management tools from which information ranging from flood prediction to groundwater discharges can be determined.

4.5 Hydrographs

4.5.1 Basic Description and Interpretation

A graph showing streamflow or some other water quantity through time is a **hydrograph**. Figure 4.7 shows a simple hydrograph with stream discharge on the x-axis and time on the y-axis. The time units can be chosen so as to show streamflow variations over periods of a few hours up to many years. The area below the curve is proportional to the quantity of stream water available at that location over a given time period. Hydrographs provide much valuable information about drainage basins, flow characteristics of streams, groundwater, and regional water resources. Hydrographs find extensive applications in flood forecasting, crop/irrigation needs, river navigation, hydropower generation, groundwater studies, and ecological investigations.

Stream discharge typically increases in response to significant runoff events and decreases during periods of little runoff. This produces the ups and downs seen on Figure 4.7. Each pronounced "hill" on the

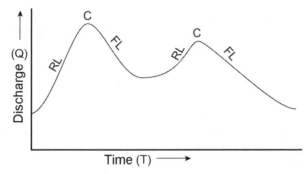

Figure 4.7. A plot of discharge (streamflow) vs. time is a hydrograph. This example shows two high-water episodes (flood waves). C = crest of a flood wave; FL = falling limb or recession curve; RL = rising limb.

graph represents an episode of increased streamflow consisting of an increase in discharge (the rising limb), a period or point of maximum flow (the peak or **crest**), and a period of decreasing discharge (the falling limb; also called a **recession curve**).

A single high-water event such as depicted on the hydrograph of Figure 4.8 is called a **flood wave**. The rising limb will usually be steeper than the falling limb. The steeper the rising limb, the more rapidly the stream discharge is increasing. Sometimes, especially in small drainage basins, a sharp increase in the slope of the rising limb can be discerned on hydrographs. This change in slope, such as inflection point A on Figure 4.8, indicates the approximate time at which the infiltration capacity of soils in the upstream runoff area is reached. In other words, the ground is now largely saturated, rainfall has exceeded the infiltration capacity of most soils, and overland flow is initiated producing an increase in the voume of water being delivered to the stream.

The falling limb will generally be less steep than the rising limb, indicating that floodwaters recede less rapidly than they rise in most cases. Ideally, the waters will recede quite rapidly at first, then more slowly, producing an inflection point (B on Figure 4.8) in the recession curve. This inflection point will be more prominent in small- to medium-sized basins and represents the point where overland flow ceases. The slope change is usually not as obvious as in this idealized example because overland flow doesn't stop at the same time in all parts of a basin. After this, the streamflow is sustained by groundwater discharge and no longer receives input from overland flow and interflow.

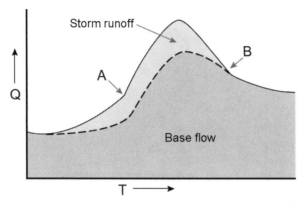

Figure 4.8. Hydrograph of an idealized flood wave. The changes in slope at A and B represent the onset (A) and the cessation (B) of overland flow. The darker shaded area is base flow (groundwater input to the stream) and the lighter shaded area within the flood wave is the storm (surface) runoff contribution to the stream discharge. In Britain, direct runoff is often called "quickflow."

The amount of streamflow which is contributed by groundwater is called **base flow**. During and following distinct runoff events, base flow will be quite high reflecting high discharge from temporary springs, storm seepage (interflow), and saturated or flooded areas near streams. Barring additional rainfall or snowmelt, the base flow will continue to decrease exponentially as groundwater seeps into the stream channel at an ever-decreasing rate. This is because, as groundwater levels decrease, less hydrostatic pressure exists to force water movement through the subsurface material. Due to the large amount of water stored below the surface and its leisurely migration through rock and regolith, groundwater alone can keep many streams flowing through extended periods of drought. The base flow or recession curve segments from numerous hydrographs can be combined to draw a general **base flow recession curve,** or master depletion curve, characteristic of a given gaging station and its drainage basin. This curve gives us the groundwater input to a stream over a lengthy period of time (Figure 4.9). Such a curve enables the hydrologist to predict stream and groundwater discharge and duration during droughts — that is, how much water will be discharged and for how long — a valuable water supply planning tool.

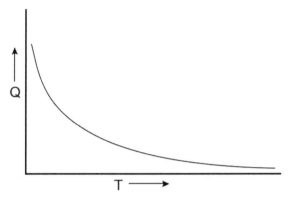

Figure 4.9. Base flow recession curve.

4.5.2 Additional Uses of Hydrographs

Much additional information relevant to groundwater can be gleaned from stream hydrographs. Hydrograph A in Figure 4.10 shows a "pointy" flood wave characterized by rapidly rising and falling waters. Generally, the higher the flood crest, the lower the storage capacity of the area contributing discharge to the stream. **Storage capacity** refers to the terrain's ability to absorb, retain, or detain rainfall and runoff. Streams with high, narrow flood waves are often called "flashy" and are prone to flash flooding. Flash floods are common in small drainage basins, especially in arid or semiarid environments. Little groundwater recharge can occur in such areas due to the rapid runoff rate.

In humid regions, hydrograph B on Figure 4.10, more permeable soils, denser vegetative cover, and other factors will inhibit runoff and produce a less pronounced flood wave. All else being equal — rainfall events, slopes, rock types, basin size, and so on — streams in arid regions will crest more rapidly, attain a higher crest, have much shorter-lived base flow (if any), and have a shorter response time than streams in humid regions. Response time, or **lag time**, refers to the amount of time between the rain event and the flood wave. It may be measured as the time differential between the centers of precipitation and runoff or between the peak (maximum) rainfall and runoff as shown on Figure 4.10. In general, lag time increases with increasing basin size and humidity. The greater the lag time for similar sized basins, the more water is probably infiltrating to the subsurface and the more recharge the groundwater is receiving.

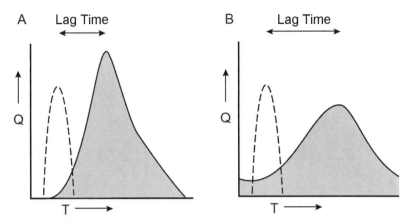

Figure 4.10. Hydrographs comparing discharge for a small stream basin in (A) an arid region and (B) a humid region in response to a given rain event. The dashed line represents the rainfall per unit time; the solid line the discharge per unit time. The time elapsed between the rainfall and the resulting stream discharge is the lag time.

Figure 4.11 illustrates stream responses for four different rainfall events in a given basin. In A, the rainfall event had no significant impact upon a typical base flow curve. This indicates that rainfall was less than the infiltration rate of the basin soils and that a soil moisture deficit continues. Except for the small amount of rain that fell directly into the stream, all the rainfall was soaked up by the soils.

In graph B, the very gentle increase in discharge may indicate that the rainfall exceeded the moisture deficit of the soil, but did not exceed the infiltration rate. Hence little surface runoff was produced but the excess infiltrated water made its way into the stream, probably via interflow, increasing the base flow discharge. Runoff produced when the soil can hold no additional water is sometimes referred to as **saturation overland flow** and is most common in forests where thick litter is present (see also figures 4.3 and 6.7).

Graph C of Figure 4.11 shows a sharp runoff peak accompanied by no increase in base flow. This suggests the rain was intense enough to exceed infiltration capacities and generate overland flow. However, the soil moisture deficit remained — the rain event was probably brief, all infiltrated water was retained as soil moisture, and no groundwater input was produced.

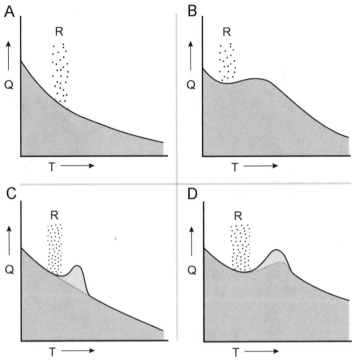

Figure 4.11. Four hydrographs illustrating the impact of various rainfall events on stream discharge. "R" indicates the rainfall event. **A.** Rainfall < infiltration rate; soil moisture deficit continues; base flow remains the same. **B.** Rainfall < infiltration rate; soil moisture deficit exceeded; base flow increases. **C.** Rainfall > infiltration rate; soil moisture deficit continues; base flow (darker shaded area) remains the same. **D.** Rainfall > infiltration rate; soil moisture deficit exceeded; base flow (darker shaded area) increases. The lighter shaded areas on **C** and **D** indicate direct surface runoff that reaches the stream.

Graph D typifies a situation in which the rainfall exceeded both the soil infiltration capacity and the moisture deficit, thus yielding both direct runoff and an increase in base flow to the stream.

Another example in which hydrograph analysis can be very useful in groundwater studies is illustrated in Figure 4.12, which shows a typical **annual hydrograph** for a temperate humid region such as the eastern US. The lowest discharges over the year can be connected to create a line representing the minimum groundwater recharge to the stream at that location. In the Figure 4.12 example, the base flow reaches a minimum in late September or early October. With the pronounced decrease in evapotranspiration in late fall and winter and an increase in cold fronts bringing rain and snow, infiltration increases, producing a rise in groundwater levels and base flow to streams. Groundwater discharge into the stream tends to increase until spring when plant growth and increasing temperatures reduce infiltration rates and cause base flow to gradually decrease. Annual hydrographs over a span of years can detect and quantify important trends in groundwater resources, climate, long-term impacts of land use, and other influences. Annual hydrographs can be used to help characterize drainage basins and regions. For example, areas with heavy winter snowfalls or dramatic wet and dry seasons would yield a different annual hydrograph from the one shown in Figure 4.12. Additional information on hydrograph use is provided in many of our references [96, 108, 185, 241, 352, 423, 555].

4.6 Lakes

A **lake** is any inland body of water occupying a depression and of sufficient size and depth to prevent plant growth from taking root across its entire surface [198]. Lakes are short-lived features, geologically speaking. In most lakes, stream erosion and deposition constantly reduce the water volume of lakes. Where surface water exits a lake, erosion occurs, gradually lowering the threshold and the lake level. Where surface water and other types of runoff enter the lake, sediment will be transported into the lake. Organic matter, wind-blown deposits, salts, and

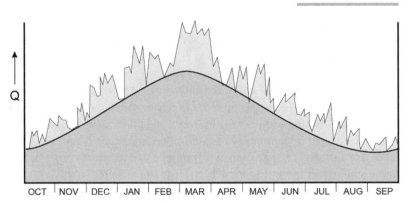

Figure 4.12. An annual hydrograph for a humid temperate area. The upper curve represents stream discharge measurements with their many flood waves (peaks). The smooth lower curve is based upon the low discharges and is a good representation of base flow into the stream over the course of a year.

other materials may also contribute to the infilling of the basin. Hence, most lakes will become shallower in time and will then pass through a wetland phase prior to becoming "dry" land.

Lakes may be fresh or saline, permanent or intermittent, influent or effluent, and boast a wide range of natural or man-made origins. Their water budget may depend mainly on streams or groundwater. In some areas, water-hungry phreatophytes such as willow trees and mesquite may be a major source of water loss.

4.6.1 Relationships Between Lakes and Groundwater

Lakes are frequently classified according to the origin of the depression they occupy. Was it created by tectonic activity, volcanism, glacial processes, landslides, weathering, or some other process? Hydrologically, we can classify lakes based upon their relationship with groundwater.

Some lakes, often called **seepage lakes**, both receive from, and lose most of their water to, groundwater. A lake that receives water from, and is wholly or partially maintained by, groundwater inflow can be called a **discharge lake**, analogous to an effluent stream that receives water from the ground. A **recharge lake** is one that recharges the groundwater and is thereby analogous to an influent stream, and a **through-flow lake** is one which both receives from and discharges significant quantities of water to groundwater (Figure 4.13) [7]. Many of the groundwater interactions described for lakes can also be applied to other terrestrial wet areas such as wetlands, lagoons, and intermittent ponds.

The water level in most lakes can be viewed as a window in, or an exposure of, groundwater and the water table. As with permanent streams, the immediately adjacent water table will be at the same elevation as the lake water as shown in Figure 4.13A, C, and D. Limited interaction between groundwater and lake water will occur in areas close to the shoreline as the water levels of both lake and adjacent groundwater fluctuate in response to such factors as precipitation, runoff input and output, and nearby groundwater withdrawals by wells and phreatophytes. Many recharge lakes will be temporary or intermittent in nature. These "losing" lakes are influent features and will produce a mound or a rise in the underlying water table (Figure 4.13B). If the lake water supply is large enough and the infiltration rate is rapid enough, the water table may rise to the surface to meet the lake (Figure 4.13C).

As with streams, the discharge-recharge conditions can change with variations in seasons and water budgets. For example, Figure 4.14 provides both cross-sectional and map views of the relationship between

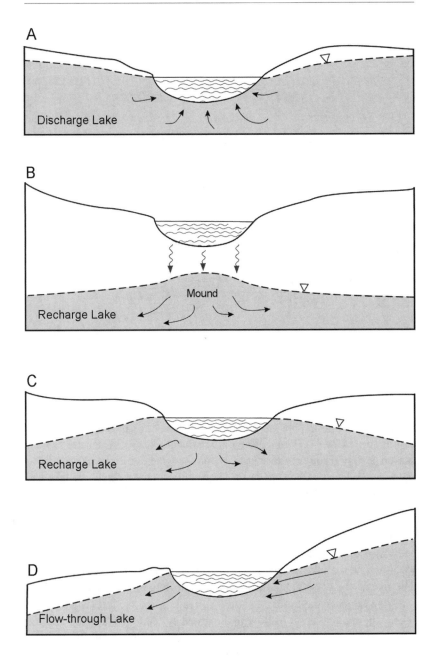

Figure 4.13. Four relationships between groundwater and lakes [7].

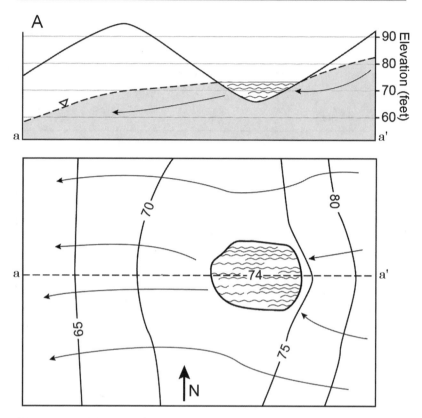

Figure 4.14 (above and facing page). Cross-sectional and groundwater contour map views of a lake during dry and wet seasons. **A.** During the dry season, a flow-through lake is present and the water table slopes steadily to the west. **B.** During the wet season, the lake becomes a discharge lake and the adjacent water table slopes toward the lake.

---

surface and subsurface water at a small lake during both dry and wet seasons. During the wet season (Figure 4.14B), the higher groundwater levels cause the lake to change from a through-flow to a discharge lake. The rise of the water table during wet conditions produces a groundwater ridge beneath the higher terrain — a ridge — to the left (west) of the lake, causing a reversal of flow in the area between the ridge top and the lake. The lake itself becomes a low area or depression in the water table and a site for groundwater discharge. Note that the flow line arrows on the water table contour maps show the shallow groundwater flowing directly downslope — perpendicular to the water table contours.

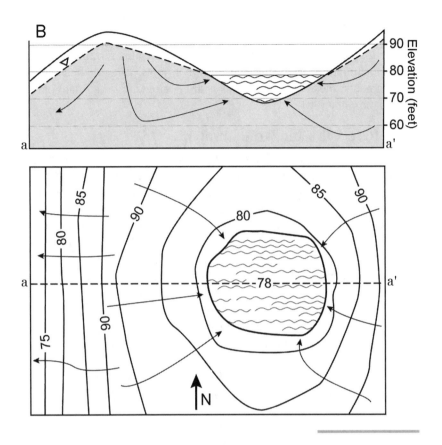

The underlying geology exerts a profound impact on the interplay between groundwater and surface water. For example, the presence of a permeable zone of rock or regolith not far below a lake will accelerate downward seepage of water from the lake — that is, it favors a recharge lake. Impermeable zones will inhibit such water loss and tend to favor or maintain a discharge (gaining) lake. Many hydrogeological factors will influence groundwater movement near a lake or other surface water body including topography, directional permeability, regional water slope, lake depth, and the size, shape, and positioning of rock or regolith units.

The term **vernal pools** has been applied to seasonal ponds or intermittent lakes which contain water only part of the year. Vernal pools are usually small and shallow. Most will owe their existence to conditions in which (1) the water table is temporarily high enough to intersect depressed areas of the land surface, or (2) runoff inflow exceeds infiltration from the depression causing standing water to be present. In the first situation, the pool will be gaining water from the groundwater; in the second, it will be losing water to the ground. Recently glaciated terrains provide ample locations for the formation of vernal pools. Like all freshwater environments, these intermittent lakes are ecologically important parts of the landscape [80].

4.6.2 Reservoirs and Groundwater

Large man-made impoundments, most of which are called **reservoirs**, are a special type of "lake." For obvious reasons, most will be located in low-lying groundwater discharge areas, often behind a dam across a river valley. When the reservoir is filling, the impounded surface water will begin infiltrating into the ground, increasing groundwater storage, raising the water table, and dramatically altering the pre-reservoir steady state relationship between surface water and groundwater. In most situations, the streams are effluent and the rise of the adjacent water table will gradually expand laterally outward from the reservoir area.

As this occurs, major changes in groundwater flow direction and volume will occur. A major groundwater recharge area is suddenly created where a discharge area previously existed. This often generates new discharge areas, and some may be many miles from the reservoir (Figure 4.15). New springs and seeps may form and existing springs often increase flow. Formerly productive forests and croplands may become waterlogged, and evaporative losses where the water table approaches the surface can cause damaging salt buildup in soils. Slopes often become unstable and mass movements result from the increase in fluid pressure due to the rise of groundwater. In effect, the groundwater adds weight and decreases coherency within earth materials. Ecosystem alterations, contamination of well water with mud and other contaminants, and many other consequences are possible. The combination of evaporation and infiltration may significantly reduce valuable surface water supplies downstream from a dam, especially in dry regions. Permanent reversals in groundwater flow direction, sometimes over large areas, are not uncommon.

4.7 Wetlands

Many arguments — legal, political, and environmental — have ensued over what constitutes a wetland. For our purposes, a **wetland** is a vegetated area where the ground is wet or moist all or much of the

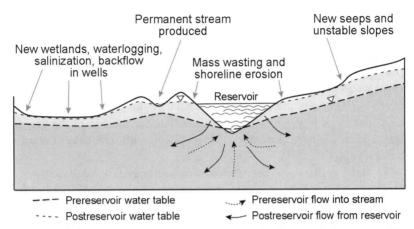

Figure 4.15. Some reservoir impacts associated with groundwater. In this case the stream where the reservoir now is was once an important groundwater discharge zone. Following reservoir construction, the stream valley becomes a major recharge area.

time. Where the water table and the ground surface are in close proximity, or tend to merge, saturated soils will be present and a wetland will exist. Shallow surface water is often present. Like lakes, wetlands provide an opening to the groundwater, and the inflow and outflow relationships between groundwater and surface water will vary with local conditions. Like streams and lakes, wetlands may be permanent, intermittent (seasonal), or ephemeral.

Wetlands are characterized by shallow water, oxygen-poor (anaerobic) soils, and water-tolerant (hydrophytic) vegetation. Among the more common terms associated with various types of wetlands are swamps, bogs, fens, marshes, sloughs, bayous, and quagmires. They are found in tundra; on river floodplains; along coasts in sites such as mangroves, deltas, lagoons, and estuaries; and wherever else high water tables or sufficient standing or slow-moving surface waters produce shallow wet surface conditions. The Florida Everglades (Plate 8, Top) is one of the planet's most famous wetlands. Sixty percent of the Everglades National Park is less than 3 feet above sea level. Canals and levees have drained about half the original Everglades and rising sea levels force salt water ever deeper into what remains. A multi-billion dollar plan to protect the area and restore natural groundwater flow to the Everglades ecosystem is underway [162].

Wetlands occupy about 6% of Earth's land surface and store 20% of its carbon. Many, from the tropics to the polar regions, are underlain by thick deposits of peat. Under the water-saturated conditions, oxidation and decomposition are suppressed allowing the accumulation of carbon-rich organic matter called peat. Destruction of the peat — for example, from melting permafrost in polar regions and expanding human intrusions in the tropics — releases large quantities of the greenhouse gases methane and carbon dioxide, which further exacerbates global warming.

Many wetlands, especially small inland ones, are associated with perched water tables — that is, they are connected to saturated zones which lie above the main water table. Thousands also exist in cold tundra environments where they are perched atop permafrost. The boreal forest belt south of the tundra is an extensive area of mostly low relief, much of it underlain by impermeable rock and regolith such as glacial till and old lake beds — a very favorable environment for wetland formation [120]. Canada's boreal forest has been called the world's most water-rich area and is estimated to contain about 25% of the world's freshwater wetlands [425].

Wetland habitats are among the most biologically important on Earth. Important wetland functions include water filtration and purification, water storage and groundwater recharge, and life-supporting habitat for millions of birds and other species. Wetlands purify water and recharge aquifers. They reduce flooding by holding back excess runoff and by buffering coastal areas from ocean storms and waves. Loss of wetlands in the New Orleans area was likely the major reason that the storm surge from 2005's Hurricane Katrina was able to overrun the levees and flood the city.

Through much of human history, the value of wetlands has been poorly appreciated. People have tended to regard swampy areas as soggy, unpleasant, mosquito-infested wastelands. Some 60% of the world's wetlands have been obliterated over the last 100 years. Most wetland destruction has been caused by agriculture but other activities, including dams, canals, groundwater pumping, urban sprawl, peat mining, and pollution, have all taken a toll.

Example: The Haihe River Wetlands

The Haihe is the third largest river system in China. The Haihe River wetlands, which once covered 3,800 km² (1,465 mi²), have been diminished by more than 80%, to 538 km² or 207 mi², over the past five decades according to China's Xinhua news agency. Chinese experts attribute most of the wetland losses to overuse of groundwater and rapidly expanding development along the river.

4.8 Springs

4.8.1 Introduction

Many ancient peoples believed that the oceans were the direct source of groundwater. One idea was that water entered openings in the sea floor, flowed through underground rivers up into the landmasses and emerged in springs. How else to account for great floods along desert rivers such as the Nile when no local rains could account for them? By the seventeenth century, comparisons of actual measurements of the water volume produced by rainfall with river discharge measurements were beginning to debunk this idea [70].

A **spring** is the place where a concentrated discharge of groundwater flows onto the ground surface or into another body of water — Figure 4.16 and the cover of this book provide photographs of some prominent springs. If the outflow of water is diffuse rather than concentrated, it is called a **seep**, or **seepage area**. Seepage flow tends to be slow and dispersed, but springs and seeps both represent a localized discharge of groundwater.

The water flow from a spring may be a trickle or a deluge. Springs are a common yet rather dramatic expression of the mysterious ocean of subsurface waters and have always fascinated people. Thousands of springs scattered about Earth are regarded as holy, while others have decidedly unholy or satanic reputations, especially those with poisonous, smelly, or sulfurous waters. Springs need not be sacred or damned to attract attention. Water which has traveled considerable distances through subsurface rock will tend to reflect the chemistry of those rocks. The results are waters which may indeed provide certain health benefits, or problems. Cold spring water in limestone areas, for example, may aid indigestion because it often contains considerable calcium bicarbonate, an antacid. Warm spring water in the same area has probably circulated longer and more deeply, causing it to lose its bicarbonate while becoming enriched in calcium and magnesium sulfate. Result: the water tends to act like a laxative and aids constipation [70].

Figure 4.16. Different types of springs. **A.** Morning Glory Pool in Yellowstone National Park, Wyoming, is the surface expression of a hot thermal spring. **B.** Burney Falls in northern California consists mostly of contact springs which emerge from interbeds in lava. **C.** Aerial view of Big Springs, in eastern Idaho, which discharges some 120 million gpd from basaltic lava flows and

is a major source of water for the Henrys Fork River. **D.** Big Spring, south of Van Buren, Missouri, is a karst spring and represents a resurgence of groundwater from a large limestone cavern system. This spring discharges an average of approximately 303 million gpd (469 cfs; 13.3 m³/sec).

Early peoples learned that waters of certain springs aided the sick or even cured diseases. Archeological investigations show that springs were often present where ancient peoples settled. Where fresh surface waters were not present or not dependable, springs became a necessity for human habitation. Many springs gained far-flung reputations as miraculous. Sterility, arthritis, dyspepsia, liver diseases, and aging are among the many ailments which have often been treated with special spring waters. Even among supposedly savvy modern consumers, the use of "spring" water is a big and successful selling point for bottled waters — whether or not it actually comes from a true spring. Many are the elaborate resorts which have, and still do, owe their existence to healing spring waters, and millions have traveled great distances to "take the waters."

4.8.2 Types of Springs

The two basic types of springs are nongravitational and gravitational.

A. Nongravity Springs

Nongravity (nongravitational) springs are caused by water rising to the surface as a result of forces other than gravity. Most nongravity springs are due to subsurface heating and are called thermal, or geothermal, springs (Figure 4.16A). Heating of water above 4°C causes expansion and lowered density causing the heated water to rise. A **thermal spring** is one whose water temperature is higher than that of the local groundwater — or local average annual air temperature, which is typically the same as that of the groundwater. In popular jargon, thermal springs are usually called **warm springs** if their temperature is below that of the human body or **hot springs** if their temperature is above that of the human body.

Thermal springs in nonvolcanic areas are usually associated with deep (1,500-3,000 m) fracture and fault zones. The warm water is a product of Earth's **geothermal gradient**, which is the change in temperature with depth below the surface. The gradient varies greatly from area to area but averages about 25°C of temperature increase for each kilometer of depth. When deep groundwater finds a relatively easy pathway to the surface along the heavily fractured rock, the heated waters may rise and discharge at the surface as thermal springs (Figure 4.17). Two good examples of this type are Hot Springs, Virginia, site of the renowned Homestead resort, and the more humble Warm Springs, located 5 miles north of Hot Springs. Hot Springs' water temperature is about 104°F and Warm Springs' is about 98°F [186].

136

The majority of thermal springs are found in areas where the geo-thermal gradient is higher than average. These are often areas of active volcanic activity, but they will occur any place where hot masses of magma or rock are found at shallow depths. The localized heating gen-erates large convection currents to develop in the groundwater, bringing heated water to the surface where rising currents are concentrated. A wide variety of thermal features are associated with the heated groundwater. Please see Section 8.13 for additional information and illustrations.

B. Gravity (Gravitational) Springs

Most common springs are **gravity springs** which result from nor-mal phreatic water flowage induced by gravity. Five major types are worthy of mention here.

Depression springs are those which occur where the slope of the land surface intersects the water table. They will usually be found at the base of a steep slope — at the bottom of a cliff, foot of a valley-side slope, or the base of an alluvial terrace (Figure 4.18A).

Contact springs occur at the contact between a permeable and an impermeable earth material. Perched water often gives rise to contact springs. If an impermeable unit, such as a shale or clay bed, underlies a

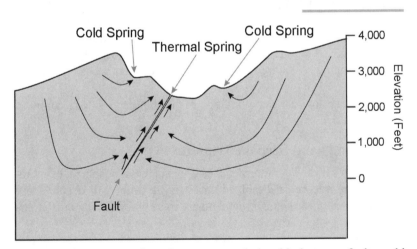

Figure 4.17. Cross-section of a common relationship between faults, cold (shallow water) and thermal (deep water) springs, and groundwater flow in a nonvolcanic area. Arrows indicate very simplified flow paths — the actual paths of deeply circulating groundwater may be very irregular as groundwater threads its way through high-permeability rock and fracture zones.

more permeable material, water will build up atop the impermeable unit and discharge as a line of springs or seeps where the contact intersects the ground surface (figures 4.18B and 4.19). Because the impermeable unit inhibits water from entering underlying rock or soil, a zone of aeration often exists below or within the impermeable layer. Numerous spring outlets may be present, reflecting more permeable zones, such as bedding planes, in the earth material (Plate 8, Bottom).

Shallow, temporary, or intermittent springs and seeps often occur atop the clay-rich B horizons of soils or above other impermeable near-surface deposits (Figure 4.19). Faults which bring rocks of differing permeabilities into contact may generate lines of springs (figures 2.15A and 4.18C). In arid regions, such faults may be identified on maps by the linear trend of the springs or by the vegetation lines which they generate. Mass wasting deposits often create conditions which produce either contact or depression springs, especially at the toe of the deposits (Figure 4.18G and H).

Fracture springs exist where water exits the ground via enlarged fractures — joints, bedding planes, faults, and so forth (Figure 4.18D).

Tubular springs are very similar to fracture springs except the openings are rounded, usually lava tubes or solutional channels in easily dissolved rock such as limestone (Figure 4.18E).

Artesian springs form where water is forced to the surface from an underlying unit in which the water is confined and under pressure (Section 8.2.3). Fractures or other zones of high permeability in the overlying, confining rocks are needed to allow the water access to the surface (Figure 4.18F).

Some springs are a combination of the above types; for example, a tubular artesian spring.

4.8.3 Spring and Seepage Deposits

When subsurface water reaches or nears the atmosphere, evaporation and the release of dissolved gases in the water will occur. These processes may force some mineral matter to be precipitated out from the

Figure 4.18. Common gravity springs. **A.** Depression spring. **B.** Stratigraphic ▶ contact spring. **C.** Fault contact spring. **D.** Fracture spring. **E.** Tubular (solutional) spring. **F.** Artesian spring. **G** and **H.** Springs associated with mass wasting deposits; water for these springs may also be perched rather than connected to the main water table.

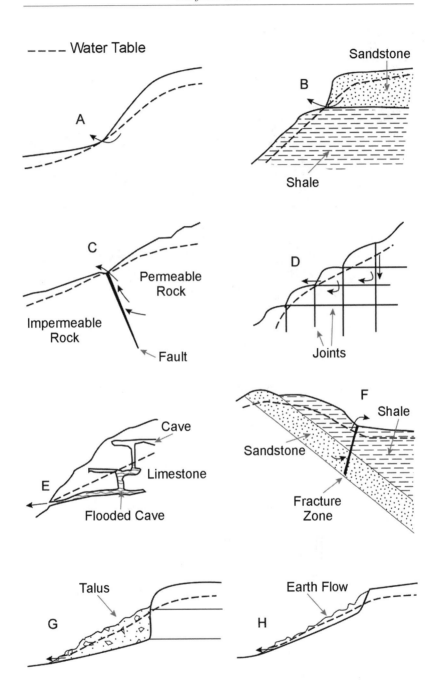

Figure 4.19. A line of springs and seeps in Madison Valley, Montana, marks the contact between permeable overlying gravels (glacial outwash) and the underlying less-permeable clay-rich sediments (lake deposits).

water. If the water contains abundant dissolved matter, the mineral deposits can become very large and even build up in or along streams many miles from the groundwater source (Figure 4.20A). Most large deposits consist of calcium carbonate in the form of **tufa** (a rather soft, porous deposit) and/or **travertine** (a dense, banded deposit). Deposits are especially voluminous where groundwater has circulated through extensive limestone layers (Figure 4.20B) and around thermal springs.

Occasionally, mineral deposits can completely plug up the spring opening, forming a dam of sorts. In arid regions such as the Middle East, water may be located by savvy individuals who have learned to recognize these deposits. Break the mineral seal and the water comes gushing miraculously forth. Perhaps this was how Moses, who was very familiar with the desert environment, produced water when he struck a rock and generated water for the thirsty and rebellious Israelites when crossing the Sinai desert.

4.8.4 Degradation of Springs

Needless to say, anything which impairs the groundwater quality or lowers the water table is likely to have a profound impact upon waters

Figure 4.20. Deposits along streams produced by mineral-laden groundwater. **A.** A small tufa dam (rimstone pool) along Falls Creek in Falls Ridge Nature Conservancy Preserve, Virginia. **B.** Sparse waters fall over a large cliff at the lower edge of a massive deposit of tufa and travertine left by mineral laden waters at Sitting Bull Falls, New Mexico.

which "spring" forth from those groundwater bodies. Many of the world's major springs are now gone, imperiled, or greatly degraded due to development, pollution, and depletion of water resources. When Las Vegas, Nevada, was first founded, springs were everywhere and the water supply seemed unending. Today the springs are long-gone and the water-stressed city is reaching out for water from sources far and wide. Situations similar to this have been repeated around the world as ever-increasing withdrawals of groundwater continue to severely deplete valuable springs and wetlands of their water supply.

Example: Florida Springs

Most of Florida's 700-plus identified springs are tubular springs, fed by an intricate subterranean network of solutional conduits in the underlying limestone. Many of these subsurface waterways are connected to the surface via the depressions called sinkholes (Section 8.5.5). Some sinkholes gather surface water which feeds the groundwater, others intersect the water table and contain lakes, and some contain major springs. Florida's springs include the largest single-orifice spring in the country, Alapaha Rise, which discharges an average of 802 ft^3 of water per second. The extraordinary growth of Florida's population, agriculture, and associated development has resulted in severe threats to most springs. Developments often divert surface waters, overpump groundwater, generate pollution, and obliterate sinkholes. Wherever they occur, sinkholes have been popular places to dispose of construction debris and trash, often polluting the groundwater in the process. Even tourism, and the associated litter and trampling of the ground, has severely degraded many popular springs. Florida alone has spent millions of dollars to try to rehabilitate wounded springs [211, 309].

5
Vadose Water

The unsaturated zone is a key linkage between atmospheric moisture, groundwater, and eventual seepage of groundwater to streams, lakes, and the oceans.

— Gary L. Guymon

5.1 Influences on Infiltration Rates

Subsurface water which lies above the water table is known as vadose water. This water cannot be withdrawn for direct human use, but its presence is critical, directly or indirectly, to all life on the surface of Earth, and most water that falls on land areas must migrate through this zone to reach the water table and become true groundwater.

Nearly all the water below the land surface but above sea level is meteoric water — water that fell from the atmosphere via precipitation. Part of the meteoric water will infiltrate, or percolate, into the subsurface — how much varies depending upon vegetation, soil characteristics, and related properties. The infiltration rate is a measure of how rapidly this water enters the subsurface. The many factors which influence the infiltration rate may be summarized as follows.

5.1.1 Soil Properties

Soil was defined in Section 2.6.4. Soil acts like a thin membrane across which matter and energy are exchanged between the surface and subsurface environments. In addition to its critical role in sustaining life at Earth's surface, soil strongly influences the quantity and quality of the matter, especially the water, which passes through it. Its influence on groundwater is often overlooked but the growing sub-specialty of hydropedology, which melds soil science and hydrology, should serve to correct this oversight.

The term "soil properties" is widely used in reference to the characteristics of the surface materials (Table 2.3), usually the upper few feet of the regolith, and are especially important in determining infiltration rates. Important soil properties include:

- texture — particle sizes;
- fabric — the sorting and orientation of soil particles;
- physical structure — the way soil breaks apart — blocky, granular, columnar, prismatic, flaky, and so on;
- biologic structures — mostly roots and animal holes or burrows;
- antecedent soil moisture — the moisture content in the soil remaining from previous wetting events; and
- soil surface conditions — hard-baked clay, loose, gravelly, recently plowed, and others.

Such characteristics as small pore spaces, poor sorting (a wide variety of particle sizes), moisture remaining from a previous rain, and the presence of ice can decrease infiltration rates. Large interconnected pores, coarse textures, and organic matter all tend to increase infiltration by allowing excess water to pass more easily through the soil.

5.1.2 Rainfall Characteristics

Moderate rainfall events usually encourage high infiltration rates. Lengthy rains cause clays to swell, decreasing the size of openings and lowering infiltration rates. Brief rains tend to be largely absorbed by evaporation and transpiration. Heavy rains encourage higher runoff and lower infiltration rates. Raindrops striking the ground surface compact soil and fine particles moved by their impacts plug soil openings, both of which decrease infiltration rates. Intense rainfall packs loose soil and disperses small particles. Splash erosion from raindrop impact with exposed soil can disturb 100 tons of soil per acre during a violent storm.

5.1.3 Vegetation

Vegetative cover and litter influence infiltration in numerous ways, including shielding soil from direct raindrop impact and splash erosion, slowing down raindrop velocity, providing organic matter, encouraging wildlife (including burrowing mammals, worms, and insects), and reducing runoff velocity. Partially decomposed organic matter in soil holds soil particles together in small, friable (easily pulverized) clumps. Most organic-rich soil retains sufficient moisture for crops and also allows enough infiltration to avoid waterlogging. Virtually any activity which diminishes vegetative cover — trampling, off-road vehicles, fires, logging, and others — will tend to decrease infiltration rates. Negative impacts of devegetation include decreases in soil moisture, decreases in groundwater recharge, increases in erosion, increases in flooding, and more severe drought conditions during dry spells.

5.1.4 Land Use

It should be obvious that human uses of the land can have enormous impacts on infiltration and runoff rates. Cities now cover much land with impervious rooftops and pavement where forests and grasslands once lay. Plowed lands and clearcut forests have greatly diminished infiltration capacities. In addition to the destruction of plant cover and root networks, plowing often brings impermeable clay-rich subsoils to the surface. In northern Mississippi, 16 times more runoff may flow from cultivated lands than from pine forests and the erosion rates may be over 1,000 times greater. More subtle land uses, such as light recreation and grazing, can still have very significant impacts. The infiltration rate on well-managed grazing land will often be several times greater than on poorly managed grazing land [108].

5.1.5 Topography

Topography encompasses the character of a terrain, including the magnitude and orientation of slopes, and the spatial distribution of flatlands, depressions, valley sides, water bodies, and other features of the landscape. Gently sloping terrain which encourages slow runoff or otherwise detains runoff will permit higher percentages of water to enter the subsurface, as will the presence of depressions.

5.2 True Infiltration Capacity

In general, infiltration rates will be highest after a long dry spell when antecedent soil moisture is at a minimum. Most soils will have a high initial infiltration rate. As rainfall continues, factors such as the increase in soil moisture content, swelling of clays, and the filling of openings by fine particles will produce a decrease in the rate of infiltration. As shown on Figure 5.1, a steady, minimal infiltration rate will soon be attained. This is often called the **true infiltration capacity**. In general, the coarser and looser the material, the greater the true infiltration rate will be. For example, tests on row crops show that minimum infiltration rates vary from about 0 to 1 mm/hr in clays to 12 mm/hr in deep sands and loess [275].

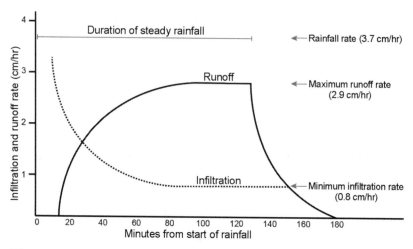

Figure 5.1. Idealized graph showing the infiltration and runoff rates during a steady rainfall. Both the infiltration and runoff rates change rapidly at first, then level off when the true infiltration capacity is reached. Ideally, the runoff and infiltration rates should equal the rainfall rate [108].

Soil infiltration rates can be measured using a metal **infiltration ring**, which consists of a pipe 15 to 30 centimeters in diameter. The pipe is driven about 5 centimeters into the ground and water is then added to the standing part of the pipe. By carefully measuring the decline in the water level over time, and adding water as needed, the rate of water infiltration can be determined. An outer pipe may also be driven into the soil to prevent lateral seepage of the water, which would exaggerate the rate of infiltration.

5.3 Water in the Zones of Aeration and Saturation

5.3.1 Terminology

As noted previously, subsurface water occurs in two major zones or environments, one saturated and one unsaturated. These are often described as an unsaturated **zone of aeration** in which the pore spaces of the earth material contain a mixture of gas (air) and water, and a **zone of saturation** in which the matrix pores are filled with water.

As noted in Section 3.8, the **water table** represents the surface of the true groundwater. The water table has no volume. Hence it is not correct to say one gets water "from the water table." Below the water table, water is able to migrate under the forces of gravity because it is under positive pressure; that is, it experiences a pressure greater than atmospheric pressure. It is this water which must be tapped to obtain water from a well. If an unlined well or pit is dug to below the water table, water will seep into the well and eventually stabilize at the level of the water table. The terms "groundwater" and **phreatic water** refer to this subsurface water which saturates its environment and moves in response to hydrostatic pressure.

Water above the water table is under "negative" pressure (that is, less than atmospheric pressure) and is often called **vadose water**. With the exception of areas temporarily saturated during major infiltration events and a zone of water immediately above the water table held in place by capillary forces (Section 5.5.3), vadose water shares its subsurface regime with "vacant" (gas-filled) pore spaces.

In recent years, some geologists and hydrogeologists have recommended abandoning the use of the terms vadose and phreatic in favor of water in the unsaturated zone and water in the saturated zone. This can be confusing because, as noted above, the "unsaturated zone" as commonly defined includes saturated material. Defining the water table as the top surface of the saturated zone is also confusing and inaccurate. Vadose and phreatic are brief, convenient terms which continue to find wide use.

5.3.2 General Characteristics of the Water Table

In most areas, the water table tends to mimic the surface terrain, but is more subdued. Its elevation will increase below hills and ridges and decrease below valleys and lowlands, often intersecting the surface topography wherever permanent streams or other water bodies are present (figures 3.1, 3.9-3.11, and 5.2). Thus, one can expect groundwater to lie farther below the surface on a hill and considerably closer to the surface along a valley bottom. One can think of the surface of most streams and lakes as an "exposure" of the water table or the groundwater. As noted above, an inverted triangle (∇) is often used on cross-sections and diagrams to identify the water table. Note on Figure 5.2 that the water table is continuous with the water level in lakes, streams, and other permanent water features. As the groundwater level decreases during droughts, so does the water level in these surface features.

The water table will slope toward a stream or lake which is receiving water from the groundwater — for example, toward an effluent stream

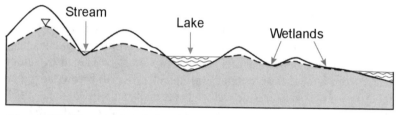

Figure 5.2. Water table relationship to permanent (effluent) surface water features.

(figures 4.5A and 5.2). The surface of an influent stream, on the other hand, will lie at a higher level than the nearby water table (Figure 4.5B and C). As noted in Chapter 4, it is not uncommon for a water body to gain water in some areas and lose it in others.

5.4 Characteristics of Vadose Water

5.4.1 Negative Pressure

As noted above, vadose water is not free to migrate into a well or onto the surface as a spring. Unlike water below the water table, no positive fluid pressure exists to force the water in the zone of aeration from the earth material. The pressure is negative (less than atmospheric pressure). The less water present in the vadose zone, the stronger the negative pressure is and the stronger will be the tendency of the material to attract or absorb water. In other words, the drier a material, the stronger the capillary forces will be. When vadose water is lost, it will be depleted first from the larger pore spaces where capillary forces are not as strong. As the material dries out, the finer pore spaces cling ever more tightly to the remaining water. The capillary forces holding the water are sometimes referred to as suction or tensional forces. The moisture present in the zone of aeration is under tension, held in place, and cannot flow unless conditions change, such as when water is added from precipitation.

This pressure can be measured with a **tensiometer**, which determines tensional (suctional) forces in the soil by measuring how much water is drawn from a tube into the soil.

5.4.2 Four Types of Vadose Water

Three categories of liquid vadose water are often present in the zone of aeration: hygroscopic water, capillary water, and gravity water.

Hygroscopic water is held as thin films on the surfaces of rock or soil particles by a strong molecular attraction between the mineral matter and the water. This water is generally very small in volume, unavailable to plants, and not very significant. **Capillary water** is held in open spaces by a combination of water's adhesive and cohesive forces. When the weight of water present exceeds the capillary forces holding the water in place, the excess water becomes **gravity water** and percolates downward toward the water table. A fourth form of vadose water, **water vapor**, can also be present in the vadose zone. Hygroscopic and capillary water can be vaporized under drying conditions.

5.5 Three Zones of Vadose Water

Vadose water is present in three major zones or belts: soil moisture, the intermediate zone, and the capillary fringe (Figure 5.3).

5.5.1 Soil Moisture Belt

Soil moisture refers to water present from the ground surface down to the lower limit of plant roots. This upper part of the unsaturated zone is often called the belt of soil water. Soil moisture represents a tiny amount (<0.002%) of Earth's total water, but it is vital to the survival of most plants, hence to nearly all life on land. Its impacts on weathering, scenery, soil formation, and the chemistry of both ground and surface waters are enormous. The upper one meter of soil in the US is estimated to contain some 630 billion cubic meters of water. This moisture is gradually depleted by evaporation and transpiration. When plants cannot extract further water from the soil, they begin to wilt. The quantity of water present when wilting commences is termed the **wilting point**. It generally requires a dry spell of 1 to 3 months to deplete all the moisture in the belt of soil water.

The total amount of water a soil can hold by capillary force is called the **field capacity** for that soil. The difference in water content between the field capacity and the wilting point represents water that is available to plants (Figure 5.4). Decreases in crop yields are often seen when the soil water content falls below a critical level — usually 40 to 70% of the soil water available to plants, depending on the soil characteristics and the crop. Field capacity depends mainly on the texture (particle size) of the soil material, with smaller-grained soils containing progressively more moisture. Note on Figure 5.4 that the medium-grained soils provide the most plant-available water, an important factor for agricultural purposes. The increasing rise in the wilting point

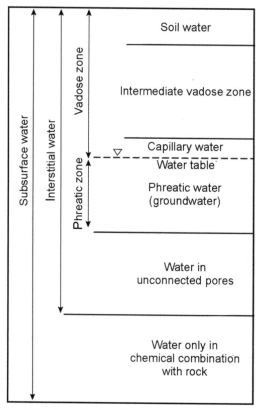

Figure 5.3. Classification of subsurface water.

curve reflects the greater water-retaining capacity of the finer-grained soils [108, 422].

Especially important is the **soil moisture cycle** which depicts the changes in available soil moisture through the year. A typical soil moisture cycle for a humid mid-latitude area in the Northern Hemisphere with warm summers and cold winters is shown in Figure 5.5. Note the build-up in soil moisture from fall to early spring, a result of the cold temperatures and the dormancy in plant growth. The early spring surplus in April typically produces muddy conditions and high runoff. Then warming conditions and rapid plant growth lead to heavy evapotranspiration demands and the soil moisture declines to a late summer-early fall deficiency. The minor "hills" on the graph indicate rain events restoring soil moisture.

Soil moisture is a critical parameter in crop-growing regions. Soil moisture needs to be considered when deciding on irrigation needs, most suitable crops to plant, the best time to plant a given crop, and other important factors. Hence, it is useful to classify agricultural areas based on soil-moisture characteristics [387, 564]. Water content is also very important in determining the behavior of soils for many construction and engineering purposes.

The amount of moisture in a soil can be measured in several ways. A representative sample of the soil can be collected and weighed, placed in an oven and dried out, then weighed again. Other methods include use of tensiometers, electrical resistivity, and neutron probes. **Electrical resistivity** instruments measure the ability of a soil to conduct an electric current; electrical conductivity generally increases with moisture content. **Neutron probes** detect neutrons from a source — usually isotopes of radium and beryllium — after they have passed through a soil

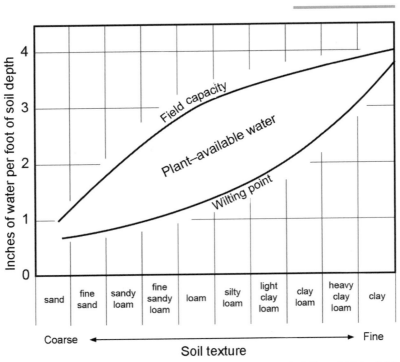

Figure 5.4. Relationships between soil texture, water-holding ability, field capacity, and wilting point. The field capacity is an average, as it can vary considerably for a given soil texture, especially for the finer-grained soils [422].

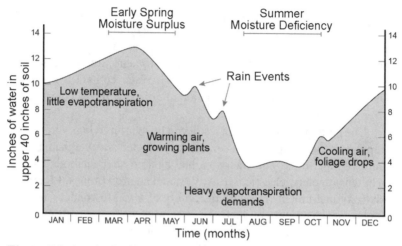

Figure 5.5. A typical soil moisture cycle for a humid temperate mid-latitude area [387].

sample. The fewer the neutrons making it through the soil, the more water is present in the soil.

5.5.2 Intermediate Belt

Below the soil moisture belt is the **intermediate belt** of vadose water. This zone may range from zero to several hundred feet in thickness. As in the soil moisture belt, gravity will pull excess water downward toward the water table once the field capacity of the material is exceeded. As water content increases above the field capacity level, the volume of water the material can transmit will increase. The excess water percolates downward from the surface as a wave of moisture. With the cessation of infiltration into the ground surface, the excess water will gradually drain out. Earth materials which do not allow soil drainage to occur readily will remain saturated for a period of time, creating a zone of perched water and waterlogged conditions. Even relatively brief periods of waterlogging can prove very destructive to buildings, septic tanks, crops, and other valuable commodities.

5.5.3 The Capillary Fringe

The **capillary fringe** sits atop the water table and consists of water held up by capillary tension. The thickness of the fringe can vary from negligible in very coarse sediments to several meters in very fine-grained

152

materials. Generally it will be on the order of one centimeter in well-sorted sand and gravel and two feet in clay. Due to the heterogeneous nature of many natural earth materials, the upper boundary of the capillary fringe can be very irregular. Although the fringe is saturated, it is not true groundwater because the water is not under positive pressure and is not free to migrate in response to hydrostatic pressure. Thus water from the capillary fringe would not enter a well.

6 Phreatic Water

Or the water of the garden will run off underground so that thou wilt never be able to find it.

— Koran, Sura 18:41

6.1 Hydrostatic Pressure and Phreatic Water

Earth's mass creates a strong gravitational pull on all nearby matter. Within a fluid such as air or water, this force produces a confining pressure which pushes in from all sides. **Atmospheric pressure** is the downward force caused by the weight of the atmosphere. Below the surface of a continuous water body, the weight of water at higher elevations must be added to the atmospheric pressure. The pressure exerted by water at any given point within a body of water is **hydrostatic pressure**. **Phreatic water** is water below the water table which moves in response to the forces of gravity and hydrostatic pressure (Figure 5.3). As used in this book and in many hydrogeologic contexts, phreatic water is synonymous with "groundwater."

The hydrostatic pressure in groundwater is greater than atmospheric pressure and is caused by the weight of water at higher levels in the body of groundwater. The **water table** marks the upper surface of phreatic water and also represents the surface of atmospheric pressure: that is, the location where the groundwater's hydrostatic pressure equals the weight of the overlying blanket of air. If the water below the water table were not under pressure greater than the atmospheric pressure, water could not enter a well but would be held back by the force exerted by Earth's blanket of air.

The presence of water or other reasonably heavy fluids within a material has strong impacts on the behavior of the material. Objects, even large heavy objects like ocean liners and tankers, float in the ocean because the water exerts an upward force equal to the weight of the displaced water. When water saturates a sediment or rock material, the water exerts a buoyant force which tends to lift up particles. This force is often called **fluid pressure** or pore-water pressure and is considered a negative force because it operates in the opposite direction of gravity. Hence, in a sediment or other material, the grain-to-grain forces between adjacent particles or surfaces are reduced by the presence of water. This internally weakens the material, making it less cohesive and less stable. Hence, regolith and rock are more liable to undergo movements or slippage when saturated with water. The term **effective stress** (P_e) indicates the difference between the gravitational force (geostatic pressure) (P_g) in an earth material and the fluid pressure (P_f).

$$P_e = P_g - P_f$$

Most groundwater moves in long, gently curved paths controlled by the pull of gravity on the water and the differences in hydrostatic pressure within the groundwater reservoir, as shown in Figure 3.11A. Except where fairly large, connected openings are present, phreatic water attempting to migrate through regolith and rock encounters great resistance and in most situations its movement, by human standards, is painfully slow. A typical flow rate for groundwater in most solid earth materials might be around 0.0000001 m/s (10^{-7} m/s) which is only about 3 m/yr (10 ft/yr). Most actual flow rates vary from less than 1 m/yr to over 15 m/yr. Much hydrogeology focuses upon the direction, velocity, and quantity of groundwater that journeys unseen through the millions of cubic kilometers of rock and soil lying at shallow depths beneath Earth's surface.

6.2 Deeper Subsurface Waters

Below the phreatic zone, water is believed to exist mostly in unconnected pores or in chemical combination with rock (Figure 5.3). The lower boundary of phreatic water is indistinct and may range from as little as 500 feet below the surface in granitic rock to 50,000 feet in some sedimentary rock sequences and heavily fractured rock. Very little free water is present deeper than a few miles below the land surface. In most, but not all, situations, high confining pressures and rock flowage will eliminate nearly all pores at such depths.

6.3 Types of Phreatic Water

Phreatic water which is open to the zone of aeration and the atmosphere — that is, whose movement is not restricted by some impermeable zone — is **unconfined water**. This water has a "normal" water table as shown in Figure 3.11A. If some relatively impermeable material overlies and is in contact with the groundwater, inhibiting its normal migration, it is called **confined water**. The presence of an impermeable confining bed holds back groundwater attempting to move toward areas of lower pressure, usually toward the ground surface. Thus pressure builds up in the water below the confining zone. Groundwater under confining pressure is also called **artesian water**.

A zone of saturation is often formed above an impermeable unit which is located above the normal water table. Under these conditions, a zone of saturation with its own water table will be separated from the underlying water table by a zone of aeration. We refer to such overlying zones of groundwater as **perched water**. The three common types of phreatic water are illustrated in Figure 6.1.

Connate water is groundwater which has been out of contact with the surface for a very long period of time — millions of years. It often consists of water which was trapped in sediments when they were being deposited. Any "old" (thousands of years or more) groundwater is sometimes called **fossil water**.

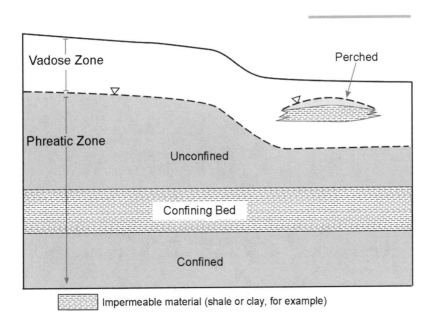

Figure 6.1. Cross-section showing three types of phreatic water bodies: perched, unconfined, and confined.

6.4 The Water Table

6.4.1 Introduction

The water table tends to reflect the topography of the ground surface, especially in humid to subhumid areas, but is more subdued (figures 3.11A and 5.2). A line of high points on the water table occurs below areas of recharge and is called a **groundwater divide**. Major groundwater divides usually lie roughly below the topographic drainage divide, but may be offset as shown on Figure 6.2 due to such major influences as subsurface geology and localized recharge areas, and by lesser factors such as directional properties in the rock (tilted strata, aligned pores, and so forth), differing rates of precipitation and infiltration, or snowmelt on the overlying slopes. The groundwater divide can be extended into the subsurface, shown by the dotted vertical lines on Figure 6.2, where it represents an irregular plane of divergent groundwater flow. In effect, this divide represents the boundaries of distinct

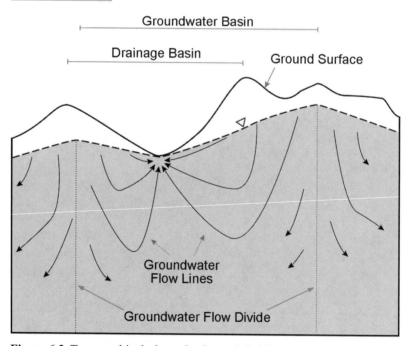

Figure 6.2. Topographic drainage basins and divides do not always coincide with groundwater basins.

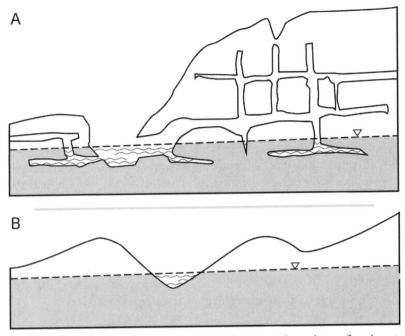

A

B

Figure 6.3. Nearly flat water tables can exist even where the surface is not level.

groundwater flow systems, often referred to as **groundwater basins** or flow cells.

The lowest areas on the local water table will usually be streams or other permanent surface water bodies into which the groundwater discharges. In arid regions, however, a groundwater ridge and divide will often be present below influent streams and lakes (figures 4.5 and 4.13).

In areas where the regolith or rock is especially permeable, water may drain rapidly downward producing a water table that is nearly flat much of the time even though the terrain is not flat. Examples include karst areas where solutional conduits are abundant (Figure 6.3A) and areas underlain by very permeable sands or gravels (Figure 6.3B). In arid regions with insignificant infiltration in local highlands, groundwater will eventually vacate the highlands leaving a nearly flat water table.

The **slope** or inclination of the water table will be quite gentle in most areas. The location and slope of the water table provide critical information for many hydrogeological studies.

Where the water table intersects the ground surface, water will be evident as a stream, lake, swamp, spring, or related water feature. These hydrologic surface features were discussed in Chapter 4. Groundwater discharge areas provide a base level for the local water table. A **base level** is an elevation or surface which erosional or depositional processes strive to reach. Surface water bodies such as streams and lakes frequently serve as local base levels for the water table over much of Earth's land surface. Nearby groundwater flows toward, and discharges into, these low-lying areas. Base level represents a surface of equilibrium, but one which is rarely maintained for any length of time on an active planet due to ongoing activities such as the recycling of water, erosion, and the tectonic movements of the solid earth. For example, as a stream erodes more deeply into the earth, the local base level for the groundwater drops accordingly. If all activities which increase the terrain's elevation — mainly tectonic uplift and volcanism — were to cease, continents — and the water table — would be reduced in a few tens of millions of years to a nearly level plain at sea level. Thus sea level is often called the **ultimate base level** and all others **local** or **temporary base levels**.

6.4.2 Water Table Fluctuations

The water table rises and falls in response to recharge and discharge. For example, in a mid-latitude area such as the north-central US, water tables will be low near the end of a cold winter followed by twenty or so weeks of recharge as infiltration from snowmelt and spring rains replenish the groundwater. Typical seasonal fluctuations vary greatly depending upon local geology and weather, but average roughly two to three feet. All else being equal, the rate of water table lowering, and hence local stream discharge, during periods of reduced recharging, such as droughts and freezing weather, can be accurately predicted based upon previous observations. Changes in depth of the water table tend to be greatest below hills and uplands and least in valley bottoms and lowlands (figures 4.14 and 6.4). In the US, information on seasonal high and low water tables is often available in the form of publications and maps from agencies such as the Natural Resources Conservation Service, Soil and Water Conservation Districts, university Cooperative Extension Services, and local water boards.

In the US, over 20,000 groundwater observation wells are used to keep tabs on groundwater supplies. The water table level may be measured relative to any convenient datum plane, such as elevation relative to mean sea level, depth below ground surface, or depth below some

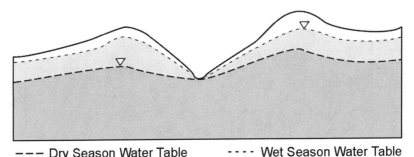

– – – Dry Season Water Table   - - - - Wet Season Water Table

Figure 6.4. The water table level can fluctuate considerably in wet and dry conditions.

established surface feature. A common practice is to graph water table levels vs. time (a groundwater hydrograph) to show groundwater trends and aid water supply predictions (figures 6.5 and 6.6). The trend of the discharge curves on Figure 6.5 can be projected to predict water table levels and groundwater supplies following lengthy periods of drought. This extended discharge curve is called a **groundwater recession curve**. Every aquifer has its own characteristic recession curve.

Longer time intervals can reveal important trends such as the decline of water table shown in Figure 6.6. The annual cycles on Figure 6.6 show distinct increases in water levels (recharge periods) followed by longer declines where discharge exceeds recharge. This curve is characteristic of a humid temperate area with winter/spring recharge similar to the soil moisture curve in Figure 5.5.

Most fluctuations in the water table will be gradual, reflecting the slow movement of groundwater through earth materials. However, exceptions do occur. Recent studies have shown that groundwater contributes much more to storm runoff than was believed in the past. This may be due in part to subsurface flow (storm drainage or interflow) through near-surface soils made more permeable by the presence of litter, fractures, root channels, animal burrows, and the like.

Another factor involves a rapid rise in the water table and the resulting increase in hydrostatic pressure in shallow groundwater near streams. In most humid and subhumid areas, the water table lies close to the ground surface along valley bottoms, both those containing active streams and ephemeral valleys. Once water percolating through the zone of aeration reaches the top of the capillary fringe, the capillary fringe zone is readily converted into phreatic water, effectively raising the level

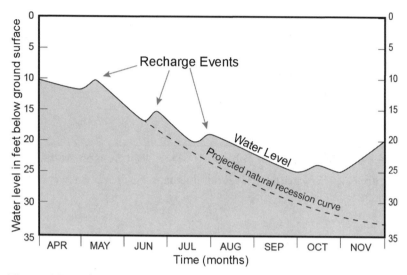

Figure 6.5. Typical groundwater hydrograph of water level changes though time in a well. This shows the decline (recession) in the water table during the spring-summer growing season in a humid temperate region. The natural groundwater recession curve is constructed by extending the curve to show the anticipated decline of the water table should no recharge occur [177].

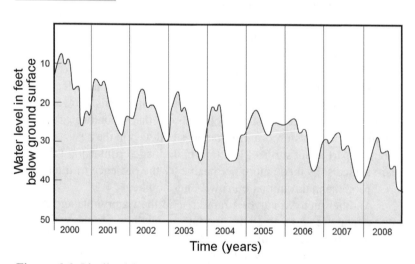

Figure 6.6. Idealized long-term hydrograph of the water table in a well. Annual recharge-discharge cycles are clearly shown as is a long-term decline in the water table [177].

of the water table (Figure 4.3). In low swales and valley bottoms this change can occur quite soon after the onset of rainfall or snowmelt, producing an acceleration of groundwater discharge and considerably increasing the area over which that discharge occurs. The result can be a rapid and significant increase in wetland area and streamflow. Figure 6.7 illustrates the increase in discharge area during a wet phase for a small idealized drainage basin in a humid temperate area. During normal or fairly dry conditions, the only discharge will be into the stream channels. During a wet period, a large increase in the area of groundwater discharge (seepage) occurs as indicated by the shaded areas on Figure 6.7 [108].

6.4.3 Human Impacts on the Water Table

The ways in which human activities impact the water table and the groundwater supply are almost unlimited. They include not only large-scale disruptions such as climate change and removal of massive volumes of groundwater, but also localized influences such as excavations and farm ponds. Even seemingly minor disturbances in groundwater flow systems can yield significant impacts including shifting of groundwater divides, changes in flow rates and directions, and serious reductions or amplifications of surface water supplies. This section provides examples of impacts on the water table resulting from common human undertakings.

A. Lowering the Water Table

Removal of groundwater by whatever means will almost always produce declines in the elevation of the water table. Direct pumping of groundwater is the most important way in which human activities deplete groundwater and lower the water table. In heavily pumped areas, water tables have often been lowered by many hundreds of feet. The consequences of groundwater depletion are covered in Section 12.3.

Any cut or excavation which intersects the water table will tend to lower the nearby water table and, initially at least, provide a discharge area. Excavations for roadcuts, building sites, tunnels, mines, and related ventures typically provide ditches, conduits, or other means of transporting excess water from the site. The extent of impacts depends mostly upon the size and depth of the excavation, the topography, and the elevation of the water table.

Impacts from simple surface cuts tend to be most severe where the terrain is nearly flat or gently sloping and the water table is close to the surface. Discharge from the intercepted groundwater into the excavated

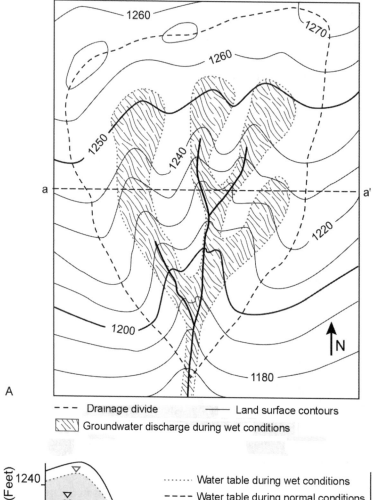

A

- - - Drainage divide   —— Land surface contours

⟦shading⟧ Groundwater discharge during wet conditions

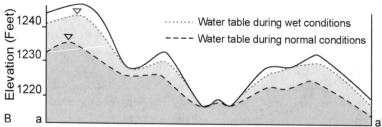

········· Water table during wet conditions

- - - Water table during normal conditions

B

Figure 6.7. A. Topographic map of a small idealized drainage basin showing the increase in groundwater discharge area during a wet period (shaded area). The dotted line is the drainage divide outlining the drainage basin. **B**. Cross-section for location a-a' on the map showing the position of the water table during normal (lower, dashed line) and wet conditions (higher, dotted line) [108].

area will proceed at a diminishing rate until a new equilibrium is achieved (Figure 6.8A). The lowering of the water table will slowly expand outward and lower the water levels in wells and surface water bodies such as streams and wetlands. In some cases, an aquifer may be intercepted or "beheaded" by deep excavations such as roadcuts (Plate 8, Bottom), quarries, and mines, thereby cutting off the water supply to downgradient water systems, as shown on Figure 6.8B.

If influent (losing) streams suffer reduced flow from upstream water withdrawals, or other losses such as evaporation from reservoirs, the amount of water recharging groundwater will also diminish. If a lake or marsh is drained, the water table will be lowered. Subsurface mining, quarrying, and drilling activities often intersect water-carrying strata, disrupting the flow of phreatic water. Such actions have serious implications for water users and sensitive ecosystems, although the negative impacts may not be apparent for many years due to the slow movement of groundwater.

The water table is especially sensitive to disruption in arid and semiarid regions. For example, during the 1860s and 1870s, many stream valleys and drainage basins in Arizona and New Mexico had high water tables which supported lush grasses, shade trees, streams, and ponds.

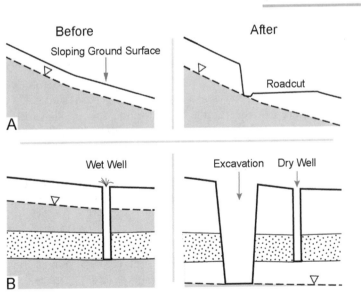

Figure 6.8. Impact of excavations on groundwater. **A.** Lowering of water table. **B.** Beheading of aquifer.

165

Figure 6.9. View down Dead Juniper Wash, Black Mesa, Arizona. The erosion of the inner gully has occurred since the 1880s. The cause of the renewed erosion is believed to be climate change (drier, warmer) and/or vegetation losses related to overgrazing. In either case, results include lowering of water table and increased erosion.

By the 1880s, the area was becoming significantly more arid. Though some feel a natural climate change may have been involved, considerable evidence suggests that the major cause was a loss of vegetative cover due to overgrazing by cattle and sheep. This resulted in accelerated runoff (more floods) and erosion along with reduced groundwater recharge leading to a drop in the water table. Soon the grasses and trees were gone. In their place were deep gullies and desert scrub brush (Figure 6.9). This is but one of many examples of the important but often unappreciated relationship between land use and water resources.

B. Raising the Water Table

Man-made features such as reservoirs, lagoons, canals, and irrigation systems will cause the local water table to rise. For those concerned with diminishing water resources, raising the water table may seem like a positive development, but such is not always the case.

Wetlands are important ecosystems providing many benefits. However, in locations where the natural water table was lower, a rise of the water table can cause waterlogging and salinization of farmlands, both of which can be deadly to crops and native vegetation. Proper drainage on agricultural lands is extremely important. Much of the finest cropland consists of fairly level lowlands where the water table is close to the surface. Even a slight change in elevation of either the water table or the bottom of a channel can have important repercussions. If the water table is too near the surface, roots can rot, salts can build up in the soil, and excess water can seep to the surface causing increased soil erosion among other problems. Over 20% (more than 110 million acres) of US cropland is in need of drainage improvements to improve production or conserve soil. Drainage ditches or pipes below the surface can alleviate these problems. Subsurface drains in the US Midwest are often 30 to 40 feet deep and placed 20 to 80 feet apart. Similar drainage adjustments are often required to prevent subsurface water problems such as structural damages, flooded basements, and unstable slopes around buildings, roadways, golf courses, and numerous other sites. Figure 6.10 illustrates three common ways of lowering the local water table to avoid or minimize potential water damage. If a drainageway has no surface outlet, a sump and a pump can be installed to remove the water.

Mass wasting, increased solutioning and corrosion, damage to structures (buildings, underground tanks, and pipelines, for example), and numerous other problems are associated with rises in the water table. In Egypt, famous archeological sites including the Temples of Karnak and the Valley of Kings/Queens, have been threatened by an elevated water table brought on by higher flows in the Nile River due to controlled flows from the Aswan High Dam, the irrigation of sugar cane fields, and sewer seepage. For example, when the water table is high during irrigation, the sandstones of the temples absorb the water. When the water level drops, salt in the water crystallizes as the water evaporates. Growth of the tiny crystals pries the sand grains apart and the rock disintegrates, weakening massive stonework that had withstood thousands of years of normal weathering. Meanwhile, in Venice, Italy, one suggestion for correcting the notorious downsinking of that city with its famous canals, islands, and bridges is to inject seawater beneath the city in an effort to raise it by as much as a foot. Unfortunately, undoing the damage caused by altering water tables is far more difficult than causing the damage.

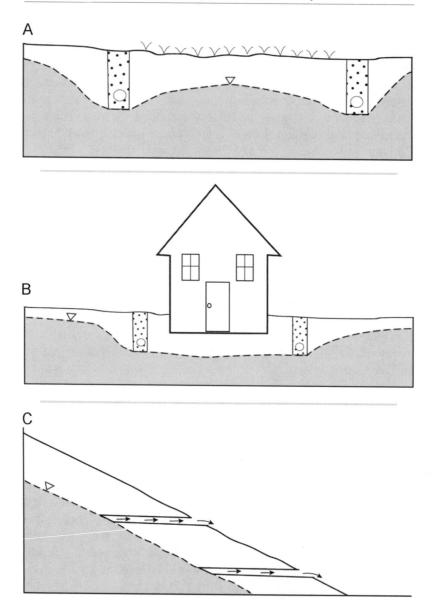

Figure 6.10. Three common methods for lowering the water table to prevent damage. **A.** Trenches filled with gravel and/or perforated drainage pipes can prevent waterlogging of crops. **B.** Trenches of permeable gravel (French drains) can protect building foundations from water damage. **C.** Perforated pipes remove excess water from slopes, helping to stabilize the material and reduce mass wasting.

6.5 Porosity

Porosity was introduced in Chapter 2 and is defined as the ratio of the total volume of openings (V_p) in a material to the total volume (V_t) of the material:

$$P = \frac{V_p}{V_t}$$

Porosity values are often given in percent. Multiply by 100% to make a ratio a percent. A common method of determining porosity is to weigh a saturated sample of the material, such as soil, then dry the sample in an oven and weigh it again. The difference in weight represents the water content which can easily be converted to volume (for water, 1 g = 1 cm³) and divided by the total volume of the original sample to give porosity. For all practical purposes, the water volume equals the pore volume.

Example: Solving a Problem

If 500 cm³ of gravel has a mass of 1000 grams when saturated and 900 grams when completely dry, what is its porosity?

The mass of the water in the sample is 1000 g − 900 g = 100 g, which equals 100 cm³. Hence it's porosity is: $P = V_p/V_t$ = 100 cm³/500 cm³ = 0.20. The porosity of the gravel is 0.20 or 20%.

Porosities of earth materials can vary from almost 0% (solid granite) to over 90% (peat), but usually range from 25 to 45%. Table 2.4 provides porosity values for some common earth materials.

Porosity in earth materials is determined by the:

- size, shape, and arrangement of rock and regolith grains;
- degree of compaction and cementation; and
- presence of fractures, solution cavities, and other openings.

Four general types of pores are commonly encountered. Figure 2.9 provides several illustrations of conditions which influence porosity.

1. **Openings between individual rock or soil particles.** Porosity tends to be high in well-sorted sediment but is reduced considerably in poorly sorted sediment as the finer grains fill the spaces between larger grains (Figure 2.3). A similar reduction in porosity occurs during cementation and

compaction of sediment. Bear in mind that the fragments themselves may have high or low porosity, thus influencing overall porosity. The high porosity of clays is due largely to the irregular size and poor packing of the tiny fragments. Clay fragments typically hold electric charges. The repulsion between like charges creates many open spaces among the fragments. Rocks with a crystalline texture such as granite and some limestones may have near-zero porosity as the growth of crystals often fills up all available space.

2. **Gas holes (vesicles).** These openings are common in the upper part of lava flows and in pyroclastic rocks where volatiles were attempting to escape from recently erupted, rapidly cooling volcanic material.

3. **Fractures and cracks.** These may be primary rock features such as bedding planes or secondary features such as joints and faults.

4. **Solutional openings and related features.** These generally consist of caves, conduits, and small solutional pockets (**vugs**). Numerous other weathering and erosional processes can also cause openings to develop in rocks, especially along preexisting zones of weakness.

The ability to predict how much groundwater is available in a given area, and for how long, is a critical factor in water management. Many approaches have been used to help determine groundwater availability in the natural environment — for example, for crops, during droughts, from wells or springs, or to sustain streamflow. Some of the more commonly used parameters are noted below.

The term **effective porosity** is sometimes used to refer to interconnected pore space; it is a measure of how effective the pores are in allowing water migration through the material, usually an aquifer. In unconsolidated sediments, effective porosity will be close to total porosity. In many lithified materials, many pore spaces will not be connected; hence, the effective porosity will often be much lower than total porosity. Effective porosity is closely related to permeability.

Specific retention (S_r) is the volume of water a material is capable of retaining (V_{wr}) — by capillary force, in isolated pores, or by other means — compared to the total volume of the material (V_t):

$$S_r = \frac{V_{wr}}{V_t}$$

Specific yield (S_y) is the volume of water which will flow out of a saturated material by gravity flow (V_{wg}) compared to the total volume of the material (V_t):

$$S_y = \frac{V_{wg}}{V_t}$$

These two terms may be indicated as ratios or percentages. Specific yield represents the ratio of water draining, or pumped, from a material to the total volume of the material. The porosity of a material equals the sum of specific retention and specific yield:

$$P = S_r + S_y$$

Specific yield for common sediment sizes are shown in Table 6.1. As the grain size of a material gets larger, the specific yield will get closer to the total porosity. This is due mainly to the smaller total surface area of the grains and the accompanying reduction in water retained by capillary force.

Example: Solving a Problem

If a sample of saturated regolith has a total volume of 400 cm³ and 48 cm³ of water drains out of it, what is the specific yield of the regolith?

Using the above formula, we find that $S_y = V_{wg}/V_t = 48$ cm³/400 cm³ = 0.12 or 12%.

The specific yield is 12%. If the porosity of this same regolith sample is 20%, that would mean that its specific retention would be 8%: $P = S_r + S_y$. Therefore, 20% = S_r + 12% and S_r = 20% – 12% = 8%.

The terms **storativity** and **storage coefficient** refer to the total amount of water that might be obtained from a given volume of earth material. Storativity is usually applied to aquifers and is defined as the quantity of water released, or absorbed, per unit surface area per unit change in the water level (head). A storativity ratio of 0.05 means that 5% of the volume of the saturated material can be released as water. Storativity may be determined by a pumping test, for example by using the Theis method (Section 7.7.4). The actual volume of water released or taken in by an aquifer (ΔV) can be calculated by multiplying the storativity ratio (S) by the areal extent of the aquifer (A) by the change in water level (ΔH):

$$\Delta V = SA(\Delta H)$$

Table 6.1. Representative Specific Yield Values for Some Common Earth Materials

MATERIAL	SPECIFIC YIELD (%)
Peat	44
Sands and gravels	23–28
Sandstone	21–27
Loess	18
Limestone	14
Siltstone	12
Silt	8
Clay	3

Source: [205].

Example: Applying the Equations

Tests indicate that a sandy unconfined aquifer has an average porosity of 0.20 (20%) and a specific yield of 0.08 (8%).

Using this information and the relationships noted above, one may assume a storativity of 0.08 — that is, 8% of the aquifer's saturated volume will be drainable water.

The specific retention will be 0.12 (12%): if $P = S_r + S_y$, then $S_r = P - S_y = 0.20 - 0.08 = 0.12$.

If we divide the specific yield by the porosity, we learn that 40% of the water in the aquifer may be withdrawn for our use: 0.08/0.20 = 0.40 and 0.40 × 100% = 40%.

If our sandy aquifer has an average saturated thickness of 20 meters (66 feet) over an area of 30 km² (30,000,000 m² or 11.6 mi²), the total saturated volume would be 20 m × 30,000,000 m² or 600,000,000 m³.

Twenty percent of this, or 120,000,000 m³, is pore space occupied by groundwater and 40% of that, or 48,000,000 m³, is potentially retrievable for human use. Note that this same result can be obtained by multiplying the total saturated volume by the storativity: 600 million m³ × 0.08 = 48 million m³.

> A cubic meter contains 264.2 gallons, so we are talking about 12,681,600,000 gallons (48 billion liters) of water.
>
> This example gives some idea of the vast quantities of water that are stored in the subsurface. Of course, withdrawing it would deplete the supply unless water from precipitation or from nearby subsurface sources was being added to this aquifer at rates equal to or greater than the withdrawal rate.

6.6 Permeability and Hydraulic Conductivity

Permeability (perviousness) is the fluid conductivity of a material; that is, the ease with which a material will transmit a fluid — such as groundwater. For the fluid to be transmitted, unequal forces must exist within the fluid in order to drive the water through the material (often referred to as the medium or matrix). The "forces" refer to the confining force resulting from the pull of gravity on water which is present at higher elevations within the body of water. Pressure generated by the weight of higher-level water increases with depth below the surface of a body of water, as it does with any other fluid such as air. As noted previously, the general term for the force exerted by water at any location within a standing body of water is **hydrostatic pressure**.

Permeability depends on the same factors as porosity with connectivity among pores and grain size being especially important. Fine grains contain more surface area to which water may adhere and contain smaller openings between the grains (hence more friction), and thus have lower permeability than more coarse-grained sediments. **Specific (intrinsic) permeability** gives the relationship between water movement and pore size:

$$k = Cd^2$$

where k = specific permeability, C = a dimensionless constant determined by the geometrical properties of the material, and d = the diameter of pore spaces (or grain size).

Hence, the finer-grained the material (and the smaller the value of d in the equation), the lower the permeability and the slower the rate of water migration through the material. As noted above, the interconnectedness of pores (related to C) is also critical to permeability as water must have avenues along which to move from one place to another.

Properties of the fluid may be added to the specific permeability equation to arrive at the actual flow rate of water, or any other fluid,

173

through a material. This gives us a parameter often called the **coefficient of permeability** in older books but now generally referred to as **hydraulic conductivity**. In equation form:

$$K = Cd^2 \frac{fg}{n}$$

where K = hydraulic conductivity, f = density of fluid (1 g/cm³ for pure water), g = pull of gravity (9.8 m/s/s), and n = viscosity of fluid (0.01 g/s/cm for pure water). C and d remain as defined above.

Hydraulic conductivity, which can be thought of as the rate at which groundwater moves through a medium, can vary immensely in different media materials as shown on Figure 6.11. High hydraulic conductivities on the order of 103 m/day (1,000 m/day; 3,300 ft/day) are not uncommon in cavernous limestones, gravel, and highly fractured basalt. At the other extreme, unfractured shales and crystalline rocks (including some basalts, granites, and gneisses) may have K values of only 10^{-8} (0.00000001) m/day or even less. In general, groundwater moves very slowly, typically from 1.5 m/day to a few cm/year.

Even within a given rock type, the range of hydraulic conductivities can differ greatly depending upon degrees of fracturing, cementation, compaction, and related factors. The range will tend to be largest in crystalline rocks and smallest in sedimentary materials. For impermeable rocks in which groundwater migration will be largely via fractures, equations have been developed which will allow hydraulic conductivity to be estimated based upon measurements such as the average spacing of fractures (for example, the number of joints per unit distance) and the average width of the fractures. Flow through a fracture will generally be proportional to the cube of the fracture opening.

Water movement through a material also typically varies greatly with the total volume of material being considered. For a particular rock

---

Figure 6.11. Range of common hydraulic conductivities for various earth ▶ materials. The rate of movement of water through many materials varies considerably, depending upon such factors as sorting, particle size, fractures, and interconnections between openings. "Massive" refers to an earth material unbroken by prominent joints, bedding planes, and other openings. Dolomite conductivities will be similar to limestone. Scale is provided in gpd/ft² (top) and m/day (bottom). Meters per day is the same as cubic meters of water passing through an area of one square meter per day [103, 108, 133, 175, 192, 402].

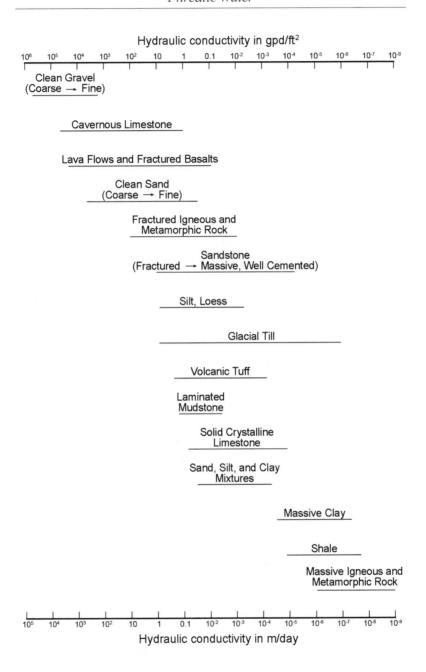

type such as a sandstone, the hydraulic conductivity — or, for that matter, the permeability or porosity — may be quite consistent throughout that unit. But if the sandstone unit contains numerous layers of sandstone and interbedded shales, one will get quite different values. On a still larger scale, if other nearby materials such as limestones, intrusive rocks, and fractured zones are included, the average conductivity, permeability, and other values will again change. This helps explain why, although hydraulic conductivity can be estimated using grain size and various models and by laboratory tests on samples taken from the field, the most meaningful values will be obtained using actual field tests, usually made by withdrawing water from one well and observing the rate at which water levels decline in nearby monitoring wells. In general, the larger the volume of earth material being considered, the greater the hydraulic conductivity and related parameters will be.

Hydraulic conductivity may be expressed in many ways:

- as **velocity** (distance per unit time, or D/t) using units such as ft/day, m/day, or cm/hr;
- as the **volume** of water per unit time passing through a given cross-sectional area using units such as $m^3/hr/m^2$, gal/day/ft^2, or gpd/ft^2 ;
- as **meinzers**, an English System unit of permeability. A meinzer is the rate of flow of water in gallons per day through a cross-section of 1 ft^2 under a hydraulic gradient of 1 — that is, a water table slope of 1 vertical foot per horizontal foot — at a temperature of 60°F; and
- as **darcies**, the Standard Metric System (SI) unit of permeability. One darcy is equal to 1 cm^3 of water per second flowing through 1 cm^3 of material under a pressure differential of 1 atmosphere. In actual practice, the millidarcy (0.001 darcy) is often used.

An instrument used to measure permeability and hydraulic conductivity is a **permeameter**. Figure 6.12 illustrates two laboratory permeameters. A sample of the material is placed in a cylindrical container between two highly pervious plates. The sample is thoroughly saturated. Water at a higher elevation in a container or standpipe is allowed to flow through the material and is then collected and measured. The hydraulic pressure can be controlled by the height of the water column in the standpipe. For coarse-grained (high permeability) materials, the pressure is usually held constant by keeping the water level (or head) in the standpipe at the same height (a constant-head test). For fine-grained materials where the flow rate is very slow, the water level is allowed to fall for several hours (a falling-head test). The results can be used to calculate the water flow rate through the material.

In the natural environment, the materials groundwater moves through cannot be directly observed and frequently vary both vertically and horizontally even over short distances. The permeability of one particular medium, or at one point in a material, is of limited value for determining overall water movement in a complex subsurface environment. One way of obtaining a better perspective on groundwater movement within a

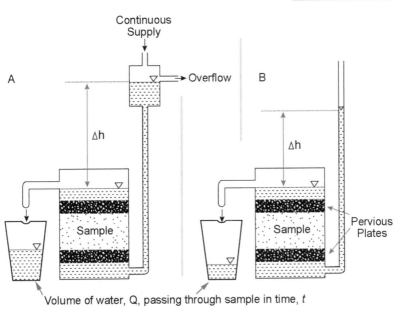

Figure 6.12. Permeameters. Water, driven by pressure generated by the differences in water levels (Δh), moves from the standpipe through the sample of material being tested. The sample material is saturated and sandwiched between two pervious plates. The cross-sectional area of the sample and the rate or volume of water moving through the sample can be used to determine the permeability (or hydraulic conductivity) of the sample. **A.** Constant-head permeameter. This permeameter keeps the water in the standpipe at a constant height (head, elevation) to produce a constant rate of seepage through the sample. This is used for coarser-grained samples. **B.** Falling-head permeameter. This allows water to slowly seep for several hours through the sample as the water in the standpipe drops, reducing Δh. This provides better results for fine-grained, relatively impermeable samples.

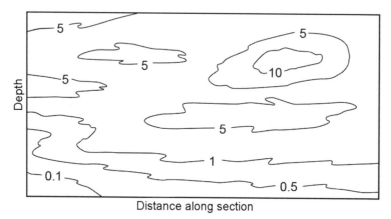

Figure 6.13. Cross-sectional view of hydraulic conductivity. This example shows layers and lenses of higher permeability sandy sediment in the upper area with decreasing conductivity toward the bottom and lower left. The contour values are in 10^{-3} cm/sec (thousandths of a centimeter per second) [103, 192].

given subsurface unit (such as an aquifer, saturated regolith, or group of strata) is to determine hydraulic conductivity for numerous points in the unit. For example, numerous samples taken from a line of borings at various depths can be used to construct a cross-section which shows conductivity along that section, usually using contours to provide an overview of the properties of the unit as shown in Figure 6.13. Such localized sections, as well as maps which may cover entire aquifers, are convenient and useful water management tools. Another useful approach involves injecting tracers such as dyes and radioactive elements into a well and measuring the time required for the tracer to reach one or more observation points such as other wells or springs. The distance between wells is then divided by the time required by the tracer to determine the flow rate.

Transmissivity is another useful way to express the mass movement of water through complex subsurface materials. **Transmissivity** is the rate at which water is transmitted through a unit length, usually the depth or thickness, of an aquifer or related water-bearing geologic formation under a hydraulic gradient of one. For a hydraulic gradient of one, the vertical and horizontal distances the water flows will be equal to produce a slope of 45°. In equation form, transmissivity is the product of the hydraulic conductivity and the aquifer thickness:

$$T = Kb$$

where T = transmissivity, K = hydraulic conductivity, and b = saturated thickness of material.

Transmissivity is used most often to determine the volume of water that can be transmitted horizontally through an aquifer that is confined between two impermeable units. True values for both permeability and transmissivity represent the flow rate measured at right angles to the flow direction. The higher the transmissivity value, the higher the overall permeability and the larger the amount of water that can pass through a representative unit area of the aquifer [100, 122, 185, 423].

Example: Solving a Problem

Determine the transmissivity of a confined aquifer that has a hydraulic conductivity of 0.25 m/day and a saturated thickness of 12 meters: $T = Kb = (0.25 \text{ m/day} \times 12 \text{ m}) = 3 \text{ m}^2/\text{day}$.

To change the answer into the volume of water being transmitted, multiply this answer by the width of the part of the aquifer being studied. For example, if the width of this aquifer lying below a property is 200 meters, then, letting w = width, the amount of water passing through that part of the aquifer will be: $Q = Tw = (3 \text{ m}^2/\text{day})(200 \text{ m}) = 600 \text{ m}^3/\text{day}$.

6.7 Darcy's Law

Someone told me that each equation I included in the book would halve the sales.

— Stephen Hawking

The most useful approach for calculating groundwater flow rates is provided by Darcy's Law, named after a nineteenth century French hydraulic engineer, Henry Darcy. Darcy needed to determine what size sand filters would be needed to purify the water supply for the city of Dijon. He first had to find out how much water would flow through porous sand filters of the appropriate sizes. He built a device in which water from an upper reservoir (inflow on Figure 6.14) would flow through a filter — basically a cylinder filled with sand — and into a lower reservoir (outflow on Figure 6.14). By varying the water level in the upper reservoir, he could increase or decrease the force (hydraulic pressure or head) on water seeping through the sand. He noted that as the pressure (that is, the difference in elevation of the water at the upper and lower ends of the filter — Δh in the figure) increased, proportionally more water flowed through the filter, and vice versa. Also, when he increased the flow path length by increasing the length of his sand filter — Δl on Figure 6.14 — he noted that proportionally less water flowed through the filter, and vice versa. Soon it became apparent that he didn't need to tediously construct any more sand filter contraptions because he could easily predict how much water would move through the sand with a simple mathematical calculation (or "model," if you prefer). Of course, the flow would be different for materials other than the particular sand he was using. Darcy concluded that the property of the material which determined how rapidly water could seep through it was permeability and that, for a given material such as pure sand of a given grain size, it could be quantified as a constant, "K." He had discovered the basic law of modern hydrology, **Darcy's Law**, which may be stated as follows: the

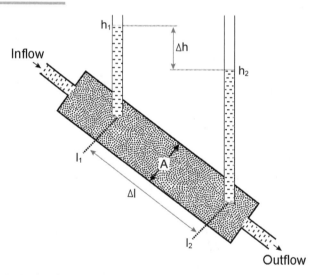

Figure 6.14. Sketch of a typical set-up to demonstrate Darcy's Law. A cylinder was filled with sand through which water flowed from an upper reservoir (inflow) to a lower reservoir (outflow). The two stand-pipes measure the difference in hydraulic head (Δh) and the volume of water moving through a cylinder of fixed cross-sectional area (A) can be collected and measured. Note similarities with the permeameters of Figure 6.12.

flow of a liquid through a porous medium is directly proportional to the pressure and inversely proportional to the length of the flow path.

Remember, all water below a water table is under hydrostatic pressure due to the weight of overlying water pushing down on it, just as the weight of water in Darcy's upper reservoir pushed down on his sand filter. This driving force or pressure is **hydraulic head** (or just head). **Head** can be thought of as a measure of the height to which the hydrostatic pressure will lift, or support, a column of water, such as the water in the standpipes in Figure 6.14. The standpipes are basically piezometers (Section 6.8). The height, or head, is usually given as elevation above mean sea level.

Most communities have large tanks of drinking water which sit in elevated areas. Their high position provides the pressure (head) to force the water to flow through pipes to your home and from your faucet (Figure 6.15). The difference in elevation from one place to another provides the "push," driving the water to move, be it groundwater migrating slowly through natural earth materials or reservoir water flowing through a pipe. If no difference in head exists, groundwater cannot flow. The change in elevation from one location to another is the **hydraulic gradient** (i). For unconfined water at or near the water table, "i" equals the slope of the water table and this is used in most problems and examples. Specifically,

$$i = \frac{\Delta h}{L}$$

where Δh = difference in height (elevation) of the water table between any two locations, or difference in head between any two locations, and L = length of the water flow path.

This equation represents Darcy's Law. It simply says that the water flow is proportional to the difference in head divided by the distance between those locations. The water flow rate can be given in terms of velocity (such as m/day or ft/yr) or quantity (such as m^3/yr or gal/day). This proportion is often given in equations as difference in elevation ($h_1 - h_2$) divided by distance apart ($l_1 - l_2$):

$$\frac{h_1 - h_2}{l_1 - l_2} \quad \text{or} \quad \frac{\Delta h}{\Delta l} \quad \text{or sometimes simplified to} \quad \frac{h}{L}$$

as illustrated on Figure 6.16. Figure 6.16 shows two open boreholes and the level of the water table in each. This is very similar to the upper and lower standpipes of Darcy's apparatus (Figure 6.14). In many actual

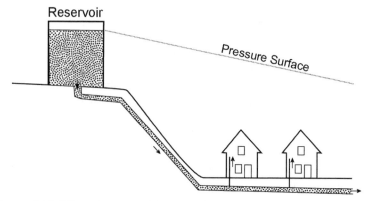

Figure 6.15. Water is pumped into reservoirs where the higher elevation provides the pressure or head to move water through pipes and into homes. Even if water is not being used by others, the water pressure (or elevation to which the water can rise) will diminish with distance from the reservoir due to frictional losses and leakage as shown by the sloping pressure surface.

situations, the elevation difference ($h_1 - h_2$) will be small compared to the length of the flow path between the two locations ($l_1 - l_2$), and the difference between a gently sloping flow path length and the horizontal map distance ($d_1 - d_2$) will be so small that map distance (Δd) can be used in calculating the hydraulic gradient without significantly affecting the results.

In Figure 6.16, if the flow path distance (Δl, or L) is 500 feet and the elevation (head) difference (Δh) is 5 feet, the hydraulic gradient would be 0.01, meaning the head along the water table decreases 0.01 foot for every 1 foot of length:

$$i = \Delta h/L = 5/500 = 0.01$$

If we wish to know how fast water is likely to move through a material (that is, its velocity), we simply need to know the permeability of the transmitting material and multiply that by the slope (i). Darcy's Law then can be stated as:

$$v = Ki \quad \text{or} \quad v = K(h/L)$$

where v = velocity, K = hydraulic conductivity, i = hydraulic gradient, h = head, and L = length of slope.

Some prefer to place a negative sign before the right side of these equations (for example, $v = -Ki$). This is because the groundwater flows from higher to lower elevations and the negative indicates that the water's elevation is decreasing.

If a value for effective porosity related to interconnected pore space (n_e) is known, a more accurate determination can be made by incorporating it into the equation as follows:

$$v = \frac{Ki}{n_e}$$

If we wish to use the quantity, or volume, of water rather than velocity, we can modify the equation $v = Ki$ by substituting Q/A for v. The quantity of water equals velocity times the cross-sectional area or $Q = vA$, just as in streamflow. Hence, $v = Q/A$. Now $v = Ki$ can be written as $Q/A = Ki$. By solving this for Q we can now state Darcy's Law as follows:

$$Q = KAi \quad \text{or} \quad KA\left(\frac{h}{L}\right)$$

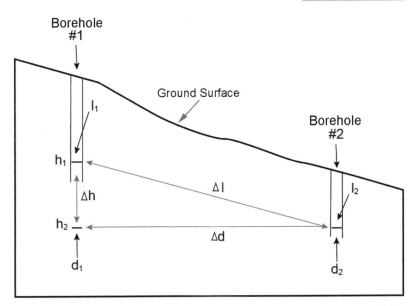

Figure 6.16. Relationship of units commonly used with Darcy's Law: Δd is horizontal (map) distance; Δh is head (difference in height of the water level in the two borings); Δl is the length (or distance) as measured along the presumed flow path (parallel to the slope).

where Q = volume of water and A = cross-sectional area. This simple adjustment to Darcy's Law allows us to determine how much water is moving or is stored in the ground. This relationship was determined by **Charles Theis** in the US in the 1930s and was another revolutionary step for hydrologic studies. Theis took a basic heat flow (thermal conductivity) equation from physics and applied it to water flow and found that it worked.

The quantities Q, A, v, and i can often be measured in the field and from maps or cross-sections. These values can then be used to compute the hydraulic conductivity or permeability of the material the water flows through: solving the above equations for K, we obtain:

$$K = \frac{Q}{Ai} \quad \text{or} \quad K = \frac{QL}{Ah} \quad \text{or} \quad K = \frac{v}{i} \quad \text{or} \quad K = \frac{vL}{h}$$

As can be seen, Darcy's Law can be manipulated in many ways to measure groundwater flow in various situations, depending upon what parameters one has measurements for. This has resulted in thousands of important uses [100, 122, 133, 185, 192, 369, 390, 423]. With modern computer technology, many sophisticated models have been devised allowing ever more accurate determinations of water behavior under various, often highly complex, conditions.

Example: Using the Equation

Figures 6.12A and 6.14 will help to visualize the values used in this problem. A sample of a sandy aquifer is placed in a constant-head permeameter. The sample is 60 centimeters long and has a cross-sectional area of 30 cm². If 140 cm³ of water flows through the permeameter in 70 seconds and the difference in hydraulic head (Δh) between the water levels at the inflow and outflow reservoirs is 20 centimeters, what is the hydraulic conductivity of this sample?

We will use K = Q/Ai. Q is the discharge rate: Q = 140 cm³/70s = 2 cm³/s. A is the cross-sectional area: A = 30 cm². i is the hydraulic gradient: i = Δh/L = 20 cm/60 cm = 1/3.

Putting this together and doing some elementary math, we find our hydraulic conductivity to be: K = Q/Ai = 2 cm³/s × 1/ 30 cm² × 3/1 = 0.20 cm/s.

However, caution must be applied! Be aware that the results, though valuable, are still only averages and estimates. The actual flow of water through the masses of unseen earth material beneath our feet can vary greatly from one place to another due to the heterogeneous nature of most regolith and rock. The presence of fractures, unpredictable openings, irregularities in strata, zones of weathering within rock, and the like can lead to rapidly changing porosities and permeabilities. In addition, permeability is often greater in one direction than in another due to the orientation of fractures or grains. The term **isotropic** is often applied to conditions which are equal in all directions. **Anisotropic** refers to directionally unequal properties. In actual field conditions, permeability and hydraulic conductivity are often anisotropic. For example, they will tend to be greater parallel to the stratification of sedimentary rocks and to foliation in metamorphic rock. Vertical conductivity will be considerably enhanced in any material possessing good vertical jointing.

In detailed studies, it may be necessary to determine water flows through various types of materials which are often themselves heterogeneous, and in different directions (north-south, east-west, vertically, and so forth) within those materials. In detail, the actual velocity of groundwater is nonuniform with countless accelerations, decelerations, and directional changes.

Yet another precaution: Darcy's Law applies only to **laminar** flow — smooth, parallel water flow — not to **turbulent** flow — rough, irregular flow (Figure 6.17). Most groundwater flow is slow and laminar, but important exceptions occur in caves, large fractures, and in materials of very high permeability — such as clean gravels — with steep hydraulic gradients.

Thankfully, for many hydrogeologic studies, reasonable estimates of average groundwater movement are all we need and the information and equations provided above will suffice.

6.8 Piezometric Pressure and Groundwater Migration

To determine the groundwater head at any desired place in the phreatic zone, a simple device called a piezometer is used. A **piezometer** ("pressure" + "measure") is simply a solid-walled, open-ended pipe or tube (Figure 6.18). It is placed in a hole which penetrates the groundwater to a desired depth. Water can enter only at the bottom of the pipe, usually through slots in or near a conical cap, and the level to which that water rises in the pipe is a measure of the water pressure or head at the bottom of the pipe. The water level in the piezometer is usually given as

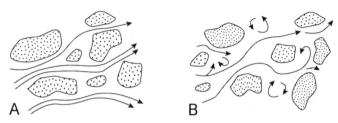

A   B

Figure 6.17. Close-up views demonstrating laminar and turbulent groundwater flow. **A.** Laminar flow is characterized by smooth distinct flow lines. **B.** Turbulent flow is more erratic and less efficient, with frequent changes in both direction and velocity.

elevation above mean sea level. Most piezometers are less than 10 centimeters (4 inches) in diameter and range from less than a meter to hundreds of meters in length.

The head, or elevation to which groundwater in a piezometer will rise, may be broken down into two parts. Elevation is usually measured relative to mean sea level, but for convenience and because the precise elevation may not be readily known for a given location, it may instead be measured relative to some solid nearby reference point or benchmark, such as a building foundation or concrete abutment. The **elevation head** is the elevation at the bottom of the piezometer and the **pressure head** is the length of the water column in the piezometer. The velocity of the groundwater also exerts a force which can add to the head, but this can be ignored except where rapid flow through conduits or large fractures is occurring. For most conditions, adding the elevation and pressure head gives the total hydraulic head present at the bottom of the piezometer.

Figure 6.18 shows two piezometers and their relation to the ground surface, water table, and sea level: h_e is the elevation head or height above sea level, X marks the bottom of the piezometer (the place at which the head is being measured), and h_p represents the pressure head or height to which the water pressure at point X has raised the water in the tube. Thus, total head (H) is the sum of elevation head and pressure head, or the elevation of the water level in the tube:

$$H = h_e + h_p$$

If the elevation at the top of piezometer A is 70 meters above sea level and the piezometer has a length of 10 meters and the water level in the piezometer lies 1 meter below the top of the piezometer as shown in Figure 6.19, we can determine the values of the elevation head (h_e), pressure head (h_p), and total head (H) as follows:

h_e = elevation at top – elevation at bottom
$h_e = 70 - 10 = 60$ meters

h_p = length of piezometer – depth of water in piezometer
$h_p = 10 - 1 = 9$ meters

$H = h_e + h_p$
$H = 60 + 9 = 69$ meters

Note that the water level in piezometer A of Figure 6.18 is higher than the water table. Assuming homogeneous conditions, this indicates that the water pressure or hydraulic head is increasing with depth at this point. This will cause the groundwater flow to be directed upward toward the surface. Hence, this location is probably near a site of groundwater discharge. At piezometer B, the water piezometer water level is lower than the water table indicating a decrease in pressure downward,

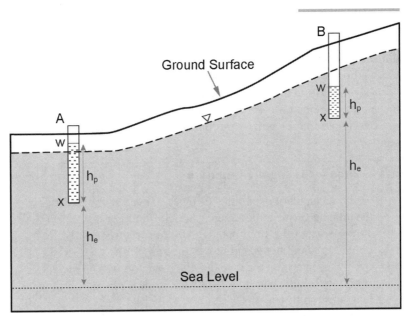

Figure 6.18. Cross-section showing two piezometers, A and B. W = water level in piezometer; X = bottom of piezometer (where head is being measured); h_p = pressure head; h_e = elevation head.

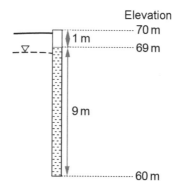

Figure 6.19. Piezometer A from Figure 6.18 with numerical values in meters.

strongly suggesting this is a recharge area with groundwater flowing generally downward.

Hydrogeology textbooks variously refer to total head as **piezometric pressure**, piezometric potential, or potentiometric pressure. Groups of piezometers ("piezometer nests") are usually required to obtain an accurate perspective of head at a project site. Piezometers need to be placed at different locations both laterally and vertically to obtain a three-dimensional view of hydraulic head distribution within the aquifer or other groundwater body of interest.

By measuring the water elevation (piezometric pressure) in two or more piezometers, one can determine the hydraulic gradient between the two locations, or within the particular water-bearing unit being studied.

Examples: Using the Equation

1. If calculations similar to those above determined that the total head (piezometric pressure) at B in Figure 16.18 was 77 meters and the flow path was 90 meters, what is the hydraulic gradient between the two piezometers?

It was determined above that the head at A was 69 meters. Hydraulic gradient is the difference in head divided by the length of the flow path:

$$i = \Delta h/L$$
$$i = (77 - 69)/90 = 0.09$$

---

2. If the water table at piezometer A in Figure 6.19 lies 1.6 meters below the top of the piezometer, what is the vertical hydraulic gradient at this location, that is, what is the gradient between the bottom of the piezometer and the overlying water table?

The head at the water table is the elevation of the water table, which is 70 – 1.6 = 68.4 meters. At the bottom of the piezometer, the head is 69 meters as determined above. The vertical length of flow path (L) between the two locations is 68.4 – 60 = 8.4 meters. Hydraulic gradient is the difference in head divided by the length of the flow path, hence:

$$i = \Delta h/L$$
$$i = (69 - 68.4)/(68.4 - 60) = 0.6/8.4 = 0.07$$

The direction of the hydraulic gradient is upward because the deeper location has the higher head — pressure decreases upward.

Numerous calculations of this type often need to be made to characterize groundwater flow conditions. The math is simple but vitally important to our understanding of groundwater behavior — and careless errors are easy to make. Various additional calculations may be necessary; for example, to determine the elevation at the piezometer top or, in the case of saline groundwater, to compensate for water density variations.

If numerous data points are obtained, the points can be placed on a map or cross-section and contour lines can be drawn. Contours of a **piezometric** (or **potentiometric**) **surface** can then be constructed for the area under study (Figure 6.20). The slope of the piezometric surface is the **piezometric gradient**. On a **piezometric surface map**, the contours represent lines of equal head in the groundwater body and are called **equipotential lines**. For unconfined groundwater, the piezometric surface map is basically a **water table map**, because the head at the water table equals its elevation relative to sea level — as in figures 3.11B and 4.14 for example. With confined groundwater, the piezometric surface represents pressure within the confined unit and will bear little or no relation to the water table or the ground surface (Section 8.2.3). Piezometric surface contour maps are a graphic presentation of the hydraulic gradient (i). Changes in the spacing of the contours represent a change in the hydraulic gradient.

The groundwater flow direction in isotropic materials of roughly uniform permeability will always be directly downgradient — from higher to lower elevation and orthogonal (perpendicular) to the water table contours (equipotential lines). This is directly analogous to surface water which, barring obstructions, must flow straight downhill — traveling along the steepest gradient, perpendicular to the elevation contours on a topographic map. The flow direction for the groundwater may be shown on the map by **flow lines** drawn at right angles to the contours as shown on Figure 6.20B.

As with terrain contours, when the equipotential lines cross an effluent (water-gaining) stream in a map view, they bend upstream to form a series of Vs (or Us) pointing upstream (Figure 3.11B). These sequences of Vs represent a trough or valley in the equipotential surface. The stream at center of the V is the groundwater discharge zone and the elevations along the stream will coincide with the water table elevations. With influent (water-losing) streams, however, a gentle ridge may be present in the underlying water table (Figure 4.5B) causing the contours to bend downstream. In general, groundwater flow, and thus flow lines, will diverge away from recharge areas such as hills, ridges, and influent water bodies and converge as they near an area of concentrated discharge, such as a spring or an effluent stream (Figure 6.21).

Permeability may not be equal in all directions; that is, it may be anisotropic, not isotropic. As noted previously, this can result from the orientation of strata, an alignment of fractures, fragments, or pores, and other properties in the rock material that allow water to flow more easily in one direction than another. Anisotropic permeability is common in well-stratified sedimentary rocks or where a dominant joint trend influences flow, but is rarely seen in unconsolidated materials. Where anisotropic permeability occurs, the flow lines will not be perpendicular to the equipotential lines. Unless anisotropy is demonstrated, assume that flow direction will be perpendicular to the equipotential lines.

For confined aquifers, a map of a piezometric surface represents only one aquifer. The groundwater of any additional aquifers at higher

Figure 6.20. A. Water table map. The contours are drawn based upon water ▶ table elevations from boreholes at the points indicated (x). The map shows that the water table slopes to the east and southeast and that the gradient is steeper in the northwest part of the area. Contour interval is 1 meter. **B.** Same map with point data removed and flow lines (dashed) added. Piezometric (or water table) surface contours and flow lines constitute a flow net.

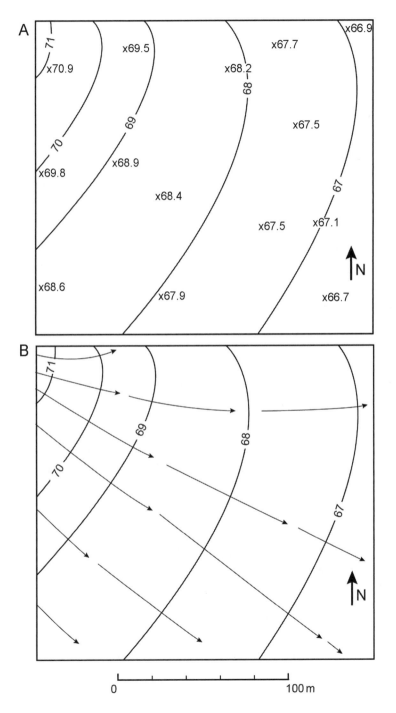

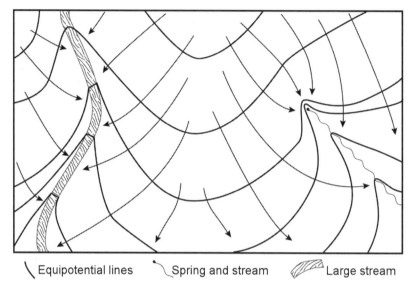

\\Equipotential lines   \\Spring and stream   ///Large stream

Figure 6.21. Flow net showing diverging groundwater flow from higher elevation recharge areas and converging flow toward discharge areas (streams and spring).

or lower elevations in the rock sequence will have different hydrostatic pressures and require separate piezometric surface maps.

A map showing both equipotential lines and flow lines at regular intervals is called a **flow net** (figures 6.20B and 6.21). Flow nets may also be shown using **hydrogeological cross-sections** (that is, in a vertical plane) as shown on Figure 6.22. Cross-sections are vertical representations drawn perpendicular to a horizontal surface. Hydrogeological sections are usually drawn parallel to the maximum groundwater flow direction. The flow lines are still perpendicular to the equipotential lines (assuming isotropic conditions) and water always moves from higher to lower pressure, moving away from recharge areas and converging at discharge areas such as streams and springs. Note that groundwater flow is upward toward the surface near discharge areas — which is where hydrostatic pressure on the groundwater is decreasing.

Hydrogeologic sections such as Figure 6.22 may be constructed based on water levels from a line of piezometers at various depths, similar to what is shown in Figure 6.23. The dotted lines on Figure 6.23 are elevation above mean sea level. The dashed lines are equipotential lines and represent the height or elevation to which water at that location will

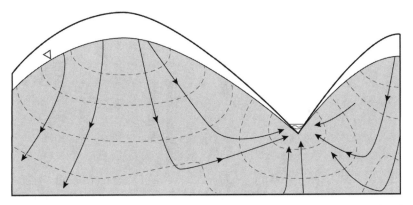

Figure 6.22. Sketch of a hydrogeological cross-section flow net in unconfined conditions. Equipotential lines are dashed, arrows are flow lines.

rise in a piezometer. Equipotential lines terminate at the water table where head equals elevation. Note that water in piezometers A and C rises to the same elevation even though they begin at different elevations and end at different depths. That is because the piezometers are measuring head on the same equipotential line. Piezometers A and B are very close but terminate at different equipotential lines; hence their hydraulic head varies and the differing pressures cause the water to rise to different levels. Hydraulic head, as shown by equipotential lines, decreases vertically beneath the recharge areas but increases beneath the discharge areas. As a result of these changes in head, the deeper a piezometer is placed beneath a recharge area, the lower the water level in the piezometer will become (in homogeneous conditions). The deeper the piezometer placement beneath a discharge area, the higher its water level tends to be, as shown by piezometers D and E on Figure 6.23.

Piezometers A, B, and C of Figure 6.23 are all in a recharge area where head decreases with depth; hence their water levels are all below the water table. Shorter piezometers on the hilltop would show increasingly smaller discrepancies between the water in the pipe and the water table until, at the water table itself, they would be the same. Recall what was said earlier: at the water table, the effective head is zero and the upward force is balanced by the downward force of atmosphere pressure; that is, the water table is the surface of atmospheric pressure and all water below it is under pressures greater than atmospheric, else the water could not rise up the open pipe. Piezometers D and E show the water level rising above the water table indicating increasing head with

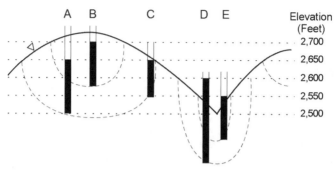

Figure 6.23. Sketch showing relationship between piezometer readings and equipotential lines in isotropic, water table conditions. For clarity, only the water table, equipotential lines (dashed), and elevation (dotted lines) are shown. A through E are piezometers. See text for discussion [191].

depth as expected in a discharge area [191]. In discharge areas, groundwater flow direction is upward toward the water table and ground surface, meaning head in this area is decreasing toward the surface and increasing with depth. Hence, we would expect piezometer water levels in discharge areas to be higher than the local water table, possibly even high enough to flow out onto the surface. Where subsurface hydraulic pressures are sufficient, water seepage onto the ground surface will occur naturally. Such would be the case for soggy areas along an effluent stream (Figure 4.3).

Water levels in piezometers and wells are often shown with their water levels at the water table. But this will be the case only if the hydraulic head which exists at the bottom of the piezometer equals the head at the water table. Ideally, the head should coincide with the elevation where the equipotential line at the piezometer's intake meets the water table as shown on Figure 6.23; this may not always be exact because of small pressure losses due to friction along the pipe, similar to the loss in water pressure along pipes delivering water from an elevated storage tank to a house.

Figure 6.24 provides simple flow net illustrations for three common groundwater conditions: isotropic, anisotropic, and a confined aquifer. Except in areas of significant discharge or recharge, the flow tends to be parallel to the confining beds in confined aquifers and the equipotential lines are perpendicular to the aquifer boundaries.

Flow nets have many uses such as predicting contamination plume migration and determining the volume of water moving through the subsurface. A **flow net analysis** may be performed to compute the quantity of water migrating through a subsurface unit if the average permeability of the unit is known. For a given cell of a flow net (Figure 6.24A), one may know or can often determine the difference in head (h), distance between equipotential lines (L), distance between the flow lines (w), permeability (K), and thickness or depth of the aquifer (y). The quantity (Q) of water moving between any two flow lines for this unit can then be calculated using Darcy's Law for volume — Q = KA h/L: quantity = hydraulic conductivity × area × hydraulic gradient (h/L) — which will give us the equation:

$$Q = K(w)(y) \frac{(h)}{L}$$

If flow lines form squares with the equipotential lines, as they do in isotropic materials, w and L will be equal so they can be divided out and the equation becomes:

$$Q = K(y)(\Delta H)$$

The total amount of water migrating beneath a large area can be computed by multiplying Q by the number of widths, or "flow channels," present.

All this looks rather complicated and some very complex-looking equations can be constructed if one is so inclined. But bear in mind that all we are doing is applying Darcy's Law to a real situation. Always

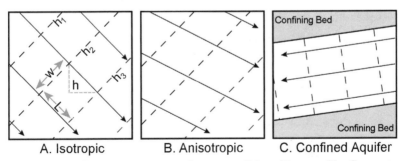

| A. Isotropic | B. Anisotropic | C. Confined Aquifer |

Figure 6.24. Three common groundwater conditions illustrated by flow nets. Dashed lines are equipotential lines, solid arrows are flow lines. On A, the width (w), length (L), and head difference (h, change in head from h_2 to h_3) are shown for the flow net of one cell.

strive to understand and remember the fairly simple underlying principles and the many numerical details that often must be dealt with will
tend to fall into place.

6.9 Groundwater Flow Systems

Note in figures 3.11B and 6.22 that groundwater tends to travel in
long curved paths, a reflection of the downward pull of gravity and the
hydrostatic force within the water which encourages water to move toward areas of discharge where pressure is being released, so to speak.
Water entering the phreatic zone may flow only a short distance before
being discharged back to the surface, OR it can undertake a great journey requiring thousands of years to complete, depending on where it
enters and exits the groundwater system. The major agent in creating
and maintaining hydrostatic head and hence in determining groundwater flow rates and directions is topography. King noted how the water
table imitated the overlying topography, but on a more subdued scale
[218]. Without **relief**, or differences in elevation from one place to another, pressure differences are minimized and very little movement of
groundwater can occur. The relief of the water table is maintained by
recharge, which in turn is maintained by precipitation.

Three groundwater flow systems are generally recognized (Figure
6.25), as envisioned by Toth [392]. These systems are highly dependent
upon the configuration of the water table, along with all the factors influencing the water table, especially topography. The situations described
below are idealized and represent unconfined phreatic water in homogeneous materials. In homogeneous materials, intensity (rate and volume)
of groundwater flow tends to decrease with depth due to more frictional
losses and longer flow paths.

1. **Local flow systems** have recharge and discharge areas at
   adjacent topographic highs and lows, as in Figure 6.22. If
   no local relief sufficient to impact the water table exists,
   local flow systems will not be present. The area covered
   by local systems is on the order of tens of square kilometers. The smaller the local flow system, the larger the variations in water table levels in response to weather, pumpage,
   and other nearby recharge and discharge events. This is
   analogous to streams: a small stream experiences far greater
   discharge changes during local rain events than large
   streams in the same area. Water table fluctuations, along

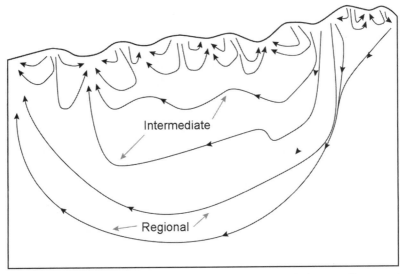

Figure 6.25. Cross-section showing simplified local, intermediate, and regional groundwater flow systems. Intermediate and regional flow lines are identified; all others are local [392].

with corresponding alterations in hydraulic head and groundwater flow lines, will also tend to be greater in rugged terrain — that is, areas of high relief.

The groundwater drainage divide, stagnant or slow-flow regions, and discharge locations tend to isolate the groundwater flow into discrete flow units or cells with little opportunity for mixing with other units (figures 6.2 and 6.26A). The flow of groundwater is normally downward, or away from, the water table in the upper parts of slopes but begins converging toward the water table as discharge areas are neared.

2. **Intermediate flow systems** are those containing one or more local systems within them (Figure 6.25).

3. **Regional flow systems** underlie areas of thousands of square kilometers and involve long-distance transport of groundwater, with recharge usually occurring near major drainage divides and discharge occurring along major river valleys or near oceans. Within such a major groundwater basin many subbasins containing local or intermediate flow

systems can develop (Figure 6.25). A regional, or long-distance, slope is needed for such a flow system to form. As regional gradients are common, at least part of the groundwater resurfacing at major discharge areas will probably have an origin far removed from the discharge point. The origin can often be revealed by chemical analyses and/ or age-dating of the water.

Water involved in long-distance regional flow systems can remain in the ground many thousands of years. Water in contact with rock or regolith slowly dissolves mineral matter. Thus the longer that contact, the more dissolved solids one can expect in the groundwater, all else being equal. Total dissolved solids (TDS) also tend to be high under extensive flat areas which, with little local relief, have little head to drive groundwater movement. Thus flow velocity is low and the residence time for groundwater is long beneath most extensive flatlands.

6.10 Additional Influences on Groundwater Flow

The generalized flow systems described above provide a good perspective from which to approach groundwater movements. But they are simplified, unlike the real subsurface environment through which water migrates. In this section, we consider some of the complicating influences upon, and the impacts of, groundwater flow.

6.10.1 Topography

In areas of little or no relief, groundwater flow is apt to be nearly parallel to the water table and ground surface (Figure 6.26B). Note that the equipotential lines between the centers of recharge and discharge are nearly vertical, indicating that head remains the same with increasing depth. The water level in a piezometer installed where equipotential lines are vertical would equal the local water table regardless of its depth.

If the local relief is relatively insignificant and a regional slope exists, only a regional flow system may be present, as in Figure 6.26B. Such conditions are common on the broad plains which border many low-lying coasts and inland areas, such as the Atlantic Coastal Plain and the Great Plains of the US. If both local and regional relief are present, local, intermediate, and regional systems may all be present. If a large

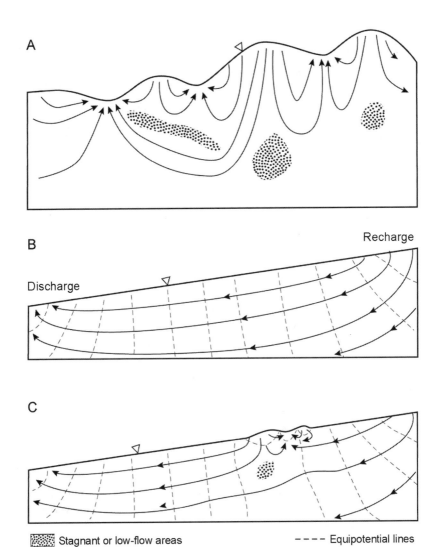

Figure 6.26. Examples of groundwater flow systems. **A.** Water table with significant relief. **B.** Water table with no local relief. **C.** Water table similar to B showing impact of small local relief.

region is virtually flat, the underlying water table will tend to be flat and little circulation will occur. A high water table in such a region will often produce waterlogged areas. Minor topographic highs and lows can greatly influence the groundwater flow systems as shown on Figure 6.26C, as can differences in infiltration rates and permeability [100].

In some areas, as noted previously, the water table can be nearly horizontal in spite of surface topography (Figure 6.3). This occurs mainly in very permeable materials — for example, sand dunes, cavernous limestone, and gravels — and in arid regions where the infiltration rate from highlands is insignificant and where, without recharge, groundwater eventually vacates the highlands and the water table levels out.

Another general rule is that the greater the relief, the greater the depth of the flow system: that is, water will circulate to greater depths in areas of high relief (Figure 6.26A). As the ruggedness of a terrain increases, local flow systems will tend to be more abundant. Where two or more flow systems move away from each other, areas of low-flow or stagnant groundwater may form (Figure 6.26A).

6.10.2 Geology and Structure

The geology and structure of the subsurface greatly influences permeability and will complicate groundwater flow. Unraveling the intricacies of flow in complex areas requires an abundance of data on rock types, distribution, structures, and hydrogeologic characteristics. Where adequate information is available, various quantitative methods can be employed to compute water flow values.

Anisotropic characteristics of the earth materials can cause groundwater to flow preferentially in the direction of the aligned features. For example, horizontal strata will encourage horizontal water movement and a high water table if relatively impermeable layers exist near the surface. Vertical fractures or strata will encourage vertical groundwater flow, deeper circulation paths, and a lower water table than would otherwise be. The combination of topographic irregularities and geological variations can produce unexpected groundwater flow patterns. Impermeable zones serve as barriers and groundwater will divert around them or pool up behind them. Low permeability zones lying perpendicular to groundwater flow lines can act like dams and impede the flow, causing water to back up and rise to the surface, or form a subsurface "groundwater cascade" where it descends abruptly to a lower level. A similar condition is illustrated in Figure 6.27A where perched water "cascades" through the vadose zone to join the underlying groundwater, causing a mound in its water table. At the left side of Figure 6.27A, note how the flow lines diverge around relatively impermeable material and converge to concentrate flow through permeable material. Figure 6.27B shows a confined aquifer with flow parallel to the aquifer boundaries and flow. In its upper part, flow through limestone is directed along joints and bedding planes enlarged by solution. Figure 6.27C shows one possible impact of a displacement along a fault upon the groundwater flow [100].

6.10.3 Infiltrating Water and Refraction

Under unconfined conditions, groundwater flow trends generally downward away from the land surface (and water table) in the recharge areas and upward toward the land surface in the lower-lying discharge areas. The upper 50 to 75% of a hillslope usually represents the recharge zone. However, virtually all illustrations greatly exaggerate the relief, making slopes appear much steeper than they really are. If this were not done, most cross-sections of the real terrain and the water table would resemble a nearly straight line. Most of the time, and in most areas, the shallow groundwater flow tends to be parallel to the water table. This changes when water is infiltrating into the phreatic zone from above. Gravity water seeping down from the vadose zone adds pressure and causes a downward deflection of the groundwater (Figure 6.28B). Hence the direction, as well as the velocity, of groundwater flow can vary significantly depending upon the local infiltration and recharge rates, which in turn are determined by such factors as rainfall, snowmelt, and human interferences. Human impacts include slope changes, devegetation, and construction of reservoirs, parking lots, roads, and buildings.

Similar **refraction**, the bending of flow lines, occurs whenever groundwater migrates around (Figure 6.27A) or passes through (Figure 6.29) materials of differing hydraulic conductivities. For groundwater crossing a boundary, the amount of refraction is proportional to the difference in the permeability coefficients of the two materials, just as light is bent when passing through transparent materials of differing densities. A line perpendicular to the contact between the materials is called a **normal** — the dotted line in Figure 6.29. Flow lines will bend toward the normal when water moves into a lower permeability material (more resistance to flow, slower flow rate) and away from the normal when water migrates into a material with higher permeability (the upper and lower contacts respectively on Figure 6.29). Note how this refraction results in flow lines that are closer together in higher permeability materials, indicating greater flow rates through those materials.

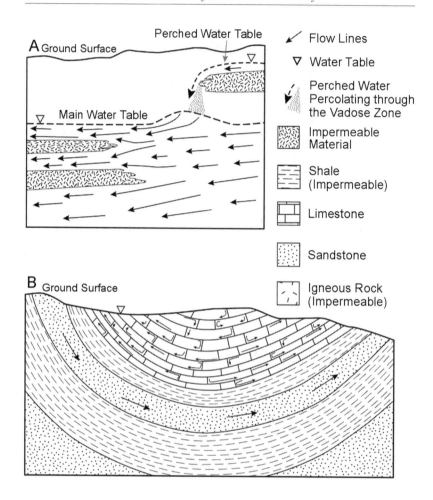

A Ground Surface

Perched Water Table

Main Water Table

↙ Flow Lines

▽ Water Table

Perched Water Percolating through the Vadose Zone

Impermeable Material

Shale (Impermeable)

Limestone

Sandstone

Igneous Rock (Impermeable)

B Ground Surface

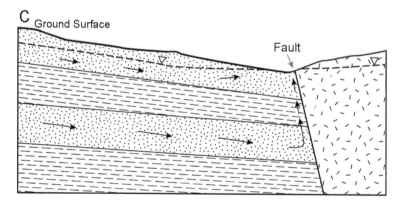

C Ground Surface

Fault

6.10.4 Impact of Permeability on Flow Rate and Direction

The dominant flow direction in aquifers which are sandwiched between impermeable layers will be parallel to the confining units and be independent of overlying topography. Note that the equipotential lines on Figure 6.24C cut straight across the confined aquifer. Hence confined water flow tends to be quite uniform across the aquifer.

Groundwater prefers the path of least resistance. Any layers or zones of high permeability material which connect to a discharge area will act like conduits and nearby groundwater will tend to converge toward these more conductive units (Figure 6.27A). The flow will tend to diverge around areas of lower permeability, such as a pocket of clay.

Various methods have been used to determine the preferential flow paths of groundwater through heterogeneous materials. A common approach utilizes the changing chemical content of the water as it flows through subsurface materials. As noted previously, groundwater in contact with rock matter will become enriched in certain elements. In general, the longer the contact, the higher the total dissolved solids in the

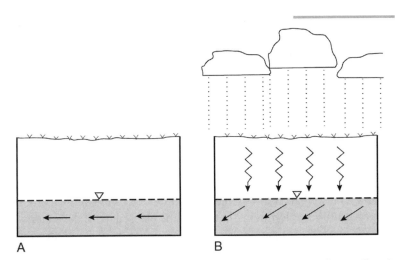

Figure 6.28. A. With no water being added from above, groundwater flow is often parallel to the water table. **B.** When water infiltrating through the vadose zone joins the groundwater, the flow is directed downward.

◀ **Figure 6.27.** Three examples of the impacts of geologic structures and rock types on groundwater flow. The flow lines represent only the dominant groundwater movements as determined by high permeability zones.

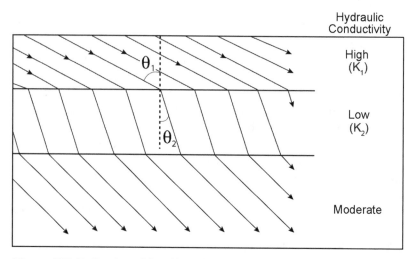

Figure 6.29. Refraction of flow lines as groundwater moves through materials of differing hydraulic conductivity (permeability). The ratio between the two angles (incoming and outgoing flow lines with the normal) is equal to the ratio of the corresponding hydraulic conductivities of the two materials. The dotted line shows the normal line and the angles (θ_1 and θ_2) made with a flow line for the top two units. K_1 and K_2 are the hydraulic conductivities of those two materials. The equation for this relationship is usually stated as:

$$\frac{K_1}{K_2} = \frac{\tan\theta_1}{\tan\theta_2}$$

groundwater. The more slowly the water moves, the more contact and the more enriched the water will be in elements peculiar to that rock. Hence the chemistry of the groundwater can often be directly related to the water's flow rate through a given type of rock. If radioactive isotopes are present, the ratio of one radioisotope to its breakdown product may be useful in determining both the time elapsed since the water was last in contact with a particular rock unit or the rate of flow through an aquifer.

7 Wells

A well is a hydraulic structure which, when properly designed and constructed, permits the economic withdrawal of water from a water-bearing formation.

— Fletcher G. Driscoll

7.1 Accessing Phreatic Water

A water **well** is any artificial excavation dug or drilled into the ground to access water. A **cistern** is an artificial depression or tank used for collecting and holding water. Most water wells are deep circular shafts or holes whose purpose is to retrieve water or gather information on groundwater. Hence they must penetrate the phreatic water. The function of most water wells is to remove groundwater for use at the surface. Hand-dug wells have been used since antiquity; some were excavated with digging and boring devices powered by humans or other animals (figures 1.1 and 7.1A). Hard labor and related difficulties limited the depth of most early wells. If the earth materials were not too resistant, a few early well drillers were able to laboriously attain depths of hundreds of feet using special boring machines and drill bits. With the invention of powerful devices utilizing petroleum and electricity in the late nineteenth century, drilling wells and retrieving groundwater rapidly became much easier than ever before (Figure 7.1B).

7.1.1 Well Functions

Wells are usually vertical holes, but they may also be horizontal or angled holes. For example, many small water-carrying fractures are vertical and a well which is drilled at an angle will intersect more fractures and produce more water than a vertical well could. Wells may be classified based on their function as follows.

1. **Supply wells.** These are intended to retrieve water from the ground for agriculture, homes, cities, industries, and other users.

Figure 7.1. A. Primitive hand-dug well in Sierra Leone. **B.** Local residents welcome water from a new electric-powered tube well in Pakistan.

2. **Extraction wells**. This term is commonly used in reference to wells whose purpose is to remove groundwater because the water may pose a problem or danger. Examples are pumping of water to aid water-logged cropland, remove contaminated water, and reduce destabilizing water pressure inside dams, at building sites, or near unstable slopes.

3. **Monitoring** (or **observation**) **wells**. These wells are used to check groundwater levels and obtain samples for water quality tests.

4. **Injection wells**. These wells are used to pour or force liquids, usually water or waste material, into the subsurface. An injection well used to help replenish groundwater is usually called a **recharge well** (Section 13.2.6C).

7.1.2 Pumps

A pump serves to transfer energy from a power source to a fluid, thereby creating flow or simply creating greater pressures on the fluid.

— Fletcher G. Driscoll

Pumps are devices which transfer both potential and kinetic energy to a fluid. The potential energy is usually in the form of increased head (elevation) or pressure and the kinetic energy is generally an increase in velocity or water movement. The function of most groundwater pumps is to lift water from a well to the surface and to the desired destination. Early efforts to remove well water date back 3,000 years and often involved direct lifting by humans or other animals using buckets with ropes and pulleys. Later efforts employed counterweights to aid the lifting or plungers which could be operated with a handle to draw water from the depths using suction. Manual pumps continue to find use and new versions have been marketed for use by poor farmers in rural Africa and elsewhere. Windmills were often employed as the energy source to lift water from a deep well (Plate 9, Bottom). Modern motorized pumps may use centrifugal force, powerful jets of fluid, suction, and other techniques to withdraw water.

By the late nineteenth century, centrifugal pumps powered by steam engines came into use. In the 1890s in California, electricity from hydropower was first used to power a centrifugal pump. The centrifugal pumps employed suction to lift the water from the well and could only lift the water a vertical distance of about 8 meters (26 feet). Three more important technological developments soon led to a revolution in the abstraction of groundwater: multi-stage vertical shaft turbine pumps, petroleum fuels, and alternating current electricity. Powerful electric and diesel turbine pumps used impellers submerged in the well and could lift water several hundred meters (Figure 7.2). An impeller is a device containing vanes or blades which rapidly rotate to force a fluid in a desired direction. The first turbine pump was installed in Chino, California, in 1907.

Today, a wide variety of pumps are available, including screw, squeeze, jet, air-life, rotary, and reciprocating pumps. **Constant-displacement pumps** produce a consistent quantity of water, regardless of such factors as the depth to water. The depth from which these pumps can lift water is usually limited to around 7 meters (23 feet) because they rely on

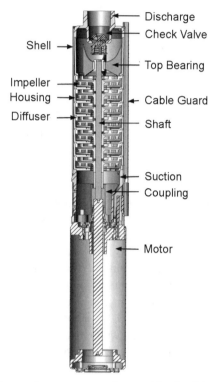

Discharge
Check Valve
Shell
Top Bearing
Impeller
Housing
Cable Guard
Diffuser
Shaft
Suction
Coupling
Motor

Figure 7.2. A modern water pump manufactured by Sta-Rite Industries. This pump is designed to operate within the well. Reprinted with permission; copyright 2012, Sta-Rite Industries.

suction and atmospheric pressure to raise water to the surface. **Variable-displacement pumps** adjust their rate of pumping based upon the head (pressure) which must be overcome to lift water to the surface. As head increases, the pumping rate decreases. This head results mainly from the vertical height the water must be lifted and the frictional forces ("friction head") which must be overcome during pumping. The most widely used variable-displacement pumps are centrifugal designs.

7.1.3 The Cone of Depression

For unconfined conditions, the original water table level prior to pumping is the **static water level**. When pumping begins, the elevation of water in the well decreases, or is "drawn down," at a pace determined by the rate of pumping and the rate of groundwater flow into the well.

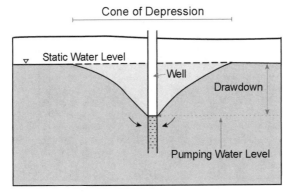

Figure 7.3. Cross-section showing a cone of depression produced by a pumping well. The original (static) water level is shown by the dashed line.

Surrounding groundwater flows toward the emptied part of the well and seeps into the well. The water closest to the well occupies smallest volume and can enter the well almost immediately. The farther from the well the groundwater, the more volume it occupies and the more slowly it will evacuate its pores. As a result, a conical zone of aeration forms around the emptying well and the slope of the cone increases toward the well. The indentation in the water table that this radial migration of water to the well produces is the **cone of depression**. In general, the more impermeable the earth materials and the more rapid the rate of withdrawal, the more rapidly the water level in the well will decline and the steeper the sides of the cone of depression. The vertical distance from the static water level to the water level in a pumping well is **drawdown** as shown on Figure 7.3.

When water is initially withdrawn from a well, the withdrawal rate exceeds the rate at which groundwater can flow into the well. Hence the water level in the well will decline. As water drains from the material surrounding the well and is pumped out, the cone of depression deepens and expands outward. The steeper the slope, the higher the hydraulic gradient and the faster the surrounding groundwater will move toward the well, all else being equal. The pumping rate, hydraulic conductivity, groundwater flow rate and direction, and storativity all help determine the shape and growth of a cone of depression. As pumping continues, the water level in the well continues to drop and the nearby water table declines as the cone spreads outward. As long as the water level in the well continues to decline, some of the incoming water represents water

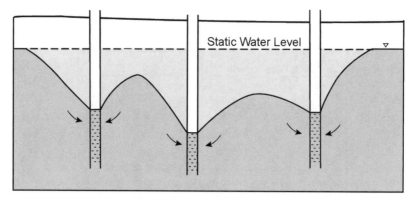

Figure 7.4. Overlapping cones of depression from three pumping wells.

that was stored in the aquifer. If a well is pumped too hard (aquifer yield rate is exceeded), or during drought, water levels in the well will continue to drop and the pump will end up sucking air.

As the areal extent of the cone of depression increases, the average slope of the water table toward the well decreases and the water level in the well may stabilize. The increased area of groundwater access helps compensate for the decrease in hydraulic gradient (slope) as the cone enlarges. If the pumping rate remains constant, a steady state will eventually be reached in which drawdown and the cone remain fairly stationary and the withdrawal rate for the well equals the recharge rate. Ideally, this indicates that an equilibrium state is attained and both drawdown and the cone of depression have achieved stability. Under these stable conditions, the water source is groundwater movement through the aquifer and additional depletion of aquifer storage is not occurring. This means that the water withdrawn will be coming from either an increase in groundwater recharge or, more likely, a decrease in groundwater discharges.

However, pumping rates will often vary, as will groundwater flow conditions, and a true equilibrium may never be attained. Groundwater flow can be greatly altered by other nearby pumping wells, each of which will have its own cone of depression. Cones of depression from adjacent wells will often merge, forming a **composite cone**, and lowering the water table over a larger area as shown on Figure 7.4.

Most of the information in this section is relevant for confined as well as unconfined conditions. Confined aquifers lie below the water table and no cone of unsaturated material forms. Instead, a cone of depression forms in the aquifer's piezometric surface where it represents decreasing hydrostatic pressure in the aquifer resulting from the water withdrawal (Figure 7.5).

7.1.4 Areas of Influence and Contribution

In large wells, the cone of depression may extend several miles outward and can take years to equilibrate. The outer limit of the cone defines the **area**, or **zone, of influence** of the well. This represents the area in which the piezometric surface (or water table for unconfined conditions) has been lowered. The area over which the surface declines can vary from a few tens of feet in diameter for low-yield wells in unconfined aquifers to tens of miles for large, heavily pumped wells in confined aquifers. Nearby water-bearing formations, lakes, streams, and other water sources within the area of influence may lose water to the pumping well. Heavily pumped, deep wells often cause smaller, shallower wells within their area of influence to dry up (Figure 7.6). They can also cause poor quality shallow groundwater to migrate downward where it can contaminate the waters of deeper aquifers.

Nice symmetrical cones of depression as in figures 7.3-7.5 result when the natural groundwater flow is very slow — in homogeneous material, the area encompassed by these cones will be close to a circle with the

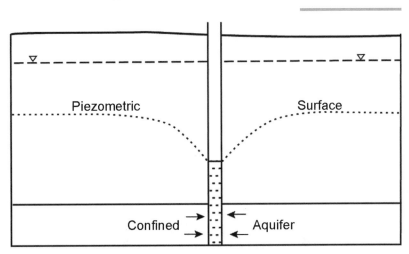

Figure 7.5. Cone of depression in the piezometric surface of a confined aquifer. Water enters the well only in the confined aquifer. (The static elevation of the piezometric surface depends upon the hydrostatic pressure in the aquifer. In this example, it lies in the overlying confining unit. For a flowing artesian well, it would be above the ground surface.)

Area of Influence

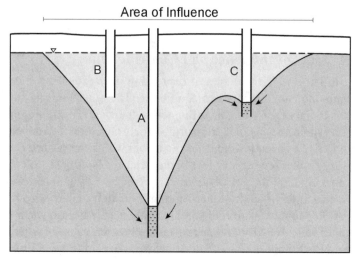

Figure 7.6. The expanding area of influence (cone of depression) of the deep well (A) has caused well B to completely dry up and has dramatically reduced the yield of well C. Dashed line is static water level.

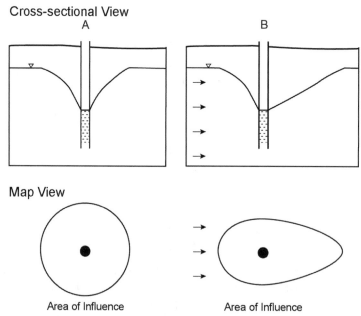

Figure 7.7. Comparison of areas of influence for groundwater with negligible flow (A) vs. persistent flow in a given direction (B).

pumping well in the center (Figure 7.7A). If the groundwater flow rate is persistent in a given direction, the cones will not be symmetrical and the area of influence will be roughly elliptical or tear-drop in shape with the pumping well located toward the upcurrent part of the area (Figure 7.7B).

A closely related term, **capture zone**, or **zone of contribution**, refers specifically to that part of an aquifer which has contributed water to a pumping well. This zone will extend beyond the zone of influence in the upgradient direction and its extent will increase with time. In other words, the longer a well has been in operation, the farther upgradient it will have drawn water from. Hence it is often called a time-related capture zone. Figure 7.8 illustrates a standard water table condition in which the zone of contribution has extended all the way to the groundwater divide. In most, but not all, situations, the upper limit of the capture zone can be considered to be the groundwater drainage divide.

The shape of both the capture zone and area of influence are strongly influenced by the groundwater flow direction and velocity as well as the local geology, such as rock types and structures. In the rare case where the water table is flat, no flow is occurring, and the aquifer material is homogeneous, the shapes would be circular as in Figure 7.7A. When the groundwater is flowing in a given direction, as it usually is, the shapes will be elongated parallel to the groundwater flow with the pumping well located in the upgradient part of the zone of influence (figures 7.7B and 7.8). The faster the groundwater flow, the more elongate the zones of influence and contribution. Note that contamination could enter the zone of influence but not reach the well, as at point x on Figure 7.8 (map view). However, any contamination in the capture zone (at point y, for example) could eventually reach the well, even if the contamination occurred far outside the area of influence.

7.2 Wellhead Protection

The surface and subsurface areas supplying water to a well, or to a group of wells, is the **wellhead protection area**. Its purpose is to protect the contributing water supply from chemical and biological pollution and to secure the actual well from any threats. Standards exist in many countries to assure that wells are properly constructed using approved materials. Regulations may also specify such precautions as buffer zones and well abandonment procedures.

In the US, wellhead protection programs often focus on establishing (1) a remedial action zone to shield wells from any pollutant releases, (2) an attenuation zone to allow reduction of contamination to acceptable levels at the well, and (3) a well-field management zone which incorporates the wells' present and future recharge zone [403]. To determine the potential threat from any contamination introduced into the well management zone, such factors as the distance to the well, contaminant travel time to the well, flow boundaries, and ability of the earth materials to reduce contaminant levels ("assimilative capacity") must be carefully considered.

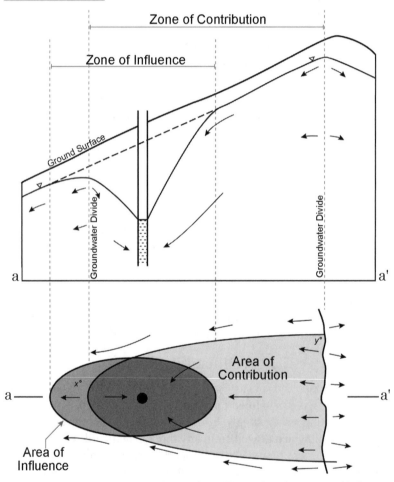

Figure 7.8. Cross-sectional and map views illustrating the zones of influence and contribution for a pumping well. Water table (unconfined aquifer) conditions in homogeneous materials are assumed. Arrows indicate groundwater movement.

Each well site is unique and risk assessment is often difficult. For example, groundwater and contaminant travel times may be far shorter during wet periods, with their high water tables, than during normal or drought conditions, especially if flow through conduits or fractures are involved. Even flow directions may change dramatically due to elevated water tables or a sudden surge of liquid contaminant. In general, all unconfined aquifers run a high risk of contamination as do confined aquifers within about a hundred feet of the surface.

Relationships between aquifers are important. Aquitards or confining units are not completely impermeable and water can move through these units, especially if fractures are present. If the head or piezometric surface for a confined aquifer lies above an overlying unconfined aquifer, water flow from the confined aquifer would be directed upward and contamination would be unlikely to spread from the overlying aquifer to the confined aquifer. However, if the confined aquifer's head lies below that of the unconfined aquifer — that is, if its piezometric surface drops below the water table as it does around the pumping well in Figure 7.9 — the pressure gradient is reversed and water (and contaminants) can migrate downward into the confined aquifer.

Determining the surface and subsurface areas needing protection and managing the siting of wells for various uses are the two major challenges for wellhead protection efforts. Defining the area which requires protection from contamination involves careful delineation of the zones of influence and contribution along with consideration of the aquifer characteristics and all possible sources of pollution including land use and seepage from surface water bodies or from other aquifers in the area. Numerous methods for delineating a wellhead protection area may be employed, including analyses of pumping tests, local groundwater and aquifer properties, hydrogeological maps, geophysical investigations, and sophisticated flow models. These methods can become quite costly. Depending upon the area under study, an experienced hydrogeologist may be able to provide good estimates of the wellhead protection area based upon sound knowledge of the site conditions and hydrogeological principles.

7.3 Water Supply Wells

7.3.1 General Well Protocols

The method(s) employed in drilling and installing any well will depend upon such considerations as the well location, site accessibility, drilling costs and time, equipment availability, surface and subsurface

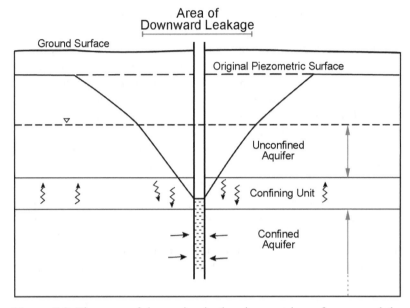

Figure 7.9. The cone of depression in the piezometric surface around the pumping well has fallen below the water table of the overlying unconfined aquifer, allowing leakage through the confining unit to seep downward into the confined aquifer. Where the piezometric surface lies above the water table, any seepage would be upward due to higher hydrostatic pressure in the confined aquifer, as indicated by the squiggly arrows [403].

characteristics, and the purpose of the well. Drilling equipment should always be thoroughly cleaned prior to drilling a new hole to prevent contamination and careful records should be kept providing information on well construction, subsurface materials encountered, hydrology, pumps employed, and tests performed.

For water supply wells, well location is especially important. In general, wells drilled in lowlands and along valley bottoms will produce the most water and those on narrow uplands the least. Efforts are being made to establish international standards for groundwater protection. Tens of thousands of failed, broken, poorly contrived, and improperly abandoned wells puncture the landscape of countries around the world. Properly constructing wells is of great importance if contamination is to be avoided, yet such information has often been lacking in the developing world. Stephen Schneider has published an excellent guide to help fill that gap [345]. His recommendations include locating the well outside flood-prone areas and at least 150 meters (500 feet) from solid waste landfills, 30 meters (100 feet) from human waste disposal or confined animal feeding areas, and 15 meters (50 feet) from food or wastewater disposal areas. Numerous publications provide detailed information on well design; Driscoll has long been the classic text [103].

7.3.2 Well Construction and Design

Well design will vary greatly depending upon the purpose, anticipated yield, rock and regolith characteristics, local regulations, and other site-specific considerations. Figure 7.10 is a very general schematic construction diagram for a water supply well. The well **casing** refers to any pipe or coating used to line or support a well. The casing keeps the hole open and prevents unwanted materials such as sediment, water, and contaminants from interfering with drilling and from entering a completed well. Multiple casings are used in some wells. In solid competent rock, a casing may not be necessary, but most wells, especially in soft or incompletely lithified materials, would collapse or become contaminated without it. The top of the casing should extend at least 20 centimeters (8 inches) above the ground surface. In unconsolidated materials, the casing should extend about 9 meters (30 feet) down from the surface to prevent contamination. The casing can be made of various materials. Polyvinyl chloride

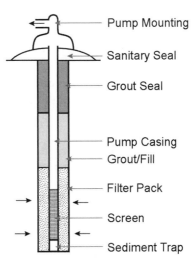

Figure 7.10. A simple water well schematic.

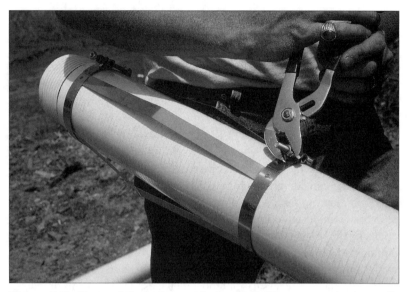

Figure 7.11. Photo of the bottom end of a small-diameter monitoring well. At the left is a cap to prevent debris from entering the well. The cap is screwed onto a screen containing narrow slots that will permit water to enter the well. The metal device being attached to the well screen is a stabilizer — its purpose is to keep the well centered in the borehole while sand, grout, or other materials are poured into the annulus (the space between the sides of the borehole and the well).

(PVC) or stainless steel are commonly used in small diameter wells. The casing comes in segments which can be screwed, glued, or welded together. A solid casing tube is often called a **riser** or **riser pipe**.

A well **screen** is a perforated or slotted section of casing that is placed where water will enter the well (Figure 7.11). The purpose of the screen is to permit groundwater to enter the well while keeping coarse debris outside. The length of screen used may vary from 5 feet or less to 100 feet or more. A well may have more than one screened interval to access different aquifers.

The space between the casing and the side of the borehole is the **annulus**. The annulus is filled with various materials whose purposes include aiding or preventing water from entering the well, preventing contaminants from migrating along the annulus, removing sediment and other impurities from water entering the well, and supporting the casing and borehole walls. In loose materials, the screen needs to be surrounded by a **filter**, or **filter pack**, to prevent soil and rock particles from muddying the water and clogging the screen slots. A typical filter consists of glass beads, quartz sand, or gravel poured or injected into the well so that it surrounds the screen on all sides. The filter should extend a foot or more above the screen top to prevent overlying material from entering the well. Sometimes the packing materials will become stuck in the annular area without falling to the bottom. To prevent this problem, called bridging, a special tube (**tremie pipe**) can be inserted into the well and material injected at the proper depth through the tube. Devices are available to keep a well centered in the borehole as the sand or other surrounding materials are added (Figure 7.11).

The remainder of the annulus above the filter pack is usually filled with grout and/or other suitable fill material. **Grout** is usually a moistened mix of cement, bentonite (a clay mineral), and/or concrete which hardens to an impermeable mass. All wells should have a grout seal at the upper part of the annulus to prevent surface contaminants from entering the well. The top of the well is shielded by an impermeable seal (cap or pad) of grout which extends about a meter out from the casing. When a well is no longer in use, it should be completely grouted to reduce interchange between different zones of subsurface waters and introduction of contaminants from the surface. If the top of the well is in an exposed location, it will need to be protected by a shelter such as a well house, manhole, or locked metal box.

7.3.3 Pump Installation

It is important that the pump chosen is suitable for its task. A pump may lack the power to withdraw adequate water. On the other hand, if a pump extracts too much water, damage to the well, aquifer, and pump may all result. Pumps may be located outside or inside a well. An outside pump operates a shaft which has been placed in the well. Near the bottom of the shaft are impellers which rotate rapidly, forcing water up the well to the surface. Compact submersible pumps fit completely inside the well itself.

7.3.4 Well Development

Once constructed, a well must be **developed** or purged to remove sediment and other impurities from the cracks and pore spaces around the well. This may be accomplished by several methods including hand purging with a bailer (Figure 7.12) or plunger for small, narrow-diameter

Figure 7.12. The hollow PVC cylinder in the bucket is a hand bailer. This one contains gasoline-contaminated water. At the left of the bucket is the monitoring well with a protective manhole rim and the top of the PVC well riser visible. To the upper right of the bucket is a locking cap which fits on the top of the well riser.

wells. Most **bailers** are simple cylinders with a valve at the lower end which opens to allow water to enter as the bailer is lowered into the water and closes to retain the water when the bailer is raised.

For most water supply wells, development involves rapid pumping of water and forcing jets of water or air into the well through a high-pressure hose. The latter method, called high velocity jetting, is widely employed, often alternating repeatedly with heavy pumping. Developing the well increases transmissivity around the screen and improves the quality of water entering the well. Developing a well can improve the yield of a well by as much as 200 to 300%.

Pumping rates vary greatly from 15 gpm (57 L/min) or less to more than 3,000 gpm (11,400 L/min) and depend upon the transmissivity of the aquifer, the depth of groundwater, the size and design of the well, and the power of the pump. If it was possible to have a pump operating at 100% efficiency — which it isn't; the maximum efficiency is around 70% — a 1 horsepower pump could lift 2 cubic feet of water 1 vertical foot in 1 second [68].

220

Other operations for water supply wells often involve sampling and chemical testing of water and disinfecting the well to kill bacteria or other unwanted organisms which may have been introduced during well construction.

7.4 Monitoring Wells

7.4.1 Introduction

Monitoring wells provide valuable information on water quality, water levels, and hydrologic properties in the local groundwater. Most monitoring wells provide water samples to determine the identity, concentration, and location of impurities in groundwater.

7.4.2 Purpose

Monitoring, or observation, wells serve many purposes; they can be used to:

- obtain background data on the hydrologic conditions of a region, including changes in water quality and water levels over time. Information from the wells may be collected and made available by various government agencies such as the US Environmental Protection Agency (EPA), USGS, and various state and local water and health agencies.
- determine if pollutants from underground storage tanks (USTs), landfills, industries, or other sites are being released;
- monitor clean aquifers for possible contaminants, especially if they are active sources of drinking water;
- determine the magnitude, extent, and migration rate of pollutants at a site;
- measure drawdown around pumping wells to obtain data from which hydraulic conductivity and related properties may be calculated; and
- provide vital groundwater data for groundwater chemistry and behavior research, court cases, regulatory requirements, and related uses.

7.4.3 Construction Details

Figure 7.13A shows a typical monitoring well. The construction is similar to a water supply well, but monitoring wells tend to be more numerous, smaller in diameter, and shallower. Figure 7.14 shows a

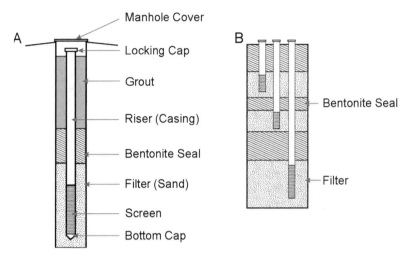

Figure 7.13. A. Typical monitoring well schematic. **B.** Simplified schematic of a cluster or nest of three monitoring wells within one borehole. In this borehole, samples can be collected from water at three different levels. For example, the upper screen may be sampling unconfined water in regolith, the two lower screens water from two confined aquifers. In such a case, the seals are placed adjacent to confining units to prevent mingling of the different groundwaters.

monitoring well being installed. Their function is not to access a large source of water, but to check on the condition of subsurface water.

Above the filter a plug, or seal, of impermeable material, such as bentonite clay, is emplaced to prevent contaminated water from entering the well from above. The clay often comes as pellets which can be poured into the annulus. The pellets will expand into a solid mass of clay after water is added. The filter pack should extend at least 0.6 meter (2 feet) above the well screen top and the overlying seal should be about 1 meter (3 feet) thick. The material filling the annulus above the seal may consist of clean cuttings from the borehole or, preferably, grout. The ground surface around the top of the well should be sealed off with a flush-mounted or slightly elevated concrete pad and the well itself protected by a steel collar and locked manhole. The riser should be provided with a locking, leak-proof cap. These measures will discourage vandalism and infiltration of surface water to the well.

Accurate construction details on the well, as shown on a good schematic (Figure 7.13), are essential if sampling data from the well are to be considered reliable. This in turn requires keeping accurate records during construction of the well in the field.

Normally, one monitoring well occupies a borehole. However, it is possible to place additional wells in a single borehole to obtain samples from different depths in the groundwater. For example, samples from several depths and locations may be needed in locations where multiple aquifers, fracture zones, or perched water tables exist (Figure 7.13B). Samples from different levels in a given aquifer may also be needed due to the presence of impurities, some of which are heavier than water and sink, and some of which are lighter and tend to remain near the top of the aquifer.

A good monitoring well needs to be properly constructed of durable materials and capable of retrieving groundwater samples which

Figure 7.14. A monitoring well being installed.

accurately reflect the quality of the water from the proper depth at that location. Specifics on standard construction methods and materials are published by several organizations, with those by the American Society for Testing and Materials (ASTM) being widely accepted in the US.

7.4.4 Surveying

The well should be surveyed and its location and elevation, usually to a specified reference point atop the well casing, carefully determined. Depth to the water table is especially important and should be measured to the nearest 3 mm (0.01 foot). In many areas the water table gradient is very low and only slight differences in elevation may determine the local groundwater flow direction. Numerous devices are available for measuring the depth to groundwater in a well, ranging from simple chalk-covered measuring tapes to sophisticated electrical sensor probes.

7.4.5 Well Placement

Proper location of monitoring wells will be determined by the specific characteristics of the site and requires a good understanding of basic hydrogeology. Wells used to check for leaks from an active UST, as at a gasoline station, are often placed close to the tanks, or even within an outer containment structure holding several USTs. With frequent checking, this permits rapid detection of any spills from faulty valves, line leaks, overfills, defective tanks, and the like.

Wells intended to detect possible contamination around a larger site such as a landfill or industrial facility are often installed several meters downgradient from the border of the site. When contamination originates at a point, such as a leak in a containment vessel or line, a contaminant plume forms which expands as it moves downgradient in the groundwater. If monitoring wells are not carefully located with respect to groundwater flow rates and direction, they may not pick up the contamination; for example, a contaminant plume may exit the site in the space between adjacent wells (Figure 7.15). If the wells are placed too far away, the contamination will not be detected until it has spread and affected a large area. Once contamination is detected, the source must be ascertained and additional wells installed to define the extent of the contamination.

Monitoring wells may also be placed in the vadose zone to detect gaseous contaminants. For example, vadose wells are often used to monitor soils above petroleum contaminated groundwater and below landfills.

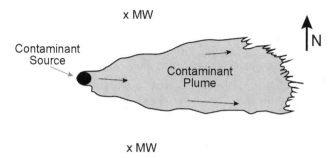

Figure 7.15. Map sketch showing monitoring wells placed too close to a point source, and too far apart, to detect a groundwater pollution plume.

7.5 Installation Methods

Wells may also be classified by their installation or construction method. A general review of well construction methods follows. Many variations of these methods exist.

7.5.1 Dug Wells

Throughout most of human history, wells were dug using simple hand tools, initially of stone, then metal picks and shovels. The earliest wells were probably just shallow holes scraped into loose regolith in a moist area or a streambed using sticks and hands. Dug wells tend to be of wide diameter and shallow depth, generally under 10 feet, and are vulnerable to surface contamination (7.1A). Once saturated sediments are encountered, the walls of a simple dug well tend to collapse. Ancient peoples such as the Mesopotamians soon learned to support the walls of their wells by lining them with stones. This allowed a much larger and more permanent water source, an important advance in the development of many early civilizations (Figure 1.1).

Smaller diameter wells can be hand-dug using augers. A **bucket auger** consists of a hollow cylinder (the bucket), often about 10 centimeters in diameter and 20 centimeters long with cutting blades at the lower end. The bucket is connected to a steel rod equipped with handles so that the device may be rotated by hand. As the auger is twisted into the soil, cuttings collect in the bucket and it must be periodically lifted from the hole and the cuttings removed. This can be hard work and is limited to relatively soft, cohesive soils without large rocks. The advantages are low cost and portability.

7.5.2 Drilled Wells

Most deep, high capacity wells are constructed by hammering or rotating a **drill bit**, the hard cutting-end piece, into rock material to produce a deep circular hole. Early drilling methods were slow and laborious. The development of fast, efficient well drilling had to wait until a convenient energy source was found to replace human or other animal labor. The portable gasoline engine provided the energy, and a strong new economic incentive, the search for more petroleum, provided the profit motive which led to a rapid expansion in drilling technology. The first successful oil well was drilled by Edwin L. Drake near Titusville, Pennsylvania, in 1859; improvements in percussion and rotary drilling technology rapidly ensued.

In the **cable tool (percussion, spudder) method**, a chisel-edged bit is hammered into the ground. Broken or pulverized material (cuttings) are removed by lifting them to the surface in elongate buckets called bailers. Cable-tool drilling rigs are rugged and versatile but slow and ornery to operate — for example, the bit and lengths of pipe often get stuck in the hole and the deeper one goes, the more difficult the drilling process becomes. Percussion drilling probably dates back to at least the tenth century A.D.

In the **rotary method**, a rapidly rotating hollow bit bores into rock as high-pressure drilling fluid — which may be water, air, foam, or special fluids — is forced down an inner tube, through holes in the bit, then back to the surface via an outer hollow cylinder, taking the cuttings with it (Figure 7.16). The cuttings are separated out and the fluid recirculated. The circulating fluid provides drill hole support, lubrication and cooling for the drill bit, and continual removal of ground rock and debris. The outer cylinder also serves as a temporary casing, preventing collapse of the walls during drilling. Primitive rotary, or "churn," drilling was probably utilized by the Chinese over 1,000 years ago.

Rotary drilling is the most frequently used method of well drilling in hydrogeologic work. Several types of rotary drilling are available; they are fast but costly. The rotary-percussion method combines the two methods noted above and is very effective in hard rock. An air percussion rig is shown in operation on Figure 7.17. A reverse-circulation rotary method is useful in unconsolidated materials.

7.5.3 Bored Wells

For bored wells, a hand- or power-driven **auger**, basically a large corkscrew, is rotated into the earth to bore a hole to the groundwater,

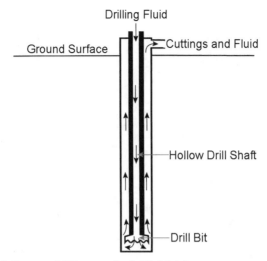

Figure 7.16. Rotary drilling method. Fluid (air, water, water mixed with clay, etc.) is forced down the central conduit, through the drill bit, and up the annulus carrying drilling cuttings.

much like a drill penetrating wood. When the first auger, or auger "flight," has penetrated to its maximum depth, additional augers are attached to the first until the desired depth is attained. Augers operate effectively in soft materials that don't cave in readily. Cuttings migrate to the surface along the outside screw threads as the auger is rotated into the earth.

Power-driven **hollow-stem augering** is especially useful in contamination investigations in unconsolidated materials because one can collect continuous, undisturbed samples of the earth material as the drilling proceeds. The drilling is accomplished by auger rotation. The bottom of the auger has cutting blades and a bit, attached to a steel rod lowered through the hollow augers, which help advance the hole. To collect a sample, the bit or plug is removed and a hollow steel collection tube is attached to the steel rod and lowered into the hollow-stem auger. Several sampling devices are available. Among the most popular are the single-pieced **Shelby tube** and a **split-spoon sampler**, which can be opened up at the drill site to reveal the sample (Figure 7.18). The tubes have a sharpened lower end and are pounded into the soil with a standard hammering device. The number of blows required to drive the tube a given distance during a Standard Penetration Test provides useful information about the strength and other properties of the earth

Figure 7.17. Air percussion drilling rig in operation in a quarry in Virginia.

material being sampled [383]. The more blows per foot, the tougher the material.

When the desired depth is reached, the well materials, usually a perforated "screen" and a solid "riser," can be inserted directly into the hollow stem of the auger. The auger is then removed, or "unscrewed," by rotating in the opposite direction, just like a wood screw. Sand and other well material can be placed into the annulus, the space around the well, via the hollow stem of the auger as it is being removed.

Most auger drills are driven by a gasoline or diesel powered engine mounted on the back of the drilling rig (Figure 7.19). Portable hollow-stem drill rigs use smaller augers, are quite flexible and can be used inside buildings and in other tight locations not accessible to a standard drilling rig truck. Many can drill at angles. Auger rigs are extremely useful in soft rock and regolith but tend to be prone to breakdowns and hence costly [423].

7.5.4 Driven Wells

The hole of driven wells is created by driving, usually by hammering, lengths of pipe into the ground. Driven wells are usually shallow and small in diameter, up to about 10 centimeters. This method is fast

Figure 7.18. Split spoon sampler. As the sampling device is pounded into the ground, unconsolidated material will collect in the hollow cylinder. It can then be split apart to reveal relatively undisturbed material for examination.

and inexpensive but only useful in fine- to medium-grained unconsolidated materials.

7.5.5 Jetted Wells

To construct a jetted well, a powerful downward-directed stream of water is used with a drill rod and wedge-like drill bit to excavate unconsolidated materials. The casing conducts sediment and water back to the surface as the well is deepened. Like driven wells, jetted wells are generally shallow, small diameter, fast, inexpensive, and unable to provide undisturbed soil samples.

7.5.6 Horizontal Wells

Horizontal wells are just that, holes or excavations to collect water and constructed with a gentle-to-horizontal slope. Examples include:
1. **Horizontal pipes**: Horizontal or low-gradient conduits may be drilled or pounded into slopes to collect seepage water from the vadose zone or to penetrate phreatic water, thus producing a gravity spring (Figure 7.20A).

Figure 7.19. Hollow-stem auger drilling rig with boom raised. The augers can be seen on the truck bed.

2. **Infiltration galleries**: These are typically shallow, wide, gently sloping tunnels or corridors designed to collect water. The water may be groundwater or gravity water percolating downward through the zone of aeration. Infiltration galleries are often placed in alluvial deposits near or below rivers (Figure 7.20B), especially in dry climates, where they collect fresh water from influent streams. A **qanat** (or ganat) is a subsurface tunnel built to gather and transfer groundwater from higher to lower elevations. Qanats were constructed in many areas of northern Africa and the Middle East (Figure 7.21 and Plate 10, Top). They are effective at gathering water from alluvial fans in arid regions (Figure 7.20C). In northern Mesopotamia, the Assyrians constructed extensive qanats to penetrate the phreatic zone and harvest groundwater from the sediments. They apparently learned this technology from the Armenians whom they invaded around 714 B.C. Some 22,000 of these passages were hand-constructed in alluvial deposits as early as 3,000 years ago. These remarkable engineering feats still provide

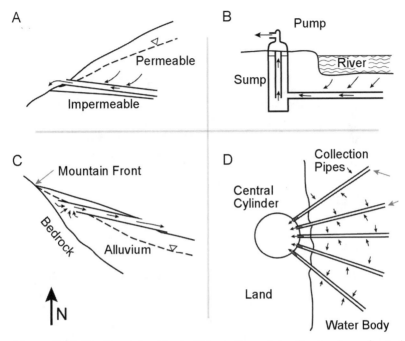

Figure 7.20. Horizontal wells. A. This well consists of a simple perforated tube inserted into an aquifer. The slight downward slope of the well is to prevent air pockets or vacuum conditions from interfering with the water flow through the well. **B.** Example of an infiltration gallery below a stream bed. In favorable locations, numerous horizontal wells may be installed. **C.** Cross-section of alluvial fan with qanat. Large infiltration galleries (qanats) consist of corridors or tunnels constructed in alluvial deposits at the foot of mountain ranges are an ancient and efficient way of obtaining water, especially in arid regions. **D.** Map sketch of a collector well located near the bank of a stream or lake. These wells utilize numerous spoke-like horizontal extension pipes to collect water, usually from below a large water body. A cross-section through this well perpendicular to the stream bank would closely resemble example B.

much of the water used in Iran today. Qanat tunnels range up to 30 kilometers (18 miles) in length and 250 meters (825 feet) in depth, though the dimensions of most are much more modest [256, 389].

3. **Collector wells:** These consist of a large, vertical central well sealed at the bottom and equipped with radiating

Figure 7.21. Two photographs of qanats near Ouarzazate in Morocco. **A.** Many qanats must be regularly cleared of collected sediment. The hills dotting this arid plain are piles of earth removed from underlying qanats which in this area consist of numerous small water-transport corridors. **B.** View down into a qanat.

collector pipes to help gather groundwater. The example in Figure 7.20D shows the collector pipes extending under the adjacent body of water. Collector wells are effective in floodplains, even under rivers or lakes. Their initial cost is high, but their high yield and low maintenance can make them good investments for large water users such as cities.

7.5.7 Special Techniques

Certain special techniques may be used to better access an aquifer or to improve the aquifer yield in the vicinity of a well. In **directional drilling**, the boring is done at an angle rather than vertically. Alternately, the boring may begin vertically and is gradually curved as drilling proceeds. **Enhanced recovery** usually involves **hydraulic fracturing**, or **hydrofracking**, in which water, sand, and chemicals are forced into the well under high pressure to flush out fine particles and increase the size of existing fractures to improve water flow into a supply well. The sand helps keep the fractures open, increasing permeability. Older wells may also be "fracked" to help remove built-up sediment and encrustations. These methods are also commonly applied, albeit on a larger scale, in oil and natural gas wells.

7.5.8 Borehole Logs

Drilling has two major functions in most groundwater investigations. One is to install the well and the other is to obtain information about subsurface materials at the site. The latter requires keeping accurate information on the earth materials encountered during drilling. This information is recorded in a **log**. It may be called a driller's, geologist's, or boring log depending upon who has recorded the information. Driller's logs are generally the least informative; the usefulness of other logs depends upon how accurately and carefully the person creating the log observes and describes the material being retrieved. The information which can be gathered depends upon the drilling method. Most informative will be methods which can secure relatively intact samples or cores of the material being penetrated. Hollow-stem augering can provide continuous, little-disturbed samples of soft materials which can be examined in the field and saved for later study or analysis. Rock cores can be extracted by most rotary drilling.

Retrieving cores from deep boreholes is time-consuming and entails additional expense but the information gathered can contribute greatly to our knowledge of the subsurface. Among the information that may be obtained from borehole logs are direct observations of the properties of subsurface materials, location of water tables and moisture zones, occurrence and nature of contaminants, data on rate of penetration or hardness of the material being drilled, presence of cavities, and similar information related to the subsurface. Figure 7.22 provides a brief description of materials encountered in the borehole of a hollow-stem auger boring log. Depending upon the purpose of the boring, a log should also include such information as boring number, location, date, elevation, driller's name, client's name, boring method, odors detected, resistance to auger penetration, and other observations.

Many faster, more sophisticated drilling methods provide only badly disturbed "cuttings" or fragments of subsurface material. Some useful information about the material (lithology, possible contamination, and so forth) can still be gleaned from the cuttings.

A variety of geophysical survey probes can gather further important information from boreholes. These instruments are lowered into the borehole where they can measure small changes in borehole diameter, electrical properties of the material, natural radiation emissions, temperature, and other parameters which aid in interpreting geologic and hydrologic properties of the subsurface materials (Section 13.4.2).

7.6 Influences on Water Levels in Wells

The most obvious impact on the water table in or near a well will be the cone of depression produced by water withdrawal. Important information about the well's capacity and the surrounding aquifer can be obtained by analyzing the behavior of water levels around a pumping well. Nearby observation wells are often the best way to obtain water level data. Water in the pumping well is disturbed by the pumping and the water itself may not be accessible due to pump equipment located in the well shaft. Figure 7.23 is a graph showing the drawdown observed in a nearby observation well, or in the well itself. Note that the rate of drawdown is rapid at first, then diminishes and approaches an equilibrium state. When pumping stops, the water level rises, rapidly at first, then more slowly as the original equilibrium level is neared. The logarithmic fall and rise of the water permits transmissivity of the material surrounding the well to be calculated.

Additional, usually subtle, influences on the elevation of the water table commonly occur, as shown at the left side of Figure 7.23. In some cases, such influences may need to be compensated for to obtain accurate results from pumping tests. These influences include the following.

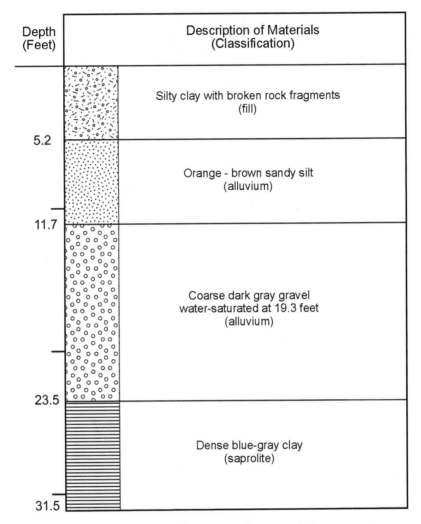

Depth (Feet)	Description of Materials (Classification)
	Silty clay with broken rock fragments (fill)
5.2	
	Orange - brown sandy silt (alluvium)
11.7	
	Coarse dark gray gravel water-saturated at 19.3 feet (alluvium)
23.5	
	Dense blue-gray clay (saprolite)
31.5	

Auger refusal on gray shale
at 31.5 feet

Figure 7.22. A typical log for a hollow-stem auger borehole, briefly describing the subsurface materials encountered during drilling. The description and depth may be augmented with additional description, drilling details, elevation values, air quality measurements of the samples, and so forth, depending on the purpose of the project.

1. **Earthquakes.** Groundwater may reflect geologic events. Monitoring water levels and water composition has long been used as a possible indication of stress buildup and other changes within the earth and may even presage an earthquake. Seismic waves moving through the earth often produce alternating episodes of compression and expansion which cause sudden fluctuations of equal amplitude in the water level. The initial arrival of waves may produce a larger fluctuation. On December 26, 2004, an earthquake near Indonesia triggered a devastating tsunami that killed some 180,000 people. Thirty-two minutes after the quake occurred, a monitoring well in Missouri, on the other side of Earth, recorded a sudden rise of 8.5 feet in the groundwater. Shock waves from the quake apparently compressed the local rock, a cavernous limestone, causing the rise.

2. **Wind.** Gusty winds blowing across an open well may produce a thick fuzzy line on a water level graph representing small, very rapid water level changes caused by corresponding variations in air pressure in the well.

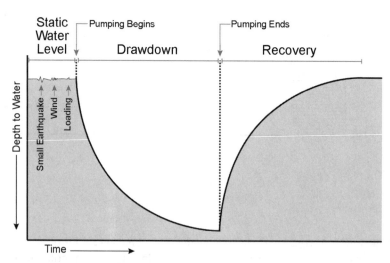

Figure 7.23. Water level readings showing minor influences, drawdown, and recovery curves in a well, or a nearby observation well. The time involved will usually be a matter of hours or days.

3. **Temporary loading.** Changes in the pressure exerted upon the local ground can cause brief increases in the water level, usually without a corresponding decrease. Heavy trucks or trains often produce this effect.
4. **Changes in the elevation of nearby surface water bodies.** In coastal environments, the water table may slowly rise and fall along with the tides. Fluctuations in lake and reservoir levels will produce a similar effect.
5. **Barometric pressure.** The higher the atmospheric pressure, the lower the water table.

7.7 Pumping Tests

Pumping tests are designed to determine the hydraulic characteristics and behavior of wells and the nearby earth materials from which the groundwater is derived. As such, they provide vitally important information about water supply prospects, well capacity, aquifer properties, and the movement of groundwater (and potential contaminants) in the immediate vicinity of a well. Many types of tests exist and details about pump types, pumping rates, field equipment, field measurements, and the many techniques and calculations which can be involved can be obtained from well supply companies and in various texts [103, 122, 402]. Pumping tests can be very costly to conduct and interpreting the data can be complex. The test wells and their relation to the aquifer, interference from other nearby wells, heterogeneities in the earth material, and other potential influences must be considered. Some common pumping tests are outlined below.

7.7.1 Aquifer Pumping Tests

Drawdown data as illustrated in Figure 7.23 are best obtained using a pump that can quickly withdraw water from the well. In most pumping tests, water is pumped from the well at a steady rate and the water level in the well, and/or in close-by observation wells, is carefully measured through time. The rate of drawdown itself can be used to provide approximate values for such properties as hydraulic conductivity, storage coefficient, and transmissivity. Data from observation/monitoring wells within the cone of depression can also be used to predict drawdown in the main well under various pumping conditions.

Ideally, water levels should be monitored for several weeks prior to a pumping test so that irregularities in local water levels due to rainfall, barometric pressure, and other influences can be determined and compensated for in the pump test results. Preliminary pumping is useful so that pump yield, drawdown, impacts on nearby observation wells, and related issues can be anticipated. The water table should have returned to the normal static water level before the test begins; in many areas, a minimum of 24 hours for confined aquifers and 72 hours for unconfined aquifers is recommended. When the test begins, drawdown will be rapid and may need to be measured every few seconds. If an automatic recording device is not available, field personnel need to synchronize watches and be prepared to rapidly record data. When the water level begins to stabilize, measurement intervals can be extended to several minutes or even an hour or two.

If an aquifer is being tested, the wells providing the pumping test data should ideally penetrate the entire aquifer. Water being pumped from the well is monitored to assure a constant rate of discharge. The water must either be contained or released at a distance so that the water cannot recharge local groundwater and flow back into the well being tested.

When the pumping test is completed, it is useful to continue recording the water level as it rises. This is sometimes called a **reverse aquifer pumping test**. These recovery measurements will ideally be the mirror image of the drawdown measurements, and may provide more dependable data than during drawdown which may be influenced by irregular pumping rates or groundwater perturbations due to the pumping.

Another variation is the **step drawdown** test in which successively higher pumping rates are employed, measuring drawdown at each rate or "step." This may involve several steps, each lasting an hour or two. In general, constant rate pumping tests are preferable but the step drawdown test can be useful in determining sustained yield and in wells experiencing turbulent flow.

7.7.2 Well Loss and Efficiency

The water level in a pumping well that is experiencing drawdown will differ from that in the surrounding geologic material or aquifer. Time is required for water to drain from the earth material, pass through perforations in the casing, and flow into the well. Therefore, the drawdown in the immediately adjacent aquifer material will lag behind that in the withdrawal well itself (Figure 7.24). This difference is called **well loss**. The ratio between the outside (aquifer) drawdown and the inside (well) drawdown is a measure of the **efficiency** of the well. Efficiencies in excess of 70% are regarded as good. Obviously, to obtain

238

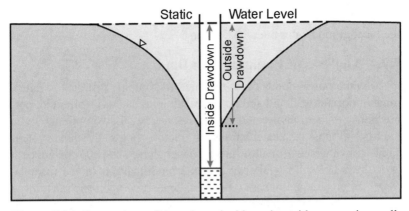

Figure 7.24. Comparison of drawdown inside and outside a pumping well.

these parameters, both the withdrawal well and at least one very close observation well need to be monitored during the pumping test.

7.7.3 Specific Capacity and Safe Yield

The **specific capacity** (C_s) of a well is the discharge from a pumping well (Q) divided by drawdown (D_d).

$$C_s = \frac{Q}{D_d}$$

It is a measure of the productivity, or water yield, of a well or an aquifer and is measured as volume per unit time per unit drawdown (such as m³/day/min, ft³/day/ft, or gal/min/ft). The specific capacity often declines over time reflecting a reduction in transmissivity. This may be caused by an overall lowering of the water table or by "well losses." **Well losses** refer to reduced water yield due to well-related problems such as water leaks, deterioration of the well screen or riser, and clogging of the screen or pump intake with sediment.

The term **safe yield** refers to the annual quantity of water that can be taken from a well without causing undesirable consequences such as lowering the water table, interfering with the withdrawal rights of others, or allowing low-quality water to migrate into good water. When the safe yield of a well is exceeded by overpumping, immediate impacts at that well usually include decreased well yields and increased costs. This is mainly because the water level in the well drops and water must be pumped a greater distance to the surface. Although no specific parameters define what safe yield is, it remains a useful planning tool for estimating the local groundwater budget (Section 3.9.2).

7.7.4 Analyses of Pumping Test Data

Numerous methods can be applied to pumping test data to determine important well and aquifer characteristics such as well yield, permeability, transmissivity, and storativity. Darcy's Law continues to be the basis of most well calculations, but factors such as the three-dimensional convergence of shallow groundwater along a convex-upward path as it flows toward a well require some modifications of the formula. Many different equations may be used, depending upon such factors as the available data, number and location of wells providing that data, aquifer properties, the goals of the investigation, and even the units being used (m/day, ft³/hour, and so forth).

For example, the following equation provides the relationships for steady flow from an unconfined aquifer into a pumping well in which the water-receiving (screened) part of the well extends throughout the entire saturated thickness of the aquifer. If the well is not screened through the entire saturated zone, additional water from below or above the screened part will move toward the well further complicating any calculations. The equation also requires obtaining data from two observation wells within the cone of depression as shown on Figure 7.25. Under these conditions, this equation produces a good approximation of the hydraulic conductivity of the aquifer material, and of other parameters, depending upon what is known or can be reasonably estimated:

$$K = \frac{Q \log R/r}{1.366(H^2 - h^2)}$$

where K is the hydraulic conductivity of the aquifer in m/day, Q is the pumping rate or well yield in m³/day, R and r are the respective distances (or radii) from the pumping well to the farther and closer monitoring wells, and H and h are the head (or saturated thickness) of the aquifer at the two monitoring wells [103, 192, 369].

For a confined aquifer, the following equation (or a variation thereof), often referred to as the **Theim, Dupuit,** or **equilibrium equation**, may be used:

$$K = \frac{Q \log R/r}{2.73b(H - h)}$$

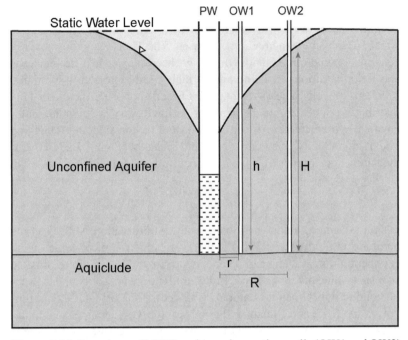

Figure 7.25. Pumping well (PW) and two observation wells (OW1 and OW2) within the cone of depression are needed for many aquifer calculations. This example labels the parameters for an unconfined aquifer: h and H represent the head for OW1 and OW2, respectively, while r and R are the respective radii (distance from the pumping well) for OW1 and OW2.

where K is in m/day, Q is the pumping rate in m³/day, R and r are the radial distances of the farther and closer wells, b is the thickness of the aquifer in meters, and H and h represent the piezometric head in the farther and closer wells respectively.

These equations and most others require certain conditions such as a stabilized cone of depression, flat piezometric surface, laminar flow, and aquifer uniformity to be completely valid, but the errors caused by not meeting these conditions are usually minor and do not seriously detract from the usefulness of the equations.

Often it is not feasible to wait for equilibrium (steady-state) conditions to develop due to the time required for stabilization. Fortunately, pumping tests may be conducted before the cone of depression has stabilized — for example, during purging of a well. Under these **nonequilibrium** conditions, the slope of the cone, and hence the head and flow rates, are constantly evolving. In hydrogeological jargon, the resulting groundwater movement is often called **transient flow**. In this situation, the **Theis** method may be used. The Theis technique actually consists of numerous methods which have been adapted to differing needs and field conditions. It is the most widely used approach to hydraulic problems of wells. The Theis method is based upon the principle that the distribution of head around a pumping well will vary in a regular, mathematically predictable manner, as indicated by the smoothly changing rate of slope seen during drawdown and recharge (Figure 7.23). One of the simplest examples of a Theis nonequilibrium equation is:

$$s = \frac{Q\,W(u)}{4\pi T}$$

where: s is the drawdown in meters in an observation well; Q is the pumping rate in m^3/day; W(u) is the "well function of u" which is an exponential integral and can be obtained from published tables; π is the standard value, pi (3.14); and T is the aquifer transmissivity, the hydraulic conductivity times the saturated thickness. The original method involves more advanced math and graphical (curve-matching) manipulations but numerous simplified and reasonably accurate modifications have been devised [100, 103, 192, 369, 422, 423].

7.7.5 Slug Tests

Full-scale pumping tests can require considerable time and expense. A much faster, more convenient, and low-cost alternative is the slug test. A **slug test**, or bail-down test, is a procedure in which a known quantity of water, the slug, is rapidly added or removed from a well and the return to a static water level is carefully monitored. In small wells, the water is often removed by hand using a bailer. The faster the water returns to its original level, the higher the hydraulic conductivity of the material in the immediate vicinity of the well screen. Several varieties of slug tests exist, among which the Hvorslev and the Bouwer and Rice methods are widely used by consultants. They are especially useful in obtaining hydrologic information on subsurface materials from monitoring wells in low-permeability materials, for example, near waste-disposal sites or leaking USTs. Slug test data are valid only for a small area near the well and are not as reliable as pumping test data. The procedures involve rapid removal or addition of a slug of water from a well or piezometer, carefully measuring the water level as it recovers, computing the ratio of each water-level measurement to the original (static) water level, and plotting this ratio on the log scale of semilogarithmic paper vs. time on the arithmetic scale. A straight line is then fitted to the plotted points and the information from that plot, along with such data as well radius, borehole radius, and well screen length, is used to compute permeability of the material around the well.

A large number of equations may be used to determine important hydrogeological parameters under various circumstances such as differing aquifer types, groundwater flow conditions, field conditions, and assumptions. An abundance of information and applications for well data, both practical and theoretical, are available, among them the sources referenced here [47, 100, 103, 185, 228, 273, 348, 369, 390, 422, 423].

8
Aquifers and Hydrogeologic Regions

In order to deal effectively with the principles of occurrence and movement of ground water in a large, geologically complex area like North America, subareas that have similar ground-water conditions must first be delineated.

— Ralph C. Heath

8.1 Definitions and Properties of Aquifers

An **aquifer** is a groundwater storage reservoir that comprises one or more rock or regolith units and is capable of yielding a usable quantity of water, such as to a well or a spring. The quantity of water regarded as usable or significant, of course, will depend upon the intended use. One gallon per minute may suffice for a single family home, but an irrigation farmer or industry may require a minimum of hundreds of gallons per minute. The term "aquifer" is commonly used to indicate any existing or potential groundwater source. The major prerequisites for a good aquifer are fairly large volume, high permeability, and a moderate-to-high specific yield (the drainable or effective porosity). These properties depend upon the size, shape, volume, and connectivity of the openings in the aquifer material. Aquifers are vital water sources and perform both storage and conduit (transport) functions. Most aquifers transmit water at from 1.5 m/day to 1.5 m/yr. Sandstone formations provide the best storage sites for retrievable groundwater and yield the most water among the bedrock aquifers. Overall, the largest quantities of water are removed annually from the more accessible and shallow alluvial deposits. As water tables fall and water shortages become more acute, water resource scientists are focusing more on mapping and determining the potential of deeper, underutilized aquifers such as the Guarani aquifer underlying parts of Argentina, Brazil, Paraguay, and Uruguay and the Kalahari/Karoo aquifers of Namibia, Botswana, and South Africa. Figure 8.1 provides locations for most of the world's major aquifers and Table 8.1 identifies the aquifers.

Table 8.1. Major Aquifers of the World

WESTERN HEMISPHERE

1.	Northern Great Plains / Interior Plains Aquifer	4.	High Plains-Ogallala Aquifer
2.	Cambro-Ordovician Aquifer System	5.	Gulf Coastal Plains Aquifer System
3.	California Central Valley Aquifer System	6.	Amazonas Basin
		7.	Maranhao Basin
		8.	Guarani Aquifer System

EASTERN HEMISPHERE

9.	Senegalo-Mauritanian Basin	22.	Parisian Basin
10.	Taoudeni-Tanezrouft Basin	23.	East European Aquifer System.
11.	Northwest Sahara Aquifer System (NWSAS)	24.	North Caucasus Basin
12.	Murzuk-Djado Basin	25.	Pechora Basin
13.	Nubian Sandstone Aquifer System (NAS)	26.	West Siberian Artesian Basin
14.	Iullemeden-Irhazer Aquifer System	27.	Tunguss Basin
15.	Chad Basin	28.	Angara-Lena Artesian Basin
16.	Sudd Basin (Umm Ruwaba Aquifer)	29.	Yakut Basin
17.	Ogaden-Juba Basin	30.	Tarim Basin
18.	Congo Intracratonic Basin	31.	Songliao Basin
19.	Northern Kalahari Basin	32.	North China Plain Aquifer System
20.	Southeast Kalahari Basin	33.	Arabian Aquifer System
21.	Karoo Basin	34.	Indus Basin
		35.	Ganges-Brahmaputra Basin
		36.	Canning Basin
		37.	Great Artesian Basin

Notes: Numerals in this table correspond to those in Figure 8.1. Source: [430].

Figure 8.1. Map showing location of major aquifers of the world. ▶

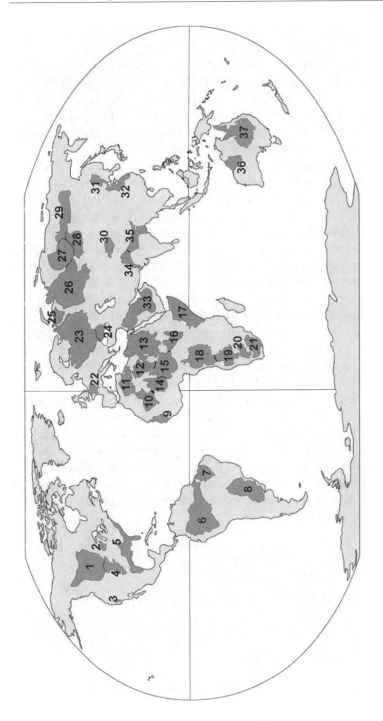

As described previously, the water which can be extracted sustainably from an aquifer depends upon there being sufficient precipitation and recharge to balance water losses. In addition, prolonged decreases in precipitation can be expected to reduce an aquifer's water volume, prolonged increases to augment the volume. How rapidly the quantity of groundwater increases or decreases will also depend upon discharge rates, including pumping, and the hydraulic gradient, storage coefficient, and hydraulic conductivity of the aquifer.

An **aquiclude** is a geologic unit of low permeability which prevents or severely limits groundwater flow. A related term is **aquitard** which refers to a geological unit which retards groundwater flow. The terms can generally be considered synonymous. Many prefer to use the term **confining bed** as a synonym for both aquitard and aquiclude. A confining unit in one location may actually be considered an aquifer elsewhere. For example, glacial till is rich in clay and produces low well yields, but in areas where materials with high permeability are lacking, till may be the best available source for groundwater.

Another related term, **hydrostratigraphic unit**, refers to a unit or group of earth materials, usually rock formations, which can be conveniently grouped based upon their hydrologic characteristics. Hydrogeologists often consider an important group of aquifers along with their confining beds to be a hydrostratigraphic unit.

The terms first defined in Sections 6.5 through 6.8 are extremely important in the study of aquifers, as are the well data reviewed in Chapter 7. To recap, transmissivity and storativity refer to actual geologic units of a given thickness and allow us to calculate respectively the flow rate and the water volume yield in an aquifer. The **storativity** (S) of an aquifer refers to the volume of water (ΔV) the aquifer will yield or absorb per unit surface area (A) per unit change in head (ΔH). Mathematically, we can say:

$$S = \frac{\left(\frac{\Delta V}{A}\right)}{\Delta H}$$

By getting rid of the complex fraction, we have

$$S = \frac{\Delta V}{A\Delta H}$$

By solving this for ΔV, we have

$$\Delta V = SA\Delta H$$

This is the same formula given at the end of Section 6.5. We can use this formula to calculate how much water might be obtained from aquifers whose storativity is roughly known. Storativity equals specific yield for unconfined aquifers. If the hydrostatic pressure is increased, the aquifer will yield a correspondingly greater volume of water; if decreased, the yield will diminish accordingly. The same is true for the storativity and area values.

Example: Using the Equation

If a confined aquifer has a storativity of 0.004, how much water can be obtained if the hydraulic head is decreased by 6 meters in an area of 2 km^2? Units need to be consistent, so converting the km^2 into m^2 yields 2,000,000 m^2. Then:

$$\Delta V = SA\Delta H = 0.004 \times 2{,}000{,}000 \text{ m}^2 \times 6 \text{ m} = 48{,}000 \text{ m}^3$$
(12,682,000 gallons).

8.2. Types of Aquifers

As an aquifer, I abide by nature's wishes and not by human wishes and expectations.

— Harry E. LeGrand, Sr.

8.2.1 Classifying Aquifers

Aquifers can be classified in various ways, including size, depth, geographic setting, water yield, rock or sediment type, and hydrologic characteristics such as groundwater flow and pressure conditions. The material the aquifer consists of is commonly used to group aquifers. In its simplest form, this gives us three big categories: sedimentary rock, igneous and metamorphic rock, and unconsolidated aquifers. Aquifers which can produce moderate to high yields of water underlie approximately half of the US. In general, the most productive wells tend to be in unconsolidated materials, usually sand and gravel, followed by sandstones, carbonate rocks, and volcanic rocks. Descriptions of the media in which groundwater occurs are provided in Sections 8.5 through 8.8. Distinctive geographic locations and environments are reviewed in Sections 8.9 through 8.14.

Hydrogeologists generally recognize three basic types of aquifers based upon the groundwater's relationship to the subsurface environment: these are unconfined, perched, and confined aquifers.

8.2.1 Unconfined Aquifers

An **unconfined aquifer** is an aquifer whose water is exposed via pores to atmosphere (figures 3.11, 6.1-6.4). Unconfined groundwater can be thought of as any groundwater that has a water table. Unconfined groundwater is also commonly referred to as a "normal," "open," or "water table" condition. The storage coefficient of an unconfined aquifer is almost identical to the specific yield because the water is supplied by normal gravity flow. In an unconfined aquifer, groundwater depletion can be thought of as the desaturation of its pores.

8.2.2 Perched Aquifers

A **perched aquifer** is an unconfined aquifer in which the zone of saturation is separated from an underlying water table by a zone of aeration. The water is often simply called perched water and will be found overlying zones of low permeability which are present above the main water table (figures 3.9 and 6.1).

8.2.3 Confined Aquifers

A **confined aquifer** is an aquifer which is isolated from the atmosphere by an aquiclude, an impermeable zone directly overlying the water in the aquifer (Figure 6.1). Confined aquifers are also called **artesian aquifers**. Wells getting water from confined aquifers are **artesian wells**. The term "artesian" comes from Artois in the former lowland country of Flanders where early wells penetrated through shales to access the abundant groundwater below. Hydrostatic pressure or head in the confined water will always exceed the anticipated pressure of unconfined water at the same location. If the pressure is high enough and an open conduit is present, the water can rise through the overlying rock and soil and emerge at the surface as a **flowing artesian spring** or **well** (Figure 8.2). Where subsurface geology is favorable, flowing artesian conditions can exist over surprisingly large areas as in the US Great Plains and Atlantic Coastal Plain, and the Great Artesian Basin of Australia.

In confined phreatic water, water in a borehole will always rise above the base of the confining layer indicating that the confined water is under pressure, just as the water confined in the pipes leading from a holding tank to your faucet is under pressure (Figure 6.15). Groundwater flowing through a confined aquifer can flow upward as long as adequate pressure exists, just as water flows upward through pipes to a faucet in your home, and forms the ice pyramid seen on Plate 10,

Figure 8.2. When water is confined and under sufficient pressure, gravitational force alone will produce a constant flow of water. Here, groundwater gushes from a pipe in southwestern Virginia.

Bottom. The elevation to which the water will rise in a standing tube (piezometer) or well reflects the pressure (head) of the confined water; it is also the level of the piezometric surface (artesian pressure surface) at that location in the aquifer. Figure 8.3 illustrates an idealized piezometric surface for a confined aquifer. Note that flowing artesian conditions exist where the artesian pressure surface lies above the ground surface. The downward slope of the surface reflects the loss of head by leakage into the overlying shale and by frictional losses during flow.

Water tends to flow through a confined aquifer parallel to the confining boundaries (Figure 6.24C), much like water through a pipe. Just

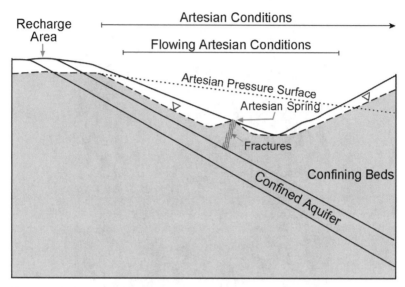

Figure 8.3. Cross-section showing an artesian aquifer. Inclined sedimentary rock strata commonly give rise to artesian conditions.

as water pipes develop leaks, so do the confining beds. The term **leaky confined aquifer** is used for confined aquifers that receive or lose significant amounts of water from surrounding formations. Such additions and detractions can greatly complicate calculations.

The piezometric surface will rise and fall in response to changes of the volume, hence to the weight and pressure, of water in the confined aquifer, just as the water table does in an unconfined aquifer. Pumping water from confined water reduces the internal pressure, although the actual aquifer material is not usually dewatered as with water table conditions. Because pressure is reduced around wells pumping water from a confined aquifer, cones of depression form in the piezometric surface as shown in Figure 7.5. If pumped strongly enough to cause dewatering, unconfined conditions would exist at that location.

It seems illogical that water can be taken from a place, yet that place remains full of water. Part of the explanation lies in realizing that whenever the hydrostatic pressure in the water increases, the force it exerts causes the rock material to actually expand somewhat — that is, its pore volume enlarges. For example, if additional water is added, the pressure will cause any existing fractures to widen to accommodate the extra matter, and this helps explain how lubricating a fault zone with fluids can precipitate an earthquake.

When water is taken from a confined aquifer, the water does not just vacate the pore spaces by gravity flow as it does in an unconfined aquifer; instead, water comes from:

- water squeezed from the aquifer due to compaction;
- water that expands due to reduced pressure in the aquifer;
- water moving through the aquifer toward the well; and
- water forced from surrounding aquicludes by compaction [103, 267].

The quantity of water provided by the above processes is typically much smaller and less predictable than that released by gravity drainage in an unconfined aquifer. Of course, some compaction or settling will occur as an unconfined aquifer is dewatered also, but, compared to the water yield from gravity flow, this compaction produces an insignificant increase in the water that can be "squeezed" from the aquifer. Hence, storativity (Sections 6.5, 8.1) is relatively small for confined aquifers. A typical confined storativity value might be around 0.0001, compared to 0.1 for unconfined aquifers. As 0.1 is 1,000 times larger than 0.0001, we would expect to get about 1,000 times more water from the unconfined aquifer for a given change in head, or for a given decrease in the water level in a piezometer [100, 177]. Potential water yield from a confined aquifer is often predicted using the concept of specific storage. **Specific storage** is the volume of water that a given volume of the aquifer can take in or release in response to a change in the pressure head in the aquifer.

When water is removed from an aquifer, hydrostatic pressure drops and the material will undergo contraction or compaction, that is, its pore volume decreases. However, part of the porosity loss which occurs when an aquifer is desaturated will be permanent. This decrease in storativity is often called "lost storage" and results from the fact that not all the compaction occurring in the aquifer is recoverable. This reduction in pore space is due to **non-elastic deformation** meaning the material cannot fully "rebound" to its original shape, not unlike an old sunken mattress which retains the impression of its occupant. When non-elastic compression occurs, some of the aquifer's original porosity and storativity is permanently lost. Table 8.2 shows the pore volume loss for five major US aquifers. Note that nearly 80% of the storage space of the three confined aquifers was lost due to non-elastic deformation [278].

Table 8.2. Groundwater Depletion and Related Information on Five Aquifer Basins in the United States

Aquifer[1]	Area (km²)	Time Period[2]	Volume of Water Withdrawn (km³)	Volume of Pore Space Lost (km³)
Dakota Aquifer System	171,000	1880–1980	19.7	4.9
Atlantic Coastal Plain	44,000	1891–1980	4.5	3.5
San Joaquin Valley	9,730	1925–1970	—.[a]	17.2
High Plains Aquifer	443,000	1949–1997	243.0	Negligible
South Central Arizona	8,070	1915–1973	80.2	Negligible

[1] The Dakota, Atlantic, and San Joaquin are confined aquifers; the remaining two are unconfined.
[2] Time represents the period during which the reported depletion occurred.
[a] Data for this cell are lacking.
Sources: [189, 225, 262, 278].

8.3 Surficial Processes and Groundwater

8.3.1 Introduction

The remainder of this chapter focuses on relationships between groundwater and the Earth environment. This section focuses on the significant impacts of subsurface water on the landscape. The problems subsurface water can create, such as loss of cropland and damage to made-made structures, are widespread and extremely costly. If these problems are to be mitigated, more attention needs to be paid to where infiltration occurs and the destination of that water.

The occurrence and behavior of groundwater is profoundly influenced by such factors as rock type and structure, terrain, and climate and those factors are in turn influenced by subsurface water in a classic reciprocal relationship. None of the many processes involved act in isolation; all act and interact concurrently to constantly modify the surface of our planet.

As noted in Chapter 2, numerous important denudational (wearing away) and constructional (building up) processes participate in shaping Earth's landscapes. The most familiar and direct expressions of groundwater such as springs, seeps, streams, wetlands, and lakes occur where groundwater intersects the surface and these have been discussed above.

If the groundwater is perched or experiences large fluctuations, these features will often be intermittent or ephemeral. Not nearly so widely recognized or well understood is the profound role shallow groundwater plays in the creation of many of Earth's major landforms. Subsurface waters induce accelerated weathering of rock material, produce surface and near-surface runoff, and are therefore intimately associated with the initiation and evolution of landforms around the world. The following three sections, 8.3.2 through 8.3.4, serve to illustrate some groundwater impacts on the major surficial processes of weathering, mass wasting, and erosion.

We will focus on the weathering and erosional impacts of groundwater in terrestrial environments, but similar effects appear to be significant in submarine environments. Where groundwater emerges from the seafloor, sudden changes in slope, unstable conditions, submarine valleys, and scarps are likely to result.

8.3.2 Weathering and Groundwater

Weathering, the ubiquitous in-place breakdown of rock by chemical and mechanical processes, is a critical step in the modification of any landscape. Weathering, both directly and indirectly, generates the raw materials for the vast quantities of regolith which blanket most of the planet's solid surface. Water plays an essential role in nearly all weathering and soil formation, and most of that water will be subsurface water. Subsurface water provides the medium within which the slow but relentless eating away of rock occurs.

If groundwater possesses little motion, it may become saturated with salts and actually help shield rock from additional weathering. Mineral salts build up in the soils due to evaporation as the water approaches the atmosphere, a process called **salinization**. Even minor amounts of some salts can make soil unsuitable for most crops. Salinization of the soil seriously impairs over 20% of the world's irrigated cropland and has caused abandonment of millions of additional acres due to extreme salinization from past irrigation. In some areas, especially arid or semi-arid regions, extensive deposits can accumulate from evaporating ground and/or surface water, producing salt flats (playas, salinas, sabkhas), thick cemented horizons (duracrusts, caliche), and other significant mineral deposits (Plate 11 and Figure 8.4). Even minute quantities of salts in water can greatly accelerate the rate of weathering by **exudation** or salt weathering. During exudation, salt crystals grow in the interstices between mineral grains as water evaporates, loosening the grains and leading to granular disintegration of the rock.

Figure 8.4. In dry regions, deposition of calcium carbonate in soil from the evaporation of groundwater may cement soil particles together and form thick deposits of caliche as in this exposure in western Washington. See Plate 11 for other examples of mineral deposits from evaporating water in dry regions.

Where a zone of perched groundwater intersects the ground surface, a line of seeps will occur (Plate 8, Bottom, and Figure 4.19). Even though many such seeps will be intermittent, the topographic impacts can be significant. Where a tough, thick but permeable rock such as sandstone lies above a weak but impermeable rock such as shale, accelerated chemical and physical weathering along the seepage zone produces considerable rubble which is removed by erosion or mass wasting leaving a hollowed-out area where the water has exited the rock. This can create large alcoves and shelter caves along cliffs (Figure 8.5A). Natural arches often form where weathering and rockfall at the back of a shelter cave creates an opening. Some weathered and eroded openings can extend through solid rock such as sandstone and granite, forming lengthy caves, often along intersecting fractures where groundwater flow is concentrated (Figure 8.5B) [16, 184].

The water table is often close to the surface at the base of scarps and steep slopes. Discharge to the surface in such areas is common, resulting in enhanced weathering and slope retreat at both large and small

Figure 8.5. A. Large shelter caves were often used as dwelling places by early Native Americans. This shows the Cliff Palace in Mesa Verde National Park, Colorado. **B.** View from inside a weathering cave in sandstone, Utah.

Figure 8.6. Removal of sediment from the base of many slopes is accomplished primarily by runoff produced from rainfall or groundwater discharge during wet periods. The smooth, gentle light-colored surface surrounding the base of this curved hill in the North Dakota badlands is a small erosional surface (pediment) over which sediment will be transported when water is present.

scales (Figure 8.6). The weathering, combined with erosion of loose debris by groundwater, runoff, and wind, helps maintain a sharp change in slope over long time periods. Many inactive escarpments (large scarps), knicklines (small, abrupt slope changes), cavernous hollows, and related features in arid and semiarid regions today exhibit evidence of basal weathering and retreat related to the discharge of groundwater during wetter periods of the past. Slope retreat is a major factor in the formation of extensive gently sloping areas called pediments, which may be the most extensive landforms on Earth.

Groundwater also plays a vital role in periglacial environments which make up about 20% of Earth's land area (Section 8.14). Here, another type of weathering, frost action, is the major process influencing the landscape.

8.3.3 Erosion by Groundwater

Groundwater contributes to erosion by promoting chemical reactions and transporting matter as ions, molecules, and small particles. Fluvial processes have traditionally been considered the most important overall erosional force on land while the impacts of subsurface waters are emphasized only in special situations, such as karst (Section 8.5.5). But consider this: in most land areas of the world, infiltration capacities far exceed rainfall intensities. Hence subsurface water volumes, even at very shallow depths, typically will exceed the volume of surface runoff. Consequently, more water will move through the shallow subsurface environment on its way to streams, lakes, and other watery surface destinations than will flow overland. It is easy to neglect subterranean flow because it is not generally visible and its impacts are often not immediately apparent.

Erosion of rock particles requires entrainment (picking up the particles) and transport (moving them from one location to another). To do so, the subsurface water itself must be moving, which usually requires saturation and hydrostatic force. Where the groundwater discharges to the surface, a force, sometimes called **seepage pressure**, is applied which can dislodge loose particles and carry them off. This erosion, aided and abetted by weathering as noted above, is usually most pronounced at the base of a slope or in a hollow, where groundwater seepage is common. The slope or hollow will migrate upgradient as groundwater outflow continues to remove sediment, just as streams extend themselves upstream by erosion. The term **scarp retreat** is often applied to the eroding back of steeper slope elements. **Headwall sapping** refers to the gnawing away at the head of a gully, box canyon, stream, or alcove due to the emergence of groundwater, either as a spring or as diffuse seepage. The headwall is the sharp declivity at the head of the stream or gully as seen at the left side of Figure 8.7. Although more frequently seen in unconsolidated materials, sapping also occurs in bedrock where the loose particles are produced by a variety of weathering processes and can then be transported away. In resistant materials, narrow, steep-sided box canyons may be produced by the combination of headwall sapping and stream erosion (Figure 8.7).

The term **seepage erosion** refers to erosion by diffuse groundwater emerging from the matrix of rock or regolith. This process is frequently critical in the maintenance of sharp changes in slope, as at the base of a hollow, scarp, or where a valley side meets a floodplain. Where

Figure 8.7. Aerial photo of a box canyon near the Snake River in southern Idaho. Headwall sapping by a spring emerging from the basalt bedrock has produced a steep narrow canyon.

seepage is more concentrated, more rapid weathering and erosion will ensue. Springs and areas of high seepage will experience accelerated sapping and the headwall will migrate upgradient, eventually forming a valley. Much of the loose debris which often collects at the base of a headwalls, valley sides, and other steep slopes, is washed away by run-off during heavier rainfall or snowmelt events. In soft material, seepage erosion may form wide-floored valleys or basins (arroyos, wadis). Many factors will influence seepage erosion and headwall sapping, among them topographic slope and the orientation, structure, cohesiveness, rainfall characteristics, and hydrologic properties of subsurface materials. Although the overall significance of groundwater erosion on the formation of stream networks continues to be controversial, its impact certainly appears to be considerable.

Discrete conduits in an earth material through which water flows are called **pipes**, and the process is called **piping**. The term **tunnel scour** has also been used to describe concentrated subsurface flow along conduits [107]. Piping can affect both hard and soft earth materials but is most effective in unconsolidated sediments containing a fair amount of silt and clay. Pipes develop when a substantial amount of meteoric water

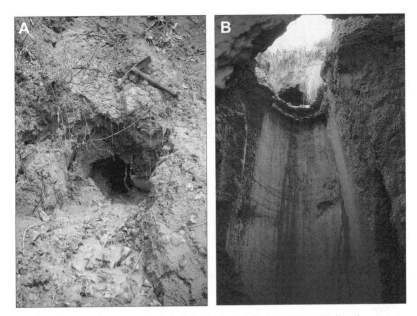

Figure 8.8. A. Piping in glacial till in the Tioughnioga River Valley in upstate New York. **B.** View up at the headwall of a large pipe in western North Dakota. The end of another pipe can be seen through the opening.

infiltrates downward into the ground, then encounters a zone of somewhat greater permeability along which it can flow laterally downgradient toward an outlet. At the outlet, any area of concentrated seepage will result in disproportionate removal of grains forming an opening which will be extended headward into the mass of material (Figure 8.8A). Maintaining an open conduit requires enough upgradient water to generate flowage, sufficient gradient and flow velocity to dislodge sediment, and material with enough cohesion to maintain the passageways. Pipe formation is enhanced if larger openings such as shrinkage cracks, animal burrows, old roots, and other water pathways are present in the recharge area. If an impermeable zone — such as a clay-rich layer or an old soil horizon — is encountered as water migrates downward, water will be concentrated atop it and move downgradient. This perched water condition is highly conducive to pipe development also. Pipes eventually collapse. The resulting debris may be removed by surface water flow and a gully may replace the former pipe. On the other hand, partial collapse of steep-sided gullies may help form some tunnels.

Piping occurs in all types of climates and may provide half or more of the streamflow in some temperate and subtropical areas. Piping tends to occur in patches where topographic and geologic conditions are favorable. It is most easily observed in semiarid regions, especially badlands, where extensive pipes large enough to be walked through may occur (Figure 8.8B). Sections of the pipes may collapse producing sinkholes and yielding a terrain called **pseudokarst** due to its resemblance to true (solutional) karst. Such terrains tend to be short-lived and can be extensively altered by a single major rain event.

Humans can exacerbate piping by such activities as devegetation, irrigation, and slope alteration. Piping causes considerable damage to roadways, buildings, and other structures. The collapse of Teton Dam in Wyoming in 1976 was a result of water entering the fill material of the dam from the adjoining, heavily fractured, basaltic bedrock. Pipes formed in the fill, rapidly grew in size, and soon the recently completed 307-foot-high dam was breached. The ensuing flood caused eleven deaths and as much as two billion dollars in damages.

8.3.4 Mass Wasting and Groundwater

Mass wasting processes such as flowing and sliding of earth materials down slopes are greatly enhanced by the presence of water. Subsurface water can cause materials to become unstable and move in several ways.

1. The interstitial **pore-water pressure** generated by water within a material is considered a positive pressure in that it acts against, or reduces, the frictional forces which hold the material together. More than any other single factor, this reduction in the internal strength and cohesion can cause materials to exceed the stability threshold, leading to landslides or other mass movements.
2. Water in large pores, fractures, and other openings also decreases the frictional forces. The force exerted by water in larger openings has been called cleft water pressure.
3. The water adds weight to unstable earth materials.
4. Water reacts in various ways with minerals in the slope material to accelerate weathering and yield less stable conditions. For example, clays are readily converted into soft, slippery slurries which can lead to sliding and flowing of the materials holding up a slope.

5. As noted in Section 8.3.3, seepage pressure represents yet another stress which can result in subsurface and surface erosion, undermining the material and leading to loss of support and slope failure [78].

Needless to say, rainfall events, antecedent moisture content, earthquakes, and other "triggers" are important in inducing mass movements. Anything which causes the local water table to rise and saturate more earth material is likely to generate unstable conditions along slopes. Irrigation of upgradient areas and the construction of reservoirs are two common activities which often lead to destabilized slopes. The areas around large reservoirs are especially susceptible to slope failures — China's massive Three Gorges Dam reservoir is notorious for its landslides. In 1963 in northern Italy, the reservoir behind Viaont Dam, then the world's highest dam at 265 meters (870 feet) was filling for the first time. As water from the rising water infiltrated into steeply inclined layers of limestone and shale along the valley side, pore pressure increased and 270 million m³ of rock broke loose and slammed into the reservoir just above the dam. The displaced water formed a giant wave 245 meters high that overtopped the dam and rushed downstream causing a catastrophic flood in which some 2,500 people lost their lives. Those in charge of the project were charged with criminal negligence and the chief engineer took his own life [308].

8.4 Introduction to Hydrogeologic Regions

Infinite diversity exists in aquifers and other hydrologic features. No two places on Earth are identical, be it on or under the surface. No adequate substitute exists for in-depth investigation of a specific site. Even so, certain similarities over large areas allow us to distinguish regions which share important hydrologic characteristics. These distinctive areas may be called groundwater regions, aquifer systems, or hydrogeological provinces. As with so many such attempts at generalizing or categorizing, disputes over how to divide and classify the terrain, or even whether it makes sense to try to do so, are abundant. Some prefer to simply use river drainage basins, or parts thereof, as the basic hydrogeologic region (Figure 8.9, Table 8.3). Others base the identification of such regions primarily upon underlying geologic rock type and structure. Climate or topography may also be considered the decisive influence in classifying a hydrologic region.

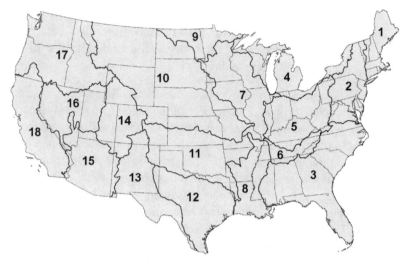

Figure 8.9. Map of surface drainage basins in the conterminous United States.

Table 8.3. Surface Drainage Regions of the Conterminous United States

1.	New England	12.	Texas-Gulf
2.	Mid-Atlantic	13.	Rio Grande
3.	South Atlantic-Gulf	14.	Upper Colorado
4.	Great Lakes	15.	Lower Colorado
5.	Ohio	16.	Great Basin
6.	Tennessee	17.	Pacific Northwest
7.	Upper Mississippi	18.	California
8.	Lower Mississippi	19.	Alaska[a]
9.	Souris-Red-Rainy	20.	Hawaii[a]
10.	Missouri	21.	Caribbean[a]
11.	Arkansas-White-Red		

[a] These regions are not shown on this map but are included in the system upon which this map is based. The numerals in this table correspond to those in Figure 8.9. Sources: [189, 225, 262, 278].

In the US, an early and admirable attempt to delineate groundwater provinces was that of Oscar E. Meinzer. Meinzer discerned 21 such regions [264] which were later reorganized into ten, plus Alaska and Hawaii [563]. Another refinement was introduced in 1982 by Ralph C. Heath and the US Geological Survey [174]. Heath determined his regions by considering five major factors: (1) groundwater aquifers and aquitards, (2) pore characteristics, (3) composition of the aquifer(s), (4) aquifer storage and transmissivity, and (5) recharge/discharge conditions [176]. Using these five characteristics, North America was divided into 28 groundwater regions, many of which are listed in Table 8.4 and shown on Figure 8.10. Note the differences between these groundwater-based areas and the surface water-based areas of Figure 8.9. Information on groundwater regions and major aquifers in many parts of the world is often incomplete or not dependable, but this is changing as indicated by the information on major world aquifers in Figure 8.1 and Table 8.1. More detailed aquifer maps can be accessed on the WHYMAP website [430].

Regional hydrologic characteristics are determined by dozens of factors related to the rock's genesis and geologic history, as well as the rock's current chemical and physical environment. Such generalizations provide a useful perspective on the anticipated groundwater conditions in any given area. In the organization below, some of the more important

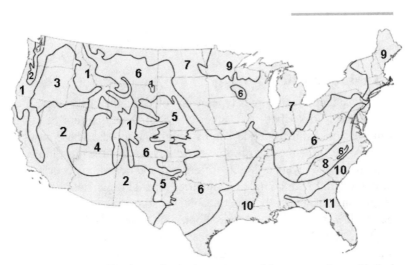

Figure 8.10. Map of hydrogeological provinces of the conterminous United States.

Table 8.4. Hydrogeologic Provinces of the United States

1.	Western Mountain Ranges	9.	Northeast and
2.	Alluvial Basins		Superior Uplands
3.	Columbia Lava Plateau	10.	Atlantic and Gulf
4.	Colorado Plateau and		Coastal Plain
	Wyoming Basin	11.	Southeast Coastal Plain
5.	High Plains	12.	Alluvial Valleys[a]
6.	Nonglaciated Central	13.	Hawaii
7.	Glaciated Central	14.	Alaska
8.	Piedmont and Blue Ridge	15.	Puerto Rico and Virgin Islands

[a] The Alluvial Valleys region incorporates the alluvial floodplains and contiguous lowlands along many stream systems in the conterminous United States, most extensively those of the Mississippi River system. This entire region lies within the conterminous United States, but its many elements are linear and discontinuous, and are not shown on Figure 8.10. Numerals in this table correspond to those in Figure 8.10. Source: [176].

influences which geologic lithology/structure and geographic environment are likely to exert upon groundwater behavior are examined. Some overlap among these categories is unavoidable.

8.5 Sedimentary Rock

8.5.1 Introduction

Basic sedimentary rock types were noted and their hydrologic properties briefly described in Chapter 2. About three-quarters of Earth's land surface is directly underlain by sedimentary rock. These rocks include some of the most permeable as well as some of the most impermeable rocks, and layers of highly differing properties often occur in close proximity and with complex geometries (spatial organization). For example, shale is generally impermeable, yet some fractured shales are as permeable as a clean sandstone. Some limestones can be so tight and impermeable that not a drop of water will enter a borehole below the water table, yet others will produce torrents of water.

The most widespread sedimentary rock aquifers consist of sandstones, although conglomerates, limestones, and even coal beds may form important aquifers in some areas. Sandstone seems like a simple rock, but as with all rocks — as with all nature — appearances can be deceiving. The size and shape of sandstones vary from small lenses to vast sheets covering hundreds of square miles. The composition of the sands, their cementation, their structural details, and other characteristics can vary greatly, and as those properties change, so do the hydrologic properties. Many extensive sandstone formations were deposited in a coastal environment or as wind deposits on land. Sandstones deposited on land and near shorelines tend to be more variable than those deposited in offshore environments.

Shale, the most abundant sedimentary rock, has generally high porosity, low permeability, and typically behaves as an aquitard or barrier to groundwater flow. The more deeply buried the shale, the more compact and impermeable, and the less porous, it becomes. Shales near the surface can have porosities as high as 50%; at depths of more than 5,000 meters, porosities will usually be in the 10% range. Primary permeability is typically low, but fracturing can increase permeability considerably.

Deep sedimentary formations, or those associated with nearby rock salt, often contain saline or briny water.

Example: The Great Artesian Basin of Australia

Australia's Great Artesian Basin (#37 on Figure 8.1) consists of water-bearing Mesozoic sandstones interlayered with relatively impermeable siltstones and shales. The strata range up to 3,000 meters in thickness and form a large complex synclinal structure. The rocks are exposed in the east and have an overall tilt toward the southwest, which is also the dominant groundwater flow direction. It underlies some 1.7 million km^2 (656,370 mi^2) of eastern Australia, contains roughly 65 million GL (gigaliters) of water — over 820 times more than all the surface water of Australia — and supports more than two billion US dollars worth of production from agriculture, mining, and tourism. Unfortunately, the aquifer is deep — up to 2 kilometers (1.2 miles) below the surface — making wells unfeasible in many areas. As of 2008, an estimated 87 million ML had been withdrawn, reducing water pressure and causing the loss of over 1,000 springs and a third of the installed artesian wells.

267

Over 90% of the water removed has been wasted, largely by evaporation in the hot, arid climate. Efforts were started in 1990 to reduce the waste, mainly by replacing tens of thousands of kilometers of open drainage ditches with pipelines, using modern computer technology, and improving livestock management. Controversies over water supply, increasing aridity related to global warming, and the feasibility of greater reliance on the aquifer are likely to continue [307].

8.5.2 Horizontal Sedimentary Rocks

Where the sequence of sedimentary rocks is relatively horizontal and undeformed, groundwater occurrence is more predictable than in most other areas due to the fact that water-related properties are determined mainly by the sedimentary characteristics of the rock itself rather than by structural influences such as folding, faulting, and fracturing. Predictable characteristics may persist over very large areas underlain

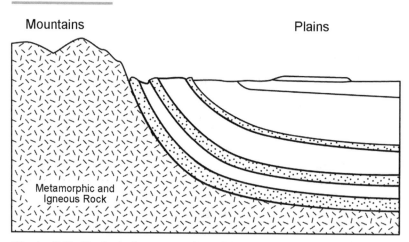

Figure 8.11. Geological cross-section of a common situation which often produces extensive confined aquifers, as in the US Great Plains. Uplift in the mountains at the left is accompanied by erosion. Sediment is deposited on adjacent lowlands. Ongoing uplift over many millions of years causes the sedimentary rock strata to dip away from the uplifted area. Continued erosion truncates the uplifted sedimentary rock near the mountains, producing excellent conditions for groundwater recharge and downgradient artesian conditions. See also Figure 8.12.

by the sedimentary rock aquifers, such as the St. Peter Sandstone of the central US which underlies some 750,000 km^2 (290,000 mi^2). Horizontal hydraulic conductivity will tend to be greater than vertical conductivity due to the presence of horizontal bedding planes and the elongation of grains resulting from compression by the weight of overlying sediment. Sandstone aquifers in nearly horizontal strata are common. Examples include North America's Dakota aquifer, northern Africa's **Nubian Sandstone aquifer** complex (Section 14.2.2) and South America's **Guarani aquifer** (Section 14.2.5), which are among the largest aquifers on Earth.

8.5.3 Homoclinal Sedimentary Rocks

A **homocline** is a geologic structure in which layered rock is uniformly inclined over an extensive area. For our purposes here, the rocks need not be uniform in dip — only the overall inclination need be in the same general direction. Extensive areas underlain by tilted sedimentary rock are often found below the plains which border mountainous terrain and coasts where their permeable units provide excellent aquifers, many of them artesian. There are several reasons for this. As mountainous areas are slowly raised during orogenies, the adjacent strata are also uplifted and thus dip away from the mountains. Figure 8.11 illustrates a condition similar to the US Great Plains. At the same time that mountains are rising, large quantities of sediment are often shed onto adjacent lowlands. Figure 8.12 is a photograph of the far western part of the Great Plains which shows the gentle inclination to the right (east), away from the uplifted mountainous regions to the west. Plate 12, Top, was taken close to the border between the Great Plains and the Rocky Mountains where the tilting of the sedimentary strata is much more pronounced.

Even without active mountain building (orogeny), isostatic uplift tends to occur as rock is eroded from highlands, assuring a continuing supply of sediment and causing their strata to dip gently away from the uplifted area, as in the US Atlantic Coastal Plain (Figure 8.13). Most of the sediments are transported into an ocean, an arm of an ocean or other sizable water body, or an inland basin where their weight causes crustal downsinking, further adding to the tilt of the strata. Under these conditions, an extensive plain underlain by a wedge of sedimentary units dipping away from uplands and toward the areas subsidence will often form. The older underlying layers, having experienced more years of tilting, will be more steeply inclined (Figure 8.13). The wedge thickens and its sediment becomes finer-grained, and hence less permeable, toward the sea.

Figure 8.12. View north along "the Gangplank," a part of the "High Plains" near Cheyenne, Wyoming, in which the gentle eastward inclination of the sedimentary strata away from the mountains is clearly reflected in the landscape.

Coastal plains often have widespread, productive aquifers consisting largely of sandy units deposited by wave action near beaches or by streams. Other deposits include silt, clay, stream gravels, marine limestones, peat (from marshlands), and salt (from evaporation in tidal flats and enclosed basins). Such complexity results from the slow but constant transgressions and regressions of the sea during the past few millions, or tens of millions, of years. During a **transgression**, the sea encroaches upon the continent; during a **regression**, the sea recedes. These fluctuations result in repetitive layers of contrasting permeability, often sands and shales — an ideal setting for widespread artesian conditions. Numerous aquifers may occur in a given area. The deeper the aquifers, the farther inland their recharge zone tends to be. Faults and gentle folds also may be present and can have important local impacts upon groundwater.

Topographic relief resulting from the slope of the overlying terrain provides the hydraulic head for artesian conditions. In areas near the coast, that relief was much greater during glacials (when sea level was some 300 feet lower than today) which enabled fresh water to flush out saline water left by the transgressions and also to build up fresh groundwater deposits in areas currently beneath the ocean. In some areas, the

Mountains   Coastal Plain   Ocean

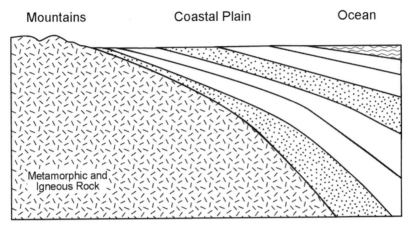

Figure 8.13. Idealized geologic cross-section of inclined strata underlying the Atlantic Coastal Plain. A combination of isostatic uplift of ancient eroding mountain masses (left side of cross-section) and subsidence in coastal areas of extensive deposition (right side) produces homoclinal strata and excellent conditions for artesian aquifer development.

pressure in confined coastal plain aquifers has been so great that electric generators and flour mills were operated by the water bursting forth from below [100, 122].

> **Example: Atlantic and Gulf Coastal Plain Aquifers**
>
> The deposits of the US Atlantic and Gulf coastal plains range in age from the Jurassic to Recent (Table 2.1) and in thickness from 0 to nearly 7 kilometers [122, 173, 271]. Most of the sediments are clays and sands. The sands form excellent aquifers and the clays provide confining beds to produce widespread artesian conditions. Figure 8.13 is a greatly simplified cross-section based on the Atlantic Coastal Plain.
>
> Recharge is mainly from infiltration where permeable materials occur at the surface. Fresh groundwater typically occurs to depths of at least 300 meters (660 feet) on the coastal plains and may extend several miles out to sea in deep aquifers. Where the confined artesian aquifers encounter saline groundwater, the artesian pressure surface dips rapidly down because of the increased density of the saline water. Groundwater discharge

is mainly to streams and low-lying wetlands — or directly to the ocean.

Most flow paths are local with only an estimated 3% total recharge reaching deeper parts of the aquifers [18]. Because of the gentle dip of the land surface and the underlying strata, the boundaries between artesian and nonartesian groundwater can vary significantly due to such factors as seasonal changes, pumping rates, and surface land uses which affect infiltration and recharge rates.

The southeastern part of the Atlantic Coastal Plain differs in that it is underlain by the cavernous limestone of the **Floridan aquifer**, described at the end of Section 8.5.5. Although most aquifers continue to be major water sources for the coastal plains with yields often in the 50 gpm (273 m³/d) range, others have experienced extensive depletion and contamination due to human interventions (Sections 8.9 and 10.4.2D) [103].

8.5.4 Folded Sedimentary Rocks

Folding (Section 2.8.4) produces local structures which exert a profound influence on groundwater movement. Hence detailed knowledge of the local geology is required to determine groundwater movements and areas of recharge and discharge. Large regional aquifers of high yield generally do not occur in areas where the rocks have undergone considerable folding. Hydraulic gradients are often high and groundwater will generally flow along rather complex paths from the high to low elevations, usually from ridges into adjacent valleys. Secondary permeability produced by the fractures generated during tectonic deformation play an important role in determining the groundwater flow paths. In the US Valley and Ridge Physiographic Province, coarse clastic rock and cavernous carbonate bedrock (limestones and dolomites) and regolith form the major aquifers and groundwater reservoirs. Large springs are quite common where karst occurs in discharge areas.

8.5.5 Carbonate Rocks and Karst

A **karst aquifer** is one in which solution has significantly modified the groundwater flow paths. It has been estimated that 25% of the world's population depends on karst aquifers for fresh water. Because of the importance and uniqueness of karst hydrology, this topic merits fairly detailed coverage here.

The common carbonate rocks, limestone ($CaCO_3$) and dolomite ($CaMg[CO_3]_2$), lie at or very near the surface of about 20% of Earth's land surface. Carbonate aquifers supply about 22% of US public groundwater supply and are the most widely used bedrock aquifers in many countries [244]. Dolomite is very similar to limestone and most of what is said about limestone also applies to dolomite. Dolomite tends to be harder and somewhat less soluble. The two rocks are often found together and grade into each other, depending upon the amount of magnesium (Mg) present. These two carbonate rocks exhibit more hydrogeologic variability than any other major rock group [45]. Not only do the common carbonate rocks come in an exceptionally large number of different physical types, the permeability and porosity of the rock itself is constantly being altered by solution and deposition as groundwater migrates through it. The changes in the subsurface features and processes are closely associated with, and proceed contemporaneously with, the evolution of the overlying landscape. It is not surprising that the literature, terminology, and controversies regarding carbonates and karst are vast [125, 222, 229, 428].

A limestone may begin as an accumulation of sand grains or shells along a seashore or a reef with primary porosities of 40 to 70%. Most, however will be formed in warm seas as a chemical precipitate and, when lithified by compaction, cementation, and recrystallization, will consist of very small grains or interlocking crystals having very low primary porosity and permeability.

Young limestones, those a few tens of millions of years old or less, such as those in Florida, usually have high primary permeability and make excellent water-producers. Yields are commonly in the hundreds of gallons per minute range, and 20,000 gpm or more is not unheard of. Dense old limestones and dolomites, however, may approach zero permeability. Old limestones may still provide abundant water from solutional openings developed along bedding planes and fractures where groundwater flow is concentrated. Hence two distinct and different permeabilities exist: the primary permeability of the rock itself, and the secondary solutional permeability. Most wells will encounter only the rock which typically constitutes over 99% of the formation volume.

A generalized equation for the solution of limestone is as follows:

$$CaCO_3 + H_2O + CO_2 \rightarrow Ca^{+2} + 2HCO_3^{-1}$$

In words, this says calcium carbonate (limestone) + water + carbon dioxide yields calcium ions + bicarbonate ions. Note that carbon dioxide, the most important gas contributing to global warming, is taken out of the atmosphere — many suspect the dissolution of limestone to be an underappreciated sink for atmospheric carbon [204, 233].

As noted previously, rainwater is slightly acidic due to the solution of atmospheric carbon dioxide in water. Due to the release of carbon dioxide by plant roots and during decay of organic matter, the concentration of this gas in soil water is far higher than in the atmosphere. Infiltrating water picks up abundant carbon dioxide in the soil, producing an abundance of carbonic acid (H_2CO_3) which can then chemically react with (dissolve) underlying limestone, forming soluble calcium and bicarbonate ions. When the Ca^{+2} and HCO_3^{-1} solutes in groundwater are high and the water encounters an environment containing much lower levels of CO_2, this reaction is driven the other way (right to left on the formula given above): carbon dioxide gas is emitted, forcing precipitation of $CaCO_3$. This results in the infilling of pore spaces which decreases permeability and porosity. In air-filled caves, it forms the travertine deposits which decorate many caves as stalactites, stalagmites, and flowstone.

Where solutional openings have formed, the rock must have been exposed to one or more reasonably robust and long-lived episodes of groundwater circulation. If the circulation occurs for sufficient time, in strong rock, and over distances of at least a few kilometers, caves are likely to develop. A **cave** or **cavern** is a subsurface conduit or opening large enough for a human to pass through, that is, about a meter or more in diameter.

The formation of limestone and dolomite caves is complex and far from uniform. Generally, caves form where acidic water moves rapidly through soluble rock. This requires throughflow of water from a recharge area to a downgradient discharge location.

Water containing abundant carbonic acid and infiltrating downward from an organic-rich soil will rapidly dissolve limestone as soon as it is encountered. The initial rate of dissolution will decrease quickly as the carbonic acid is used up and the water approaches saturation with calcium carbonate. The travel distance for this to occur can vary from only a millimeter to 10 meters or more. Solution doesn't cease as the water continues its journey, however. The solution rate simply decreases in proportion to the amount of carbonic acid remaining in the water. Hence, the initial dissolution rates are very fast, but a much longer period of slower dissolution usually ensues as the water continues to move through the rock to its discharge point. This often results in greatly enlarged joints and fractures near the surface where the infiltrating water is highly charged with CO_2. These enlarged near-surface openings, often in the form of fissures and funnels, will rapidly decrease in size with depth as CO_2 is used up (figures 2.2I and 8.14A and B). These openings are usually filled in with insoluble rock debris and soil and are not easily seen except in cliffs or roadcuts. As water continues downward into the unsaturated zone, it will slowly continue to enlarge openings.

The openings in the unsaturated (vadose) zone are often near-vertical shafts, chimneys, and clefts formed along fracture surfaces. These precipitous passageways always slope downward, often forming a series of deep subsurface gorges. When a chimney or other vadose opening becomes large enough to transmit soil from above, mass wasting and pipes will begin removing the sediment. This often signals the start of sinkhole formation on the surface (Figure 8.14C). Vast amounts of sediment from the overlying regolith and from surface streams are transported through cave systems, sometimes completely filling them in.

When the saturated zone is reached, the water will continue to enlarge openings wherever its flow is concentrated, though lateral flow now tends to dominate. It is not unusual for phreatic passages to rise in the downstream direction — just as water under pressure can move upwards. The larger openings will pass more water and thus can grow faster than smaller openings, most of which will be abandoned as their water becomes relatively stagnant. Eventually, as larger pathways continue pirating water from their smaller neighbors, a small number of large openings will become dominant pathways carrying water to a discharge point, usually a spring, the point of lowest head. The location of the spring may be controlled by the level of a local downcutting river, by a stratigraphic unit (for example, an impermeable unit supporting a large perched water table), or by faults and other geological factors. Each major subsurface drainageway typically has its own discharge point, and that outlet largely determines the potentiometric surface for that drainage system. As a result, the regional water table may be highly irregular or discontinuous and its elevation can vary rapidly in karst areas — for example, in response to water recharge or pressure variations. Similar unusual characteristics are apparent in the sparse surface waters of karst. Streams may emerge abruptly from a cave, or disappear into a cave or other openings. Even lakes can appear, or disappear quite suddenly when

Figure 8.14. A. The joints in this limestone surface near Syracuse, New York, have been enlarged by solution and other weathering processes. **B.** Removal of regolith has exposed enlarged fissures and intervening pinnacles and ridges in this dolomite bedrock near Roanoke, Virginia. **C.** Small sinkhole in a field near Roanoke, Virginia. **D.** Sudden collapse into an underlying cavern is a serious environmental hazard in some areas. This collapse sink opened up in Florida following lowering of the water table due to drought and groundwater withdrawals.

the groundwater levels are subject to major fluctuations. Lake Chernika (Cerknisko), with a maximum surface area of over 25 km^2, is the largest natural lake in Slovenia, but during the dry summers, it often disappears completely through underwater drainageways. It is a serious error to assume that groundwater behavior in karst will be similar to that of "normal" or non-karst areas where permeabilities tend to be relatively uniform.

Studies indicate roughly a few thousand to a hundred thousand years is required to develop large vadose shafts and attain a 1-centimeter-wide path in the phreatic zone. Once attained, the rate of pathway enlargement in the phreatic zone tends to increase considerably [300]. In general, enlargement rates will decrease with increasing length of the flow path and increase with increasing discharge rates and CO_2 concentration.

About 80% of caves exhibit a branching pattern similar to surface streams. These form where soluble rock is exposed at the ground surface and concentrated recharge has occurred through localized openings in the vadose zone, usually sinkholes. If a more homogeneous rock unit covers the limestone, recharge will tend to be uniform and dispersed, not concentrated. Thus all parts of the limestone receive equal input of surface water and distinct pathways give way to a maze-like configuration of cave passageways. Damming of a cave branch, for example, by collapse or sedimentation, will also produce a local maze. The blocked water will occupy all parts of the rock around the blockage, rather than being concentrated along the major flow path, and maze passages will eventually develop in that location.

Numerous other processes can influence subsurface dissolution of rock. Here are some examples.

1. Additional CO_2 can be added to the water from the air in vadose passages, increasing its ability to dissolve rock. The subsurface air will have more CO_2 — that is, it will have a higher CO_2 partial pressure — due to diffusion from overlying soil and from release of CO_2 from infiltrating water. In addition, organic matter is often present and will release CO_2 as it is oxidized.

2. Large increases in flow volume during heavy rain or snowmelt events will increase the dissolution rate.

3. Hydrogen sulfide from brines, volcanic activities, reduction of gypsum, anaerobic decomposition of organic matter, and other sources can greatly increase the acidity and aggressiveness of water leading to rapid dissolution. Some cave

systems, including those of Carlsbad Caverns National Park in New Mexico, almost certainly owe their origin to water rich in sulfuric acid seeping upward from below. If the source of the water is deep-seated — if the cave-forming water came from below — it is termed a **hypogenic** cave. If the groundwater movement results from surface recharge areas, it is an **epigenic cave**. Hypogenic cave origins are relatively rare and require special conditions. In the Carlsbad Caverns example, the area is arid and the adjoining basin contains abundant petroleum hydrocarbons (oil and gas) overlain by deposits containing abundant sulfate minerals (mostly gypsum). These deposits underwent chemical reactions to produce sulfuric acid water which migrated upward along with the hydrocarbons. The hypogenic water invaded massive limestones where the acid dissolved huge chambers from the rock. Upward migration of acidic waters is unlikely to occur in wet climates because downward seeping (epigenic) waters tend to dominate subsurface water movements.

4. Any number of other changes in the chemical environment may be encountered as water moves through rock. For example, when waters containing different amounts of solute are mixed, the resulting solution will be unsaturated, even if both original solutions were saturated. Such mixing can cause significant additional dissolution, even deep underground.

5. Changes in the physical environment can have profound impacts. If a significant change in the base level of local surface waters occurs, due, for example, to rapid stream downcutting or damming of the stream, one set of cave passageways may be abandoned and another produced at a different level.

Where rock with well developed solutional openings occurs near the surface, **karst** topography is produced. Roughly 7 to 10% of the global land surface is karst. Karst can be classified in several ways, including types of landforms present, climate, rock type, surface cover, and relations to other rock types. Most karst occurs in limestone and its close relative dolomite, although gypsum also forms extensive karst in some areas, such as the Carlsbad-Roswell area of New Mexico. To form good karst, subsurface water flow needs to be localized along planar fractures such as joints, bedding planes, and faults. Lacking localized flow paths, solution of rock would be more uniform and major conduits would not develop. Solution along zones of higher permeability removes rock matter. Solution is especially pronounced at the intersections between planar features, and this is where the largest caves and the major groundwater flows are likely to be found. The karst landscape is characterized by abundant enclosed surface depressions called **sinkholes** and a lack of surface streams. Sinkholes and other depressions form where solution is more rapid and where gradual subsidence or collapse into underlying voids has occurred (Figure 8.14C and D).

Groundwater in karst tends to move rapidly (>100 m/day) through subsurface conduits and caves. Streams may occupy passageways in the vadose zone and phreatic water flow is determined by the solutional pathways. Darcy's Law does not apply. Infiltration rates can be very fast if open conduits are present in recharge areas. But in most places, insoluble minerals from the soluble rock itself or from other nearby rocks will litter much of the surface and plug up openings to the subsurface, greatly increasing recharge time to days or weeks [429]. The water is typically hard — high in calcium and magnesium. Groundwater often discharges to the surface via springs in karst areas. For a considerable distance upgradient from major springs, a trough will usually be present in the water table indicating groundwater convergence upon the zones of major conduit formation [100].

Due to the rapid dissolution of rock, the denudation of carbonate terrains in humid and temperate regions tends to be considerably faster than for terrain on other rock types where mass wasting and fluvial erosion tend to dominate.

Karst is notorious for an array of environmental problems: dams often will not hold water; the groundwater is very vulnerable to pollution from surface activities and the pollution spreads rapidly; and the formation of sinkholes damages highways, buildings, subsurface utility lines, and other structures. Where drought or human activities such as groundwater withdrawals, mining, and construction projects lower the water table, subsidence problems are often greatly exacerbated. When the water table is lowered, buoyant support of overlying rock and regolith is lost, and subsurface mass wasting and erosion of the regolith increases. Piping, downward soil migration, and fluvial erosion accelerate, rapidly enlarging sinkholes. Sudden subsidence (collapse) into large underlying caverns following the lowering of the water table is a serious problem in many karst areas (Figure 8.14D).

Example: The Floridan Aquifer

This huge karst aquifer extends from Florida into low-lying parts of Alabama, Georgia, and South Carolina. This aquifer is recharged by abundant rainfall in the lake-dotted karst terrain of central Florida and much of its discharge is via large springs which in turn support vital streams and ecosystems (Plate 8, Top and Plate 9, Top). Florida is said to contain the largest concentration of springs in the world. At one time they literally burst up from the ground but today, most are imperiled or have dried up. Overextraction of groundwater, nitrate pollution, saline intrusion, and mining are among the threats to Florida's springs and watery ecosystems [309]. Due to human extraction of groundwater many of the springs are drying up. Catastrophic subsidence of the ground surface is an ongoing threat, especially during droughts (Figure 8.14D).

Some four billion gallons of groundwater are pumped from the Floridan aquifer annually. A million gpd from a single, inexpensive 150-foot-deep well is not unusual. The water supply is huge and easily accessible and has supported much of the rapid economic growth of the Sunbelt for the past five decades. The first supply wells for Savannah, Georgia, were drilled in 1884 and the use of the aquifer's groundwater rose sharply from then on. Savannah was withdrawing some 90 million gpd from the aquifer by the late twentieth century and the cone of depression for the Savannah wells had lowered the water table to more than 80 feet below mean sea level in the city and to some 20 feet below sea level along the coastline, 15 miles to the southeast. As a result, salty sea water was seeping into the Floridan aquifer threatening the water supply for coastal communities and resorts. This forced various areas to limit their withdrawal of groundwater and increase reliance upon surface water such as the Savannah River [70].

Other important karst aquifers include the Edwards aquifer in Texas which provides water for about two million people, the Madison limestone beneath the Northern Great Plains, and the Dinaric karst of Slovenia, Croatia, Bosnia, and Herzegovina [38]. The stony limestone terrain of the Dinaric region is where the term "karst" (kars or kras in the native language) originated. The **Dinaric karst aquifer system** is the subject of an important UN project to apply sustainable integrated management principles to a transboundary freshwater karst aquifer.

8.6 Plutonic and Metamorphic Rock

8.6.1 Introduction

Metamorphic rocks and intrusive igneous rocks underlie about 20% of Earth's land area and generally make poor aquifers. The crystalline (interlocking) nature of the minerals in these rocks produces low primary porosity and permeability. Thick, extensive zones of moderate to highly permeable rock such as found in sedimentary or volcanic rock are lacking. Most groundwater will occur within roughly 100 meters of the surface where weathering of rock has increased porosity and permeability. In areas of plutonic and metamorphic rock not modified by glaciation or recent mountain-building processes, such as the Piedmont-Blue Ridge region of the eastern US, each permanent stream tends to be the discharge zone for a small groundwater basin whose outline closely matches that of the stream's drainage basin [238]. Hence, numerous small, discrete groundwater basins are present with the flow directed toward the nearest stream. Intermediate or regional groundwater basins may be present with water circulating through the fractures in the bedrock, but the volume of water moving through these larger basins is probably very small [393]. The Piedmont water table is often close to the surface near valley bottoms and can lie ten meters or more below the surface of hills.

8.6.2 Groundwater Sources: Regolith and Bedrock

Groundwater in plutonic and metamorphic terrains will generally be found in two contrasting subsurface environments: regolith consisting largely of in-place weathered bedrock (saprolite) and fractured bedrock (Figure 8.15). Weathering produces a mantle of saprolite whose thickness varies from zero to a few tens of meters (100 feet), although it can extend to over a hundred meters (330 feet) below the surface in favorable locations. The saprolite in plutonic and metamorphic rock is typically clay-rich and granular in texture. Incompletely weathered rock (corestones) may be present within the saprolite, especially close to bedrock (Figure 2.6B). Saprolite will be thicker on more easily weathered rocks, such as mafic rock and schist, which tend to underlie lower-lying parts of the terrain. Saprolite is also thicker where the rock is more fractured. If bedrock outcrops are not present, the saprolite will probably be

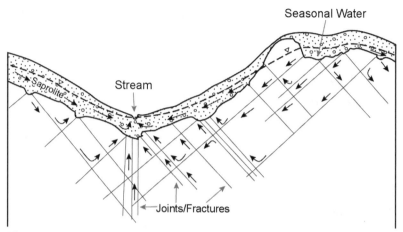

Figure 8.15. Geologic cross-section showing movement of groundwater (arrows) through massive igneous or metamorphic rock and saprolite. Flow in these rocks is mainly along fractures (joints, faults, shear zones).

relatively thick, and the water table will tend to lie fairly deep within the saprolite. Rock outcrops, springs, and thin saprolite will be more common in more resistant, less fractured rock.

8.6.3 Importance of Fractures

Fractures can increase porosity by a few percent and permeability by many hundreds of percent. Most bedrock wells in plutonic and metamorphic rocks will be shallow, under 100 meters in depth, except along deep fracture and fault zones. This is because fracture size and density, and hence well yields, decrease rapidly with depth except along major fault zones. The orientation, surface roughness, and interconnections of fractures will also impact permeability.

Most fractures are associated with unloading (exfoliation and sheeting joints) or tectonic movements within the rock mass. The latter category includes steeply dipping fault zones, overthrust faults, gravity sliding, and shear zones. Unless detailed geologic studies have been done, knowledge of the subsurface location and character of major fault and fracture zones is generally lacking. Faults often influence groundwater migration by cutting across aquifers or by production of impermeable pulverized, partially cemented, or welded rock. Where soluble rock or abundant open fractures accompany the fault, the fault may provide a zone of high permeability along which groundwater can migrate great distances.

Where fracture zones intersect the surface, they often produce linear trends, especially where they formed along inclined fault or shear zones where bedrock stresses were concentrated. Stream valleys and other low elevation landforms often follow these trends. These low-elevation linear trends, and especially their intersections, are especially promising sites for a good water supply. Recognizing such trends by studying aerial photographs and topographic maps will aid in finding the best locations for water supply wells. In some places fractures exist at depths of over 100 meters and can produce excellent yields.

8.6.4 Felsic vs. Mafic Rock

The lighter colored, felsic igneous and metamorphic rocks, sometimes grouped together as "granitic" rock, tend to produce soft water which is slightly acidic and contains very little dissolved mineral matter (total dissolved solids are usually less than 100 mg/L). The darker-colored mafic rocks (gabbro, hornblende gneiss, diorite) generally produce hard, somewhat alkaline, water which often contains more than twice the dissolved mineral matter that the granitic rocks contain. Overall, the water is usually of excellent quality but well yields are low. The sustained yield of most wells in metamorphic and intrusive crystalline rock ranges from 0.3 to 6.7 L/s (5 to 106 gpm), quantities which would be deemed quite pathetic in areas of high-yielding aquifers [238]. If marble is present, solutional conduits may provide additional water but they can be difficult to locate. Blasting and hydrofracturing can improve well yields.

The tabular intrusions, sills and dikes, are often small and less permeable than the rocks they occur in. Hence, they can influence groundwater flow by producing barriers and confining beds.

8.7 Volcanic Rock

Volcanic rocks come in two basic types: lavas and pyroclastics. Abrupt, local changes in hydrologic properties are common due to rapid changes in permeability and porosity. Many highly productive springs and wells will be found in volcanic rocks. At the other extreme, some volcanic rocks are highly impermeable and have been considered as disposal sites for toxic and radioactive wastes.

8.7.1 Lava Rock

Most volcanic rocks are formed from lava flows and their hydrologic properties can vary greatly, even within a single lava flow. Primary porosity and permeability is often quite high due to the presence of rubbly zones at the top and bottom of a flow, cracks produced by shrinkage during cooling, stress fractures generated as the flow was cooling and still moving over uneven terrain, vesicles formed by air trapped during solidification, and lava tubes formed when molten lava escaped from inside a partially consolidated flow. The highly permeable basalts of the Hawaiian Islands, combined with that area's high rainfall, produce excellent aquifers with exceptionally high transmissivities (up to 100,000 m^2/day) and hydraulic conductivities (up to 3,000 m/day). The zones between lava flows are the most important sources of water. Liquid lava is viscous and cools rapidly at the base of an active flow. Thus it cannot effectively fill the many openings in underlying surfaces, which often contain loose sediment, weathered rock rubble, exploited bedrock fractures, and other irregularities. The combination of simultaneous motion and hardening also produces extensive fractures and associated openings in the base of the lava. Sediment often accumulates on top of a lava flow and is then buried by a later flow. The resulting **interbeds** may contain alluvium and form excellent aquifers. On the other hand, if clays and silts from standing water are present, the interbeds can be quite impermeable and often have perched groundwater overlying them. Lava rocks are thus similar to sedimentary rocks in that most major zones of high permeability will be parallel to the layers.

The most important factor in finding water in lava terrain is often the location of impermeable zones which help to localize groundwater. The groundwater zones are often perched well above the main water table, which can be very deep, even 1,000 meters or more. Impermeable zones may consist of fine-grained volcanic ash, fine-grained interbeds, buried soils, dikes which cut across the lava flows, or dense, relatively unbroken zones of rock in the middle part of the flows.

The water tends to be of good quality but harder and higher in total dissolved solids than water from plutonic and metamorphic rock. Water near hot springs and active volcanoes is likely to contain natural pollutants. Groundwater is often vulnerable to pollution due to high permeability.

Basalts are the most abundant and permeable of the lava rocks. Where permeable zones between flows are exposed in downgradient areas, large springs are quite common (Figure 4.16B and C). In some areas, such as the Columbia Plateau in the northwestern US and the Deccan Traps of India, hundreds of repeated outpourings of basaltic lavas have built up extensive plateaus underlain by nearly horizontal lava flows

(Figure 2.2D). Horizontal transmissivity can be extremely high along the many zones between lava flows.

> ## Example: The Snake River Plain Aquifer
>
> In southern Idaho, the Snake River flows through a series of small but precipitous canyons cut into an arid plain. The Snake River Plain, an eastward extension of the Columbia Plateau, is underlain by hundreds of feet of flood basalts created by at least 120 separate eruptions of fluid lavas over the past 1.6 million years or so (figures 2.2C and 8.16). These basalts have high primary permeability and porosity, mainly along heavily fractured zones near the top and bottom of lava flows. Thin beds of lake deposits, stream sediments, and rubble are present between many of the flows. Much of the groundwater flow occurs along the irregular sand and gravel sediments and weathered zones between flows. Water from the Rocky Mountains to the north flows down upon the plain and rapidly infiltrates the basalts where it continues its journey to the south and southwest along subterranean routes through the lavas (Figure 8.17). Most groundwater movement is nearly horizontal, parallel to the lava flows, along zones of high hydraulic conductivity (150-1,500 m/day). Most of the water moves through the upper 100 meters of the aquifer and discharges at numerous springs along the Snake River, notably at an area known as the Thousand Springs (Plate 12, Bottom), where 11 first-order springs occur along a 65-kilometer (39-mile) stretch of the Snake River. Today, a significant amount of the aquifer recharge is from the hundreds of thousands of acres of irrigated cropland and the leaky canals which serve them [438]. Studies by the Idaho Department of Water Resources indicate that water storage in the eastern Snake River Plain aquifer has been declining by perhaps 225,000 acre-feet annually since 1980. A comprehensive management plan exists but funding to address concerns over aquifer depletion has been lacking.
>
> Concerns have often been expressed regarding the Idaho National Engineering Laboratory (INEL), site of the world's first commercial electric-generating nuclear reactor. INEL is located near the northern edge of the Snake River Plain, 160 kilometers (100 miles) upgradient from the Thousand

Figure 8.16. Aerial view of the Snake River Plain, Idaho. Darker areas are more recent lava flows.

Springs. The site produced nuclear reactors for ships and re-processed spent fuel rods. By 1953, some 200 million gallons of radioactive wastewater was being generated annually and was disposed of in the Snake River Plain aquifer via injection wells. Thankfully, it appears that most of the radionuclides, which include plutonium, strontium, and cesium, were insoluble and became trapped in the rock. Tritium (H-3) is part of the water itself but studies indicate that it will decay to negligible levels before reaching the surface environment.

8.7.2 Pyroclastic Rock

As with lava rocks, the hydraulic properties of pyroclastics can vary greatly. Some pyroclastic rocks consist of very coarse conglomerations of cinder and sediment deposited by streams and mass movements near sites of violent eruptions (Figure 2.2H). These rocks can possess very high porosity and permeability. Other rocks form when hot ash and debris from violent eruptions sweep down the slopes of a volcano and leave a deposit called an ash-flow tuff. Repeated eruptions can produce

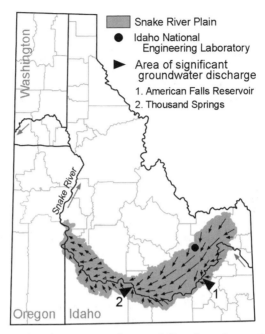

Figure 8.17. Map showing extent and general direction of groundwater flow in the Snake River aquifer.

thick, extensive deposits of partially fused rock which will become less permeable with depth due to compaction. Interbeds, shrinkage joints, and related properties can produce zones of high hydraulic conductivity, especially near the tops of the ash flows. More densely welded parts of the flows, usually the middle and lower parts, often exhibit very low primary permeability but are still quite susceptible to fracturing.

8.8 Unconsolidated Sediment

We have pumped 170 feet off the (High Plains) aquifer,
that's gone. There's just a little tick of water at the bottom.

— Lawrence Withers, a farmer near Sublette, Kansas

8.8.1 Introduction

Most of Earth's surface is directly underlain by unconsolidated material or regolith, as opposed to solid rock. Much of this blanket of material consists of thin blankets of saprolite, colluvium, or sedimentary deposits which are of limited use as aquifers. However, many areas exist where the regolith is of sufficient thickness and permeability to yield important quantities of groundwater. Indeed, some 90% of developed aquifers are in unconsolidated materials, usually sand and gravel. Most are small in extent compared to major rock aquifers. Five important categories of unconsolidated aquifers are discussed below.

8.8.2 Alluvial Valleys

Mature streams will deposit a large quantity of sediment along their valleys as they wander from side to side across the width of the valley floor. These valley floor deposits, often accompanied by higher-level alluvial terrace deposits, form many of the world's best-producing aquifers. Streams in cold or arid environments tend to transport large quantities of coarse sediment (sand and gravel) and develop a **braided** pattern (Plate 13, Top). The channels of these streams tend to be wide, shallow, and full of gravel bars which the stream waters thread their way through. The deposits formed by these streams consist of fairly uniform sheets of sand and gravel. In warmer, more humid areas where vegetation is present, more clays will be present and streams tend to form **meandering** channels which snake their way along the floodplain floor (Plate 13, Bottom). The deposits formed by these streams will contain abundant fine sediment (silt and clay) deposited on the river plain during floods. The actual stream channels will yield curving elongate deposits of sand and gravel which reflect the shape and changing positions of the channel. Some features of a meandering stream floodplain are shown on Figure 8.18.

The alluvial deposits underlying floodplains contain large volumes of good quality water at shallow depth. In many locations, river alluvium is readily recharged from the nearby river and its tributaries during high flow periods, local precipitation and runoff, and the surrounding bedrock. Infiltration of meteoric water is the most important source of recharge in large floodplains and where extensive alluvial terraces are present. Most discharge is into the trunk stream and its major tributaries, although seepage into bedrock, pumping, and/or evapotranspiration dominate in some areas. Compared to river water, the alluvial groundwater is typically more dependable, more uniform both physically and chemically, less polluted, and not subject to the many vagaries of river flow. Floodplain aquifers act much like giant sponges, absorbing water during rainfall and flooding events and yielding that water back to the stream

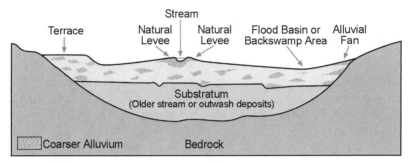

Figure 8.18. Cross-sectional sketch showing some features of a typical floodplain environment for a meandering stream. The bodies of coarser alluvium within the upper unit or "topstratum" consist primarily of buried stream channel deposits, levee deposits, and alluvial fan deposits near the valley side.

during dry periods. The total amount of water stored in floodplain alluvium at any one time can easily be hundreds or thousands of times greater than the water contained in the river. In spite of this, river alluvium has often been underexploited as a water source. One major exception to this pattern is Europe, where the rivers themselves have long experienced pollution problems.

Most of the world's major rivers and their associated deposits were strongly influenced by the Pleistocene glaciations, both inland and near sea level. Many river valleys were sites of extensive sediment deposition during the melting stages of glacial periods, especially in high-elevation and mid-latitude areas. An abundance of coarse rubble was generated by accelerated mechanical weathering and the glaciers themselves transported and deposited vast quantities of sediment. Much of the sediment was picked up by glacial meltwaters and deposited as permeable outwash along valleys downstream from the melting ice. It is not unusual for these sediments to have accumulated to depths of a few hundred meters (several hundred feet). Meltwater deposits tend to be coarser, and thus more permeable, near the bottom and become gradually finer upward.

Impacts were even more pronounced in coastal areas. During the lengthy Pleistocene glacial episodes, sea level fell by some 130 meters (430 feet), exposing large tracts of land and causing erosion along the lower parts of rivers entering the sea. During interglacials, sea level rose and inundated the sensitive, low-lying environments near river mouths.

At the close of the latest glacial episode, about 12,000 years ago, sea level began to rise and the lower parts of river valleys filled with water, forming estuaries, bays, and related features

Younger deposits, sometimes called "topstratum," resulting from river deposition in post-Pleistocene time overlie older river and meltwater deposits ("substratum") in most places (Figure 8.18) [358]. These recent sediments range from highly permeable sands and gravels deposited in the river channels themselves to clays deposited in low-lying flood basins and backswamp areas. Sands and gravels are deposited by the rapidly moving water in meandering stream channels and the finer sediments are washed away, leaving elongate deposits ("shoestring sands") and lenses which possess excellent hydraulic conductivity and storativity. However, most young (Holocene age) valley floor sediments consist of fine silts and clays deposited by slowly moving water as it spread over the floodplain during floods. In general, the recent floodplain deposits tend to have low permeabilities and act as a partially confining bed for groundwater in the underlying aquifer.

The water table near the river will rise and fall with changes in the river level. Farther from the river, the water table tends to be quite stable, and is often higher than near the river due to runoff from the adjacent uplands and small streams. The water is often fairly hard with total dissolved solids averaging around 500 mg/L for the Mississippi River aquifer. River deposits are the major aquifers in much of the US Central Lowlands.

Most alluvium in the lower reaches of large rivers consists of old delta deposits overlain by more recent floodplain alluvium. Near the mouths of many major rivers, subsidence has been occurring for millions of years, thus preserving older sediments, usually of Tertiary age, in large synclinal structures (Figure 8.19). These older underlying units also may contain important aquifers.

Streams are very dynamic features and, over time, their waters may be pirated by other streams or otherwise seriously disrupted by events ranging from climatic change to tectonic and volcanic activities to human interferences. Numerous abandoned stream valleys and deposits exist, and their alluvium provides excellent aquifers in some areas, although their recharge rates tend to be lower than in active stream valleys.

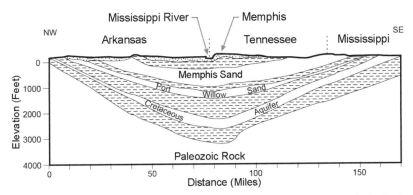

Figure 8.19. Geological cross-section of deposits in the lower Mississippi Valley showing aquifers and the broad synclinal structure underlying the valley. Vertical relief is greatly exaggerated. Clay-rich confining beds are shown by a dashed pattern, young alluvium by a dotted pattern.

Example: The Memphis Sand and Mississippi River Valley Aquifers

Most of the water used by millions of people along the lower Mississippi River comes from the alluvial aquifers lying beneath the river's floodplain. One of the major river valley aquifers is the **Memphis Sand**, or **Sparta**, aquifer which underlies parts of the states of Mississippi, Arkansas, and Tennessee (Figure 8.19). It is included in the Mississippi embayment aquifer system which contains several aquifers and confining beds. The aquifer is part of the Clairborne Group of sediments and was deposited during the Eocene Epoch [406]. The Memphis Sand consists of very fine to very coarse sand and, where not eroded, ranges from 400 to 900 feet in thickness [301]. It is estimated to contain up to a trillion gallons of good quality water. The aquifer is exposed at the surface along the eastern side of the large synclinal structure underlying the Mississippi embayment. Where no overlying clay-rich deposits are present, as shown here along the right side of the Figure 8.19 cross-section, the aquifer is vulnerable to pollution from hazardous wastes, leaking tanks, and other sources.

Since the mid-1960s, the Memphis Sand has been heavily pumped for use in the City of Memphis and its suburbs. Most

291

of the extraction has been by the Memphis Light, Gas, and Water utility, which currently withdraws some 160-200 million gpd from the aquifer to provide drinking water for over a million people in the Memphis area. If they had to use Mississippi River water, it would require costly treatment. These heavy, long-term withdrawals have produced a large, expanding cone of depression which extends across the state line into Mississippi and has become a source of contention among Mississippi, Memphis, and the utility company. The natural groundwater flow apparently is from Mississippi into Tennessee, and the aquifer's water has never been allocated among its various users, further complicating the issue. The fact remains that the water table is dropping in rapidly growing DeSoto County in Mississippi, and that state claims that at least part of the decline is due to the Memphis utility's extraction. In essence, they believe that Memphis is stealing Mississippi's water. In the ensuing court case, Mississippi requested a billion dollars in water-loss damages. The case was pursued to the US Supreme Court but, on January 1, 2010, the Court refused to hear the case. This was a major disappointment for many water managers and others who were hoping that the court would help clarify such murky issues as "ownership" and "use" of groundwater [62].

The **Mississippi River Valley aquifer** consists of Quaternary-age alluvial deposits which tend to become coarser with depth. It is represented by the thin, uppermost unit with the dotted pattern on Figure 8.19. This aquifer overlies the Tertiary deposits and is hydraulically connected to the river, meaning there is relatively free interchange of water between the river and the aquifer — the aquifer absorbs water during floods and contributes water to the river during normal flow. Although much smaller than the Memphis Sand and other Tertiary aquifers, it continues to provide water to farms and residents. Where the aquifer is pumped heavily, the river will continue to lose water to the aquifer, recharging it.

8.8.3 Alluvial Plains

Many stream deposits are not confined to the floodplains of one or two major rivers, but are spread out upon plains. The sheet-like alluvial deposits which result are the products of numerous streams, along with some reworking by wind, and are most frequently located near coasts and/or adjacent to high-elevation regions. These deposits are very similar to, and may be gradational with, the homoclinal sedimentary rocks described in Section 8.5.3.

Example: High Plains Aquifer

The higher, western part of the Great Plains is the High Plains (Figure 8.12). This region received alluvial sediment which was eroded from the Rocky Mountains during the early Miocene to the early Pliocene epochs. Extensive parts of this vast alluvial blanket still remain and the water-yielding parts are known as the Ogallala aquifer, or more properly, the **High Plains** aquifer (#4 on Figure 8.1). The aquifer lies at or near the ground surface and is composed primarily of sands and gravels of an important regional hydrogeological unit, the **Ogallala Formation**. The Ogallala consists mostly of sandy alluvium which was deposited over five million years ago by streams flowing eastward onto the plains from the Rocky Mountains. Parts of the Ogallala also contain lake clays, coarse gravels, wind-deposited sands, and freshwater limestones. Consequently, its hydrogeologic properties vary considerably from place to place. The formation underlies parts of eight states and encompasses an area of some 445,000 km2 and is often, and erroneously, called the world's largest aquifer. The total water stored in the aquifer in 2007 was estimated to be about 2.9 billion acre-feet (3.58 trillion m^3). The deposits dip gently eastward at about 3 m/km (16 ft/mi), a result of regional tilting, and the groundwater flows west to east at about 0.3 meter (1 foot) per day. Saturated maximum thickness varies from less than 30 meters (100 feet) in west Texas to more than 300 meters (1,000 feet) in western Nebraska. The physical and chemical properties of the formation are quite uniform; over 80% of the water has less than 500 mg/L total dissolved solids [86]. Recharge is minimal in the south, 0.03 in/yr in parts of Texas, and reaches a maximum of about 6 in/yr in Nebraska where two-thirds of the aquifer's water is stored. In the Sand Hills region of Nebraska, the High Plains aquifer lies at or near the surface and still produces flowing artesian wells. A

---

proposed petroleum pipeline carrying petroleum from Canada's tar sands operations in Alberta to ports in Texas would cross the Nebraska section of the aquifer, raising water quality concerns [434].

The economic value of the High Plains aquifer to the semi-arid Great Plains and to the entire nation has been enormous. It has provided water for nearly a fifth of all irrigated land in the US. As much as 40% of US beef cattle have depended upon grain irrigated by its waters. Following the Civil War, Ogallala water from many springs and hand-dug wells was widely used but extensive flood irrigation was not practical due to the rolling topography. Truly large scale exploitation began with develop of center-pivot irrigation in the 1950s. From 1950 to 1980, agricultural pumpage in the High Plains increased from around 651 billion gal/yr to 7.5 trillion gal/yr. In 1980, some 170,000 wells were producing 18 million acre-feet of water to irrigate 13 million acres and water levels in much of Texas and Oklahoma had declined 50 or more feet. Faced with this lowering of the water table and more costly pumping, certain conservation measures were implemented, including the use of low-pressure nozzles to cut evaporation and irrigating only when needed [70]. Irrigated land in the southern Great Plains has decreased by more than 24% since 1980 [55, 313]. According to some estimates, the aquifer is still being depleted eight times faster than nature can recharge it [246]. By 2007, overall (area-weighted) decline in the water level of the aquifer was calculated to be 14 feet [261]. The total decline in water storage in the aquifer was about 270 million acre-feet, or a 9% decrease from its natural, predevelopment state. More recent surveys have yielded similar results — an 8% loss was obtained using the Gravity Recovery and Climate Experiment (GRACE) satellite data (Section 13.4.2). This seems like a small decline, but the decline varies greatly from one area to another and even small decreases in groundwater can have very large impacts, including, for example, increased pumping costs and surface water depletion. Many springs, streams, their attendant ecosystems, and even small communities in the plains have disappeared completely. Larger communities such as Lubbock, Texas, and

Ulysses, Kansas, have considered costly plans to import water from distant sources and many farmers have been forced to make due with less water or do what others have already done and abandon agriculture completely.

8.8.4 Alluvial Basins

A substantial amount of terrain in the western US and elsewhere around the world is dominated by large basins or valleys, most of which have been formed in the recent geologic past as a result of large downward displacements along normal faults. Adjacent to the basins are steeply rising mountain ranges in which the bedrock has been upfaulted, often by several miles relative to the corresponding bedrock beneath the adjoining basins (Figure 8.20). The most notable examples occur in areas of crustal tension where downfaulted blocks produce deep basins which often have no outlet. Famous examples include the Dead Sea basin in the Middle East and Death Valley in the southwestern US. Other important basins may be synclinal (downfolded) in origin. Weathering and erosion in the mountains produce sediment which is carried by streams and deposited in the adjacent basins. As erosion removes sediment from

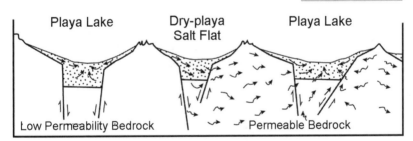

Figure 8.20. Simplified cross-section of characteristic basin-and-range structure showing common groundwater flow paths. The dotted pattern indicates basin fill sediments. Flow paths in the bedrock are irregular to represent movement along fractures and solutional conduits. Single-barb arrows indicate relative fault movements. The water table is not shown but it would reach the surface at the playa lakes (groundwater discharge area); it would rarely reach the surface where dry playas exist. The basins shown here are characterized by internal drainage (no significant water discharge to outside areas) as in the Great Basin of the western US. Vertical relief greatly exaggerated.

adjacent mountain ranges, additional uplift of the ranges is encouraged because of their reduced mass. At the same time, downsinking of the basin occurs partly due to the increasing weight of sediment. Both the uplifting of mountains and downsinking of the basins are examples of isostatic adjustment.

Where streams leave a mountainous terrain and enter onto a relatively flat surface, the loss of gradient forces the streams to deposit their sediment load quite rapidly, building up fan-shaped deposits which frequently merge to form a broad alluvial apron (*bajada*) at the base of the mountains (Figure 2.8B). Alluvial fans and aprons often comprise most of the deposits found in alluvial basins and along the base of major elevated regions. The sediments tend to be very coarse and poorly sorted near the highlands, reflecting deposition during periodic flash flood events. Finer-grained sediment is carried farther toward the center of the basins where they may be interbedded with lake deposits — silt, clay, and evaporites (salts). Over time, as fault movements, mountain erosion, and basin deposition continue, thousands of meters of sediment can accumulate in such basins and troughs, though most are less than 1,000 meters (3,300 feet) in thickness.

Where these basins lack stream or subsurface outlets, the water will remain confined in the subsurface, sometimes reaching the surface where a lake forms. In arid regions, these **closed basins** will often contain saline lakes or salt flats — known by many names including playas, alkali flats, and salinas — in their lowest elevations (Plate 11, Top, and Figure 8.21). The presence of salt and clay deposits produces low permeability and saline groundwater in the central parts of many basins.

Where basins are drained by a through-flowing stream, much of the finer sediment gets carried out of the area leaving behind better sorted and more permeable deposits which have higher hydraulic conductivities and specific yields. Although sediment can vary rapidly vertically and horizontally, overall hydrogeologic properties of many alluvial basins are quite consistent and can be reliably predicted [86].

The **Basin and Range Province**, which extends from Idaho and Oregon southward deep into Mexico, provides many classic examples of fault-block terrain and alluvial basins (figures 8.20 and 8.21). Most of the water contained in the basin sediments of the western US and many other dry region basins is fossil water dating from the glacial episodes of the Quaternary Period when these areas experienced a climate characterized by high precipitation. Due to water infiltration during the wet glacials and the large accumulations of permeable sediment, excellent

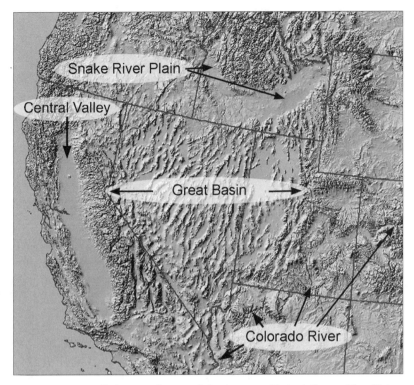

Figure 8.21. Relief map of part of the western United States identifying important regions described in text.

aquifers containing billions of gallons of fresh water are present in most basins. During the glacials, many basins held large freshwater lakes. As the climate gradually became arid during interglacials, the lake water evaporated, concentrating the salts contained in the water. As a result, in the central parts of many basins, salt deposits and saline water are present both on the surface and at depth (Figure 8.22). Great Salt Lake in Utah is a shrunken remnant of a much larger lake. Much of the water remaining in the subsurface of these basins is fresh water, however. But it is also fossil water inherited from a previous climatic regime — a nonrenewable resource. This is an inconvenient reality all too often ignored by the humans who now populate these basins.

In today's arid climate, groundwater recharge is minimal in most basins and occurs primarily from seepage into sediment aprons near the mountain fronts. The high ranges of the US Basin and Range province

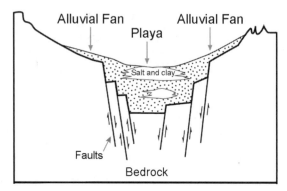

Figure 8.22. Idealized cross-section of fill material in a closed basin such as the one at the left in Figure 8.20. In this case, the basin is isolated and its lowest part often contained a lake or a salt flat. Hence the salt and clay in the center of the basin fill. This impermeable sediment grades outward into sandy alluvium which gets coarser near the mountains. Each basin is different. Some have streams flowing through them, depositing alluvium in the central area, others contain extensive volcanic deposits.

often receive moderate rainfall (25 in/yr or more) due to the rain shadow effect (Figure 3.5). The adjacent basins receive very little rain (6 in/yr or less), setting the stage for a distinctive hydrogeologic regime. When streams emerge from the mountains, they lose most of their discharge to the ground by percolation into the coarse, permeable sediment near the base of the mountains. Once underground, the water will slowly migrate downgradient away from the mountains. The water table will also tend to be closer to the surface near the mountains. The apex of alluvial fans is generally the best place to find shallow groundwater supplies. The average depth to water in these sediment-filled alluvial basins can vary enormously, from less than 100 feet to over 1,000 feet in areas of great tectonic activity, such as along the southern California coast.

Low-lying basins near the Pacific coast often served as arms of the sea in the past and may contain salt-water and marine sediments in their older, deeper deposits. The large lowland valleys and basins, such as the Central Valley of California, Puget Sound Lowland, and Willamette Valley, are mostly underlain by deeply subsided synclinal or tilted rock. Large quantities of fresh groundwater are present in the younger sediments and tens of thousands of wells have withdrawn vast quantities of groundwater from many of these lowlands, helping to support some of the largest agricultural and urban developments in the US.

The present-day natural recharge of most alluvial basins is limited. If withdrawals are balanced by recharge from local influent streams and nearby mountain precipitation, the water table will remain stable. Unfortunately, withdrawals generally exceed recharge many fold, and the water table drops as the groundwater is mined. In populated basins such as the Salt River Valley where Phoenix, Arizona, is located, groundwater pumpage may exceed a billion gallons per year.

Example: The Central Valley of California

California water will never be managed sustainably until we bring the state's groundwater under public management.
— Peter Gleick, 2012

California's water history is incredibly complex. It includes the violent 1907-1913 conflict over Los Angeles' ruthless appropriation of water from Owens Valley via a 233-mile aqueduct, and continues with the current disputes over ongoing water transfers and their budget-busting costs.

The Central Valley of California occupies some 20,000 mi^2 in the low central part of a huge trough bordered by the massive Sierra Nevada range on the east and the young Coastal Ranges on the west (Figure 8.23). The valley has been subsiding and accumulating sediments for some 120 million years. It is underlain by a large synclinal structure containing up to 15,000 meters (50,000 feet) of sedimentary rock and sediment. The upper layers of these sediments contain many coarse sands shed from the nearby mountains. The sands are interbedded with clays and form excellent aquifers (#3 on Figure 8.1). The older, underlying sediments are marine in origin. The northern third of the valley is drained by the Sacramento River and most of the southern part by the San Joaquin River.

The major supply of fresh groundwater occurs in the upper 300 meters (1,000 feet) of the sediments, although in some areas it occurs to depths of more than 1,000 meters (3,300 feet) [185]. The natural groundwater flow generally was from areas of recharge in the bordering mountains toward the central part of the valley, then north or south parallel to the San Joaquin or Sacramento rivers, respectively.

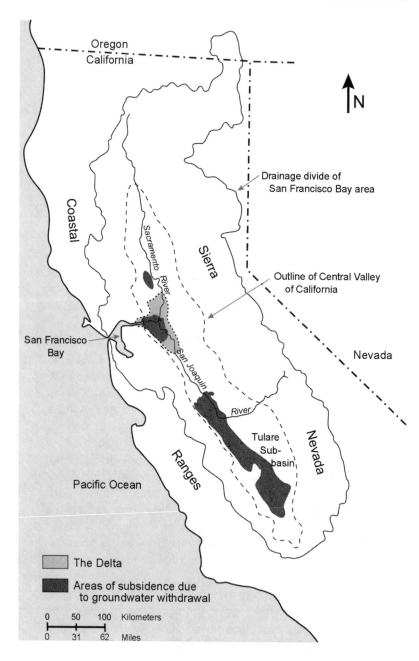

Figure 8.23. Sketch map showing relevant features of the Central Valley of California.

With its level terrain, warm temperatures, and fertile soils, the Central Valley was to become the most productive agricultural area on the planet by the early part of the twentieth century, producing about $40 billion of products annually. The Central Valley is the largest supplier of vegetable produce, fruit, and nuts for America's supermarkets. California accounts for nearly 25% of US irrigation water use and 18% of total US groundwater withdrawals. Agriculture consumes 85% of the fresh water used in the state, yet accounts for only about 3% of the state's economic production. Like most basins surrounded by mountains, annual rainfall in the valley is sparse — generally limited to 10 inches or less, not nearly enough to produce crops in this climate.

But groundwater was plentiful, or so it seemed. In the 1880s, flowing artesian springs and wetlands were abundant. Some springs would yield in excess of 3,800 m³ (more than a million gallons) of water per day. By the end of the nineteenth century, agricultural extractions had depleted the upper part of the aquifers and artesian flow was limited or nonexistent. Water also was delivered to fields via canals and ditches from local rivers such as the San Joaquin. With the development of modern drilling techniques around the turn of the century, deeper groundwater became available and agricultural production exploded. As more efficient wells and pumps came into use, the water table continued to drop. Soon, withdrawals of hundreds of millions of gallons per day were vastly exceeding recharge. By 1977, water tables had declined by over 120 meters (400 feet) in parts of the San Joaquin Valley. Sands and gravels in the aquifers were dewatered and intervening clays slowly gave up their water. Within the deeper groundwater hydraulic head decreased, sediment grains rearranged, porosity declined, and the sediments compacted yielding the largest volume of land subsidence ever attributed to water withdrawal — as much as 29 feet (Section 12.3.3). Wells collapsed or were left standing high and dry above the sinking ground surface, while concrete cracked and damaged buildings and canals.

It was obvious by the 1960s that water from farther afield would be needed if the valley's multi-billion-dollar agricultural economy was to survive. Today, the State Water Project, Central Valley Project, Colorado River Aqueduct, and other undertakings entailing many hundreds of miles of canals, tunnels, and other conduits along with dams, reservoirs, and related facilities, transfer water from northern California rivers, the Colorado River, and other locations into the valley. This costly and complex network delivers millions of acre-feet of water annually to thirsty fields and cities in southern California [128]. Imported water soon became the most used water source for agriculture, and the water was applied liberally, some say extravagantly, to fields. Much of the excess water seeped into the ground where it caused the uppermost water table, a perched water table overlying a zone of impermeable clay, to rapidly rise, bringing with it salts dissolved by the water. This created waterlogging and salinization problems in some croplands. To save crops from these two threats, subsurface drains were installed under many fields to carry off the excess water and salts. However, this water was now contaminated by high levels of salts often containing selenium. High concentrations of selenium occur in the Coast Ranges and are thus present in the sediments underlying the valley. Oxygen in the water combines with selenium to create selenate, a very soluble, hence mobile, form of selenium. Selenium is highly toxic to many wildlife and, by 1983, thousands of waterfowl were dying in wildlife refuges fed by streams receiving runoff from the croplands [70].

The San Joaquin and Sacramento rivers join to form a large estuarine-delta complex from which their waters flow west to San Francisco Bay (Figure 8.23). Two huge pumping stations in the delta suck fresh water from the southern end of the delta and distribute some 7.5 million acre-feet of it southward to dozens of California cities via the State Water Project and to farmers in the arid San Joaquin Valley. The delta's water loss poses serious threats to the estuary's fish populations, ecosystems, and the many people who depend upon these for their livelihood. The original elevation of the delta region was sea level, but compaction following the conversion of most of the marshland to cropland caused some 3 to 5 meters (10 to 16 feet) of subsidence, which in turn led to the construction of a massive system of some 1,700 kilometers (1,100 miles) of levees to protect the sunken farmlands. Even in a stable region, this would be an unsustainable situation. In earthquake-prone California, during a time of global warming and rising sea levels, the delta levee system is precarious to say the least. A major earthquake could leave millions of people with no dependable water supply. Numerous proposals, projects, and plans attempting to protect the delta ecosystem while meeting water needs to the south continue to be discussed and argued about [281]. One, the Bay Delta Conservation Plan, hopes to transfer water from the Sacramento River via a 65-kilometer-long tunnel, but analyses reveal numerous deficiencies in the 150-million-dollar plan [412].

Droughts are a recurring phenomenon in the Central Valley of California, and when they do occur, river discharge shrinks and agriculture must rely on heavier groundwater withdrawals. During the drought of 1977, 80% of the water required by agriculture came from wells in the San Joaquin Valley. Nine thousand wells were drilled in the valley in that year alone. The result was a precipitous decline in water levels and renewed compaction of underlying sediment, reversing a 10-year trend of rising water levels [103, 119].

Today, perhaps half the irrigation water in the valley is provided by groundwater and the resource continues its decline. The US National Aeronautics and Space Administration (NASA) satellite findings indicated that the water content in the Sacramento and San Joaquin drainage basins decreased by more than 30 km^3 from 2003 to 2009 [232]. The San Joaquin basin was losing 3.5 km^3 (2.8 million acre-ft) of water annually, most of it due to groundwater pumping. California has very little state regulation of groundwater. Attempts to limit withdrawals have routinely been defeated by wealthy, politically connected agribusiness interests, the same interests that have benefited from decades of public spending on costly water transfer projects [543]. In many cases, water provided to wealthy irrigators and land developers at public expense is sold back to the public at exceptionally high prices. At the end of the twentieth century, some 70% of the profits from farming in the Central Valley were attributed to taxpayer subsidies

[95]. In 2011, California's debt for publicly subsidized water-related projects exceeded $30 billion. Another long and severe drought, which was finally alleviated somewhat by heavy mountain precipitation in 2011, forced cuts (up to 85%) in water deliveries and increased pressure to have the public approve another multi-billion dollar bond to transport still more water southward to support agriculture and desert subdivisions [312, 354]. California's severe economic problems are closely linked to its large and growing water supply expenses [461]. The situation, financially and environmentally, is unsustainable. Unfortunately, unsustainable water use cleverly and misleadingly promoted by sustained pressure of special interest groups and their pro-growth-at-all-costs allies in government is a scenario all too often repeated in the US and elsewhere.

8.8.5 Glacial Deposits

Roughly a third of the land area of Earth was covered by ice during the glacial episodes of the Quaternary. The repeated glaciations had profound impacts on surficial processes and the deposits they yielded around the world. For example, as glaciers formed and melted, sea level declined and rose by a total of at least 130 meters (430 feet). Our focus here is on the sediment left by the glaciers themselves. North America alone has some 13 million km² of glacial deposits (Figure 8.24) [377].

Hydraulic conductivities of glacial deposits vary enormously with excellent conductivity in outwash (often roughly 1 m/day) and very low conductivity in clayey lake deposits and compact tills (0.0001 m/day). All can vary considerably depending upon such factors as texture (grain sizes), weathering, and fracturing. For example, conductivity in loess can vary from about 1-0.000001 m/day. **Loess** is common in or near areas of extensive glaciation. It consists of silt — fine particles winnowed from outwash deposits by wind and then deposited somewhere downwind. Porosities can exceed 50%. The chemistry of water in glacial deposits will depend largely upon the composition, texture, water residence time, conductivity, weathering, and related properties of the different deposits.

Due to the interplay between advancing and retreating ice masses, repeated melting and refreezing, large changes in the volume of water present at different seasons, and other fluctuating conditions, the sediment making up glacial deposits can vary greatly within a small area.

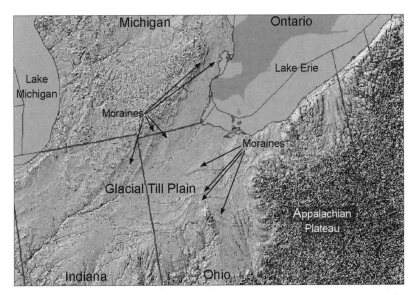

Figure 8.24. Relief map showing topography produced by glacial activity in the states of Indiana, Michigan, and Ohio.

Where deposits accumulate in contact with ice, numerous small to medium sized bodies of both till and outwash are likely to occur. Beneath ice sheets, extensive plains underlain by a thick mantle of till are common. Most tills, ice-marginal lake sediments, and loess deposits will be quite impermeable and poor groundwater sources. However, permeable sand and gravel bodies produced by melting ice commonly occur within till deposits and may be large enough to serve as aquifers. Some tills, especially sandy tills and those which accumulated on top of the ice, are sufficiently permeable to provide a modest amount of water to a well.

Glacial outwash generally makes excellent aquifers. Beyond the glacier margin, extensive deposits of sand and gravel outwash will accumulate as **outwash plains** or **valley trains** — valley floors filled with outwash. Enormous quantities of sediment were washed out of glaciers that once covered 30% of North America. The glacial meltwaters left thousands of now abandoned channels lined by permeable sands and gravels. As noted in Section 8.8.2, where meltwaters from the glaciers occupied valleys beyond the ice margins, sediment-laden waters deposited sand and gravel, often to depths exceeding 100 meters. In other places broad outwash plains were built up by melting glaciers. All tend to be excellent aquifers. Typical sustainable yields from outwash in Wisconsin are on the order of 350-1500 L/min compared to less than 10 L/min in crystalline bedrock. Glaciers sometimes overrode outwash, depositing till on top of it, creating confined aquifers.

8.9 Coastal Environments

Coastal areas bordering salt-water bodies require special attention by hydrogeologists because of the interactions between fresh and salt water. Nearly all coastal environments, including islands, will have saline sea water lying below fresh groundwater.

8.9.1 Relations between Fresh and Salt Water

Fresh water, with a mass of approximately 1.000 g/cm^3, is less dense than sea water, which has an average mass of about 1.025 g/cm^3. When simplified to whole numbers, the ratio of the mass of fresh water to salt water becomes 40:41. The less dense fresh water will float atop saline water where the two come into contact. The zone of mixing between the two is usually quite narrow due to the lack of strong currents and turbulent flow in groundwater.

For an island in the ocean, the fresh groundwater forms a fat lens, not unlike a bubble, surrounded by the overlying zone of aeration and the underlying salt water (Figure 8.25). This floating body of fresh groundwater is often termed **basal water**. The 40:41 density ratio means that, for every foot the water table of the island stands above sea level, the fresh-/salt-water contact will lie 40 times deeper below sea level. In equation form:

$$z = 40h$$

where z represents the relief (vertical distance) between sea level and the fresh-/salt-water contact and h is the elevation of the water table above mean sea level. This relationship is known as the **Ghyben-Herzberg ratio**, after the two scientists who, working independently, first defined it. Thus, if the maximum elevation of the water table was 6 meters, one would expect to find the bottom of the bubble — that is, the place where salt and fresh water come into contact — at an elevation of –240 meters (240 meters below sea level), and the total maximum thickness of the freshwater bubble would be 246 meters. A similar relationship will exist everywhere on the island, as well as on peninsu-

PLATE 1

Top: Abundant rainfall and warm temperatures yield lush, verdant vegetation as seen here along the path to La Mina Falls in the Sierra de Luquillo cloud forest of Puerto Rico.

Bottom: In stark contrast to the cloud forest, the Atacama Desert in northern Chile is one of the driest and most barren places on Earth. Yet, even here, life persists. Prehistoric human activity is evident from the intaglios on the distant hills.

PLATE 2

Top: This aerial view shows evidence of tectonic activity along the Forellen fault in the northern Teton Range, Wyoming. The ancient Precambrian rocks on the right were thrust upward many thousands of feet relative to the younger layered Paleozoic rocks on the left along a zone of movement called a fault.

Bottom: Mount Saint Helens, Washington, shown here before its 1980 eruption, is an excellent example of a large, young "stratocone" volcano made of lava flows and ejected material.

PLATE 3

THE GROS VENTRE SLIDE

BEFORE YOU LIE THE REMNANTS OF ONE OF THE LARGEST EARTH MOVEMENTS IN THE WORLD.

ON JUNE 23, 1925, EARTH, ROCK AND DEBRIS MOVED RAPIDLY FROM AN ALTI– TUDE OF 9000 FEET, ACROSS THE VALLEY BOTTOM AND UP THE SLOPE OF THE RED BLUFFS BEHIND YOU. THE ACTION LASTED ONLY MINUTES BUT A RIVER WAS DAMMED AND THE LANDSCAPE CHANGED.

GROS VENTRE SLIDE GEOLOGICAL AREA
TETON National Forest

Top: Rocks of various size break loose from the cliffs and fall or tumble down to form the lower slopes shown in this view of the Killdeer Mountains in North Dakota. This rock debris will continue to weather as it slowly migrates farther downslope, mainly by the imperceptible process called creep.

Bottom: The higher end of the Gros Ventre Slide in northwestern Wyoming lies 2,000 feet above the valley floor. Like a number of other large rock and debris slides, this one dammed a river, impounding a lake that was 200 feet deep and five miles long.

PLATE 4

Top: This unconformity is located along the Shoshone River near Cody, Wyoming. The tilted underlying strata were eroded and the overlying gravels were deposited on the eroded surface to form an angular unconformity. One of the numerous mineral springs along this section of the river is visible in the center of this view.

Bottom: The rectangular jointing in limestone shown here is located along the Bonnechere River, Ontario, Canada.

PLATE 5

Top: Turtle Rock in the Laramie Range, Wyoming, exhibits good exfoliation jointing in granite.

Bottom: This roadcut along Interstate 81 near Tremont, Pennsylvania, reveals a symmetrical syncline in sedimentary strata.

PLATE 6

Top: This view looks west across Jackson Hole at the Teton Range, Grand Teton National Park, Wyoming. The abrupt rise and straight mountain front, or escarpment, is characteristic of many geologically young fault-block mountains.

Bottom: This view in Big Bend National Park looks south along the border between the United States (left) and Mexico (right). This is a desert environment with sparse vegetation except at the lower right where phreatophytes, including many tamarisk, crowd the floodplain of the Rio Grande. The cliffs consist of resistant sandstone on the uplifted side of a fault.

PLATE 7

Top left: The Chateaugay River in northern New York state is, at this location, a permanent stream in a bedrock gorge.

Top right: Capitol Gorge in Capitol Reef National Park, Utah, is an intermittent stream valley in a bedrock gorge of similar size to that in the photograph at left.

Bottom: This small ephemeral valley in glacial deposits near Jordan, New York, will contain running water only following a heavy or sustained rainfall.

PLATE 8

Top: The Florida Everglades is an extensive region over which the water table and the ground surface occur at nearly the same elevation. The Everglades was once the largest wetland environment in the United States.

Bottom: Ice shown here is from freezing perched groundwater emerging from sedimentary rocks in a roadcut along Interstate 81 near McAdoo, Pennsylvania.

PLATE 9

Top: Saint Johns River in Florida, like many other rivers in the state, is fed by numerous tubular springs emerging from the limestone bedrock.

Bottom: This working windmill was located north of Cheyenne, Wyoming. Thousands of such windmills were once scattered across the Great Plains of the United States. This one probably was pumping water from the far western part of the High Plains aquifer.

PLATE 10

Top: Pulleys are shown in use here to haul dirt to the surface during routine qanat cleaning operations near Ouarzazate, Morocco.

Bottom: This ice cone formed from groundwater discharge spray in the western Altiplano in Bolivia. Residents and travelers alike come here to fill buckets with ice for personal and commercial uses, including cooling drinks and food on the Arica-La Paz railway that once ran between La Paz, Bolivia, and Arica, Chile.

PLATE 11

Top: Evaporating water has left a deposit of salt along the edge of this saline pond, or playa lake, in Death Valley, California.

Bottom: The evaporation of mineral-laden groundwater has left white salt deposits covering part of the ground in this seepage area in western North Dakota.

PLATE 12

Top: Looking north in Red Rocks Park near Denver, Colorado, Precambrian rock of the mountains is seen at the upper left and red sedimentary rock of the Fountain Formation is seen dipping to the east (right) at the right. Outcrops of tilted permeable bedrock often provide important aquifer recharge areas.

Bottom: The Thousand Springs area is located along the north side of the Snake River in southern Idaho. These springs, part of which are shown here, represent the resurgence of surface water which entered the region's basalt deposits many miles upgradient.

PLATE 13

Top: This aerial view shows a typical braided stream channel in the Northern Rocky Mountains of Montana.

Bottom: Large meanders along the James River near Buchanan, Virginia, are shown in this aerial view.

PLATE 14

Top: Mineral deposits have formed a large terrace decorated with rimstone pools, flowstone, and associated features at Minerva Springs in Yellowstone National Park, Wyoming.

Bottom: The big thermal spring at Thermopolis, Wyoming, is often said to be the world's largest with a discharge of 18.6 million gallons of water daily at a temperature of 135 degrees Fahrenheit.

PLATE 15

Top left: Acid mine drainage is shown here emerging from the old Vulcan Mine in northern Idaho. The acidic effluent is often called "yellow boy" due to the yellow-to-red colors imparted to it by oxidized iron.

Top right: Agriculture is by far the greatest consumer of water among all human enterprises. Here, groundwater is shown gushing from pipes in fields in southern California.

Bottom: This grassy dike near the western coast of The Netherlands protects the reclaimed land to the left from the higher seawater at the right.

PLATE 16

Top: This pipeline in the sparsely populated Altiplano of Bolivia carries groundwater westward to Chile where it is used in agriculture.

Bottom: The "dunes" section of the All-American Canal is shown in this photograph taken January 4, 1985. At that time, large volumes of water were leaking from the unlined canal and flowing southward, underground, into Mexico, benefiting both Mexican farmers and natural ecosystems along the way.

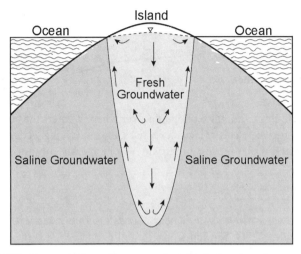

Figure 8.25. Cross-section of an oceanic island showing the groundwater lens of fresh groundwater (basal water) surrounded by saline groundwater.

las and in coastal areas, assuming fairly static conditions and homogeneous permeable materials [173].

In similar fashion, rivers entering the ocean will have an underlying tongue of salt water extending upriver below the fresh water (Figure 8.26). The balance between salt and fresh water in coastal areas is quite delicate. The water table as well as the underlying salt-water contact tend to rise and fall with tides, much like a float. World-wide rises in sea level will likewise produce an overall rise in groundwater levels along coasts as well as landward encroachment of salt water in the subsurface and on the surface, diminishing the available freshwater supply. With increased sea levels, tides will tend to sweep the tongue of salt water ever farther up river where the water can then seep into the river bed and contaminate local groundwater. If river discharge is diminished by such factors as upstream withdrawals, evaporation from reservoirs, climate change, or dry seasons, the salt-water tongue will also advance upstream. The tongue of seawater can penetrate many miles up a low-gradient river. In coastal areas which contain effluent rivers flowing over permeable material to the sea, a pronounced ridge tends to be produced in the fresh/salt groundwater boundary below the river due to groundwater flow toward the river (Figure 8.27A). Thus, in some conditions, saline groundwater can replace fresh water both from above and from below. In time,

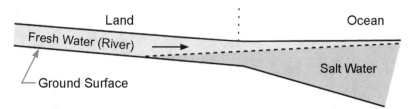

Figure 8.26. Longitudinal section of a river where it enters the ocean. If the river discharge decreases or if sea level rises, the underlying wedge or tongue of salt water will migrate upstream where it can contaminate fresh groundwater.

the groundwater flow system near a coastal-zone river will resemble that in Figure 8.27B. Similar impacts will occur, albeit more slowly, in coastal aquifers. One estimate (in New Jersey) is that a two-foot rise in sea level will cause a gradual landward migration of salt water of one to four miles per century in local artesian aquifers [173]. Ongoing sea level rise from global warming will obviously have serious impacts on groundwater in coastal regions.

Where rivers enter the ocean or other standing water bodies, deposition produces **deltas**. The surface of deltas is nearly flat. They may be deposited mostly inland where sediment has filled in a drowned river mouth as in the Mekong and San Joaquin deltas, or they may protrude outward into the water body as do the Nile and Mississippi deltas. In most active deltas, the water table is very shallow, the groundwater is fresh, the sediment is permeable, and the soil is suitable for crops. Consequently, many deltas are vital crop production areas and are often heavily populated. Unfortunately, their location and construction makes them highly vulnerable to such problems as seawater intrusion, subsidence, flooding, and coastal erosion.

> **Example: The Nile Delta**
>
> The Nile Delta, shaped like the Greek letter Δ and from whence the term delta is derived, provides an excellent example of the difficulties faced on these unique landforms today. Within the delta, the Nile River divides into numerous smaller channels (distributaries) and its water is further split by thousands of canals and irrigation ditches. Nearly all of Egypt's 84 million people live amidst this complex network

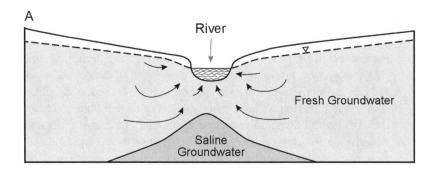

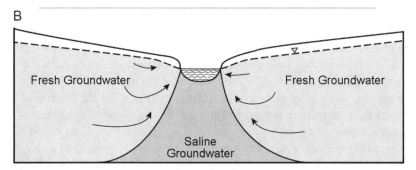

Figure 8.27. A. Transverse section of an effluent river in a low-lying coastal area near the ocean showing the underlying ridge in saline groundwater. **B.** The same scene after salt water has migrated up the river channel. Infiltration of saline water from above and upwelling from below has eliminated all fresh water from beneath the river.

on the delta or along low-lying plains adjacent to the Nile River. Most are farmers who utilize every drop of the surface water so that fresh water rarely, if ever, now reaches the Mediterranean Sea. Consequently, thousands of wells, two-thirds of them illegal, have been drilled. Loss of underlying water has accelerated subsidence; parts of the delta are sinking by nearly a centimeter per year. Warming climate may cause the Mediterranean to rise by nearly a meter by mid-century. This would flood a third of the delta and devastate the country's economy [37]. In Alexandria, the largest city on the Mediterranean Sea with a population of more than 4 million people, even a quarter-meter rise in sea level would reportedly place over half the city's population and industry below sea level.

8.9.2 Human Impacts

Degradation of coastal environments and their freshwater resources has been accelerating. Valuable coastal ecosystems, including salt marshes, mangroves, and seagrasses, are disappearing at about 2% per year [83]. In recent decades coastal populations have exploded and those populations have had to rely increasingly on groundwater obtained from wells. Coastal withdrawals can produce surprisingly large disruptions in the groundwater interface between fresh and salt water. As the Ghyben-Herzberg relation shows, any reduction in head will produce a rise in the underlying fresh-/salt-water interface. For example, when pumping a well, for every foot of downward displacement in the water table, a corresponding 40 feet of upward displacement would eventually tend to occur in the underlying fresh-/salt-water boundary. As shown on Figure 8.28, a reverse cone of depression forms at the salt-water boundary below a pumping well. Hence even minor overpumping of coastal fresh water can yield large impacts and end up contaminating freshwater supplies from salt-water intrusion. On a larger scale, withdrawal of fresh groundwater along coasts has caused extensive landward migration of the underlying salt water, forcing abandonment of thousands of wells as fresh groundwater is replaced by salt water (Figure 8.29). This will occur in both confined and unconfined aquifers and only by carefully regulating pumping, or recharging the aquifers with fresh water, will saline-water intrusion be prevented.

Mixing of the subsurface salt and fresh waters will occur if strong groundwater flows are generated, most often by heavy pumping. The mixing often creates zones or lenses of brackish groundwater. One way to inhibit this mixing — and the accelerated depletion of the available freshwater supply — is double-pumping, in which a corresponding quantity of saline water is pumped as the fresh water is pumped, thus maintaining a balance between the two masses.

Many coastal areas, especially in tropical and humid temperate areas, contain extensive freshwater wetlands. These swamps and marshes were once regarded as wastelands. Even today, the desire to drain them to create land for agricultural, industrial, or other profitable uses is strong. These wetlands are major sources for fresh water along the coasts, not to mention their value as ecosystems and in purifying water. When drained, freshwater recharge near the coast is greatly reduced and saline-water encroachment often replaces or contaminates the fresh groundwater as shown in Figure 8.30.

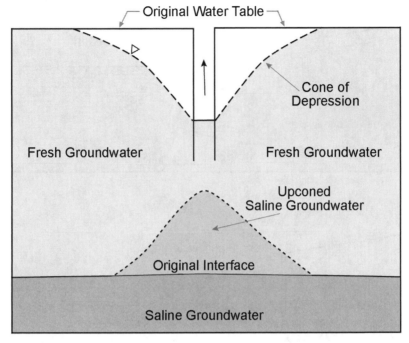

Figure 8.28. Inverse cone of depression in underlying saline water produced by pumping of fresh water. Recall that saline or brackish groundwater often underlies fresh water well away from coastal regions.

In arid coastal regions, the fresh water may exist only in a thin, nearly horizontal zone, only a few centimeters thick in some cases, that overlies the saline groundwater. Most wells will be useless in such situations, but horizontal collector galleries (Section 7.5.6) may be able to provide a usable albeit limited water supply without causing negative impacts. If elevated areas are present, such as sand dunes or other hilly regions, a lens of fresh water may be present below them. Its size will be determined by such factors as local rainfall quantities and infiltration rates.

8.10 Mountainous Terrain

Mountainous regions tend to be characterized by highly varied topography and bedrock geology, heavier rainfall and snowfall, glaciers, permafrost, heightened sensitivity to climate change, and other characteristics which are of great hydrologic significance to surrounding

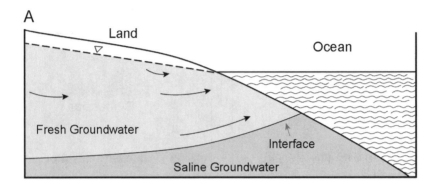

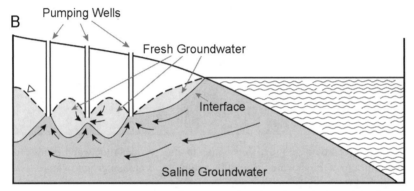

Figure 8.29. A. Hydrogeological cross-section showing relation of fresh and saline groundwater in an undisturbed coastal area. **B.** The same area after excessive well withdrawal of fresh water. The fresh groundwater resource has been severely reduced. Due to upconing, the two outside wells are now pumping saline water. The middle well still is still accessing fresh water, possibly because it hasn't been pumping as long as the other wells, or is withdrawing considerably less water. The impact of mixing is not shown, but would further diminish the remaining fresh groundwater supply.

areas. Although mountainous terrains are recognized as important groundwater source areas, most studies have focused on surface water influences. As noted previously, the higher the relief of a terrain, the deeper the circulation of groundwater will likely be. Deep groundwater movement, combined with the high heat flow and active geology of many young mountainous regions, means that temperature and tectonic stress influences may also have to be considered. Large contrasts in precipitation

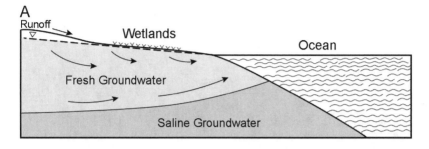

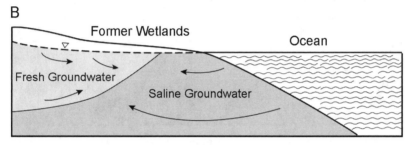

Figure 8.30. A. Normal conditions along a low-lying coast bordered by freshwater wetlands. Infiltrating fresh water recharges the underlying groundwater. **B.** The same area following draining of the wetlands, lowering of the water table, and related freshwater diversions (for development, agriculture, etc.). The loss of freshwater recharge near the coast permits saline groundwater encroachment.

are common over fairly short distances in the major high-relief mountains of temperate regions with abundant rain and snow at high elevations and much drier conditions prevailing in larger basins and valleys of lower elevations. Stoss (windward) slopes are likely to receive far more precipitation than lee (downwind) slopes. Runoff tends to be highly seasonal with heavy flows during the spring melting season and greatly reduced flow the rest of the year, except for heavy summer storms which carry a threat of flash floods. The complexities of mountainous regions create many irregularities in recharge rates and hydraulic conductivity distribution in the subsurface. Groundwater flow systems will be correspondingly complex and often difficult to decipher. Most groundwater in mountainous terrain will come from unconsolidated, mainly alluvial and glacial, deposits in intermontane valleys and basins. Groundwater in the mountains themselves is often limited in quantity, although springs adequate for small local use tend to occur frequently [100].

Figure 8.31. Snow- and ice-covered mountains such as the Andes, seen here near La Paz, Bolivia, provide water to millions of people around the world.

The precipitation falling upon the high mountainous regions of Earth has long been the primary source of water supplying rivers upon which hundreds of millions of people depend (Figure 8.31). Most of the water collects as snow and ice, to be released gradually during the spring and summer seasons. The Himalayan Mountains have long been referred to as the water towers of Asia. In the western US approximately 75% of the water supply for cities, towns, and agriculture comes from the mountain snowpack [25]. In addition to rising temperatures, dust deposition absorbs additional solar energy thus accelerating the melting of mountain snow and ice. Due to the spread of deserts and increased human activities in desert areas, deposition of dust in mountains is increasing. In the Rocky Mountains, dust levels are around five times greater than they were prior to the mid-nineteenth century. The dust promotes earlier melting of the snowpack than temperature increase alone would. This creates an ecological imbalance because plant growth responds to temperature, not dust [376]. A warming climate threatens to continue increasing temperatures and dust, further reducing this vital water supply (Section 12.6).

8.11 Arid Environments

Many regard arid regions and deserts as wastelands lacking water. As the iconoclastic environmentalist Edward Abbey was fond of pointing out, most arid and semiarid regions have just the right amount of water to sustain vibrant ecosystems in which the lifeforms are well adapted to the prevailing conditions. As with tropical rainforests, indigenous peoples had successfully utilized these areas for many centuries (Plate 1, Bottom). Alluvial fans near mountains and talus deposits may harbor usable, albeit limited, supplies of groundwater (figures 4.18G and 7.20C). In the great deserts such as the Sahara, oases exist where groundwater is present in or near the surface (Figure 8.32). As noted previously, many arid regions were quite wet during the glacials of the Quaternary Period and copious amounts of groundwater accrued. But that water is "fossil" water, the product of a bygone era, and once consumed, cannot be replaced under the current climatic regime in which evapotranspiration potentials of arid regions far outstrip precipitation. With little to no recent recharge, groundwater circulation is slow and salts often build up in the water as well as in sediment from which mineral-bearing water has evaporated. **Salinization** (Section 8.3.2) is a common

Figure 8.32. An oasis in Morocco.

Figure 8.33. A sprinkling system in operation in an arid Basin and Range setting north of Enterprise, Utah.

result of crop irrigation in arid and semiarid climates and has degraded millions of acres of cropland around the world. Irrigating fields in areas with high evaporation rates (Figure 8.33) causes salts to accumulate in the soil, eventually rendering them unable to support plant growth [313].

Nearly all arid and semiarid regions have experienced significant irreversible damage resulting from exploding populations, modern technologies, and ever-increasing demands on these delicately balanced environments. Many dryland regions have been made to yield bountiful harvests by bringing in water from other locations or by pumping local groundwater. Often, the successes are short-lived, especially where they depend upon the mining of groundwater or where agriculture is not very carefully adapted to the local environment. Overgrazing, plowing of fragile grassland, and other unsustainable land uses lead to excessive runoff, soil erosion, and surface and ground water depletion. **Desertification** is the conversion of once-productive land to a devegetated, desert-like condition. The threat of desertification is most severe in semiarid regions where livestock grazing and attempts at large-scale farming readily lead to salinization of soil and soil depletion by water and wind erosion. Desertification is especially widespread in northwestern China and the African Sahel. It is one of the most severe environmental problems and a potential threat to the survival of roughly a third of Earth's population (Figure 8.34) [469].

Example: The Southwestern United States

The southwestern US provides many excellent examples of water use and misuse in an arid environment. Enticed by climate, spectacular scenery, and unending promotions, millions have flocked here making it the fastest-growing region of the country. It is also the "water-poorest." Evidence suggests that the region was unusually wet (that is, not as dry as usual) for much of the twentieth century and worsening droughts were anticipated even without climate warming, which is expected to increase the area's aridity. As noted previously, most groundwater in the region is fossil water accumulated during Quaternary glacial episodes when abundant rainfall and lakes existed. Under today's climate, groundwater recharge is very low which has led to extensive mining of groundwater.

Diminishing groundwater led in turn to increased reliance upon the limited surface waters of the region, especially the Colorado River (Figure 8.21) which now supplies water to some 27 million people in seven states and Mexico. The Colorado rises in the Rocky Mountains and carves some of Earth's most spectacular canyons as it crosses the Colorado Plateau on its way to the Gulf of California. But it is becoming

---

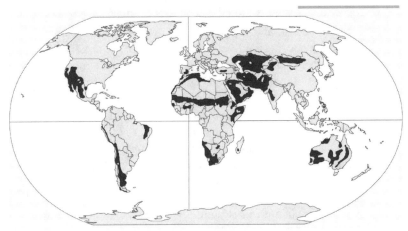

Figure 8.34. Map showing extent of desertification around the world.

increasingly obvious that the river's water is badly over-allocated. The water supply depends upon storage behind the many dams along the river — those reservoirs contain some 60 million acre-feet of water, nearly four times the average annual discharge of the river. When such factors as evaporation and infiltration losses from the reservoirs, human withdrawals, and the very real possibility of longer and more severe droughts are considered, it is possible that the river's two largest reservoirs, Lake Mead behind Boulder Dam and Lake Powell behind Glen Canyon Dam, could dry up completely in the not-too-distant future — by 2057 according to some calculations [23, 24].

Numerous books and countless articles have been written about the water problems in the southwestern US. It began with the prescient writings of John Wesley Powell (1834-1902), the first man to explore the great canyons of the Colorado River and later head of the US Geological Survey, who warned of the water limitations of this region [318]. Marc Reisner's *Cadillac Desert: The American West and its Disappearing Water*, first published in 1986 [326], is regarded as a seminal classic, and James Lawrence Powell's *Dead Pool* (2008) [317] and Stephen Grace's *Dam Nation* (2012) [160], provide sobering updates to the problems elucidated by Reisner. Numerous scientific articles provide additional insights, including a set of eight papers on climate change and water in southwestern North America, first published in the December 14, 2010 Online Early Edition of the Proceedings of the National Academy of Science [335].

Nevertheless, and in spite of the growing water scarcity and recent housing and economic problems, it is generally assumed that population growth and resource consumption in this region will continue unabated. California alone continues to grow by some half million people a year despite increasingly desperate water problems (Section 8.8.4). Local authorities and politicians persist in encouraging growth even as they complain of water scarcity. Many promoters continue to encourage massive water diversion projects which would transfer water from such far-away places as the Pacific Northwest, Canada, and the Mississippi River to the thirsty southwest. The costs of such projects would be phenomenal, even if the monumental environmental disruptions were ignored.

Example: The Great Basin Aquifer

At the same time that Mississippi and Tennessee were having legal squabbles over use of the Memphis Sand aquifer (Section 8.8.2), a battle involving the states of Utah and Nevada and numerous concerned individuals was brewing over nonreplenishable groundwater in the Basin and Range Province. As discussed in Section 8.8.4, most major groundwater supplies in the southwestern US are found beneath arid alluvial basins and valleys. Most of Nevada and western Utah lie within an area called the **Great Basin** (Figure 8.21), a section of the Basin and Range characterized by internal drainage — no streams flow out of this area and eventually into an ocean. The groundwater in the many basins is sometimes collectively called the **Great Basin aquifer**.

The Las Vegas area in southern Nevada contains 70% of the state's population [163]. It lies in a desert basin and receives only about four inches of precipitation annually. Seemingly oblivious to their hydrologic insecurity, Vegas' population exploded 50% (to 1.9 million) from 1999 to 2007. Some still expect the population of Las Vegas to almost double to 3.6 million by 2035. Despite a number of water-saving efforts, per capita water use was 254 gallons per day in the late 2000s when other western cities such as Long Beach and Seattle were using only about 105 gallons per day. To prepare for looming water shortages and anticipated future growth, in 1989 the Southern Nevada Water Authority laid claim to groundwater reserves in five major desert basins near Great Basin National Park. The project intended to pump tens of thousands of acre-feet of water from the ground and transport it southward to the Las Vegas region via a $3.5 billion, 300-mile-long pipeline.

A Bureau of Land Management assessment indicated the anticipated yearly removal of some 57 billion gallons of groundwater would lower water tables 50 to 200 feet, cause more than five feet of ground subsidence over hundreds of square miles, eliminate or reduce water for over 8,000 acres of wetlands, 305 springs, and 112 miles of streams and impact hundreds of existing water rights. Local agriculture, wildlife

habitat, and even air quality, from dust generated when vegetation dies for lack of water, would be severely impacted.
Local farmers and residents were not happy and hundreds filed
protests. The Nevada Supreme Court ruled in January 2010
that the plan violated the rights of people in target basins such
as Spring Valley who had long protested the pipeline plan.
This temporarily negated access to the pipeline water which
had been awarded to Las Vegas, but, like most large-scale water
engineering proposals, this controversy, often called "the Great
Las Vegas Water Grab," is far from over [163, 320].

8.12 Cold Environments

The term **permafrost** refers to a condition in which near-surface
earth materials have experienced subfreezing temperatures averaging
below 0°C for two or more years in succession. Consequently, water in
the upper part of the regolith or rock will be in a frozen state. These
permafrost conditions may be continuous, as in colder areas to the north,
or discontinuous. Permafrost may extend to a depth of 1,000 meters (3,300
feet) or more in the coldest areas. Nearly a fifth of Earth's land area is
permafrost. Water in permafrost will exist primarily as ice. The ice matrix forms a near-surface layer of low permeability and tends to eliminate shallow aquifers as dependable sources of groundwater. However,
liquid water can exist above, within, and below the permafrost. The behavior of this water is generally more irregular and less predictable than
in temperate or tropical climates [367].

Abundant water may be present atop the permafrost during the
melting season. This is perched water which comes from the melting of
the "**active layer**," the upper meter or so of frozen ground (Figure 8.35).
The active layer or zone may produce water for as little as two months of
the year and the water quality is likely to be questionable.

Water within the discontinuous permafrost zone occurs locally in
areas of unfrozen ground or **taliks**. The most significant of these warmer,
insulated pockets and zones will be found beneath large lakes and along
major river valleys (Figure 8.35). Where permeable materials are present,
good water supplies often occur below the permafrost. Subpermafrost
alluvial deposits and karst provide excellent water supplies in some areas. These underlying water tables may fluctuate considerably due to
seasonal variations in temperatures and rainfall.

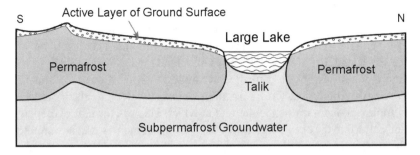

Figure 8.35. Cross-section in Arctic permafrost region showing the active layer, permafrost zone, and a talik (unfrozen ground) lying below a large lake. Note that the permafrost is thinner beneath warmer, south-facing slopes.

Farther north where permafrost is thicker and continuous, fresh-water aquifers are increasingly rare. Water quality can also vary widely. As with groundwater anywhere, residence time of the groundwater and the chemistry of the aquifers strongly influence the water quality. An added factor influences water quality in permafrost areas. When ice is melting, the nearly pure meltwater will have exceptionally low levels of dissolved matter. But the exclusion of minerals during the freezing process can also cause water within and below permafrost to be very high in dissolved minerals. Hence much subpermafrost water will be brackish or saline. Water mineralization is unlikely to be a problem where the subpermafrost groundwater flow is rapid or permafrost is uncommon.

Groundwater recharge and discharge in permafrost areas tends to be sporadic and localized. Most terrestrial discharge occurs along major rivers, below large lakes, and in a few large springs. Where heavy local discharge is occurring, large masses of ice often build up during winters. Where springs occur in permafrost or other liquid water sources exist, as happens at the close of the melting season, **ice lenses** may grow from freezing waters forming **frost blisters** on the surface. Because freezing occurs from the surface downward, the underlying water is trapped by ice above and ice below. As the water continues to freeze, expansion occurs and pressure builds. This can result in sudden repeated ruptures of the frost blisters. A similar, more persistent, condition produces larger, more permanent hills (**pingos**) which may exceed 50 meters in height.

Permafrost is a unique environment and special precautions need to be taken when such areas are developed. Factors such as the expansion and contraction of ice during repeated freeze-thaw cycles and the melting of ice under pressure require that buildings and other structures be specially designed to accommodate these processes.

Glaciers cover large parts of cold environments. The vast tracts of ice covering most of Antarctica and Greenland are basically cold deserts. Large quantities of liquid fresh water underlie parts of these ice sheets, especially Antarctica. The interactions of liquid water and glacial ice are complex and can influence the rate at which glaciers form, move, melt, and calve into the oceans. Satellite observations of melting glaciers around the world, including the marginal portions of the Greenland and Antarctic ice sheets, indicate that meltwater rapidly reaches the base of the ice where it can greatly accelerate the glaciers' movement (Section 12.6.2B).

8.13 Geothermal Areas

In general, groundwater within about 10 meters (33 feet) of the surface will reflect seasonal temperature variations. Below this, groundwater temperature will tend to increase in association with Earth's natural rate of temperature increase with depth — the **geothermal gradient**. On average, temperature in the upper crust increases about 30°C for every kilometer in depth. This geothermal gradient varies considerably from one place to another. It tends to be low in old, compact rock such as that found in the Precambrian shield areas (9.1°C/km in the Canadian Shield) and high in areas of active mountain building, volcanic activity, and young poorly consolidated sediment and rock (36°C/km in the Mississippi delta area). The higher the geothermal gradient, the more rapidly heat is escaping from Earth's interior, a phenomenon called **heat flow**. The heat flow at Earth's surface will be low in areas like Precambrian shields (perhaps 1 calorie/cm²/s) but can be eight or more times higher where hot rock and magma approach the surface. Groundwater is an important factor in heat transport and distribution within Earth [100]. Ascending groundwater in discharge areas will tend to accelerate heat flow and descending groundwater in recharge areas will decrease heat flow. Any groundwater that is significantly warmer than normal for its surroundings can be called **hydrothermal water**.

Areas of high heat flow produce unique groundwater conditions. **Thermal** (or **geothermal**) **areas** (Figure 8.36) usually occur in volcanic areas where a body of magma or hot rock is present at shallow depth. If groundwater is able to circulate to considerable depth (1,500-3,000 meters; a few thousand feet) over such a geological heat source, convection currents will often develop (Figure 8.37). Most of the water is meteoric

Figure 8.36. An aerial view of the world's largest geyser basin, the Norris Basin in Yellowstone National Park, Wyoming. Geyser basins are characterized by numerous hot springs, fumaroles, geysers, and related thermal features fed by hot rising groundwater. The deposits left by the mineral-laden waters form the white area seen on the photo.

water which enters the ground in recharge areas around the margins of the thermal area and descends under hydrostatic pressure, usually along fracture and faults. Deep in Earth's crust it becomes superheated to temperatures well above the surface boiling point. The resulting expansion and pressure causes the heated water to rise toward the surface where much of it will be discharged. Note that the major driving mechanism here is thermal rather than the hydrostatic pressure which causes normal springs and artesian conditions. The hydrothermal waters tend to be heavily laden with dissolved minerals. When these hot waters encounter the cold, low-pressure surface environment, a wide variety of attractive precipitates including rimstone pools, pinnacles, and draperies are often deposited (Plate 14, Top).

If a spring's temperature is noticeably higher than the mean annual temperature in the area where it occurs, it is called a **thermal spring**. Thermal springs may be classified as either hot or warm. Really hot springs with temperatures above 150°C occur where the water is heated by hot igneous rock or magma bodies that have been recently intruded at shallow depths (Plate 14, Bottom). Warm springs, with water usually

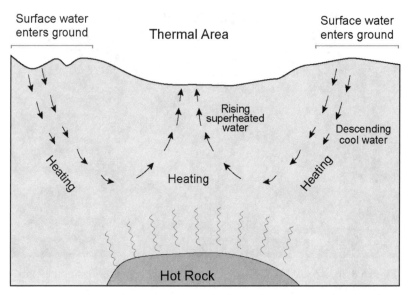

Figure 8.37. Schematic cross-section of a thermal area. Meteoric water from the surface enters permeable ground and circulates to great depth where it is heated to well above the boiling point by hot rock, often a cooling magma chamber. Fractures and faults associated with magma intrusion and associated volcanic activity often provide ready pathways along which the groundwater can circulate [389].

less than 90°C, can also occur where faults and other zones of high permeability allow hot fluids from deep in the crust access to the near-surface environment, such as the thermal springs scattered through the middle Appalachians near the Virginia/West Virginia border (figures 4.17 and 8.38A). Some thermal springs are intermittent or highly variable in flow due to fluctuations in subsurface pressure and heat conditions.

Thermal areas may exhibit a wide variety of hot springs, including various pools, geysers, fumaroles, mud pots, and related phenomena. **Geysers** result when hot groundwater and steam occupy large pore spaces connected by constricted channels. The large pores result from numerous fractures as well as solution by the rising hot waters. Ongoing heating at depth produces superheated groundwater in which temperatures exceed the normal boiling point. This produces expansion of the water and steam (bubbles) begin to form. The expansion forces water to the surface through a trunk conduit (Figure 8.39). As water begins to spill out onto the surface, it reduces the pressure on the very hot underlying water allowing some of that water to begin flashing into steam, pushing more water upward. As water continues to evacuate the system, the rapidly accelerating expansion of water into steam violently forces the overlying water and steam to the surface where it erupts into the air as a fountain (Figure 8.38B). When the force is spent, water runs off or seeps back into the earth and another cycle of gradual heat buildup begins. Some geyser fountains attain heights of nearly 200 feet. If limited water

Figure 8.38. A. Warm Springs, Virginia. On a frosty morning, clouds of steam rise from the warm (98°F) springs along Warm Springs Creek. Figure 4.17 provides a simplified cross-section of the geology that gives rise to these springs. **B.** Daisy Geyser in full eruption, Yellowstone National Park, Wyoming.

is available a soupy suspension of fine rock particles may be produced and exhibited at the surface as a boiling mud pot or mud volcano. Hot steam escaping through openings to the surface forms **fumaroles**. Geologically speaking, geysers and related phenomena are short-lived, delicate features which are easily destroyed by human activities such as exploratory drilling, geothermal energy projects, and groundwater withdrawal.

As noted previously, groundwater has a profound effect on the stability of earth materials. It has been suggested that geothermal heating resulting in an upward movement of groundwater may be an important factor in causing some major landslides, especially in steep volcanic terrains. For example, in July of 1888, the northern flank of Bandai Volcano in Japan suddenly collapsed, killing 461 people. No volcanic or

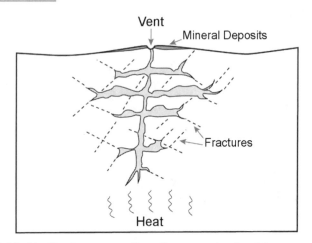

Figure 8.39. Idealized cross-section of a geyser's plumbing system. An eruption cycle begins when the conduits and chambers shown are full of water. The water is heated to well above the boiling point by geothermal heat. With continued heating, the water expands; steam and bubbles form and collect at constrictions and in the upper parts of the chambers. Eventually the thermal forces of expansion exceed the force of the overlying water and water migrates up the central conduit and begins to overflow at the surface. This reduces pressure in the underlying system, inducing further vaporization and expansion which proceeds at a rapidly accelerating pace and climaxes in a violent ejection of water and steam at the surface (an erupting geyser). Surface waters then begin to re-enter the system and the cycle is renewed. Deposition of mineral deposits within the system, earthquakes, or human interventions may cause the cycle to end.

near-surface magmatic activity appeared to be involved. Magma a few kilometers below the surface may have caused the rise of heated groundwater. The resulting increase in fluid pressure probably reduced the stability of the materials underlying the mountain slope, leading to its catastrophic failure. Over 200 large amphitheaters representing similar slope collapses are known, at least some of which may be due primarily to elevated fluid pressures generated by groundwater [355].

Hydrothermal solutions are important in the formation of many major ore deposits, including copper, lead, zinc, gold, and uranium. Over time, vast quantities of elements can be transported as solutes by hot circulating groundwater. Most of the valuable elements are dissolved as the water migrates through various rock formations. When the mineral-laden water encounters conditions which encourage deposition of a certain chemical species, it becomes concentrated in a valuable ore deposit.

Hot subsurface waters, fresh water or brines, may be harnessed to produce **geothermal energy** for heating or electricity generation. Italy, Iceland, and the Geysers Region in northern California are among the areas known for their utilization of geothermal energy. If the water temperatures are above 150°C, it is often feasible to generate electricity. At lower temperatures, the hydrothermal waters can be used for space heating and various industrial processes. Where favorable conditions exist, it is also possible to heat water using excess energy produced at power plants or other energy generating systems, then store the heated water in a convenient aquifer or other subsurface storage unit for later use. Hot dry rock can also be used for energy production but requires that water from an outside source be circulated to retrieve the heat.

Although some problems, including high initial cost, release of hazardous gases, land subsidence, and earthquakes can be associated with geothermal energy production, this is an alternative energy source whose potential is enormous. Unfortunately its potential has been vastly underutilized, but this may be changing with the growing shortage of fossil fuels and the emergence of new low-temperature geothermal technologies [102].

8.14 Water in Deep, High-Pressure Environments

Groundwater studies focus upon the fresh groundwater supplies which people commonly depend upon. This water generally lies within a few hundred meters of the surface where compaction and related geologic processes are less likely to have seriously diminished porosity and permeability. However, groundwater is present in numerous localities at depths of several hundred meters or more. Although conditions at greater depths, 2 kilometers or more below the surface, cannot generally be directly measured, free water can and does exist in such environments, although its overall abundance and importance as a water source remain controversial (Section 13.5.3). Most of this deep groundwater will be brackish or briny, but in favorable environments, significant quantities of fresh water may occur.

Several origins for deep groundwater are possible. Most sediment is deposited in vast quantities in large, subsiding basins in a salt-water environment. As thousands of meters of sediment accumulate over millions of years, compaction occurs and the ever-increasing pressure generated by overlying sediment squeezes most of the pore water out of the underlying sediment. Additional forces such as horizontal compression associated with plate tectonics may also add to the pressure. The water that remains in these abnormally high pressure environments will increase in volume due to expansion — a result of the high temperatures typical of such environments — which further increases hydrostatic pressure. Water in an abnormally high temperature/pressure environment is sometimes referred to as **thermobaric water** [100]. As compaction and confining pressures increase, water continues to be forced from the lower parts of the deposit, assuming permeability is sufficient to allow migration. The general flow direction of this water will be away from areas of maximum pressure, and upward. This pressurized water may accumulate in traps produced by impermeable materials, not unlike petroleum, or continue upward to intermix with meteoric waters (Figure 8.40). If highly pressurized groundwater is encountered by drilling, it may form a gusher, even blowing well casings and equipment high into the air. If unconsolidated sediment mixes with highly pressurized water, upward-migrating masses of fluid sediment (sedimentary intrusions), mud volcanoes, and related phenomena may result.

> **Example: Lusi**
>
> A spectacular example of a **mud volcano** named Lusi first erupted near Sidoarjo in Indonesia in May of 2006. Six years later it was still going strong and had obliterated numerous homes, factories, roads, and rice paddies, displacing at least 40,000 people and killing 15. Lusi's origins are still being debated but it appears that a deep exploratory well penetrated an impermeable rock zone, then encountered highly pressurized

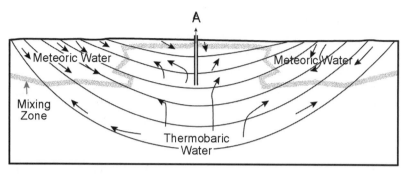

Figure 8.40. Simplified schematic of a deep, active depositional basin. The deep water is hot and under high pressure (thermobaric water) which causes it to migrate toward lower pressure areas, generally upward, where it will eventually mix with meteoric water from the surface. If a well drilled at location A encountered a confined, high-pressure aquifer, a water gusher would be one likely result [100].

water which rushed upward carrying with it vast quantities of overlying muddy sediment. Some believe that it will continue spewing mud for decades and result in extensive subsidence of the ground surface.

Many highly pressurized groundwater areas are located where large masses of sediment have been rapidly deposited in the recent geologic past, such as today's major river deltas. These deposits are often poorly compacted and the presence of pressurized, often saline, water supports a large part of the overlying sediment. Pockets of deep (17 kilometers) high-pressure water trapped beneath impermeable cap rocks in the US Gulf Coast area may have temperatures of 300°C or more. If this water, whether fresh or saline, is removed by pumping, considerable subsidence of the overburden and hence the ground surface, can be anticipated, as has occurred in the Houston area [271].

At depth, free water may be released from hydrous minerals such as amphiboles by pressure and chemical reactions. Subduction of tectonic plates may also carry seawater-bearing rock to depths approaching 100 kilometers (60 miles). The presence of this water can strongly influence geologic activities, including earthquakes, the migration of solid and liquid rock masses, volcanism, chemical reactions, and mass wasting along ocean trenches [328]. The pressure within a trapped fluid opposes the frictional forces between rock masses within the earth, and can destabilize those masses as a result, thus greatly increasing the likelihood of faulting which aids the subduction process and generates deep earthquakes.

Deep water is often unregulated under the assumption that it is isolated from surface water and does not impact "water supplies" as such. As water demands increase and readily accessible sources are depleted, deep groundwater becomes an ever more attractive possibility as a water supply, especially in arid locations. Large-scale pumping and desalinization of deep brackish water is viewed as a viable option in many areas. In New Mexico, for example, billions of acre-feet of brackish water are estimated to lie at depths of 760 meters (2,500 feet) or more in alluvial basins.

When considering large-scale mining of, or injection into, deep groundwater, we should remember one of the basic rules of ecology, as stated by ecologist Barry Commoner, namely that everything is connected to everything else. For example, extraction of deep brackish water, even where separated from overlying fresh water by aquicludes, could yield a number of problems. The pumping will alter pressure distribution in the groundwater and surrounding rock material. Pressure changes could produce fracturing of the aquiclude, opening connections between aquifers. During pumping of the deep water, fresh water may seep into lower brackish aquifers, depleting the freshwater reserves with attendant consequences such as lowering of water tables and drying up of surface water supplies. When pumping is not occurring, and especially when forcibly injecting fluids to the deep subsurface, the tendency would be for brackish water to migrate upward toward fresh water. The wells themselves provide an avenue for potential migration of contaminants. Even when properly installed, well casings and seals deteriorate in time. The alterations of hydrostatic pressure conditions produced by accessing deep waters, or other resources in these high-pressure environments, would be almost immediate, but the negative impacts on freshwater supplies could take many years, or centuries, to become apparent.

Thousands of deep wells have been used to inject liquid wastes deep below the surface under high pressure and have often been linked to increased earthquake activity. A similar situation occurs when large reservoirs, 100 meters or more in depth, are filled. The added weight and increased fluid pressure generated in the subsurface is believed to trigger slippage along subsurface zones of weakness. Please see Section 10.3.7 for additional information on this topic.

Groundwater Chemistry

*It is now generally recognized that the quality of ground-
water is just as important as its quantity.*

— David Keith Todd (1980)

9.1 Isotopes of Hydrogen and Oxygen

Some basic chemistry was introduced in Chapter 1. This chapter
will provide additional information important in the study of groundwater. Water problems during the industrial age have consisted of a double
whammy: increasing demand for fresh water coupled with increasing
contamination of water. The quality of water is every bit as essential as
its quantity. To grasp issues of water quality, some knowledge of water
chemistry has become ever more important for those involved with the
planning, management, and protection of the resource as well as the
general reader. This is a highly complex field and our limited coverage
here is intended only to provide a starting point and a perspective. Some
explanations are necessarily simplified.

Pure water is mostly O-16 and H-1, the common isotopes of oxygen and hydrogen. Minor amounts of O-17, O-18, H-2 (deuterium), and
H-3 (tritium) are also usually present. The relative quantities (ratios) of
certain isotopes provide important information about the origin, age,
and evolution of water. The concentrations of isotopes change during
processes like evaporation, adhesion, condensation, and migration
through different subsurface materials and are sensitive to environmental conditions such as temperature and pressure. For example, a water
molecule containing a heavier oxygen isotope such as O-18 will not
evaporate as readily as normal O-16 — it's more difficult, it requires
more energy — for the heavier molecule to vaporize. This causes the
water to be enriched in O-18 and the vapor to be depleted in O-18. The
evaporation of the heavier molecules will be even more difficult to achieve
as temperatures drop. Hence the ratio of O-18 to O-16 in water can be

used to suggest the origin of a water sample as well as the temperature of the water's previous environment.

Tritium is a short-lived radioisotope with a half-life of 12.4 years. Small amounts of tritium are produced naturally by cosmic ray bombardment in the atmosphere. Due to atomic bomb testing from about 1952-1963, tritium in rainfall around the world increased from ten-fold to over a thousand-fold, depending on location. Hence, when factoring in its natural decay rate, the amount of tritium in groundwater will give some indication as to its time of origin. Tritium has been used mostly to distinguish between water originating before and after the start of nuclear bomb testing. If no tritium is detected in groundwater, that water has presumably been out of contact with the atmosphere since at least 1952.

9.2 Natural Impurities in Groundwater

9.2.1 Introduction

Natural water is almost never completely pure. Recall that water is the universal solvent (Section 1.4.8) and can be expected to contain solutes. Evaporated water consists of pure water molecules, but upon condensation, liquid water evaporated into the atmosphere will immediately begin to scavenge impurities, including the important gases oxygen and carbon dioxide. Rain and snow in inland areas typically contain only around 10 mg/L of dissolved solids, most from pollution or dust particles about which condensation or sublimation of water occurred. Precipitation near oceans or other salt sources can contain 100 mg/L or more of dissolved mineral matter, consisting mostly of ions of sodium, chlorine, magnesium, and sulfate derived from wind-blown particles or sea spray.

Impurities may have either beneficial or harmful impacts upon the environment and human health, depending upon the specific chemicals and their concentrations. Some constituents, such as fluorine, iron, and zinc, can be beneficial at low concentrations but become troublesome at high concentrations. Some broad categories of water impurities are listed in Table 9.1. More detailed information on groundwater pollutants is provided in the next chapter.

9.2.2 Gases and Organic Matter

As soon as meteoric water reaches the ground surface and begins to infiltrate, it will commence to pick up additional solutes from gases in the soil and the minerals the water comes into contact with. The gases dissolved in water have important roles to play. Oxygen in water is

Table 9.1. Selected Water Impurity Categories and Impacts

CATEGORY

IMPACTS

Acidity (low pH from acids)
> Corrosion, release of toxic metals, toxic (especially to young aquatic organisms)

Hardness (Ca and Mg salts)
> Produces scale, interferes with many processes (cleansing, dyeing, etc.)

Metalloids (As, Be)
> Toxic, probable carcinogens

Metals
> Many are toxic (e.g., Pb, Hg, Se, Cd); others (e.g., Mb, I, Zn) are essential nutrients at low concentrations

Nutrients (fertilizers; animal and industrial waste; detergents)
> Eutrophication and depletion of oxygen; nitrates are a major groundwater pollutant in agricultural areas

Organic compounds (huge category including additives, pesticides, pharmaceuticals, solvents)
> Toxic, many carcinogens; cause endocrine disruption and hormonal imbalances in humans and wildlife

Pathogens (mainly protozoa, bacteria, viruses)
> Major causes of diseases, infections

Radionuclides
> Toxic, cancer, birth defects, mutations

Salinity (inorganic salts; total dissolved solids [TDS])
> Renders fresh water unusable for many plants and animals

Turbidity (suspended matter)
> Reduces penetration by light, renders water unusable for many uses (e.g., drinking, industrial processes), may contain pollutants

Sources: [250, 251, 299, 548].

essential for aquatic animal life and carbon dioxide is needed for plants, especially algae. Carbon dioxide creates a weak acid, carbonic acid, in water which greatly increases groundwater's ability to dissolve minerals. The solubility of gases, a high energy state, will increase with decreasing temperatures.

Carbon dioxide and oxygen are the major gases present in groundwater. By far the most abundant naturally occurring organic compounds in water are fulvic acid and humic acid, both derived from the decomposition of plant material. If organic matter has been decaying under oxygen-poor conditions, hydrogen sulfide and methane will often be present. The amount of dissolved gases and organic matter in subsurface water will typically decrease with depth and distance from their sources. Oxygen will be removed from groundwater fairly rapidly. Not only is oxygen highly reactive in general, but microbes quickly consume it during the decomposition of organic matter. It was once thought that microorganisms were rare in groundwater, but that idea has been proven false over the last few decades.

9.2.3 Major Constituents

The natural solutes contained in groundwater can come from almost any substance the water has had contact with, including the air, soil, rock, and organic matter. Generally, most groundwater will contain seven to nine common chemical species — dissolved ions and molecules — from among the following: Ca^{2+}, Mg^{2+}, Na^{1+}, K^{1+}, SO_4^{2-}, HCO_3^{1-}, CO_3^{2-}, Cl^{1-}, H_4SiO_4, N_2 [88, 100]. These are considered **major constituents** of groundwater and are often present at more than 5 mg/L. All are ions except the last two. H_4SiO_4 is often indicated in reports as SiO_2. The bicarbonate and carbonate ions (HCO_3^{1-} and CO_3^{2-}) are reported as **total alkalinity**. Calcium usually has the highest concentration in most fresh water with magnesium often second in abundance. Together, sometimes with Fe^{2+}, they account for water **hardness** (Section 9.3.3).

9.2.4 Minor Constituents

Minor constituents are boron, carbonate, fluoride, iron, oxygen, nitrate, potassium, strontium, bromide, and carbon dioxide [88]. These commonly are present in groundwater at concentrations of 0.01 to 10 mg/L.

9.2.5 Trace Constituents

Trace constituents, generally in concentrations less than 0.01 mg/L, are also normally present in groundwater. Among the more common natural trace contaminants are As, Ti, I, B^{3+}, Fe^{2+}, and NO_3^{1-}. Some, including the heavy metals, can constitute serious health hazards. Many trace pollutants which elicit concern emanate from human operations such as mines or waste disposal sites and rarely travel long distances through groundwater from their source. Natural trace elements such as arsenic and fluoride are important groundwater pollutants in some areas.

9.2.6 Conditions of Equilibrium and Inequilibrium

Nature abhors an imbalance. As noted previously, the many ongoing processes in nature are always attempting to establish a balance, an equilibrium. If a large cube of salt is placed in a glass of pure water, it will begin to dissolve quite rapidly. As the salt content of the water builds up, the rate of solution will decrease until the water is saturated with salt. At saturation, the equilibrium point has been reached and no additional solution of the remaining salt will occur, all else remaining equal. If groundwater is not saturated — is not in equilibrium with — a soluble mineral, it will continue to dissolve that mineral, assuming conditions such as temperature do not change. If the water becomes oversaturated, as by loss of water through evaporation, it will tend to precipitate or deposit that mineral to reach a balance. So it is with all the chemical activities described below. The tendency to achieve balance between the various solutes in water and the surrounding environment are the driving forces behind the chemical reactions in water. In a true equilibrium, no energy is available to alter the quantity or quality of the matter present. But only under relatively long-term, static conditions will an equilibrium be likely to occur in groundwater.

As groundwater moves through the subsurface, it comes into contact with differing materials and conditions, that is, its chemical and physical environment changes. The speed at which chemical reactions occur can vary from seconds to millions of years. Compared to the very slow rate of most groundwater flow, the majority of important chemical reactions are relatively fast. Groundwater is often in a partial equilibrium state. Certain solutes will have had time to achieve equilibrium with the current environment, but others will be somewhat out of equilibrium. Hence the water quality slowly changes through time via such processes as solution, ion exchange, mineral precipitation, oxidation, and reduction. Dissolved mineral constituents in groundwater generally increase with the length of the flow path and the subsurface **residence time**, the time the water has been in contact with rock materials. In general, water from a distant recharge area can be expected to contain more impurities than water from a local recharge area. Very generally, as rainwater enters the soil and migrates ever greater distances through the subsurface, the following trends are often observed. Carbon dioxide from decaying organic matter is added in the soil zone, along with impurities such as nitrates, phosphates, and potassium which are generally present in agricultural areas. In the lower vadose zone, calcium and magnesium carbonates undergo solution into bicarbonates. Once in the phreatic zone, bacterial action tends to reduce the amount of oxygen present — the water becomes increasingly anoxic (low in oxygen). In deeper groundwater, iron and manganese enter into solution and may later be deposited as sulphide precipitates. If clays are encountered, calcium ions tend to be replaced by sodium ions. At even greater depths, saline water is often encountered and significant groundwater migration may cease [185].

9.3 Important Chemical Reactions and Processes

9.3.1 Introduction

A wide variety of physical, chemical, and biological processes are responsible for transferring mass (water, particles, ions, molecules, and so forth) in the subsurface environment. The chemical processes involved in groundwater's role in moving and altering materials are often complex and require considerable background in chemistry.

The influencing factors encompass both long-term, large-scale considerations (a regional overview) as well as the more immediate, local considerations (site-specific factors). The regional overview may include the source or recharge area of the water, the materials the water has flowed through, flow rates, flow paths, and mixing with other water sources and contaminants. The site-specific concerns include local land uses, topography, mineralogy, flow rates and directions, and nearby areas of recharge and discharge.

The processes listed below are by no means exclusive of each other. Many processes and reactions occur together and simultaneously — for example, dissolution can produce acids which may trigger an oxidation reaction which may be accompanied by still other processes. Our purpose here is to provide an overview of the most important processes along with a few prime examples.

9.3.2 Dissolution and Exsolution

A. Influences on Solubility

Dissolution and exsolution basically refer to solution and precipitation, and were introduced in Chapter 1. Much of the chemical makeup of groundwater can be attributed to the dissolution of minerals as the water migrates through the subsurface. The exchange of gases in the vadose zone is an important first step in determining the chemistry of the groundwater below. In particular, carbon dioxide dissolved in water produces carbonic acid, a mild acid, which greatly increases water's ability to mobilize and transport mineral matter. Oxygen, which water dissolves both in and above the vadose zone, will also be important in determining chemical reactions in shallow groundwater.

As groundwater migrates through different subsurface lithologies, the environmental and equilibrium conditions vary. This can cause the water to dissolve a mineral in one location and precipitate it in another, or trade one group of ions for another. Over time, enormous quantities of matter have been transported by groundwater solution and precipitation with great impacts upon nearly all natural phenomena from soil and rock formation to climate. In general, the deeper the groundwater and the longer it has been in the subsurface, the more mineral matter it will contain. Another influence is groundwater temperature, which increases as one goes deeper by an average of roughly 0.6°C/30.5 m or 1°F/100 ft. The higher temperature allows deeper water to hold more solute.

Rock and regolith are made up of minerals, which are basically inorganic chemicals formed from positively and negatively charged ions. When groundwater encounters a mineral, its dipolar water molecules are attracted to the charged parts of the mineral molecules where they can neutralize the forces bonding the mineral ions together, releasing the ions from the solid mineral. As noted previously, the process of dissolution will continue until the water is saturated. However, saturation is often not attained because groundwater is typically moving, thus being constantly refreshed. Equilibrium is most likely to be attained if the water moves very slowly and the minerals present are quite soluble, such as calcite (limestone) or halite (rock salt).

The solubility of materials varies greatly. Some 95% by volume of the common crustal minerals are silicates and these are only slightly soluble in water. The common carbonate minerals, limestone and dolomite, are far more soluble and hence their ions (Ca^{2+}, Mg^{2+}, CO_3^{2-}) are frequently present in groundwater. For organic chemicals, the larger the molecules, the less soluble they tend to be. Solubility also varies significantly depending upon the placement of a single atom on a complex organic molecule which may have dozens or hundreds of atoms. Chemical environment, temperature, and pressure all affect solubility.

B. Electrical Conductance and TDS

Pure water has very low electrical conductance, but because ions carry electric charges, the presence of ions increases the amount of electric current that can pass through the water. Thus, the higher the **specific electrical conductance** or **conductivity**, the greater the number of ions present and the higher the mineral content of the water. Electrical conductance of water is usually measured in units called siemens (S).

The ability of water to conduct an electrical current can be used to estimate the amount of dissolved mineral matter the water contains. This quantity is often called **total dissolved solids (TDS)**. Conductivity of a water sample can be conveniently measured in the field with a conductivity (or resistivity) meter. To determine TDS (in mg/L) in most groundwater, the conductivity value in microsiemens (μS) at 25°C is multiplied by a factor ranging from roughly 0.5 (acidic waters) to 0.8 (saline waters). The factor varies depending on the types of ions present but averages around 0.65 for most groundwater [103, 423]. Thus, the TDS of water with a conductance of 1,000 μS is approximately 650 mg/L (1,000 × 0.65). Note, however, that not everyone defines a solution the same way. Some groups, such as the American Public Health Association, consider anything which passes through a 0.45 micrometer (μm) pore diameter filter to be a "dissolved" substance.

As implied above, some ions conduct electricity better than others, and not all the mineral matter in water is ionized. Hence, conductivity provides only an estimate of the TDS. A more accurate determination can be made in the laboratory by completely evaporating a sample of water and weighing the residue which remains.

C. Exsolution

Exsolution is the reverse of dissolution. It often occurs where near-surface water undergoes evaporation resulting in the deposition of salts, especially in arid and semiarid climates. A repetitious cycle of dissolution and precipitation of gypsum ($CaSO_4 \cdot 2H_2O$) is common in many arid and semiarid regions such as the Great Plains of the US and Canada. Annual evaporation exceeds precipitation in such areas and most water that infiltrates the soil will evaporate leaving behind a precipitate of gypsum. During most years, gypsum will accumulate in the soil, but during exceptionally wet events, water heavily laden with dissolved gypsum ($Ca^{2+} + SO_4^{2-}$) can migrate downward and enter the groundwater [100].

When groundwater approaches the surface, water will also be lost by evaporation. An important example is salinization of soils caused by evaporation of irrigation water (Section 8.3.2). Natural saline seeps are common in many parts of the world (Plate 11, Bottom). Infiltration of irrigation water often causes the underlying water table to rise. Once again, the result is evaporation, deposition of dissolved mineral matter, and a probable salinization problem.

Exsolution from groundwater or from infiltrating water in the vadose zone is an important process in the formation of sedimentary rocks and indurated soil horizons, called **duricrusts**, such as caliche (Figure 8.4). **Caliche** is one of several terms — others include calcrete, hardpan, and, in India, *kandar* — for hard cemented sediment and soil. The cementing agent is often calcium carbonate (limestone), but gypsum, nitrates, sulfates, and other materials can also form caliche. Due to higher rates of evaporation, the most extensive deposits, often over a meter thick, will be found in arid and semiarid regions such as the Edwards Plateau of Texas.

9.3.3 Acid-Base Reactions

Acid-base reactions are chemical changes involving a transfer of protons (hydrogen ions, H+). Acids are substances which tend to lose protons and bases tend to gain protons (and produce hydroxide ions; Section 1.4.10). The strength of an acid or base depends upon the extent to which the protons are lost or gained.

In groundwater recharge areas, water dissolves carbon dioxide and nitrogen oxides, mostly from the air in the pore spaces of organic soils. The mildly acidic groundwater which results is more chemically active than pure water, especially at picking up calcium and bicarbonate ions from the solution of common minerals such as feldspar and calcite. As the water migrates through the subsurface, it dissolves additional mineral matter and tends to become less acidic. The pH of most groundwater will vary from about 6 to 8.5 with more acidic conditions generally nearer the surface or sources of contamination, whether natural or man-made, and more basic conditions in areas with abundant limestone or dolomite. Stronger acidity (pH less than 6) in groundwater usually indicates pollution. Even slightly acidic water can threaten aquatic life, lead to significant corrosion of metal pipes, and release harmful metals into drinking water.

Alkaline (high pH) water results mainly from the metal ions calcium and magnesium, which are usually produced by carbonation, a reaction with carbonic acid in water. The amount of calcium and magnesium ions in water is commonly expressed as **hardness**. Areas underlain by limestone and dolomite are likely to have hard water. Hard water tends to build up deposits (scale) on materials with which it is in contact (the water faucet, pipes, glasses, and others), especially where evaporation forces some of the mineral matter to precipitate out. Hard water also reacts with soap to form insoluble compounds — soap scum, another precipitate — which inhibit the sudsing action and make washing difficult. Definitions of hard and soft vary. One classification defines "soft" water as containing 0 to 75 mg/L $CaCO_3$ while water containing over 300 mg/L $CaCO_3$ is "very hard." Another considers anything over 60 mg/L $CaCO_3$ to be "hard" [198].

The pH of water is easily determined with pH meters and special indicators, including fluids or papers which turn color to indicate the pH.

9.3.4 Reduction/Oxidation

Oxidation is often defined as a chemical reaction in which oxygen is a reactant — for example, when iron combines with oxygen to form iron oxide (rust). Oxygen has a strong affinity for electrons to complete its outer shell. Given half a chance, oxygen will grab an available electron; that is, it is an **electron acceptor**. The iron (in iron oxide) or hydrogen (in water) tend to lose their electrons to the oxygen and are called **electron donors** which have been "oxidized" by the **oxidant** (oxygen). Chemists consider any chemical which accepts electrons to be an oxidant and the process of removing electrons from a molecule or ion is defined as **oxidation**.

Consider an iron ion which has lost two electrons leaving it with a charge of +2 (Fe^{2+}). If Fe^{2+} loses an additional electron, it will become "oxidized" to an Fe^{3+} ion. The chemical equation for this simple change in ionic state is:

$$Fe^{2+} \rightarrow Fe^{3+} + e^- \qquad \text{(Equation 9.1)}$$

This oxidation reaction, as written here, is often called a "half-reaction" because it only shows what is happening to the iron. The superscripts ($^{2+}$, $^{3+}$, $^-$) represent the ions' charges and are often called "oxidation numbers." Note that the charges on both sides of the equation balance.

The addition of electrons to a molecule or ion is **reduction**. The reverse of the above reaction,

$$Fe^{3+} + e^- \rightarrow Fe^{2+} \qquad \text{(Equation 9.2)}$$

is reduction; the iron has gained an electron, or been "reduced." Remember that most chemical reactions are reversible, depending upon the chemical environment. Reduction and oxidation always occur in tandem; that is, the reduction of one chemical species such as a molecule or ion, is accompanied by the oxidation of another. As such, they are often called **redox** reactions. A simple example is the reaction between sodium metal and chlorine gas:

$$2Na + Cl_2 \rightarrow 2NaCl \qquad \text{(Equation 9.3)}$$

In this reaction, each uncharged atom of sodium loses an electron to the chlorine to form sodium chloride salt. If we write this as two half reactions we can more clearly see the transfer of electrons:

$$2Na \rightarrow 2Na^+ + 2e^- \qquad \text{(Equation 9.4)}$$
(sodium is oxidized; loses two electrons)

$$Cl^2 + 2e^- \rightarrow 2Cl^- \qquad \text{(Equation 9.5)}$$
(chlorine is reduced; gains two electrons)

Any chemical able to donate electrons to another is often called a **reducing agent**, a chemical that accepts electrons is an **oxidizing agent**. Note that the reducing agent is itself oxidized during the reaction, and vice versa.

The elements in the upper right of the periodic table (Table 1.2) have the greatest tendency to gain electrons and are strong oxidizing agents. Elements in the lower left exhibit the greatest tendency to lose electrons and are strong reducing agents. Atoms which have little or no tendency to transfer (gain or lose) electrons are more stable (less active chemically) and will often be found in nature a pure elements.

Oxidation is important in the breakdown (biodegradation) of many organic compounds. A simplified equation for this reaction is:

$$CH_2O + O_2 \rightarrow CO_2 + H_2O \qquad \text{(Equation 9.6)}$$

Here, the biomass (CH_2O) is oxidized and the O_2 is reduced during the reaction.

Another consequential oxidation reaction occurs when common sulfide minerals such as pyrite (FeS_2) are present. Pyrite is typically present in coal. When exposed to oxygen, as during the mining and combustion of coal, the sulfur is oxidized to form the sulfate ion, $(SO_4)^{-2}$. This produces a strong acid, sulfuric acid, in water and is the source of two very serious problems, **acid fallout** from the use of coal as a fuel and **acid mine drainage** from mining areas (Section 10.3.8). Acidic groundwater frequently pollutes groundwater supplies in coal mining areas such as Appalachia where coal beds often serve as aquifers. Acid fallout alters soil and groundwater chemistry over large areas affected by coal-burning power plants.

Reduction-oxidation reactions involve electron transfers and acid-base reactions involve hydrogen ion (proton) transfers. Just as pH defines the proton presence and activity, a similar value, **pE**, is used to define electron activity in a solution. The higher the electron activity in an aqueous solution, the more the chemicals that are present, including water itself, will tend to accept electrons and be reduced. Hence the common term, **reducing environment**. When the electron activity is low, conditions represent an **oxidizing environment** — picture, for example, an abundance of electron-grabbers like oxygen and chlorine wiping out free-roaming electrons.

As with pH, pE is technically defined as the negative log of electron activity. And as with pH, where lower values mean higher proton activity, the lower the values on the pE scale, the higher the electron activity. The actual pE values can be calculated by measuring the electron transfer potential (EP) in volts, basically a measure of the force which produces an electric current, a flow of electrons. This can be done by measuring the current between two electrodes placed in a solution, then converting this value to pE numbers by the equation $pE = EP/0.0591$. The pE values range from a low of about — 6 (a very electron-rich, highly reduced environment) to a high of about 13 (an electron-poor, highly oxidized environment). Comparing pH and pE is useful in determining the conditions under which different chemicals will be stable in a water solution. For example, at high pH and pE many metals exist as ions, but at lower values, they are likely to form insoluble compounds and precipitate out of the solution. Thus, in the reducing environment of deeper groundwater where sulfates are reduced to sulfides, metals combine with the sulfide ions to produce insoluble metal sulfides.

This process removes many hazardous metals from groundwater and forms important ore deposits.

Groundwater that has been in the subsurface for some time typically provides a reducing environment because the water's oxygen, which was dissolved in the water in the near-surface environment, has been used up during chemical reactions as the water migrated through regolith and rock. This often results in conditions which are alkaline, anoxic (low oxygen), and low pE where abundant free electrons exist since few oxidizing agents are present to take them up. A common example is groundwater containing high levels of iron. In many places the groundwater used in homes contains many Fe^{2+} ions in solution. This results in unsightly orange stains in sinks and on clothes. This stain is a precipitate which forms when the iron ions undergo oxidation to form iron hydroxide:

$$Fe^{2+} + 3H_2O \rightarrow Fe(OH)_3 + 3H^+ + e^- \quad \text{(Equation 9.7)}$$

As in Equation 9.1 above, the iron has lost an electron and is oxidized from Fe^{2+} to Fe^{3+}. The Fe^{3+} combined with hydroxide ions from water, leaving behind three hydrogen ions and forming the insoluble precipitate, $Fe(OH)_3$. This occurred because the groundwater was pumped to the surface where an oxidizing environment existed, causing the Fe^{2+} ion to lose an additional electron to the oxygen in the hydroxide ion to become Fe^{3+}. Because this oxidized iron now exists as part of the iron hydroxide molecule — which precipitates out of solution — it is not written as Fe^{3+} in the equation.

Redox conditions will change as groundwater flows through different subsurface environments. These conditions will have significant impacts upon many substances in the water including carbon-containing gases, metal ions, and solids containing sulfur or metals. For example, where organic matter is present, its oxidization generates carbon dioxide which influences acidity and yields carbonate or bicarbonate ions.

Most redox reactions are mediated by microorganisms. The microorganisms, usually bacteria, act as catalysts which speed up what would otherwise be a very slow reaction rate. A **catalyst** is any substance which alters the rate of a chemical reaction. Microorganisms are ubiquitous in the subsurface where they are usually found in cracks and attached to the surfaces of mineral grains. The tiny organisms utilize the energy emitted during reactions. Redox reactions are an important means of cleaning up organic contaminants in groundwater and considerable effort has been expended to find microscopic "bugs" which will accelerate the degradation of pollutants.

9.3.5 Hydrolysis and Hydration

A reaction, such as that shown in equation Equation 9.7 above, in which water is a reactant and its molecules are broken apart, is called **hydrolysis**. Hydrolysis plays a significant role in many reactions, including the chemical breakdown of silicate minerals, the biodegradation of organic matter in water, and many other organic reactions, including metabolic processes in our bodies.

Don't confuse hydrolysis with **hydration**, which refers to the addition of complete water molecules to a substance. For example, SiO_2 is silica (the mineral quartz); when quartz gets hydrated, it becomes opal and has the formula $SiO_2(H_2O)_n$. The n subscript means that the number of water molecules present can vary. Adding water to molecules typically leads to expansion of the material and its loss causes shrinkage. Shrink-and-swell cycles, especially in clays, greatly accelerate the deterioration of many materials, and are responsible for billions of dollars in damage annually to roads, buildings, and other structures.

9.3.6 Complexation Reactions

Many elements and simple ions in water will bond with other chemicals, including water molecules, hydroxide ions, and organic species. This bonding is important because it can greatly impact the mobility, fate, and even the toxicity of many elements. For example, it will influence how easily an element can be dissolved and migrate through groundwater, how readily it can be incorporated into a sediment or the tissue of an organism, and how toxic it will be in a living organism. In chemistry, a **complex** is a compound or ion that exists in combination with one or more other ions or molecules. **Complexation** simply refers to the process of forming these complex chemicals. The most important group of complexation agents in nature are the humic substances formed during the decomposition of vegetation. These occur in shallow groundwater but are far more abundant in surface waters.

A complex usually refers to species containing metals which have bonded with one or more other ions or molecules. The **heavy metals** are especially perilous to human health. For example, a cadmium ion (Cd^{2+}) may combine with one or more cyanide ions (CN^-) to form complexes such as $CdCN^+$, $Cd(CN)_2$, or $Cd(CN)_3^-$. Lead is very insoluble in soil but if it "complexes" with chlorine, which might come from the overuse of road salt, it forms a highly soluble and mobile lead chloride complex ($PbCl_4^{-2}$). One of the most notorious examples involves mercury. Complexation of mercury is produced when the actions of microorganisms combine it with methane to yield a hazardous methylmercury complex. Cadmium, lead, and mercury are all very dangerous heavy metals and complexation helps explain how they migrate and spread through aqueous environments.

A special type of complex involves **chelating agents** which can bond with metals at more than one place on the ion; the process is called **chelation**. The resulting chelates tend to be quite stable and are important in providing necessary minerals to organisms. For example, the iron and oxygen needed by our bodies and which make our blood red are carried by a chelate called hemoglobin. Another critically important chelate, this one containing the metal magnesium, is chlorophyll, which enables photosynthesis to occur in green plants. Chelating agents can be used to remove toxic metals from wastes or from the human body.

9.3.7 Adsorption and Desorption

Some chemical reactions in groundwater occur entirely in the liquid phase. Most, however, will involve interactions with gases, solids, and organisms. Many important changes occur on the surfaces of solids the water comes into contact with. **Adsorption** is the adhesion of a substance to a solid surface; the material doing the adsorption is the **adsorbent**. The reverse process, which occurs when a substance (ion, molecule, or tiny particle) leaves the surface of the adsorbent, is called **desorption**. Some books use the term **sorption** to refer to either process.

Some molecules strongly resist water and are called **hydrophobic** (water-hating). These substances will tend to seek surfaces to cling to or will precipitate from an aqueous state. The term **partitioning** refers to the tendency of a chemical to attach to, or "sorb," a solid. Partitioning is very useful in determining how readily a given chemical will be leached from a site or adsorbed by the material the groundwater flows through [422]. Locating chemical species which will encourage hydrophobic behavior or adsorption is an important approach for **attenuating** (reducing) hazardous contaminants in water, as in seepage from landfills and nuclear waste sites.

Clays are especially effective at adsorbing a variety of contaminants from subsurface waters. Clays consist of tiny plates which have a very large surface area to which ions can adhere. More about clays in the next section.

9.3.8 Ion Exchange

The term **ion exchange** generally refers to the displacement or replacement of a cation or anion from the surface of a solid. This is especially important in clays, which often pick up a net negative charge by ion replacement. Clays adsorb cations more readily than anions. Silicon and aluminum ions in clays can be replaced by metal ions of similar size but lesser charge. The resulting negative charge tends to attract positive cations which accumulate on the surfaces of clay layers. These cations can then be exchanged with other cations in water. The quantity of exchangeable cations per 100 grams of dry clay is called the **cation-exchange capacity**. In general, cations of higher valency (oxidation number) will replace those of lower valency in or on solids encountered by groundwater [250, 423].

Due to their cation-exchange capacity, clays can have considerable influence on the chemistry of groundwater. For example, as groundwater comes into contact with clay minerals in the subsurface, it tends to pick up sodium ions in exchange for calcium and magnesium ions — that is, the calcium and magnesium replace sodium in the clay, releasing sodium ions to the water. During this process, calcite or dolomite are precipitated out, forming the cement which often binds sediment grains together and fills in fractures and other voids in solid rock. Another result is that in many discharge areas, sodium and chloride ions will be common. This natural "softening" of groundwater is the most important cation exchange reaction.

Example: The Atlantic Coastal Plain

The Atlantic Coastal Plain aquifers (Figure 8.13) provide an excellent example of ion exchange. In the recharge areas, the water typically contains a moderate amount of calcium and bicarbonate ions. As the groundwater migrates eastward through the sandy aquifers, it dissolves increasing amounts of sodium, chlorine, and bicarbonate from the sediment it passes through [70]. Calcium ions (Ca^{2+}) have a stronger charge and therefore one calcium ion tends to replace two sodium ions (Na^+) on the surface of clay minerals. Hence the water becomes depleted in calcium and enriched in sodium as it moves along. As a result, the downgradient parts of the Coastal Plain aquifers provide rather flat-tasting water containing high sodium concentrations. A liter of groundwater in downgradient

---

locations such as Charleston, South Carolina, may contain 500 mg/L or more of sodium which makes for a significant addition to the maximum daily sodium intake of 3,300 mg recommended by the USDA. The sodium makes the water very soft, and this water is suspected of contributing to hypertension and higher incidences of heart disease in people drinking it.

Deep groundwater is likely to be old, up to a few tens of thousands of years old, and rich in dissolved constituents. Bicarbonate-rich waters from near the surface are often transformed to sulfate-rich waters and then to highly saline brines as groundwater circulates deeper into the earth. The deep groundwater often loses sulfate ions in exchange for chlorine ions, resulting in the precipitation of sulfide minerals. The water remaining will often form a brine and be hot due to geothermal heating. The formation of brines is aided by the presence of impermeable, clay-rich rock which impedes the passage of dissolved ions, helping to produce the brines. Perhaps half of all groundwater is both deep and saline [268].

As with all chemical processes, the actual ions gained or lost by groundwater will depend upon such factors as the minerals present in rock and soil, flow time and velocity, mixing of waters, and the subsurface chemical environment.

9.3.9 Mixing

Mixing refers to the interaction of waters, and other liquids, of differing chemical content. This is an ongoing process resulting from groundwater's constant recharge, migration, and discharge. As water percolates through subsurface formations, it undergoes constant chemical evolution in response to the changing conditions it encounters. The changes are usually gradual and subtle, but may be more dramatic if environmental conditions change suddenly, as during the subsurface injection of wastes, oil drilling, and geologic events such as floods or earthquakes. Examples of special concern include the invasion of fresh water by contaminated leachate from surface pollution sources and the mixing of fresh water with salt water from deep below the surface or from seawater (sections 8.9 and 10.4.2D).

When differing subsurface waters are brought together, a zone of mixing produced by mechanical dispersion and diffusion will be generated between the two water types. The mixing zone may be fairly uniform or highly irregular, especially where major differences in permeability exist.

Immiscible liquids — liquids which do not form homogeneous mixtures with water, such as petroleum products and other nonaqueous phase liquids (Section 10.4.3) — often will form tiny droplets which can migrate along with groundwater.

9.3.10 Particle Transport

Another way in which groundwater movement transfers matter from place to place is by transporting small particles. The particles include colloids, exceptionally large molecules (such as those of humic substances), bacteria, viruses, and mineral fragments. The particles carried by subsurface waters in the vadose and phreatic zones are important because they aid in the formation of soils and certain ore deposits. The particles themselves may be major pollutants or may have major pollutants attached to them [100].

9.3.11 Volatization

Volatization is the tendency of a substance to change into a vapor. This process is especially important when dealing with organic pollutants in or near the vadose zone. For example, fuels such as gasoline frequently contaminate soils and groundwater. The vapors from such volatile materials can be used to indicate the presence of pollution. They can also be extremely dangerous. Petroleum products are less dense than water. If a large petroleum spill reaches the water table, a substantial amount of the fuel will float atop the groundwater and migrate downslope. Fumes from the floating fuel, called "free product," can enter buildings where they create a health threat and an explosion hazard.

Soils polluted with volatile materials such as gasoline can be remediated by aerating them on the surface or forcing air through the subsurface soils. When sampling volatile pollutants dissolved in water, the samples need to be placed in sealed vials with no air space to prevent vaporization from the water.

9.3.12 Isotopic Processes

Radioactive elements undergo constant change or decay as their nuclei trend toward a more stable state. Because the decay rate is unique and unchanging, they act like natural timepieces of the environment. Radioisotopes are everywhere, including in groundwater where they can represent anything from a health threat to an elegant method for learning about the age and history of our planet and its resources. Water can be age-dated by using such isotopes as H-3, C-14, Si-32, and Co-36. By measuring and comparing tiny quantities of certain isotopes we can distinguish between water originating over land, over the sea, and in seawater, or even the latitude from which the water came. This is possible in part because the mass of the isotopes affects such behaviors as the rates at which they will be precipitated from the atmosphere or transferred between groundwater and minerals, and the temperatures at which they become incorporated into sediments or ice. Radioisotopes are very useful in tracing the movement of water through the ground and determining the groundwater's previous history. Due to the nature of radioactivity, some radioactive elements, such as radon, can also be serious pollutants (Section 10.4.11).

10

Groundwater Pollution

Filthy water cannot be washed.

— West African proverb

10.1 Historical Perspectives

Humans are blessed with some remarkable qualities, among them are a capacity for intelligence, ingenuity, and persistence. In spite of this, we can also be stupifyingly foolish. For striking examples of both, we need look no further than our long and ongoing struggle to provide water for our needs. Most people know enough not to ingest foul-smelling water, rotten food, excrement, and other unpleasant things. Yet, down through thousands of years of human history, people have dumped such unpleasant things into their water supplies, then proceeded to drink the water, become ill, and wonder what happened. Often the "evil" was blamed on something supernatural, especially if groundwater was involved. Even today, close to 90% of the wastewater of developing nations is discharged directly into local waterways, often the same water impoverished people use for washing, drinking, and cooking. Is it any wonder that water-borne diseases take the lives of millions every year?

During the Dark Ages, the major contaminant, at least in European nations, was human waste generated by the communities themselves. Although it had long been recognized in Islamic cultures, it wasn't until the mid-1800s that human illnesses and death were widely linked to the wastes which fouled the rivers in most of Europe. This belated awakening led to the development of "sanitary science" in England and elsewhere. By the end of the nineteenth century it was apparent that reducing exposure to sewage also reduced illness and death in the general population [256].

With the explosion of industry and the generation of thousands of new synthetic chemicals in the twentieth century, the pollution of water increased exponentially. As earlier folks did with their human and household wastes, industry initially discarded its wastes into the nearest

351

convenient hole or stream with little thought as to what would then happen to it, or to the water into which it was discharged. After all, the primary concern of most industries was, and is, to survive and thrive in the marketplace, not the local stream habitat or hydrogeology. Two world wars, "Cold War" competition, and many other conflicts and priorities added to the rush to grow, produce, and develop in the US and around the world. Governments, military and defense facilities, chemical factories, petroleum companies, agricultural interests — all had more pressing concerns than water pollution. Wastes were to be gotten rid of in the fastest, easiest, cheapest way possible. Raw wastes of all kinds were placed in unlined seepage ponds, forced down wells, and discharged into streams and lakes.

When the magnitude of the problems became too obvious to ignore, governments began to enact laws to prevent and correct pollution problems. An important step in promoting awareness of the importance of clean water and human impacts on the hydrologic cycle was the UN-sponsored International Hydrologic Decade (1965-1974). In the US, the problems began to be addressed by a series of important federal laws, including the National Environmental Policy Act of 1969, the Federal Water Pollution Control Act of 1972, the Safe Drinking Water Act of 1974, the Resource Conservation and Recovery Act of 1976, the Clean Water Act Amendments of 1977, the Comprehensive Environmental Response, Compensation, and Liability Act of 1980 (CERCLA), the Hazardous and Solid Waste Amendments of 1984, and the Superfund Amendments and Reauthorization Act of 1986. Most other nations, developed and developing, have enacted laws, codes, rules, and related instruments similar to those noted above in efforts to protect their water resources. Great Britain passed its Control of Pollution Act in 1974. Today's European Union summarized its policies in the Blueprint to Safeguard Europe's Water Resources. Like most efforts, the Blueprint aims to preserve water quality and quantity and also ensure economic prosperity. It is supported by the European Innovation Partnership on Water, which was launched in May of 2012. China's 1979 Environmental Protection Law is similar to corresponding US laws but, as in many developing nations, the regulations have had limited impact due to lack of enforcement and the pace of industrialization. Section 12.4.2 provides additional information on water laws, many of which include pollution controls.

By the mid-1980s, sophisticated waste isolation and treatment technologies were being developed. Meanwhile, the UN sponsored the International Drinking Water Supply and Sanitation Decade from 1981-1990, which led to a large, albeit far from adequate, effort to bring safe drinking water and sanitation services to those lacking it [256]. At its close, some 1.8 billion humans still were without access to sanitation and 1.3 billion lacked access to clean water, a reflection of the magnitude of the problem and the difficulties of finding workable solutions for a vast population that continues to expand. As of 2009, an estimated 2.5 billion humans, two in every five, lacked proper sanitation and some 900 million lacked clean water. The UN Environment Program notes that more than half of the people occupying the world's hospital beds are suffering from water-related illnesses. This in spite of thousands of regulations, projects, and related efforts around the world which have been aimed at alleviating these sad conditions. In many areas, the greatest need is for some simple, reliable, and affordable tools such as equipment, tests, and techniques which local inhabitants can use to better inform and protect themselves.

Unfortunately, most regulations focus on restricting pollution and waste disposal at the surface and pay little heed to groundwater. This has tended to encourage subsurface waste disposal, further jeopardizing groundwater. Groundwater will be increasingly sought as a major water supply, and that will require improved protections, more hydrogeological expertise, and better funding to access, manage, and protect the resource. As of this writing, most governments are facing serious financial difficulties and support for important efforts, ranging from research projects to regulatory reform and enforcement to aid for the needy, is declining.

Prior to the mid-1970s, little to no regulation existed relating to the disposal of hazardous wastes into the ground. It was generally assumed that the "earth" had an almost unlimited capacity to absorb and purify wastes. Subsurface wastes would not travel far, and if they did, the water carrying them would soon be purified as it seeped through soil and rock. Earth materials are indeed an effective filter and help to remove contaminants, including microorganisms and organic particles, from water. Additional factors such as chemical reactions and bacteria may also aid the purification of water. Bacteria can metabolize many common dissolved pollutants, often converting carbon and nitrogen compounds into harmless carbon dioxide and nitrogen gas. However, purification capacities and rates are limited and easily exceeded. Thousands of communities have had to abandon once-pristine groundwater supplies because the assimilative capacity of the groundwater system was overloaded with impurities.

Like Humpty Dumpty, basically an example of the Second Law of Thermodynamics, groundwater cannot be easily returned to its original state once excess quantities of pollutants have made their way into the subsurface. Decades of ignorance and neglect, and unknown thousands of waste disposal sites constitute a large obstacle to overcome. Groundwater cleanup costs can be enormous and, even with the best current technology, some sites will require many centuries before the water will be restored to its original quality.

Corrective actions such as cleanup or containment of contaminated groundwater, where feasible, often require long periods of time and are expensive: one estimate is a minimum of $1 trillion to address the worst sites in the US over the next 30 years. Three basic approaches to corrective action are to (1) contain or isolate the contaminants, (2) remove the contaminants, and (3) treat the contaminants *in situ* (in place).

Most damage done to aquifers is irreversible except over a very long time span. As the International Association of Hydrogeologists puts it, "Prevention is the only credible strategy." Prevention of groundwater contamination — and other major environmental threats — will require a profound change from the current resource-depleting, fossil fuel- and synthetic chemical-dominated global economy to one based on renewable energy, efficiency, and a concern for the rights and lives of all people and the environment that supports them. While terrorist attacks generate far more publicity and fear, persistent environmental, resource, and social deterioration, and the unrest and conflict they generate, represent far greater threats to the future of humanity.

10.2 Overview

The air and water grow heavier with the debris of our spectacular civilization.

— Lyndon Baines Johnson

The terms "pollution" and "contamination" are inconsistently used in both popular and scientific publications. Water **pollution** refers to any water quality change that produces a harmful impact upon lifeforms or has negative impacts on water use. Water **contamination**, on the other hand, may refer to any substances not generally expected, or to impurities in general. In other words, pollutants are harmful whereas contaminants may or may not be harmful. Pollutants may consist of specific chemicals (organic or inorganic), biological entities (such as disease-producing organisms), or other physical phenomena (such as heat or sediment). Pollutants may be directly toxic, toxic only beyond a certain level, or completely nontoxic. Nontoxic pollutants include normally harmless materials which can degrade water quality under some conditions, such as the presence of too much sediment or organic matter in the water.

Pathogens in water cause more than two million human deaths each year, most of them children less than five years of age living in poor developing nations. Even in the US, some 20 million humans are made ill each year from waterborne organisms. Despite the magnitude of these **biological pollutants**, we do have the ability, if not the will, to provide adequate sanitation and prevent all this suffering and death.

In contrast, the overall impacts of **chemical pollutants** are poorly understood, but may well be as great or greater than the biological contaminants. A chemical water pollutant can be thought of as an impurity which is present in sufficient quantity to produce degradation of an environment or cause negative effects on organisms, including humans. Evaluating chemical pollution, once it has been recognized, involves two major steps: (1) determining the extent of, and exposure to, the pollutants; and (2) evaluating the behavior and impacts of the pollutants in the environment — be that a human body or a lake. One commonly used index of toxicity is **LD50**: lethal dose 50. This is the amount of a poison which will cause death in 50% of a group of organisms. Already we can see that deciding what should be considered a pollutant can be a tricky, complicated, and controversial undertaking [349].

Now consider this. Well over 100,000 registered chemicals are in use, and tens of thousands of those are in wide daily use around much of the world. More than 300 million tons of synthetic compounds enter the world's freshwater supply each year from industrial and consumer wastes, along with more millions of tons of pesticides, fertilizers, medicines, solvents, manure, salts, acids, oils, radioactive wastes, and other potentially hazardous materials. These pollutants come from millions of sites around the world, among which are industrial plants, individual homes, landfills, pipelines, agricultural activities, vehicles and roadways, storage tanks, mining operations, toxic waste disposal sites, smokestacks, wells, and natural sources. Keeping track of all this and understanding the long-term impacts and interactions is an impossible task. Most countries attempt to identify and place limits on the pollutants that appear most commonly in waste products and drinking water, and that show up frequently in food and are known to produce health problems. The US EPA's list of 129 priority pollutants is one such list (Table 10.1).

The impacts of pollution upon human health may be **acute** (short-term) or **chronic** (long-term). Chronic effects can be difficult to assess due to such factors as low concentrations of pollutants, uncertainties

Table 10.1. Priority Pollutants

1.	Acenaphthene	34.	2,4-dimethylphenol
2.	Acrolein	35.	2,4-dinitrotoluene
3.	Acrylonitrile	36.	2,6-dinitrotoluene
4.	Benzene	37.	1,2-diphenylhydrazine
5.	Benzidine	38.	Ethylbenzene
6.	Carbon tetrachloride	39.	Fluoranthene
7.	Chlorobenzene	40.	4-chlorophenyl phenyl ether
8.	1,2,4-trichlorobenzene	41.	4-bromophenyl phenyl ether
9.	Hexachlorobenzene	42.	Bis(2-chloroisopropyl) ether
10.	1,2-dichloroethane	43.	Bis(2-chloroethoxy) methane
11.	1,1,1-trichloreothane	44.	Methylene chloride
12.	Hexachloroethane	45.	Methyl chloride
13.	1,1-dichloroethane	46.	Methyl bromide
14.	1,1,2-trichloroethane	47.	Bromoform
15.	1,1,2,2-tetrachloroethane	48.	Dichlorobromomethane
16.	Chloroethane	49.	REMOVED
17.	REMOVED	50.	REMOVED
18.	Bis(2-chloroethyl) ether	51.	Chlorodibromomethane
19.	2-chloroethyl vinyl ethers	52.	Hexachlorobutadiene
20.	2-chloronaphthalene	53.	Hexachlorocyclopentadiene
21.	2,4,6-trichlorophenol	54.	Isophorone
22.	Parachlorometa cresol	55.	Naphthalene
23.	Chloroform	56.	Nitrobenzene
24.	2-chlorophenol	57.	2-nitrophenol
25.	1,2-dichlorobenzene	58.	4-nitrophenol
26.	1,3-dichlorobenzene	59.	2,4-dinitrophenol
27.	1,4-dichlorobenzene	60.	4,6-dinitro-o-cresol
28.	3,3-dichlorobenzidine	61.	N-nitrosodimethylamine
29.	1,1-dichloroethylene	62.	N-nitrosodiphenylamine
30.	1,2-trans-dichloroethylene	63.	N-nitrosodi-n-propylamine
31.	2,4-dichlorophenol	64.	Pentachlorophenol
32.	1,2-dichloropropane	65.	Phenol
33.	1,2-dichloropropylene	66.	Bis(2-ethylhexyl) phthalate

Table 10.1, continued

67.	Butyl benzyl phthalate	99.	Endrin aldehyde
68.	Di-n-butyl phthalate	100.	Heptachlor
69.	Di-n-octyl phthalate	101.	Heptachlor epoxide
70.	Diethyl phthalate	102.	Alpha-BHC
71.	Dimethyl phthalate	103.	Beta-BHC
72.	Benzo(a)anthracene	104.	Gamma-BHC
73.	Benzo(a)pyrene	105.	Delta-BHC
74.	Benzo(b)fluoranthene	106.	PCB–1242 (Arochlor 1242)
75.	Benzo(k)fluoranthene	107.	PCB–1254 (Arochlor 1254)
76.	Chrysene	108.	PCB–1221 (Arochlor 1221)
77.	Acenaphthylene	109.	PCB–1232 (Arochlor 1232)
78.	Anthracene	110.	PCB–1248 (Arochlor 1248)
79.	Benzo(ghi)perylene	111.	PCB–1260 (Arochlor 1260)
80.	Fluorene	112.	PCB–1016 (Arochlor 1016)
81.	Phenanthrene	113.	Toxaphene
82.	Dibenzo(a,h)anthracene	114.	Antimony
83.	Indeno(1,2,3-cd)pyrene	115.	Arsenic
84.	Pyrene	116.	Asbestos
85.	Tetrachloroethylene	117.	Beryllium
86.	Toluene	118.	Cadmium
87.	Trichloroethylene	119.	Chromium
88.	Vinyl chloride	120.	Copper
89.	Aldrin	121.	Cyanide, Total
90.	Dieldrin	122.	Lead
91.	Chlordane	123.	Mercury
92.	4,4-DDT	124.	Nickel
93.	4,4-DDE	125.	Selenium
94.	4,4-DDD	126.	Silver
95.	Alpha-endosulfan	127.	Thallium
96.	Beta-endosulfan	128.	Zinc
97.	Endosulfan sulfate	129.	2,3,7,8-TCDD
98.	Endrin		

Notes: Priority pollutants are a set of chemical pollutants regulated by the US Environmental Protection Agency, and for which analytical test methods have been developed. The current list of 129 Priority Pollutants, shown here, can also be found in *Appendix A to 40 CFR Part 423*. Source: [517, *http://water.epa.gov/scitech/methods/cwa/pollutants.cfm*].

about exposure, subtle early symptoms, and long latency periods between exposure and symptoms. Epidemiologic studies attempt to correlate illnesses with probable exposures. Unfortunately, knowledge of long-term health impacts for most potential pollutants, including those widespread in the environment, is rudimentary. Many standards, such as those of the US Safe Drinking Water Act, are routinely violated and are badly outdated. The standards fail to include many hazardous new chemicals and do not incorporate knowledge of damages that we now know can occur at much lower concentrations than believed when the lists were originally compiled. Roughly 20 million Americans are estimated to become ill each year from drinking contaminated drinking water.

In short, we are all guinea pigs. For some pollutants such as radioactive materials, the hazard is cumulative and even a small added exposure means a greater risk. For others, the threat is short-term and only exposure above a certain level is dangerous. Improving water quality safety can be a difficult task as many industries and individuals oppose attempts to set higher safety standards, citing reasons such as cost, inconvenience, and the need for additional studies.

About 15% of the US population obtains its drinking water from private wells. Recent analyses find that some 20% of these well waters will exceed recommended human health benchmarks. Water from private wells is infrequently analyzed and is more likely than surface water to be contaminated [204]. The pollutants which most often violate health-related standards are elemental trace elements, especially manganese, arsenic, uranium, and radon. Reasonably accurate overviews of groundwater pollution are difficult to come by, even in the advanced nations. A recent (2012) survey in the US found a minimum of 126,000 sites where groundwater pollution from chemicals was being treated but where the pollution levels were still too high to allow closure. The minimum cost of bringing those concentrations to acceptable levels is estimated at $110 billion to $127 billion [279].

To ascertain the quality of water, samples need to be carefully collected and analyzed. In the US, the EPA has established enforceable standards, called **maximum contaminant levels** (**MCLs**) for various pollutants. All states are required to adhere to these standards, but may set stricter MCLs if they feel they are needed. Many other contaminants have suggested MCLs, which are recommendations, not requirements. Violations of standards are common, enforcement is weak, and fines are rarely imposed. Appendix C provides the MCLs for selected contaminants and includes brief comments on the health impacts and sources of the chemicals listed.

10.3 Sources of Groundwater Pollution

Was it not enough for you to drink the clearest water,
that you had to foul the remainder with your feet?

— Ezekiel 34:18

10.3.1 Introduction

Groundwater pollution is generated in many ways. It may come from existing natural sources such as seawater or rock and soil units which contain hazardous chemicals. Most groundwater pollution, however, is created from potentially hazardous substances, natural or artificial, introduced into an environment by human activities. The contaminating material may come from any number of sources among which are land applications of pesticides, fertilizers, road salt, and wastes; storage facilities on the surface of the ground or below it (waste lagoons, tanks, and so forth); extraction of resources such as mining and oil drilling; intentional disposal of wastes (injection wells and landfills); industrial accidents; and accidental spills during handling and transport.

Among the more specific sources of groundwater pollutants are landfills, USTs, waste lagoons and other impoundments, petroleum extraction wells, pipelines, septic tank systems, injection wells, cropland, animal feedlots, industrial facilities, polluted surface waters, urbanized areas, construction sites, homes and gardens, vehicle accidents, salt-water bodies, natural rock and soil, polluted air, military installations, runoff from croplands and city streets, and virtually any potentially hazardous substance spilled on, dumped on, or buried within the ground [29]. Some of the more important sources are briefly described in sections 10.3.3 through 10.3.8 below.

In developed nations, we tend to take the safety of our water for granted. However, many widely used and important water sources in these developed nations are very poorly protected. Small quantities of certain extremely hazardous biological agents and chemicals can pollute huge quantities of water. The danger to major surface reservoirs should be obvious, but subsurface waters are also vulnerable. Where aquifers are important sources of water and the groundwater flow is rapid, the possibility of intentional contamination by irresponsible parties, such as mentally disturbed persons or terrorists, should not be ignored [148, 534].

10.3.2 Nature of the Pollution Event

The pollutants may enter groundwater from a **point source** — a specific location such as a factory, pipe, waste lagoon, or underground tank — or from a **nonpoint source** such as fields, roadways, or the atmosphere. Point sources often yield a well-defined plume. Nonpoint sources tend to be more difficult to identify and control and tend to produce widespread contamination with widely varying concentrations.

The way in which pollutants enter the ground is an important consideration. If the pollution was generated by a short-term event, such as a single spill or leakage over a brief time period, the term **pulse loading** is sometimes applied. **Continuous source loading** refers to long-term leakage, often over many years. Also of concern is the **loading rate**, the rate at which pollution enters the subsurface. Was it a long-term leak of steady volume and concentration, or did the volumes and concentrations of pollutants vary widely through time, and were those variations a result of weather conditions (affecting the rate of leaching from a landfill), of direct addition of pollutants (different release or dumping times of toxics), or some other cause?

10.3.3 Storage Tanks

Large quantities of hazardous liquids are stored in aboveground and underground tanks. Millions of tanks around the world have leaked, polluting soils and water. By the mid-1990s over two million commercial USTs existed in the US. Most were not designed to last more than 10 or 20 years. Estimates during the last 30 years suggest that over a half million USTs, most containing volatile petroleum products, are probably leaking at any one time in the US. A study in Silicon Valley in California found 85% of the tanks had leaks. One gallon of gasoline can contaminate a million gallons of water. Many leaking facilities were not discovered until considerable contaminant had escaped and many remain to be discovered. Leakage also occurs frequently in faulty lines or valves associated with UST systems. Despite efforts to upgrade or properly abandon tanks, many contaminated sites were never discovered, reported, investigated, or properly remediated. Upgrades designed to prevent or minimize future tank spills include special spill guards, corrosion protection, containment units, and automatic monitoring devices.

Spills at refineries and during fuel pumping and transfers are fairly common. One of the largest petroleum releases is the estimated 17 to 30 million gallons from oil refineries and tanks in Greenpoint, NY. The oil contaminated over 50 acres of soil, then seeped into Newtown Creek between Brooklyn and Queens, and from there flowed into New York Harbor. After many years of litigation, the owner, Exxon-Mobil, signed an agreement in 2010 with the state of New York to address the spill and pay $25 million in fines.

10.3.4 Landfills

Water infiltrating through waste disposal sites, mostly sanitary landfills and miscellaneous "dumps," will pick up contaminants. **Leachate** is contaminated groundwater. The contaminants are usually derived from materials through which the water has migrated. The term is most commonly applied to water that has picked up (leached) pollutants while percolating through solid wastes, as in a landfill. To reduce groundwater pollution, landfills are generally required to provide a covering (cap) and liners (along the sides and bottom) made of impermeable materials such as synthetic fabrics, plastics, and clay in order to prevent water from entering and leaving the accumulated waste material. Unfortunately, all caps and liners will eventually fail, but the waste itself will remain hazardous for centuries, especially without water to accelerate decomposition. Many modern landfills have leachate collection systems consisting of perforated pipes placed in gravel beds, usually just above the bottom liner. The purpose is to transport leachate to a collection point where it can be confined and treated.

The US has more than 3,000 active sanitary landfills and well over 10,000 abandoned municipal landfills according to the EPA. Approximately 80% are believed to have leaks. Worldwide, known and unknown "dump sites," ranging from large industrial landfills to local garbage piles, number in the millions.

10.3.5 Septic Systems

Waste water from the typical household contains many pollutants of which the most common are bacteria, viruses, nitrates, and phosphates. Where sewer lines are not accessible, **septic systems** are used. Over a trillion gallons of water is probably entering the ground from some 30 million septic systems in the US [29, 122]. Most home septic systems consist of an underground tank into which household wastewater is discharged. Most solids settle out in the tank where anaerobic bacteria break them down. The liquid moves on into a network of perforated pipes. From there water percolates downward to the water table, ideally being purified along the way by filtration and aerobic decomposition. Many septic systems fail due to inadequate design (for example, discharge rates that are not matched to hydraulic conductivities of underlying soil), poor location (for example, too close to the water table), clogged or leaking tanks and pipes, and chemicals which kill the tank bacteria. Often there are simply too many septic systems in a local area for the all the collective discharge to be purified. Alternatives to septic systems such as aerobic spray systems and composting toilets are being used more frequently. In many parts of the world, privies and outhouses are still widely used. The effluent seeping from sewage constitutes a major health threat (Section 10.4.6).

10.3.6 Storage Ponds and Land Applications

Hundreds of thousands of impoundments containing wastes from a wide range of activities from mining to agriculture are scattered throughout the world. These sites pose a serious threat to both surface and ground water.

Example: Coal Ash

Power plants in the US generate some 140 million tons of coal ash annually. The EPA has documented hazardous levels of arsenic, lead, mercury, radioactive isotopes, and numerous other pollutants in the ash. The ash is stored at thousands of active and inactive sites, including impoundments along valleys, various lagoons and ponds, landfills, abandoned mines, and other "fills." Groundwater pollution has been documented at dozens of sites, but many lack any monitoring. The hazards associated with coal ash impoundments received long-overdue attention when a 40-acre Tennessee Valley Authority coal ash pond near Kingston, Tennessee, ruptured on December 22, 2008. Over a billion gallons of semi-liquid coal ash sludge inundated some 300 acres of land, destroying homes and contaminating streams. Numerous environmental organizations are pressuring the EPA to regulate coal ash as a hazardous waste.

In properly applied quantities, treated sewage and other liquefied organic wastes can act as fertilizers when applied to land. But excessive application results in polluted runoff, which is the largest single source of surface water pollution in many areas, and downward seepage often contaminates groundwater. Huge quantities of sewage are produced at confined animal facilities, especially large factory farms housing hundreds to tens of thousands of animals. One cow generates about as much waste as eighteen people, and thousands may be housed in a single dairy or meat-producing facility. The US Clean Water Act of 1972 generally does not regulate pollutants which are not from a point source. Hence farm wastes are poorly regulated. Pathogens from sewage and chemical pollutants from fertilizer and pesticide applications have severely polluted groundwater in many agricultural areas.

Croplands are a major source of groundwater pollution, primarily from pesticides and nitrogen fertilizers. For example, a substantial number of schools with their own water supply wells have been found to have contamination, especially if they are located in an agricultural area. Some 8 to 11% of US schools have wells, and water from one in five of these violated the Safe Drinking Water Act in the past decade [59].

An underappreciated source of pollution originates from the application of pesticides and fertilizers to lawns and gardens in residential areas. The quantities applied were estimated to have exceeded 45 million kg annually in the early 2000s [316]. On average, homeowners have been found to use ten times more pesticide per acre than farmers.

10.3.7 Wells

A. Deep Extraction Wells

As noted in Section 7.1.1, wells have many functions. In addition to active and inactive water wells, millions of oil wells, natural gas wells, waste injection wells, unsuccessful exploration wells, and other borings penetrate deep into Earth's outer skin. The boreholes and the disturbed rock immediately around them can provide conduits for fluid migration. Polluted groundwater can easily contaminate clean water via the pathways provided by old wells. Deep water is often saline and contains numerous hazardous chemicals. Due to its highly pressurized state, it can force its way up well shafts and pollute overlying zones of fresh groundwater, or even be extruded, geyser-like onto the surface. Most wells, both active and abandoned, have casings and concrete/clay seals to prevent underlying waters from contaminating the fresh groundwater above, but improper installation, defective casings, deterioration over time, and related problems inevitably occur. Result: leakage is widespread (Figure 10.1).

Recent innovations allow wells designed to access crude oil, natural gas, water, or other materials to be drilled ever deeper into high pressure environments (Section 8.14). These wells represent a growing concern, one vividly demonstrated by the April 20, 2010, Deepwater Horizon disaster in the Gulf of Mexico in which a deep offshore well experienced a blowout, killing 11 people and spilling 200 million gallons of crude oil. Land-based wells — often thousands of feet deep and intended to carry fluids other than potable water — represent a serious potential source of groundwater pollution.

Potential threats to groundwater supplies exist during all deep well operations, including oil, natural gas, and deep groundwater drilling. Deep wells need to be carefully constructed to insure that the hazardous substances they carry do not threaten people's safety, freshwater supplies, and the general environment. But care takes time, and the scale of such operations has been increasing at unprecedented rates.

Example: Hydrofracking

Since about 2008, deep drilling has increased dramatically in many parts of the US where deep shales containing petroleum in the form of natural gas or liquid petroleum, occur. The shales typically lie more than 1,000 feet below the surface and obtaining the petroleum product from them involves combining advanced techniques in horizontal drilling and hydraulic fracturing (Section 7.5.7). This is not the old standard

---

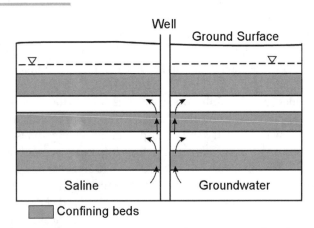

Figure 10.1. Saline groundwater may migrate up a well and contaminate overlying aquifers as a result of improper construction (poor grouting and sealants), deterioration, fracturing of nearby rock during drilling, injection of high pressure fluids, and other conditions.

water well fracturing and purging but a far more potent and complex technology which owes its origins largely to industrial oil field procedures — one of the more accurate names for this method is "high-volume slickwater hydraulic fracturing from long laterals." The common terms applied to it are simply hydrofracking or "fracking." In this technique, a mix of water, sand, and chemicals is forced down a well under high pressure to pry open tight joints in the shale and release the petroleum trapped within the rock. The sand helps keep fractures open.

Constructing even a few of these wells is a multi-million-dollar endeavor and very energy intensive. The well drilling begins vertically, then, often over a distance of about a quarter mile, the borehole is curved to extend laterally along the petroleum-bearing layers. One drilling pad may contain a dozen or more deep wells, and each well may require more than a million gallons of water to which is added sand, gelling agents, lubricants, biocides, cleansers, acids, and other chemicals.

Local water supplies may be threatened by overuse as well as by contamination from waste waters either at the surface or from migration of deep saline water upward into aquifers. The water which comes back out of the wells, called produced water, is usually highly toxic and contains high levels of radioactive radium, salts, and other pollutants. Produced water must be contained or treated, either on site or elsewhere (Section 10.3.7B). Unknowns such as the specific chemicals used, the location and extent of existing subsurface faults and fractures, and the disruptions accompanying the hydrofracturing itself, which entails using small explosive charges, make it difficult to evaluate the potential environmental impacts of the operations [81].

Groundwater near existing gas wells tends to have higher levels of methane (the major component of the natural gas), occasionally enough to burst into flame when a flame is held near an open water faucet. It is usually not clear if the methane is migrating upward along the well casings, through fractures, or from some other source. Due to the high pressures and fracturing operations that accompany hydrofracking, it is certainly possible that polluting gases and liquids will migrate upward through any available openings and pose threats to overlying water supplies. The time for such migration to occur is highly variable and is but one of many contestable issues.

Hydrofracking of impermeable petroleum-bearing bedrock is a large-scale industrial development and with it comes an abundance of truck traffic, workers, construction, and related activities which generate considerable stress, both environmental and financial, upon local governments, schools, and residents. Residents in gas producing areas complain frequently of air pollution, illness, well-water contamination, noise, deteriorating roadways, increased crime, and other problems related to the sudden increase in local development [81, 414].

The Marcellus Shale is one of the largest shale gas formations. It underlies large parts of New York, Pennsylvania, West Virginia, Ohio, and adjacent states. Hydrofracking the Marcellus has become a major controversy which exemplifies many pros and cons of the issue. Some welcome the increase in local jobs and associated economic benefits that development of this resource can bring to an area. Others point out that the US needs to become more energy independent, and natural gas generates considerably less carbon dioxide than coal or liquid petroleum, and may be our best bet for a needed bridge between the fossil fuel age and the anticipated green energy future [181]. Recent government prognoses suggest that the US could become the major petroleum producing nation due to the ongoing surge in production from hydrofracking. Other studies indicate that these estimates are overstated, noting that each well accesses a relatively small volume of rock and that the volume of gas retrieved decreases rapidly [193].

The Williston Basin area of western North Dakota and adjacent parts of Montana and Saskatchewan is underlain by the Bakken Formation, an oil-rich shale which may contain over 2 billion barrels of oil which can be retrieved using hydrofracking. An estimated 2,500 new wells are expected to be drilled annually over the next two decades or so in the Williston region. Each well requires some 2 million gallons (7.6 million L) of water for which state agencies issue permits. The water sources are a contentious issue. Most permits granted thus far involve pumping groundwater which threatens

to deplete aquifers and induce salt-water intrusion from below. Surface water is scarce except for the Missouri River and
the state is negotiating with the US Army Corps of Engineers
over allocation of its water.

The North Dakota oil drilling rush has already transformed
small communities, which in some cases are seeing their population double in just a few years. The huge influx of new people,
mostly male workers, is accompanied by sudden increases in
crime, traffic, rental costs, housing and schooling needs, and
related problems with which local governments and residents
are ill-prepared to cope.

The most accessible, least costly reserves of nonrenewable resources tend to be exploited first. Over the last century, humanity has
been depleting these resources at a ferocious, and still accelerating, rate.
Recently developed technologies such as hydrofracking, deep offshore
drilling, and massive strip mining enable us to continue retrieving ever
greater amounts of many important resources. But such achievements
come at a price which often includes ever increasing economic, environmental, and social costs, and the risks associated therewith. Even as the
rush continues, some hard questions remain unanswered, especially where
fossil fuels are concerned. For example, are the total long-term costs
greater than the benefits, will the total energy invested in some enterprises exceed the useful energy we get out of those efforts, and what are
the climatic consequences of these activities?

B. Deep-Well Injection

Injecting hazardous liquid wastes into deep subsurface formations
has long been a standard disposal method. But the process is fraught
with uncertainties. The liquids are pumped into the ground under high
pressure which alters the existing hydrostatic pressure distribution thus
affecting groundwater flow patterns. The subsurface pore spaces aren't
empty, the fluids already present must go somewhere. The high pressure
can force deep saline waters and the wastes themselves upward and outward along permeable rock zones or old boreholes, polluting freshwater aquifers. Thousands of examples of deep-well injection gone
awry can be cited. Consequences may include blowing nearby well
casings sky-high, the reappearance of injected wastes many miles
away, and earthquakes generated by the increase in subsurface hydraulic pressure.

In addition to contamination issues, use of deep fluid injection wells correlates closely with increased earthquake activity, as near Denver, Colorado, where fluid injection beginning in 1962 at the Rocky Mountain Arsenal generated a well documented series of earthquakes in an area that had been quake-free for nearly 80 years [190]. Most such earthquakes occur contemporaneously with injection, suggesting that the subsurface rock was easily displaced and/or that old dormant fault zones were reactivated. For example, on November 5, 2011, the largest earthquake ever to occur in Oklahoma with a magnitude of 5.6 caused considerable damage, including the destruction of 14 homes. Evidence strongly suggests that this and numerous other recent earthquake swarms in Oklahoma and elsewhere have been triggered by the injection of wastewaters from hydrofracking [30].

C. Well Abandonment

When any well has outlived its purpose, it needs to be properly abandoned. The well borehole, casing, liners, grout, and adjacent disturbed rock provide a conduit along which contaminants may migrate and pollute freshwater supplies. Hence wells must be thoroughly sealed (plugged) to prevent, insofar as possible, (1) surface water from moving downward along the well, (2) poor-quality water from migrating from one aquifer to another, (3) hazardous fluids (petroleum products, wastes, gases, and so forth) from migrating upward from deeper high pressure environments, and (4) loss of confining pressure or other alterations of the preexisting hydrogeological conditions. Failure to properly construct and abandon wells has created many dangerous incidents and represents both immediate and long-term threats to groundwater resources.

10.3.8 Mining Operations

Tens of thousands of abandoned or inactive mines exist just in the US (Plate 15, Top Left). The extraction of mineral matter from the solid earth entails subsurface disruptions and can have profound impacts on groundwater quality and flow paths. Solid and liquid wastes have often been "disposed of" in old mines, posing additional threats to groundwater. Mining exposes minerals to air, inducing chemical reactions, especially oxidation, which may continue to generate hazardous pollutants indefinitely. Mining waste piles, waste lagoons, and processing by-products can also leach pollutants to the groundwater. Millions of acre-feet of water lie in old mining pit ponds scattered around the world and many have contaminated the water of nearby aquifers. The plume from the huge Bingham Canyon mine in Utah has rendered the water beneath an area of some 72 mi^2 too polluted for drinking.

10.4 Common Groundwater Pollutants

Pollution is a crime compounded of ignorance and avarice.

— Lord Ritchie-Calder

10.4.1 Introduction

Thousands of water pollutants have been recognized and enormous quantities of information about them are published each year. The pollutants include a vast array of organic and inorganic chemicals along with infectious agents, oxygen-depleting waste materials, sediment, radioactive substances, and heat [29, 103, 423]. The term **macropollutant** is often used for common pollutants often present in large concentrations such as salts, acids, nutrients, or natural organic matter. The impacts of macropollutants are often well understood. **Micropollutants** are present in very small concentrations, but tend to be ubiquitous, and some are capable of producing harmful effects even at the picogram (a trillionth of a gram) per liter range. Micropollutants include numerous synthetic substances, pharmaceuticals, and trace elements. Cities and industries are believed to generate wastewater containing more than 300 million tons of synthetic compounds each year. Their interactions, distribution, and overall impacts on health and the environment are often poorly understood.

Sufficient documentation does not exist to accurately state the percentage of groundwater that is polluted, locally or globally. But what has been documented is unsettling. For example, in virtually all areas where agriculture is widespread, nitrate levels in groundwater exceed recommended MCLs (Appendix C). And nitrate concentrations are increasing rapidly because of an ongoing explosion in nitrogen fertilizer use. Pesticides are also widespread in groundwater — in 2006, the USGS reported finding the herbicide atrazine in 24% of roughly 18,000 private wells tested [156, 519]. The long-term combined health impacts of even minute quantities of such chemicals on children are especially worrisome.

Privately owned wells are of special concern. Some 50 million Americans depend upon them, but their wells are infrequently tested for contaminants and are less secure and shallower than public supply wells.

Adding to the concerns is the realization that huge quantities of pollutants already exist in countless locations around the world where they are insidiously migrating toward, or through, vital groundwater supplies.

Many ways of categorizing hazardous contaminants can be formulated — see, for example, Appendix C, which also provides information on the health impacts and sources of drinking water contaminants. The following groupings were chosen for convenience and simplicity and some overlap is unavoidable. Methods for treating and mitigating subsurface pollution are covered in Section 11.3.8.

10.4.2 Acids, Bases, and Salts

Acids, bases, and salts are common inorganic chemical species (Section 1.4.10) that frequently become serious pollutants when excess quantities are present in water. Their presence depends upon how much of the chemical has had contact with the water and how soluble the chemical is. Once dissolved in water, the pollution will tend to migrate along with the groundwater flow, a process called **advection**.

A. Acid Mine Drainage

The major acidity problem is **acid mine drainage** produced by the mining of sulfur-bearing earth materials such as metal sulfide ores and coal. The most widespread problems occur in coal-mining areas. Sulfide minerals are typically present as impurities in coal, most commonly as pyrite (FeS_2). When exposed to air, oxygen, with the aid of microorganisms, reacts with the pyrite to yield an abundance of hydrogen and sulfate ions in the presence of water. The result is sulfuric acid. The acidic waters often contain numerous other contaminants as well, especially metals. The acid water migrates through the rock or along old mined areas where it can contaminate aquifers and/or discharge to the surface where it becomes a severe threat to streams and other surface waters (Plate 15, Top Left). Acidic waters also seep from mining waste piles and storage lagoons. Acid mine drainage is extremely difficult to control and can persist for centuries.

B. Acid Precipitation

A similar acidification process occurs when sulfur or nitrogen oxides are released to the atmosphere when coal and other fuels burn. The gases react with atmospheric water to produce sulfuric or nitric acid. The result is known as **acid precipitation**, which includes dry acid fallout (usually sulfate particulates), acid rain, acid fog, and acid snow. In soils, the acidic waters can leach away important nutrients such as calcium and magnesium while releasing harmful elements such as aluminum. Increasing acidity of groundwater is a concern in many areas of high acid precipitation.

Bases can produce excess alkalinity but this is not as serious a problem as acidification. Human activities which disturb soil or rock containing alkaline materials can release excess bases to the environment.

C. Fluorine and Chlorine

Fluorine (F) is a very reactive nonmetal, as are all the halogens. It forms many hazardous compounds including fluoride (F^-) salts and fluorinated synthetic organics. A very small amount of fluorine can help fight tooth decay. The EPA upper limits for fluoride in drinking water vary from 1.4 to 2.4 mg/L, depending upon how much water people drink — people drink more in warmer than cooler climates. Too much fluoride (>4.5 mg/L) can cause **fluorosis**, characterized by tooth mottling, skin cancers, and crippling bone damage, among other problems. Though most groundwater contains very little fluoride, it is a natural contaminant of bedrock aquifers in some areas. The groundwater serving perhaps 70 million people in northern China and 30 million in India contains dangerous fluoride levels. Some 62 million people in India are afflicted by fluorosis [144]. The fluoride added to dozens of consumer products also ends up in water.

Chlorine (Cl) is chemically very similar to fluorine, but much more abundant. Like fluorine, it forms both inorganic salts and many hazardous organic chemicals (Section 10.4.4). Chloride (Cl^-) is the dominant ion in seawater at some 19,000 mg/L. In fresh groundwater, it is usually present at about 5 to 13 mg/L. Chloride is very mobile in groundwater and can travel great distances.

D. Sodium Chloride

Many salts can cause problems. Sodium, magnesium, and calcium sulfates from saline seeps are a problem in many semiarid regions, including the western US. However, when the term "**salt**" is used in common language, it typically refers to sodium chloride — also known as table salt, NaCl (mineral name: halite), and rock salt. In this section, unless otherwise stated, "salt" will refer to sodium chloride. Sodium chloride is the most common of many highly soluble minerals which can contribute ions to water, often rendering it unusable. In many areas, especially along low-lying coasts, salt has become a major threat to groundwater supplies due to landward migration of seawater (Section 8.9).

Of all the water impurities from deeper in the earth, the most troublesome is naturally occurring salt. Rock salt is a common sedimentary rock and tends to become more abundant with depth due to the solutioning of near-surface salt deposits by fresh waters of meteoric origin. In addition, it is believed that much of the water present in sedimentary rock is seawater which has been trapped in the formations as connate, or formation water, since their deposition [137]. Thus, in many parts of the world, fresh groundwater is underlain, often at fairly shallow depths, by saline groundwater. Some two-thirds of the US is underlain by aquifers containing over 1,000 mg/L salt. Common terms expressing the degree of saltiness in water are defined in Section 1.7.

D-1: Sources

The major sources of salt contamination in surface and subsurface waters are:

1. **Seawater.** Ocean waters may migrate landward in coastal areas contaminating both ground and surface waters.
2. **Connate water.** This is often seawater from the distant past which was trapped in sediment and failed to be expelled during lithification.
3. **Bedrock formations containing rock salt.**
4. **Surface or near-surface concentrations of salt** formed by evaporation in arid regions.
5. **Human activities.** Among the activities which can generate and/ or release excess amounts of saline wastes are drilling for oil and natural gas, irrigation, desalination of water, and numerous industries. Some 20% of the world's irrigated land has been damaged by salt accumulation in soil (salinization). Salt contamination of surface and subsurface water is a problem in cold areas which use large quantities of road salt. During the winter, up to 11 tonnes/km (19.5 tons/mi) of salt are applied per single lane of roadway in some northern areas of the US [268].

D-2: Causes

The basic causes of salt pollution in groundwater often involve:

1. **Reversal of groundwater gradient and flow.** This is a major cause of seawater encroachment into freshwater aquifers, and has become a major problem in coastal areas around the world. Fresh water flowing toward the ocean exerts hydrostatic pressure which prevents seawater from

flowing landward. As discussed in Section 8.9, overpumping of groundwater in coastal areas can reduce the seaward flow of fresh water and induce a landward flow of seawater (figures 8.29 and 8.30). Overpumping of groundwater in inland areas can cause the upwelling of underlying salty groundwater (Figure 8.28).

Application of large quantities of fresh water at the ground surface can cause major changes in groundwater flow. Two common causes are construction of large reservoirs and irrigation. Evaporation of irrigation waters has led to salt buildup which has degraded over 50 million hectares of cropland worldwide [141]. Reservoir water increases hydrostatic pressure in nearby groundwater which can cause saline subsurface waters to migrate into formerly freshwater aquifers, or rise toward the surface in nearby areas where evaporation can cause salt buildup in soils. The latter situation has produced disastrous salinization of many croplands of the Murray-Darling River basin of Australia.

2. **Destruction of natural barriers.** The "barrier" which prevents salt water from contaminating fresh water can be as simple as a natural undisturbed ground surface, the seaward movement of fresh water, or an impermeable zone of rock. Disturbance of any such barrier may yield major changes in the behavior of groundwater. Deep well drilling (Section 10.3.7), underground mining, large excavations, and related operations often penetrate numerous confining layers, thus breaching barriers (Figure 10.1). Disturbance or contamination of the ground surface due to flooding of low-lying coastal areas from rising sea levels, storms, and tsunamis can cause extensive saline pollution of fresh groundwater. The Asian tsunami of December 26, 2004, which killed more than 31,000 people in Sri Lanka, polluted or otherwise destroyed some 40,000 wells near that country's coast. Seawater moved as much as 1.5 kilometers (0.9 mile) inland, pouring down shallow, often hand-dug, wells and seeping into the permeable regolith. Efforts to pump out the seawater often drew in additional saline water from below.

3. **Disposal or use of saline wastes.** Many saline wastes are generated by industrial processes and drilling for oil and

natural gas. These are often held in ponds or lagoons which may leak or overflow. Toxic fluids, including high-salinity wastes, are often disposed of by deep-well injection (Section 10.3.7B). Large quantities of solid salt may accumulate from certain industries or at desalination plants where it can easily produce saline leachate and threaten local groundwater.

D-3: Controls

Common methods of controlling contamination of water resources by salt (and other pollutants) are briefly described below. More than one method may be employed simultaneously at a given site.

1. **Reduced groundwater withdrawal.** Where groundwater withdrawal is generating the problem, as in seawater encroachment along a coast, reducing withdrawals and demand, or finding alternative water sources will help alleviate the problem.

2. **Extraction barriers.** This entails using a line of pumping wells to extract unwanted or polluted water and to produce a trough in the water table, thus preventing further landward encroachment of saline water (Figure 10.2A).

3. **Artificial recharge.** A series of recharge (infiltration) basins or injection wells along a coast will create a ridge in the water table. The hydraulic gradient will then be away from the ridge, creating in effect a pressure ridge which can block the migration of salty water from the sea or other sources (Figure 10.2B). Extraction and recharge methods are most effective if the unconfined aquifer is underlain by impermeable material at shallow depth. Figure 10.2C is an example of artificial recharge in a confined aquifer.

4. **Modify pumping patterns.** This often involves reducing withdrawal rates at locations where saline encroachment is a threat or changing pumping locations, usually to wells located farther inland. If the salt-water intrusion is not too severe, such tactics may minimize or eliminate the problem.

5. **Impermeable subsurface barriers.** It may be feasible to construct a trench filled with impermeable material completely through the vertical extent of the aquifer, thus blocking the intruding saline water or other contaminants.

6. **Elimination of pollution source.** If the pollution source is small and localized, eliminating it may be the best option.

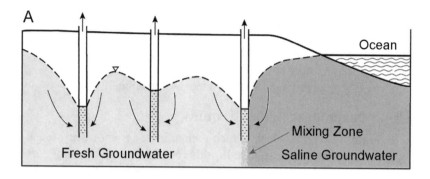

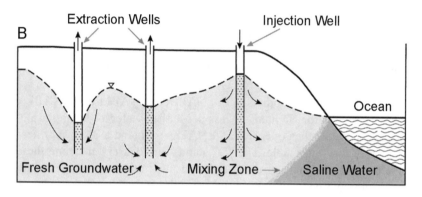

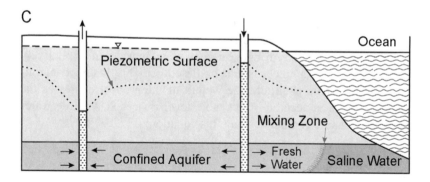

Figure 10.2. Simple cross-sections illustrating the use of extraction or injection wells to inhibit salt-water encroachment into aquifers along a coast. **A.** An extraction barrier for an unconfined aquifer using pumping wells. **B.** An injection well barrier for an unconfined aquifer. **C.** An injection well barrier for a confined aquifer.

375

Obviously, this would not be feasible for seawater encroachment along a coast!

7. **Desalination.** Pumping and treating groundwater to remove the salt may be an option in some situations, but desalination is costly and energy-intensive (Section 12.7.4A).

10.4.3 Nonaqueous-Phase Liquids

Many of the chemicals which contaminate groundwater are categorized as **nonaqueous-phase liquids (NAPLs)**. Unlike many common salts and related chemicals noted above, these pollutants do not dissolve readily in water, but persist in phases separate from water. The term **immiscible** often is often used to describe such fluids — fluids which do not dissolve, or dissolve only to a limited degree, when mixed, such as water and oil. Determining the transport and fate of such fluids is considerably more difficult than is the case with soluble materials.

Two important subdivisions of NAPL are **LNAPLs** and **DNAPLs**. The "L" stands for "lighter" — less dense than water, or having a specific gravity less than one. Hence, LNAPLs will tend to float at or near the top of the water table. The "D" stands for "denser," meaning these liquids will sink through the water. The most important LNAPLs are petroleum hydrocarbon fuels such as gasoline, diesel, jet fuel, kerosene, and heating oil. DNAPLs include many widely used organic chemicals. Information on specific NAPLs is provided in the following sections.

LNAPLs tend to follow the shallow groundwater flow near the water table as shown in Figure 10.3. An LNAPL which reaches the water table, or the capillary fringe, can float atop the water in its relatively pure state as, for example, gasoline or diesel fuel. This floating contaminant is called **free product**. The weight of the product depresses the water table. If an accurate water table level is needed, the true water table level can be computed using this equation:

$$d_w = d_m - tg$$

where d_w is the corrected depth to water, d_m is the measured depth to water, t is the thickness of the free product and g is the specific gravity of the product [192]. Note on Figure 10.3 that three additional contaminant phases will be present in addition to the floating liquid product: the vadose zone will retain some liquid contaminant as well as a vapor phase and a dissolved phase will form a contaminant plume in the groundwater.

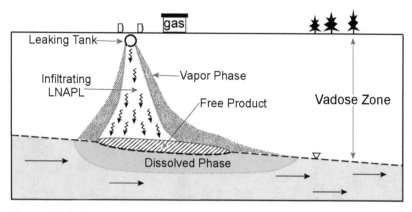

Figure 10.3. Cross-sectional sketch of an LNAPL leak showing movement of the contaminant and the various phases which can develop: a residual (liquid) phase adhering to regolith or rock particles along the contaminant path in the vadose zone, a vapor phase, free product atop the water table, and a dissolved phase in the groundwater. The contaminant source here is a leaking underground gasoline tank.

If DNAPLs are present, they will sink downward through a permeable material until they encounter an aquitard. When an aquitard is encountered, the contaminant will accumulate in a pool and/or migrate downslope along the upper contact of the impermeable material, all the while releasing vapor contaminants into the vadose zone and dissolved contaminants into the groundwater. The example shown on Figure 10.4 illustrates the complex and often unexpected migration routes that subsurface DNAPLs may follow. DNAPLs may also form globules which separate from the main mass. These can migrate deep into the earth making extraction especially difficult.

10.4.4 Organic Compounds

Vast numbers of organic compounds are in use. Note that most of the EPA's priority pollutants (Table 10.1) are organics. Appendix C provides information on some of the more common organics. Organic compounds consist mostly of synthetic chemicals along with the natural petroleum products. Many are pollutants. They can be subdivided or classified in many ways based upon chemistry, behavior, health impacts, analytical approaches, origin, or other characteristics [100, 551]. Some important, and often overlapping, categories of organic compounds are discussed below.

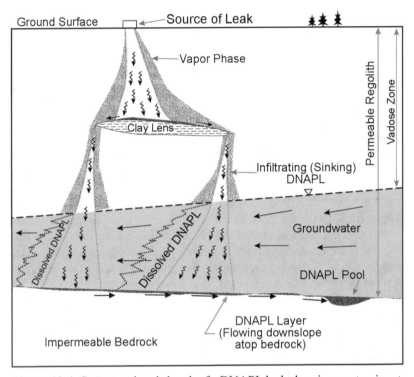

Figure 10.4. Cross-sectional sketch of a DNAPL leak showing contaminant movement through the subsurface and the associated contaminant phases. In this situation, the DNAPL pollutant encounters an impermeable clay lens in the vadose zone, spreads out atop it, then proceeds downward and into groundwater in two separate paths. Once an impermeable barrier (bedrock in this example) is reached, it spreads out and migrates downslope (opposite the direction of groundwater flow and dissolved DNAPL in this case), eventually pooling up in any low areas atop the bedrock. Each situation is different and requires careful investigation. Possible contaminant sources include waste disposal sites, underground tanks, and surface spills.

Many organic compounds are volatile, meaning they vaporize readily — hence the huge category of **volatile organic chemicals/compounds (VOCs)**. VOCs were present in about half the wells sampled near US cities between 1985 and 1995. Health effects are poorly understood but we know even tiny amounts, as low as the parts per trillion range, can be dangerous, especially to young children and fetuses. Included in this category are **hydrocarbons**, compounds made of hydrogen and carbon. Most hydrocarbons are associated with **petroleum** (literally "rock oil") and its many derivatives. Natural petroleum products include gases such as methane (natural gas, CH_4), liquid crude oil, and solid hydrocarbons such as asphalt, tar, and kerogin.

Many pollutants, including common petroleum products, are mixtures of numerous compounds, some of which are at least partially soluble. Gasoline contains approximately 150 different compounds. Four common chemicals which pose potential health threats and are present in most liquid petroleum fuels are benzene, toluene, ethyl benzene, and xylene — often abbreviated **BTEX**. All are aromatic hydrocarbons soluble in water. In groundwater, these soluble constituents will form a plume which migrates with the groundwater flow. Many petroleum compounds are volatile and will form a **vapor phase** in the unsaturated zone as shown on figures 10.3 and 10.4. An especially troublesome and widespread groundwater pollutant is methyl tertiary butyl ether (**MTBE**). MTBE has been added to gasoline since 1990 to lessen carbon monoxide emissions. MTBE is very soluble in water, migrates rapidly, is not easily degraded or adsorbed, and even a part per billion can render water unfit for drinking [156].

Most VOCs are NAPLs, including the **chlorinated hydrocarbons** — hydrocarbons in which chlorine atoms have replaced one or more hydrogen atoms — and petrochemicals. Nearly all chlorinated hydrocarbons, including trichloroethene (TCE), polychlorinated biphenyls (PCBs), trichloroethylene, and carbon tetrachloride, are dangerous pollutants (Appendix C). TCE, a strong degreasing solvent extensively used by the military and by industry, and perchlorate, a rocket-fuel chemical, are especially pernicious and have contaminated numerous sites, resulting in very costly, long-term cleanup efforts. These chemicals present numerous threats to human health and wildlife, including cancers, impairment of the nervous system, and reproductive problems. Tens of thousands of such chemicals, which include many plastics, solvents, and adhesives, are produced and are frequently encountered in groundwater. For example, the US uses some two million kg of septic system VOCs annually; 34 billion liters of solvents and other highly hazardous wastes are injected directly into deep groundwater in the US each year; half the groundwater in England and 29% of wells near US urban areas contain multiple VOCs.

Aliphatic hydrocarbons have chains of carbon atoms and are classified based upon the bonds between the carbon (alkanes: single bond; alkenes: double bond; alkynes: triple bond). Most are DNAPLs. As with many organics, they tend to be especially hazardous to health if they are halogenated — that is, if they contain halogen atoms such as fluorine and chlorine. The **aromatic hydrocarbons** are DNAPLs characterized by a closed carbon ring structure, can pose significant health threats, and are difficult to clean up and decompose.

The **polycyclic aromatic hydrocarbons** (**PAHs**) have numerous rings ("many cycles") and are among the major pollutants found in petroleum. PAHs, such as benzopyrene and naphthalene, are a huge category of suspected carcinogens and have become ubiquitous in the environment. They are present in thousands of common products and are released from industries, power plants, and motor vehicles (tail pipes and tires). Although generally of more concern as air pollutants, runoff and infiltrated water from urban areas can contain very high concentrations of PAHs. PAH concentrations of around 23 mg/kg can produce adverse impacts on aquatic organisms. Ordinary runoff from parking lots often contains over double this amount of PAHs, and runoff from lots treated with coal tar-based sealants have been found to contain 3,500 mg/kg.

The **polychlorinated biphenyls** (**PCBs**) and related compounds were widely used in the past in transformers and capacitors, and as plasticizers, among other uses. Huge quantities were leaked or dumped onto and into soils of the vadose zone. The lighter-weight constituents are gradually lost by evaporation and water transport. Ironically, those vaporized factions have reappeared at relatively high concentrations in remote Arctic regions where the cold climate apparently causes the vapors to condense. Although production in the US was halted by the Toxic Substances Control Act of 1976, and nearly all other nations have discontinued their manufacture, PCBs are very stable in the environment and continue to persist as serious pollutants.

The chronic, long-term health impacts of even low levels of these organic pollutants, including synergistic effects (combined impacts), remain uncertain but extremely troublesome. Hundreds of studies on various organics document their harmful impacts to fish and wildlife. In humans, a vast array of health problems from nervous ailments to cancer to cardiovascular disease are related to exposure to organic chemicals. Because many synthetic organics mimic hormones and disrupt animals' endocrine systems, they are especially dangerous during the early stages of development (the fetus, the young). Among numerous books detailing these impacts is the pioneering effort by Colborn, Dumanoski, and Myers [79].

10.4.5 Pesticides

Pesticides is another very large category of chemicals, many of which are NAPLs. Most pesticides are organic compounds. All are designed to kill organisms regarded as pests. We have pesticides designed to kill plants (herbicides), insects (insecticides), fungi (fungicides), fish (piscicides), rodents (rodenticides), and many others. Most newer pesticides are less persistent than older ones but are also more soluble, making them more likely to enter groundwater. Nematicides (roundworm killers such as aldicarb) often contaminate groundwater because they are designed to move easily through soil and reach nematodes attacking plant roots. Herbicides are by far the most widely used pesticides and their use escalated markedly during the past few decades as they replaced cultivation for weed control.

Hundreds of individual pesticide compounds are invading surface and ground waters; the US EPA has drinking water standards for only 33, and those levels have not been proven safe and are often exceeded. A New York Times investigation in 2009 found that the Clean Water Act had been violated more than 506,000 times since 2004 [104, 105]. Atrazine, a herbicide which is banned in the European Union, was found, often at very high levels, in 40% of the groundwater of agricultural areas sampled by the USGS. Concentrations as low as 0.1 ppb can produce gender deformities in frogs — the EPA allows 30 times that level in drinking water [366]. Some 80 million pounds of atrazine are used annually in the US. **Dioxins** are a notorious by-product of pesticide manufacturing. The most notable dioxin is TCDD, a stable, persistent chemical highly toxic to many animals. The LD50 level of TCDD for male guinea pigs — that is, the dosage which would be lethal to 50% of the individuals in the population — is a mere 0.6 ìg/kg of body mass.

10.4.6 Pathogens

A **pathogen** is any agent that causes disease. Pathogenic organisms include viruses, fecal bacteria, protozoa, and parasites. Most disease-causing organisms and infectious agents enter water via sewage or septic systems. Animal feedlots, paper mills, food processing plants, slaughterhouses, and hospital wastes are other important sources. Numerous disease outbreaks have been linked to pathogens. In poor nations, the World Health Organization estimates that some 80% of all disease is related to drinking water made unsafe by human wastes at a cost of some 25,000 lives every day.

In addition to human feces, the sewage delivered to a treatment plant often contains a witches brew of other foul ingredients such as detergents, industrial wastes, oil and grease, household chemicals, and discarded medicines. Common primary and secondary treatment will remove most oxygen-demanding substances, oil, grease, and solids. More costly tertiary treatments are needed to remove many hazardous metals, salts, and organics. Millions of tons of sewage sludge, often containing hazardous chemicals rendering it unsafe for land application or other uses, create a huge disposal problem.

Groundwater contamination by pathogens most often originates from land-disposal of sewage, including septic tank leakage, leachates from landfills and other disposal sites, and agricultural wastes, especially from large confined animal facilities. Microscopic organisms, mainly bacteria and viruses, can persist for several months in favorable subsurface environments. Europe suggests a waiting time of 50 days to one year to protect wellheads if viruses and pathogenic bacteria are known to be present in the well water.

10.4.7 Nutrients

A **nutrient** can be broadly defined as any substance required by an organism for its maintenance and growth. Most aqueous nutrients will be simple dissolved inorganic ions such as nitrates or ammonia, although some exist as organic forms or even as trace elements. Most enter surface and ground water via sewage, livestock excrement, and fertilizer applications.

Nitrogen is an essential plant nutrient, but in its elemental state (N_2, the major component of air), it is quite inactive. To be used by plants, nitrogen needs to be converted chemically into another form, usually the **nitrate** radical (NO_3^{-1}), by a process called nitrogen fixation. Most such conversion occurs in nature when nitrogen-fixing bacteria combine nitrogen with hydrogen to produce ammonia (NH_3) and then with oxygen to produce nitrate radicals. Nitrates are used by plants in building complex organic molecules (amino acids, then proteins and peptides).

Human "fixation" has created a huge overload of nitrates in the environment, contributing to acid fallout (Section 10.4.2B) and widespread water pollution. Human activities convert nitrogen into nitrates during high-temperature combustion and manufacture of fertilizers. In both cases, nitrogen combines with oxygen to produce nitrates, which are water-soluble and very mobile. Nitrogen-rich wastes from the air, fertilizers, manure, and septic systems contaminate both surface and groundwater in many urban and agricultural areas. An overload of nutrients in surface waters results in excess growth of aquatic plant material, especially algae. When the plants die, decomposition by aerobic bacteria depletes the water of oxygen resulting in foul, oxygen-depleted "dead zones" incapable of supporting life, a process called **eutrophication**.

Nitrates from fertilizer use in agricultural areas often contaminate underlying groundwater. The EPA maximum concentration level is 10 mg/L. Nitrates exceed 100 mg/L in groundwater in parts of Nebraska and other farming areas, and is usually about 30 mg/L in effluent from US sewage treatment plants. In addition to fertilizer use, the simple act of converting natural soils to croplands leads to the oxidation of the abundant nitrogen in organic matter in the soil, generating more nitrates.

Nitrates in drinking water reduce the ability of blood to carry oxygen resulting in "blue-baby syndrome." In addition, nitrates and the compounds they may form can cause miscarriages, and are implicated in cancers, lymphoma, and other ailments. High nitrate levels in water can harm crops, a process similar to the damage acid rain causes to the soils and forests of the eastern US (Section 10.4.2A). Nitrate pollution of groundwater has become a worldwide problem. For example, over half the wells in northern China have excess nitrates and nitrates are present at 5 to 15 times the safe levels in groundwater in India's most important agricultural areas.

Phosphorous is another important plant nutrient which is a pollutant in some areas. Its impacts are similar to those of nitrates. Major sources of phosphorous include overapplication of fertilizers and organic wastes to crops, seepage from septic systems, and industry.

The actual concentration of pollutants such as nitrates in groundwater will depend upon such factors as soil/rock composition and permeability in both the vadose and phreatic zones, depth to the water table, and where, when, and how much pollutant is released. Nutrient pollution from nitrogen and phosphorous could be minimized by carefully matching fertilizer applications to the plants' specific requirements.

10.4.8 Elemental Pollutants

Pure elements are often present in water but usually at very low levels of a few parts per million or less. Most are metals and are considered **trace elements** (Section 9.2.5). Some elements are valuable nutrients at low concentrations but become toxic at moderately high levels. Elements which tend to be very toxic to virtually all living organisms are beryllium, bromine, silver, mercury, lead, radon, actinium, and uranium, along with all elements heavier than uranium; see also under Inorganic Chemicals in Appendix C.

Moderately toxic elements include vanadium, chromium, copper, selenium, palladium, tin, osmium, thallium, polonium, and cerium. Many of these are so rare they do not constitute a significant pollution problem. Among the other troublesome elements in groundwater are fluorine and chlorine (Section 10.4.2C); sodium, which can pose a health threat for those on low-sodium diets; and boron, which can damage some crops and is a frequent groundwater contaminant in the Mediterranean basin.

A. Heavy Metals

Metals in an aquatic environment often link up with organic chemicals including fats, proteins, acids, and synthetic compounds. Such complexes can increase or decrease the toxicity of the metal and greatly influence its movement through the ecosystem, or through an organism like the human body. Tin forms the largest number of organically bound metals and is present in many pesticides, including many used to keep slime and other organisms from the walls of conduits and cooling towers or to help preserve wood, leather, and textiles [250].

Among the most serious elemental pollutants are certain metals, especially the **heavy metals** such as mercury, lead, and cadmium, which tend to be located in the lower right part of the periodic table (Table 1.2). These metallic elements can attack organisms in numerous ways. For example, they have a strong affinity for sulfur and can disrupt sulfur bonds in enzymes. Heavy metals may bind to cell membranes where they inhibit transport of important nutrients through cell walls. They can combine with a wide variety of ions and molecules. Whether in a pure elemental state or as compounds, they tend to be highly toxic to many life forms. In even mildly acidic water, lead readily leaches from old pipes, solders, brass, and other lead-containing materials, making it a major contaminant in drinking water in many places. Thankfully, heavy metals are not common or widespread groundwater pollutants, although local exceptions do exist. These metals tend to adsorb strongly to clays, reducing their presence in groundwater.

B. Metalloids

Arsenic, that old favorite in murder mysteries, is a highly toxic **metalloid**, a term given to elements which are borderline between metals and nonmetals. Among the visible signs of arsenic poisoning are blackened skin, scaling on feet and hands, skin mottling and open lesions which can lead to gangrene. Additional health impacts include lethargy, nervous disorders, and possible brain damage.

Although only about 2 to 5 ppm are present in Earth's crust, large amounts have been released to the environment from the burning of fossil fuels, especially coal, and by the mining and refining of copper, gold, and lead. Arsenic also has been concentrated and released as a consequence of its numerous uses, including in various pesticides, wood preservatives, and even in human embalming fluids. Pre-WW II pesticides often contained highly toxic arsenic compounds. Many of these uses have now been banned in most countries, but arsenic continues to be among the most persistent and dangerous of groundwater pollutants.

Where present naturally in earth materials, arsenic often contaminates vast quantities of groundwater as has occurred in heavily populated parts of Asia and Latin America, where over 100 million people drink water exceeding the WHO limit of 10 ìg of arsenic per liter (10 ppb). Arsenic is readily converted into mobile and toxic methyl derivatives. Acute arsenic poisoning results from ingestion of more than 100 mg, and chronic poisoning can occur by drinking water containing much lower levels. In 2001, the EPA found that more than 4,000 US public water supply systems would need to upgrade their treatment to meet the 10 ppb standard for arsenic.

Arsenic, fluoride, and other contaminants in drinking water represent ongoing threats to tens of millions of people around the world, even in developed nations such as the US. Extensive testing of thousands of well-water samples, careful groundwater monitoring programs, and enforcement of protective measures are needed to combat such problems and avoid mass poisonings.

Selenium and antimony are other metalloids which can occur in groundwater and often pose threats to both humans and wildlife, especially where the elements are present in local bedrock and regolith.

Example: Arsenic Poisoning in South Asia

In Bangladesh and several Indian states, especially West Bengal, surface water contamination forced people to turn to groundwater beginning in the 1970s. The groundwater wasn't tested for arsenic which turned out to be a natural pollutant in many areas where it was present at levels from 5 to 100 times

---

the recommended levels. Just in Bangladesh, some 75 million people have been exposed to high levels of arsenic in what has been called the largest mass poisoning in history. The arsenic occurs in sediments deposited on floodplains and deltas by rivers draining the Himalayans [121]. In Bangladesh, the shallow groundwater tends to be high in arsenic while most deeper water contains little arsenic. Heavy pumping from deep agricultural wells threatens to draw the arsenic-laden waters downward.

10.4.9 Particulates

Too much sediment or particulate matter from any source smothers aquatic life and makes the water unusable for most human needs. This is mainly a surface-water problem, but it also affects groundwater in many areas, especially near mines, construction sites, sewer lines, deep drilling sites, and septic systems, and wherever groundwater flows through large subsurface openings. Particulate problems are usually localized near wells where they degrade water quality and reduce permeability near the well, decreasing water input. Particulates often serve as carriers of toxic chemicals, bacteria, and other harmful substances.

10.4.10 Heat (Thermal Pollution)

Heat, mainly from the huge amount of water used for cooling at power plants and major industries, increases chemical reactions, depletes oxygen, and eliminates many temperature-sensitive species of animal and plant life. Nearly half the water withdrawn from all sources in the US is used for cooling in electric power plants. This is primarily a surface-water problem.

10.4.11 Radioactive Materials

Radioactive isotopes are serious groundwater and surface-water contaminants in many parts of the world. The nuclear power and weapons industries are the major generators. Radioisotopes may be released during uranium mining, uranium enrichment and fuel fabrication, power plant operation (where many additional radioisotopes are generated during the fission reaction), reprocessing of spent fuel, and waste disposal operations. Numerous nuclear weapons facilities and test sites are also important sources of radioactive contaminants. Groundwater has been polluted at many locations, including the Yucca Flat test site in Nevada where hundreds of underground nuclear weapons were detonated, contaminating an estimated 1.6 trillion gallons of groundwater [411].

Naturally occurring radioisotopes also occur in dangerous quantities in some areas, including along the Colorado River which provides water for Los Angeles, nearly all of southern Nevada, and many other downstream areas. Some 1,100 uranium mining claims exist within five miles of the Grand Canyon. Mining of the uranium deposits in this area and farther upriver has the potential of releasing more radioactive pollutants, either to surface streams or to groundwater which feed many springs along the Colorado River. Considerable uncertainty remains as to the transport and fate of some important radionuclides. For example, actinides such as plutonium appear capable of groundwater migration by attaching to minute nanometer-sized particles in colloids [291].

Radioactive substances are especially hazardous due to the insidious and often deadly impacts of the **ionizing radiation** emitted by their unstable nuclei. The high energy of this radiation can strip electrons from molecules, disrupting the delicate biochemistry of cells and leading to cancer (**carcinogenic** impacts), mutations in future offspring (**mutagenic** impacts), and birth defects (**teratogenic** impacts). The dose of radioactivity considered "safe" has continuously been decreased as more is learned of its effects on living organisms. The dosage regarded as safe by the US Atomic Energy Commission in the early 1950s was over 10,000 times greater than today's "safe" dose. Most studies indicate that the damage is cumulative, highly dependent upon an individual's susceptibility, and that no such thing as a "safe" dosage exists. Radioisotopes which are interchangeable with elements normally present in living organisms are especially hazardous. Radium is of special concern in drinking water, especially in uranium-mining areas.

Radon (Rn-222) is a common naturally occurring radionuclide in groundwater. Radon has a half-life of 3.8 days and is one of the breakdown products of uranium, which occurs in many common rocks. Because radon forms a gas at low pressures near the atmosphere, it can migrate through rock and soil and accumulate in homes where it can be a health hazard. Radon decays into another hazardous radioisotope, lead-210, which has a half-life of 22 years. The EPA considers no level of radon as "safe" and estimates that over 20,000 deaths are caused annually in the US by exposure to radon in indoor air. Meanwhile, in Japan and elsewhere, thousands patronize **radon springs** and baths where they believe it can cure a wide array of ills from hemorrhoids to high blood pressure. Despite advertising brochures promoting bathing rooms "pumped full of radon," the radon levels from such springs are actually very low.

Radon content is often used to estimate groundwater flow rates, the time that water has been in a stream, and the time elapsed since groundwater was in contact with radon-rich rock.

10.4.12 Medicines and Related Substances

In recent years, numerous studies have revealed that illegal drugs, pain killers, hormones, cancer drugs, and related chemicals appear to be ubiquitous at trace levels in US waters, including drinking water. Even though concentrations are low, concern is growing because of the sensitivity of many people and the fact that minute quantities and synergistic effects of these chemicals have been shown capable of potentially serious health impacts and ecological consequences, including impairment of human cell growth and reproductive damage to numerous aquatic animal species. Of special concern is the rise of antibiotic bacterial resistance due to the ongoing presence of these pharmaceutical ingredients in the environment.

The major source was initially thought to be consumer use of medicines. Over three billion prescriptions are written in the US each year. People flush millions of unused pills and pharmaceutical products down the toilet or otherwise carelessly discard them. In addition, much medicine is incompletely metabolized in the body. The excess will be excreted from the body and eventually adds to the environmental burden. Additional millions of pounds of drugs and contaminated packaging are disposed of, usually "down the drain," by the 5,700 hospitals and 45,000 long-term-care facilities in the US.

Most pharmaceuticals used in developed nations are manufactured in developing nations where regulations are often weak and poorly enforced. For example, villagers have complained for years about contamination from drugs and other pollutants in streams and well water near Patancheru, India, where some 90 drug factories are concentrated. Alarmingly high levels of a wide variety of drugs have been found in samples taken from treated wastewater at Patancheru [252]. Regulations on drug factories are much stricter in developed nations, but even there, only selected pharmaceuticals are tested for. Illegal dumping of medicines and related substances is another ongoing problem.

10.4.13 Miscellaneous Inorganics

A variety of inorganic chemical pollutants exist which do not fit neatly into the above categories. Five of the most important are listed below.

1. **Cyanide.** The cyanide radical (CN–) forms deadly compounds with many metal ions. In water, it tends to be present as HCN, a weak but very toxic acid used in gas chamber executions in the US. Cyanides are widely used in industry, especially for metal cleaning, electroplating, and mineral processing.

2. **Ammonia.** Ammonia often forms from the decay of nitrogenous organic waste and is a normal constituent of groundwater in a reducing environment.

3. **Hydrogen Sulfide.** Hydrogen sulfide (H_2S) is a deadly gas often emitted during the anaerobic decay of sulfur-containing organic matter and the precipitation of metallic sulfides. It is a common component of many industrial wastes and is readily recognized by its rotten-eggs odor.

4. **Carbon Dioxide.** In addition to its impact as a greenhouse gas (Section 12.6), excessive carbon dioxide can be harmful to aquatic life. Its increase in the atmosphere causes more to enter ocean waters where it forms carbonic acid and increases the acidity of seawater. This has potentially devastating impacts upon marine species, for example, by reducing the ability of plankton and other organisms to produce their shells and exoskeletons.

5. **Asbestos.** The presence of asbestos fibers in drinking water have raised concern in several regions, but its health impacts remain uncertain.

10.5 Contaminant Transport and Fate

Out of sight, out of mind.

— Anonymous

10.5.1 Introduction

The movement of mass (molecules, ions, and particles) through groundwater is influenced by the many chemical processes noted in Chapter 9. The actual transport of these materials occurs primarily by

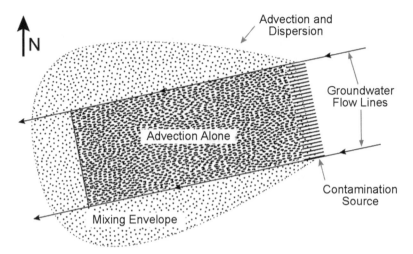

Figure 10.5. Idealized map view of a contaminant plume and its mixing zone or envelope. This shows the distribution of a contaminant in moving groundwater by advection alone (shaded area between the groundwater flow lines) and by advection and dispersion (entire area within the dotted line).

two processes: **advection**, which consists of being carried along by the groundwater flow itself, and **dispersion** (or, hydrodynamic dispersion), which consists of spreading out of the groundwater and its solutes by physical mixing and diffusion. Localized pollution sources, such as a landfill or leaking underground tank, often produce a continuous contaminant release in the form of a distinct plume generated by both advection and dispersion (Figure 10.5). The transport and dispersion of many pollutants, including organic chemicals and metals, can be accelerated considerably by such factors as the presence of organic solvents, colloids, and large macromolecules [100, 133, 423]. In some cases the pollutant migration rate can exceed that of the groundwater.

10.5.2 Advection

Advection is controlled by the same basic factors that determine groundwater flow rates and directions: topography, subsurface materials, and water recharge and discharge, among others. For the most part, impurities carried by the groundwater will be carried along by advection in the same direction and at the same rate as the water itself. How rapidly any impurity is transported depends upon the hydraulic gradient, hydraulic conductivity, and the interconnectedness of the pores (effective porosity), according to Darcy's Law:

$$v = (\frac{K}{n_e})(\frac{h}{l})$$

The higher the hydraulic conductivity (K) and hydraulic gradient (i = h/l), the faster the flow; the higher the effective porosity (n_e), the slower the flow. Other influences, mostly on a micro-scale, may alter the relative rate of water and solute flow, but they are usually of minor importance. For example, electrical charges on ions and matrix minerals can affect the movement of some ions and microcurrents in pores and can alter the water's flow rate [100].

10.5.3 Dispersion

Dispersion produces a zone of mixing between the normal groundwater and any invading water such as a contaminant plume. This mixing envelope will increase the size of the plume as the contaminant migrates downcurrent by advection (Figure 10.5). The concentration of pollutants in the mixing zone will decrease with time and distance from the source. Pollutant concentration can be indicated on both maps and cross-sections using contours as shown on Figure 10.6.

Physical (or **mechanical**) **mixing** produces dispersion by the many small-scale changes in flow velocity and direction produced as the water maneuvers through pore spaces and fractures in the earth material. The water will flow faster through larger openings (less flow resistance) and near the center of any openings (Figure 10.6C). The water also must constantly change direction as it migrates around grains and areas of less permeable material in the soil or rock matrix (Figure 10.6B). Rock/regolith type and structure, permeability, and pore size, shape, and distribution obviously will influence physical mixing.

Diffusion refers to the migration of any solute from areas of higher concentration to areas of lower concentration, like a drop of dye spreading out in a basin of water. Physical mixing requires water movement; diffusion does not. Most diffusion is slow and becomes a significant factor only where groundwater flow rates are very slow, but in those situations, it can allow harmful substances to contaminate areas where moving groundwater cannot penetrate.

In areas of steady groundwater flow, the upcurrent dispersion is usually negligible and maximum dispersion will be directly downcurrent. As a leachate plume moves downcurrent from a source, its pollutants

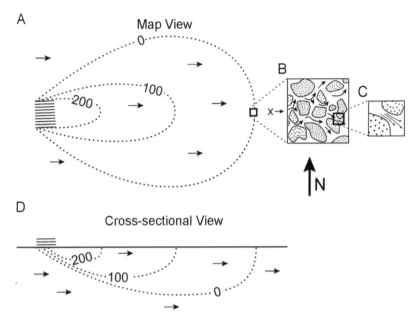

Figure 10.6. Contaminant plumes. **A.** Map view of a contamination plume with concentration contours. Groundwater flow (arrows) is to the east. For this idealized sketch, we assume (1) the contaminant is less dense than water, (2) a constant release of contaminant from the source, and (3) homogeneous earth materials (e.g., sand). **B.** Enlargement of the front of the plume showing a point source injection of contaminated water (point x) and how it will spread out as it moves between the grains of a sediment. **C.** Further enlargement of the water flow between two grains. Due to friction, the flow is reduced near the grains and faster in the center. This aids diffusion of the solute. **D.** A cross-sectional view of the plume seen in A, showing concentration contours.

will spread out as water moves along small twisting flow paths around grains and through fractures and other openings in the earth material. **Longitudinal dispersion** (or "dispersivity") refers to dispersion and mixing in the direction of the groundwater flow path. **Transverse horizontal dispersion** refers to lateral spreading perpendicular to the flow direction (to the north and south on Figure 10.6A) and **transverse vertical dispersion** refers to vertical spreading perpendicular to longitudinal dispersion (Figure 10.6D). In general, longitudinal dispersion tends to be about 10 times more rapid than transverse horizontal dispersion, which in turn occurs roughly at 10 to 100 times the rate of transverse vertical dispersion.

Dispersion will be considerably influenced and often restricted by the presence of impermeable materials and other inhomogeneities in the matrix materials. If fractures are the major pathways for groundwater movement, variations in the fracture size, density, and connections, along with diffusion of contaminants into the rock, are all likely to influence dispersion.

10.5.4 Influences on Transport

Dispersion and advection rates and directions will be influenced by the characteristics of the medium and the impurities being carried by the groundwater. For example, some solutes, called "**conservative**," will not react with the groundwater or be attracted by the medium. Others, called "**reactive**," tend to interact with the medium, or with groundwater and its contents. Adsorption onto clay particles is an especially effective means of reducing groundwater impurities. Conservative solutes include nitrate, chloride, and bromide ions. Reactive solutes include many synthetic organics and cations. The extent of interaction may be indicated by a **retardation factor**. A retardation factor of three means that a reactive solute will travel at one-third the velocity of the groundwater. The more reactive a material, the higher its retardation factor and the more slowly it will migrate through the water. A retardation factor of "one" would indicate a conservative solute moving at the same rate as the groundwater.

Adsorption, the tendency of a solute to be adsorbed by the medium it passes through, is indicated by the **distribution coefficient**. The value of this coefficient can be determined in the laboratory by saturating samples of a given soil with water containing differing concentrations of specific solutes and then comparing the solution concentrations with the resulting soil concentrations. The result is a value, such as eight milliliters of solute retained per gram of soil, indicating the tendency of the solute to attach to the material it passes through.

Attenuation refers to those processes which reduce the concentration of contaminants as they travel through a medium over time. Specifically, our concern is the reduction of groundwater impurities as the water migrates through regolith or rock. Recognizing the attenuation processes such as adsorption, absorption, dilution, oxidation, and other transformations is a vital part of determining the fate and the potential risks of groundwater contaminants. The soil/rock types encountered and the chemical reactions which occur during transport can significantly influence the pollutant types and concentrations. For example, polluted source areas such as landfills often have a strong reducing environment but, as the leachate migrates away from the source, more oxidizing conditions will be encountered. This can trigger various reactions including the conversion of ammonia into nitrate and the precipitation of soluble metal ions.

Understanding these processes is important in determining how much waste can be released in an area without impacting groundwater. This knowledge is necessary if operations involving landfills, sewers, septic tanks, waste lagoons, and land spreading of wastes are to proceed safely. Although the details of contaminant degradation in the vadose and phreatic zones must be left for more advanced explanations, some of the more important considerations in pollution attenuation will be briefly noted here.

Attenuation of hazardous contaminants is typically more effective in the unsaturated zone than in the saturated zone, a result of the presence of oxygen and aerobic bacteria, and of more effective absorption and ion exchange on the extensive interfaces which exist between solid, liquid, and gas phases. In most places, before becoming groundwater, meteoric water falling to Earth must pass through a blanket of soil or regolith. A productive agricultural soil typically will contain roughly 35% air by volume. The oxygen content of this soil air will be significantly less, and the carbon dioxide content far more, than in the atmosphere. Organic matter and humus will usually be less than 5% of the soil mass. However, this humic material has a strong affinity for many solutes and can absorb many organic compounds, heavy cations, and other impurities, albeit in limited amounts. Soil sorption of pollutants such as pesticides may increase or decrease the rate of degradation of the pollutants. Degradation in soil occurs mainly through the action of organisms, especially microbes, and chemical reactions.

Inorganic chemical pollutants include some of the most troublesome and ubiquitous groundwater pollutants, such as arsenic, sodium chloride, ammonia, and nitrates. Inorganics in the vadose zone are retarded primarily by denitrification, adsorption, bacterial decomposition, chelation, and chemical precipitation. Many metals have relatively low solubility and are adsorbed readily, for example, by clays or organic matter. Oxidizing conditions in soil or water encourage precipitation of many metals while reducing conditions favor breakdown of nitrates. In groundwater, dispersion and dilution tend to have the greatest overall impact on attenuating inorganic pollutants.

Synthetics, including many pesticides, solvents, and miscellaneous hydrocarbons, are the major concerns among the organic chemical pollutants. Factors influencing their degradation rates include the nature and quantity of contaminants, their solubility and miscibility in water, oxygen content, temperature, pH, and, of course, the subsurface geology. The presence of beneficial microorganisms can greatly accelerate the degradation of organic contaminants. Many factors influence the elimination of harmful microorganisms including the kinds of organisms present, pH, temperature, dissolved organic carbon, oxygen levels, and clay content.

10.5.5 Contaminant Plumes

The shape of a contaminant plume is determined mainly by advection. The more reactive the contaminants, the smaller the plume will be. This is because reactive contaminants will tend to be captured or immobilized during migration.

Loading variations (Section 10.3.2) will have considerable impact upon the plume and its contents. If the contaminant release is continuous and the contaminant strength consistent, the plume will be connected to the source at the upgradient end and the contaminant concentrations in the plume will increase as one nears that source (figures 10.6A and D and 10.7A). If the contamination ceases, groundwater flow will eventually replace contaminated water near the source with clean water and we will have a disconnected plume, or "slug," that will migrate downgradient (Figure 10.7B). Contaminant concentrations in the isolated, slowly expanding "slug" will decrease over time. If contaminant releases and concentrations have been intermittent or fluctuating widely, several "slugs" of varying concentrations may be present (Figure 10.7C). The size and shape of plumes will also be influenced by the source. Some releases are from a single point source such as a factory discharge or UST, others from several point sources, and still others from an extensive, diffuse source such as spreading wastes on the land surface or leakage from dozens of septic tanks.

The size and direction of movement within a groundwater plume are determined by all those factors which influence the groundwater flow as well as by the nature of the contaminants in the plume [100, 347]. Generally, the more rapid the groundwater flow rate, the more elongate the plume will be (Figure 10.8). Variations in hydraulic conductivities of rock and soil, location of aquitards, presence of large pores such as open fractures, the shape of the water table and piezometric surface, structural variations in the medium, local areas of recharge or discharge, and the nature of the contaminant source will all affect the size, shape, and

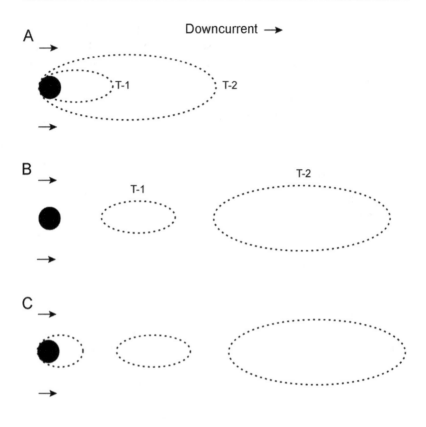

Figure 10.7. Map sketches of simple relations between contaminant releases and resulting plumes. The solid dots represent the contaminant source, arrows indicate groundwater flow direction. **A.** When release of a contaminant is continuous, the plume increases in size through time and remains attached to the source. T-1 indicates plume position after a designated time interval since contamination began. T-2 shows the same plume at a later time. **B.** If a single brief contaminant release occurs, the contamination plume will become detached from the source and migrate downcurrent as a slug (location T-1). As the slug moves downcurrent, its size will increase (location T-2) and its contaminant concentration will decrease. **C.** If releases are discontinuous or fluctuating in contaminant concentration, various contaminant slugs of different sizes may be present. The slugs may be separate as shown or connected by a zone of lesser concentration.

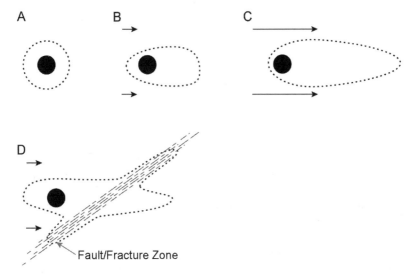

Figure 10.8. Map sketches of the impact of groundwater flow rates and directions on contaminant plumes. Solid circles represent the contaminant source; arrows indicate groundwater flow direction (the longer the arrow, the faster the flow). **A.** If groundwater is stagnant, contamination will slowly spread outward equally in all directions (assuming homogeneous conditions) to form a circular plume. **B.** If groundwater flows slowly, a relatively fat oblong plume will result. **C.** If groundwater flows rapidly, a highly elongated plume forms. **D.** Changes in permeability can have a strong impact on plumes. In this example, a fault or fracture zone of higher permeability is intersected by the plume, significantly altering its shape.

migration direction of the plume (Figure 10.8D). If no groundwater movement is occurring and homogeneous conditions exist, dispersion will tend to occur equally in all directions and the contaminant zone would be circular as in Figure 10.8A.

Delineating a plume and predicting the ultimate disposition of its contaminants can be especially difficult in karst or heavily fractured materials where groundwater flow may be very rapid and concentrated along large irregular pathways. In these situations groundwater and contaminant flow may be highly irregular, but will tend to converge toward a major flow path such as a stream, cave or large fracture system, if such exists (Figure 10.9).

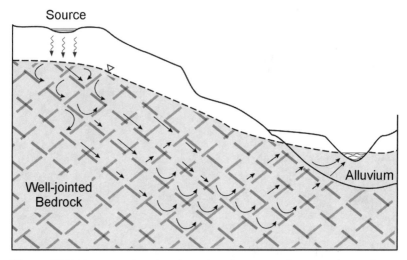

Source

Well-jointed Bedrock

Alluvium

Figure 10.9. Cross-section showing migration route of a contaminant plume (arrows) through well-jointed bedrock, then to alluvium, and finally discharging into a stream.

10.5.6 Monitoring Contaminant Plumes

A. Determining Plume Limits and Movement

The shape and extent of plumes are usually determined from sampling results at monitoring wells as illustrated in Figure 10.10. Plume migration is determined largely by groundwater flow paths; for example, their movement will be downgradient and perpendicular to the piezometric contour lines in relatively homogeneous materials.

Accurately determining the extent of the plume and its contaminant concentrations requires proper siting and construction of monitoring wells. To determine the limits of a plume, it is necessary to locate monitoring wells near the edges of the plume, both within and outside of the plume (Figure 10.10). The more wells, the more accurate the delineation of the plume and its contents. Testing samples from these wells over time will provide important data on the rate of plume spreading and changes in contaminant levels. Once a reasonably clear outline of the plume is established, additional sampling wells placed along the center line of the plume will aid in determining contaminant levels, plume thickness, and how these change through time. It may also be worth installing additional sampling points perpendicular to the center line or at other

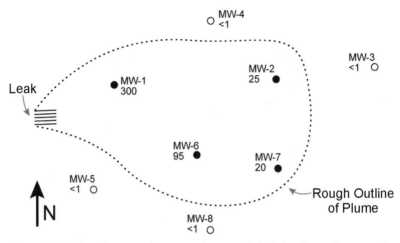

Figure 10.10. In this example, a petroleum tank leak has been discovered. Initially, an estimate of the water table slope and groundwater flow direction is made (eastward in this example), then a monitoring well (MW-1) is installed, usually several meters downgradient from the leak. Contamination is found in MW-1. Based on that result, seven additional wells, MW-2 through 8, are installed to roughly determine the extent of the plume. Analytical results for total petroleum hydrocarbons are indicated for each well in ppm. An open circle represents no apparent contamination, darkened circles represent contaminated water.

points, depending upon the nature of the contamination and the plume characteristics.

By using available sources of information about the elevation of the water table (including water levels in wells and nearby effluent streams, springs, and lakes) along with the local surface topography, one can construct a reasonably accurate contour map of the local water table. Water table (piezometric) contours can then be drawn and the movement of a contaminant plume can be predicted. In Figure 10.11, leachate from the landfill will move eastward toward the stream and possibly south into a cone of depression where it may contaminate the well water. Concentration levels of pollutants can also be indicated using contours. If a confined aquifer is involved, a similar contour map can be drawn for its piezometric surface and pollutant distribution.

Every contamination site is unique and no single approach will be appropriate for all. In complex conditions, data from deeper wells may

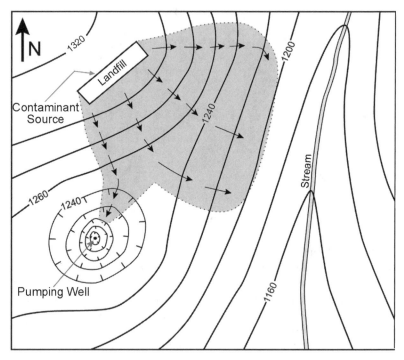

Figure 10.11. Map of a leachate plume from a landfill. The leachate will migrate downgradient, spreading by advection and dispersion. Water table contours are in feet above mean sea level and the contour interval is 20 feet. Note the cone of depression around a pumping water well. Arrows represent anticipated leachate movement. The contamination threatens both the well water and the stream. If adequate data are available, concentration of contaminant(s) can be indicated by another set of contours, or by shading.

be needed to determine contaminant pathways. Figure 10.12 shows how contamination may end up migrating in unexpected directions depending upon subsurface conditions.

If a site is characterized by highly irregular flow, as in karst or fractured media, monitoring locations will vary considerably from the above suggestions. Using tracers such as dyes and checking local discharge areas such as springs is a recommended approach under these conditions.

B. Plume Sampling

Obtaining samples from a contaminant plume involves more than just properly locating monitoring wells. The design and installation of

W

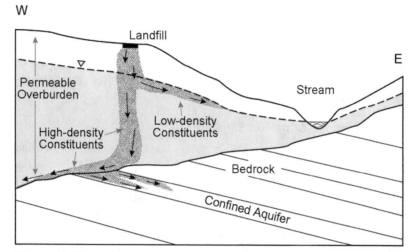

Figure 10.12. A cross-sectional view provides a different perspective of a relation such as that of the landfill and the stream in Figure 10.11. Arrows indicate movement of pollutants. The light constituents (those less dense than water) are carried eastward along the top of the water table with unconfined aquifer flow. The heavier constituents continue to sink downward until relatively impermeable bedrock is encountered. They then migrate west along the sloping bedrock, encountering a confined aquifer which provides an additional pathway eastward for the contamination.

monitoring and extraction wells will depend upon the behavior of the contaminants present. The sampling location of each well must be considered. Contaminant concentrations vary both vertically and laterally within a plume. Hence it is often necessary to carefully select where to take samples within the plume. Understanding interactions between the natural earth materials and the pollutants can aid greatly in determining what chemicals to test for. Chemical reactions between the medium and the contaminants will often produce by-products, usually ions, which migrate more rapidly than the actual contaminants. Detection of these by-products provides advance warning that contamination is approaching.

Determining the vertical changes in concentration from the top to the bottom of a plume is often the most difficult type of sampling, as it requires obtaining samples from different depths within the plume. If a well is constructed with a screen that extends throughout the entire thickness of the plume, a sample will represent a crude average of the contamination throughout that part of the plume. To determine the vertical distribution of the contaminant, "point samples" will need to be gathered from specific depths in the plume. This is possible by constructing multiple wells or piezometers with very narrow intake areas or by use of multilevel sampling devices which can collect samples from various depths within a single well.

10.5.7 Vadose Zone Contamination

Most pollution sources will be located near the ground surface and above the water table. A plume of contamination will spread from the source(s) down into the zone of aeration (vadose zone), generally expanding outward as it proceeds. The dominant direction of movement will be downward under the direct influence of gravity. However, if one or more relatively impermeable layers (aquitards) are present, the contamination will tend to spread out laterally atop the aquitards. If the vadose plume reaches the water table, it will then become the source of a groundwater contamination plume (figures 10.3 and 10.4).

An adequate number of borings with continuous sampling of the soil or rock materials will be needed to determine the lateral and vertical extent of the contamination. When the plume has been delineated, a course of action will be decided based upon the nature and quantity of the pollutants and the risks they pose at that specific site. The action may be to do nothing if the pollution poses no threat to health, groundwater, or environment; to remove and treat contaminated material; or to undertake *in situ* remediation.

Vapor phase contamination in the vadose zone is a special concern. Vapor contaminant pathways trend upward allowing hazardous gases to enter buildings. Monitoring to detect volatile pollutants in the vadose zone is an important part of many contamination investigations. Vapor surveys and profiles can help determine the extent and potential risk of such common ground pollutants as gasoline, perchlorate, and PCE.

> **Example: Hanford Nuclear Facility**
>
> In some areas, the vadose zone is capable of accumulating large quantities of pollutants. At the Hanford Nuclear Facility, a 1,517 km^2 (586 mi^2) site in Washington state, the largest environmental clean-up in US history is underway. The purpose of this decades-old, multibillion-dollar effort is to treat

and immobilize some 200,000 m³ of radioactive wastes from the production of nuclear weapons. These wastes are highly corrosive and boiling hot due to the release of heat from radionuclide breakdown. The wastes were placed in poorly constructed tanks which have repeatedly leaked their hellish contents into the ground — new leaks continue to be discovered [206]. Hundreds of millions of liters of hazardous wastes have escaped containment and seeped into the vadose zone over the past several decades. The radioactivity has rendered some 240 mi² of the site uninhabitable. The great variety, large volume, and hazardous nature of the contaminants and their proximity to the Columbia River make this one of the highest-risk sites in the nation. Some two million curies of radioactivity and hundreds of thousands of tons of waste are believed to have been captured in the thick stratified units of the vadose zone, but some, including carbon tetrachloride, tritium, and nitrate have reached underlying groundwater. Complex interactions make the transport and fate of such pollutants as uranium and organic compounds extremely difficult to predict and quantify. Processes which must be considered include ion exchange, surface complexation reactions, precipitation, and dissolution and how these impact and alter the many chemical contaminants present. Studies of the complex interactions between infiltrating water, climate, the stratified sediment, and the pollutants have been ongoing for over three decades, but much remains to be learned, and to be done [310, 444, 516].

11 Applied Hydrogeology

Our knowledge of Earth's water environment at the surface and shallow subsurface remains appallingly insufficient.

— Jay Famiglietti, 2012

11.1 Putting Hydrogeology to Work

Most of this book concerns basic occurrences and behavior of groundwater, sometimes called "**theoretical**" hydrogeology. In this chapter, some of the practical activities related to groundwater, usually referred to as "**applied**" hydrogeology, are introduced. This information provides insight into the real world of hydrogeology investigations for the prospective hydrogeologist and provides valuable information on groundwater projects for other readers.

Practicing hydrogeologists and other water professionals are required to put their knowledge into action. They have responsibilities to the public, the organization they work for, and the clients who hire them. As noted at the beginning of this book, water is an absolute essential whose importance cannot be overstated. Actions which impact its quantity and quality can have great and grave consequences and need to be based upon solid information and understanding.

Hydrogeologists are, and will continue to be, in high demand. Due to the vital importance and vulnerability of water resources, hydrogeologic studies incur an exceptionally heavy responsibility and those individuals who engage in such investigations must always keep this in mind, be s/he a field assistant, technician, project manager, or company president. If investigations involving water supply and quality have not been competently carried out, decisions will be based upon defective information and the results can be costly, tragic, and/or fatal. Too many mishaps, both large and small, have resulted from inadequate hydrogeologic knowledge and input. The products of insufficient investigation or knowledge of subsurface water range from failing dams to collapsing highways to sinking cities to releases of toxic pollutants.

Having said that, it is important to realize that our knowledge is never complete and every undertaking represents a balance between the ideal and the reality. The ideal is to gain maximum knowledge of any situation before proceeding, but nature's infinite variables, along with real-world time and cost constraints, make the ideal unobtainable. Due largely to the complex and hidden characteristics of subsurface waters, this frustrating compromise between what we wish we knew and what we must quickly do is something all practicing hydrogeologists must deal with repeatedly. Meanwhile, the need to preserve, conserve, and restore groundwater is growing at an unprecedented rate around the world. That growth will almost certainly continue to accelerate.

Purely hydrogeological goals can range widely, but will often concern a water supply or a potential threat to water supplies. Most hydrogeologic studies involve four major steps; they should: (1) obtain the basic background information, (2) gather the necessary site-specific data, (3) organize this information into a coherent concept or overview of site conditions, and (4) use this information to realize the project goals.

1. **Background information.** Background information involves gathering preliminary information about the local geology (lithology, structure, geomorphic setting, and so forth) and hydrology (water occurrence, movement, and chemistry) as well as any pertinent information about nearby sites which may influence, or be influenced by, the project (pollution sources, sensitive ecosystems, utility corridors, and population centers, among others). Important geologic information may be obtained from topographic maps, geologic maps and sections, aerial photographs, previous reports on the study area, and direct observation (preliminary field study). Hydrologic data often includes information on surface water, groundwater, and soil/regolith characteristics. Both geologic and hydrologic information can be obtained from the journals and related publications of professional societies, reports of consulting and engineering firms, reports and files of national and local government agencies, university departments, the Internet, and numerous other organizations (References, II - Miscellaneous).

2. **Site specific data.** This refers to more detailed information obtained by on-site field investigations and from previous in-depth studies conducted at or near the site. This may

involve soil and water sampling, drilling to determine subsurface conditions, data from nearby wells and surface water features, geophysical surveys, and interviews.

3. **Organize the data.** The third step involves synthesizing or conceptualizing the assembled information: putting it all together, making sense of it, and deciding how to proceed. For example, how many wells are needed, where, how deep, what size, and how should they be constructed? It often requires the ability to organize large masses of data in an accessible and concise manner, then to use those data to arrive at relevant conclusions. This requires having a well-founded model, or conceptual framework, of the overall hydrogeological environment upon which to base site activities.

4. **Action plan.** This involves putting the information to work, determining how to proceed. Once actual site operations commence, the work plan may need to be modified based upon new information discovered during drilling or other activities.

The actual projects or activities which may require hydrogeologic input are virtually without limit. Almost any operation which alters Earth's surface is likely to produce some effects on both surface and ground waters. Construction (highways, large buildings, housing developments, pipelines), surface water projects (dams, river channelization or restoration, canals, coastal structures), agriculture, almost all situations involving land and water pollution, ecological restoration, and dozens of other operations will potentially impact, and be impacted by, subsurface waters.

11.2 Prerequisites for the Applied Hydrogeologist

Maintain your professionalism at all times.

— William J. Stone

11.2.1 Knowledge

A solid qualitative grasp of basic concepts of both geology and hydrology is essential. This entails understanding the concepts and using accurate terminology. Science is a never ending quest and a good scientist never stops studying and learning. Staying abreast of current advances and trends is part of the job. A broad liberal arts background which expands knowledge beyond one's field of expertise can be extremely valuable. Health, ecology, engineering, and many other fields of knowledge may be critical to the success of a project.

Virtually every hydrogeologist will be faced with situations which were never covered or anticipated during standard coursework and training, nor during the planning phase of a project. The person in charge of field operations will often need to make on-site decisions and modifications. This requires knowledge, confidence, and a clear, well-founded concept of the site conditions.

An ever-expanding list of basic textbooks and related references is available and many are listed in this book (References, I - Publications).

11.2.2 Field Experience

Experience with a broad array of field methods and techniques is also a huge advantage. The importance of field experience cannot be overemphasized. All beginners should accompany an experienced professional at several active sites before going it alone. The background and training obtained in the classroom and field methods courses is valuable, but cannot replace hands-on experience.

Numerous texts and manuals cover field methods and applications in detail, as do many government publications, both federal and local [47, 100, 273, 378, 402, 422, 423].

11.2.3 Practical Skills

Skillful use of the "tools of the trade" is another necessity. A good field person needs familiarity with a wide array of equipment. Field equipment frequently used by hydrogeologists ranges from simple hand bailers and water testing devices to air monitoring and land surveying equipment. More complex field operations which s/he may need to participate in, or possibly take charge of, include operations involving drilling rigs, releases of hazardous materials, remediation efforts, health and safety procedures, and a variety of engineering-related activities.

Following established **safety procedures** is especially important and most employees, especially if involved in any way with contaminated sites, will be required to take an annual health and safety training class. A hydrogeologist is often in charge of field operations and is, at least to some extent, responsible for the safety of the work crew and the public. This can range from requiring that proper precautions are taken around machinery such as a drill rig to deciding when vapor releases require use of a special breathing apparatus.

408

S/he should also be adept at locating and interpreting a wide variety of documents and information sources, including reports, topographic maps, geologic maps and cross-sections, graphs, aerial photographs, and satellite imagery. Familiarity with basic office equipment, computers, and modeling programs can be a big plus.

11.2.4 Communication Skills

Communication skills, both oral and written, are another very important part of the hydrogeologists' arsenal. Obtaining work contracts may require a hydrogeologist to write a proposal outlining the anticipated work and its costs. S/he may then need to explain the proposal to the client and keep the client informed during the project. If obstacles or problems such as contamination are encountered, the impacts of these on the costs and time involved need to be evaluated and explained.

Ability to communicate across different fields, such as engineering, human health, ecology, law, and the social/political sciences, is another valuable asset. In many areas, projects must be approved by a "certified" or "professional" person, often an engineer. This person may not be an expert on groundwater and must rely upon input from the hydrologist, geologist, or other qualified persons. It is also frequently necessary to establish good working relations with local people such as town managers, public utility workers, or even members of a third-world community.

Interaction with others can become complicated. Most projects involve teams of workers. This may require sharing responsibility with others or assuming a leadership position. Good communication and cooperation always make work easier and more efficient for everyone. A qualified hydrogeologist would likely be responsible for directing the efforts of other team members. Common projects include overseeing the removal of pollution sources such as USTs, directing the drilling and installation of wells, and overseeing a complex, long-term site remediation. The hydrogeologist may also be responsible for recording the work that is done and reporting the progress in a detailed, accurate, timely, and effective manner. This requires an ability to take good notes and write good reports as discussed in Section 11.3.12.

11.2.5 Attitude

Enthusiasm for the subject matter, its value to society, and a positive attitude toward work and learning are always important, both for beginners and "old timers." Critical and imaginative thinking is a valuable asset and should be encouraged.

409

11.2.6 Efficiency

In purely practical terms, this means the ability to work effectively and produce anticipated results within budget and time restrictions. This is not always easy. It will at times prove to be impossible and the hydrogeologist will be called upon to use his communication abilities to explain the situation and justify the need for additional time and expense. Adhering to a schedule, working under scrutiny and within budget limits can be enormously frustrating, especially for the idealist. It requires the above prerequisites along with good organization, personnel management, and flexibility.

11.3 Groundwater Consulting Activities

Practicing groundwater scientists may be involved with many different activities, a selected number of which are described here.

11.3.1 Site Selection

The first step for some groundwater-related projects may require locating the most suitable site — for water supply wells or a waste-disposal site, for example. This involves a preliminary review of the areas under consideration followed by elimination of certain sites and a general ranking of the potentially suitable sites. The geological and environmental conditions of the best sites must be evaluated along with nearby locations which might influence, or be impacted by, the site project. Hydrogeologic, environmental, technical, legal, and economic aspects all need to be considered.

11.3.2 Water Supply

Many major applications of hydrogeology concern water supplies. The hydrogeologist's role can be varied. For example, s/he may be required to locate a new supply of groundwater, to assess the groundwater resources of an area, to help guide the actual extraction of water, to determine the impacts of groundwater removal, or to evaluate the sustainability of the groundwater resource under various scenarios. The water may be needed for any number of enterprises: an individual home, a city, an industry, a mining operation, or even an entire country or a large part thereof. The groundwater scientist may also be involved in an initial determination of the water requirements, well installation operations, well purging and sampling, well sterilization, pump selection, water treatment and storage needs, environmental impacts, infrastructure to deliver water to consumers, cost estimates, legal concerns, and other related matters [378].

The search for a sustainable groundwater source of suitable quantity and quality may require an original investigation by the hydrogeologist. If the area has been well-studied, s/he may be able to rely heavily upon previous reports. For example, many local entities such as counties and provinces have water resource reports available and various state and local government agencies maintain databases of wells. Well logs, geologic maps, reports, aerial photographs, and related sources will often provide much of the information needed to evaluate the groundwater potential.

Every location is unique and must be evaluated for its water potential using sound geologic and hydrologic principles. Techniques range from basic field work to computer modeling to geophysical studies.

11.3.3 Well Installation

The individual in charge of installing wells will often be responsible for well location, determining its impacts on the surrounding environment, designing the well, directing its drilling and installation, developing the well, collecting samples, and related activities. For an important project, especially if an environmental threat is involved, it would be ideal to have a fully qualified hydrogeologist to plan and oversee the installation. But, depending upon the nature of the project and the firm employed, a number of workers — including engineers, geologists, project assistants, technicians, and drillers — may be assigned to supervise and carry out the operations.

Many monitoring wells are installed to determine the severity and extent of groundwater pollution. The contamination may be a potential threat to human safety and to the environment. Hence, special care is needed during all parts of a contamination investigation. All materials used in the well, including the well itself, should be chemically inactive to avoid influencing the chemical makeup of the water. Equipment used during well drilling and installation must be thoroughly cleansed to avoid spreading contamination.

Well development involves removing water and debris from a well to restore the material around the well to its original (predrilling) condition. The most thorough development is done following construction of a well. With a new water supply well its purpose is to improve hydraulic conductivity near the well so that groundwater will flow more efficiently into the well, mainly by removing small particles. Forcing water or air

411

into the well under pressure is also utilized to aid in flushing out particles and enlarging interconnected pore spaces. A variety of procedures may be used, including surging, jetting, hydrofracking, overpumping, and backwashing [103].

11.3.4 Water Sampling

A. Overview

One of the most important jobs the hydrogeologist, or his field technician, must perform is collecting water samples which will accurately reflect the actual field conditions. Most groundwater samples are obtained from a piezometer or a well. The persons in charge of water sampling have several important duties, including to:

- determine the goals of the sampling program, what is to be tested for and why;
- decide where the samples are to be taken, how many, how often;
- be sure any preliminary operations are completed, such as properly purging a well and waiting the appropriate time period before sampling; and
- establish a good quality control program. This requires the hydrogeologist to (1) provide a record of the sampling which includes the time, date, site name, specific well or other water source; (2) assure sterility of sampling equipment and perform thorough decontamination between sampling; (3) use the correct size and type of containers with appropriate preservatives; and (4) deliver samples promptly to the laboratory with the proper paperwork and documentation.

To obtain good water samples for analysis, wells and piezometers need to be carefully placed so as to reflect the complexity and characteristics of the site. Small diameter sampling tubes or casings are desirable to minimize mixing of waters with differing contaminant concentrations. It is often necessary to obtain samples from a number of locations and at various depths. "Nests" of closely spaced wells can be used to obtain samples from different depths as can specially designed multilevel samplers. Multilevel samplers utilize various arrangements of small rigid or flexible tubes to sample water at two or more levels in a single borehole (Figure 11.1). Using these samplers is less costly but the equipment can be fussy to use and tends to be less durable than that for individual wells.

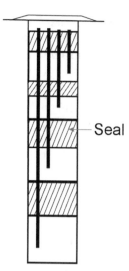

Figure 11.1. Schematic of multi-level sampling device. Two or more sampling tubes are inserted into a single borehole to allow water sampling from different depths, either within a single aquifer, or from separate aquifers. This example shows four sampling tubes with an impermeable seal (usually bentonite clay) between each to prevent mingling of waters from different aquifers. The seals may not be necessary if sampling from different depths in a single unconsolidated unit.

Seals may be needed between sample points to prevent mixing of waters from different depths. Another sampling tool is the HydroPunch® which can bore through unconsolidated materials to quickly collect a water sample without the expense of installing wells.

Water samples can be obtained by pumping or bailing water from a well or other opening to the subsurface and placing the water in an appropriate container. If initial samples indicate a contamination problem, samples will usually need to be collected from the same location over established time intervals to monitor contamination trends. Additional monitoring wells may be required to define the extent of the problem.

B. Purging

Prior to collecting water samples, a well should also be purged of several well volumes of water to remove foreign particles and solutes. This involves pumping or bailing a quantity of water from the well

413

sufficient to remove unwanted materials including sediment, drilling fluids, and miscellaneous substances resulting from the drilling and construction of the well. Later sampling involves a similar procedure because water that has been sitting for some time in a well is stagnant, may be contaminated by debris from the surface, and may not be an accurate representation of the groundwater. Thus, all wells should be purged prior to sampling by pumping or bailing three or more well volumes of water. To calculate how much water needs to be removed by hand bailing, one needs to determine the volume of water in the well and the volume of water in the bailer. The water in both the well and the bailer occupies a cylinder and the basic equation for the volume of a cylinder is:

$$V = \pi r^2 h$$

where V is the volume of water, r is the radius of the well or bailer, and h is the height of the water column in the well or the bailer. Once both volumes are known, the number of bailers of water needed to purge the necessary amount of water can be easily calculated.

When purging or sampling potentially contaminated well water, the field worker should use disposable gloves and thoroughly clean anything that contacts the contamination (including clothes and hands) before starting work on another sample. When several wells must be checked or sampled, the activity should begin with the least polluted well and proceed to the most polluted to minimize spreading contaminants. If severe pollution is present, a complete hazmat outfit with breathing apparatus may be needed.

In most monitoring wells, removal of the water can be achieved simply and inexpensively by hand with a **dedicated bailer**. The term "dedicated" means that a given bailer is used in only one well as a means of avoiding cross-contamination between wells. Most hand bailers (Figure 7.12) are long cylinders made of PVC, Teflon®, or stainless steel which can be attached to a string or rope and lowered into the well by hand. The bailer has sufficient weight to sink into the water. Water enters the bottom of the bailer as it sinks and a check valve closes to prevent the water from flowing out as it is hoisted back to the surface. Disadvantages of bailers are the time and labor involved, imprecision about the exact location of the water sample, and the possible alteration of sample chemistry by contamination or loss of gaseous contaminants while transferring water from the bailer to a sample bottle.

414

If hand purging is too laborious, a variety of pumps, including bladder, peristaltic, and electric submersible types, may be purchased or rented to purge wells and retrieve groundwater samples. If rapidly changing water quality requires frequent sampling, automatic sampling devices are also available.

C. Sample Collection

After a well is purged, samples are collected following a brief waiting period (usually 24 hours or less) to allow the water level to stabilize — that is, to return to its equilibrium level — in the well. Basic field observations such as water level in the well, time of collection, and weather conditions should be recorded. Methods employed to collect pollutants vary with the properties of the pollutant. Proper collecting protocols to maintain sample integrity and avoid cross-contamination are essential. In the US, EPA specifications are generally followed for all labeling, storage, and handling of samples.

Many parameters, including pH, conductivity, and turbidity can be measured immediately in the field using portable instruments. This has the advantage of avoiding the lag time between sample gathering and analyses — some contaminants deteriorate over time — and minimizes risks of contaminating the samples. On the other hand, some analyses can only be done in a laboratory, or will produce more reliable results than can be obtained with field equipment. Some companies have well-equipped mobile laboratories for on-site analyses.

D. Sample Containers

Suitable water containers and collecting protocols need to be employed. Actual requirements vary depending upon the contaminants being sought [284]. Sample containers need to be sterile, air-tight, and suited to the materials being collected. If testing for inorganics, plastic bottles are best because metals may be leached from glass. If organic compounds are to be tested for, glass is best because organics can interact with plastic. Certain chemicals will break down if exposed to light and must be collected in tinted glass to avoid decomposition. Some analyses require large samples, some small. If volatile compounds are to be tested for, special vials with no air space are used. Special preservatives, filters, and limited holding times are common requirements. Some samples must be kept cold to reduce deterioration. Dilute acid will help preserve some contaminants such as metals or nutrients. Most analytical laboratories will provide sampling instructions along with appropriate containers, preservatives, and other materials.

E. Sample Documentation and Transport

Immediately after collection, samples should be placed in a cooler and taken or shipped to the lab as soon as possible. Sample labels should include the site name and location (for example, Smith's Service Station, Butler, VA), sample location (for example, monitoring well #MW-4), collector's name and company, date and time collected, and chemicals to be tested for. A chain of custody is a document which should accompany each sample or group of samples. Its purpose is to keep track of the samples and help document that proper handling procedures were followed. This helps ensure accurate identification of samples, and reduces the likelihood of tampering. A **chain-of-custody** form provides information including sample identification numbers, sampling times, all transfers, arrival at the analytical lab, signatures of persons handling the samples, and other relevant information.

F. Analytical Methods

Analytical methods will vary depending upon the contaminants being tested for. Pathogens will often be cultured on a growth medium or observed directly with microscopes. Filtration and centrifuging may be employed initially to separate dissolved material from particulate material. Identification of contaminants is accomplished using various chemical analyses, x-ray diffraction, gas chromatography, mass spectroscopy, and other techniques.

G. Quality Control

The accuracy of all field and laboratory analyses needs to be periodically checked. Methods include internal lab quality control programs; **spiked samples**, including samples containing a known concentration of a chemical; **split samples**, a sample that is split in two and both samples separately analyzed, sometimes at a different laboratory; and **field blanks**, pure water that has been run through the sampling equipment. Such techniques are all part of a good quality control program and are intended to spot problems such as faulty lab equipment, improper sampling and handling procedures, and contaminated field sampling equipment.

All the expertise, effort, expense, and sophisticated modeling on Earth will not produce meaningful results if the basic data gathered in the field are not dependable. Unfortunately, sloppy field practices are not uncommon, especially with the time and budget constraints which sometimes exist. Field conditions can be very unpleasant and it is difficult at times to maintain proper procedures at subfreezing or painfully hot temperatures, or when battling wind and rain and mud along with any number of other distractions.

11.3.5 Site Characterizations

A **site characterization** is an investigation whose purpose is to describe the relevant conditions at particular location. The characterization provides the basic information which will determine what work needs to be done to address the situation, be that containing a plume of groundwater contamination or locating a new supply of groundwater. As noted in the introduction to this chapter, once the problem or purpose has been defined, the procedure will involve gathering existing information on the geology, hydrology, and chemistry of the site area, adding the results of the current site investigation, and putting all the information together to provide a reasonably accurate idea, a conceptualization, of the subsurface environment. This characterization will guide all subsequent actions such as the number, location, and depth of wells or a plan to determine the extent and nature of contamination and how to handle it.

Most site characterizations are contamination investigations. The hydrogeologist must determine the nature and extent of contamination and evaluate its impacts, present and future, on groundwater resources, as well as potential effects on ecosystems and human health. Some details on monitoring contamination plumes are provided in Section 10.5.6. Contamination projects involve more than the science, the installations, the methods to be used, the findings, and the recommendations. Beyond these are a whole slew of affairs, many of them quite frustrating to hydrogeologists and consultants, which may arise. The hydrogeologist may be responsible for determining the purpose and scope of the project, writing a proposal, preparing a budget for the study, producing regular progress reports, and interpreting the conditions for the client. Past uses of the site area often need to be investigated. Regulations, many of them written in obfuscating language by people with little understanding of groundwater science, must be plowed through. Regulators must be consulted, provided with information, their interpretations of the rules given due consideration. Forms must be filled out, permits must be applied for, and deadlines met. It may be necessary to work with numerous contractors and subcontractors, not all of whom are responsible or knowledgeable. Special equipment, maps (of subsurface utilities, for example), or personnel may need to be acquired. All activities, including communications and field procedures, should be carefully recorded, with dates and documentation. Sometimes, legal complications must be dealt with.

Groundwater experts are often asked to testify on behalf of a litigant or as an outside expert witness.

For contaminated sites, the recommended course of action is usually decided based upon an assessment of the risks to human health and the environment associated with each site. The resulting **risk-based analysis** is used to estimate the amount of effort and cost which a given site merits [6]. Risk-based analyses typically entail such undertakings as:

- determining known and potential sources of contamination;
- identifying possible migration paths and receptors such as water supply wells, surface water bodies, ecologically significant areas, and other features that could potentially be impacted by the contamination;
- collecting, analyzing, and interpreting soil and water samples;
- identifying nearby active and potential water supplies;
- evaluating the hydrologic properties of the subsurface and their influence on water and contaminant migration;
- using such information to predict the movement and fate of the contaminants, usually with the aid of computer modeling programs; or
- assess the potential impacts upon the identified environmental receptors.

11.3.6 Corrective Action Plans

Using the findings of the site characterization and/or risk-based analysis, the hydrogeologist will then recommend suitable responses to the situation. Needless to say, some response actions may need to be taken immediately — for example, when a serious threat is imminent, a pollutant is continuing to be released, or free product is present. Other actions will need to be carefully considered using the methods outlined above. These recommended actions are described in a document called a **corrective action plan (CAP)**. If contamination is severe and important water supplies are threatened, the CAP may recommend extensive remediation of an aquifer, a process that can require many years and anywhere from thousands to millions of dollars. If the contamination is minor and unlikely to pose a threat to humans or the environment, the best recommendation may be to do nothing but continue monitoring for a period of time. For example, a UST may have leaked gasoline into soils below the tank. If the soils are fairly impermeable, groundwater has not been impacted or only minimally impacted, and no local supply wells, basements, or other receptors are likely to be affected, doing nothing may be the most sensible alternative. Digging up the soils or similar actions could expose the environment and people to more risk than leaving it be. Natural capture and degradation of petroleum hydrocarbons will probably limit the contamination to the local area with minimal risk to health and environment.

11.3.7 Source Control

If soil and/or groundwater contamination is documented, the initial action is to discover and control the source, unless already known. Controlling the source may be simple or complex. If the problem is a defective valve or connection — in underground pipe lines or in a gasoline pump, for example, a simple repair job or replacement may stop the release. If a leaking underground tank is the source, it will probably need to be excavated along with heavily contaminated soil. The tank, soil, and other impacted materials must then be properly handled and disposed of or remediated.

In most areas firms exist which will pick up, treat, and/or dispose of such wastes. The consultant may still need to evaluate the extent of possible contamination in the remaining soil, usually by analyses of a series of samples. Once the degree and extent of contamination is known, any existing or potential threat can be evaluated. Additional soil excavation or in situ remediation may be recommended if a threat to groundwater or human health remains.

Larger sources of pollution, such as landfills and industrial sites, cannot be moved. The usual approach in these cases is to contain the contamination at the site by hydrologically insulating the site from the environment. Three major actions are often required (Figure 11.2A).

1. Divert surface water away from the site. This consists of altering the surface so that runoff is prevented from eroding the site area and/or transporting contaminants off site.
2. Place an **impermeable cap** over the contaminated areas to prevent meteoric water from infiltrating the wastes and forming more leachate. Caps may consist of compacted clay or an artificial cover made of special concrete, plastic, or other sealant.
3. Install **subsurface barriers** to prevent contaminated leachate from leaving the site. Where feasible, this may consist of constructing a wall-like containment structure around the entire site — a **cutoff wall**. If the local soils are suitable

and the contamination not very deep, a narrow trench up to about 80 feet in depth can be dug and filled with a thick, liquid mix, often of bentonite clay and cement. This material hardens into an impermeable solid. The resulting enclosure, often called a **slurry wall**, inhibits subsurface water (phreatic or vadose) from entering or leaving the contaminated area. In a **grout curtain**, a slurry of bentonite cement, gelatinous clay, or similar material is injected under pressure through a series of boreholes around the periphery of the site. The purpose again is to waterproof a subsurface area to prevent contaminated water from exiting the site. This technique is most successful where the soil or rock material has relatively large interconnected pores and high effective porosity. A big advantage of grout curtains over slurry walls is that the grout can be injected at great depths. A major disadvantage is that the grout slurry from neighboring boreholes may not merge, leaving open areas through which subsurface waters and contaminants can migrate. Grout can also be injected through on-site boreholes to create a seal beneath the contamination source. Grout curtains are also used extensively around dams and subsurface construction works to strengthen loose material and restrict groundwater migration. Another alternative is to drive metal sheet piling into the soil around the contaminated area. This is most suitable for soft, fine-grained soils.

If the water table intersects the contamination source, it may be necessary to install pumping wells at the site. The withdrawal of water will serve to lower the water table at the site and cause local groundwater to flow toward, rather than away from, the source of contamination (Figure 11.2B). The groundwater withdrawn can then be treated as discussed below.

11.3.8 Remediation

As noted previously, the only intelligent approach to preserving potable groundwater resources is to avoid polluting them. Given enough time, bacterial action, adsorption onto clays, filtration and other natural processes may eventually produce potable water from contaminated groundwater. But natural cleansing of contaminated soils and groundwater may

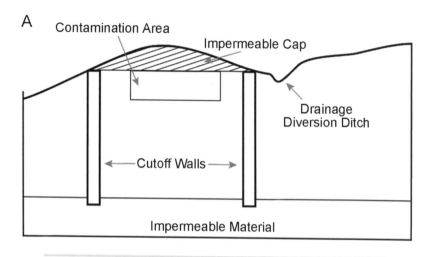

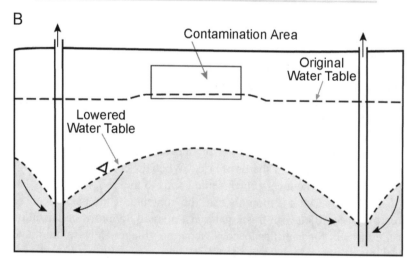

Figure 11.2. Insulating a contaminated area from the environment. **A.** Three common approaches are to provide runoff diversion, an impermeable cap, and an impermeable base with cutoff walls. **B.** If cutoff walls are impractical and the water table is high, pumping wells, sometimes in combination with an impermeable cap and runoff diversions, can be used to lower the water table and prevent contaminated groundwater from entering and exiting the site. This cross-section shows two withdrawal wells and their impact on the water table. A mound often forms in the original water table beneath old fill and waste sites due to increased infiltration rates through the disturbed (contaminated) material.

require hundreds or thousands of years. In many situations, the contamination threatens drinking water sources or surface waters and active remediation is required. Even then, restoring the water to a drinkable state will often be economically impractical or physically impossible. Remediation of contaminated groundwater has proven to be a stubborn, costly, and long-term problem. Reasons for this range from the unpredictability of pollutant migration pathways and destinations to the sheer magnitude, variety, and persistence of pollutants [349]. Minimizing the threat is often the best that can be achieved.

Remediation techniques are reviewed in depth in numerous books, symposia and conference reports, articles, and online sources [42, 73, 276, 404]. Table 11.1 lists frequently employed mitigation methods where groundwater pollution exists or is a threat. A simplified overview of common remediation approaches follows.

A. Simple Solutions

Some solutions can be remarkably simple. Arsenic is a common pollutant, both natural and human-generated, in groundwater and a major threat to human health (Section 10.4.8B). In Nepal, bacterial contamination of surface waters led to large-scale well construction, only to find the groundwater heavily contaminated with arsenic leached from bedrock — up to 700 ppb in some areas, compared to a recommended maximum of about 10 ppb. A device developed at the Massachusetts Institute of Technology uses a plastic bucket filled with layers of gravel and sand, iron nails and shards of brick. When the contaminated water is poured through the layers, the arsenic bonds to the iron, removing 96% of the arsenic. After a month's use, the contents of the bucket can be removed and filled with fresh materials. A small nonprofit organization called Filters for Families teaches Nepalese villagers how to build and use this device, which costs about $20.

Acidic groundwater from old mines is a serious problem in many regions. A widely applied approach consists of channeling the contaminated water through a system of ponds containing various plants, and/or through beds of crushed limestone. Adding materials such as mushroom compost to the limestone can improve the results. Getting just the right mix of ingredients can be a challenge, but once an effective combination is found, the system may continue to function for many years with minimal upkeep. Similar methods have been applied to contaminated water pumped from the ground.

422

Table 11.1. Groundwater Pollution Mitigation Methods

I. CONTAINMENT/ISOLATION OF CONTAMINANTS

1. Install impermeable subsurface barriers: includes grout curtains, slurry walls, or sheet steel piling walls, to isolate contaminated area or divert groundwater around it.

2. Construct surface seals (caps and liners) of clay, synthetic membranes, many other materials.

3. Alter surface drainage: uses ditches, dikes, benching, etc. to divert surface water from the contaminated area.

4. Inject or remove groundwater to alter groundwater flow direction and prevent outward migration of contaminants.

5. Encapsulation: may include all above methods. Goal is to surround contaminated material with adsorbents, absorbents, impermeable substances, synthetics; may be used in conjunction with stabilization or solidification of soil.

II. REMOVAL OF CONTAMINATED SOIL AND WATER
FOR SURFACE TREATMENT

A. Soil Treatments (excavate contaminated "soil" and treat it)

6. Solidification (making a solid mass) or stabilization (binding contaminants to solid particles): involves mixing excavated material with appropriate additives (cement, fly ash, lime, etc.).

7. Thermal treatment, including incineration (volatilization and combustion of contaminants).

8. Chemical treatments to reduce toxicity by adding appropriate chemical reactants.

9. Bioremediation: aerobic or anaerobic.

10. Soil washing using water, surfactants, solvents, etc.

11. Landfarming: spreading and tilling soils to enhance volatilization and biodegradation.

12. Composting: similar to landfarming but uses thick (up to ten feet) layers of soil containing a bulking agent such as wood chips to facilitate oxygen flow.

13. Off-site excavation and burial in a suitable location: often used in past; generally not recommended.

(continued on next page)

Table 11.1, continued

B. Water Treatments ("pump-and-treat": extract contaminated water from wells or interceptor barriers/trenches and treat)

14. Free product recovery: remove contaminants, usually petroleum products, that are floating atop the water table.

15. Air stripping and steam stripping.

16. Oxidation by chemical or biological means: may include use of highly reactive agents such ozone, hydrogen peroxide, chlorine, and permanganate.

17. Adsorption, including activated carbon adsorption.

18. Sedimentation (settling out of heavier particles) and precipitation (by transforming soluble contaminants into insoluble phases).

19. Filtration, including synthetic membranes.

20. Photochemical oxidation, co-oxidation.

21. Exposure to nonchemical stressors such as high temperatures or ultraviolet light.

III. *In Situ* Approaches (decontaminate soil and water "in place")

22. Soil-vapor extraction: induce air currents by equipping wells with vacuum blowers to suck out volatile contaminants from earth material.

23. Air sparging: force air into contaminated groundwater and remove vapors using soil-vapor extraction.

24. In-well air stripping: remove volatile contaminants by circulating and treating surrounding water as it moves through the well.

25. Bioventing: vacuum-extraction wells move air through earth materials to speed up degradation of contaminants, mainly by bacterial action.

26. Bioslurping: combination of free product recovery and bioventing.

27. Hot air, steam, and soil flushing: inject hot air, steam, and/or chemicals to increase soil temperatures, enhance vapor extraction, and capture contaminants.

28. Resistance heating and radio frequency heating: generate electrical fields and currents to heat the soil.

29. Intrinsic bioremediation: attenuation by natural processes.

30. Enhance natural bioremediation (microbial degradation) by adding oxygen, nutrients, and appropriate chemicals to the groundwater.

Table 11.1, continued

31. Introduce specially designed microorganisms which can consume or degrade contaminants.

32. Introduce abiotic reactants such as strong oxidizing agents, surfactants, zero-valent metals (usually iron filings), hydrogen, or carbon tetrachloride to encourage chemical breakdown or removal of contaminants.

33. Thermal enhancement: inject hot water or steam to accelerate removal and breakdown of contaminants.

34. Recirculation wells allow contaminated groundwater or water which has been chemically or biologically "enhanced" to be constantly recycled, expediting cleanup.

35. Reactive barriers and funnel-and-gate systems are among the methods often used in combination with abiotic or biotic bioremediation.

36. Electrochemical remediation: place electrodes in the soil to attract certain contaminants.

37. Hydraulic and pneumatic fracturing: inject water or air under high pressure into the subsurface to facilitate remediation in impermeable earth materials.

38. Stabilization or solidification of earth materials: involves injection of such substances as cement, asphalt, lime, molten glass (vitrification), organic polymers, and coal fly ash.

39. Phytoremediation: at some sites plants, especially tree roots, have been employed to attract and aid remediation of contaminants via natural biochemical processes.

IV. Non-technical (Management) Approaches

40. Source control: remove, stop, or alter contaminant sources or activities.

41. Stop or limit use of the affected water.

42. Locate alternative water supplies.

43. Continue to monitor the contaminants, evaluate risk, issue advisories to consumers, etc.

44. Do nothing (accept the risk).

Notes: Methods actually employed at a site depend upon the nature and location of the pollutants. Several approaches may be used at a given site. Sources: [29, 122, 292, 294, 349].

B. Pump-and-Treat

Pump-and-treat methods have been widely used, and sometimes overused. Polluted groundwater is pumped to the surface through one or more **extraction** (contaminant withdrawal) **wells**, run through a suitable treatment system, and returned to the ground or to surface water. Treatment methods at the surface include use of activated carbon filters to adsorb contaminants, evaporation, and biological treatment (Table 11.1). **Air stripping** is an evaporative method very effective at removing volatile organic compounds. An extraction well pumps contaminated water from the ground and the water is transferred to an air stripping tower (Figure 11.3A). In the tower, a stream of contaminated water is mixed with a stream of air moving in the opposite direction. Packing material in the tower breaks water into small droplets causing enhanced vaporization of the appropriate pollutants (Figure 11.3B)[103].

Wells must be placed so as to ensure efficient, continuous flow of contaminated water to the extraction wells. Not uncommonly, fewer extraction wells will work better than many. Too many wells improperly placed will try to draw water in opposing directions from the same place resulting in pockets of dead or stagnant groundwater which will then remain contaminated. Overpumping of extraction wells can also cause problems. For example, it can lower the water table causing floating contaminants such as diesel fuel or gasoline to be smeared widely through the soil or rock material. Many contaminants will adhere to solids where they can remain for decades, slowly yielding pollutants to the water. Properly employed and placed, extraction wells will both remove contamination and prevent or reduce off-site migration of contamination by reversing the local hydraulic gradient. Where adequate data exist, computer modeling will help determine the best locations and pumping rates for extraction wells. Extraction wells in impermeable soils will often be ineffective due to extremely slow migration rates and soil retention of

Figure 11.3. Air stripping system. **A.** General view of part of a typical air ▶ stripping set-up. Contaminated water is pumped from a well and then passes through an air stripping tower. From here the water flows to an infiltration gallery where it percolates back into the ground, encounters a cone of depression, and circulates back to the well for additional withdrawal and treatment. **B.** More detailed view of the air stripping tower. A blower forces air into the bottom and up through a packing material as contaminated water trickles downward. The air leaving the tower may need to be treated to remove pollutants.

A

Air Stripping Tower
(See Part B Below)

Water In

Infiltration Gallery
(Crushed Stone)

Contaminated
Water

Blower

Water Out

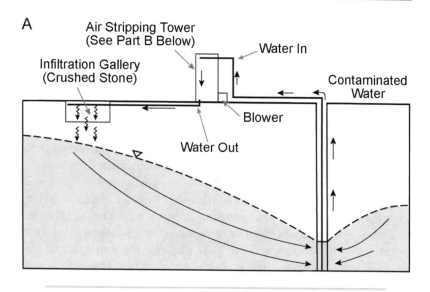

B

Air Out

Water In

Water Down

Packing Material

Air Up

Air In

Water Out

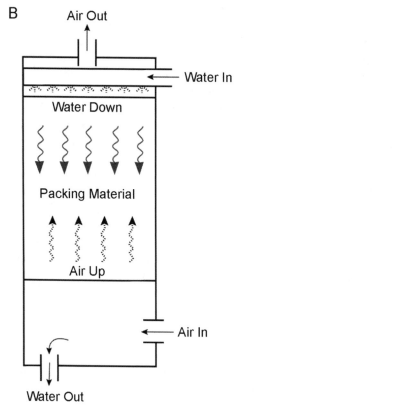

pollutants. The large number of contaminated sites, the time required for remediation (at least several years), and expense limit the usefulness of pump-and-treat methods [349].

C. Bioremediation

Bioremediation refers to the use of biological agents, usually microorganisms such as bacteria, to degrade or alter the pollutants to a nonhazardous state. They work in various ways. Many microorganisms can consume certain pollutants directly as food, converting them to harmless materials in the process. Others can produce chemicals which in turn combat certain pollutants. But it's usually not as simple as adding some bacteria to water, then pumping it into the contaminated water. The microbial metabolism needs to be suited to the task at hand. Biological remediation companies will often sample the contaminated water or soil and develop the right type and concentration of bacteria (sometimes referred to as "bugs") to best do the job.

In addition, the bacteria need a suitable environment to flourish in. This may mean adding other chemicals to the groundwater at the site to enable the bugs to thrive. For example, many bacteria require oxygen, but common molecular oxygen is not very soluble in water. Fortunately, many bacteria can make use of the oxygen in sulfates, nitrates, or other compounds which are more soluble in water. Some bacteria need methane. If air and methane are injected into an aquifer, a substantial population of methane-oxidizing bacteria can be sustained. The bacteria generate an enzyme, methane monooxygenase (MMO), which can then oxidize methane, TCE, and other pollutants. Yet another technique has injected molasses into the ground to provide a food source for bacteria which then multiply, consuming oxygen which then causes certain metals such as chromium to undergo chemical change from a hazardous to a benign form.

Mycoremediation uses the thin stringy structures called mushroom mycelium to break down toxic compounds in contaminated soil and clean up oil spills. The fruiting bodies of some fungi have been used to absorb heavy metals. Bacteria in wood chips have been used to remove excess nitrogen from water.

D. *In Situ* Remediation

In situ (in-place) **remediation** is generally achieved by injecting specially chosen mixes of bacteria, nutrients, solvents, oxygen, or other substances into the contaminated soil or groundwater to enhance and speed up biological or chemical degradation of the pollutants [292]. It can be applied to a pump-and-treat system by recycling contaminated water which has been withdrawn and treated back to the subsurface through **injection wells**. If the return flow wells are properly placed this added water will accelerate local water movement toward the extraction wells and speed removal of contaminants from the soil. The oxygen, solvents, bacteria, or other agents added to this return flow can greatly accelerate the removal and degradation of contaminants.

Soil-vapor extraction is commonly used to remove hazardous VOCs (BTEX, TCE, PCE, and many others) from the vadose zone. Most of these systems employ vacuum blowers to suck hazardous gases from carefully designed and sealed extraction wells. This generates air flow-age through the contaminated material (Figure 11.4), greatly facilitating removal of volatile pollutants. The more permeable the "soil" or regolith, the more readily the air will move and the more efficiently the vapor extraction system will perform. The extracted gas may be vented to the air, but this is not recommended unless the contaminants pose very little risk. Normally the gas will be channeled into special treatment chambers where nongaseous substances and polluted vapors are treated, usually by combustion/oxidation or adsorption [29, 100].

A number of approaches to controlling salt-water intrusion into fresh groundwater were mentioned in Section 10.4.2D-3. Many of those methods may also be applied to pollution plumes in general. Where a contamination plume is restricted to shallow groundwater, a treatment bed can be placed in the path of the plume. For example, a high-pH material such as crushed limestone sand could be placed in a deep, wall-like trench, or treatment curtain, to intercept a low-pH (acidic) plume and a highly adsorptive or ion-exchange material may be used to capture heavy metals. Cutoff walls of impermeable material may be employed to surround a contaminated area to minimize the spread of pollutants. The walls may also be used to direct polluted water into a subsurface treatment bed, trench, extraction zone, or similar area where the contamination can be mitigated. The directing walls and treatment area are often referred to as a "funnel and gate" system and the treatment bed as a "reactor."

In situ **air stripping** is an effective means of treating groundwater polluted by volatiles. Air is forced into an aquifer or other subsurface material to aid vaporization of volatile pollutants directly from the groundwater. Air stripping is often accomplished by a technique called **air sparging** in which an air stream is generated by forcing air at high pressure

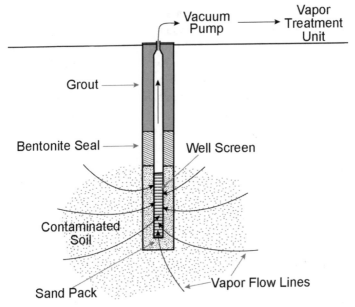

Figure 11.4. Soil vapor extraction. A pump sucks air from the contaminated soil and sends it to a treatment system. Working systems may be considerably more complex and include multiple extraction wells, vapor and pressure test probes or wells, pressure gauges, and sampling ports.

through wells into contaminated groundwater (Figure 11.5). Although its functioning has been attributed to the production of many tiny bubbles, it appears that the air actually generates many small channels through the sediment. As air streams through these passages it removes volatile contaminants, adds oxygen, and facilitates movement of contaminated water and gas towards extraction wells. The major flow paths for the vapors will be along zones of high permeability, usually fractures [1]. When the air reaches the unsaturated zone, soil-vapor extraction wells are used to withdraw the contaminated gases.

Numerous related techniques exist. Many employ various additives such as peroxide, methane, nutrients, solvents, and detergents, among others, to flush out, immobilize, or destroy the pollutants. Two examples are steam flushing, which uses hot steam instead of air, and injecting hydrogen into the contaminated zone to facilitate the chemical breakdown of chlorinated solvents. Electrical currents and radio waves can also be generated through contaminated sediment. Their energy is converted to heat which encourages additional vaporization and aids pollutant removal. Additional approaches include use of a single **recirculation well** which emits air at the bottom and withdraws the air in the upper part of the well [292, 369]. Other similar techniques make use of horizontal trenches or conduits placed within a contaminated region to facilitate access to, and elimination of, pollutants. Newer approaches to groundwater remediation range from applied genomics to subsurface imaging, but thus far, major breakthroughs have been elusive.

Which methods are most appropriate will depend upon the specific site, including hydrologic properties of the soil or rock, local geology and environment, the contaminants present, and the magnitude of the problem. Substantial time and expense are often required, even at small sites. The removal of large quantities of diverse pollutants presents a major challenge. At the Savannah River site in South Carolina where hundreds of millions of gallons of low-level radioactive wastes along with millions of pounds of chlorinated solvents and other pollutants contaminated the groundwater, a combination of horizontal wells, air stripping, and bacteria proved little more effective than pump-and-treat. Case studies of successful clean-ups are available from numerous

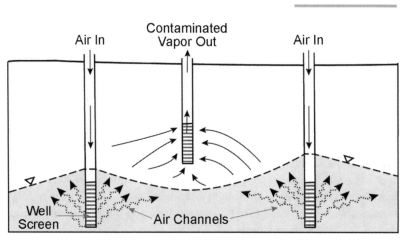

Figure 11.5. Air sparging, an *in situ* air stripping technique. This schematic shows two air injection wells and one air extraction well. The injected air moves upward through the phreatic zone collecting contaminants, then is drawn to the extraction (vacuum) well to be withdrawn and treated. The pressure and force of upward-moving air causes a rise in the water table near the injection wells.

sources, including local and federal government agencies and numerous textbooks [29, 122, 369, 404, 423].

It bears repeating that the least costly, most effective approach by far is a precautionary one which emphasizes prevention. This should entail improved management of pollutants, reduced use or replacement of hazardous substances, and development of more benign processes and substances in both industrial settings and in homes.

11.3.9 Monitoring

All of the previous eight activities may require groundwater monitoring. Most monitoring consists of keeping track of water level and quality, and how those conditions vary over time. This is mainly accomplished using monitoring wells, but existing wells, pumping tests, springs, streams, and other sources of information associated with groundwater may also be utilized. Hundreds of thousands of monitoring wells are in use around the world. Monitoring of groundwater is a major, often legally mandated, procedure for thousands of studies and projects which could impact the environment.

Large numbers of water, and possibly soil, samples may need to be gathered and tested at a project site, possibly over a period of many years. This requires a well-coordinated effort. The hydrogeologist may be in charge of the design, installation, and operation of a monitoring system, as well as evaluating and reporting results as they come in.

11.3.10 Legal Undertakings

Very little is accomplished regarding such matters as pollution prevention and clean-up without regulations and enforcement. Laws which relate to groundwater protection are often the underlying mechanism which creates the need for hydrogeological investigators. In addition, rules and standards must be met for every water supply system, well, septic system, wastewater lagoon, and other water-related items. The hydrogeologist must be thoroughly familiar with the relevant regulations and will often need to act as liaison between his employer, clients, and the enforcement agencies.

One very important law every environmental consultant should be familiar with is the 1980 **Comprehensive Environmental Response, Compensation, and Liability Act — CERCLA**, often called the "Superfund" Act. This act was passed to help determine who should be held accountable for pollution and cleanup, and to provide funds to begin cleanup at high-risk sites. The accountable party is ideally the corporation or individual who produced the pollution, but in many cases, the guilty party is unknown or no longer exists. For example, the company may have been dissolved, bankruptcy declared, or the owner is deceased. In this case, the current owner of the land or the pollution source may be held liable for the cleanup costs. If the owner can prove innocence, or that "due diligence" was exercised when purchasing the property, the Superfund will pay for cleanup. Meeting the **due diligence** standard usually means having a thorough environmental site assessment performed prior to purchase of a property to determine if any hazards are present. If soil or groundwater pollution are suspected, subsurface samples of soil and water should be collected and analyzed. Cleanup costs at a single large site can run into the tens of millions of dollars.

Lawsuits involving angry victims, defensive site operators, property owners, and large sums of money may result, and hydrogeologists may need to testify in court on behalf of one side or the other. Outside of the courtroom, they may be called upon to provide advice to attorneys, individuals, and organizations involved with or concerned about the issue.

A brief overview of groundwater and laws is provided in Section 12.4.

11.3.11 Modeling and Related Tools

Even though these predictions may not always be entirely right, they can and do give guidance to people responsible for using and protecting ground water supplies.

— Francis H. Chapelle

A. Introduction

Analyzing groundwater behavior and predicting the future distribution and concentration of groundwater contaminants are complicated procedures. In this book, we have introduced relatively simple ways of quantifying flow rates, available water quantities, and other important aspects of groundwater behavior. Unfortunately, simple math will often prove inadequate when dealing with the complexities of the real world. For example, simply pumping water from the ground will alter flow rates and directions, and transmissivity will change as drawdown occurs. Determining the amount of groundwater contamination which may reach wells located some distance from a major pollution source can involve complex variables such as the rate of contaminant introduction into the aquifer, the breakdown rates of various individual contaminants, groundwater flow rates, hydrodynamic dispersion of solutes, advective mixing with existing groundwater, the amount of sorption of contaminants onto the aquifer media and other complexities. Groundwater flow rates and direction may vary depending on seasonal and short-term weather conditions — which affect water table levels, hydrostatic pressure, and recharge-discharge rates — or the material the water flows through may differ significantly in hydrologic and chemical characteristics from place to place in both the vertical and horizontal directions. These conditions and the many possible numerical and analytical approaches to them obviously cannot be condensed into a few simple equations. Hence, a need exists for more sophisticated methods for quantitatively evaluating and predicting groundwater behavior and environmental conditions existing therein.

By the late 1960s, hydrologists were using computers to help describe and predict groundwater and contaminant behavior through time. Since then, improvements in numerical calculations and analyses have produced ever more sophisticated models to simulate groundwater behavior. Today, computer modeling is standard procedure in most hydrogeologic investigations. Many standard hydrogeology textbooks include one or more modeling programs on a disk along with coverage of the complex quantitative techniques employed in many groundwater analyses.

B. Description and Use of Models

A **model** is a tool which helps us represent a phenomenon or system. It may be a physical structure such as a scale model of a proposed building, an idea, or a simple math equation such as Darcy's Law. Models can help us understand groundwater behavior, anticipate responses to changing conditions, find discrepancies in other models, and discover where more study and data are most needed. Good models are vital tools for predicting aquifer performance over time, determining transport and fate of contaminants, and helping to manage groundwater.

A well-designed groundwater model requires an abundance of dependable data and a solid qualitative understanding of basic hydrogeology. Required information for the area of interest includes the size, shape, extent, and nature of the subsurface geologic units. Hydraulic properties of these units such as storativity, hydraulic conductivity, and head distribution need to be obtained. The location and rates of groundwater input and output for the study area are also highly desirable. Dependable measurements, such as those obtained from boreholes or hydraulic tests, may be difficult or unfeasible to obtain and estimates

434

for many parameters often must replace concrete data. A special concern is choosing well-defined boundary conditions for the area of interest. This involves determining or estimating lateral and vertical limits for the study area which are hydrogeologically meaningful and which will minimize hydrologic variances. Convenient boundaries include streams (common discharge areas) and groundwater drainage divides (where flow separation or no-flow conditions prevail) since these often define the lateral limits of groundwater basins. Computer simulations of well-defined basins will tend to yield the most dependable results. The lower boundary often has to be estimated based upon rock type and structure. The upper (near-surface) boundary, while easily located, can be difficult to quantify hydrologically due to ongoing changes in recharge and discharge rates through time. The original or natural hydrologic conditions in the study area should be estimated as accurately as possible. Where concrete data are lacking, more than one reasonable estimate are often used to simulate behavior under differing conditions or scenarios.

Once adequate data have been obtained, the study region or parts thereof may be subdivided into a network or **grid**. Two common grids consist of squares of equal area (or cubes of equal volume for 3-D models) or other geometric forms (often triangles) whose size and location are based upon convenient data-gathering points such as streams or wells (Figure 11.6). Hydrologic data for each grid subsection (that is, each square or triangular unit or cell) can then be determined and analyzed by computer. Organization of data varies based upon the specific model used. A computer sums up all the data and generates results.

But that's not all. The model needs to be calibrated. Parameters (variables such as groundwater velocity, head, streamflow) need to be selected and their values adjusted to provide the best match between predicted results and observed data. In most cases, understanding of the groundwater system is very sketchy and the calibration, or "tuning up," of the model is largely a trial and error process. Many run-throughs may be required to get a good match and validate the model.

Following calibration, one or more additional tests will often be done to verify the model's ability to reach viable conclusions. This may involve comparing the model's results with actual field data, such as an aquifer test. If the model performs successfully, it is ready to be used for "predictive analyses."

Of the many more sophisticated groundwater models, the most widely used are the MODFLOW series, the first of which was released in 1984. **MODFLOW** is readily available and has a proven track record

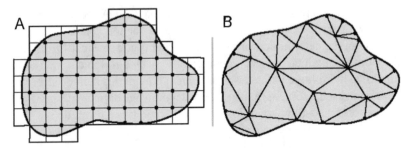

Figure 11.6. Two examples of modeling grids applied to an aquifer. In each case, the dots represent *nodes* (data input/output points). **A.** A square or rectangular grid style characterizes *finite-difference* modeling methods. The nodes may also be placed in the center of each square. **B.** These triangles, made by straight lines drawn between adjacent nodes, characterize a *finite-element* modeling method. This approach is especially useful when trying to define irregularly shaped bodies [200, 378].

and widespread support. Clear, detailed instructions, frequent training opportunities, an abundance of software, and numerous specialized versions all contribute to its popularity.

Well-designed models provide the best available estimates of groundwater conditions and behavior. They can provide critical information on future water resource supplies, information essential for intelligent management of this most precious resource. Unfortunately, a tendency to overdo computer modeling often exists. It looks and sounds impressive and can bring in extra dollars for consulting companies. Zealous regulators may ask for modeling even when it makes little sense and can provide no meaningful information.

Most models require a fairly large set of data collected over a period of time to be viable. Consider: highly sophisticated models, aided by concrete data from up-to-the-minute surveillance from satellites and radar, are used to formulate your local weather forecast also. Are they always correct? The major problem with most models is that we simply cannot know and quantify all of the nearly infinite influences which may impact the weather over the next few days, or a groundwater plume over the next few years. We cannot measure directly the changing conditions along the many hidden flow paths of the groundwater. As in all science, we continue to accumulate information and knowledge. And sure enough, as time goes on, our models and our accuracy improve. But each location is unique, and that which provided dependable results at site A may not be so dependable at site B.

C. A Caveat

Remember, models are intended to complement skills, not replace them.

— William J. Stone

Models using sophisticated math and computer programs provide useful simulations of the real world. But be careful. The best models, computerized or otherwise, are still only simulations — imitations, approximations of reality; they are not immutable and need to be taken with a grain of salt. It is important to realize that they provide a guide to groundwater behavior, not proof of future behavior or consequences. The real world of groundwater is far more complex and the actual subsurface conditions are never completely known. The best models yield results which are still only educated guesses, and remain entirely dependent upon the reliability of the data provided. As noted above, those data will inevitably be incomplete and plagued with uncertainty. The modelers themselves vary widely in the data they select and manipulate [136]. All too often, use of modeling becomes addictive and encourages a level of confidence which is unwarranted. Many investigators, especially those lacking a solid qualitative understanding of groundwater behavior, tend to rely too heavily on results spat out by a computer, responding to what Bredehoeft and Konikov [50] call an unjustified "aura of correctness."

The best approach when modeling a contamination problem is usually to use a precautionary approach, to err on the side of safety. For example, one can estimate that groundwater flow rates will fall within a certain range, based on the type of aquifer material. One could run a computer model three times using the maximum, middle, and minimum values. But if only one run is feasible, use the maximum for flow rates (which will speed up the transport rate). For adsorption rates (which tend to slow down the transport rate), use the low estimate. This way, you will overestimate the time for the contamination to reach a target, providing a margin of safety. This is analogous to building a bridge — always make the structure capable of supporting more than it will have to support. Play it safe with peoples' health and lives.

Following a few year's use, a model's predictions should also be compared to actual measured field data to determine how well it has anticipated groundwater behavior. All too often, the level of accuracy is poor.

D. GIS

A **Geographic Information System** (**GIS**) uses a computer program in which various types of information are analyzed and illustrated on maps. For example, one could show the surface landscape with buildings and underground utilities, the underlying water table, and contamination plumes complete with pollutant concentrations to provide a useful visualization of a site. GIS is used for monitoring land use changes, producing map overlays, plotting utility lines, soil and vegetation mapping, wetland delineation, three-dimensional representations, and any number of other applications which can greatly aid investigations.

11.3.12 Report Writing

Clearly communicating the procedures and results (findings, risks, recommendations, and so forth) of a study is essential. The finest efforts are worthless if their value cannot be coherently communicated to those who need the information. Many of today's college graduates have poor writing skills and in an era of unfocused multitasking and thinking, the situation threatens to deteriorate even further. The only long-term solution to this dilemma is good basic education, preferably one in which all disciplines require their students to master reasonably good writing skills. This requires a conscientious effort to improve on the part of the writer, and can be greatly aided by good report reviewing and editing.

The hydrogeologist, especially if s/he is a project manager, will probably spend more time on reports and paper work than working in the field. Just preparing a proposal for a project can involve considerable research and data gathering. It is never too early to start on a draft of the final report. Beginning a preliminary draft for the first day of field operations will help keep the work in perspective and avoid costly errors and omissions which can be easily overlooked in the busy, noisy, and occasionally frustrating field environment. Many projects proceed in phases, each one may require its own report along with periodic updates to keep all concerned parties informed.

Organization is key to a good report. Organizational details will, of course, vary depending on the type, purpose, and complexity of the report. In general, the main body of a report should contain (1) an introduction (purpose, scope of study, site location and description, and relevant background information including previous studies), (2) an explanation of methods employed (field techniques, approaches taken, equipment used, and so forth), (3) findings (results, discussion, conclusions), and possibly (4) recommendations for future work. Numerous diagrams, graphs, photographs, well logs, and related illustrations typically need to be incorporated into the report in an orderly fashion. They may be included as figures and plates within the text or placed in an appendix (or in a special pocket if too large to fit on a standard page). A good illustration can replace several paragraphs of text, but it must be clearly and accurately drawn with an informative caption and a complete legend where appropriate. In addition, title page, list of contents, an executive summary or abstract of major findings, tables, acknowledgments, references, and appendices are frequent requirements of a good report.

Documenting the work being done in the field is another aspect of hydrogeological work. Most "field notes" as such will not appear in a final report, but they provide vital on-the-spot documentation. Field notes, including drawings, provide necessary information for the report and can resolve questions which may later arise. They may also need to be submitted as evidence in the event of legal proceedings in which case field notes and reports may become public documents!

Recording accurate and thorough field notes is a demanding task, even an art. It is often said that you can never make too many field observations. Field notes encompass more than occurrences and descriptions of site conditions. They often should include a detailed log of daily activities, recording such items as weather, people spoken to, phone calls and messages, and other details telling what happened, when, and under what circumstances. Chains of custody, drilling forms and logs, and other papers may also need to be incorporated into the daily field record. When on a site, especially in unpleasant conditions (time running out, dirt and mud, wind, rain, hellish heat or frigid cold, misery), the tendency is to say, "Oh, I'll remember. Right now I've got to get out of here!" Many the field worker who has come to regret such haste, often during time- and cost-consuming revisits to a site.

11.4 Observations, Ethics, and More Caveats

Both those in the hydrogeology business and those who seek their services must consider some important questions. How much training, and of what type, should field personnel receive? How far should a service provider go to please the customer? When an individual or a business is in need of groundwater services, how do they go about it? What should they look for? The questions never end and many will have no simple or definitive answer.

11.4.1 Cost vs. Quality

An eternal problem in the world of business is the conflict between cost and quality. The people controlling the purse strings may be basically businessmen and not well versed in the scientific and technical complexities of environmental or engineering work. The customer (client) who requires hydrogeological services typically desires maximum value at minimal cost, and in some instances, may be an unwilling participant in the whole affair — for example, regulations or lawsuits may be forcing him to pay for work which he feels is unnecessary or for problems which he did not create. The service providers, especially office and project managers, on the other hand, are under pressure to maximize income (the all important "productivity") while minimizing output (time, effort, expense). That challenge is passed on to the workers they manage. This can generate pressure to get the work done as quickly as possible and cut corners in the service of increased production. This in turn can lead to such irresponsible actions as hiding potential threats to the public, failing to accurately record field findings, faking information, billing for time not used on a project, and sloppy decontamination and safety precautions. Most firms will carry some form of insurance to protect them from problems resulting from unintentional errors and unforeseen events during their work. Firms which engage in improper actions risk malpractice suits which can make it extremely difficult to obtain insurance or certification.

Some firms, as well as their clients, laboring under tight time and budget constraints and anxious to get a project completed, will discourage original thought and dismiss responsible concerns, fearing they will raise unnecessary "red flags" or reduce productivity. It may then be up to the scientist to explain (perhaps to his own firm's leaders as well as to the firm's client) the need for certain procedures and operations.

11.4.2 Real vs. Ideal

Even without pressure from above, many projects will experience unavoidable compromises between the real and the ideal. It is simply not feasible to undertake the exhaustive research which would be ideal. Be it the details of groundwater flow paths or the results of chemical analyses, substantial uncertainties will exist and the working hydrogeologist needs to be aware of these. When working with the subsurface environment, we will always have to deal with a variety of "unknowns." This is an area where experience, a solid qualitative understanding of groundwater, and the ability to communicate are invaluable.

In such cases, the scientist's reputation for dependability, efficiency, and quality work can be the deciding factor between success and failure.

11.4.3 Education

The sciences are not immune to recent academic conundrums such as grade inflation and lowering of standards. One result is that not all students of hydrogeology or a related field have achieved adequate training in the fundamental aspects of geology, the water sciences, and other relevant disciplines. Incredible as it may seem, a substantial number of individuals working in the applied groundwater field have never had a college-level course in hydrogeology, or even introductory geology. The two-day (or 10-day) seminar "courses" which many attend are no substitute for challenging full-semester college courses. One result is the plethora of poorly written reports which follow a **boiler-plate** (basically an established fill-in-the-blank) **outline** and exhibit little solid hydrogeologic understanding or context. This has become a subject of considerable concern, criticism, and controversy, especially among older practitioners and academicians [344, 378, 423].

11.4.4 Professional Qualifications

A related issue concerns the qualifications of a hydrogeologic consulting or engineering firm and its employees. Those in need of a groundwater expert or a consulting firm should choose carefully. State agencies and professional societies may provide lists of hydrogeologists or companies who have met their requirements, but they generally can't offer any council as to whom to select. Most firms will provide a list of projects and clients, but this, while helpful, is no guarantee of quality. Most clients will not have the scientific expertise to evaluate the content of hydrogeologic work. If a report was delivered on schedule at the agreed-upon price and meets their needs, they will probably be happy. Unless something goes badly awry and results in a malpractice suit, a serious examination of the quality of work performed is rarely undertaken. When interviewing a firm, ask about the educational background and experience of their groundwater people; try to speak with them directly and don't hesitate to ask hard questions. If possible, contact others who may have required similar services and ask for their recommendations.

It is unfortunate that some consulting and engineering firms will seek young, pliable employees, then assign them responsibilities for which they are not adequately prepared. In addition to being less costly to employ, office managers may prefer inexperienced employees such as a recent college graduate who can be easily controlled and taught the preferred procedures, not all of which may be scientifically or socially responsible, rather than hiring a more experienced professional. Hiring biases, especially against older, and often more knowledgeable applicants, is common in many fields, including the broad area of environmental consulting. In the applied sciences and engineering, such practices are not only unfair, they can be dangerous for the public and result in errors, some of which may have very serious consequences.

11.4.5 Limited Perspectives

Another self-serving but short-sighted tendency which often exists within any bureaucracy, be it an engineering firm or a college department, is to discourage their people, such as employees or students, from obtaining first-hand knowledge and experience from "outside" sources, preferring instead to offer their own "in-house" training sessions or courses. This is usually a bad idea. A good college department or consulting company will encourage their people to expand their horizons, experience different perspectives, and take advantage of the most reliable sources whenever possible.

11.4.6 Summary

Hydrogeologic projects frequently involve seeking a water supply, addressing contamination of soils or groundwater, or other matters which relate directly to human welfare. As such, even small projects need to be well thought out and undertaken by qualified personnel. Errors can be costly and lead to major threats to the environment and to human life.

As with all things in life, negative conditions and influences will intervene from time to time and must be dealt with. The situations mentioned here are common circumstances which people who may require services in groundwater and related arenas should be aware of. Criticisms noted here should not be applied indiscriminately. Many excellent sources of expertise are available. The sources may be individual hydrogeologists, planning agencies, engineering firms, environmental companies, governmental agencies, or nongovernmental organizations. These observations and caveats are intended to aid in finding well qualified providers and to provide awareness of certain conditions and limitations which often exist.

The engineering and consulting firms engaged in groundwater work vary greatly in size, focus, and quality. A firm should be selected carefully as poor quality work is not uncommon in groundwater-related projects. Time and money are always big concerns: firms want to maximize profits while minimizing time and effort. Their clients are seeking maximum effort and results at minimum cost. Reports often reveal poor understanding of fundamentals of geology and hydrology, a very limited perspective, and bad writing. Some of this is due to basic lack of knowledge and experience, such as not knowing what information to gather, where to find it, or how to interpret and use the information. This in turn relates to inadequacies in education and/or training. The uncritical, routine "cookbook" approach frequently prevails in the real world of consulting, engineering, and other applied science. Individuals with little expertise and background can rapidly churn out reports with the aid of computer models and boiler plates. Those aids, while useful, are no substitute for solid knowledge, critical thought, field experience, and accountability [384].

12
Contemporary Groundwater Supply Issues

The magnitude of the global freshwater crisis and the risks associated with it have been greatly underestimated.

— Thomas S. Axworthy and Bob Sandford

12.1 Overview: A Water Stressed World

And it never failed that during the dry years the people forgot about the rich years, and during the wet years they lost all memory of the dry years. It was always that way.

— John Steinbeck, *East of Eden*

12.1.1 Introduction

This chapter provides an introduction to contemporary water resource issues with an emphasis on groundwater. If a sense of urgency and an advocacy approach is noted, that is intentional. All too many scientists have failed to meet their obligations to society, preferring to restrict themselves to their ivory towers, or seek only maximized income for their efforts, rather than maximizing the good they might do. For more detailed, nontechnical coverage of specific water resource issues, numerous fine publications can be recommended and many are included in the References [22, 65, 70, 95, 124, 150, 155, 156, 160, 243, 258, 303, 317, 320, 431, 445, among others].

Of roughly 1,360 million km³ (326 million mi³) of water on earth, less than 0.3% is fresh water available for withdrawal, and it would be unwise or unfeasible to remove most of that water due to such factors as cost, temporal and spatial irregularities in water availability, and in-place water requirements such as the integrity and function of ecosystems, navigation, and hydroelectric power needs. The remaining 99.7% of water on the planet is salt water, locked up in glaciers, or otherwise not readily available or usable. Withdrawal of water from rivers, lakes, and aquifers has tripled over the past 50 years and demand for fresh water is growing by over 60 billion m³/yr. Of the reasonably accessible fresh water, over half is already appropriated by humans, and removal of this water, be it from surface or groundwater, is producing numerous severe impacts. The natural replacement of surface waters by the water cycle is readily overwhelmed by growing demand in large areas of the world. Because of the very long renewal or recharge period for most groundwater, its withdrawal or pollution represents an immediate and long-lasting loss of freshwater resources. No one knows exactly how much groundwater exists, but it clearly has been, and continues to be, over-extracted on a massive scale in many regions of the planet, including much of India, northern China, the Middle East, Spain, and the central and southwestern US [117, 154, 283, 396, 409].

The importance of groundwater has largely been ignored and undervalued even as water tables drop, extraction costs rise, and water quality deteriorates. The policies, rules, organizations, and controls needed for intelligent governance of groundwater resources have been likewise neglected or remained inadequate even as groundwater withdrawals have jumped from perhaps 100 km³/yr in 1950 to 800 km³/yr in 2010. Easily obtained groundwater has produced great benefits to millions of people. Worldwide, more than 50% of drinking water, 43% of global irrigation water, and a large portion of industrial water use are currently dependent on groundwater [431]. But, when the resource is being depleted, the benefits cannot continue indefinitely. Like a bank account with more money constantly being removed than is coming in, or a debt-ridden individual who continues borrowing, a day of reckoning will come. Global water debts are growing, and as with unsound financial dealings, the "bubble" will burst. For many countries, including those containing over half the world's population, temporarily available water and affordable fossil fuels have enabled impressive increases in food production. But, the readily available water for many of the world's major croplands is fast disappearing and this, along with increasing energy costs, changing climates, and other concerns, could lead to terrible consequences unless strong actions are undertaken immediately [57].

Through most of human history, water shortages were generally localized, brief, and rare. In today's world of unprecedented need and

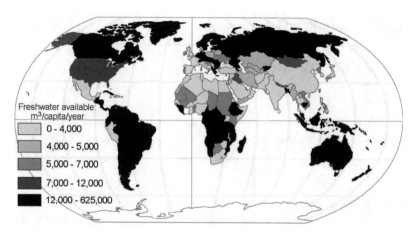

Figure 12.1. Map of world per capita water availability.

demand, shortages are widespread and protracted with no easy remedies in sight. Never in Earth's history has one species so dominated the use and consumption of essential natural resources as humankind does to-day. The consensus is clear: a water crisis of global proportions looms, and is well underway in many areas.

Figure 12.1 is a map of per capita water availability. A region or country in which an annual average of less than 1,700 m^3 of water is available to each person is considered to be water stressed, if the annual supplies drop below 1,000 m^3/person, it is called a water scarcity. The UN Environmental Program (UNEP) estimates that two of every three people will live in water-stressed areas by the year 2025 [397]. The OECD estimates that 47%, or some 3.9 billion people, will live in high water stress areas by 2030, and Vörösmarty, *et al.* [419] conclude that the water security of 80% of the world's population is at high risk. Little doubt can exist that groundwater depletion alone poses a serious threat to both national and local food supplies [58, 260, 283]. Global water scarcity is increasingly recognized as an international security issue [227, 283]. Despite these sobering considerations, most experts believe that sufficient water is available to meet human needs. But to meet those needs, water must be used more wisely, more productively, than at present. And humanity as a whole must respond far more responsibly and effectively than our species has ever done in the past when confronted with major threats to survival. Only time will tell if an adequate response will occur, and time is growing frighteningly short [33].

12.1.2 Complications

> *We are building up a horrible legacy for our children and grandchildren.*
>
> — Granger Morgan

Water supply problems are complicated by numerous factors of both natural and anthropogenic origin. Some are briefly reviewed below.

A. Resource Depletion

Although water is constantly recycled, if it is used more rapidly in a given place than can be replenished by the hydrologic cycle, the resource will be depleted. Even where groundwater recharge rates are not exceeded by withdrawals, negative impacts can be expected from the alteration of established equilibrium conditions produced by any interference in the natural water cycle. This is exactly what is happening with increasing frequency around much of the world. With the rapidly increasing exploitation and pollution of surface water in recent decades, demands for groundwater have increased exponentially and it has become overexploited in nearly all areas of Earth which lack abundant, potable surface water supplies. The most immediate result is a dramatic decline of subsurface water levels. To provide one extreme example, some of the sandstone aquifers that generated flowing artesian wells in Chicago in the nineteenth century now have water levels more than 150 meters (490 feet) below the surface [87]. Overall, the total groundwater depletion in the world's sub-humid to arid areas is estimated to have increased from about 126 km^3/yr in 1960 to 283 km^3/yr in 2000 [421]. Another study estimates global groundwater depletion from 1900 to 2008 to be approximately 4,500 km^3. The rate of depletion continues to accelerate but that trend should reverse as the resource dwindles [224]. Groundwater demand has been estimated to be about 6% of the annual global recharge, which may imply that abundant water remains [144]. But much of the recharge occurs where groundwater is not needed or not accessible, as noted in Section 1.1.5.

B. Distribution of Water and People

Huge amounts of water may be accessible in places quite unsuited to other basic human wants and needs, such as the Amazon Basin or near melting glaciers. Many places highly desirable for human settlement — those with pleasant climates or good soils, for example — may lack the water to support high populations or sustained agriculture.

Millions of people are now settled in regions which lack sufficient water to meet their needs. This is especially true of arid and semiarid environments, many of which are experiencing rapid population growth despite water shortages. The majority of people lacking access to a safe drinking water supply are rural residents [333]. The amount of water replenished in any time period can also vary dramatically. Some areas are drenched with excess rains during one part of the year and dry as the proverbial bone at other times.

C. Competition

Competition for water is growing. Agriculture, rapidly growing urban areas, business and industry, energy, recreation, fisheries, navigation — all have their water requirements. Other factors, such as continued population growth, global warming and the accompanying changes in water distribution, political and cultural differences, or the recalcitrance of people toward moving from their homelands or having to adapt a different lifestyle, further complicate the issue. Underlying it all is the essential need to maintain healthy, life-supporting ecosystems. Providing adequate water while avoiding major conflicts and widespread suffering will not be easy.

D. Inefficiency

In nations around the world, profligate waste of precious water resources has been the norm for decades. Countless government programs have subsidized wasteful water use and most continue to do so even when a crisis is plainly imminent. Vast amounts of "unaccounted-for-water" go to waste each year during standard operations by users ranging from industry to homeowners to the water utilities themselves. Huge increases in the efficiency of water use are possible in nearly all areas.

E. Inequitable Access

The basic unfairness which pervades so many human endeavors pertains also to water. Well-intentioned rules to provide water to small farmers and ranchers in the US and elsewhere have been manipulated by those with wealth and influence into advantages for huge agribusiness interests. In like manner, influential individuals, industries, and organizations see to it that they have safe, abundant, low-cost water for themselves while the less fortunate lack potable water and sanitary conditions. In many developing nations, the poor must pay far more for water than the rich.

F. Changing Environments

The natural environment was generally quite consistent and moderate during the time in which modern industrialized civilizations took root. Most changes which occurred tended to be gradual and "greener pastures" — or should we say "bluer horizons?" — existed for those with the arrogance and strength to take them from the weak. In today's crowded world, nearly all desirable, productive environments are being utilized, and usually overexploited. In addition, human influences, from land use to climate change (Section 12.6), are generating many abnormally rapid changes in water quality, availability, and distribution.

G. Attitude

Once again, human myths, denial, and related perceptions and misconceptions complicate the issue. While impoverished young women in Africa must walk many miles each day carrying heavy vessels to obtain essential water, more fortunate consumers often regard water as a basically free and unlimited resource to which they are entitled. A problematic attitude on the part of many water resource engineers and managers concerns stationarity, the concept or assumption that natural conditions will vary only within established limits. The degree of variation in streamflow, groundwater recharge, and rainfall, for example, is typically based upon data gathered in the very recent past. Such predictable fluctuations cannot be relied upon, especially in a world of changing climates.

H. Foolish Choices

All too often, decisions impacting water resources are based upon short-sighted goals and lack adequate objective, science-based input. Due to the intimate association between politics and wealth in many countries, powerful self-serving interests strongly influence the use and fate of human, financial, and natural resources. The results are often environmentally destructive practices including large, poorly planned water projects, unsustainable agriculture, deforestation, and warfare. Unwise choices are frequently aided and abetted by outdated and foolish laws, poorly educated citizens, unfounded technological optimism, and economic pressures.

12.2 Water Use

*Water is the forgotten keystone to solving so many of the
world's ills.·*

— Letter, *Washington Post* (March, 2010) by four
interfaith leaders: Reverend Aykazian, Rabbi Bemporad,
Reverend Kowalski, and Imam Naqvi

Water is the lifeblood of all organisms. Water, or the lack thereof,
is a critical factor in the world's greatest ills, including disease, malnutrition, women's needs and rights, warfare, and poverty. Human water
needs extend well beyond that required to sustain our physical bodies.
Nearly all businesses, industries, energy generation, and related undertakings require a dependable supply of water if they are to function successfully. Past human use of water has often been plagued, and continues to be plagued, by incredible wastefulness and uninformed decision
making as documented in countless articles and books [22, 65, 156, 326].

12.2.1 Estimating Water Use and Availability

*The loss of stationarity that is occurring is likely to be
far more costly than what has ever been projected.*

— Mike Hightower

Average water availability for large regions of Earth is often regarded as well known and reasonably stable, but more specific and localized data on groundwater withdrawals, recharge and discharge,
streamflow, or total use and consumption of water are likely to be spotty,
even in advanced nations. Virtually no states or nations have achieved
the desired levels of water data needed to make properly informed decisions. Many less advanced countries lack the ability to collect, organize,
and publish basic water resource data. Methods for estimating water
resources vary depending upon such factors as available data, assumptions, funding, expertise, and climate. The reliability of data on water
supply and use from many countries is very poor [150]. In general, arid
countries will use the average infiltration rate (as a percent of average
annual precipitation) to arrive at an estimated groundwater recharge value.
For humid countries, base flow into streams is often used to estimate
groundwater storage. Even where abundant data exist, only probabili-
ties can be provided as to where, when, and how much water may be
available in a given location, or within a specific time-frame, or for a

certain use. In this new era of over use and changing climates, we can no longer depend upon past estimates and assumptions regarding water availability — that is, the stationarity approach. Section 3.9 describes methods for determining a hydrologic budget. As with any sensitive issue, we should be aware that some estimates of water use, supply, and need will be politicized, biased, or otherwise manipulated. And even when they are not, some will accuse those who created the estimates of such.

In spite of the incompleteness of much water data, sufficient information has been gathered to provide some vital perspectives on water resource and use issues (tables 1.6, 3.1, 3.2, and 12.1). From the human perspective, the most precious and accessible water by far is liquid fresh water. Of this, 96 to 99% lies below the ground surface, depending on which estimate one uses. The remainder is shared among the lakes, rivers, atmosphere, and organisms of the planet. Global annual recharge of groundwater has been estimated at 11,500 km^3/yr by Giordano and at 12,600 km^3/yr by Doll (Table 12.1) [99, 144, 535, 538]. These estimates suggest that approximately 104,700 km^3/yr, 12% of the total land precipitation, will become groundwater.

Table 12.1. Global Renewable Freshwater Resources and Use

FRESHWATER RESOURCE OR USE	GLOBAL TOTAL (KM^3/YEAR)
Precipitation on land (excluding Antarctica)	104,700
Evapotranspiration of precipitation from agricultural land	5,300
Runoff	38,800
Withdrawals for irrigation	2,900
Withdrawals for thermal power plant cooling	530
Withdrawals for households	340
Withdrawals for manufacturing	250
Withdrawals for human use	4,020
Groundwater recharge	12,600
Groundwater withdrawals	1,100

Notes: These data represent estimates of the average long-term freshwater flow or movement through parts of the global water cycle (precipitation, runoff, and groundwater recharge), including human uses of that water. Source: [99].

12.2.2 The Water Footprint

Since it takes a thousand tons of water to produce a ton
of grain, the most efficient way to import water is as grain.

— Lester R. Brown

The Dutch researcher, Arjen Hoekstra, developed the useful concept of a water footprint [118]. A water footprint is the total quantity of
water an entity uses to sustain itself, be it an individual, an industry, or
an entire nation — for example, all the water a nation uses to support its
population, lifestyle, and industries. The average person in a developed
nation uses about a gallon of water daily for drinking but requires another 800 gallons a day to provide the food s/he eats. Consuming a pound
of beef is, in effect, tantamount to consuming the 1,857 gallons of water
that was required to produce that pound of beef. Many developed nations receive much of their water needs indirectly via the many products
they import. Britain imports two-thirds of its water footprint. The hidden water demands of products (Table 12.2) from agricultural commodities to zinc and other metals are often called "virtual water."

Table 12.2 provides some examples of the water footprint for various products. These figures are averages because the water used will
vary considerably due to where and how the products are produced. The
US water footprint is about 2,500 m^3/capita/year (656,000 gal/cap/yr),
largest in the world, and four times that of Yemen (probably the world's
smallest), three times that of China, and twice that of the United King-
dom [314]. The US is also the world's leading virtual water exporter
[231]. The global water footprint is roughly 8 trillion m^3/yr. An
individual's water footprint can be calculated on the website
www.waterfootprint.org.

The UN estimates that some 450 trillion gallons of virtual water,
or 40% of the world's total consumption, are traded annually. Large transfers of water are common within nations also and frequently lead to
bitter disputes. By importing more virtual water from water-rich to water-poor areas, the water will support a larger population. However, the
global water debt will continue to increase because aquifers and other
water sources are still being depleted, especially in the world's most
important agricultural areas. The water footprint concept could be made
more useful if water sources and environmental implications are incorporated into it [98]. For example, is the water used to produce a product
coming entirely from dependable rainfall, or from an aquifer which is

Table 12.2. Examples of Average Estimated Water Footprints

PRODUCT	LITERS OF WATER
Mug of Tea (250 mL)	30
Cup of Coffee (125 mL)	130
Pint of Beer (568 mL)	170
Glass of Milk (250 mL)	255
One Slice of Bread	60
One Apple	125
Egg (60 g)	200
Cheese (250 g)	1,265
Chocolate Bar (100 g)	1,700
One Hamburger	2,400
One Steak (250 g)	3,850
Sugar from Beets (1 kg)	920
Sugar from Cane (1 kg)	1,780
Wheat (1 kg)	1,827
Meat: Chicken (1 kg)	4,330
Meat: Pig (1kg)	5,990
Cotton Fabric (1 kg)	10,000
Meat: Beef Cattle (1 kg)	15,400
One Cotton Shirt	2,500
One Pair of Blue Jeans	8,000
One Automobile	50,000

Notes: Metric-English equivalents: 29.6 mL = 1 fluid ounce; 28.3 g = 1 avoirdupois ounce; 1 kg = 2.2 lbs. Source: [527].

being rapidly depleted? With improving means of assessing water use in different regions, it may be possible to develop a non-renewable water footprint.

In a closely related development, the last decade has seen an alarming increase in the acquisition of land and water by corporations and nations which can afford it. Nations, including China, Saudi Arabia, India, and the US purchase or lease land and water in other nations, basically using other nations' resources to meet their own needs. The governments of many poor and developing nations want to encourage rapid economic growth and welcome these investments, but the land and water provided to incoming industries is often taken from local residents who already lack adequate water and food. Much of the appropriated land and water is used for industrial-scale mechanized agriculture, mining projects, and other environmentally disruptive activities. Based upon recent reported "land grabs," it is estimated that, globally, some 450 billion m^3 of water has been appropriated from 47 billion hectares of land for crop and livestock production [332]. Local inhabitants are frequently displaced and have no control over the land they have traditionally relied upon. Land and water "grabs" are a growing concern, especially in Africa [58, 161, 304]. Large scale land acquisitions by foreign investors are a relatively new development and reflect increasing competition for Earth's diminishing vital resources. Without fair oversight and regulation, conflicts with local populations are likely to increase.

The concept of a groundwater footprint has recently been introduced to amplify and complement the value of methods such as water and ecological footprints. The groundwater footprint is defined as the area necessary to sustain groundwater use and groundwater-dependent ecosystem services [145]. The groundwater footprint can be used to assess the use, recharge, and ecological value of entire aquifers. The global groundwater footprint is estimated to be some 3.5 times the actual area of aquifers. In other words, we are withdrawing 3.5 times more water than the aquifers can continue to provide. Some 1.7 billion people depend upon groundwater in areas where that resource cannot continue to meet human and ecosystem requirements. Groundwater footprint evaluations provide additional documentation of the overexploitation of aquifers in important agricultural areas. They also show that, in many areas, including South America, Africa, and Siberia, groundwater is abundant but its present and potential use is limited by such factors as ample surface water, a lack of arable land, sparse human population, inadequate technology, and politics.

12.2.3 Water Use vs. Consumption

Terms such as withdrawal, use, and consumption are often used interchangeably, but they are not the same. Groundwater withdrawals indicate the water removed from a well, and are variously referred to as extractions, abstractions, or simply pumpage. More generally, water withdrawals refer to the total amount of water removed from all water sources (streams, lakes, oceans, groundwater, and so forth), even if most of that water is returned directly to its source. How water is employed, applied,

Figure 12.2. A. A communal water source in Afghanistan. **B.** Woman in Upper Nile, Sudan, carries a 5-gallon jerry can during her daily hike to secure water. Five gallons of water weighs 42 pounds. Every day, many women and young girls must walk several miles, barefoot, sometimes for many hours, to obtain the water essential for survival. The available water is often contaminated and their journeys are often dangerous due to military activities and little law enforcement.

or exploited is its use (Figure 12.2A). Water that is consumed during use refers to water that is not soon returned to its source. Water which generates power in a hydroelectric dam or turns a mill stone is used but not consumed during that use. Water withdrawn from a well or a stream that is evaporated or transpired during use is consumed. Water withdrawals can easily remain stationary or even decrease while consumption/depletion of the resource continues. Water may be used and returned to the source, but in a degraded state — due, for example, to heating or pollutants — thus diminishing the value of the water resource. Table 12.1 gives estimates of global water resources and use and Table 12.3 provides data on water use in the US.

12.2.4 Human Requirements and Use

> *Humans build their societies around consumption of fossil water long buried in the earth, and these societies, being based on temporary resources, face the problem of being temporary themselves.*
>
> — Charles Bowden, 1977

Life as we understand it cannot exist without water. Human life and most human activities depend directly or indirectly on water. The human body is roughly 65% water by weight; it varies depending on age and sex. The human lung is 90% water, blood 83%, a newborn baby nearly 80%. A loss of only 6 to 7% of our body's water is fatal in 1 to 5 days. Each person must replace by ingestion as food or water, an average of 2.6 liters (5.5 pints) every day, that being the amount lost by perspiration, excretion, and exhalation. Water to provide for a person's total food requirements is on the order of 3,000 liters per day [315].

Great discrepancies exist between what is needed and what is used. Actual human water consumption is heavily dependent upon life style, and some life styles, like some businesses, thrive on waste. The fresh water delivered by utilities to homes in the US averages some 150 gpd/person, though in some upscale communities it can reach 500 gpd [22]. Annual freshwater withdrawals vary wildly from country to country, from less than 1 to over 2,000 m^3/per/yr, according to the Pacific Institute's latest compilation [150]. In developing nations, the poor often must walk many miles every day to obtain essential water. This difficult work is done primarily by women and young girls (Figure 12.2B). The total time that they spend on this endeavor is estimated at some 73 billion hours per year, most of that in Africa. Not only is this back-breaking work, it is

Table 12.3. Water Use in the United States, 2005

USE	PERCENT OF TOTAL	MILLIONS OF GALLONS PER DAY
Public Supply	11	44,200
Domestic	1	3,660
Irrigation	31	128,000
Livestock	<1	2,140
Aquaculture	2	8,780
Industrial	4	18,200
Mining	1	4,020
Thermoelectric	49	201,000
Total	100	410,000

Notes: About 410,000 million gallons per day (Mgal/d) of water was withdrawn for use in the United States during 2005. About 80% of the total (328,000 Mgal/d) withdrawal was from surface water, and about 82% of the surface water withdrawn was freshwater. The remaining 20% (82,600 Mgal/d) was withdrawn from groundwater, of which about 96% was freshwater. If withdrawals for thermoelectric power in 2005 are excluded, withdrawals were 210,000 Mgal/d, of which 129,000 Mgal/d (62%) was supplied by surface water and 80,700 Mgal/d (38%) was supplied by groundwater [544].

often fraught with danger and denies millions of women the ability to earn wages, obtain an education, and otherwise improve their lives and contribute to their societies.

12.2.5 Health and Sanitation Requirements

Sanitation isn't a priority for funders; it's still not easy to talk about it.

— Anais Mourey

Sanitation has not been emphasized in this book because it is largely a surface water problem. However, impure surface waters often contaminate the groundwater and many solutions to the inexcusable conditions in which many must live will involve groundwater use. The major environmental killer of people is polluted water. Roughly 700 million people lack access to a safe drinking water source and some 2.5 to 3.0 billion lack improved sanitation facilities. The WHO has estimated that some 2.2 million children under the age of 5 die every year due to unsafe water, poor hygiene, and inadequate sanitation, most of which is due to fecal contamination of surface waters [41, 397]. The two major UN Millennium Development Goals of 2002 were to cut in half the number of people lacking drinkable water and sanitation by 2015. In early 2012, the Joint Monitoring Programme of the UN Children's Fund (UNICEF) [511] and WHO [536] announced that the first goal had been met with nearly 90% of the world's population having access to potable drinking water. Such estimates are based upon so-called "improved" water sources such as public taps, piped-in water, and collected rainwater, which are assumed to be safe. Some of that water has been shown to be unsafe to drink and even when it is, contamination after obtaining the water and other factors may render the water unsafe [15]. Other estimates suggest that 28% of the global population (1.8 billion people) lacked safe drinking water in 2010 [296]. The goal for halving sanitation has fallen far short. It is likely that some 40% of the world's population currently lacks access to toilets and two-thirds of the world population, more than 5 billion people, are expected to be without basic public sewerage in 2030 [465]. The situation is especially dire in Sub-Saharan Africa [522]. Even in the US, the poor often lack adequate sanitary facilities and are increasingly denied access to those facilities. For example, some 13% of Native American households lack safe water and/or a safe way to dispose of wastewater [89].

12.2.6 Specific Water Uses

The United States Geological Survey has published summaries of the best estimates of water use in the US every five years since 1950. The water use data are based upon a plethora of information sources and utilize numerous methods of estimating water use. The effort required to accumulate and organize the data often results in a delay of four or more years before the final statistics are published. Table 12.3 summarizes some of the USGS data on water usage in the United States in the year 2005.

Globally, roughly 50% of domestic water, 40% of self-supplied industry water, and 20% of irrigation water is from groundwater (Table 12.1). Many uses do not fit conveniently into, and may be excluded from, the categories listed below. For example, as Barnett [22] points out, vast quantities of water, up to 19 trillion gallons, are used to maintain the grass found around homes, on sports fields, and along highways in the US. Collectively, these lawn-like areas occupy more acreage than any other "crop" in the US and are an important source of groundwater pollution due to heavy pesticide and fertilizer use!

A. Agriculture/Irrigation

Many articles and much research emphasize the need to increase agricultural output. But food cannot be supplied without soil and water, and both resources continue to be depleted at unsustainable rates (Plate 15, Top right). If human populations and human expectations continue to grow around the world as anticipated, agriculture will be forced to conserve soil and use water far more efficiently (Section 13.2.3). This will require major changes in how we grow our food and in what many people eat [54, 56, 58, 374].

Agriculture accounts for roughly 68% of global water use, industrial use about 15%, energy generation 10%, domestic use 4%, and evaporation from reservoirs 3% [57, 283, 374]. Agriculture consumes about 93% of the water humans use with industrial and domestic use equally sharing the remaining 7% [283]. Major agricultural water users such as the US, China, and India rely heavily on groundwater and diversions from rivers; half of this water use is probably nonrenewable. Section 12.2.7 focuses on the important relationships between food, water, and energy.

Ideally, irrigation refers to all water withdrawn to sustain plant growth and includes water used for field crops, orchards, golf courses, nurseries, parks, and other plant-supporting facilities and endeavors. In addition to direct watering of plants, the USGS statistics include water used for chemical applications, harvesting, field preparation, salt leaching, frost protection, and related tasks. This water may be self-supplied or may come from such entities as government agencies, irrigation districts, companies, and cooperatives. Most of the world's irrigated land is in Asia — some 80% of China's, and 60% of India's, grain harvest depend upon irrigation [58].

B. Energy

Thermoelectric-power water use refers to the large quantities of water withdrawn to generate electricity using steam-driven turbine generators, as in standard fossil-fuel or nuclear power plants (Table 12.3). Most of this water is used for cooling and then returned to the source, so little is consumed. In the US, over 99% of this water comes from surface supplies.

C. Public Supplies

On Table 12.3, "public supplies" refers to water withdrawn by public and private water suppliers and delivered to users. The water users include private homeowners, commercial businesses, industries, and public services. Public suppliers provide water to some 260 million people in the US, 85% of the population. Tap water in developed nations is generally a safe and reliable source of potable water. Purification often involves use of chlorine to kill microorganisms. Chlorine can react with other impurities to produce potentially harmful chemicals as well as impart an unpleasant taste to the water. This, and heavy promotion, has led many people to turn to bottled water for drinking (Section 13.3.2D).

D. Industry

The industrial use category pertains to water withdrawn by industry for its own use. The uses include fabricating, processing, washing, cooling, incorporation into products, transporting, diluting, and sanitation needs.

E. Aquaculture

This is the water used in the growing of finfish and shellfish for food, sport, conservation, and other uses. This water was included in the livestock category in pre-2000 USGS water use surveys.

F. Domestic

Some 15% of the US population in 2002, 43.5 million people, mostly rural, supplied their own water, 98% from groundwater.

G. Mining

Mining refers to the extraction of mineral resources (solid, liquid, or gas) from the earth. Most resources are taken from the solid earth, but a small quantity of salts are extracted from saline-water bodies such as the Dead Sea and the Great Salt Lake. Because water used for quarrying, milling, and related activities need not be pure, most of the groundwater used in mining is saline.

H. Livestock

This is water used for watering livestock in pastures and in associated farm/feedlot operations.

12.2.7 The Water-Food-Energy Nexus

The centrality of fresh water to our needs for food, for fuel, for fiber is taking center stage in what has become a crowded, environmentally stressed world.

— Mindy Lubber

Energy is vital to the economy and the quality of life in all nations, and producing that energy requires water. Conversely, or perversely, depending upon one's outlook, providing that water requires energy, and the water consumed by energy production may increase 3- or 4-fold by 2035 in the US, and by even greater amounts in rapidly developing nations [33]. Consider: pumping and treating water in the US uses over 50 billion kilowatt-hours of energy each year at a cost of billions of dollars, and each kilowatt-hour of coal-generated electricity demands about 25 gallons of water. A recent study found that obtaining, storing, treating, and delivering water for use accounts for at least 12.6% of total US energy consumption [339]. Water is often a limiting factor in obtaining energy from new sources such as organic shales and tar sands. Numerous plans for power plants, regardless of their energy source, have been curtailed due to insufficient water. The energy needed to treat and deliver water can represent up to 80% of the cost of the energy a plant generates [341]. The water transferred from northern California to support agriculture in southern California (Section 8.8.4) consumes some 2.4 kilowatt-hours of electricity for every cubic meter (264 gallons). Approximately 20% of California's electricity consumption is for the transport, storage, and treatment of water. About 2 kilowatt-hours of electricity is needed to desalinate 1 cubic meter of seawater [314]. The statistics demonstrate that obtaining water for any purpose is requiring ever-rising expenditures of energy, be it for deeper wells, importing water from distant sources, or special techniques such as desalination.

Huge volumes of water pass through the cooling towers of fossil fuel and nuclear electric generating plants. Although about 93% of the water is returned to the environment, it is returned at a much warmer temperature than it was withdrawn at. The heat, a form of thermal pollution, damages ecosystems, increases evaporation, and often limits other uses for the water. In general, it should benefit water productivity and conservation if fossil fuel and nuclear plants are replaced by renewable energy sources, especially solar. However, even green energy sources are not exempt from the water hex. For example, a number of centralized solar facilities planned for the arid western US are facing opposition because of their high water demand in a water-poor area. Improved conservation and greater efficiency in all operations that use energy and water will be necessary if future needs are to be met.

Between 1961 and 2004, world population increased at roughly 2.0% per year while crop yields increased at 2.3% per year. This was achieved mainly by a doubling of the irrigated land area which in turn relied heavily upon increased groundwater withdrawals and fertilizer applications, both of which are energy-intensive and unsustainable. World food demand is expected to grow by as much as 50% by 2030, and perhaps double by 2050. Hunger and malnutrition decreased until 1996, then began rising. By 2009, it was estimated that over a billion people lacked sufficient food and over two billion suffered chronic nutrient deficiencies [290]. In 2012, Save the Children [505] estimated that, over the next 15 years, some 450 million children were likely to be physically and mentally stunted without additional efforts to reduce malnutrition. Economics, conflicts, poor distribution, and related problems strongly influence these trends. But the productivity of major agricultural regions around the world, including China, India, North Africa, the Middle East, and the US, is threatened by a more fundamental problem: groundwater depletion [140].

Globally, agriculture has become increasingly dependent upon groundwater in the last few decades. Millions of farmers are withdrawing groundwater with no oversight or control. This has yielded short-term benefits and helped feed billions, but those benefits cannot be sustained [144]. Many factors, including population growth, an explosion of middle-class consumers, ground/surface water depletion, pollution, and cropland losses due to development, desertification, and salinization are eating away at the gains provided by the "green revolution" and easily exploited water sources [313]. Water users will increasingly be pitted against each other in their quest for diminishing supplies. Due to the greater political power of cities and industries, the major loser is expected to be agriculture. But this in turn may pose a threat to local, national, and global food security [253].

World grain production peaked at 339 kg/person in 1984, then began falling. It is worth repeating that over half the world's irrigated cropland is in Asia, mainly China and India, along with about half the world's population. Some 80% of China's grain is from irrigated lands and over 50% of India's [55, 471]. These crops are heavily dependent upon overpumping groundwater. As that water supply diminishes, so also will the food supplies made possible by that water. Due in part to water scarcity, China has rapidly become the world's leading importer of many grains, placing heavy pressure on the world grain market and increasing the cost of grain.

One cubic meter of water weighs 2,205 pounds. Withdrawing groundwater from ever-greater depths is requiring ever-greater amounts of energy, contributing to higher food prices. That energy comes mostly from electricity generated by coal or diesel fuel, the cost of which is often heavily subsidized by governments. Using these fossil fuels produces more greenhouse gases which are likely to alter climates in ways which will further diminish the supply of both food and water.

In large, rapidly advancing nations such as China, India, and Brazil, poverty has been dramatically reduced in recent years. One result is that growing numbers of affluent people are increasing their consumption of foods, especially meats, which require far more water than direct grain consumption (Table 12.2). In addition, such factors as growing population, use of grain crops for automotive fuel, continuing excessive consumption in most developed nations, and market speculation add to the pressure on, and cost of, food supplies. These trends make it very difficult for poor nations to meet their food needs. Some believe that the recent disturbing trends in agricultural yields, productive land, energy, and water supply may represent the leading edge of a quantum shift from a world of surplus resources to one of scarcity. A warming climate exacerbates the problem; global food supplies need to double by 2050, yet every degree increase in global temperature has thus far led to a roughly 10% decline in the yields of major crops [167].

Surprisingly, these vital links between water and energy and food are often neglected. As with so many other water issues, we can afford to neglect them no longer. To look at this depressing scenario from a more positive perspective, the efficiency of food production will improve with every drop of water conserved, conserving water will help conserve energy, and energy conservation will help conserve water.

12.2.8 Groundwater Availability: The "Safe Yield" Myth

Quantifying the long-term availability of groundwater is difficult. All too often, water managers will assume that, once a water budget had been calculated or a groundwater "steady-state" condition defined, they can base future dependable withdrawals upon these models [48]. Terms such as "sustainable withdrawal" are often used to imply that negative impacts will never occur if groundwater removal is held below a certain limit, that limit commonly being the recharge rate. But there will always be impacts. Most obviously, the water pumped out of an aquifer represents an artificial discharge which is bound to decrease natural discharge rates, all else remaining unchanged. The impacts may be subtle or dramatic, and they may not become apparent for many years due to the slow flow rate of most groundwater. Pumping water from the earth inevitably produces an imbalance which will be compensated for by (1) a loss of groundwater storage, (2) decreases in discharge rates, and/or (3) increases in recharge rates, as pointed out by Theis in 1940 [386]. The water removed alters the groundwater conditions, invalidating the original steady state equilibrium between recharge and discharge rates. If recharge does not increase, removing groundwater will decrease discharges at downgradient wetlands, springs, streams, and wells and/or groundwater storage will be depleted. At best, a new balance or steady-state between recharge and discharge may eventually be attained at withdrawal rates which yield minimal negative impacts. In some situations, pumpage may even increase recharge by allowing additional water to enter the aquifer from the surface or from surrounding rock, but this still constitutes a water loss from another location.

The term safe yield [235] has been widely used by some water managers, hydrologists, environmentalists, and others to indicate the maximum sustainable rate of groundwater withdrawal, and is typically based only on anticipated recharge rates. This simplistic approach ignores basic groundwater behavior, especially the value of groundwater discharge, and has resulted in severe deterioration of water resources. Establishing the impacts of groundwater withdrawal should include consideration of such factors as annual recharge rates, seasonal fluctuations, climatic variability, economic viability, long-term water quality, variations in withdrawal rates, legal aspects, ecological impacts, other water demands which may impact the groundwater supply, and the always changing nature of these factors themselves. After thinking about it, we may justifiably conclude that "safe" or "sustainable" yield is too unwieldy a concept to be meaningful. Nonetheless, estimates of water availability are often required. Hydrogeologists who must attempt to quantify future withdrawal capacities often focus upon a basin-wide approach utilizing sophisticated models to simulate water supply and demand conditions over time. Such efforts can benefit from the participation of ecologists, economists, engineers, and other qualified experts who are familiar with the locale.

12.3 Impacts of Groundwater Depletion

The earth dries up and withers, the world languished and withers, the exalted of the earth languish. The earth lies under its inhabitants; for they have transgressed the laws, violated the statutes, and broken the everlasting covenant. Therefore a curse consumes the earth; its people must bear their guilt.

— Isaiah 24:4-6.

The following sections review several major impacts produced by the extraction and mining of groundwater.

12.3.1 Declining Water Supplies

The gap between rising water use and the sustainable yield of aquifers grows larger each year, which means the drop in water tables each year is greater than the year before.

— Lester R. Brown

A. Surface Water Depletion

In almost every situation where groundwater is depleted, surface waters will also suffer. The amount of surface water suitable for most human requirements is decreasing in much of the world due to excessive withdrawals, inefficient use of water, land abuses such as devegetation, and contamination. Essentially all available water is put to human use in some drainage basins. Many major rivers often dry up, at least part of the year, before reaching their destination, including the Yellow, Amu Darya, Colorado, and Nile. Overall, an astounding 55% or more of the normal total river flow to the oceans now fails to reach the sea as a consequence of human uses and activities.

Groundwater withdrawals often cause the base flow to streams, springs, and wetlands to diminish or cease completely. The water table is lowered and groundwater discharge rates diminish [21]. Marshlands, lakes, and other previously wet areas can dry up causing entire ecosystems to perish. Effluent streams become influent (Figure 4.6). Consequences range from species extinction to salt-water incursions in coastal areas. Groundwater overdraft has reduced surface water supplies around much of the world. Water navigation to ports located along rivers and estuaries can be seriously impeded by the reduced flow. Without the

466

extra water to dilute pollutants, formerly innocuous contaminants can become serious threats in surface waters. Important and delicate coastal waters, especially in partly enclosed areas such as estuaries, lagoons, bays, and seas, often suffer serious damage, directly from the more concentrated pollutants being delivered to them, and from increased saltiness due to the decrease in fresh water input (Section 8.9). When fresh river-water flow to the ocean decreases, the delicate balance between fresh- and salt-water shifts, causing a wedge of salt water to migrate upstream along the river bed (Figure 8.26). The salt water, being denser than fresh water, can then seep downward through the river bed and contaminate fresh groundwater supplies. Industries such as fishing, shellfishing, and tourism frequently suffer dramatic declines.

Example: San Pedro River

The San Pedro River in Arizona is considered the last wild, undammed desert river of note in the southwestern US. It supports the finest example remaining of a cottonwood-willow forest, the rarest forest type in North America (Figure 12.3). The forest in turn supports a thriving ecosystem, including dozens of species of breeding birds. In addition to contending with phreatophytes and drought, the river and all that depends upon it is threatened by excessive groundwater pumping. Wells in the upper part of the San Pedro already extract an estimated 6,000 acre-feet of nonreplenishable groundwater annually. The aquifer supplying the lower San Pedro with base flow is being overdrawn by some 11,000 acre-feet per year by a nearby Army base, Fort Huachuca. The expanding cone of depression is approaching the river. Meanwhile, the base is planning its own major expansion. In 2011, a court decision found that, in spite of numerous water-conserving efforts, the groundwater pumping plan devised by the US Army and the Fish and Wildlife Service for Fort Huachuca would not provide adequate protection for the river [69]. In addition, as this is being written, the Arizona Department of Water Resources is considering allowing the construction of thousands of new homes in the Sierra Vista region which would withdraw more thousands of acre-feet of water annually. Arizona state law does not recognize legal connections between a river and its recharge sources [132].

Figure 12.3. View along the San Pedro River in southern Arizona. Phreatophyte vegetation here consists largely of cottonwoods and willows.

B. Groundwater Depletion

Global estimates of groundwater resource supply and demand remain sketchy and incomplete [144, 283, 313, 421]. The data provided in Table 1.6 reveal that groundwater stores about 96 times more liquid fresh water than does surface water: 10,530,000 km³ for groundwater vs. 110,120 km³ for lakes, wetlands, and rivers [295]. Due in part to the decrease in usable surface water and the availability of sophisticated new drilling and pumping technologies, worldwide groundwater withdrawals have surged in the last quarter century, with especially large increases in the developing world. Models used by Wada, *et al.* [421] indicate that annual groundwater depletion in arid to sub-humid regions increased from approximately 126 km³ (30 mi³) in 1960 to 283 km³ (68 mi³) in 2000. They estimate the 2000 figure at roughly 39% of the total global annual groundwater extraction of some 726 km³. In view of these data, and recent groundwater resource evaluations and trends, it is probable that the current global groundwater overdraft exceeds 1,000 km³ annually.

As a result, a huge and growing deficit of groundwater removed but not replaced is being created and water tables are declining in virtually all major agricultural and most urban areas of the world. Due to the slow movement of most groundwater, this water supply cannot be renewed except over a significant period of time, typically hundreds to thousands of years. The rate of depletion continues to increase, although increasing costs as the readily pumped groundwater disappears, should help to reduce the depletion rate and encourage conservation.

12.3.2 Decrease in Groundwater Quality

Extraction of groundwater far exceeds recharge in many parts of the world, including most of the vital food producing regions. When reserves of fresh, potable groundwater are depleted, contamination of both surface and ground water becomes ever more likely, even where human-generated contamination is not present. As noted previously, deeper groundwater has typically been in contact with rock for a longer period of time and will contain higher levels of mineral impurities, including salt, metals, fluoride, and many other contaminants.

Seawater intrusion is a major problem from groundwater overdraft in coastal areas around the world, degrading both water and soil. In the US, the Atlantic and Gulf coasts are most susceptible to this. The water supply for hundreds of thousands of people, their farmlands, and communities in many areas of India and China is threatened by salt-water intrusion.

12.3.3 Subsidence

Subsidence refers to the lowering of the ground surface. Recall that, because of its buoyancy effect, water is capable of floating ships weighing many tons. If large quantities of water, or other fluids, are removed from earth materials, the decrease in fluid mass and pore pressure causes a loss of support, resulting in compaction. In coarse-grained sediments, the amount of compaction is small, mainly because large grains can support the added weight caused by the water loss. If water returns to the sediment, the compaction will be reversed. This is often referred to as recoverable or elastic compaction. In fine-grained sediments like clays and silts, however, the tiny fragments are much more compressible and contain a relatively greater volume of water. As fine sediment slowly dries out, it decreases in volume, or shrinks, considerably. Density increases, squeezing out still more water. The resulting reduction in volume is largely nonrecoverable and is called inelastic compaction. As this happens, the ground surface above will settle downward — subside. The specific minerals present also influence compaction. One of the most common and highly compactable clay minerals is montmorillonite.

Draining wetlands can cause subsidence due to the compaction and oxidation of organic soils rich in peat. Peat consists of vegetable matter which has partially decomposed in a saturated, oxygen-poor environment such as a swamp or bog. When the water table is lowered, atmospheric oxygen enters the organic-rich matter allowing the growth of microorganisms which consume the organic debris. The result is release of large quantities of carbon dioxide and subsidence of the land surface. This appears to be the major cause of the subsidence of the Sacramento-San Joaquin Delta complex in California. Much of this important farming area is below sea level and facing growing threats from water diversions, rising seas, and related problems (Section 8.8.4).

Example: The Netherlands

The Netherlands, where the remarkable system of dikes, piers, and gates has been keeping the sea at bay for many decades, provides another example. The coastal region was originally above sea level and composed largely of peat bogs (fens) and lakes. Embankments were built along rivers, depriving the lowlands of stream deposits which had countered natural subsidence. The lakes and fen meadows were drained to create land suitable for agriculture, and peat and clay were mined commercially. The water loss, oxidation of peat, and lack of sediment deposition resulted in lowering of the land surface. Soon the water table was at the surface again, interfering with farming. To drain the water, deeper channels and sluiceways were constructed, windmills (Figure 12.4) were built to pump water from shallow wells, and the land sank further. Today parts of the Netherlands are 6 meters (20 feet) below sea level, the subsidence continues, sea level is slowly rising, and the lowlands must be protected by an ever more complex and precarious system of great dikes, dams, canals, and related structures (Plate 15, Bottom).

The amount of land subsidence resulting from dewatering an aquifer, also called hydrocompaction, can be estimated by a simple equation,

$$C = kb\Delta h$$

Figure 12.4. A windmill in The Netherlands. Built in the mid-nineteenth century near Groningen, this mill kept water from accumulating in polders, artificially drained wetlands that were located below sea level.

where C is the total compaction, k is a compressibility constant which depends upon the material, b is the thickness of the material, and Δh is the decrease in water level.

Example: Solving a Problem

The water table of a 2,500-foot-thick sandy aquifer in an arid basin in Nevada has declined by 300 feet. How much subsidence can be anticipated at the ground surface? From tables, we find that the compressibility of a sandy aquifer is about 0.00001/ft (10^{-5}/ft). Thus,

$$C = 0.00001/\text{ft} \times 2500 \text{ ft} \times 300 \text{ ft} = 7.5 \text{ ft}.$$

Subsidence related to the mining of groundwater has caused serious problems around the world. More than 50 cities in China have serious subsidence problems due to overextraction of groundwater, according to the Xinhua news agency [246]. Shanghai, China's largest city, has been sinking for about a century — its business center has subsided at least 2.6 meters (8.5 feet) since 1921. The city now diverts surface water into underlying aquifers and plans to limit groundwater withdrawals by 2015 to reduce the problem. In the US, more than 80% of subsidence is attributed primarily to groundwater extraction [246]. Figure 12.5 shows the extent of this subsidence, most of which is due to the inelastic compaction of clays.

Due to such factors as well locations and withdrawals, land surface uses, changes in aquifer composition, structural irregularities, and relations to underlying materials such as buried masses of bedrock lying beneath unconsolidated sediments, subsidence will often not be uniform over an area nor will it occur at the same rate in all places. Collapse into underlying caverns due to a lowered water table is a serious threat in some karst areas (Figure 8.14D). Some of the most severe problems result from irregular rates of subsidence. Where bedrock lies closer to the surface, subsidence will be less than where it is buried more deeply. This often generates tension in the earth material causing fissures to open up at the surface (Figure 12.6B). Subsidence can result in extensive damage to wells, canals, levees, buildings, and other structures.

In low-lying coastal regions, subsidence can be especially devastating. Many such environments are already experiencing downsinking due to the compaction of underlying sediment and tectonic subsidence — isostatic adjustments caused by the accumulation of land-derived sediment in coastal areas. Factors such as increasing population, rising sea levels, potential storm surges and tsunamis, ongoing groundwater withdrawals, and salt-water intrusion all combine to yield an insidious, and accelerating, increase in the risks associated with coastal environments around the world.

Examples: Subsidence

Many hundreds of examples of dramatic subsidence are known, including nearly all areas where extensive water table declines have occurred and most of the world's major deltas. Three prominent areas are noted here.

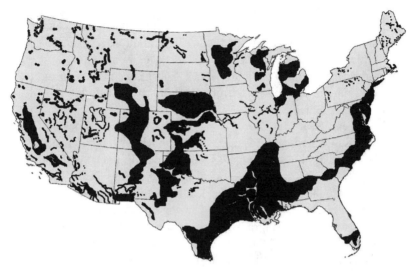

Figure 12.5. Map of areas in the US subsiding due to groundwater extraction.

San Joaquin Valley. The Central Valley of California (Section 8.8.4) contains some of the most extensive recent land subsidence, by volume, in the world. More than 13,500 km² of land in the southern part the San Joaquin Valley has subsided more than 0.3 meters (1 foot), largely a result of the lowering of the water table due to groundwater pumping and the resultant compaction of clays. Figure 12.6A illustrates an impressive demonstration of 52 years (1925-1977) of subsidence in the Valley.

Mexico City. Five hundred years ago, a lake occupied the basin where the capital of Mexico now sits. Soon the Spaniards began draining the waters for settlements and agriculture. In recent decades population growth has been explosive and today some 22 million people occupy Mexico City and its environs. About 75% of their water now comes from groundwater which is being withdrawn three times faster than it can be replenished. Most runoff rapidly flows from the area through artificial channels and tunnels. The removal of water from the underlying sediments has caused consolidation of the clays, leading to subsidence of 9 meters (30 feet) or more in parts of Mexico City. Irregularities in underlying sediment result in differing rates of subsidence. The results include leaning and sunken buildings, fractured foundations, and related damages which have made Mexico City a favorite textbook example of subsidence problems (Figure 12.6C). Subsidence in some areas continues at rates varying from 1 mm to more than 400 mm (16 in.) annually [246].

Dead Sea. The Dead Sea has shrunk by a third since the 1960s due mainly to diversion of Jordan River water by Israel and Jordan. Thousands of sinks have opened up along the shore due to the lowering of the local base level (the Dead Sea). Fresh groundwater, as it migrates down to the lower base level, dissolves underlying salt beds, causing collapse in overlying sediments. Various proposals have been promulgated to take water from the Red Sea (Gulf of Aquaba) and transport it by canals, tunnels, or pipelines to the Dead Sea. This requires transferring seawater more than 100 miles through a tectonically active rift zone in a politically volatile part of the world at a cost of up to $15 billion. Environmental risks are considerable, especially contamination of fresh groundwater by seawater leakage. The most feasible approach appears to be by pipeline with an associated desalination plant [441]. Without stabilization of its water level by such a project, the Dead Sea is expected shrink by another third by the end of the century.

12.3.4 Miscellaneous Impacts

The impacts noted above can severely threaten human welfare and local ecosystems which, in some situations, may require nearly complete abandonment of a region. Alternatives, such as importing water or desalinization, will be economically unfeasible for many regions.

Secondary or indirect impacts are often underestimated. For example, natural vegetation is among the first victims of a lowered water table. Plants are especially vulnerable in arid to subhumid climates, and will die when their roots can no longer reach water. The loss of vegetation leads to the loss of agricultural production and wildlife, increased runoff, excessive erosion, and flooding. Wind erosion of devegetated land produces air laden with dust and associated pollutants which can yield negative impacts ranging from human health and visibility to climate alterations and accelerated rates of glacier melting. Any of which may lead to still further disruptions.

Figure 12.6. Examples of subsidence. **A.** Famous photo showing a telephone pole on which the elevation of the ground surface in past years is given. From 1925 to 1977, when the photo was taken, the land surface at this location subsided about 9 meters (30 feet) due to overextraction of groundwater. Reduced groundwater pumping and use of surface water for irrigation since 1977 has limited additional subsidence to less than a meter. The man standing next to the pole is Joseph Poland, a USGS scientist who pinpointed this location of maximum subsidence. located southwest of Mendota, California. **B.** A ground fissure in Arizona. **C.** Excess groundwater extraction has lowered the water table causing many structural problems in Mexico City. Note the tilt of the cathedral at the left in this photo.

One of the unexpected impacts has to do with building foundations. Many low lying wetlands adjacent to water bodies have been filled in and built upon, including large sections of cities such as Amsterdam, Stockholm, Milwaukee, and Boston. As long as the water table remains at the same level as when buildings were constructed, wooden building supports will continue to bear their load, often for centuries. But when the water level drops, pilings and other supports quickly rot. In Boston, the value of properties supported by pilings is estimated at perhaps $10 billion. Lowered groundwater levels caused by pumping, the presence of many impermeable surfaces, and leakage into subsurface sewer lines, subways, and other infrastructures threaten valuable and historic properties in Boston and many other cities.

12.4 Ethical and Legal Issues

You are piling up a heritage of conflict and litigation on water rights for there is not sufficient water to supply the land.

— John Wesley Powell, 1893

12.4.1 Is Water a Human Right?

Who owns water? Local governments, national governments, individuals, companies? Whoever claims it first? Whoever demonstrates a need for it? Or should no person or group be allowed to possess and profit from a resource that is essential to everyone's survival? Should water be regarded as a universal human right, or a commodity to be bought and sold to those who can afford it? Is it morally acceptable that people should suffer and die because they can't afford clean water? But if it's to be a basic right, will a legal morass follow as citizens, governments, and corporations file lawsuits to retain or obtain what they feel are their rights [19]? Who provides oversight and determines what is essential and fair? Such questions never end. Because life itself depends upon water, issues of ownership and distribution quickly become moral as well as much-debated political, economic, ecologic, and legal issues. Numerous individuals have discussed these issues in depth [20, 22, 68, 147, 320, 379].

The UN and the World Bank have generally considered water a human need but not a right; if it is a need, it can be sold and traded like any other marketable item. Most water experts, including scientists, lean toward regarding water as a basic human right. The need for sanitary conditions which are affordable, safe, and which protect human dignity are inextricably related to water. Many believe the right to water must also incorporate a right to sanitation, especially in view of the degrading conditions which continue to exist in much of the developing world. The US Agency for International Development's (USAID) [515] Water, Sanitation and Hygiene (WaSH) initiative focuses on providing sanitation services to the world's poor.

Equitable, workable solutions to ethical issues will require a combination of approaches. At a minimum, those approaches should include maintaining a supply of water suitable for human consumption and sanitation requirements, realistic charges for water, and guaranteeing sufficient water to meet everyone's essential needs. Essential needs do not include watering the lawn, washing the car, or filling a swimming pool. A recommended approach is to establish essential water needs and guarantee these at no cost, or at a cost that even the poorest can afford, then apply rapidly escalating charges for all usage above that essential minimum. A similar approach can be applied for industries and other businesses. Providing additional water at unrealistically low cost encourages waste and corruption.

A multilateral treaty adopted by the UN in 1976, the International Covenant on Economic, Social and Cultural Rights, includes the right to an adequate standard of living and to health, neither of which are possible without access to a safe and adequate supply of water. More recently, numerous local governments and nations have declared water to be a human right. At the 2000 World Water Forum in The Hague, an alliance of environmentalists, indigenous peoples, farmers, and other sympathizers calling itself the Blue Planet Project demanded that water as a human right be considered. In 2005, Uruguay became the first nation to outlaw water privatization, declaring water a "constitutional right" and a "public good."

At the close of the World Water Forum in Mexico City in March, 2006, a declaration on the importance of clean water was agreed to by 148 countries. In a separate statement, Bolivia, Cuba, Venezuela, and Uruguay noted their desire to see water considered a human right, not just a need. Bolivian Water Minister Abel Mamani is quoted by Reuters: "You can't use a thing as important as water, which is synonymous with life, to make money." International resolutions supporting the right to clean drinking water and sanitation generally have been supported by all lower-income (developing) nations while the wealthier nations abstain. On July 29, 2010, the UN General Assembly unanimously voted to view water as a basic human right.

In the final analysis, water rights and supplies, climate change, pollution, and other environmental challenges are fundamentally moral issues which require us to consider the condition of the world we leave to our descendants [274].

12.4.2 Water Law

> *Because the existence, origin, movement and course of such waters, and the causes which govern and direct their movement, are so secret, occult and concealed that any attempt to administer any set of legal rules in respect to them would be, therefore, practically impossible.*
>
> — from the 1861 Ohio Frasier vs. Brown decision regarding "underground waters percolating, oozing or filtrating through the earth."

A. Introduction

Rules and guidelines concerning water can be found in the earliest legal records we have, such as the Code of King Hammurabi (1795-1750 B.C.). In general, private property is governed by jus civile (civil law) and critical natural resources by jus gentium (the law of all peoples). Beginning in the seventeenth century, surface waters were often regulated under the latter and considered as public property. Groundwater was generally assumed to belong to the overlying land owner and was ignored in legal proceedings until excessive withdrawals courtesy of the turbine pump (Section 7.1.2) began producing alarming drops in groundwater levels and interference with neighboring wells in the early twentieth century. Even today, water laws continue to be focused strongly on surface waters, often ignoring groundwater altogether. Rules regarding the use and distribution of both surface and subsurface water resources remain deeply flawed around much of the world, and solid, objective scientific input is often completely lacking. Part of the problem lies in the nature of water itself. How does one fairly legislate a resource which exists as groundwater under one person's property, enters the surface as a spring on someone else's property, becomes a stream which then flows into another property, only to infiltrate again to the subsurface and contribute to the water supply for an entire community, and so on? And there are the many transboundary aquifers and drainage basins to consider. All too often, antiquated laws have become obstacles to improved management of water, especially groundwater.

The Boundary Waters Treaty of 1909 provided a framework and rules for managing water resource issues between the US and Canada, the first of numerous such agreements, many centering on the Great Lakes. In Canada, the Constitution Act of 1867 allowed water policies be instituted by provinces or local governments, with the federal government providing expertise if requested. In Australia, like Canada, responsibility for water resources rests with the states, cities, and other governing entities. Australia's Water Act of 2007 provides funding to address current water-related problems, including infrastructure, irrigation, and environmental needs [178]. In contrast, Mexico places responsibility for water resources on the federal government. Development of a legal framework for water resources began in 1926 with the creation of the National Irrigation Commission and Irrigation Law. The Mexican Institute of Water Technology was founded in 1986 to perform research and educate individuals in the science and management of water. This was followed in 1992 with an updated National Water Law [68].

Other nations have followed similar paths with extensive, ongoing attempts to better manage their precious water resources. South Africa's 1998 National Water Act was praised for recognizing human and environmental rights. The European Union Water Framework Directive of 2000 is an attempt to provide a central water policy guide for member nations, especially in the areas of ecology, governance, and economics. The Russian Federation Water Code No. 174-ф3 focuses on water resource protection and integrated water management on a regional scale [75]. Of course, it is one thing to approve policies and establish regulations, and quite another to implement and enforce them fully and fairly.

B. Water Law in the United States

The Nation's policy is no policy; its vision is no vision.
— Gerald E. Galloway, 2003

The nation needs a 21st century water policy.
— Peter H. Gleick and Juliet Christian-Smith, 2012

In the water-rich eastern United States, the legal right to use water is governed mainly by the riparian doctrine. This doctrine declares that all property owners bordering a water body such as a stream or lake have equal rights to the water and must share the resource. Each owner may withdraw "reasonable" but limited quantities of the water for use on his riparian property; he cannot sell or export that water for use elsewhere.

In the largely arid or semiarid western US a completely different doctrine, called prior appropriation evolved beginning in the 1850s. Much of the impetus for this rule was a government eager to provide incentives which would encourage economic growth. Water rights were gained by being the first to take water and apply it for a beneficial use, such as mining or irrigation. The water right can be lost if the water is no longer being used, but no restrictions exist on where the water may be used in a given state and the user's property need not border the water body. If the water is transferred across a state line, it is often allocated by legally binding "compacts," such as that which divides Colorado River water between seven states. Prior appropriation has been a first-come-first-served, use-it-or-lose-it proposition in which water belongs to whatever party first laid claim to it. As such, it has encouraged much selling, transfer, and waste of water, even during droughts.

Prior appropriation and related legal rules often encourage waste of water while denying water for more efficient uses. A Texas law allows unlimited pumping of groundwater as long as the water is put to some undefined "reasonable" use. Many states have laws forbidding the reuse of the "greywater" left from household uses — such as washing clothes and dishes, bathing, and so forth — or even rainwater. Inefficient water users are often allowed to continue wasteful practices while efficient users are denied water simply because their water claims postdate those of inefficient users. Various institutionalized subsidies provide water at ridiculously low cost, encouraging waste. Changing such entrenched inefficiencies is difficult because the beneficiaries are often politically powerful.

Prior appropriation and riparian rights have long existed concurrently in several western states, and in at least two eastern states, Mississippi and Florida. Except for certain very old claims, most western states have appropriated all water falling within their borders as state property rendering it illegal for any other party, such as an individual landowner, to collect or use even the water running off their roofs. This is beginning to change as water scarcity becomes ever more apparent. Two 2009 Colorado laws legalized rainwater catchment under certain circumstances for the first time ever. Some western states and cities are now encouraging, or even mandating, installation of rainwater capture devices.

The 1861 *Frazier vs. Brown* decision quoted at the start of this section on Water Law followed the precedent of an 1843 English court decision which permitted a landowner to pump as much groundwater from beneath his property as desired, regardless of damage to neighboring properties. This became known as the "English rule." In 1862, a New Hampshire ruling recognized the rights of adjacent landowners and restricted use of groundwater to a reasonable amount. This became the "American rule." Many versions of these rules have ensued, including a 1984 repeal of the *Frazier vs. Brown* decision.

Laws concerning water in the US continue to vary greatly from place to place. Ideally, federal laws may be strengthened but not weakened by states. Water is regarded as both a public resource and a private property right. The US Congress last enacted general water legislation in the 1965 Water Resources Planning Act. Since then, bits and pieces of water legislation have arisen by amendments of rules for a bewildering array of programs and projects. The rules will differ depending upon the governing body and its focus, whether regional rules, local ordinances, contracts, treaties, or otherwise. The result is an unwieldy jumble of regulations with widely divergent intents, and often completely at odds with the principles of basic water science. Nearly all regulations are inadequate at protecting the environment and many encourage resource-degrading practices and waste. Laws in many US states and in other nations often allow individuals or corporations to profit greatly while depleting water resources, leaving the public to pay the immediate and long-term costs.

Groundwater in particular continues to be treated as private property in most western states. Responsibility for water quantity and/or quality is often dispersed among numerous local, state, and federal agencies and it's often unclear where authority lies, or if a legal authority even exists. Databases of water violations are often inaccurate. Confusion and inconsistencies abound and it is sometimes painfully obvious that the lawmakers understood little about water. Existing legal tenets are often a morass of outdated, poorly planned rules exacerbated by grandfathered water rights and perverse subsidies which continue to encourage waste and discriminate against efficient use [172]. Many difficult situations date back to the nineteenth century when settlers were granted legal rights to certain amounts of groundwater. As with prior appropriation of surface waters, these rights were made without any scientific basis and with little concern for future changes in water needs. Those needs are well manifest now, and pressure to implement rules which will preserve the resources and encourage sustainable use is growing. But holders of old water rights promote short-term economic benefits and have no intention of relinquishing them without a fight. Legal stalemates and quagmires often result.

Rules concerning groundwater are especially weak, and often non-existent. It has been commonly assumed, for example, that groundwater is inexhaustible. The popular concept of "reasonable use" of groundwater by all participants encourages overuse of the common resource, as does the exemption of "small" wells, such as domestic wells, from any regulation. Such approaches ignore the cumulative impact of such withdrawals from millions of small wells — some of which will extract over a million gallons of groundwater annually [156]. In the western US alone, hundreds of thousands of active wells are exempt from any controls or metering, making it impossible to know how much groundwater is being withdrawn. Recently, several state supreme courts have declared that land owners have a property right to the groundwater beneath their land, making comprehensive water resource oversight and management very difficult if not impossible. Environmental repercussions of such loose policies are generally ignored. Yet changing even antiquated and clearly harmful laws and legal protocols can be a daunting task requiring years of haggling over user rights and other details. Meanwhile, the water resource often continues to be decimated.

12.4.3 Legal Reform

Legal cases, decisions, and concepts are riddled with unscientific and ill-defined terms such as 'percolating waters,' 'subflow,' and 'overlying rights.'

— Luna B. Leopold

If water is to be used smartly and efficiently with minimal environmental impact, many antiquated laws need to be eliminated and new ones instituted. Thankfully, the tangled legalities of water are slowly improving. Governmental bodies, from the local to the international, are beginning to address legal aspects of groundwater law. For example, the 2000 Water Framework Directive of the European Union follows a growing and well-advised approach which entails considering surface water, groundwater, and ecosystems as interconnected parts of the hydrologic system. International water laws tend to incorporate two major ideas: (1) states are equal under the law, and (2) the benefits of shared waters should be allocated equally [257]. Regarding the latter concern, the UN International Law Commission [514] has spent years preparing its Articles on the Law of Transboundary Aquifers. International attempts to officially recognize water as a human right have been blocked, mainly by the US and Canada. Additional legal complications involve transfers of water supply responsibilities from public agencies to private, for-profit businesses (Section 13.3.2D) and the marketing of groundwater [28].

Fortunately, obstructive legalities can be avoided by a variety of methods. Agricultural interests often preceded the vast expansion of urban areas and thus established water rights early on. In many areas, including much of the western US, large agricultural interests tend to be favored by those responsible for overseeing water resource allocations. However, individuals and organizations are often able to transfer their water rights to others. Many farmers in water-stressed areas are finding it more profitable to sell their water rights than to produce crops. In other cases, local authorities, aided by consumer education, are succeeding in placing caps on water use. For example, San Antonio, Texas, cut per capita water use by more than 40% when limits were placed on groundwater pumping from the Edwards aquifer in an effort to conserve this precious resource.

12.5 Water Conflicts

People are desperate and will fight to death for a cup of water.

— Tom Osbeck, missionary at the Jesus-in-Haiti Ministry school

12.5.1 Introduction: Is Water for Fighting Over?

Whiskey's for drinking. Water's for fighting over.

— attributed to Mark Twain

Throughout human history, water has been a major source of both conflict and cooperation. It can be a weapon of war or a tool for peace. Because water serves so many essential needs, water use is unavoidably a source of competition and controversy, and thus a frequent cause of friction between users, be they nations, industries, or individuals. Households, agriculture, manufacturing, mining, navigation, fishing, recreation, ecosystems — all require water and must often share the same sources. Water stresses and rivalries, generated by increasing demand and dwindling supplies, can yield instability and conflict between nations and, even more commonly, within a nation [153]. Hundreds of millions of the poor lack adequate water. Agriculture is under growing pressure to use less water as rapidly growing cities cry out for more. Corporations are realizing that water access is essential to success and must be seriously considered when developing strategies for the future [342]. Nations and businesses that have the financial ability to do so are buying up or manipulating water resources, often to the detriment of other, more needy users.

In the past, major conflicts over water have been relatively rare, probably because, unlike an individually owned piece of land, water is more commonly regarded as a communal resource. As such it is often managed by some agency or organization in whose decisions the diverse water interests can all participate. It would seem that water-poor regions would experience more conflict, but this is not usually true, largely because residents of dry areas have learned to adapt to the limited water supply by negotiating agreements. By establishing an orderly and fair process, the resource can be managed without violent conflict. Hence, water can become a means of establishing communication and cooperation between and among nations. When violence does occur, it tends to be because the institutions managing water resources failed to do so fairly or wisely. Needless to say, to manage fairly and wisely, dependable hydrogeological and meteorological data are essential.

Due to the sheer numbers of people now populating Earth, the continuing expansion of that population, and the growing scarcity of usable water supplies throughout the world, many are concerned that resource wars, especially over fresh water, may become much more common in the near future [365]. Such conflicts may be more likely to develop within nations than between them. Because water is essential and water insecurity is growing, water stress is seen as a growing security challenge. A classified 2012 National Intelligence Estimate requested by Secretary of State Hillary Clinton confirms that defense agencies increasingly see water as a focal point of possible future conflicts both between and within nations. Water supply facilities such as dams, reservoirs, and distribution systems are also ill prepared to defend against terrorism, either by direct physical assault (bombs, poisons) or indirectly via the use of malicious computer software ("malware"). It remains to be seen whether water will provide an avenue for cooperation or a fount of conflict, and possibly warfare, in the troubled future that awaits [148, 283, 365, 396].

12.5.2 Transboundary Water Bodies

Many of the wars in this century were about oil, but wars of the next century will be over water.

— Ismail Serageldin

When a water resource such as a lake, river, or aquifer is shared by more than one political entity, it is termed a transboundary condition. Transboundary issues can become especially thorny. The distribution and use of interstate water resources is a rapidly growing problem which will need to be addressed by nations and local governments around the world (Section 13.3). Water disputes often persist for decades during which time the interested parties are unlikely to correct inequalities and problems of supply and quality [153, 436]. About 60% of the world's river flow is shared by two or more countries. The record goes to the Danube River which is shared by no fewer than 17 nations, but the Nile, Tigris-Euphrates, Himalayan rivers, and dozens of others pose potential problems among those sharing the waters.

For obvious reasons, most disputes to date have involved surface water, but as aquifers become better delineated and their waters more valuable, groundwater disputes are becoming more frequent. International Alert [553], a British nonprofit organization, has identified 46 countries with nearly 3 billion people where water and climate stresses threaten conflict by 2025 [350]. At least 273 significant international aquifers have been identified. Figure 8.1 provides locations of Earth's major aquifers. For examples of aquifer disputes and agreements, see sections 8.8.2 (Memphis Sand), 8.11 (Great Basin), 14.2.2 (Nubian Sandstone), and 14.2.5 (Guarani aquifer).

12.5.3 Reducing Conflict

Here we have facts to face, not pleasant ones. Is the end a picture of people not facing a fact that stares them in the face?

— Robert Simpson

Water and food are essential to human security and survival. If conflict is to be avoided, both of these needs must be met. In the short term, the need can be met by importing virtual water as food and other goods. This, in essence, expands the water supply of the importing nation. But, as noted previously, this may occur at the expense of less fortunate people in other nations, thus increasing the potential for conflict. Effective guidance, aid, and possible intervention by an outside authority such as the UN can help greatly to seek just solutions and avoid violent disputes.

One big step in reducing potential conflicts, and water resource problems in general, would be to redefine and redirect "growth." The prevailing attitude among politicians, city managers, most economists, and other members of the status quo, seems to be that growth means more of everything — more money, more material goods, more people even where the existing population cannot be adequately provided for. Policies are needed which encourage people to live in locations containing the water and resources to support them, but in many locations around the world the opposite trend has prevailed for decades. Despite an obvious lack of water and the vast expense and problems resulting from large-scale water transfers, virtually no nation or sizable region has taken adequate steps to address the situation. To do so may require difficult and unpopular steps including stabilizing or reducing population, decreasing water use, improving water efficiency and infrastructure, and inducing people to relocate. But not doing so could prove the undoing of entire nations. Regions cannot prosper and survive if vital natural support systems, especially water supplies, are not available and sustainable [56].

12.6 Climate Change

We are losing control of our ability to get a handle on the global warming problem.

— Andrew Weaver

12.6.1 Introduction

The consequences of climate change are stressors that can ignite a volatile mix of underlying causes that erupt into revolution.

— Anne-Marie Slaughter

It has long been known that certain gases in Earth's atmosphere, such as carbon dioxide, methane, and water vapor, absorb outgoing heat radiation (infrared radiation), thus keeping the lower atmosphere, the troposphere, much warmer than it would otherwise be. These heat-intercepting atmospheric chemicals are called greenhouse gasses. Carbon dioxide is the most influential greenhouse gas. It normally constitutes only about 0.03%, or 300 ppm, of our atmosphere by volume, but that tiny amount results in average near-ground air temperatures some 36°C (65°F) warmer than they would be without the CO_2. At current atmospheric concentrations, a one ppm CO_2 increase appears to produce a temperature increase of about 0.12°C.

For the last 2.5 million years of Earth's history, the climate has undergone repeated swings from cold "glacials" to warm "interglacials" (Section 2.3). The cold glacial episodes were only some 5°C (9°F) colder than the warm interglacials, yet that small temperature change coincided with enormous changes in the surficial environment — for example, glaciers covered 200% more land area and sea level was over 100 meters (330 feet) lower than during interglacials. Thus it would appear that even relatively small changes in greenhouse gasses and global temperatures will produce very large, and relatively rapid, impacts on our living environment [53]. We should bear in mind that long-term climatic fluctuations are influenced by additional factors, such as Earth's distance from the sun, solar energy output, and episodes of intense volcanism on Earth.

The Industrial Revolution was brought about primarily through the widespread use of cheap energy provided by the carbon-based fossil fuels coal and petroleum, and most of today's energy is still derived from fossil fuel combustion. When the fuel is burned, oxygen chemically combines with carbon to release carbon dioxide gas to the atmosphere. In 2011, the world pumped some 38 billion tons of CO_2 into the air, an increase of about a billion tons over 2010. Estimates of the pre-industrial level of atmospheric CO_2 range from 270 to 290 ppm. By 2012, atmospheric CO_2 had risen to approximately 395 ppm and the rate of increase was accelerating — from an average increase of 1.5 ppm during the 1990s to a 2.3 ppm increase from 2009 to 2010 [537]. Studies of Earth's past indicate that these increases in CO_2 release are unprecedented. If this accelerating trend continues, the CO_2 content of the atmosphere would be around 1,000 ppm by volume by the year 2100 [217]. Geological data indicate that the last time atmospheric CO_2 was at that level (over 30 million years ago), it required tens of millions of years to decrease CO_2 to the normal levels of the recent past (around 300 ppm). Even if all excess greenhouse gas emissions could be stopped immediately, the existing increases will likely have serious impacts for centuries to come.

Unfortunately, and in spite of international efforts to address the issue, the rise in atmospheric CO_2 concentration is unlikely to cease, much less be reduced, for at least a few decades. Worldwide, energy use is projected to increase at about 1.6% per year until 2030 [484], and it appears that much of that increase will be from fossil fuels. Developed nations such as the US continue to emphasize economic growth and consumerism which rely heavily on fossil fuels and developing nations, especially China and India, are voraciously consuming coal and other fossil fuels at increasing rates to feed their rapidly growing economies [204]. Plans are afoot to increase coal exports from the US to China and India while Canada, the US, China, and others look to even dirtier fossil fuels such as those extracted from the Athabasca tar sands of Canada. If governments continue to subsidize fossil fuels and fail to mount a massive effort to develop more benign energy and economic engines, ever more alarming consequences can be expected.

In the intertwined ecosystems of Earth's biosphere, changes trigger changes which trigger still more changes in ever-expanding progressions. When changing conditions attain a critical point at which a normal equilibrium state is disrupted, we say a threshold or "tipping point" has been reached. For a structure such as a bridge or a chair, if the threshold beyond which it can no longer support weight is exceeded, the structure will rapidly deteriorate or collapse. Similar changes occur in the far more complex arenas of ecosystems and climate. Thresholds can be crossed without our knowledge, leading to imbalances which could drastically alter environmental conditions for untold thousands of years. Long-term, systemic changes in natural cycles and processes with profound worldwide impacts already appear to be underway in ice sheets, tropical rainforests, regional weather patterns, and the oceans. Significant, often dramatic, increases in average near-surface temperatures of the atmosphere, soils, and water bodies, are well documented. Global warming is causing changes affecting all surface processes and all areas of Earth. Natural processes from rainfall patterns to animal migrations are being altered in ways which are poorly understood. Abrupt and possibly catastrophic changes in the way natural systems operate pose unprecedented threats to humanity [110].

12.6.2 Impacts of Global Warming on Water Resources

If the system tips over, that would have catastrophic effects on human activities and populations over wide areas.

— Edward Cook

The cost of acting goes far higher the longer we wait — we can't wait any longer to avoid the worst and be judged immoral by coming generations.

— James Hansen

A. Overview

Overwhelming evidence indicates that Earth's climates are changing but, as with all that is yet to be, the impacts on water supply cannot be "predocumented." Climate change doesn't alter the amount of water on Earth. Due to growing human water demand, water shortages would exist with or without global warming. But changing climates will certainly cause some major disruptions of the water cycle with resulting redistribution of water, especially of vital freshwater supplies. Precipitation patterns will be altered, evaporation rates will increase in most areas, surface waters will be reapportioned, sea level will rise, and groundwater budgets and flow patterns will change. In general, it appears that an intensification of the water cycle is underway due to the warming climate. The rate of global water cycling has generally increased about twice as fast as most models have predicted [242]. Specifically, an increase in greenhouse gases is producing more precipitation where it is already wet and less precipitation where it is dry [109]. Global trends also reveal increases in precipitation intensity with increasing temperature [417].

Changes in climate will have serious repercussions upon nearly everything from ecosystems to manufacturing facilities. The primary driver of the current warming trend is excess carbon dioxide emitted to the atmosphere by fossil fuel combustion. Paleoclimatic evidence clearly shows that increases in atmospheric CO_2 leads to global warming [91, 357, 437]. Human-generated CO_2 will likely continue to impact Earth's environment for at least the next few centuries, and possibly for millions of years, even if all human-induced greenhouse gas emissions could be halted immediately. However, details as to just how climate change will influence a given area remain unclear. Dozens of models exist but the complexity of weather patterns is such that determining the specific impacts on a localized region is generally not possible. Incorporating the almost infinite number of fluctuating, interacting small-scale, medium-scale, and large-scale influences into any model is extraordinarily difficult, although the projections continue to improve. Predicting precipitation change is especially difficult [213].

While climate change still involves many uncertainties, the overwhelming judgment of scientific communities around the world is that the impacts will be largely negative. Thus far, most models have underestimated those impacts. Feedback mechanisms in particular can have reinforcing or perpetuating effects which are difficult to predict (Section 12.6.2B).

In general, we anticipate an ongoing increase in average temperatures in most near-surface systems, both on land and water, along with the advance of warmer temperature zones to higher latitudes and higher elevations, with accompanying disruptions in the hydrologic cycle and regional ecosystems. By 2006, many scientists and governments agreed that the average global temperature increase should not exceed 2°C if severe impacts were to be avoided. Unfortunately, known fossil fuel reserves far exceed the amount capable of yielding sufficient CO_2 to exceed the 2°C threshold, should they be burned [263]. And we are burning them. Temperatures have been increasing more rapidly than anticipated and an increase in the global mean temperature of 3°C by 2050 is not unrealistic.

Although no one event can be attributed to warming, an overall increase in severe storms, droughts, and floods is anticipated, and apparently is underway. Substantial increases in major weather-related disasters are well documented and there appears to be little doubt that global warming is increasing the probability of such events. Statistical analyses suggest that high-temperature events such as the 2003 European and 2010 Russia/Mid-East heat waves which cost many thousands of lives, are strongly linked to global warming, as were the ongoing (2012-2013) droughts, which at times affected over 60% of the US. The probability of very hot summers occurring is some ten times greater than it was a few decades ago [169]. To a large extent the global increase in severe weather activity occurs because higher temperatures increase evaporation which puts more energy, as heat of vaporization (Section 1.4.3), into the atmosphere. Thus far, the changes induced by increases in the mean global temperature have been occurring much more rapidly than anticipated and the impacts on surface waters and human water supply needs are already profound. Yet these disturbing effects represent only the beginning, and far more serious disruptions are very likely in the near future [168, 169].

Existing and anticipated future decreases in available surface water are encouraging increased exploitation of groundwater [394]. The impacts of climate change upon groundwater resources will take longer to be manifest due to slow response times. Any decrease in groundwater recharge could have serious repercussions in vulnerable areas such as North Africa, southwestern Africa, and northeastern Brazil [99]. Much food production depends heavily on groundwater and the total water available for crops will likely be reduced by global warming. Increasing temperatures in many of the most populated areas of the world, including tropical, temperate, and semiarid regions will tend to depress crop production even as additional stresses such as the growth of population and inefficient consumption of livestock continue [27].

What can be done to solve or at least alleviate the impacts of global warming? Literally thousands of articles, reports, and books have been written about the impacts, documented and anticipated, of climate change. Many publications and organizations focus strongly on how to reduce or limit the release of greenhouse gases; others emphasize the need to recognize that climate change will likely continue and we must plan how we will accommodate, or adapt to, the conditions which will result. Those conditions may well include severe health and ecological impacts, massive food and water shortages, and the direct threat of rising seas to coastal areas and the resulting displacement of millions of people [56, 169, 566].

As for solutions or mitigation, most would agree that vastly increasing conservation and efficiency in all enterprises which utilize energy and water, planting trees while reducing deforestation and desertification, and developing alternate energy sources while reducing fossil fuel use are among the most imperative adaptations which humanity must undertake posthaste. Numerous plans for achieving this have been proposed. A widely quoted paper by Pacala and Socolow [298] proposed seven massive campaigns, called stabilization "wedges," which they thought might stabilize rising carbon emissions at 2004 levels by 2054. Eight years later, annual global emissions had increased from seven to ten billion tons. A recent reevaluation of the idea posits that we now need to employ nine basic wedges with an additional 12 wedges, each representing massive efforts, just to keep from continuing to increase emissions plus another ten wedges if we hope to reduce and eliminate carbon emissions in 50 years [219]. If meaningful progress is to occur, it will require some mega-scale alterations in economies, consumption, taxation, spending priorities, and planning [221]. One approach, recommended by climate expert James Hansen, involves a gradually increasing fee on carbon emissions to be collected from fossil fuel companies [169]. He suggests redistributing the fees to individual citizens, except for the excessive energy users, to compensate for increased energy costs.

Thus far the political will to act forcefully enough to have significant impact has been lacking. For example, during the 2012 US presidential campaign, for the first time since the 1980s, climate change and environmental concerns in general were essentially ignored completely. Numerous citizen organizations have been pressing for more "official" action for decades. In 2011, the World Resources Institute, UN Development Program, UN Environmental Program, and World Bank released a special report to guide governments in addressing the issue of climate change [9]. On the other hand, special interests whose profits could be threatened by reduced fossil fuel consumption and mitigation efforts continue — especially in the US — a massive, well-funded effort to spread confusion and untruths about the whole issue of global warming [221].

Anticipated impacts of global warming on specific climatic and topographic regions are briefly reviewed below.

B. Polar Regions

The high northern latitudes are proving to be more sensitive to global warming than any other large region. Some parts of Alaska have experienced average temperature increases as high as 5°C (9°F) and the growing season has lengthened by as much as 50% over the last 6 decades. Among the less desirable results of this temperature increase are the loss of an estimated 15% of Arctic permafrost, an area three times that of California, since the 1970s and a decrease in Arctic sea ice cover of roughly 8% per decade. Some 24% of the terrain in the northern hemisphere contains permafrost [399]. Permafrost provides the foundation for buildings and other structures. Melting of permafrost produces damage to man-made structures from unstable ground, losses of traditional hunting and fishing grounds of indigenous peoples, and loss of key feeding and breeding grounds for polar bears, walruses, seabirds, and other wildlife.

Numerous positive feedback mechanisms tend to reinforce the warming. Positive feedback amplifies a process; negative feedback reverses or slows down a process. Positive feedback appears to dominate the global warming scenario. For example, more atmospheric carbon dioxide appears to favor soil microorganisms which release additional methane and nitrous oxide, both powerful greenhouse gases. In cold polar areas, warmer temperatures reduce ice and snow cover leaving more open water and ground which in turn increase absorption of the sun's heat during summer. Reduced snow and ice cover anywhere means a decrease in the albedo (reflectivity) of the surface, resulting in more solar heating. Ice and snow reflect some 80% of incoming sunlight, but water and land generally absorb 80% of that energy, turning it into heat. Increased air temperatures are often accompanied by increased precipitation due to more evaporation over open water and rising air currents. Rain attacks permafrost directly in contrast to snow which insulates the ground from the frigid winter air. Rain, along with higher air and surface water temperatures, reduce permafrost from above while groundwater eats at it from below. Positive feedbacks are stronger in the Arctic and help explain why the Arctic has warmed more rapidly than other Earth regions, a process called "Arctic amplification." Arctic warming in turn influences weather patterns in temperate regions hundreds of miles to the south, causing weather systems to move more slowly, which can mean longer droughts, heat waves, or storm events [131].

Permafrost contains vast quantities of partially decayed organic matter and accompanying gases, isolating them from the atmosphere. The decay of organic matter in soils releases both CO_2 and methane, another greenhouse gas whose impact on warming is about 21 times greater than CO_2. The thawing of permafrost releases large quantities of these gasses, further exacerbating the warming trend. Release of huge stores of methane that have long been trapped in the permafrost, below frozen lakes, and in sea sediments is a growing concern. The Russian Academy of Science reports finding hundreds of methane gas plumes, some 1,000 meters in diameter, bubbling up out of parts of the Arctic Ocean formerly covered by ice.

Groundwater in permafrost areas (Section 8.12) is highly sensitive to disruption. This can lead to important changes in groundwater volume, temperature, and flow rates. It is expected that soil moisture will continue to decrease while temperatures, precipitation, runoff, and evapotranspiration increase. The ecological impacts of warming in cold regions are likely to be severe and are only beginning to be documented [130]. Measurements indicate that flows into the Arctic Ocean have increased by about 10% and the melting of all forms of ice in the north

Polar region continues to accelerate [12, 139]. Recent losses of Arctic sea ice suggest that an ice-free Arctic Sea could occur within 10 years [214].

An ice sheet, or continental glacier, is a land-based glacier greater than 50,000 km^2 in area. Today, only two locations, Antarctica and Greenland, support ice sheets. The ice flows outward in all directions from the areas of greatest thickness. Maximum thickness is approximately 4,500 meters in Antarctica and 3,300 meters in Greenland. A comprehensive study of numerous observations from 2005 to 2012 indicated that these ice sheets were losing ice at a rate some 344 billion tons per year, more than three times the estimated losses in the 1990s [359].

The Greenland Ice Sheet is undergoing the most rapid losses, increasing from an average of some 50 billion tons per year in 1995-2000 to some 263 billion tons in 2005-2010 [12]. The ongoing acceleration of melting is the greatest concern [209]. If greenhouse gas emissions are not rapidly reduced, many experts fear that extensive deterioration of the ice sheets, accompanied by changes in oceanic circulation patterns and threats to ecosystems and human lives around the world, are likely to result. In July 2012, surface melting was occurring over more than 98% of the Greenland Ice Sheet [287]. A regional temperature rise of only 3°C could result in the melting of the entire ice sheet, which would increase global sea levels by 7.2 meters (24 feet).

Antarctica has seen the least temperature increase of any continent and the massive East Antarctic Ice Sheet remains quite stable, even gaining some ice. However, in West Antarctica, especially the Antarctic Peninsula, rising air and seawater temperatures have caused the ice shelves to lose thousands of square kilometers of ice. These impacts appear to be closely related to an intensification and southerly (poleward) migration of the belt of westerly winds which encircle Antarctica. The strength of these winds stirs up the ocean waters leading to more melting of ice shelves and a probable reduction in the water's ability to store greenhouse gases. The tightening belt of wind also helps bottle up cold air over the central part of Antarctica.

Why this is occurring appears to be related to global warming at lower latitudes and especially to the presence of the Antarctic ozone hole [215, 237 ,424]. A zone of ozone in the upper atmosphere absorbs ultraviolet radiation from the Sun, protecting Earth's surface from this hazardous radiation. Chlorofluorocarbons (CFCs) are stable, nontoxic chemicals that were widely used in refrigeration units and aerosols. In the 1970s, it was found that CFCs were destroying the protective ozone and their use was phased out. However CFCs still linger in the atmosphere and continue to deplete ozone, especially over cold areas where the breakdown of ozone is greatly accelerated by atmospheric ice particles. Hence the ozone hole over Antarctica. When ozone over the Antarctic is at its lowest during the austral spring, little ultraviolet radiation can be absorbed and released to the atmosphere as heat. As a result, the atmosphere over the continent is colder, which appears to keep the East Antarctic Ice Sheet cold and increases the temperature contrast between the continent and the warm encircling westerly winds. This in turn intensifies the velocity of the westerly winds with wide-ranging impacts which are still far from being fully understood. The winds are now pushing warmer water towards the Antarctic, melting the vast ice shelves from below [180, 322]. This in turn has led to major increases in the thickness and rate of flow of outlet glaciers. West Antarctic glaciers are discharging some 60% more water than is accumulating in their catchment areas.

C. Alpine Regions

Most mountain ranges of sufficient height and latitude to extend into the alpine and tundra climatic zones are experiencing double the average rate of global temperature increase. Alpine glaciers and snowfields are disappearing at unprecedented rates around the world. Although many mountain glaciers have been slowly retreating since the eighteenth century, the rate of melting has accelerated greatly in recent decades.

Data from mountain terrain around the world reveal similar trends. Studies at the National Snow and Ice Data Center in Colorado indicate that, by the mid-2000s, the duration of snow cover in the Rockies had already been reduced by some 20 to 35 days a year. Montana's Glacier National Park may lose all its glaciers by 2030 and the famous snow cap of Africa's Mount Kilimanjaro may be gone within ten years. Glaciers in Italy's Alps could be gone within 30 years.

Large parts of the world rely on mountain precipitation and melting snow and ice to keep rivers flowing, recharge groundwater, and provide water for agriculture, cities, hydroelectric power, navigation, and other vital needs (Figure 8.31) [63]. Many of Earth's major rivers and substantial amounts of groundwater originate in alpine areas. Glaciers and ice fields are especially important in maintaining water supply during the warm, dry months. Dry season flow is vital to crop production, and often for hydroelectric power. Alpine glaciers have been called the "water towers of the world" and "reservoirs in the sky." Glacial meltwater supports some 40% of the world's irrigation. In most of the western US, mountain snowpack is estimated to provide about 90% of the spring, summer, and fall water. Anticipated warming of 2 to 3°C by 2050 in the Sierra Nevada and Cascade Mountains may produce a 50 to 70% decrease in snowpack and cause maximum stream discharge to peak a month earlier. In Lima, Peru, where six million people depend upon the snow-fed Rimac River for drinking water, snowpack loses could cause the Rimac to run dry half the year within two decades. The world's largest ice mass in the tropics, the Quelccaya Ice Cap of Peru, is rapidly disappearing and may be gone by the time you read this [82]. Similar changes are likely in the Hindu Kush and Himalayan-Tibet region of Asia where the glaciers and snowpack provide summer water for half the world's population. Like many cold regions, recent temperature increases in the Himalayas, about 2°C in two decades, have been about double the world average [280]. Even a small 1°C increase in temperature can result in much more rain than snow, causing increased flooding during the wet season and reduced flow during the dry season when agricultural demands are highest. Global warming could spell the end of that once-dependable supply.

Particulate air pollutants are a special concern, especially in alpine environments. For example, some estimate that black carbon particles, or soot, contribute significantly to global warming by absorbing sunlight and the energy reflected by clouds. These particles average only around 100 nanometers in diameter but they play a significant role in warming the climate by absorbing sunlight, brightening clouds, and darkening highly reflective surfaces such as ice and snow [39]. Human activities are continuing to increase the concentrations of these materials in the atmosphere. Black carbon is generated whenever fossil fuels and other organic matter is burned without effective emission controls. Asia's "great brown cloud," produced in large part by the burning of wood, cow dung, and diesel fuel, threatens the health of millions of people. Black carbon particulates are carried high into the mountains and appear to be accelerating the melting rates of Himalayan glaciers [562]. Particulate impacts on glaciers are cumulative. During the melting season, meltwater runs off, leaving the soot and other particulates behind. Hence glacier melting rates tend to increase as the years pass.

In the western US, studies indicate that "dust fall" over the past 100 years was five to seven times heavier than at any other time in the last 5,000 years. Much of this atmospheric dust resulted from desertification caused by widespread overgrazing (devegetation) of the land by livestock. Dust from croplands and worsening drought conditions related to global warming are exacerbating the dust problem. Like soot, dark dust particles deposited on mountain snowpack absorb sunlight, increasing the melting rate and shortening the duration of snow cover. Particulates, which can be transported thousands of miles, contribute significantly to increased springtime flooding, reduced streamflow in summer and fall, and reduced groundwater recharge.

D. Dry Regions

Arid and semiarid regions, already experiencing considerable water stress, are expected to become drier and hotter. Droughts, such as those recently plaguing southern Australia, Africa, and the southwestern US, could represent the onset of a profound change to a much more arid climate for those areas. In other arid regions, such as those closer to the tropics, an increase in rainfall is possible which could lead to more infiltration and increased groundwater recharge. Increased runoff with flooding and erosion is another possible consequence, especially if wise land use is not practiced.

Wide-spread desertification, in which productive land is degraded to an unproductive desert-like state, began in the mid-nineteenth century and has continued to the present, especially in semiarid regions. Increases in human population and the associated overgrazing, poor farming methods, deforestation, and mining are among the major causes. Most climate models indicate that large areas, including the southwestern US, will likely experience drier and warmer conditions due to the migration of arid climate zones to higher latitudes. This means less soil moisture, lower groundwater recharge rates, less surface water, and more airborne particulates. Impacts such as groundwater depletion, reductions in total runoff and base flow to streams, increased evaporation, and related climatic factors could conceivably dry up major reservoirs, destroy most agriculture, and make many semiarid regions virtually uninhabitable.

E. Coastal Areas

Melting ice and thermal expansion of ocean waters are causing a rise in sea level. In addition, the extraction of groundwater may be contributing as much as 25% of the total sea-level rise, considering that the extracted water will soon find its way to the ocean [421]. Since 1880, the overall rise has been approximately 20 centimeters (8 inches). Recent studies estimate that sea level will rise an additional 0.3 meters (12 inches) by 2050, and up to 2.1 meters (7 feet) or more by 2100 [12, 77].

If recent trends continue, even these estimates are likely to be found to be too conservative. In either case, coastal lowlands which are now home to millions of people, including entire cities, will be submerged and nearly all coastal wetlands could perish by the end of the century. Storm surges will be greatly amplified, doubling and tripling the frequency of major coastal flooding events [77] such as that seen during Hurricane Sandy in the New York City and New Jersey areas in 2012 [60]. Continued melting of Greenland ice, ocean currents, and shoreline configurations cause sea level rise to be greater in many mid-latitude areas including the east coast of North America.

Even a moderate rise in sea level or intensity of storm surges could drastically alter the delicate balance between fresh and salt water in rivers, wetlands, estuaries, bays, and lagoons, threatening their valuable ecosystems. When storm surges cause extensive flooding of low-lying coastal areas, the seawater increases the salinity of both groundwater and soil, posing a serious threat to agriculture and human health [220]. Heavily populated deltas such as those of the Ganges-Brahmaputra and Nile rivers will be especially vulnerable. Already, it is feared that rising salinity in drinking water threatens the health of many living in rural coastal regions such as Bangladesh [418].

F. Tropics

Atmospheric warming appears to increase weather extremes in tropical areas such that rainfall increases significantly during warm phases and decreases during cooler phases. Overall, river discharges and other freshwater resources are decreasing in many mid-to-low latitude areas, where most of the world's population lives. From 1948 to 2004, freshwater discharge to the Pacific and Indian oceans decreased by 6 and 3% respectively.

Another concern is the possibility of permanent dieback of tropical forests. Warming dries forests and may cause more El Niños, warming phases in the Pacific Ocean, which tend to reduce rains in the Amazon, the world's largest tropical forest and an area often called "Earth's lung" for the large role it plays in regulating atmospheric CO_2 and climate. In addition, direct human impacts are increasing in tropical forests. Forest destruction in the Amazon doubled from 1994 to 2004, up to some 9,000 mi^2/yr, a result of increases in cattle ranching, agribusiness plantations (especially soy fields), slash and burn agriculture, timbering, road building, and settlements. Satellite observations indicated an average of some 600 fires were started each day in the Amazon in 2004.

498

Deforested terrain means less evapotranspiration resulting in reduced moisture in the air and less rainfall. This may produce a permanent reduction of forest vegetation and its uptake of CO_2 even as the burning and decaying vegetation releases excess CO_2 to the atmosphere. Drought conditions appear to be increasing in the Amazon where two 100-year droughts have been recorded in the last five years.

G. Temperate Regions

One of the few anticipated benefits of the warming trend may be a longer growing season for the northern temperate regions. Snow cover during May and June in North America and Eurasia has been decreasing at an accelerating rate [93]. Less fortunate impacts, which many believe are already occurring, include an increase inthe frequency and magnitude of droughts, heat waves, violent storms, and rain events. This could be quite pronounced in northern temperate regions, where cold air masses from the north clash with warm, humid air masses from the south. For much of Europe and the US, this will likely yield earlier and heavier winter runoff with increased flooding, decreased runoff during summer when demand is high, reduced groundwater recharge, and disruptions in such areas as biodiversity, navigation, hydropower generation, and tourism [346].

In more southerly parts of temperate zones, including the southeastern US, protracted megadroughts are a real possibility. The northward migration of numerous plants and animals, including disease-carrying organisms, raises major concerns for both human and ecological health.

H. Oceans

The impacts of rising sea levels on coastal regions were noted above. Groundwater withdrawal is one of several factors contributing to the rise [336, 421]. The oceans themselves are also responding in other ways to the warming trend. Ocean waters are absorbing both heat and CO_2 from the atmosphere, becoming warmer and more acidic. Even small changes in temperature and acidity can threaten entire oceanic ecosystems, especially coral reefs. The oceans are a major CO_2 sink but warmer water generally decreases the amount of CO_2 the water can absorb, another positive feedback. Climate change also alters ocean circulation and temperature patterns, such as the El Niño and La Niña phenomena in the central Pacific and the Atlantic Meridional Overturning Circulation, all of which have profound impacts upon weather conditions around much of the world.

Facing the Challenge

All the flowers of all the tomorrows are in the seeds of today.

— Chinese proverb

13.1 Addressing the Problems

There are encouraging signs that sustainable groundwater management will eventually materialize out of sheer necessity.

— T. N. Narasimhan

Many problems associated with human overuse and misuse of water have been noted. We now review actions and approaches for correcting, mitigating, or adapting to those problems. Unfortunately, water squandered by pollution, waste, and misuse cannot be easily replaced. The water cycle will often require decades or even thousands of years to replenish a lost water resource, and some losses may be permanent. Magic bullets do not exist. All earthly resources are limited in some ways. When human populations and their demands on resources were less, it was easy to ignore those limits. We no longer have that luxury. We will either learn to recognize and respect limitations and do what is necessary to live within those limits or we, and our descendants, will soon pay a fearsome price for our unsustainable exploitation and abuse of the basic natural resources necessary to the survival of life on this tiny planet. Indeed, hundreds of millions of Earth's less fortunate citizens are already paying that price.

Faced with huge and growing human populations, water demands that increase two to three times faster than population, falling water tables, disappearing rivers, degraded farmland, pollution, changing climates, governmental inertia, and the like, the situation may seem hopeless. But the finest human achievements have often arisen in the face of monumental threats. And remember, water is a renewable and reusable resource, and the waste of water is still rampant. As with so many of our twenty-first century problems, water crises can be resolved, if enough people will rise to the challenge. This must entail increasing water productivity through conservation and more efficient use. This in turn will require substantial improvements in knowledge, planning, and cooperation. Better hydrogeological data and modeling are also needed.

To properly address groundwater problems, a maintainable, resilient, whole-systems response that fairly balances the many needs is required. Responsible solutions are possible, but toes will be stepped on and practitioners will have to grapple with powerful special interests. More often than not, implementing remedies to water problems will involve altering long-standing policies and behaviors. From Arizona to India, hydrogeologists have identified looming water supply problems and suggested appropriate changes during the last 60 or more years. Yet in most cases, little or nothing has been done to meet the challenge.

Most resource crises are ultimately a consequence of mismanagement, greed, and ignorance. Solutions will require addressing these and other social issues in addition to the hard science. Sufficient water still exists to meet human needs, but we must learn to use that water wisely and efficiently, and policies must embody oft-neglected qualities such as adaptability, sustainability, and resilience. Hence many of the corrective actions noted below are basically conservation or efficiency measures. Much overlap exists among the actions noted below. In most situations, a combination of several approaches will be required to attain a successful and sustainable water supply.

13.2 Conservation

The challenge, therefore, is to overcome the need for competition and to find ways to harmonize the water requirements with those of the natural environment.

— Gabriel Eckstein

It is now quite clear that conservation of freshwater supplies is no longer an option, but a necessity. In efforts to address the water crisis, conservation should always come first. Conservation means maximizing the use of any resource over the long term. Conservation approaches are virtually unlimited and extend from the small choices and actions of each individual to worldwide cooperative efforts. We know vast amounts of groundwater still remain, but it is often not where the greatest needs are, and the pumping and long-distance transport of such water are often rendered unwise due to high costs, environmental impacts, and widespread opposition. The answers to many water crises are to do a much better job of preserving, conserving, and managing the water we have where we have it.

Conservation of any resource has often been denigrated by some as unrealistic, anti-growth, the province of daydreamers and hippies . . . . Behind much of this bias often lurks a simple truth. Over the short term, both money and power can be more readily attained by maximizing the exploitation and sale of water, oil, metals, timber, and other resources than by conserving them. The underlying market-oriented principle of many businesses, to maximize short-term gains, often by over-exploiting valuable resources, is inherently at odds with the conservation ethic. The anti-conservation forces are wealthy and politically powerful, often having become that way through the wasteful exploitation of the very resources that are now becoming scarce. Exacerbating the situation are a plethora of firmly entrenched subsidies, legal squabbles, and obsolete, self-serving attitudes which encourage and help maintain many wasteful practices. And politicians find that promising new water supplies is easier to sell to a gullible public than encouraging conservation.

The ensuing list of selected water-conserving techniques is by no means complete. The categories will often overlap. For example, pricing water so as to encourage conservation applies equally to agricultural, industrial, or domestic use and could be listed as both a management and a conservation tool. Deciding upon what conservation approach to use can be a challenge. Stream water diverted in one location to recharge groundwater may mean less water or poorer quality water for people downstream. All possibilities should be carefully considered before embarking on a project. Effective water conservation requires intelligent management at all levels and the legal authority and commitment to enforce decisions.

13.2.1 Pollution Control

Preventing pollution of groundwater (Chapter 10) is an essential first step in conserving this resource. Once polluted, it can require centuries to restore the water quality (Section 11.3.8). Hence prevention must be a priority.

Controlling air pollution will also have great benefits for water. Many air pollutants will end up in water. Reducing all greenhouse gasses and many particulates will slow the climatic changes which threaten groundwater in coastal regions and in many other locations around the world.

13.2.2 Improved Water Efficiency

Many vital food-producing areas are depleting aquifers and surface waters at an alarming rate. All available water needs to be used in the most efficient manner possible. This entails many of the methods given in the following sections, including the use of more water efficient irrigation techniques, improved crop selections, gathering rainwater, recycling water, and recharging aquifers with any available excess water. For example, studies have found that the most water-hungry state, California, in the most water-consuming nation, the US, could cut water use significantly — up to 50% — and still meet its water needs and even save money in the process [142]. These studies consider readily available water conservation methods. Upfront costs are often needed but the payback time is typically only one to four years. Outdoor water demand in the thirsty western US could be reduced by as much as 75% — up to 88% if rainwater harvesting is included [240].

13.2.3 Agricultural Improvements

Water and food are inseparable. Globally, agriculture withdraws some 70% of the available water and accounts for 80 to 90% of the total water consumption [293]. Much agricultural water is used very inefficiently, and government subsidies frequently encourage inefficient practices in spite of overwhelming evidence of waste. Once a practice, however ill-advised and destructive, becomes institutionalized and has powerful vested interests wishing to continue it, it is an exceptionally difficult and lengthy task to change it. But change it we must. Many of the world's major food-growing regions are dependent upon groundwater. Most of that groundwater use is unsustainable. Soon, water tables decline and ever-deeper wells are needed. The results often include the drying up of millions of shallow wells, most belonging to small farmers; the loss of surface water resources such as springs, wetlands, rivers, lakes; large increases in the energy costs of obtaining groundwater from depths which may exceed a kilometer (3,280 feet); and declining water quality. The escalating environmental and economic costs of developing additional water supplies are severe and contribute further to a troubling food/water future.

The consumption of water to produce food will have to be cut by half or more if anticipated future human needs are to be met. This need is being approached in several ways. Currently, 1 tonne (1 m³) of irrigation water is needed to produce approximately 1 kg of grain. This can be greatly improved by methods ranging from market incentives to adoption of efficient irrigation technologies. Competing needs, declining reserves, and increasing costs of water are already forcing more efficient agricultural water use in many areas. Some specific approaches are briefly described below.

A. Ecologically Sound Agriculture

Vast areas of land in all parts of the world have deteriorated due to unsustainable agricultural practices. Is it wise to raise water-hungry crops in deserts? Perhaps we should adapt our agriculture to the climate instead. Arid and semiarid areas, usually grasslands, have been especially victimized by widespread agricultural abuses resulting in devegetation, soil erosion, accelerated runoff and diminished groundwater recharge, flooding, desertification, and related problems. In some areas, the natural resilience of the ecosystem and its accompanying hydrologic cycle, have been so weakened that restoration to a productive regime may be impossible. However, ecologically sound management strategies can restore many deteriorated lands to both a healthy environment and economic viability. In other cases, agriculture can be relocated to areas more amenable to the crop, be it livestock or grain. In the early 2000s, alfalfa, a low-value crop contributing less than 1% to the state economy, was consuming about 25% of California's irrigation water. This makes little ecological or economic sense. Many management techniques are available, but must be suitably adapted to local conditions. Examples include organic farming, no-till farming, limited and well-planned livestock grazing, preservation of open space, restoration of riparian and wetland tracts, planting of multiple crops and avoidance of monoculture, and use of perennial crops whenever possible rather than annual crops [157, 158, 490].

B. Water-Efficient Crops

The urgent need to produce more crops from dry lands was emphasized in the April 2000 Millennium Address of the UN Secretary-General. Water-poor areas such as northern China and Egypt are phasing out rice in favor of less water needy plants [55]. Much research focuses on the very complex matter of finding, breeding, or engineering crop species which require less water or mature more rapidly.

For example, plants with longer coleoptiles (seed sprouts) can be sown deeper where moisture is better **retained** [547]. Some rice can be grown with only about a quarter of the water currently used (500 L/kg vs. 2000 L/kg) [488].

C. Salt-Tolerant Crops

Salinization of soils is a major ongoing problem which has resulted in the loss of tens of millions of acres of once-productive land (Section 8.11). The volume of brackish water present under or on Earth's land areas is roughly equal to the volume of fresh water, and 97% of all water is saline seawater. Brackish groundwater has salt concentrations of 1 to 50% that of seawater. Saline waters can be desalinized, of course, but this is usually too costly and energy-intensive to provide the large quantities of water needed to produce crops. If we can learn to make better use of these vast stores of salty water to produce food and other useful crops, it would be a great advance. Roughly 1% of land plant species can be grown in brackish water or salinized soils [331]. A number of these plants have potential crop value. Other plants are known that can actually take up excess salt. By combining our use of such plant species, or genetically engineering new species which exhibit such abilities, it may be possible to greatly expand crop production on salinized land or even improve salt-degraded lands. This is a complex yet promising field for additional research.

D. Irrigation Improvements

Because irrigation consumes most of the water used by humans, improvements in the efficiency of irrigation are essential. Traditional **flood irrigation** consists of transporting water from a source such as a river, lake, or well to the fields through a series of canals and ditches. At the fields, water may be periodically spread uniformly across the fields (flood method) or carried to the crops in small trenches (furrow method). **Sprinkler irrigation** applies water over the top of crops using a system of pipes, sprinkler nozzles, pumps, and associated hardware (Figure 8.33). Sprinkler systems may be portable, rotate about a fixed pivot, or be completely immobile. The term **microirrigation** refers to the use of drip irrigation and micro-sprinklers. Of the 61.9 million acres irrigated in the US in 2000, 29.4 million was flood irrigation, 28.3 million was sprinkler irrigation, and about 4.2 million was microirrigation.

Leaks in delivery systems and evaporation lead to large water losses, up to 75% or more, in surface water irrigation. Such factors as humidity, temperature, soil type, and terrain also affect efficiency. Efficient surface irrigation systems, as practiced in Israel, Japan, and Taiwan, for example, may utilize as much as 60% of the water, but this method of irrigation requires careful management.

Irrigation improvements include the following:

1. **Low-pressure sprinkler systems.** Traditional sprinklers produced a fine mist of water under high pressure which greatly increases evaporation loses. The best low-pressure nozzles reportedly can cut water use by 50 to 80%.

2. **Drip irrigation.** Drip irrigation is the most efficient method, generally reducing water use by 50% or more over flood or furrow methods, and often raising crop yields as well. In this method, surface or subsurface pipes carry water directly to the roots of plants. On the negative side, this type of drip irrigation costs at least 30% more than standard methods, often consumes more energy, and requires clean water to avoid clogging. It is also more labor-intensive, but this can be an advantage, since underemployment is a problem in many rural areas around the world. Much simpler drip irrigation methods are appropriate for small farms and may pay for themselves in a year or less. These systems typically employ slightly elevated water containers with flexible plastic tubing to carry water to the plants by gravity flow. These easy-to-use, movable units can greatly increase water and crop productivity. As of 2000, only Cyprus, Israel, and Jordan made extensive use of drip irrigation; the method was used on only about 4% of US cropland and on less than 1% of the cropland in India and China.

3. **Schedule irrigation more effectively.** Water use can be adjusted based upon planting schedules, crop variety, weather conditions, and when in the growth cycle water is required.

E. Miscellaneous Adaptations

Traditional societies have developed many clever techniques for adapting to local environments. In the rush to mechanized farming, many of these methods have been neglected. Methods of adaptation include ingenious devices designed to collect water from fog by condensation on water-attracting membranes, combining crops with tree plantings, hillside terraces, making use of resilient crop species more compatible with local conditions, and a variety of simple but surprisingly effective storage and rainwater harvesting techniques (Section 13.2.6B).

13.2.4 Land Conservation

In many cases, this broad category will encompass agricultural, urban, and other categories listed separately here. The restoration, preservation, and conservation of forests, grasslands, wetlands, and other natural ecosystems is essential if the supply and quality of both surface and subsurface water supplies are to be maintained. Many cities are protecting forested drainage basins because the value of the water provided by those areas is saving them billions of dollars in water supply and treatment costs. Especially important to groundwater supplies is pollution control and maintenance of vegetative cover in recharge areas.

For land conservation efforts to succeed, it is vital that all stakeholders work together. Where farmers, foresters, environmentalists, commercial interests, ranchers, industry, and others have recognized the mutual benefits of intelligent land use and formed partnerships to achieve that goal, the results have been most impressive [343].

Example: Edwards Aquifer

The Edwards aquifer (Figure 13.1) provides high quality drinking water to more than two million people in the San Antonio area of south-central Texas. It is a highly permeable limestone karst aquifer some 500 feet thick and 3,600 mi^2 in areal extent. Surface water runs south and east off higher elevation areas, the Edwards Plateau and Llano Hills, and onto a lengthy strip of land where the limestone outcrops at the surface — the recharge zone. The recharge zone occurs along the Balcones fault zone where numerous faults provide abundant, nearly vertical fractures. Surface waters infiltrate through sinkholes and fissures into the aquifer. Some water returns to the surface as springs along the base of the fault zone escarpment but most continues its journey through complex subsurface conduits and fractures. Confining beds provide ideal conditions for an artesian aquifer. Annual aquifer recharge in the San Antonio area varies greatly from a few tens of millions (circa 40,000 acre-feet) to over two billion m^3 (1,700,000 acre-feet) [208]. The city withdraws an average of 450,000 acre-feet annually from the Edwards aquifer.

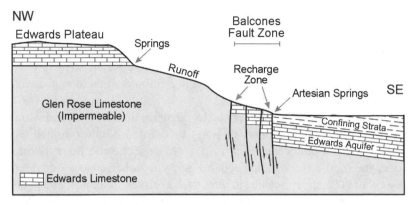

Figure 13.1. Geological cross-section of geology along the Balcones fault zone near San Antonio, Texas. Surface water enters the highly permeable Edwards Limestone on the plateau at the left and flows southeastward as groundwater, then as surface water (runoff), before seeping back into the permeable limestone along the fault zone.

Like other karst aquifers, the Edwards is very vulnerable to pollution, and the area's human population is one of the fastest growing in the nation. A major aquifer-protection plan has involved dramatically reducing water use, buying land outright, and especially purchasing easements. The conservation easements allow landowners to retain their land and pays them for agreeing to use good conservation techniques and to never subdivide or develop their properties. Most of the money has come from a voter-approved one-eighth-cent sales tax in San Antonio which has raised over $140 million to protect the aquifer. Thus far, some 21% (125,000 acres) of the recharge zone has been protected [202]. As a result of San Antonio's various water conservation efforts, Cynthia Barnett, in her book *Blue Revolution*, considered it the only US city to have achieved a community-wide water ethic [22].

13.2.5 Urban and Residential Conservation

In 1950, 29% of the world's population lived in cities. By 2008, UN data indicated that 50% of all people had become city dwellers and the world's urban population would increase another 50%, to 5 billion, by 2030. The number of city dwellers who will be unable to obtain needed water inside the city is expected to swell from some 150 million in 2010 to about 1 billion by mid-century. In a classic Catch-22, as growing cities demand an ever-larger share of the available water, farmers have been forced to do with less water, forcing millions of them to abandon agriculture and flock to the cities.

Urban areas are characterized by intensive domestic and industrial use of water. Huge amounts of water are wasted in cities around the world, a result of decades of infrastructure neglect, wasteful consumption, and inefficient planning and design. Many urban areas are covered by about 90% impermeable surfaces such as roads, buildings, and parking lots which generate huge volumes of polluted runoff, exacerbate flooding, and rob underlying groundwater of its recharge. Even suburban residential areas with home lots averaging one-third acre are roughly 35% impermeable. In Mexico City, it is estimated that for every square meter of land urbanized, some 170 liters of recharge are lost annually; the water lost for every hectare (2.5 acres) that gets urbanized is sufficient to supply the water needs of 500 families [507]. The areas surrounding cities also consume surprisingly high quantities of water. Lawn watering is a regular activity on an estimated 30 million acres of suburban residences in the US.

With education, effort, and funding, water waste can be dramatically reduced as cities from San Antonio to Singapore have shown. Many methods exist for increasing the productivity of available water, be it in a home, place of business, or major industrial site, as indicated by the following examples.

A. Runoff Control

Reducing polluted runoff and recharging groundwater is a major part of movements promoting the greening of urban and residential areas. Examples include: reducing paved areas and replacing pavement with permeable surfaces such as crushed stone and porous cements; cluster housing with more open, vegetated areas; redirecting runoff into rain gardens, woodlots, or infiltration basins; rooftop rainwater harvesting in which water from roofs is channeled into cisterns or various infiltration areas [455, 507]. It has been well documented that these and related efforts can increase groundwater recharge and generate good jobs while saving cities many hundreds of millions of dollars in water supply, flood prevention, and related costs. The Alliance for Water Efficiency estimates that a $10 billion investment in conservation methods such as installing water efficient equipment (toilets, washing machines, and so forth), channeling runoff for irrigation, and replacing leaking water lines would yield a gross domestic product increase of up to $15 billion [433].

B. Water Reuse

Some industries have long used the same water over and over. Significant conservation can be achieved if urban and residential planners begin encouraging this practice. For example, some states have relaxed the rules for reuse of "greywater" by home owners. In a water-scarce location, using a large quantity of water once, often polluting it in the process, then sending it on its way makes little sense. Such methods dilute and disperse pollutants, which is especially irresponsible when pathogens are involved. Water can be recycled and treated repeatedly for nearly all nonconsumptive uses (residential, municipal, and industrial) by adopting a closed-loop water-handling system. In such a system, only water which is lost — through direct human/animal consumption, leakage, evaporation, incorporation into products, or other means — must be restored to the system.

C. Water-Saving Appliances

Many appliances and related devices used in both home and businesses are incredibly wasteful. For example, thousands of eating establishments from restaurants to coffee and ice cream shops use constantly running water in "dipper wells" to rinse utensils, wasting billions of gallons each year. More water-efficient alternatives are available, among them special spray nozzles and dishwashers.

Of special interest, in view of the vast numbers of people lacking sanitary facilities, is the traditional toilet. So-called "modern" methods of handling human wastes as used in most of the developed world combine vast amounts of good, usually drinking-quality, water with human wastes, contaminating the water. Then all this water must be transported away and treated to remove and reconcentrate the wastes. The treatment is often incomplete and contaminated water from the treatment plants and sewer lines often overflows into streams and onto city streets. This is widely seen as an effective system and many developing countries seek to copy it. However, this system is costly (too costly for many developing nations), contaminates and wastes water, interferes with nutrient cycles, and can spread disease [56].

In the exploding cities of the low-income nations, sewage can be handled far more efficiently and economically with modern dry toilets, which use no water and generate a valuable fertilizer. Many of these facilities separate urine, to be used as a fertilizer supplement, from solid waste [55]. The solids are retained in a simple odorless composter which can accept other organic wastes as well. Following composting, the condensed wastes yield a rich humus that can be returned to soil. These devices are now employed extensively in a number of nations and many designs have been approved for use by the US EPA.

D. Landscaping

About a third of all commercial, industrial, and institutional water use is devoted to the urban landscape, and much of that water is wasted. Using plants adapted to the local climate and better design of vegetated and open areas can greatly reduce water use in cities. This does not mean reducing greenery in cities; quite the opposite in fact. Among the good and growing trends in many urban areas around the world is the use of open areas, rooftops, walls, and similar locations for vegetation, including food crops.

13.2.6 Groundwater Augmentation

Numerous techniques are available that can increase or replenish the groundwater supply without generating or importing additional water for a water-poor region. These methods make better use of the available water by retaining or capturing more of it. In many places, local governments help plan and implement such projects.

A. Water Spreading Techniques

This refers to practices which disperse water widely over a permeable surface to increase the amount of water that will infiltrate and add to groundwater supplies. In reality, irrigation by inefficient flooding of cropland has become a major source of groundwater recharge in most croplands. Unfortunately, fertilizers and pesticides may accompany the infiltrating water, contaminating the groundwater. Water spreading is also achieved by standard dams, which will obviously add to the groundwater in the areas immediately surrounding the reservoir. As noted in Section 4.6.2, the costs and benefits yielded by large dams have been long debated. Objective analyses find that the damages done often outweigh the benefits gained. With the growing concern over less dependable water supplies which may accompany climate change, storing water behind large dams is receiving increased attention, to the dismay of many conservationists.

Water can be stored and, more importantly, conserved without large dams. The method may be as simple as scarifying the ground surface to increase infiltration rates and surface water detention. Small terraces, ridges, or furrows along the contour of hillslopes is an ancient and effective method of inhibiting runoff, controlling soil erosion, and encouraging infiltration. Stream water may be channeled onto level permeable surfaces such as the adjacent floodplain. Low ridges or embankments placed across a floodplain or in the stream itself will detain water and encourage infiltration.

B. Water Collecting Techniques

A wide variety of basins, pits, troughs, and small dams are used to collect general runoff as well as reclaimed wastewater, storm water, and diverted stream water. The purpose is to allow water to percolate downward and replenish the underlying groundwater. **Recharge basins** (percolation basins, infiltration fields) and smaller, deeper **recharge pits** should be located well above the water table and lined with gravel or other permeable material. They are most often used in developed areas where residential, commercial, and highway runoff is directed by culverts or channels into constructed depressions of various sizes — the largest may exceed 13 hectares (32 acres) in area and 13 meters (43 feet) in depth. A recharge mound will form in the water table below the recharge pit (Figure 13.2).

A closely related approach involves **rainwater harvesting** techniques. Water collection and storage devices can be built in or near fields, homes, and large buildings. The "devices" can be as simple as small terraces or berms of soil and rock constructed perpendicular to the ground slope in agricultural areas or fairly sophisticated systems for collecting, storing, transporting, and using precipitation in urban environments.

Small dams along drainageways, hillside furrows, planting trees, maintaining ground cover, and other simple techniques are being used with great success in rural parts of Sub-Saharan Africa, India, and elsewhere. Small dams and trenches can gather rainwater, retard runoff, reduce soil erosion, and increase infiltration rates in recharge zones. The water collected may be used immediately, stored in various central containment facilities (Figure 13.3), allowed to infiltrate and replenish groundwater, or any combination of these. It is estimated that rainwater harvesting methods could increase food production two- or three-fold in some areas such as Sub-Saharan Africa [467].

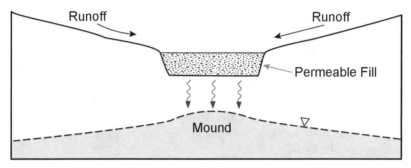

Figure 13.2. Cross-sectional sketch of a recharge basin. Runoff is directed into the basin which has been excavated and partially filled with gravel, crushed stone, or another highly permeable material.

In urban areas, **rooftop harvesting** of rainwater can collect and make available for recharge 70 to 90% of the precipitation compared to natural recharge rates of perhaps 3% in a semiarid regions and 30% in humid regions. All such techniques need to be well designed and intelligently operated. Filtration or disinfection will often be needed if the water is to be used for drinking, and problems associated with standing waters, such as mosquitoes and mold, need to be avoided.

In many developing nations, springs and shallow wells are going dry, even where deep well extraction is not occurring. In Himalayan villages and elsewhere, deforestation, changes in precipitation patterns (some related to climate change), loss of snowpack, and related influences are reducing aquifer recharge. If recharge areas are not known, methods such as radioisotopic analyses of water have been used to match groundwater discharge waters to rain water, thus locating the recharge areas where efforts to improve recharge can then be undertaken.

Fresh water can also be collected where it enters the sea. A membrane can be installed to separate the fresh and salt water, producing an "ocean reservoir" of fresh water which can be transported back to the land and put to use.

C. Recharge Wells

Recharge wells are injection wells which pump water collected from the surface directly to the subsurface for the purpose of adding to the groundwater supply and maintaining pressure in the groundwater reservoir. These are frequently used to recharge deep confined aquifers and to protect fresh water by preventing the inland migration of salt water in coastal areas (Figure 10.2B and C).

Recharge wells can create problems if contaminated runoff is injected or surface pollution seeps down along the well. Injection wells may also be designed specifically to dispose of hazardous wastes (Section 10.3.7B).

D. Groundwater Storage

Capturing water during wet periods and safely storing it for use during droughts and periods of high demand has been practiced since ancient times. Where the subsurface conditions are favorable, underground water storage or **groundwater banking** can be an efficient way to secure large quantities of water for future use. A subsurface "**water bank**" can be especially valuable in areas where the water supply varies greatly from one season to another. Such factors as location, the water source, recharge methods, aquifer leakage, and related factors require careful evaluation if the effort is to be successful.

Figure 13.3. Rainwater harvesting. Residents in the Marwar region of India gather to obtain water during the long dry season from structures such as this which store water collected during the monsoon season. Declining water tables and poor land use have forced many thousands to leave regions such as this, but rainwater collection, revegetation, water retention devices, and other methods are slowly reversing much past damage and providing necessary water to citizens.

Example: The Kern Water Bank

The Kern Water Bank in the southern San Joaquin Valley of California has been called the largest underground water storage facility in the US. Water transported from rivers in northern California is stored in the large alluvial fan of the Kern River. The water capacity of this sandy fan deposit is estimated at over 300 billion gallons, and it is considered an ecologically and economically preferable alternative to more dams and surface reservoirs. Unfortunately the water bank has been mired in lawsuits and controversy over who now owns the water, who can use it, how to use it, and how fast they should be allowed to use it [164]. Additional information on California water issues is presented in Section 8.8.4.

13.2.7 Industrial Improvements

Industries provide the goods and services which people require. This includes everything from basic foodstuffs and water to energy and financial services to construction and manufactured products. Industries have enormous impacts both as polluters and as consumers of essential resources. Many industries have made great advances in water efficiency, but much more can still be achieved, especially in such areas as waste stream separation, pollutant removal, and recycling of treated water in a closed system. It would also be of great benefit if both businesses and governments would recognize that economies cannot grow indefinitely and aim instead for a sensible, sustainable, and environmentally sound level of development and resource consumption.

13.2.8 Infrastructure Improvements

Infrastructure includes all the supportive installations, facilities, equipment, and services needed to obtain and deliver water. Water infrastructures are in desperate need of improvement in most of the world. In some areas, including much of Africa, water is present but the wells, storage facilities, delivery lines, and related structures to make it available to most people are lacking. Where infrastructure is present, it is often crumbling, causing enormous waste of water. Leakage and illegal connections to delivery systems removes some 40 to 70% of the water in parts of the developing world [316, 436]. The situation often isn't much better in developed nations. Leaks alone cause London to lose a third of its water supply [46]. In the US, over 250,000 significant water-line breaks occur each year and approximately a trillion gallons of untreated water escapes from dilapidated water systems, yet the federal investment in water infrastructure has been declining for decades. Current estimates place the cost of upgrading and maintaining the US water, wastewater, and storm water infrastructure at roughly $600 to $700 billion over the next 20 years [254]. The American Society of Civil Engineers gave an overall failing grade of "D" for the condition and performance of 15 major US infrastructure systems and noted that drinking water was among the worst [5, 106].

In 2009, the UN estimated the total worldwide investment required to build and maintain water supply, irrigation, and sanitation needs at between $92.4 and $148 billion annually, and this is likely an underestimate. These needs represent an awesome challenge in an era of global financial crises and related stresses. And yet, in comparison to the more than 1 trillion dollars per year cost for all US military-related expenditures and the $7.7 trillion the US government (Federal Reserve) provided to rescue its financial institutions during the 2007-2009 economic crisis, these costs do not seem so extravagant, and might well do far more to benefit worldwide security and promote peace than the usual military actions and financial shenanigans have been able to accomplish during the past several decades.

13.2.9 Consumer Habits

As with political change and improvement, conservation needs to begin with people. Profits are enhanced by high consumption of products from food to electricity to toys. Producing all these things requires water. Advertising, pricing, and clever marketing generally encourage excessive and wasteful consumption. Most people, from the US to China, fail to see the connection between their consumer habits and major looming problems such as climate change and water supply. Habit and its stubborn associate, denial, are very difficult to change, especially in a brief time period. But this is a large part of what needs to be accomplished if the problems facing humanity are to be successfully dealt with. Altering overall consumer attitudes and habits is a large challenge. Here are four areas with great potential for advancing consumer conservation:

A. Education

An obvious starting place is improved environmental and resource education in schools around the world. Whether due to ignorance, apathy, or human nature, most individuals tend to consume wastefully until a crisis forces change. One hopeful sign may be found among the growing numbers of informed and concerned individuals who have organized grassroots movements in many regions of the world. Many movements are impelled by necessity and peoples' desire to regain control over their own lives and the resources they depend upon.

B. Food

Modification of food consumption trends can reduce water consumption. For example, 1 pound of beef requires about seven pounds of grain which in turn requires some 840 gallons of water. When all water requirements are added up, some 1,860 gallons of water were used to produce that pound of beef [172]. If the 300 million Americans could reduce their livestock consumption by just 12.5%, from 800 to 700 kg grain-equivalent per person, it would mean a reduction in the grain fed to livestock of 30 million tons, which translates to a water savings of 30 billion tons, enough to provide food for 100 million people at an average annual world grain consumption level of 300 kg per person [55]. Yet most humans, especially in rapidly developing nations such as China and India, are consuming more meat. A related issue is food transport distances. Most standard produce sold in US markets is now transported well over a thousand miles. Vast quantities of energy and water are required to transport the food found in our supermarkets. These trends need to be reversed. Many are becoming aware that eating more locally grown crops will save considerable energy in addition to aiding local economies. Consumers need to be more conscious of the water demands of food — that is, virtual water (Table 12.2). For example, 1 kg of chicken needs 3,500 L of water to produce, but 1 kg of beef requires 43,000 L; rice needs 1,600 L/kg, corn 650 L/kg, and so on. By eating less meat and more fruits, grains, and vegetables, consumers will not only help conserve water, they will improve their health.

C. Non-Food Consumer Products

In one way or another, directly or indirectly, almost everything we use requires water. Water-efficient appliances and devices, from washing machines to shower heads, help to conserve water. Construction materials, clothing, electronics, energy consumption — all have a water footprint which, if made known, can help guide better consumer choices. Some nations are adopting water efficiency standards and labeling. Governments could help by providing consumer incentives such as tax breaks or rebates for buying more efficient products.

D. Landscaping

Green grassy lawns occupy some three times more acreage than any other crop in the US [314]. Those lawns and their accompanying vegetation consume huge quantities of water, especially in the dry western states. As with consumer products, many cities, faced with water shortages, are beginning to offer residents rebates and other "perks" for converting lawns to native plants.

13.2.10 Legal Actions

If conservation is to be effective, it needs to be backed by fair, intelligent, and enforced legal requirements. Information on this important topic is provided in Section 12.4.

13.3 Water Resource Management

In particular, the links between groundwater management, economic development, and land-use planning have rarely been recognized.

— Stephen Foster and Mohamed Ait-Kadi

13.3.1 Overview

The use of groundwater has exploded in the last few decades. Unfortunately, water policies, especially regarding groundwater, have failed to provide an effective, science-based framework to deal with the water crises which are emerging around the world. Management policies have too often reflected short-term political and economic interests driven by pro-growth motives with little regard to the long-term viability and sustainability of the resource and without understanding the many negative impacts which result from bad decisions and ill-conceived projects. Water resource management often has consisted of a patchwork of inconsistent schemes and regulations which tend to ignore the long-term viability of the resource and the environment. Many well-intentioned projects to aid people of water-stressed areas in developing nations have failed due to such factors as inappropriate technologies, inadequate long-term planning, and a failure to educate or train local people. For example, many thousands of hand pumps have been provided to the poor in rural areas but the majority of such pumps have often been found to be broken down or unusable at any one time [333, 504].

A troublesome trend has been for governments of developing nations to sell their most precious natural resources, including entire rivers and aquifers, to transnational companies to help relieve their debt. One can find African water resources for sale online. Meanwhile, hundreds of millions of the less fortunate masses are left with no say in the management of their water and no access to a safe or adequate water supply — and hundreds of millions more in over a hundred countries are financially burdened with unreasonably high water costs. Large corporations that control most of the world's marketing, finances, and resources are rapidly developing policies to secure water to provide income or to meet their anticipated future water requirements. Water offsets (providing water aid in one area in exchange for water exploited elsewhere), sophisticated mapping of water resources, water footprint analysis, and related approaches are being widely employed.

Effective governance of water resources is absolutely necessary if fair, intelligent use of water supplies is to be achieved and maintained. A well-executed comprehensive management plan, fairly administered, and backed by solid science and a good practical legal framework, can reduce human conflicts and ecological damages while efficiently utilizing the available water supply. Policies will need to consider economic, environmental, and social concerns, including such thorny problems as long-term climate change, population growth, and the ecological health of planetary life-support systems. A current catch-phrase for such a well-coordinated, holistic approach is "**integrated water resources management**," which the Global Water Partnership defines as a "process which promotes the coordinated development and management of water, land, and related resources in order to maximize the resultant economic and social welfare in an equitable manner without compromising the sustainability of vital ecosystems." All this sounds fine. Making it work is the problem, especially where groundwater is involved. Groundwater is an unseen commons, and millions of individual well owners are already withdrawing it and feel they have a right to it. Establishing partnerships with all the stakeholders and achieving fair integrated management of groundwater resources is a huge challenge [129, 431].

13.3.2 Important Management Issues

A. Planning

Too often, plans are approved, policies are implemented, and projects are undertaken without considering the total, long-term impacts on water and other vital natural resources. Water regulators and officials tend to be overly conservative in thinking when fresh, original approaches are needed. The impacts of urban growth, agriculture, industrial complexes, energy generation, and other developments on water supply and quality need to be understood and integrated during the planning stage. The relationships between water and other major endeavors should be considered before projects are allowed to proceed.

The size and location of groundwater supply wells can be planned so that other resources such as nearby wells, valuable wetlands, or streams are not adversely affected. It is often better to locate wells within a recharge area rather than near sensitive discharge points. Water pumping can be coordinated so as to avoid unnecessary withdrawals or excessive short-term withdrawals. Water demands can be moderated by cooperative scheduling of withdrawals for various crop, industrial, or residential uses. This can often be accomplished with only minor changes in when the various users take their water. Other approaches require more detailed efforts. For example, the Qinxu Groundwater Management System in China allocates to each farmer in the county a quantity of sustainable water he can withdraw. Farmers are given a swipe card to use for wells in the county, all well use is carefully monitored, and users are charged. Farmers may trade unused water and those who exceed their quota must pay an additional fee [410].

Many nations continue to rely on controlling nature with large hydro-engineering projects such as dams, diversions, and irrigation schemes. Organizations such as the World Bank and powerful private interests have also encouraged large projects. With proper planning, some dams can store excess water during high flow periods, alleviating flooding, and release that water during low flow periods. But all too often large water projects have actually reduced the total water supply while causing severe environmental impacts. For example, dams intended to provide more water to an area may lose vast quantities of precious water to evaporation and infiltration into bedrock. Or they may dramatically alter groundwater flow regimes resulting in serious problems for water users over a large area. All large water projects need sound hydrogeological input to assure that impairment of water and land resources are minimized. With global warming likely to reduce water supplies in many areas, some believe increasing water storage capacity, usually by building large dams, should be a priority. Some abhor all dams; others recommend only small dams. Only by objective analyses of individual projects by knowledgeable individuals will the best solutions be found.

B. Cooperation

It is not unusual for scientists and informed experts to meet, review the known facts, and reach an agreement. Unfortunately, these people usually don't decide policy. When the powers-that-be meet, narrow political views, self-serving economic concerns, cultural attitudes, and other highly subjective biases are frequently foremost in the thoughts of the participants, and cooperation can be elusive. Effective management of a vital resource such as water requires a commitment to achieve progress and a willingness to allow, from the beginning, meaningful input from all impacted parties, including the "little people" who are so often left out. Governments should seek to maintain strong yet flexible programs, embrace global concerns, and encourage citizen education and participation. Intergovernmental institutions such as the UN can have a major role in promoting and regulating fair and effective cooperative efforts [32].

Water does not respect man-manipulated boundaries, political or otherwise. Many of the world's major river and groundwater basins extend over more than one country. Large-scale exploitation by one nation causes other nations to fear that they will lose their fair share of the water. This in turn can lead to hastily conceived withdrawal projects and more tension. If overexploitation, unfair distribution, pollution, and other water problems are to be solved peacefully, international cooperation on water resource management will be essential, especially in an era of growing demand and changing climate. Unfortunately, most governments in the past have been blind to the pernicious problem of groundwater depletion. Official responses to water problems to date have often been inadequate, ill-advised, and/or superficial in countries around the world.

There are some signs that this is changing. Two international efforts to address and build a consensus on water problems are the Global Water Partnership and the World Water Council, both formed in 1996. In 2000, world leaders at the UN Millennium Summit adopted a set of Millennium Development Goals (MDGs) which included cutting in half the proportion of people lacking safe drinking water access by 2015. Two years later halving the proportion without basic sanitation services was added to the MDGs (Section 12.2.5). Achieving these goals will require several billion dollars a year in water and sanitation improvements, but the economic benefits of such an investment have been estimated at seven to eight times the costs [536]. Efforts are hampered by funding shortages and corruption by large contractors, governments, and individuals. The Water Integrity Network (WIN), launched at a meeting of water experts in Stockholm in 2006, includes various groups such as Transparency International, Stockholm International Water Institute, and Aquafed, an industry group, and is working to identify and prevent corruption [460, 508, 530, 565]. The World Bank estimated that corruption causes losses of 20 to 40% of water sector finances. In yet another effort to facilitate progress, the UN General Assembly proclaimed 2005-2015 the International Decade for Action: Water for Life as a means of promoting a wide range of water initiatives. The International Association of Hydrogeologists and other groups are mapping aquifers to gather data necessary to work out agreements between nations for sharing the resource. A US Water Partnership is being created by the Global Environment and Technology Foundation and numerous other public and private organizations [475, 521]. Its purpose is to provide a platform for sharing US knowledge and resources to encourage innovative solutions to water problems, especially in the developing world.

International conferences and forums are other endeavors through which nations can discuss water issues, set goals, and arrange for cooperative action. The largest such effort is the **World Water Forum (WWF)**, which meets every three years. It is convened by a group called the World Water Council which comprises delegates from governments, nongovernmental organizations, industry, and other institutions [540]. The Fifth Forum, held in Turkey in 2009, was attended by some 33,000 people and was the first to provide at least some focus on groundwater. Consumer groups organized their own meeting called the People's Water Forum where the focus was on managing water as a common right for all people. Groundwater topics were expanded somewhat at the Sixth Forum (2012) in Marseille, France. Once again, an "Alternative WWF" forum was held and its leaders strongly criticized the main WWF for failing to support water as a human right and investigate real-life solutions while encouraging water trading and speculation. In general such meetings provide individuals with good opportunities to communicate with peers in various fields, but concrete achievements are minimal and groundwater continues to receive far less attention than it merits. Numerous consumer-oriented groups and civil society movements feel these gatherings are basically trade shows laden with business representatives primarily interested in controlling, and profiting from, water [472].

Numerous other management and development organizations or partnerships exist to aid in meeting water needs. The organizations may be national, international, or local; private business, environmental, or charitable. Examples include US Aid [515], the Global Environment and Technology Foundation [475], World Wildlife Fund [542], and the Development Bank of Southern Africa [468].

Within nations, various combinations of apathy, ignorance, incompetence, confusion, competing interests and agencies, antiquated legalities, and other "usual suspects" can stifle water resource management efforts. In the US, thousands of major water commissions, conferences, symposia, and reports, governmental and nongovernmental, have come and gone over the past century. Most have involved highly qualified people. Many reports filled with data, worthy ideas, and good suggestions have been produced. Yet actual progress has been woefully inadequate. A major part of the problem is a lack of oversight and coordination among various government agencies. Consolidating these interests into a single effective water bureau is long overdue.

Hopefully, current efforts, given impetus by an increasingly obvious need to act, will lead to improved communication, cooperation, and implementation. Water is a mutual need for all and this realization has often provided a focal point for cooperation, leading to dialogues and establishment of authorities which can manage water resources for the long-term benefit of all. Water has been almost the only point upon which some nations have been able to come to agreements on. The international water-related treaties or agreements have been signed within the past 50 years number in the hundreds, but many have been weakened by conflicting interests or yield only local results.

Many governments face severe budget deficits and operate under heavy influence from power brokers whose interests are self-serving, limited, and short-term. Providing water, especially in small developing countries, is often best accomplished on a local level through cooperation between local communities, nongovernmental organizations, businesses, development institutions, and other groups who share a need for a dependable water supply. A business cannot operate effectively without a reliable, affordable source of water. In developing nations of Africa and elsewhere, many companies, from Coca-Cola to Anglo Platinum, a mining firm, have found that working with other interested parties to provide good water for both local inhabitants and their operations can produce benefits for all.

C. Pricing

Many people still seem to believe that water simply falls out of the sky and that it should be basically free, forgetting that it costs money — hundreds of billions of dollars a year — to collect, clean, store and distribute it.

— Steve Maxwell

The price of a commodity, be it a gallon of gasoline or water, should reflect the real costs, direct and indirect, of the item. When the market fails to accurately reflect the costs of vital commodities, prices do not reflect true value, which can result in unfair pricing, pollution, wasted resources, and unsound decisions which can disrupt entire economies. Studies by the International Center for Technology Assessment concluded that if such indirect costs as oil-company tax subsidies, military protection, and health/environmental damages associated with pollution were included in the price of a gallon of gasoline, they would add $12 to every gallon [483]. As with fossil fuels, the costs of obtaining and sustaining a water supply are often far greater than suggested by the price of the water. Governments of many nations provide water and other resources at minimal cost for influential corporations. Water utilities commonly must acquiesce to pro-growth pressures by keeping consumer and business costs low.

One reflection of the pro-growth mentality is the perverse practice of **inverse pricing** where the cost per unit used decreases as more is used. Hence those who use the least, and/or practice good conservation, are penalized and pay more. More outrageous is the situation in many developing nations where water may be provided to the wealthy at a pittance while the poor must pay exorbitant prices for water of very dubious quality. In most of the US, the water supplied by public water systems is free. Users pay only a part of the costs of providing that water — administration, extraction, treatment, energy use, building and maintaining delivery lines, and so forth.

Businesses and individuals will not generally alter wasteful habits unless the price they pay increases. This was well illustrated in India where nearly free water led to huge wastage of irrigation water, along with an upsurge in waterlogged and salinated soils. Yet if water can be had only for a price, what will happen to the poor who cannot pay that price? A morally acceptable approach is to provide absolutely essential water at a minimal cost — and at no cost to those unable to afford even that — and steeply increasing the cost if users exceed their "need" limit. Ideally, the full cost of providing water should be included in the market price. The water itself should be priced based upon the scarcity of water and an evaluation of total water requirements for the region. Businesses and industries are charged for the removal and/or pollution of water supplies in about half the developed nations. This market approach discourages excess development and overuse of water. The intertwining issues of economics and water policy are complex and often controversial [445, 151].

In general, however, increasing prices for public services are seen as discouraging growth and development. Hence they are politically unpopular. The resulting government inaction encourages irresponsible water use and can ultimately prove disastrous to a region [293].

D. Privatization

One way or another, water will soon be moved around the world as oil is now.

— World Bank

Water is life. It really should not be a commodity to be bought.

— Sister Mary Zirbes

Privatization can mean many things. As used here, it refers to water that is controlled by a private entity which can then sell it to others. Water privatization most often refers to the ownership and operation of water systems by private businesses. Responsibly undertaken, privatization can be an appropriate way of providing water, but it can also be a cynical scheme to capitalize on the water crisis. Large-scale privatization of water began in the early 1990s and spread rapidly. Twenty years later, for-profit corporations owned and operated well over $200 billion worth of water systems around the world, serving nearly 10% of the population [142, 258]. Over 260 million taps now dispense water delivered by large multinational water companies. In addition, thousands of smaller entities are now engaged in the rapidly growing market of buying and selling water. Privatization may also be partial as where a municipality contracts a private company to operate part of the water system, or to design, construct, and maintain the system [156].

Organizations such as the World Bank, World Trade Organization, World Water Council, and the International Monetary Fund are closely allied with international corporations and have tended to promote free trade (marketing) of water. Beginning in the late 1990s, they would often demand that countries privatize their public water systems to obtain needed loans. International trade treaties such as NAFTA frequently require such concessions before a country can participate. Laws of supply and demand have worked well for many tradable commodities; why not for water? The position of most governments has been that water supplies should remain under public control. The state should focus on improving access to safe water, not hand the responsibility over to private profit-seeking corporations.

Even so, growing financial pressures on governments have led to large decreases in government spending on public utilities. In recent years, both developed and developing nations have often found themselves overwhelmed by internal problems, debt, insufficient funds, and public needs. The US government's spending on water infrastructure declined from 78% of the total required in 1978 to only 3% in 2008. Some believe a free enterprise system would be more competitive, efficient, and cost-effective. And some private water supply operations have functioned well. A company operating internationally and focusing exclusively on providing water may have experience and know-how which most governments lack. As such they may be able to provide water more cost-effectively and more efficiently.

Unfortunately, many experiences with privatization have resulted in unjustifiably high water prices, corruption, compromised water quality, poor service, and water cutoffs for the poor [19, 20]. Private enterprises typically base profits on a percent of expenditures. The higher the expenditures, the more profit. Efficiency and conservation rarely are a high priority. A powerful incentive exists to inflate expenditures on water delivery and treatment systems. The most notorious of many privatization failures is Cochabamba, the third largest city in Bolivia. Privatization resulted in doubling water rates and other intolerable conditions that left tens of thousands with no water at all. Months of protests and finally riots in April of 2000 forced the companies out. As a result of such experiences, privatization of public services has become a fiercely contested issue around much of the world.

Other difficulties with privatization include the facts that: (1) little incentive exists to conserve water (the more water sold, the more profit); (2) the public often will lack basic information about its water and have little input into decision-making; and (3) although often regulated by public advisory boards or commissions, such groups themselves may be strongly influenced or even controlled by the private industry.

527

The rapidly growing **bottled water** industry can be regarded as part of water privatization also. Consuming water from plastic bottles grew in a few short years to a multibillion-dollar industry selling over 178 billion liters worldwide by 2006 [142]. In the US in 2011, the average person consumed nearly 30 gallons of bottled water, typically paying a few hundred up to 10,000 times more than the cost of tap water [197]. The implication is that bottled water is safer than public water systems. Yet numerous studies show that bottled water is no safer than tap water. In many countries, including the US, government regulation of public water supplies is far more stringent than of the bottled-water industry. Many bottled waters labeled "spring" water are actually drawn from municipal water supplies. Some brands must be shipped thousands of miles to reach their customers.

The bottles themselves represent a huge cost in energy consumption — worldwide, their manufacture and transport consumes well over 100 million barrels of oil annually [549, 550], they may leach harmful chemicals into the water, and they usually end up in landfills. Numerous bottle boycott efforts are underway.

In many locations, the bottled water industry has withdrawn large amounts of groundwater which have caused substantial water table declines. Many communities are engaged in prolonged efforts to restrict such exploitation of their water supplies. Due to the influence of corporations on higher-ranking elected officials, many people find that local efforts such as town ordinances limiting bulk water extractions, zoning restrictions, placing groundwater in a public trust under local control, and similar declarations are the most effective way of preventing private companies from dominating local resources.

Example: Fiji Water

Fiji Water is one of the most chic and popular brands of bottled water. Fiji Water has been described in promotional materials as rivaling the "known and significant abilities of 'Holy Healing Waters' in Lourdes, France or Fatima, Portugal." A related blurb notes that the water's "electromagnetic field frequency enables Fiji Water to stimulate our human self-regulation system." Fiji Water does come from the Pacific island nation Fiji where, ironically, many citizens lack a clean, reliable supply of water. The company, owned by US billionaires, has near-exclusive rights to the high-quality water from a large aquifer which stretches for miles along the main island's northern coast [239].

Private companies can certainly contribute in many ways to providing safe water for the public. The deeper controversy to be addressed is whether profit-oriented enterprises should be allowed full control over essential natural resources. Because water is necessary for survival, many regard its privatization or "commodification" as a social and ethical evil. Proper management of fundamental needs, be they a nation's defense or a society's water supply, requires a level of expertise, foresight, long-term planning, and commitment to meeting basic human needs which are often not strong points with corporations whose focus is upon maximized profit, growth, and short-term return to stockholders.

13.3.3 Goals and Recommendations

Water management goals will vary depending upon the conditions existent at each location. Four desirable objectives are briefly noted below, followed by some recommendations for achieving those goals.

A. Reduce Consumption

In many areas, water consumption needs to be reduced if disastrous consequences are to be avoided. This is especially true for groundwater which is nonrenewable or only very slowly replenished. Numerous approaches can be used to achieve this end (Section 13.2). An initial, albeit difficult, step is to quantify water extraction and use. Water management agencies need to be capable of making reasonable estimates as to how much water is being used, where, and by whom. In some situations, it may be necessary to ban unnecessary, unsustainable, or wasteful water uses. At a minimum, it will be prudent in many locations to establish reasonable limits on water withdrawals based on such factors as minimal streamflows, groundwater recharge rates, competing needs, and ecological requirements. Limits on the density of wells and total groundwater withdrawals should be enforced in many areas.

B. Redistribution

Redistribution refers to changing where and how water is used. This may involve redistributing population from water-poor to water-rich areas or changing the amount of water provided for specific uses. Even with conservation and efficiency improvements, certain water uses, especially for agriculture (Section 13.2.3), will need to decrease in many parts of the world if other critical water demands are to be met. Trading, or buying and selling, of water rights can encourage higher-value water uses and provide some relief for water-stressed regions. In many countries, including the US, wasteful subsidies and other perverse economic supports should be replaced with subsidies designed to lower the cost of water-conserving consumer goods and encourage efficient use by all water users.

C. Participation

It is highly desirable that all users of water be involved in determining water management rules and share in the costs of utilizing and maintaining the supply. "All users" means affected citizens and communities, government agencies, nongovernmental organizations (environmental, labor, consumer, legal, and so forth), and business organizations (industrial, agricultural, fishing, recreational, and others). It is worth repeating that the people most harmed by water scarcity and pollution are often left out of the planning and decision-making, especially in developing nations. This is a major mistake. The poor, and especially women who are often responsible for providing water for families and communities, should be informed and involved if water supplies are to be fairly and successfully utilized. Federal governments need to coordinate and support small groups and communities, but not dictate efforts to improve water and sanitation needs.

D. Fairness

Management plans also need to be fair to all parties. For example, simply requiring every user to reduce water consumption by 30% will not hurt those who are wasteful, but it could impose severe hardship upon users who are already doing their best to conserve. A fair policy needs to anticipate the reasonable water needs of each user or group of users such as industry, agriculture, and recreation , as well as the actual use of the water, whether that use is wise in view of the available supply, and other relevant matters. Where it is not feasible to monitor, meter, and otherwise keep track of individual wells, decisions can be guided by the impacts on the groundwater resource. Methods of determining those impacts include water table monitoring, satellite measurements, and evaluation of discharge areas.

E. Recommendations

Achieving these and other worthy management goals will require the establishment of competent water agencies where none currently exist.

In a country such as the US, it may mean replacing the antiquated system of competing, overlapping agencies with one lean, efficient, and effective department, or at least appointing an influential advisor, to oversee all water issues [344, 534]. Specific recommendations for improving water management, laws, and policies include the following:

- Involve qualified scientists and other **experts**.
- Improve water **data** collection and analyses.
- Promote **public** education, participation, and responsibility; avoid top-down, centralized control, which has often led to ineffective efforts and neglect of many needs.
- Make realistic, long-term **sustainability** of the water resource(s) a primary consideration. This will entail incentives to conserve water.
- Use a **holistic** approach which considers all water-related ecological, social, and economic values. This means giving due consideration to groundwater, surface water, water quantity and quality, land use, and ecological concerns when formulating policies.
- Base water management units on **hydrologic boundaries** such as surface and groundwater basins, not political borders.
- Establish water resource **protections**. Tools for achieving protection might include prohibiting certain land uses, establishing protected areas, and encouraging astute land tradeoffs, easements, zoning, and permits.
- Establish a comprehensive, and comprehendible, **legal** framework for water resources. Laws need to recognize groundwater and include fair and enforceable rules for wells and groundwater extraction.
- Devise feasible **governance** (coordinative) structures.
- Develop **flexible** policies that can be adapted to local conditions.
- Promote **pollution prevention**. This requires better control of septic systems, land application of wastes and fertilizers, waste lagoons, deep well installation, all subsurface waste disposal operations, and so forth.
- Eliminate perverse **subsidies** which encourage water waste and discourage intelligent stewardship of natural resources. Conversely, governments should support programs which conserve and restore natural life-supporting resources. This

can be accomplished via tax relief, subsidies, or other creative funding initiatives.

- Provide realistic, dependable, long-term **financial support**. In part, funds for water-related expenditures can be provided by placing a fair and realistic price, and possibly a progressive tax, on all water use [155].

Adequate funding of water programs is essential if the above goals and recommendations are to be realized. Many developing nations (such as Yemen, Afghanistan, Nigeria, and Pakistan) and impoverished regions will need considerable outside financial aid and scientific/technological support if water security is to be achieved and chaos/collapse avoided. Many nations are politically unstable and close to collapse due in large part to growing population pressure and depletion of such vital natural resources as water, soil, and ecosystems. Failed states pose a threat to human welfare and international stability. It is in the best long-term interests of wealthy nations to aid those in need [57, 58].

13.4 Groundwater Exploration

Finding a usable supply of groundwater usually involves answering five basic questions: (1) is water present, (2) what is the biological and chemical quality of the water, (3) are permeable rocks present, (4) is a significant quantity of water in storage, and (5) is adequate local recharge of that water occurring? Techniques commonly used to find groundwater include the following.

13.4.1 Understand the Hydrogeology

The least expensive, fastest approach to hydrogeologic exploration is to make use of a well-qualified, experienced hydrogeologist, preferably one who already has some familiarity with the site area. S/he will use all available tools to learn the geology of the area, including study of previous reports, well data, maps, photographs, satellite imagery, and related information sources. Field work by a qualified geologist can be invaluable and may include measurement of streamflow and spring discharge, examination of rock outcrops, evaluation of wetlands and other water-related features, and identification of soil and vegetation types.

13.4.2 Geophysical Techniques

Geophysical methods can aid in finding and evaluating groundwater reserves by detecting differences in the physical characteristics of earth materials. Table 13.1 provides a brief summary of geophysical techniques useful in groundwater exploration. Subsurface information on rock, regolith, and groundwater can usually be obtained either from on-the-surface operations or by employing a **probe** which can be lowered into a borehole. As the probe travels along the length of the borehole, it records information on the subsurface materials present. Among the useful data that can be measured by borehole devices are hole diameter, temperature, natural radioactivity, density, magnetic properties, and responses to electric currents, sound waves, and radioactive bombardment. These data in turn can be related to the nature of the earth material around the hole [100, 103, 378, 389, 423]. Downhole geophysical logs are especially valuable in correlating subsurface properties between different boreholes. Interpreting the results requires experience to recognize the often subtle differences in properties of the materials present.

The electrical and seismic properties of subsurface materials are widely used in groundwater exploration. For the **electrical resistivity** and **electromagnetic induction** techniques, the greater the current that will pass through the earth material, the greater its conductivity and the less its resistivity. The resistance of porous materials is determined mainly by water content. Resistivity tends to be decreased, and conductivity increased, by increases in clay content, water saturation, and salinity. If boreholes and borehole probes are not available, electrodes (usually metal stakes) may be inserted into the ground and a current made to flow from one electrode to the other through the material. Electric potential, a measure of the force or pressure causing the current to flow, is analogous to the equipotential forces producing groundwater flow, and can be measured using additional electrodes and a voltmeter. The farther apart the electrodes are placed, the more deeply the current circulates. Sudden changes in the potential and thus the current flow, reflect changes in the subsurface materials. By comparing resistivity or other geophysical characteristics of subsurface materials at known depths, cross-sections can be drawn revealing the dimensions and attitude of the various rock units as shown on Figure 13.4.

In **seismic methods**, vibrations are created by pounding the earth with a heavy instrument or setting off small explosions. Vibrations from the disturbance are reflected (bounced off) or refracted (bent) as they travel through the earth, much like light traveling through different materials (air, glass, water). The refraction results from the changes in the speed of the seismic waves as they move through different materials. They tend to move most rapidly through solid igneous rock and slowly

Table 13.1. Geophysical Techniques Useful in Groundwater Studies

Technique	How it Works Frequent Uses

Electrical Resistivity

Measures a material's resistance to an electrical current.

Depth to water table and fresh-/salt-water interface, shallow stratigraphy.

Electromagnetic Induction

Measures a material's ability to conduct an electrical current (the inverse of resistivity).

Similar to electrical resistivity but faster with greater resolution; detect buried objects; mapping saline contamination plumes.

Seismic Refraction

Measures the velocity or travel time of seismic vibrations through a material.

Depth to unconfined water table; depth to bedrock or dense overburden; stratigraphy.

Seismic Reflection

Detects seismic vibrations that bounce off of surfaces to determine their location and depth.

Detailed shallow stratigraphy; mapping of bedrock at base of valley-fill aquifers.

Ground Penetrating Radar

Measures the nonconducting (dielectric) properties of a material using high-frequency electromagnetic waves.

Depth to water table; shallow stratigraphy; detect buried objects and some contaminants.

Gravimetry

Measures the density of subsurface materials.

Mapping stratigraphy and thickness of unconsolidated regolith.

Magnetometry

Detects magnetic properties of mineral matter.

Mapping formations and fractures in rock containing magnetic materials; detect magnetic objects.

Notes: This list includes methods commonly used on or above the ground surface. These are useful in determining physical properties of subsurface earth materials. Among their common uses are location of the water table and the regolith-bedrock contact. Source: [517].

534

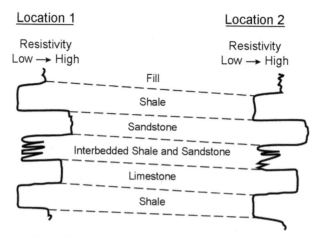

Figure 13.4. Two idealized resistivity logs showing their use in correlation of rock layers at two locations. Shales and clays conduct electric current far more efficiently (or have low resistance to the current) than limestones and sandstones and the contrast is readily seen in this hypothetical example.

through unconsolidated materials. Vibrations from the initial disturbance are detected at a series of carefully spaced recording stations (geophones: basically small seismometers) and automatically recorded for later interpretation. Seismic methods are often employed where a large area is involved. Water saturation causes a marked increase in the velocity of seismic waves (vibrations) passing through most unconsolidated materials. The sudden change in velocity at the water table produces refraction and reflection of the waves which are readily recorded by the sensitive instruments. From these data, the depth of the water table and of other significant subsurface contacts can be determined.

Ground penetrating radar uses electromagnetic waves in a similar fashion to seismic methods. An antenna directs radio wave pulses into the earth and the waves are reflected back to receiving antennas by subsurface materials of differing electrical properties. Buried objects, earth materials of varying density, water saturation, and certain chemicals (LNAPLs for example) can be detected by moving the transmitting antenna over an area. Under favorable conditions, a detailed map of the subsurface can be produced using ground penetrating radar.

Small changes in the **gravitational** pull of Earth can be used to determine changes in the mass of groundwater which lies below. **Remote sensing** can be defined as the acquisition of information via a device located at some distance from the object(s) being observed. It usually refers to aerial photographs and satellite images which use electromagnetic energy (such as visible light or infrared radiation) to view Earth's surface (Section 13.4.3). It may also include measuring geophysical properties of Earth in great detail from satellites.

Example: GRACE Satellites

Measurements made by the Gravity Recovery and Climate Experiment (GRACE) satellites, which were launched by NASA in March of 2002, can provide reasonably accurate estimates of changes in mass within the underlying terrain being surveyed [212]. GRACE uses a pair of satellites to measure slight variations in Earth's gravitational field. As one satellite passes over an area of slightly increased gravity, the gravitational pull causes it to speed up slightly relative to the second satellite, then slow down as it moves past. The same happens to the second satellite. By comparing these relative movements during repeated passes over an area, an estimate of any changes of mass in the terrain below can be made. Most such changes in mass and gravity are due to changes in amount of water on or under the region being investigated (for example, in aquifers, lakes, or soils).

GRACE has determined groundwater storage changes in several critical regions, including California and India. For example, calculations from GRACE data found a net depletion of 109 km³ of groundwater in the Indian states of Rajasthan, Punjab, and Haryana from August 2002 to October 2008. That is twice the amount of water in India's largest surface-water reservoir and indicates serious ongoing depletion of the groundwater in an area containing some 114 million residents [329]. See sections 8.8.4 and 14.2.1B for additional information on groundwater in California and India respectively.

13.4.3 Aerial Photography and Satellite Imagery

These forms of remote sensing use the electromagnetic spectrum to observe Earth's surface. Standard visible light photographs and other images can readily locate landforms, fracture zones, vegetation, watery areas, and other features often associated with groundwater. Satellite images in particular provide a global perspective of human impacts on the planet. By observing variations in vegetation, wetlands, rivers, lakes, ice fields, and other water-related features through time, satellite imagery can detect important changes in the hydrologic cycle. Interpretation of the data provides vital information on phenomena ranging from soil moisture to changing climates to groundwater recharge and discharge.

Under favorable conditions, infrared imagery can detect subsurface changes in the temperature of groundwater. This can be used to locate subaqueous springs, trace certain pollutants, or determine mixing patterns in ground and surface waters.

13.4.4 Water Witching

Water witching, or **dowsing**, consists of holding a forked stick or wand of some sort in one's hand and walking over the ground surface. The stick will supposedly be pulled downward when subsurface water lies below [389]. It is claimed that the technique can identify items as diverse as mineral resources, buried pipes, human bodies, archaeological ruins, bombs, and ghosts. "Dowsers" have been repeatedly tested by the USGS and others in terrains with hidden water containers below the surface. The results are no better than random guesses. This ancient technique has many adherents, but it is based on superstition and has no scientific basis. Like many gimmicks, however, dowsing continues to attract considerable attention, not to mention hard-earned dollars.

13.5 Alternative Water Supplies

The first thought of most upon running out of a resource is the ancient one — we'll just find more. This means getting it from some other place. Such an approach is fraught with difficulties today, not the least of which is that fresh liquid water is probably serving important needs, both ecological and human, right where it is. Of course, that has rarely stopped the more powerful from appropriating the water from the less powerful. Most efforts to produce new or alternate water supplies focus upon the following.

13.5.1 Desalination

Desalination is an (expensive) supply-side solution to a demand-side problem.

— Fred Price

The largest, most obvious alternate water supply is seawater. **Desalination** is the process of removing salt from saline waters using special filters and membranes or by evaporation. Interest in desalination has been increasing. By 2016, worldwide desalination is expected to approach 40 billion m³/yr, over twice the rate in 2008. More than 10,000 plants now exist and more than half are in the Arabian Gulf region. Costs are prohibitive for most developing nations and even in industrialized nations such as the US, numerous companies have gone bankrupt trying to construct desalination plants. The two most common methods are **thermal distillation** (boil and condense) and **reverse osmosis** (pump water across a salt-retaining membrane). Although far more efficient than thermal distillation, about half the cost of a reverse-osmosis plant is for energy; but the technology is continuing to improve and become more efficient [112]. Where water supplies are extremely low and the end use of water is high-value, desalination may be the best alternative. In most areas, costs have limited the use of desalinated water to drinking or high-priority industry. In some locations such as the Middle East and Spain, where groundwater depletion is severe, desalinated water for agricultural use has been approved.

In addition to the high cost of desalination, large quantities of salt or very salty water will need to be safely stored or disposed of. Returning extremely salty water to the sea will eliminate most sea life in the area of impact. Many sea organisms are also killed when water is pumped from the ocean to a desalination plant. The composition of seawater can change with the seasons, sometimes producing potentially hazardous by-products during desalination. Desalinated water also lacks essential nutrients such as calcium and magnesium and often contains high levels of boron, a potential threat to some crops and possibly to humans [269].

Additional treatment to add or remove certain chemicals can be undertaken to improve the quality of desalinated water. Research continues into more energy-efficient, low-cost methods [353]. These methods include utilizing waste heat, renewable energy, and the ocean itself. For example, wave energy and the temperature differential between surface and deep ocean water (low-temperature thermal desalination) are potentially valuable energy sources [31].

In general, the more saline the water, the most costly it will be to produce fresh water from it — in 2007, costs ranged from about $700 to $1,160 per acre-foot of water, to which must be added distribution costs. Except in areas of severe water shortages, better water management and conservation measures will usually prove far more cost-effective than building desalination plants [46, 152].

13.5.2 Water Transfers

Transferring large quantities of water from one area (usually wa-ter-rich) to another (usually water-poor) has long been a popular and controversial approach to water supply problems. Most often, water trans-port concerns surface waters, often over distances of hundreds or even thousands of miles, but groundwater is playing an ever-larger role, ei-ther as a recipient of water for recharge, or as a water source to be ex-ported (Plate 16, Top).

> ### Example: The All-American Canal
>
> The complex and controversial nature of many water trans-fers is well illustrated by just one section of the All-American Canal. The canal is 132 kilometers (82 miles) long and was completed in 1942. It carries about 20% of the Colorado River's water westward, mainly to croplands in the Imperial Valley of California where it has been used, often very wastefully, to irrigate crops. Evaporative losses from the canal increase the water's salinity some 30% by the time it reaches its destina-tion. In addition to evaporative losses, the unlined All-Ameri-can Canal lost nearly 70,000 acre-feet of water annually by seepage along a 14-mile section through sand dunes, shown in Plate 16, Bottom. This seepage recharged groundwater which then flowed south across the border into Mexico where, for many years, it greatly benefited Mexican farmers and the ecosystem of the Colorado River delta. In 2010, despite bitter lawsuits and controversies, a $285 million US project was completed to line the canal and prevent this "waste" of the water [156].

The most economically feasible water transfers are usually des-tined for water-stressed urban regions where the water's dollar value is higher and the quantity required is less than for agricultural uses. The purchase of agricultural water rights by urban areas or industries is already wide-spread. Large-scale water transfer schemes continue to be dusted off and promoted, or generated anew. A recent proposal by two US companies involves taking some three billion gallons of water annually from a glacial valley in Alaska and shipping it on tankers to Mumbai, India, where the water would be processed for shipment to thirsty cities in the Middle East. A related idea is to transfer fresh water across the seas in large, strong plastic bags.

Some transferred water may be used to recharge aquifers. Examples are the ongoing transfer of water from southern China to northern China and the long-simmering schemes to transport massive amounts of water from the northern US and Canada to the thirsty southwestern US. Another proposal envisioned an undersea pipeline carrying water from Alaska to California. The Great Lakes Compact, an agreement among the eight states that share the lakes, prevents water transfers to outside regions, even by bottle, but does not mention groundwater. Numerous other projects to import water to rapidly growing cities of the American southwest have been proposed [128]. Among them is piping water from the Mississippi River many hundreds of miles westward and many hundreds of feet upward to Las Vegas and other destinations.

Large transfer projects are usually expensive, energy-intensive, wasteful of water, and almost always have severe social and ecological impacts. Like dams, some have been well conceived, but most have long-term negative effects which, upon a careful and objective analysis, can easily overwhelm the benefits. Large water transfer projects will often fail to achieve long-term goals and are a poor substitute for intelligent planning based upon an understanding of water's true worth [40, 156].

Another approach is to transfer water as large **icebergs** from the high latitudes to ports in thirsty nations. Iceberg-towing ideas have been around since at least the 1820s. A million tons of iceberg might provide the annual water consumption for approximately 5,000 people. Among the obstacles to utilizing icebergs as a water source are the high costs of long-distance transport and end-point treatment and distribution, possible iceberg break-up during transport, and impacts on local coastal ecology and weather triggered by the large ice mass and its meltwater.

We should not forget the vast amounts of water are also transferred in a secondary or indirect manner in the form of commodities. As noted in section 12.2.2, when nations import food and other water-intensive commodities, they are also importing virtual water.

13.5.3 "New" Groundwater Sources

Do large quantities of potable groundwater exist which have not been exploited or discovered? Recent studies indicate that as much as 300,000 km^3 of freshwater may exist in deep **offshore aquifers**. Some are presently being renewed by recharge areas on land, but many are thought to contain mostly nonrenewable fossil water. That water accumulated during the glacials of the Quaternary Period when the continental shelves were exposed and absorbed water from precipitation or melting ice. It remains to be seen if exploitation of coastal submarine aquifers will prove feasible. In favorable locations, they could provide a worthy alternative to desalinization plants.

Another concept is that "**megawatersheds**" harboring vast quantities of fresh water await discovery and exploitation in the deep subsurface [116]. Deep megawatersheds may result when high rates of precipitation, usually in mountains, infiltrate deeply and migrate great distances laterally along fracture zones or other high permeability zones deep in the earth. These have been promoted as a new groundwater source which could increase existing freshwater supplies a hundred-fold or more. Most hydrogeologists question the originality of this idea and suggest it is more hype than substance [534]. It is well-known that very deep aquifers exist. Most are probably associated with an active or inactive (disconnected or stagnant) regional groundwater flow system (Section 6.9). Deep aqueous flow systems, especially in mountainous areas, can penetrate many kilometers into the earth and can contain large quantities of fresh water — an interesting case study of a complex system in the US Basin and Range is provided by Fetter [122]. Additional information on deep aqueous waters is provided in Section 8.14. Due to uncertainties regarding the existence, location, and expense of finding and utilizing deep freshwater aquifers, it appears they will not soon, if ever, play a major role in quenching humanity's great and growing thirst.

13.5.4 Recycling

The usable supply of water can be "increased" above that delivered by the hydrologic cycle by recycling it, sometimes over and over. Many industries use closed-loop systems along with in-house purification to keep reusing water with minimum loss. Municipal wastewater, if properly treated, represents a large underutilized source of usable, even potable, water. Orange County in California pumps 70 million gallons of advanced-treated wastewater into the ground for reuse as drinking water. The US currently recycles only about 8% of its wastewater. On a much smaller scale, numerous devices are available to capture and purify used household water, including human waste. In many locations, well-designed recycling and augmentation techniques (Section 13.2.6) may be capable of avoiding water shortages and crises.

13.6 Hydrophilanthropy

Water is the lifeblood of human existence and at the heart of civilization.

— Donald R. Coates

The term **hydrophilanthropy** refers to humanitarian actions aimed at preventing or at least reducing the misery caused by inadequate water, polluted water, and/or poor sanitation. Numerous promising initiatives, such as the US Senator Paul Simon Water for the World Act of 2005, exist, or have been proposed. Many governments, non-governmental organizations (NGOs), charitable foundations, and international agencies have considerable experience with these issues and have provided advisers, inexpensive pumps, drilling tools, water purifiers, toilets, and other aids. Unfortunately, most efforts are small compared to the vastness of the water dilemmas afflicting billions of people. And, despite growing needs, aid from wealthier nations has been declining in recent years. Various goals have been set but meeting them remains a challenge. It should be emphasized that the costs of not providing essential aid will likely far exceed the costs of doing so, even if the terrible human costs are ignored.

Many well-intended efforts are plagued by inconsistent and inadequate funding, poor advance planning, lack of sound hydrogeologic advice, broken-down equipment, and poorly informed beneficiaries. One highly touted effort, launched with a celebrity-adorned, multi-million-dollar sendoff in 2006, was the introduction of PlayPumps in Africa. These devices were basically water-pumping merry-go-rounds intended to be powered by playing children. But, among other problems, the devices were costly, prone to breakdowns, and children would need to be playing on one 27 hours a day to produce the intended quantity of water. It is clear that much greater, more levelheaded efforts are needed. Efforts must consider sustainability along with the willingness and ability of the local population to properly use and maintain water supply and sanitation systems.

14

Perspectives on Tomorrow

Without perspective, we are lost.

— Tom Athanasiou

14.1 A World Shaped by Human Influence

The future is not some place we are going to, but one we are creating. The paths are not to be found, but made, and the activity of making them changes both the maker and the destination.

— John Schaar

The hydrologic cycle appears to have been remarkably consistent over very long periods of time. Today, the dominating influence on Earth's near-surface environment, including the hydrosphere, is human activity. By 2025, humans are expected to appropriate 70% of the world's annual renewable freshwater [425]. By 2030, many expect that human global water needs will surpass sustainable water supplies by 40% [283]. Already, over half the world's people live in nations that depend upon the overpumping of groundwater to provide food [58]. As a result of this and other trends such as global warming and soil erosion, water and food security are decreasing dramatically, and the hydrologic cycle is being altered on a scale and at a rate perhaps unprecedented in Earth's history. After decades of expansion in population, the inefficient use, pollution, and outrageous waste of water, serious shortages are now affecting nations around the world. Although fertility rates have decreased about 50% since 1950, the huge number of young people assures that, barring major calamities, total human numbers will continue to increase for several decades. Human population is expected to grow from 7 billion, probably reached late in October, 2011, to 9.3 billion by 2050. Nearly all the growth will occur in those countries least able to support their citizens.

Another major factor is the ever-increasing population shift from rural areas to cities [373]. By 2008, roughly half the world's people lived in urban areas; by 2050, the number is expected to be 70%. Most of the urban growth is in poor nations where the influx is concentrated in unplanned slum areas. Such haphazard growth is overtaxing most governments' ability to provide basic water and sanitation needs. The urbanization trend presents major challenges, but with adequate planning, innovation, and investment, the challenges can be met [34].

The global impacts that humans continue to impose upon this precious little planet will not simply go away or end in 50 years or at the turn of the century. The world of the foreseeable future will be one shaped largely by human influences. Groundwater mining and pollution, climate change, and the extinction of species represent extremely protracted impairments of nature which we and our ancestors will have to live with. In time, natural processes will evolve anew, but that is of little help to humanity in our little window of time. Nor will the consequences end there. Humanity's profound impacts upon the global environment will continue to be felt for hundreds of thousands of years, so much so that many refer to the geologic epoch in which we now live as the Anthropocene.

14.2 Regional Perspectives

What are we going to do? There is no future without water.

— Mateko Mafereka, subsistence farmer in Lesotho

This section provides overviews of recent regional water supply issues and trends around the world. Table 14.1 provides a continental perspective by comparing percent of total global water supply to population. The water-to-population ratio indicates that Africa, Asia, and Europe have an overall deficiency of water while South America and Oceana have an abundance of water relative to their populations.

Table 14.2 lists the top twelve groundwater-using countries along with their estimated renewable groundwater resources and their share of global withdrawals, circa the mid-2000s. Note that countries such as Pakistan, Iran, and Saudi Arabia have exceeded the total renewable groundwater limit, and severe supply problems are almost a given. However, nations such as China and the US, although using only a small percentage of their total renewable groundwater, still have serious water supply problems. Regional data such as these make for interesting comparisons

Table 14.1. Global Water Supply and the Human Population

Continent	Water Supply (Percent of Total)	Population (Percent of Total)	Ratio: Water Supply to Population
Asia	36	60	0.6
South America	26	6	4.3
North America	15	8	1.9
Africa	11	13	0.8
Europe	8	13	0.6
Australia/Oceana	5	1	5.0

Notes: This table compares water supply and human population by continent. The two middle columns show the approximate percent of total global water supply and human population represented by each continent. Source [512].

Table 14.2. Groundwater Resources and Withdrawals

Country	Total Groundwater Withdrawals (km^3)	Total Renewable Groundwater Resources (km^3)	Percent of Global Withdrawals
India	190	419	28.9
United States	110	1,300	16.7
Pakistan	60	55	9.1
China	53	828	8.1
Iran	53	49	8.1
Mexico	25	139	3.8
Saudi Arabia	21	2	3.2
Italy	14	43	2.1
Japan	14	27	2.1
Bangladesh	11	21	1.7
Brazil	8	1,874	1.2
Turkey	8	68	1.2
All others	122	6,457	18.8
Total	658	11,282	100.0

Sources: [144, 471].

but fail to account for vitally important factors such as where water is located relative to where water is needed and how accessible it is [144].

14.2.1 Asia

> *[W]ater scarcity is set to become Asia's defining crisis by mid-century.*
>
> — Brahma Chellaney

Many regard Asia as the most water-stressed continent. Asia contains 60% of the world's population but only 36% of its liquid fresh water, and another 1.4 billion people are expected to be added by 2050. These conditions have already led to increasing dependence upon groundwater and rapidly falling water tables, a clear indication that the resource is being depleted and a water crisis is approaching. Unsustainable groundwater withdrawals and irrigation are the major causes. India, Pakistan, China, and Iran alone account for more than half the world's groundwater use (Table 14.2). Water management and use is highly inefficient, and water pollution continues to be a huge problem [71]. The most severe problem areas are the important grain-producing regions of north China and South Asia.

A. China

China, the country with the world's largest population, 1.34 billion in 2010 according to the National Bureau of Statistics of China, is fast becoming the world's largest economy with over 10 years of near double-digit economic growth and a still expanding population. Unfortunately, like many nations, in its haste to emulate the fundamentally unsustainable life style and economy of the developed nations, China has failed to adequately recognize the need to protect and conserve its most important resources — water, air, soil, and healthy ecosystems [54]. China contains approximately 20% of the world's population but only 7% of its fresh water. As of early 2013, China was facing an annual water supply shortfall of some 50 billion m^3/yr. Factors such as urban expansion, which appropriated more than 860,000 hectares of arable land annually from 1998 to 2006, increasing food consumption, and climate change pose major challenges to China's ability to feed itself [234]. The northern 60% of China is generally dry, the southern 40% wet. Most of the surface and subsurface water in both the north and south is polluted, often severely. About 70% of the population relies on groundwater for drinking, and at least 90% of China's shallow groundwater is polluted. The result is some 60,000 deaths and 190 million illnesses each year [321]. Costs to the economy are estimated at tens of billions of dollars. The State Environmental Protection Administration in 2007 reported that groundwater reserves for 9 out of 10 Chinese cities were polluted or overexploited. Excess extraction of groundwater since 1989 for the cities of Beijing, Tianjin, and Tanggu alone is estimated at more than 600 million m³/yr. Land subsidence is widespread and exceeds 3 meters (10 feet) in some locations. Because China lacks groundwater regulations, overdrafts and pollution continue to be rampant.

The Chinese government has undertaken numerous efforts to address the country's water problems, including a 10-year, $5.5 billion groundwater contamination plan, extensive dam construction, and large desalination plants. The most ambitious project involves a massive $63 billion scheme to transfer some 37 million acre-feet (45 billion m³) of water from three southern river basins to the thirsty north by 2050 [295]. The total economic, environmental, and energy costs of this project render it highly questionable [57].

Example. North China Plain Aquifers

The **North China Plain**, which occupies much of eastern China from Beijing south to Shanghai, is a vital economic and agricultural area which produces half the wheat and a third of the corn for China. Groundwater supplies some 70% of the water. Two aquifers underlie the North China Plain, the upper is replenishable, but is depleted in many areas, forcing increased pumping of the lower, fossil (nonreplenishable) aquifer. For over 30 years, water needs in this area have been met by mining groundwater, a temporary fix at best. The North China Plain contained an estimated 3.6 million water supply wells at the end of 1996. A 1997 study found 99,900 wells dry and abandoned, and another 221,900 new wells drilled [55]. The water table is being lowered at rates of 1-3 m/yr (3-10 ft/yr) under parts of the Plain. The water table in the Beijing area has dropped 20 to 40 meters and 45% (62,000 km²) of the entire plain has seen a water table drop of 10 meters or more from 1960 levels. Head has decreased up to 110 meters in the deep aquifer and some 55% of the deep groundwater table of the Plain is now below sea level, according to the China Geological Survey [246]. Total groundwater overdrafts exceed 4 billion m³/yr.

B. South Asia

The population of South Asia is expected to grow from 1.6 billion in 2011 to 2.4 billion by 2050. At the same time, some projections anticipate a reduction of nearly 25% in South Asia's wheat yield due to global warming.

India contains some 16% of the world's population but has only 4% of the world's liquid freshwater. Eighty percent of India's annual rainfall occurs during the monsoon season when floods cause an average $335 million of damage annually. India's grain production needs to double by 2050. India ranks second to China in population but 108th in per capita water availability. It is projected to overtake China as the world's most populous country by 2020. The amount of water per person in India in 2009 was well under half what it was in 1990. Two-thirds of India's 1.2 billion people already lack clean water and half its morbidity is related to water problems. The cost of inadequate sanitation was estimated to cost India some US$53.8 billion (6.4% of India's GDP) in 2006 [439].

India's water challenges are formidable [52]. It withdraws more groundwater than any other nation (Table 14.2) and 60% of its irrigation depends on groundwater. Northern India and surrounding areas have lost more groundwater storage than any other region, a net volumetric depletion of 1,361 km^3 of a world total of 4,534 km^3 (GRACE satellite example, Section 13.4.2) [224]. More than 25 million water wells, most hundreds of meters deep, have replaced the traditional shallow wells and are lowering water tables through most of the country, including the major food-producing areas of Punjab and Haryana. Aquifer overpumping began in earnest during the 1950s when modern drilling techniques and deep-well turbine pumps replaced the traditional shallow dug wells [278, 303]. Soon millions of deep "tube" wells were in operation. Indian farmers compete to dig deeper wells than neighbors causing water table declines of up to 6 meters (20 feet) per year in areas such as North Garat. Satellite gravity measurements in the mid-2000s indicated a net annual loss of some 54 km^3 of groundwater over a 2.7 million km^2 region centered on New Delhi. This region includes the world's most intensely irrigated area with a population of some 600 million — and the groundwater withdrawals are expected to continue increasing [212]. Total groundwater withdrawals probably exceed 200 km^3/yr (Table 14.2). New wells use modified petroleum-drilling methods to seek water 1,000 meters (3,300 feet) or more below the surface. In some states, half of all electricity use is to pump groundwater. In Tamil Nadu, home to 62 million Indians, 95% of the wells on small farms are dry and irrigated land has fallen by

50% in 10 years. In many areas, drinking water must be trucked in. Annual decline in the water table for India's western and southern states has been averaging some 20 cm/yr since 1995 [246]. Although some unexploited groundwater remains in eastern India, most groundwater is being mined and is not replaceable, posing a grave threat to the country's future. Regulation of the drilling has been poor to nonexistent.

The Himalayan Mountains with their many glaciers that feed the great river systems of Asia are justly known as "the water towers of Asia." But the glaciers are receding as increasing temperatures and deposition of soot and dust accelerates their melting. In the short term, this means more water, and more severe flooding, during high-flow periods. The changing climate is also producing more intense but less reliable rains during the three-month monsoon season and reduced snowfall during the winter. China's plans to place large dams on the headwaters of rivers flowing into India are a growing source of tension between these nations. At the same time, India's plans to dam rivers upon which Pakistan and Bangladesh depend threaten conflict with those nations [2].

But, like China, the Indian government is leaning toward a reliance on huge projects to "solve" its water problems. The proposed, on again-off again, $115-200 billion **Interlinking of the Rivers Project** (or, **National River Linking Project**) would move potentially four times more water than China's massive south-to-north water transfer. The entire project envisions linking 37 rivers with some 12,500 kilometers of canals to move some 178 km^3 of water from eastern India to dry western states. Benefits include flood mitigation, providing water (hence improved food production) to southern and western India, hydroelectric power generation, inland navigation routes, and employment opportunities. It has proven highly controversial and many Indian states are opposed, noting such problems as the displacement and resettlement of hundreds of thousands of people, endangering relations with Bangladesh and Pakistan, and numerous severe environmental impacts including increased salt and pollutant content of rivers downstream from irrigated areas, damage to fisheries and coastal ecology, deforestation, and soil erosion.

Some parts of Pakistan, especially its cities, also rely heavily on groundwater and withdrawals of around 60 km^3/yr probably exceed the country's total recharge (Table 14.2). Pakistan's annual per capita water availability has dropped below 1,000 m^3, less than 18% its value in 1960 and about 10% that of the US, and continues to decline [179]. Most of the available water is heavily contaminated. The USGS has been working on water-related issues with Pakistan since 1953 but a lack of data, treatment facilities, good management, funding, political stability, and regulations seriously hampers progress. Both India and Pakistan have allowed their water infrastructure to deteriorate and millions of gallons are lost each day.

Like India, millions of wells have been dug or drilled in Bangladesh. Most of Bangladesh sits upon the low-lying delta of the Ganges and Brahmaputra Rivers where rising sea levels, arsenic-laden groundwater (Section 10.4.8B), and poverty pose great challenges. Withdrawals in this region are expected to increase, even with serious efforts to reduce groundwater overdraft.

C. Middle East

Water's role has always been a vital one in the Middle East, and will be even more so in the future of this most volatile of Earth's many water-poor areas. What water is there has been severely depleted by overuse and polluted by salt, sewage, and other contaminants. Ecosystems dependent on water have been destroyed as the human population and its water demands have grown. Irrigation of wheat has been banned from many areas [55]. Satellite data indicated a loss of 144 km^3 (117 million acre-feet) of total freshwater storage from January 2003 through December 2009 in a large area of the Tigris-Euphrates drainage basin and western Iran. Of that, 90 km^3 (73 million acre-feet) was due to groundwater withdrawals, much of it during a 2007 drought. The region is expected to get dryer with climate change. Only India experiences a faster rate of groundwater depletion [420]. The fresh surface and groundwater available in the Jordan River basin is woefully inadequate to meet the needs of the existing population, and Israelis, Jordanians, and Palestinians all claim water rights [201]. Understandably, water has often been among the most contentious of the many issues which need to be negotiated in that troubled region.

Example: The Mountain, Coastal, and Gaza Aquifers

Part of the reason for the Six-Day War in 1967 was Jordan's proposed diversion of the Jordan River. As a result of that war, Israel gained control of two Palestinian territories, the West Bank and the Gaza Strip, and increased the water resources they control by about 50% (Figure 14.1) [72]. The **Mountain aquifer** underlies most of the terrain west of the Jordan River and the Dead Sea. The aquifer is recharged by

---

rainfall on the West Bank. The Mountain aquifer actually contains three separate aquifers: groundwater west of the drainage (and groundwater) divide flows west, the eastern aquifer flows east to the Jordan River and Dead Sea, and the northwest aquifer flows north-northwest. The largest and most important is the western aquifer which provides the Jerusalem-Tel Aviv area with some 360 million m^3/yr, of which Israelis have been using about 94.5% and Palestinians 5.6% [3]. Israel has withdrawn about 85% of the aquifer's annual yield, seriously depleting the groundwater. In the West Bank, 2.4 million Palestinians experience serious water shortages and drilling of new wells is severely restricted by Israel. An Israeli-Palestinian Joint Water Committee does exist but its activities and proposals appear to be dominated by Israeli interests [351]. The results have included productivity and employment losses for Palestinian farmers [253]. Following the 2006 electoral victory of the militant Hamas party in the West Bank, the US imposed sanctions cutting off water and wastewater treatment aid, worsening already bad conditions there. Over 80% of West Bank communities lack sewer connections with waste going directly to open trenches and riverbeds. Average water consumption is 8 to 10 gallons per day, a third of WHO's recommended minimum.

Between the Mountain aquifer and the Mediterranean Sea lies the **Coastal aquifer** (Figure 14.1). It has also been depleted and recharge efforts are underway. In the Gaza Strip, about 1.5 million people are entirely dependent on the **Gaza aquifer**, a shallow sandy aquifer which slopes west toward the sea. By the year 2000, overpumping had so stressed the aquifer that its water was considered unfit for human consumption due to high levels of salt, boron, and nitrate [413]. Plans to build a desalination plant in Gaza were withdrawn following the murder of US contractors in 2003 and the rise of the Hamas political party. As a result, thousands of additional illegal wells were drilled, further depleting the aquifer and accelerating seawater intrusion [381]. The Gaza aquifer is recharged by rainfall (at estimated rates of 75 to 125 million m^3/yr), subsurface flow from Israel, and leakage from pipes and irrigation, but withdrawal rates far exceed this recharge. Both

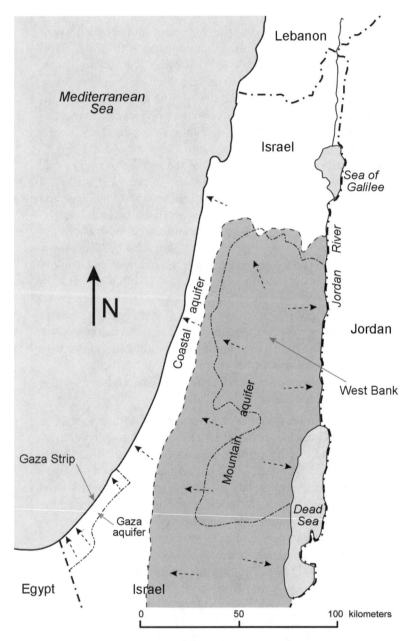

Figure 14.1. Map showing locations of the Mountain, Coastal, and Gaza aquifers in Israel. The darker shaded area is the Mountain aquifer. Dashed arrows indicate general flow of groundwater.

> Israeli and Palestinian water experts have been willing to cooperate to alleviate the dreadful conditions in Gaza and the West Bank, but political roadblocks have prevented progress [36].

Prior to the 1980s, arid Saudi Arabia was largely dependent upon imported grain. Concerns such as a possible grain embargo similar to the Arab oil embargo on the 1970s, led the Saudis to turn their attention and their oil-drilling technologies to a large "fossil aquifer," the Disi aquifer, lying deep beneath the sands of Saudi Arabia and Jordan [246]. Soon irrigated fields sprang up (Figure 14.2) and wheat production soared from 140,000 tons in 1980 to 4,100,000 in 1992. But fossil aquifers have almost no sustainable yield and by 2008, depletion of the aquifer caused the Saudis to begin phasing out wheat production, leaving their 30 million people once again dependent on imported grain [55, 57]. The Saudi's continue to withdraw large amounts of water from the aquifer and Jordan also plans to increase its extractions, another potentially contentious issue concerning a transboundary water resource.

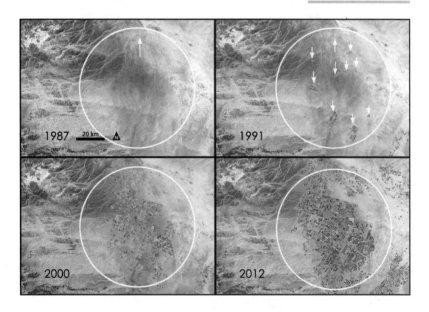

Figure 14.2. Satellite image showing the increase in irrigated croplands in the Wadi As-Sirhan Basin of northern Saudi Arabia from 1987 to 2012. Arrows identify the location of small, scattered areas of irrigation in 1987 and 1991.

At the south end of the Arabian peninsula lies Yemen, population 23 million and growing at 3% per year, one of the most water-stressed nations on Earth. Yemen relies almost entirely on groundwater and 19 of its 21 major aquifers are being depleted. Water wells in Sanaa, a city with a population over two million, exceed 1,000 meters in depth, water levels are dropping from 6 to 20 m/yr, and tap water is available only once every few days. Virtually no control of water exploitation exists and waste and pollution are excessive. Due to groundwater depletion, most grain must be imported and some 60% of Yemen's children lack adequate nutrition [57].

The great and growing gap between freshwater needs and availability in the Middle East, a gap that could quintuple by 2050, cannot be ignored much longer without potentially devastating consequences. Much better management and new water sources will be essential. According to a World Bank study [440], desalination using concentrated solar power is the most promising source for new water in the region.

14.2.2 Africa

The UN Population Division estimates that half of all population growth over the next 40 years will be in Africa where the 2010 population was 1,022,234,000 [396]. Many experts consider Earth's most water-stressed region to consist of a broad band extending from Morocco eastward across northern Africa, through the Middle East, and on to Iran. The World Bank notes that this region already has the lowest quantity of fresh water on Earth and is expected to experience growing water shortages resulting from climate change [415]. The UN estimates that the cost of water pollution and over-extraction in north Africa and the Middle East ranges from $9 billion to nearly $14 billion annually [396].

Others would add to the water-critical list the densely populated Sahel region where the Sahara Desert grudgingly gives way to grasslands to the south. In all of Sub-Saharan Africa, which could potentially account for almost 80% of world population growth by 2100, nearly 65% of the urban population lacks piped-in water [306] and about 80% of rural water supplies comes from groundwater [431]. Most must seek their water from standpipes and storage units or must purchase it from neighbors who are connected to a water system [446].

Ironically, in most of Africa, groundwater is an underutilized resource and its intelligent use could greatly improve lives. About 60% of global unused cropland is in Africa and a total of some 660,000 km^3 of groundwater is believed to underlie Africa [248]. Only about 5% of

Sub-Saharan Africa's cropland is irrigated, compared to some 55% in South Asia. Africa's water problems are a consequence of human population growth, poverty, unstable governments, lack of serviceable infrastructure, ecological degradation, and poor water management. Too many plans to aid Africa have been poorly thought-out and designed, from manual pumps which break down to large irrigation or tree-plantation schemes of little benefit to small farmers.

Large corporations and other nations, most notably China, are currently pursuing Africa's resources, often buying large tracts of land for megascale agricultural projects with little regard for local populations that depend upon the water and land [161, 304]. As Bob Geldof, founder of a large private-equity fund focusing on Africa, has stated "In the end, we all have to go to Africa. They have what we need" [306]. The best hope for Africa's people may lie in small-scale, grassroots-oriented, water-conserving, and sustainable land-use practices such as interspersing food crops with trees and utilizing traditional rainwater harvesting techniques (sections 13.2.3E and 13.2.6B) [182, 325].

Example: The Nubian Sandstone Aquifer System

The **Nubian Sandstone aquifer system** (#13 on Figure 8.1) is one of the world's largest aquifers and an excellent example of a large transboundary groundwater resource. It underlies perhaps 2,000,000 km^2 of the Sahara Desert, including most of Egypt, northeastern Chad, southeastern Libya, and northwestern Sudan [369]. This is the source of the Sahara's many famed oases. The aquifer complex consists of a thick sequence of sandstones with some overlying carbonates to the northeast. Numerous shale interbeds are present and much of the groundwater is confined. The lower regions contain saline water. The sediment was derived from Precambrian highlands to the south and ranges in age from Paleozoic to Cenozoic. Groundwater flows very slowly to the north. The saturated thickness may exceed 3,000 meters in places. The last time the aquifer received significant recharge was some 14,000 to 38,000 years ago when a moist pluvial climate existed in the Sahara region. Most of its water is much older, perhaps as much as a million years. Due to the arid climate — less than 5 millimeters of rainfall annually — essentially no recharge occurs today. The Nubian Sandstone aquifer system contains a

---

vast amount of water, perhaps 150,000 km³ of exploitable water. In some areas it may be capable of providing water for agriculture and urban use for a few centuries.

The aquifer is being pumped heavily in places by both Egypt and Libya. Egypt generally floods its fields, evaporating in one day water which required decades to accumulate. Libya's **Great Man-made River Project** is one of the world's largest groundwater mining and transfer projects. Libya is an arid country with some 80% of its population and agriculture concentrated in the northern strip along the Mediterranean coast. Wells, most over 500 meters deep, withdraw water from Nubian Sandstone aquifer units lying beneath the barren desert in the extremely arid southern part of the country. The water is carried in huge 4-meter-diameter pipelines hundreds of kilometers north to thirsty cities and crops in the coastal zone. The $25 billion dollar project anticipates withdrawing 6,180,000 m³/day (2.26 km³/yr) for at least another 50 years.

Although this aquifer system receives no recharge, in a situation such as this, the benefits of extracting nonrenewable groundwater are generally considered to far outweigh the costs [185]. Possible problems include the high cost of pumping deep water and moving it over large distances, salt buildup in croplands after years of irrigation, and the various hydrologic impacts of groundwater mining. Already, large cones of depression have formed, and upward and lateral migration of saline water is a potential threat in places. Many springs and oases have gone dry, and need to be replaced by wells as the water table declines. Impacts of heavy groundwater extraction on neighboring countries or districts need to be more carefully assessed and legal considerations addressed. The four nations sharing the Nubian Sandstone aquifer have sought to create a regional aquifer development strategy with the aid of such organizations as the Center for the Environment and Development for Arab Regions and Europe (CEDARE), the International Fund for Agricultural Development, and the Islamic Development Bank.

14.2.3 Europe

In the year 2000, the European Union approved a Water Framework Directive which requires member states to protect, restore, and enhance both surface and ground water. An additional directive in December 2006 addressed the chemical status of groundwater. Europe has made important strides toward providing oversight of its water supplies, but the ubiquitous problems of funding, environmental threats, and incomplete or inconsistent data remain. Europe's most significant impact on world water supplies is the indirect importation of water via imports of food and other products which often come from countries where water is scarce. This is true for all nations which must import much of their food.

Some 70% of the population is wholly or in part dependent on groundwater for drinking supplies. Nitrogen fertilizer, pesticides, chlorinated hydrocarbons, heavy metals, and increasing acidity are the major pollutants in groundwater. Many decades of industrialization have left more than a half-million known contaminated soil sites in Europe; the total number may be 3.5 million [470]. **Acidification** of groundwater is a problem in northern Europe. It results when sulfates and nitrates from fossil fuel combustion and fertilizers cause the pH to reach or exceed 5.5.

Although total withdrawals began decreasing in 1990, many areas, especially in eastern Europe, are still experiencing serious groundwater overdrafts resulting in salt-water intrusion, wetland damages, and related problems. Boron contamination and salt-water intrusion due to water table declines are a growing problem in most coastal areas, especially along the Mediterranean [413]. Droughts and water shortages are recurring problems in many European countries, especially in coastal areas. In Spain, groundwater has been so severely depleted, it is illegal to pump groundwater in many areas. Increases in tourism and irrigation are further depleting water resources. Global warming is expected to result in increased ecosystem vulnerability in Europe, including a general decline of precipitation in the Mediterranean region [346].

14.2.4 North America: Canada and United States

Canada is water-rich. Its vast boreal forest is the most water-rich area on Earth. Yet even here, agriculture, timbering, mining, extraction of fossil fuels (including the Athabasca tar sands), water diversions, and dams threaten the freshwater hydrologic cycle and the ecosystems which depend upon it [425].

Although water is plentiful across most of the northern US, water shortages are present and growing across much of its southern half. The southwestern US has been the fastest growing part of the country. The collapse of the economic/housing bubble in 2008 reduced or reversed the population influx in many areas, but most expect growth to continue for the region. The southwest is the most water-poor part of the country. Vast quantities of groundwater accumulated in the western US during wet glacial episodes of the past. This nonrenewable water was mined profligately to support irrigated croplands and population growth [90, 160, 317, 326, 432]. The southwestern US, including the Central Valley of California (Section 8.8.4), is facing a very strong probability of and increase in severe droughts and water shortages which will severely impact agriculture and the economy. Faced with these challenges, many agencies are proposing costly large-scale pipelines and related projects which are likely to further exacerbate the problems [128, 495].

Water problems also afflict much of the south-central and southeastern US. Extended droughts such as that of 2006-2009, are likely to become more common in these areas. As in much of the southwestern US, water supply data (hence water planning) for the southeast is based upon unusually wet years, and a warming climate will likely exacerbate the drying trend [305]. Many southeastern farmers, with political encouragement, are turning to irrigation using groundwater resulting in declining water tables.

Since the 1970s, conservation efforts in the United States have significantly improved its water productivity and numerous agencies, especially city governments, are focusing on continued productivity increases. Despite these efforts, it continues to lead all nations in per capita water use. Overall US groundwater overdrafts exceed recharge rates by at least 25%. One estimate is that more than 365 km^3 of non-renewable water was mined from just five major US groundwater systems — the High Plains aquifer, San Joaquin Valley of California, south central Arizona, the Dakota aquifer, and the Atlantic Coastal Plain — during the twentieth century (Table 8.2) [278]. This is clearly not sustainable. The lack of a comprehensive water strategy, aging water infrastructure, budget cutbacks, climate change, and population growth and distribution are among the water-related issues requiring immediate attention in the US.

14.2.5 Latin America

Dramatic declines in the water table have been documented in Mexico, including Mexico City (Section 12.3.3) and the agricultural states of Guanajuato and Sonora. Some 60% of the groundwater extracted in Mexico is endangered by overexploitation [58, 246] and the quality of public water in Mexico is notoriously suspect. One result of this is that, for many years, Mexicans have been the world's largest consumers of soda pop (248 liters per capita in 2011). Mexican bottled water sales are expected to skyrocket from $9 billion in 2011 to $13 billion in 2015 [67].

Most of South America is rich in both surface and ground water. This does not mean it has few water problems. Most nations lack strong regulations and the resources to manage water efficiently. Dam construction, mining, poor farming practices, pollution, and deforestation are among the land uses which threaten water resources. Even in the vast watery Amazon basin, freshwater ecosystems are showing troubling signs of severe and escalating degradation [66]. Data from the last 40 years indicate an ongoing decline in the average rainfall in the southern Amazon. Such findings, combined with serious droughts in 2005 and 2010 from which the Amazon rainforest has been unable to fully recover, suggests the basic functioning of Amazonian ecosystems is being impaired [334].

Millions of people near the Andes Mountain chain rely heavily on melting snow and ice, and warming temperatures are rapidly reducing this vital water supply (Figure 8.31). Observations indicate the melting rate of Andean glaciers tripled from about 1950 to 2000 [356]. Governments generally pursue rapid economic growth and welcome companies which often appropriate and pollute the fresh water that villages and farms have relied upon for decades. Violent conflicts are increasing throughout most of the continent as mining companies and various corporations hasten to exploit the resources of this rapidly developing region [368].

Example: Guarani Aquifer System

One of the world's most important aquifers, the **Guarani aquifer system**, underlies some 1.2 million km² of Brazil, Argentina, Paraguay, and Uruguay (#8 on Figure 8.1). Currently, it provides water to some 15 million people. The Gurarani appears to consist primarily of sandstone, some 90% of which is overlain and confined by basaltic lava flows. Recharge, some 166 km³/yr, is by infiltration into outcrops of the sandstone and through the overlying rocks. The volume of fresh water in the Guarani is estimated at roughly 40,000 km³. Its potential value as a water source is enormous — enough to provide 360 million people with 300 L/day/person for a very long time, but exploitation in a few localities has already caused well interferences and water table declines [426]. Much discussion about this aquifer has focused on political and social issues involving discord between international organizations,

---

mainly the World Bank; local countries and civil groups; and fears of privatization or militarism. Numerous conspiracy theories have been generated. On August 2, 2010, the four nations who share the aquifer signed an "Agreement on the Guarani Aquifer" in which they agreed to cooperate with each other regarding the aquifer while still maintaining sovereign rights. While generally weak and unspecific, it still represents a rare step in international law towards a more rational approach to transboundary groundwater resources.

F. Australia

Australia is the world's driest inhabited continent and water problems never seem far away. The 400,000 mi^2 Murray-Darling drainage basin is Australia's major food-growing region, and about 40% of its water is provided by groundwater. Heavy reliance on taxpayer-subsidized irrigation in the Murray-Darling basin has proven very costly. From 1997 to 2009, this region, and much of the country, was experiencing a devastating drought. In 2002, for the first time in recorded history, the Murray River delivered no water to the sea. Unprecedented restrictions on water use were imposed and many farmers were without irrigation water [165]. Over 10,000 families abandoned farming and billions of dollars of agricultural production was lost. Bushfires and dust storms increased. Then in late 2010 and early 2011, the rains came and flooding, mostly in Queensland, produced a shallow inland sea covering an area larger than Germany and France combined. Over 35,000 homes were inundated and 35 people lost their lives. Australia, unlike the US, assigns water licenses, not rights, but, like the western US, it had overallocated its water. Some feel that Australia's continuing expenditures on engineering solutions, such as additional water storage and infrastructure for irrigation, would be better directed to rain-fed agriculture. Having learned from the disasters of the last 14 years, the government is now aggressively pursuing water conservation strategies, water recycling, desalination, and ecosystem restoration. For example, the Murray-Darling basin plan, adopted on November 22, 2012, is considered an excellent model for balancing agricultural, environmental, and drinking water needs [123]. In Australia as elsewhere, it is likely that higher temperatures and less precipitation associated with climate change will increase water stresses in the future which possibly may lead to increased reliance on nonrenewable groundwater in the near future [178].

14.3 Challenges

To survive in the world we have transformed, we must
learn to think in a new way. As never before, the future of each
depends on the good of all.

— from a statement of 100 Nobel Peace Prize laureates,
issued 6 December, 2001.

If you don't know how to fix it, please stop breaking it.

— Severn Suzuki (age 12) and
the Environmental Children's Organization in an address
to the 1992 Earth Summit in Rio de Janeiro

14.3.1 Megascale Problems

There is no historical precedent simply because the en-
tire world has never before been so threatened.

— Lester R. Brown

Looking ahead is always a tricky business. But we must try if we are to avoid risking calamity. Despite the magnitude of the task, we do still have the ability to foresee and to forestall the challenges that loom before us. The question is whether or not sufficient numbers of us will use that ability and rise to the challenge. It will require hard work, sound knowledge, wisdom, cooperation, and some major changes in thought and policy.

Thus far, despite the mind-boggling population increase of the past century, we have avoided massive crop failures, political and social collapse, widespread warfare, and other major catastrophes which could terminate civilization as we know it. But we have done so at ever increasing cost to the basic resource support systems upon which we all ultimately rely. Fresh water is not the only victim of overuse and abuse. It needs to be viewed within the context of the many other potential "crises" now confronting humanity. Soils, fisheries, and entire ecosystems from the oceans to the world's forests are under assault as human population and demands on Earth's life-sustaining resources continue to accelerate. The result is a global problem of unprecedented magnitude and most trends indicate it can only worsen, especially when such factors as climate change, ecological impairment, frequently adverse political policies, unsustainable economic priorities, public apathy, and population growth are factored in. In 2012, the UN estimated that by 2030, the world will require at least 30% more water, 45% more energy, and

50% more food with the needs continuing to increase to 2050 and beyond [401].

Over the past century or so, as the world economy has increased some 20-fold, dozens of forms of **megascale** environmental and resource problems have been converging, altering the very chemistry and behavior of Earth's atmosphere, hydrosphere, biosphere, and outer geosphere. The impacts are weakening Earth's ecosystems and reducing their ability to cope with ongoing assaults, threatening a global collapse [57]. At the same time, human interactions have become increasingly complex, and increasingly reliant upon ever-growing consumption of energy and resources. Under these conditions, political and economic stability tend to decline. Possible solutions to the dilemmas posed likewise become ever more complex and difficult to implement [159, 568]. Such trends cannot be sustained in a finite world. Some see these megatrends generating a massive disequilibrium which can lead to both environmental and governmental collapse [97]. This is sometimes called the "panarchy theory" and it applies to social as well as natural systems.

A related approach views the entire Earth as an organism. James Lovelock's Gaia concept considers Earth a self-regulating superorganism which requires a holistic approach based more upon observation and experimentation than upon computer models and traditional studies focused upon a specific science [247].

14.3.2 Leadership and Attitudes

It is simply unimaginable that American politics as we know it today will deliver the transformative changes needed.

— Gus Speth

Massive collapse of human institutions and/or natural support systems on a global scale is not inevitable but the possibility is real and could occur in the very near future. Major changes are plainly underway in our planet's life-support systems which threaten national and international security. Some monumental changes in the business-as-usual approaches to political, economic, and environmental issues will be required if the challenges are to be met. Unfortunately, it seems apparent that very few leaders have grasped this. Endless studies and conferences have come and gone while political leaders do little more than agree to have more studies and conferences, and reaffirm pleasant-sounding intentions. For example, virtually all governments have thus far failed to address the looming issue of water scarcity. No nation has yet successfully addressed the problem of groundwater depletion, and most haven't even made a meaningful attempt. Meanwhile, the sustainable yield of aquifers continues to be outpaced ever more rapidly by increases in water consumption. If this doesn't change soon, the consequences of the groundwater issue alone could include dramatic increases in hunger, poverty, governmental instability, and conflict.

Groundwater problems cannot be realistically viewed or solved in isolation. The challenges which must be met involve not just water resources but also entire ecosystems, food supplies, energy, economics, life styles, social conditions, moral values, and so much more. Humanity faces an impending "perfect storm" of simultaneous global-scale problems: depletion of multiple natural resources, deteriorating ecosystems, unprecedented climate change, overpopulation, frail economies, cultural clashes, the threat of wars — including nuclear, to name a few. Thus far, most governments have failed miserably in their feeble attempts to deal with these issues. The experts (if there are any) do not agree on what may happen next, but they do agree that time is not on our side and large-scale efforts to address these issues must begin immediately [57, 159, 226, 372].

The more optimistic see an "intensification" of agriculture and renewed economic growth resulting from increases in the working-age population and human ingenuity. New technologies will arise as the necessity grows and megascale disasters will be avoided. Others find hope in the thousands of small movements around the world focused on social and economic justice, peace, environment, community, sustainability, and self-help.

The more pessimistic note that, among far too many people, factors such as apathy, denial, intolerance, greed, and ignorance are dominant and will continue to dictate most human actions. Destructive and unsustainable practices, including the exploitation of people and the depletion of ecosystems and resources, are likely to continue. The growing, globalized market-oriented system thus created continues to externalize and ignore the real costs of environmental degradation and resource depletion. Those who profit from such activities exert great influence and most will use their power to fight any change which threatens their control. But never-ending material growth, like cancer, cannot be maintained on a finite world and will ultimately destroy that which it feeds upon. The longer we stubbornly cling to a consumption-oriented, resource-depleting path, the more precarious our position becomes. It is becoming ever more apparent that such a system lacks resilience and cannot be sustained.

14.4 Solutions

As human beings, our greatness lies not so much in being able to remake the world — that is the myth of the "atomic age" — as in being able to remake ourselves.

— Mahatma Gandhi (1869-1948)

This all sounds very bad — doomsday at the doorstep. But that need not be. Civilization's greatest accomplishments have often come during times of great stress. Occasionally, entire nations have awakened and roused themselves in time to meet enormous challenges. This time, the threats could be terminal and solutions will require many nations acting together. Nothing short of a radical change in how we live, act, think, and do business will suffice to prevent the crises from becoming catastrophes on a scale never before experienced. Solutions lie in embracing, on a large scale, a truly responsible and holistic approach. Hard work, knowledge, adaptation, and fundamental change will be necessary. As noted previously in this book, solid science, conservation, good government, efficiency, education, and participation by local people are needed. Many approaches and specific actions which can contribute to solving our various water crises have been enunciated throughout this book. The ideas and perspectives on how to deal with these complex and unprecedented challenges come from many sources, only some of which are included in the references. Individuals whose thoughts I have found to be especially valuable include Lester Brown, Peter Gleick, Gus Speth, David Brower, Donald R. Coates, and Ralph Nader, among many others. Some keynote thoughts for countering the groundwater problems and negative megatrends now threatening humanity are briefly summarized below:

1. If the challenges facing humanity are to be met, sound science must be incorporated into government policies far more effectively than is currently the case. Political expediency must be replaced by policies based on scientific realities, moral principles, and ethical responsibility.

2. We cannot afford to continue neglecting groundwater at professional meetings, in water resource discussions, and in government policy.

3. Utilize a holistic approach. For example, groundwater planning and policies should always consider related factors such as surface waters, land use, and human need.

4. A new water conservation ethic, a "blue revolution" in the words of Cynthia Barnett [22], needs to be nurtured and developed, especially in water-wasteful nations such as the US.

5. Everywhere, the critical importance of freshwater resources needs to be promoted to all people by the media, schools, water professionals, utility companies, governments, and whatever other means are possible.

6. In many cases, the procedures we adapt must be restorative, not merely sustainable. Due to the damages already incurred, it will often be necessary "to put back more than we take" if we are to meet our responsibilities to current and future generations [8].

7. The true costs of all industrial activities should be internalized — the value of all affected resources, including land, and the total, long-term costs of all pollution and other impacts should be included in the prices charged.

8. Economic policies must change to promote conservation, resource productivity, and sustainability rather than consumerism and gross domestic product [371, 372].

9. Most governments need to adapt major policy changes NOW; slow, incremental change is insufficient and irresponsible.

10. Stronger collaborations between developed and developing nations are needed to meet the challenges involved in providing water, food, and energy for millions of additional people without further damaging the life-supporting natural environment [167].

11. Policies need to incorporate preparations for climate change, including prospects of rising sea level, ecologic and economic impacts, and more extreme weather events such as drought, flooding, violent storms, and heat waves.

12. Revise tax codes to encourage the most benign technologies and discourage polluting, unsustainable technologies. A worldwide tax on carbon emissions and other harmful side effects would be a good start [57].

13. In much of the world, the influence of money in determining governmental leaders and policies must be eliminated or greatly reduced in favor of democratic representation and intelligent, science-based decision making.

Unbridled growth, be it of human population, economies, or material commodities, has led to depletion of our most precious resources — biodiversity, fresh water, and soil. The assumptions upon which many of today's policies and economies are based are often self-serving fantasies and need to be rejected. The necessary changes will almost certainly involve major changes in life style for highly consumptive societies, infrastructure improvements, technical innovations, restructuring of financial systems, and so on. These transformations can have highly positive impacts upon both individual and societal happiness and well-being. Humanity can continue to grow in more satisfying ways such as knowledge, wisdom, and the joy that comes from helping others. Perhaps only a well-informed moral or ethical approach, incorporating a concern for, and an awareness of, the impacts of our individual and collective behavior upon others and upon future generations, has a chance of success. In reaching for a higher, more responsible, and more advanced form of society, a more rewarding and enriching future than could ever result from material consumption and growth may await.

———————————

Appendix A

Abbreviations, Acronyms, Prefixes, and Symbols Used in This Book

Abbreviations and Acronyms and Their Meanings

A	area
ASCE	American Society of Civil Engineers
ASTM	American Society for Testing and Materials
BTEX	benzene, toluene, ethyl benzene, xylene
btu	British thermal unit
C	often represents a constant value for use in math equations
C	Centigrade or Celsius
c	centi- (prefix; 0.010×)
cal	calories
CAP	corrective action plan
cap	capita (person)
CERCLA	Comprehensive Environmental Response, Compensation, and Liability Act ("Superfund" Act)
cfs	cubic feet per second
CI	contour interval
cm	centimeters
cm^2	square centimeters
cm^3	cubic centimeters
D, d	often used in formulas to indicate distance
DNAPL	dense nonaqueous phase liquid

EPA	US Environmental Protection Agency
EU	European Union
F	Fahrenheit
ft	feet
ft^2	square feet
ft^3	cubic feet
g	grams
gal	gallons
GIS	geographic information system
gpd	gallons per day
gpm	gallons per minute
GRACE	Gravity Recovery and Climate Experiment
H, h	hydraulic head or height
hr	hours
i	hydraulic gradient
in	inches
K	hydraulic conductivity
k	kilo- (prefix; 1000×)
kg	kilograms
km	kilometers
km^2	square kilometers
km^3	cubic kilometers
kwh	kilowatt-hours
L	liters

L, l	often used in formulas to indicate length	S	siemens, a unit of electrical conductance; in hydrogeology, storativity of an aquifer
LD50	lethal dose for 50% of the individuals in a group of organisms		
		s	seconds
LNAPL	light nonaqueous phase liquid	SI	*System Internationalle* (international or metric system of measurement)
m	meters		
m²	square meters	T	often indicates transmissivity in hydrogeology
m³	cubic meters		
MCL	maximum contaminant level	T, t	time
		TCE	trichloroethene
mg	milligrams	TDS	total dissolved solids
MGDs	Millennium Development Goals	TPH	total petroleum hydrocarbons
mi	miles	UK	United Kingdom
mi²	square miles	UN	United Nations
mi³	cubic miles	UNEP	United Nations Environmental Program
min	minute		
mL	milliliters	UNESCO	United Nations Educational, Scientific, and Cultural Organization
mm	millimeters		
MTBE	methyl tertiary butyl ether		
μm	micrometer, micron	UNICEF	United Nations Children's Fund
μS	microseimens		
NAFTA	North American Free Trade Agreement	US	United States
		USAID	United States Agency for International Development
NAPL	nonaqueous phase liquid		
NASA	National Aeronautics and Space Administration	USGS	United States Geological Survey
nd	no date (used if a reference source provides no date of publication)	UST	underground storage tank
		V	volume
		v	velocity
NGO	non-governmental organization	VOC	volatile organic compound/chemical
OECD	Organization for Economic Cooperation and Development	vs.	versus
		WaSH	Water, Sanitation, and Health
P	porosity		
PAHs	polycyclic aromatic hydrocarbons	WHO	World Health Organization
PCBs	polychlorinated biphenyls	WWF	World Water Forum
ppb	parts per billion	yr	year
ppm	parts per million	%	percent
PVC	polyvinylchloride	3D	three-dimensional
Q	quantity, volume, discharge		

Common Prefixes

p	pico- (trillionth part, 10^{-12})		c	centi- (hundredth part, 10^{-2})
n	nano- (billionth part, 10^{-9})		k	kilo- (thousandfold, 10^{3})
μ	micro- (millionth part, 10^{-6})		M	mega- (millionfold, 10^{6})
m	milli- (thousandth part, 10^{-3})		G	giga- (billionfold, 10^{9})

Major Symbols

°	thermal or geometric degree symbol		%	percent symbol
/	per; relationships between variables		▽	water table

Appendix B

Conversion Table for Units Used in This Book

Linear Measure
1 foot = 12 inches
1 mile = 5280 feet
1 kilometer = 1000 meters = 10^3 meters
1 millimeter = 0.001 meter = 10^{-3} meters

Area Measure
1 square mile = 640 acres
1 acre = 43,650 square feet
1 square kilometer = 100 hectares

Volume Measure
1 cubic foot = 1,728 cubic inches = 7.48 gallons
1 liter = 0.001 cubic meter = 1,000 milliliters
1 cubic centimeter = ~1 milliliter
1 cubic meter = 1,000,000 cubic centimeters = 1,000 liters
1 acre-foot = 325,851 gallons = 43,560 cubic feet

Weights and Masses
1 short ton = 2,000 pounds
1 metric ton (tonne) = 1,000 kilograms

English-Metric Conversions
1 inch = 25.4 millimeters = 2.54 centimeters
1 foot = 0.3048 meter
1 mile = 1.609 kilometers
1 acre = 0.4047 hectare
1 square mile = 2.590 square kilometers
1 cubic foot = 0.0283 cubic meter = 28.32 liters
1 acre-foot = 1,233.48 cubic meters

English-Metric Conversions *(continued)*

1 cubic mile = 4.168 cubic kilometers
1 ounce = 28.33 grams
1 pound = ~0.4536 kilograms
1 short ton = 0.9072 metric ton (tonne)

Metric-English Conversions

1 meter = 3.281 feet
1 kilometer = 3,281 feet
1 square meter = 10.764 square feet
1 hectare = 2.471 acres
1 square kilometer = 0.386 square mile = 247.1 acres
1 cubic meter = 35.3 cubic feet = 264.2 gallons
1 cubic kilometer = 0.240 cubic miles
1 liter = 0.264 gallons
1 kilogram = ~2.205 pounds
1 metric ton (tonne) = 2,204.6 pounds = 1.102 short tons

Flow Rate Conversions

1 foot/second = 0.682 miles/hour = 0.3048 meters/second
1 meter/second = 3.6 kilometers/hour = 2.237 kilometers/hour
1 liter/second = 15.9 gallons/minute = 86.4 cubic meters/day
1 cubic foot/second = 449 gallons/minute = 1.98 acre-feet/day
    = 2,450 cubic meters/day
1 cubic meter/second = 15,800 gallons/minute = 35.3 cubic feet/
    second = 70.0 acre-feet/day
1 inch of rain = 5.61 gallons/square yard = 17,150 gallons/acre

Miscellaneous Water Properties

1 liter = 1 kilogram
1 gallon = 8.33 pounds
1 imperial gallon = 10.0 pounds
1 cubic foot = 62.4 pounds
1 cubic meter = 1 tonne
Density: 1.000 grams/cubic centimeter at 4°C (39.2°F)

572

Appendix C

US Environmental Protection Agency Maximum Contaminant Levels for Drinking Water

This list provides information on the health impacts and contaminant sources for the chemicals currently on the agency's MCL list. For this listing, the EPA has organized the contaminants into the following categories: microorganisms, disinfection byproducts, disinfectants, inorganic chemicals, organic chemicals, and radionuclides. Within each category, contaminants are listed alphabetically. Definitions, footnotes, and related information are provided in the Notes at the end of the list [517, *http://water.epa.gov/drink/contaminants/*].

The list has been assembled directly from the EPA source and begins on the next page.

Microorganisms

Contaminant	MCLG[1] (mg/L)[2]	MCL or TT[1] (MG/l)[2]	Potential Health Effects from Long-Term Exposure Above the MCL (unless specified as short-term)	Sources of Contaminant in Drinking Water
Cryptosporidium	zero	TT[3]	Gastrointestinal illness (e.g. Diarrhea, vomiting, cramps)	Human and animal fecal waste
Giardia lamblia	zero	TT[3]	Gastrointestinal illness (e.g. Diarrhea, vomiting, cramps)	Human and animal fecal waste
Heterotrophic plate count	n/a	TT[3]	HPC has no health effects; it is an analytic method used to measure the variety of bacteria that are common in water. The lower the concentration of bacteria in drinking water, the better maintained the water system is.	HPC measures a range of bacteria that are naturally present in the environment.
Legionella	zero	TT[3]	Legionnaire's Disease, a type of pneumonia	Found naturally in water; multiplies in heating systems
Total Coliforms (including fecal coliform and E. Coli	zero	5.0%[4]	Not a health threat in itself; it is used to indicate whether other potentially harmful bacteria may be present[5]	Coliforms are naturally present in the environment; as well as feces; fecal coliforms and *E. coli* only come from human and animal fecal waste.
Turbidity	n/a	TT[3]	Turbidity is a measure of the cloudiness of water. It is used to indicate water quality and filtration effectiveness (e.g., whether disease-causing organisms are present). Higher turbidity levels are often associated with higher levels of disease-causing microorganisms such as viruses, parasites and some bacteria.

These organisms can cause symptoms such as nausea, cramps, diarrhea, and associated headaches. | Soil runoff |
| Viruses (enteric) | zero | TT[3] | Gastrointestinal illness (e.g., diarrhea, vomiting, cramps) | Human and animal fecal waste |

Disinfection Byproducts

Contaminant	MCLG[1] (mg/L)[2]	MCL or TT[1] (MG/l)[2]	Potential Health Effects from Long-Term Exposure Above the MCL (unless specified as short-term)	Sources of Contaminant in Drinking Water
Bromate	zero	0.010	Increased risk of cancer	Byproduct of drinking water disinfection
Chlorite	0.8	1.0	Anemia; infants & young children: nervous system effects	Byproduct of drinking water disinfection
Haloacetic acids (HAA5)	n/a[6]	0.060[7]	Increased risks of cancer	Byproduct of drinking water disinfection
Total Triholo-Methanes (TTHMs)	--> n/a[6]	--> 0.080[7]	Liver, kidney or central nervous system problems; increased risk of cancer	Byproduct of drinking water disinfection

Disinfectants

Contaminant	MCLG[1] (mg/L)[2]	MCL or TT[1] (MG/l)[2]	Potential Health Effects from Long-Term Exposure Above the MCL (unless specified as short-term)	Sources of Contaminant in Drinking Water
Chloramines	MRDLG=4[1]	MRDL=4.0[1]	Eye/nose irritation; stomach Discomfort, anemia	Water additive used to control microbes
Chlorine (as Cl[2])	MRDLG=4[1]	MRDL=4.0[1]	Eye/nose irritation; stomach Discomfort	Water additive used to control microbes
Chlorine dioxide	MRDLG=0.8[1]	MRDL=0.8[1]	Anemia; infants & young children: nervous system effects	Water additive used to control microbes

575

Inorganic Chemicals

Contaminant	MCLG[1] (mg/L)[2]	MCL or TT[1] (MG/l)[2]	Potential Health Effects from Long-Term Exposure Above the MCL (unless specified as short-term)	Sources of Contaminant in Drinking Water
Antimony	0.006	0.006	Increase in blood cholesterol; decrease in blood sugar	Discharge from petroleum refineries; fire retardants; ceramics; electronics; solder
Arsenic	0[7]	0.010 as of 1/23/06	Skin damage or problems with circulatory systems, and may have increased risk of getting cancer	Erosion of natural deposits; runoff from orchards, runoff from glass & electronics production wastes
Asbestos (fiber > 10 Micrometers)	7 million fibers per liter	7 MFL	Increased risk of developing benign intestinal polyps	Decay of asbestos cement in water mains; erosion of natural deposits
Barium	2	2	Increase in blood pressure	Discharge of drilling wastes; discharge from metal refineries; erosion of natural deposits
Beryllium	0.004	0.004	Intestinal lesions	Discharge from metal refineries and coal-burning factories; discharge from electrical, aerospace, and defense industries
Cadmium	0.005	0.005	Kidney damage	Corrosion of galvanized pipes; erosion of natural deposits; discharge from metal refineries; runoff from waste batteries and paints
Chromium (total)	0.1	0.1	Allergic dermatitis	Discharge from steel and pulp mills; erosion of natural deposits
Copper	1.3	TT[7]; Action Level = 1.3	Short term exposure: Gastrointestinal distress Long term exposure: Liver or kidney damage People with Wilson's Disease Should consult their personal Doctor if the amount of copper in their water exceeds the action level.	Corrosion of household plumbing systems; erosion of natural deposits

Cyanide (as free cyanide)	0.2	0.2	Nerve damage or thyroid problems	Discharge from steel/ metal factories; discharge from plastic and fertilizer factories
Fluoride	4.0	4.0	Bone disease (pain and tenderness of the bones); Children may get mottled teeth	Water additive which promotes strong teeth; erosion of natural deposits; discharge from fertilizer and aluminum factories
Lead	zero	TT[7]; Action Level= 0.015	Infants and children: Delays in physical or mental development; children could show slight deficits in attention span and learning disabilities Adults: Kidney problems; high blood pressure	Corrosion of household plumbing systems; erosion of natural deposits
Mercury (inorganic)	0.002	0.002	Kidney damage	Erosion of natural deposits; discharge from refineries and factories; runoff from landfills and croplands
Nitrate (measured as Nitrogen)	10	10	Infants below the age of six months who drink water containing nitrate in excess of the MCL could become seriously ill and, if untreated, may die. Symptoms include shortness of breath and blue-baby syndrome.	Runoff from fertilizer use; leaking from septic tanks, sewage; erosion of natural deposits
Selenium	0.05	0.05	Hair or fingernail loss; numbness in fingers or toes; circulatory problems	Discharge from petroleum refineries; erosion of natural deposits; discharge from mines
Thallium	0.0005	0.002	Hair loss; changes in blood; kidney, intestine, or liver problems	Leaching from one-processing sites; discharge from electronics, glass, and drug factories

Organic Chemicals

Contaminant	MCLG[1] (mg/L)[2]	MCL or TT[1] (MG/l)[2]	Potential Health Effects from Long-Term Exposure Above the MCL (unless specified as short-term)	Sources of Contaminant in Drinking Water
Acrylamide	zero	TT[8]	Nervous system or blood problems; increased risk of cancer	Added to water during sewage/waste-water treatment
Alachlor	zero	0.002	Eye, liver, kidney or spleen problems; anemia; increased risk of cancer	Runoff from herbicide used on row crops

577

<u>Atrazine</u>	0.003	0.003	Cardiovascular system or reproductive problems	Runoff from herbicide used on row crops
<u>Benzene</u>	zero	0.005	Anemia; decrease in blood platelets; increased risk of cancer	Discharge from factories; leaching from gas storage tanks and landfills
<u>Benzo(a)pyrene</u> (PAHs)	zero	0.0002	Reproductive difficulties; increased risk of cancer	Leaching from linings of water storage tanks and distribution lines
<u>Carbofuran</u>	0.04	0.04	Problems with blood, nervous system, or reproductive system	Leaching of soil fumigant used on rice and alfalfa
<u>Carbon tetrachloride</u>	zero	0.005	Liver problems; increased risk of cancer	Discharge from chemical plants and other industrial activities
<u>Chlordane</u>	zero	0.002	Liver or nervous system problems; increased risk of cancer	Residue of banned termiticide
<u>Chlorobenzene</u>	0.1	0.1	Liver or kidney problems	Discharge from chemical and agricultural chemical factories
<u>2, 4-D</u>	0.07	0.07	Kidney, liver, or adrenal gland problems	Runoff from herbicide use on row crops
<u>Dalapon</u>	0.2	0.2	Minor kidney changes	Runoff from herbicide used on rights of way
<u>1,2-Dibromo-3-chloropopane</u> (DBCP)	zero	0.0002	Reproductive difficulties; increased risk of cancer	Runoff/leaching from soil fumigant used on soybeans, cotton, pineapples, and orchards
<u>o-Dichloroben-zene</u>	0.6	0.6	Liver, kidney, or circulatory system problems	Discharge from industrial chemical factories
<u>p-Dichloroben-zene</u>	0.075	0.075	Anemia; liver, kidney or spleen damage; changes in blood	Discharge from industrial chemical factories
<u>1,2-Dichloroethane</u>	zero	0.005	Increased risk of cancer	Discharge from industrial chemical factories
<u>1,1-Dichloro-ethylene</u>	0.007	0.007	Liver problems	Discharge from industrial chemical factories
<u>Cis-1,2-Dichloro-ethylene</u>	0.07	0.07	Liver problems	Discharge from industrial chemical factories
<u>Trans-1,2-Dich-loroethylene</u>	0.1	0.1	Liver problems	Discharge from industrial chemical factories

578

Dichloromethane	zero	0.005	Liver problems; increased risk of cancer	Discharge from drug and chemical factories
1,2-Dichloro-propane	zero	0.005	Increased risk of cancer	Discharge from industrial chemical factories
Di(2-ethylhexyl) adipate	0.4	0.4	Weight loss, liver problems, or possible reproductive difficulties	Discharge from chemical factories
Di(2-ethylhexyl) phthalate	zero	0.006	Reproductive difficulties, liver or problems, increased risk of cancer	Discharge from rubber and chemical factories
Dinoseb	0.007	0.007	Reproductive difficulties	Runoff from herbicide used on soybeans and vegetables
Dioxin (2,2,7-8-TCDD)	zero	0.00000003	Reproductive difficulties; increased risk of cancer	Emissions from waste incineration and other combustion; discharge from chemical factories
Diquat	0.02	0.02	Cataracts	Runoff from herbicide use
Endothall	0.1	0.1	Stomach and intestinal problems	Runoff from herbicide use
Endrin	0.002	0.002	Liver problems	Residue of banned insecticide
Epichlorohydrin	zero	TT[8]	Increased cancer risk, and	Discharge from industrial chemical factories; an impurity of some water treatment chemicals
Ethylbenzene	0.7	0.7	Liver or kidney problems	Discharge from petroleum refineries
Ethylene dibromide	zero	0.00005	Problems with liver, stomach, reproductive system, or kidneys; increased risk of cancer	Discharge from petroleum refineries
Glyposate	0.7	0.7	Kidney problems; reproductive difficulties	Runoff from herbicide use
Heptachlor	zero	0.0004	Liver damage; increased risk of cancer	Residue of banned termiticide
Heptachlor epoxide	zero	0.0002	Liver damage; increased risk of cancer	Breakdown of heptachlor
Hexachloro-benzene	zero	0.001	Liver or kidney problems; reproductive difficulties; increased risk of cancer	Discharge from metal refineries and agricultural chemical factories
Hexachloro-cyclopentadiene	0.05	0.05	Kidney or stomach problems	Discharge from chemical factories

Lindane	0.0002	0.0002	Liver or kidney problems	Runoff/leaching from insecticide used on cattle, lumber, gardens
Methoxychlor	0.04	0.04	Reproductive difficulties	Runoff/leaching from insecticide used on fruits, vegetables, alfalfa, livestock
Oxamyl (Vydate)	0.2	0.2	Slight nervous system effects	Runoff/leaching from insecticide use on apples, potatoes, and tomatoes
Polychlorinated Biphenyls (PCBs)	zero	0.0005	Skin changes; thymus gland problems; immune deficiencies; reproductive or nervous system difficulties; increased risk of cancer	Runoff from landfills; discharge of waste chemicals
Pentachlorophenol	zero	0.001	Liver or kidney problems; increased cancer risk	Discharge from wood preserving factories
Picloram	0.5	0.5	Liver problems	Herbicide runoff
Simazine	0.004	0.004	Problems with blood	Herbicide runoff
Styrene	0.1	0.1	Liver, kidney, or circulatory system problems	Discharge from rubber and plastic factories; leaching from landfills
Tetrachloro-ethylene	zero	0.005	Liver problems; increased risk of cancer	Discharge from factories and dry cleaners
Toluene	1	1	Nervous system, kidney, or liver problems	Discharge from petroleum factories
Toxaphene	zero	0.003	Kidney, liver, or thyroid problems; increased risk of cancer	Runoff/leaching from insecticide use on cotton and cattle
2,4,5-TP (Silvex)	0.05	0.05	Liver problems	Residue of banned herbicide
1,2,4-Trichloro-benzene	0.07	0.07	Changes in adrenal glands	Discharge from textile finishing factories
1,1,1-Trichloro-ethane	0.20	0.2	Liver, nervous system, or circulatory problems	Discharge from metal degreasing sites and other factories
1,1,2-Trichloro-ethane	0.003	0.005	Liver, kidney, or immune system problems	Discharge from industrial chemical factories
Trichloroethylene	zero	0.005	Liver problems; increased risk of cancer	Discharge from metal degreasing sites and other factories
Vinyl chloride	zero	0.002	Increased risk of cancer	Leaching from PVC pipes; discharge from plastic factories

Xylenes	10	10	Nervous system	Discharge from petroleum factories; discharge from chemical factories

Radionuclides

Contaminant	MCLG[1] (mg/L)[2]	MCL or TT[1] (MG/l)[2]	Potential Health Effects from Long-Term Exposure Above the MCL (unless specified as short-term)	Sources of Contaminant in Drinking Water
Alpha particles	none[7]---- -------zero	15 picocuries per Liter (pCi/L)	Increased risk of cancer	Erosion of natural deposits of certain minerals that are radioactive and may emit a form of radiation known as alpha radiation
Beta particles	none[7]---- -------zero	4 millirems per year	Increased risk of cancer	Decay of natural and man-made deposits of certain minerals that are radioactive and may emit forms of radiation known as photons and beta radiation
Radium 226 and Radium 228 (combined)	none[7]---- -------zero	5 pCi/L	Increased risk of cancer	Erosion of natural deposits
Uranium	zero	30 ug/L as of 12/08/03	Increased risk of cancer, kidney toxicity	Erosion of natural deposits

Notes

[1] Definitions: Maximum Contaminant Level Goal (MCLG) - The level of a contaminant in drinking water below which there is no known or expected risk to health. MCLGs allow for a margin of safety and are non-enforceable public health goals. Maximum Contaminant Level (MCL) - The highest level of a contaminant that is allowed in drinking water. MCLs are set as close to MCLGs as feasible using the best available treatment technology and taking cost into consideration. MCLs are enforceable standards. Maximum Residual Disinfectant Level Goal (MRDLG) - The level of a drinking water disinfectant below which there is no known or expected risk to health. MRDLGs do not reflect the benefits of the use of disinfectants to control microbial contaminants. (TT) Treatment Technique - A required process intended to reduce the level of a contaminant in drinking water. Maximum Residual Disinfectant Level (MRDL) - The highest level of a disinfectant allowed in drinking water. There is convincing evidence that addition of a disinfectant is necessary for control of microbial contaminants.

[2] Units are in milligrams per liter (mg/L) unless otherwise noted. Milligrams per liter are equivalent to parts per million.

[3] EPA's surface water treatment rules require systems using surface water or ground water under the direct influence of surface water to (1) disinfect their water, and (2) filter their water or meet criteria for avoiding filtration so that the following contaminants are controlled at the following levels:

- *Cryptosporidium: Unfiltered systems are required to include Cryptosporidium in their existing watershed control provisions.*
- *Giardia lamblia: 99.9% removal/inactivation*

- Viruses: 99.99% removal/inactivation
- *Legionella: No limit, but EPA believes that if Giardia and viruses are removed/inactivated, according to the treatment techniques in the Surface Water Treatment Rule, Legionella will also be controlled.*
- Turbidity: For systems that use conventional or direct filtration, at no time can turbidity (cloudiness of water) go higher than 1 nephelolometric turbidity unit NTU), and samples for turbidity must be less than or equal to 0.3 NTU in at least 95 percent of the samples in any month. Systems that use filtration other than the conventional or direct filtration must follow state limits, which must include turbidity at no time exceeding 5 NTU.
- HPC: No more than 500 bacterial colonies per milliliter.
- Long Term 1 Enhanced Surface Water Treatment: Surface water systems or (GWUDI) systems serving fewer than 10,000 people must comply with the applicable Long Term 1 Enhanced Surface Water Treatment Rule provisions (e.g. turbidity standards, individual filter monitoring, *Cryptosporidium* removal requirements, updated watershed control requirements for unfiltered systems).
- *Long Term 2 Enhanced Surface Water Treatment Rule This rule applies to all surface water systems or ground water systems under the direct influence of surface water. The rule targets additional Cryptosporidium treatment requirements for higher risk systems and includes provisions to reduce risks from uncovered finished water storage facilities and to ensure that the systems maintain microbial protection as they take steps to reduce the formation of disinfection byproducts.*
- Filter Backwash Recycling; The Filter Backwash Recycling Rule requires systems that recycle to return specific recycle flows through all processes of the system's existing conventional or direct filtration system or at an alternate location approved by the state.

[4] *No more than 5.0% samples total coliform-positive in a month. (For water systems that collect fewer than 40 routine samples per month, no more than one sample can be total coliform-positive per month.) Every sample that has total coliform must be analyzed for either fecal coliforms or E. coli if two consecutive TC-positive samples, and one is also positive for E.coli fecal coliforms, system has an acute MCL violation.*

[5] Fecal coliform and E. coli are bacteria whose presence indicates that the water may be contaminated with human or animal wastes. Disease-causing microbes (pathogens) in these wastes can cause diarrhea, cramps, nausea, headaches, or other symptoms. These athogens may pose a special health risk for infants, young children, and people with severely compromised immune systems.

[6] Although there is no collective MCLG for this contaminant group, there are individual MCLGs for some of the individual contaminants:

- Trihalomethanes: bromodichloromethane (zero); bromoform (zero); dibromochloromethane (0.06 mg/L): chloroform (0.07mg/L).
- Haloacetic acids: dichloroacetic acid (zero); trichloroacetic acid (0.02 mg/L); monochloroacetic acid (0.07 mg/L). Bromoacetic acid and dibromoacetic acid are regulated with this group but have no MCLGs.

[7] Lead and copper are regulated by a Treatment Technique that requires systems to control the corrosiveness of their water. If more than 10% of tap water samples exceed the action level, water systems must take additional steps. For copper, the action level is 1.3 mg/L, and for lead is 0.015 mg/L.

[8] Each water system must certify, in writing, to the state (using third-party or manufacturer's certification) that when acrylamide and epichlorohydrin are used to treat water, the combination (or product) of dose and monomer level does not exceed the levels specified, as follows:

- Acrylamide = 0.05% dosed at 1 mg/L (or equivalent)
- Epichlorohydrin = 0.01% dosed at 20 mg/L (or equivalent)

References

I Publications

The following information sources are referred to in the text by the number which precedes them in this list. Organization is as follows: author(s), year of publication, title. source/publisher, volume (V.), number (No.), specific date, pages of article (p. 00) or pages in book (00 p.), web source — as applicable.

1. Ahlfeld, D.P., A. Dahmani, and W. Ji, 1994, A conceptual model of field behavior of air sparging, and its implications for application. Ground Water Monitoring Review, Fall, p. 132-139.

2. AlertNet, 2012, The Battle for Water. Multimedia presentation. http://www.trust.org/foundation-news/special-report-the-battle-for-water/

3. Aliewi, Amjad, 2006, The Palestinian-Israeli Management of Shared Groundwater Aquifers: Status, realities, and lessons learned. Workshop presentation, Beirut, April 24-25, 2006. www.hwe.org.ps/EventsImages/shared aquifers.pdf

4. Alley, W.M., T.E. Reilly, and O.L. Franke, 1999, Sustainability of ground-water resources. US Geological Survey Circular 1186. http://pubs.usgs.gov/circ/circ1186/html/bot.html

5. American Society of Civil Engineers (ASCE), 2009, 2009 Report Card for American Infrastructure. www.asce.org/reportcard

6. American Society for Testing and Materials (ASTM), 1995, Standard Guide for Risk-Based Corrective Action Applied at Petroleum Release Sites. ASTM, West Conshohocken, PA.

7. Anderson, M.P., and J.A. Munter, 1981, Seasonal reversals of groundwater flow around lakes and the relevance to stagnation points and lake budgets. Water Resources Research, V. 17, p. 1139-1150.

8. Anderson, Ray, and Robin White, 2011, Business Lessons from a Radical Industrialist. St Martins Griffin, New York, NY, 336 p.

9. Angell, P.S. (Ed.), 2011, World resources report 2010-2011: Decision making in a changing climate. UN Development Programme, UN Environment Program, World Bank, World Resources Institute, Washington, DC, 184 p. http://bit.ly/pzxKcn

10. Anisfeld, Shimon C, 2010, Water Resources (Foundations of Contemporary Environmental Studies Series), Island Press, Washington, DC. 352 p.

11. Annin, Peter, 2009, The Great Lakes Water Wars. Island Press, Washington, DC. 320 p.

12. Arctic Monitoring and Assessment Program (AMAP), 2011, Snow, Water, Ice, and Permafrost in the Arctic. SWIPA2011V2.pdf

13. Ayotte, J.D., J.M. Gronberg, and L.E. Apolaca, 2011, Trace-elements and radon in groundwater across the United States, 1992-2003. US Geological Survey Scientific Investigations Report 2011-5059, 115 p.

14. Back, William, Rosenshein, J.S., and Seaber, P.R., (Eds) 1988, Hydrogeology. Geological Society of America, Boulder, CO, 524 p.

15. Bain, R.E.S., et al., 2012, Accounting for water quality in monitoring access to safe drinking-water as part of the Millennium Development Goals: lessons from five countries. Bulletin of the World Health Organization, March 2012. doi:10.2471/BLT.11.094284

16. Baker, V.R., 1990, Spring sapping and valley network development, *in* Higgins, C.G., and Coates, D.R., eds., Groundwater Geomorphology: The Role of Subsurface Water in Earth-Surface Processes and Landforms. Boulder, CO, Geological Society of America Special Paper 252, p. 235-265.

17. Bakker, Karen, 2010, Privatizing Water: Governance Failure and the World's Urban Water Crisis. Cornell University Press, Ithaca, NY, 296 p.

18. Barker, R.A., 1986, Preliminary results of a steady-state ground-water flow model of the southeastern Coastal Plain aquifer system, *in* Proceedings of the Southern Regional Ground Water Conference, San Antonio, TX, p. 315-338.

19. Barlow, Maude, 2003, The world's water: a human right or a corporate good? *in* McDonald, Bernandette, and Douglas Jehl (Eds), Whose Water Is It? National Geographic Society, Washington, DC, p. 25-39.

20. Barlow, Maude and Tony Clarke, 2003, Blue Gold: The Fight to Stop the Corporate Theft of the World's Water. The New Press, New York, NY, 296 p.

21. Barlow, P.M. and S.A. Leake, 2012, Streamflow depletion by wells – Understanding and managing the effects of groundwater pumping on streamflow. US Geological Survey Circular 1376, 84p. http://publs.usgs.gov/circ/1376/

22. Barnett, Cynthia, 2011, Blue Revolution: Unmaking America's Water Crisis. Beacon Press, Boston, MA, 286 p.

23. Barnett, T.P., and D.W. Pierce, 2008, When will Lake Mead go dry? Water Resources Research 44 W03201, doi:10.1029/2007WR006704.

24. Barnett, T.P., and D.W. Pierce, 2009, Reply to comment by J.J. Barsugli, et al. Water Resources Research 45, W09602, doi:10:1029/2009WR008219.

25. Barrera, Lina, 2009, Portraits of climate change: the Rocky Mountains. World Watch, V. 22, N. 4, p. 8-16.

26. Bassington, Rick, 2006, Field Hydrogeology: Geological Field Guide, 3rd Edition. John Wiley, New York, NY, 264 p.

27. Battisti, D.S., and R.L. Naylor, 2009, Historical warnings of future food insecurity with unprecedented seasonal heat. Science, V. 323, p. 240-248.

28. Baxtresser, Dean, 2010, Antiques Roadshow: The Common Law and the Coming Age of Groundwater Marketing. Michigan Law Review, V. 108, No. 5. www.michiganlawreview.org/articles/antiques-roadshow-the-coming-age-of-groundwater-marketing.

29. Bedient, P.B., H.S. Rifai, and C.J. Newell, 1997, Ground Water Contamination, 2nd Edition. Prentice-Hall, Upper Saddle River, NJ, 604 p.

30. Behar, Michael, 2013, Whose fault? Mother Jones, V. 38, No. 2, p. 34-39, 65.

31. Bhattacharjee, Yudhijit, 2007, Turning ocean water into rain. Science V. 316, p. 1837-1838.

32. Biermann, F., et al., 2012, Navigating the Anthropocene: Improving Earth System Governance. Science, V. 335, p. 1306-1307.

33. Bigas, H. (Editor), 2012, The Global Water Crisis: Addressing an Urgent Security Issue. Papers for the InterAction Council, 2011-2012. Hamilton, Canada: UNU-INWEH. http://www.inweh.unu.edu/WaterSecurity/documents/WaterSecurity_FINAL_Aug2012.pdf

34. Birch, E.L., Afaf Meseis, and Susan Wachter, 2012, The urban water transition: Why we must address the new reality of urbanization, women, water, and sanitation in sustainable development. wH2O: The Journal of Gender and Water, V. 1, No. 1, 6-7.

35. Bloom, D.E., 2011, 7 billion and counting. Science, V. 333, p. 562-569.

36. Bohannon, John, 2006, Running out of water – and time. Science, V. 313, p. 1085-1087.

37. Bohannon, John, 2010, The Nile Delta's Sinking Future. Science, V. 327, p. 1444-1447.

38. Bonacci, Ognjen, 1987, Karst Hydrology with Special Reference to the Dinaric Karst. Springer-Verlag, Berlin, Germany, 184 p.

39. Bond, T.C., et al., 2013, Bounding the role of black carbon in the climate system: A scientific assessment. Journal of Geophysical Research – Atmospheres. onlinelibrary.wiley.com/doi/10.1002/jgrd.50171/

40. Borenstein, Seth, 2011, Too wacky? Moving water from flood to drought. Associated Press, 9 September 2011.

41. Boseley, Sarah, 2010, Sanitation for all – but not for another 300 years. http://www.guardian.co.uk/society/sarah-boseley-global-health/2010/apr/21/sanitation-diarrhoea-in-children?oo=0

42. Boulding, R.J., 2003, Practical Handbook of Soil, Vadose Zone, and Ground-Water Contamination: Assessment, Prevention, and Remediation, Second Edition. CRC Press, Boca Raton, FL, 728 p.

43. Bouwer, Herman, and R.S. Rice, 1976, A slug test for determining hydraulic conductivity of unconfined aquifers with completely or partially penetrating wells. Water Resources Research, V. 12, No. 3, p. 423-428.

44. Bowden, Charles, 1977, Killing the Hidden Waters. University of Texas Press, Austin, TX, 206 p.

45. Brahanna, J.V., et al., 1988, Carbonate rocks *in* Back, William, et al. (Eds), 1988, Hydrogeology. Geological Society of America, Boulder, CO, p. 333-352.

46. Brannan, Paul, 2008, Debunking desalination. E Magazine, V. 19, No. 2, p.16-19.

47. Brassington, Rick, 2006, Field Hydrogeology, 3rd Edition. Wiley-Interscience, New York NY, 276 p.

48. Bredehoeft, J.D., 1997, Safe yield and the water budget myth. Ground Water, V. 35, No. 6, p. 929.

49. Bredehoeft, J.D., 2002, The Water Budget Myth Revisited: Why Hydrogeologists Model. Ground Water (40)4: 340-345.

50. Bredehoeft, J.D., and L. F. Konikow, 1993, Editorial – Groundwater models: validate or invalidate. Ground Water, V 31, No. 2, p. 178-179.

51. Brichieri-Colombi, Stephen, 2009, The World Water Crisis: The Failures of Resource Management. I.B. Tauris, London, UK, 352 p.

52. Briscoe, J., and R.P.S. Malik, 2005, India's Water Economy – Bracing for a Turbulent Future. World Bank, Washington, DC, 102 p. water.worldbank.org/publications/indias-water-economy-b

53. Broecker, W.S. and Robert Kunzig, 2008, Fixing Climate: What Past Climate Changes Reveal About the Current Threat – and How to Counter It. Hill and Wang, New York, NY, 253 p.

54. Brown, Lester, 1995, Who Will Feed China? W.W. Norton, New York, NY, 165 p.

55. Brown, Lester, 2004, Outgrowing the Earth. W.W. Norton, New York, NY, 240 p.

56. Brown, Lester, 2008, Plan B 3.0: Mobilizing to Save Civilization. W.W. Norton, New York, NY, 400 p.

57. Brown, Lester, 2011, World on the Edge. W.W. Norton, New York, NY, 240 p.

58. Brown, Lester, 2012, Full Planet, Empty Plates. W.W. Norton, New York, NY, 145 p.

59. Burke, Garance, 2009, AP Impact: School drinking water contains toxins. Associated Press, 25 September 2009.

60. Burkett, V.R. and M.A. Davidson (Eds), 2012, Coastal Impacts, Adaptation and Vulnerability: A Technical Input to the 2012 National Climate Assessment. Cooperative Report to the 2013 National Climate Assessment, 150 p. usgcrp.gov/NCA/technicalinputreports/Burkett_Davidson_Coasts_Final_.pdf

61. Cairns and Patrick (Eds), 1986, Managing Water Resources. Greenwood, Westport, CT, 144 p.

62. Cameron, A.B., 2009, Mississippi vs. Memphis: A Study in Transboundary Ground Water Dispute Resolutions. Grant Law and Policy Journal 2009 Symposium, nsglc.olemiss.edu/SGLPJ/Presentations_09/Cameron.pdf

63. Carey, Mark, 2010, In the Shadow of Melting glaciers: Climate change and Andean Society. Oxford University Press, New York, NY, 288 p.

64. Carle, David, 2009, Introduction to Water in California. University of California Press, Berkeley, CA, 292 p.

65. Carr, D.E., 1966, Death of the Sweet Waters. Norton and Company, New York, NY, 257 p.

66. Castello, L., et al., 2012, The vulnerability of Amazon freshwater ecosystems. Conservation Letters, doi:10.111/conl.12008.

67. Castano, Ivan, 2012, Mexico's Water War. Forbes magazine 3/12/12. www.forbes.com/sites/ivancastano/2012/02/22/mexicos-water-war/

68. Cech, T.V., 2003, Principles of Water Resources: History, Development, Management, and Policy. John Wiley, New York, NY, 446 p.

69. Center for Biological Diversity, 2011, Compilation and analysis of 1995 to 2008 water-level data at monitoring and test wells, Fort Huachuca, AZ. www.biologicaldiversity.org/report_20110126_ACOE.pdf

70. Chapelle, F.H., 2000, The Hidden Sea: Ground Water, Springs, and Wells. National Ground Water Association, Westerville, OH, 232 p.

71. Chellaney, Brahma, 2011, Water: Asia's New Battleground. Georgetown University Press, Washington, DC, 400 p.

72. Clarke, Robin and Jannet King, 2004, The Water Atlas. The New Press, New York, NY, 127 p.

73. Cheremisinoff, N.P., 1999, Groundwater Remediation and Treatment Technologies. Noyes Publications, Westwood, NJ, 406 p.

74. Cherry, J.A., 1983, Piezometers and other permanently installed devices for groundwater quality monitoring. Proceedings: Seminar on Groundwater and Petroleum Hydrocarbons Protection, Detection, Restoration. Petroleum Association for Conservation of the Canadian Environment. Ottawa, p. IV/1-39.

75. Christian-Smith, Juilet, P.H. Gleick, and Heather Cooley, 2012, U.S. water policy reform, *in* The World's Water, Volume 7: The Biennial Report on Freshwater Resources. Island Press, Washington, DC, p. 143-155.

76. Clarke, Robin and Jannet King, 2004, The Water Atlas. Myriad Editions Limited, The New Press, New York, NY, 127 p.

77. Climate Central, 2012, Surging Seas. sealevel.climatecentral.org

78. Coates, D.R., 1981, Environmental Geology. Wiley & Sons, New York, NY, 731 p.

79. Colborn, Theo, Dianne Dumanoski, and J.P. Myers, 1996, Our Stolen Future. Dutton, New York, NY, 306 p.

80. Colburn, E.A., 2004, Vernal Pools: Natural History and Conservation. McDonald & Woodward, Granville, OH, 426 p.

81. Cooley, Heather and Kristina Donnelly, 2012, Hydraulic Fracturing and Water Resources: Separating the Frack from the Fiction. June 2012, Pacific Institute, Oakland, CA, 35 p.

82. Coontz, Robert, 2007, Wedging sustainability into public consciousness. Science, V. 315, p.1068-1069.

83. Copertino, M.S., 2011, Add coastal vegetation to the climate critical list. Nature, V. 473, p. 255.

84. Costa, J.E. and V.R. Baker, 1981, Surficial Geology: Building with the Earth. John Wiley, New York, NY, 498 p.

85. Danielson, E.W., James Levin, and Elliot Abrams, 2002, Meteorology. McGraw-Hill, New York, NY, 558 p.

86. Davis, G.H., 1988, Western alluvial valleys and the High Plains, *in* Back, William, et al. (Eds), Hydrogeology. Geological Society of America, Boulder, CO, p. 283-300.

87. Davis, S.N., 1988, Sandstones and shales, *in* Back, William, et al. (Eds), Hydrogeology. Geological Society of America, Boulder, CO, p. 323-332.

88. Davis, S.N. and R.J.M. DeWiest, 1966. Hydrogeology. John Wiley, New York, NY, 463 p.

89. de Albuquerque, Catarina, 2011, Is the Human Right to Water and Sanitation an Issue in the USA?. News release, 11 March 2011. aquadoc.typepad.com/files/un-ie-end-of-mission-statemen...

90. deBuys, William, 2011, A Great Aridness: Climate Change and the Future of the American Southwest. Oxford University Press, New York, NY, 348 p.

91. De Conto, R.M., et al., 2012, Past extreme warming events linked to massive carbon dioxide release from thawing permafrost. Nature, V. 484, p.87-91.

92. Deming, David, 2001, Introduction to Hydrogeology. McGraw-Hill, New York, NY, 480 p.

93. Derksen, C., and and R. Brown, 2012, Spring snow cover extent reductions in the 2008–2012 period exceeding climate model projections. Geophysical Research Letters, V. 39, Issue 19. DOI: 10.1029/2012GL053387

94. De Simone, L.A., P.A. Hamilton, and R.J. Gilliom, 2009, Quality of water from domestic wells in principal aquifers of the United States, 1991-2004. US Geological Survey Circular 1332, 48 p.

95. de Villiers, Marq, 1999, Water: The Fate of Our Most Precious Resource. Stoddart Publishing Co., Toronto, Canada, 352 p.

96. De Wiest, R.J.M., 1965, Geohydrology. John Wiley, New York, NY, 366 p.

97. Diamond, Jared, 2005, Collapse: How Societies Choose to Fail or Succeed. Penguin Group, New York, NY, 576 p.

98. Dicken, Sarah, 2013, Refining the water footprint concept to account for non-renewable water resources. Global Water Forum.

http://www.globalwaterforum.org/2013/01/20/

99. Doll, Petra, 2009, Vulnerability to the impact of climate change on renewable groundwater resources: a global-scale assessment. Environmental Research Letters 4, 035006, 12 p.

100. Domenico, P.A. and F.W. Schwartz, 1998, Physical and Chemical Hydrogeology. John Wiley, New York, NY, 506 p.

101. D'Odorico, Paolo, et al., 2010. Does globalization of water reduce societal resilience to drought? Geophy Res Let, 37: DOI 10.1029/2010GL043167.

102. Dorn, J.G., 2008, World geothermal power generation nearing eruption. Earth Policy Institute Plan B Update. http://www.earthpolicy.org/Updates/2008/Update74.htm

103. Driscoll, F.G., 1986, Groundwater and Wells. Johnson Filtration Systems Inc., St. Paul, MN, 1089 p.

104. Duhigg, Charles, 2009A, That tap water is legal but may be unhealthy. New York Times, 16 December 2009. www.nytimes.com/2009/12/16water.html

105. Duhigg, Charles, 2009B, Toxic Waters: Clean water laws are neglected, at a

cost in suffering. NY Times 12 September, 2009. www.nytimes.com/2009/09/12water.html

106. Duhigg, Charles, 2010, Toxic waters: Saving U.S. water and sewer systems would be costly. New York Times, 14 March 2010. www.nytimes.com/2010/03/14water.html

107. Dunne, Thomas, 1990, Hydrology, Mechanics, and Geomorphic Implications of Erosion by Subsurface Flow, *in* Higgins, C.G., and Coates, D.R. (Eds)., Groundwater Geomorphology; The Role of Subsurface Water in Earth-Surface Processes and Landforms: Boulder, Colorado, Geological Society of America Special Paper 252, p. 1-28.

108. Dunne, Thomas, and L.B. Leopold, 1978, Water in Environmental Planning. W.H. Freeman & Company, San Francisco, CA, 818 p.

109. Durack, P.J., S.E. Wijffels, and R.J. Matear, 2012, Ocean Salinities Reveal Strong Global Water Cycle Intensification During 1950 to 2000. Science, V. 336, p. 455, 458.

110. The Earth Institute at Columbia University, 2008, Synthesis and assessment product 3.4: abrupt climate change. http://www.climatescience.gov/Library/sap/sap3-4/final-report/default.htm

111. Eby, M., et al., 2009: Lifetime of Anthropogenic Climate Change: Millennial Time Scales of Potential CO2 and Surface Temperature Perturbations. Journal of Climate, V. 22, p. 2501–2511. doi: http://dx.doi.org/10.1175/2008JCLI2554.1

112. Eilmelech, Menachem, and W.A. Phillip, 2011, The future of seawater desalination: energy, technology, and the environment. Science V. 333, p.712-717.

113. Ellison, W.D., 1948, Erosion of soil by raindrops. Scientific American, V. 180, p. 40-45, Offprint 817.

114. Evans, D.M., 1970, The perils of polluting the ground, *in* Mears, Jr., Brainerd, (Ed), The nature of geology. Van Nostrand Reinhold, New York, NY, p.226-235.

115. Fagan, Brian, 2011, Elixir: A History of Water and Humankind. Bloomsbury USA, New York, NY, 416 p.

116. Falconer, Bruce, 2008, The wizard of h_2o. Mother Jones, V. 33, No. 6, p.16-19.

117. Fan, Y., H. Li, and G. Miguez-Macho, 2013, Global patterns of groundwater table depth. Science, V. 339, p. 940-943.

118. Faris, Stephan, 2009, Liquid Assets. Mother Jones, V. 34, No. 4, p. 57.

119. Farrar, C.D. and G.L. Bertoldi, 1988, Region 4, Central Valley and Pacific Coast Ranges, *in* Back, William, et al. (Eds), 1988, Hydrogeology. Geological Society of America, Boulder, CO, p. 59-67.

120. Farvolden, R.N., et al., 1988, Region 12, Precambrian Shield *in* Back, William, et al. (Eds), 1988, Hydrogeology. Geological Society of America, Boulder, CO, p. 101-114.

121. Fendorf, Scott, H.A. Michael, and Alexander van Geen, 2010, Spatial and temporal variations of groundwater arsenic in South and Southeast Asia. Science, V. 328, p. 1123-1127.

122. Fetter, C.W., 2001, Applied Hydrogeology, 4th Edition. Prentice-Hall, Upper Saddle River, NJ, 598 p.

123. Finkel, Elizabeth and Dennis Normile, 2012, River basin management plan secures water for the environment. Science, V. 338, p. 1273-1274.

124. Fishman, Charles, 2011, The Big Thirst: The Secret Life and Turbulent Future of Water. Free Press, New York, NY, 388 p.

125. Ford, D.C., and P. W. Williams, 1989, Karst Geomorphology and Hydrology. University Press, Cambridge, UK, 601 p.

126. Ford, D.C., A.N. Palmer, and W.B. White, 1988, Landform development: karst *in* Back, William, et al. (Eds), 1988, Hydrogeology. Geological Society of America, Boulder, CO, p. 401-412.

127. Foreign Policy, annually, The failed states index. July-August issues. See www.fundforpeace.org for complete index.

128. Fort, Denise, and Barry Nelson, 2012, Pipe Dreams: Water Supply and Pipeline Projects in the West. Natural Resources Defense Council, New York, NY, 46 p. www.nrdc.org/water/management/pipelines-project.asp

129. Foster, Stephen and Mohamed Ait-Kadi, 2012, Integrated Water Resources Management (IWRM): How does groundwater fit in? Hydrogeology Journal, V. 20, p. 415-418.

130. Fountain, A.G., et al., 2012, The Disappearing cryosphere: Impacts and ecosystem responses to rapid cryosphere loss. BioScience, V. 62, No. 4, p. 405-415. http://www.jstor.org/stable/10.1525/bio.2012.62.4.11

131. Francis, J.A. and S.J. Vavrus, 2012, Evidence linking Arctic amplification to extreme weather in mid-latitudes. Geophysical Research Letters, V. 39, L06801, doi:10.1029/2012GL051000.

132. Friederici, Peter, 2012, Cutting a Lifeline. Audubon, V. 114, No. 4, p. 14.

133. Freeze, F.A. and J.A. Cherry, 1979, Groundwater. Prentice-Hall, Englewood Cliffs, NJ, 604 p.

134. Freeze, R.A., and P.A. Witherspoon, 1966, Theoretical analysis of regional groundwater flow I: Analytical and numerical solutions to the mathematical model. Water Resources Research, V. 2, p. 641-656.

135. Freeze, R.A., and P.A. Witherspoon, 1967, Theoretical analysis of regional groundwater flow II: Effect of water table configuration and subsurface permeability variations. Water Resources Research, V. 3, p. 623-634.

136. Freyberg, D.L., 1988, An exercise in ground-water model calibration and prediction. Ground Water, V. 26, No. 3, p. 350-360.

137. Friedman, G.M., J.E. Sanders and D.C. Kopaska-Merkel, 1992, Principles of Sedimentary Deposits: Stratigraphy and Sedimentology. Macmillan College Division, New York, NY, 717 p.

138. Galloway, G.E., 2003, Perspectives on a national water policy. Universities' Council on Water Resources, Water Resources Update 126, p. 6-11.

139. Gardner, A.S., et al., 2011, Sharply increased mass loss from glaciers and ice caps in the Canadian Arctic Archipelago. Nature, V. 473, p. 357-360.

140. Gardner, G.T., 2006, Inspiring Progress: Religions' Contributions to Sustainable Development. W.W. Norton, New York, NY, 211 p.

141. Ghassemi, F., A.J. Jakeman, and H.A. Nix, 1995, Salinisation of Land and Water Resources: Human Causes, Extent,, Management, and Case Studies. CAB International, Wallingford, UK, 540 p.

142. Gies, Erica, 2009, Water Wars. World Watch, V.22, No. 2, p. 22-27.

143. Gilbert, Janine, Jacques Mathieu, and Fred Fournier (eds), 1997, Groundwater/Surface Water Ecotones: Biological and Hydrological Interactions and Management Options. Cambridge University Press, Cambridge, UK, 258 p.

144. Giordano, Mark, 2009, Global groundwater? Issues and solutions. Annual Review Environmental Resources, 2009. ANRV 390-EG34-07, p. 7.1-7.26. www.environ.annualreviews.org/doi:10.1146/annurev.environ.030308.100251

145. Gleeson, Tom, et al., 2012, Water balance of global aquifers revealed by groundwater footprint. Nature, V. 488, No. 7410, p. 197-200.

146. Gleick, P.H. (Ed), 1993, Water in Crisis: A Guide to the World's Fresh Water Resources. Oxford University Press, New York, NY, 504 p.

147. Gleick, P.H., 2004, The human right to water: two steps forward, one step back, *in* Gleick, et al., The World's Water 2004-2005, Island Press, Washington, DC, p.204-227.

148. Gleick, P.H., 2006, Water and terrorism *in* The World's Water, 2006-2007. Island Press, Washington, DC, p. 1-28.

149. Gleick, P.H., 2011, Bottled & Sold: The Story Behind Our Obsession With Bottled Water. Island Press, Washington, DC, 232 p.

150. Gleick, P.H., et al., 1998-2012, The World's Water, Volumes 1-7: Biennial Reports on Freshwater Resources. Island Press, Washington, DC.

151. Gleick, P.H, and Juliet Christian-Smith, 2012, A Twenty-First Century U.S. Water Policy. Oxford University Press, USA, New York, NY, 360 p.

152. Gleick, P.H., Heather Cooley, and Gary Wolff, 2006, With a grain of salt: An update on seawater desalination *in* Gleick, P.H., et al., The World's Water, 2006-2007. Island Press, Washington, DC, p. 51-89.

153. Gleick, P.H., and Matthew Heberger, 2012, Water conflict chronology *in* Gleick, P.H., et al., The World's Water, Volume 7. Island Press, Washington, DC, p. 175-216.

154. Glenn, J.C., T.J. Gordon, and Elizabeth Florescu, 2011, 2011 State of the Future. The Millennium Project, Washington, DC, 106 pages and 8,600-page CD.

155. Glennon, Robert, 2002, Water Follies: Groundwater Pumping and the Fate of America's Fresh Water. Island Press, Washington, DC, 314 p.

156. Glennon, Robert, 2009, Unquenchable: America's Water Crisis and What To Do About It. Island Press, Washington, DC, 432 p.

157. Glover, J.D., et al., 2010A, Increased food and ecosystem security via perennial grains. Science V. 328, p. 1638.

158. Glover, J.D., et al., 2010B, Perennial questions of hydrology and climate. Science, V. 330, p. 33-34.

159. Gore, Al, 2013, The Future: Six Drivers of Global Change. Random House, New York, NY, 592 p.

160. Grace, Stephen, 2012, Dam Nation: How Water Shaped the West and Will Determine its Future. Globe Pequot Press, Giulford, CT, 360 p.

161. GRAIN, 2012, Squeezing Africa Dry. Report dated 11 June 2012. http://www.grain.org/article/entries/4516-squeezing-africa-dry-behind-every-land-grab-is-a-water-grab

162. Grange, Kevin, 2012, Sea change. National Parks, V. 86, N. 4, p. 24-25.

163. Green, Emily, 2008, Quenching Las Vegas' Thirst. Five-part series published in the Las Vegas Sun on June 1, 8, 15, 22, and 29, 2008. www.lasvegassun.com/news/2008/

164. Grossi, Mark, 2010, "Chinatown II?" Water bank sued as wells go dry. The Fresno Bee, 5 September 2010. www.fresnobee.com/2010/09/05/2066738

165. Grubel, James, 2007, Australian water crisis could be worse than thought. Reuters, 16 May 2007.

166. Guymon, G. L., 1994, Unsaturated Zone Hydrology. Prentice Hall, Englewood Cliffs, NJ, 210 p.

167. Ham, Becky, 2012, In a "flattening" world, innovation must be global, S&T leaders say. Science, V. 335, p. 1593.

168. Hansen, James, 2009, Storms of My Grandchildren. Bloomsbury USA, New York, NY, 304 p.

169. Hansen, James, 2012, Game over for the climate. NY Times Op-Ed, 9 May 2012.

170. Hansen, James, Sakiko Sato, and Reto Ruedy, 2012, Perception of climate change. Proceedings of the National Academy of Science, 6 August, 2012. doi:10.1073/pnas.1205276109

171. Harder, Ben, 2002, Water for the rock. Science News, V. 161, Issue 12, p. 184. www.sciencenews.org/?M=A/view/feature/id/2577/title/Water_for_the_Rock

172. Harkinson, Josh, 2009, What's your water footprint?/Paying through the hose. Mother Jones, V. 34, No. 4, p. 54-59.

173. Harris, S.A., 1972, Hydrology, coastal terrain *in* Fairbridge, R.W. (Ed), The Encyclopedia of Geochemistry and Environmental Science. Van Nostrand Reinhold Company, New York, NY, p. 535-538.

174. Heath, R.C., 1982, Classification of ground-water systems of the United States. Ground Water, V. 20, No. 4, p. 393-401.

175. Heath, R.C., 1983 (revised 2005), Basic groundwater hydrology. US Geological Society Water Supply Paper 2220. pubs.usgs.gov/wsp/wsp2220/

176. Heath, R.C., 1988, Hydrogeologic setting of regions *in* Back, William, et al. (Eds), Hydrogeology. Geol. Society of America, Boulder, CO, p. 15-23.

177. Heath, R.C. and Trainer, F.W., 1968, Introduction to Ground-water Hydrology. John Wiley, New York, NY, 284 p.

178. Heberger, Matthew, 2012, Australia's millennium drought: impacts and responses *in* Gleick, P.H.: The World's Water, Volume 7. Island Press, Washington, DC, p. 97-125.

179. Hebert, David, 2010, Impossible odds, irrepressible hope: Pakistan's water woes and the science that can solve them. Earth Magazine. www.earthmagazine.org/earth/article/3a4-7da-a-5

180. Hellmer, H.H., et al., 2012, Twenty-first century warming of a large Antarctic ice-shelf cavity by a redirected coastal current. Nature, V. 485, p. 225-228.

181. Helm, Dieter, 2012, The Carbon Crunch. Yale University Press, New Haven, CT, 304 p.

182. Hertsgaard, Mark, 2011, A great green wall for Africa? The Nation, 21 November 2011, p. 22-26.

183. Hill, Carol, and Forti, Paolo, 1997, Cave Minerals of the World, 2nd Edition. National Speleological Society, Huntsville, AL, 463 p.

184. Higgins, C.G., 1990, Seepage-induced cliff recession and regional denudation, *in* Higgins, C.G., and Coates, D.R. (Eds), Groundwater Geomorphology; The Role of Subsurface Water in Earth-Surface Processes and Landforms: Boulder, Colorado, Geological Society of America Special Paper 252, p. 291-317.

185. Hiscock, Kevin M., 2005, Hydrogeology: Principles and Practice. Blackwell, Oxford, UK, 389 p.

186. Hobba, W.A., Jr., et al., 1979, Hydrology and geochemistry of thermal springs of the Appalachians. US Geological Society Professional Paper 1044-E, 36 p.

187. Hoekstra, V.Y. and A.K. Chapagsin, 2006, The Water Footprint of Nations. Water Resource Management, 12 p. http://www.waterfootprint.org/Reports/Hoekstra_and_Chapagain_2006.pdf

188. Hoffman, S.J., 2009, Planet Water: Investing in the World's Most Precious Resource. John Wiley, New York, NY, 368 p.

189. Holzer, T.L., 1979, Elastic expansion of lithosphere caused by groundwater depletion. Journal of Geophysical Research. onlinelibrary.wiley.com/doi/10.1029/JB084iB09p04689/pdf

190. Hsieh, P.A., and J.D. Bredehoeft, 1981, A reservoir analysis of the Denver earthquakes. Journal of Geophysical Research, V. 86, p. 903-920.

191. Hubbert, M.K., 1940, The theory of groundwater motion. Journal of Geology V. 48, No. 8, 785-944.

192. Hudak, P.F., 2000, Principles of Hydrogeology, 2nd Edition. CRC Press LLC, Boca Raton, FL, 204 p.

193. Hughes, J.D., 2012, Drill, baby, drill: Can unconventional fuels usher in a new era of energy abundance? Post Carbon Institute Report http://www.postcarbon.org/drill-baby-drill/report

194. Hunt, C.G., 1974, Natural Regions of the United States and Canada. W.H. Freeman, San Francisco, CA, 725 p.

195. Hvorslev, M.J., 1951, Time lab and soil permeability in groundwater observations. US Army Corps of Engineers, Waterway Experiment Station Bulletin 36, Vicksburg, MS.

196. Inman, Mason, 2007, The dark and mushy side of a frozen continent. Science, V. 317, p. 35-36.

197. Institute for Water and Watersheds, 2012, Bottled Water in Oregon. Oregon State University, September, 2012, www.water.oregonstate.edu.

198. Jackson, J.A. (Ed), 1997, Glossary of Geology, Fourth Edition. American Geological Institute, Alexandria, VA, 769 p.

199. Jacob, C.E., 1946, Radial flow in a leaky artesian aquifer. Transcripts of the American Geophysical Union V. 27, p. 198-208.

200. Jacobson, Michael, Michael Webster, and Kalanethy Vairavamoorthy (Eds), 2013, *The Future of Water in African Cities: Why Waste Water?* World Bank, Washington, DC, 199 p. http://water.worldbank.org/node/84190

201. Jagerskog, Anders, 2005, Water sharing between Israel, Jordan, and the Palestinians *in* Starke, Linda (Ed), State of the World 2005. W.W. Norton, New York, NY, p. 86.

202. Jenkins, Matt, 2012, Water works. The Nature Conservancy Magazine, 2012, Issue 2, p.28-43.

203. Jiang, Jia-Qian, et al., 2012, Arsenic contaminated groundwater and its treatment options in Bangladesh. International Journal of Environmental Research and Public Health, V. 10, No. 1, p. 18-46. doi:10.3390/ijerph10010018

204. Jiao, Li, and Richard Stone, 2011, China looks to balance its carbon books. Science, V. 334, p. 886-887.

205. Johnson, A.I., 1967, Specific yield-compilation of specific yields for various materials. US Geologic Survey Water Supply Paper 1662-D, 74 p.

206. Johnson, Eric, 2013, Radioactive waste leaking from six tanks at Washington state nuclear site. Reuters, Seattle, 23 February 2013.

207. Jones, F.L., 1975, Water: The history of Las Vegas – Volume 1. Las Vegas Valley Water District, Las Vegas, NV, 171 p.

208. Jorgensen, D.G., et al., 1988, Region 16, Central Nonglaciated Plains *in* Back, William, et al. (Eds), 1988, Hydrogeology. Geol. Society of America, Boulder, CO, p.141-156.

209. Joughin, Ian, R.B. Alley, and D.M. Holland, 2012, Ice-sheet response to oceanic forcing. Science, V. 338, p. 1172-1176.

210. Kasting, J.F., 2003, The origins of water on Earth. Scientific American, V. 13, No. 3, p. 28-33.

211. Kennedy, Sara, 2005, Florida focuses on saving its endangered natural springs. Associated Press, 10 January, 2005.

212. Kerr, R.A., 2009, Northern India's groundwater is going, going, going... Science, V. 325, p. 798.

213. Kerr, R.A., 2011, Vital details of global warming are eluding forecasters. Science, V. 344, p. 173-174.

214. Kerr, R.A., 2012, Ice-free Arctic Sea may be years, not decades, away. Science, V. 337, p. 1591.

215. Kerr, R.A., 2013, The psst that pierced the sky is now churning the sea. Science, V. 339, p. 500.

216. Khan, M.A., et al., 2008, Panicum turgidum, a potentially sustainable cattle feed alternative to maize for saline areas. Agriculture, Ecosystems, Environment, V. 129, Issue 4, p. 542-546.

217. Kiehl, Jeffrey, 2011, Lessons from Earth's past. Science, V. 331, p. 158-159.

218. King, F.H., 1899, Principles and conditions of the movements of groundwater. US Geological Survey 19th Annual Report., Part 2, p. 59-294.

219. Kintisch, Eli, 2013, Climate study highlights wedge issue. Science, V 339, p. 128-129.

220. Kirwan, M.L., et al., 2010 Limits on the adaptability of coastal marshes to rising sea level. Geophysical Research Letters, 1 December 2010, V. 37. doi:10.1029/2010GL045489L23401

221. Klein, Naomi, 2011, Capitalism vs. the climate. The Nation, 28 November 2011, p.11-21.

222. Klimchouk, et al., (eds), 2000, Speleogenesis: Evolution of Karst Aquifers. National Speleological Society, Huntsville, AL, 527 p.

223. Knox, R.C., D.A. Sabatini, and L.W. Canter, 1993, Subsurface Transport and Fate Processes, Lewis Publishers, Boca Raton, FL, 430 p.

224. Konikow, L.F., 2011, Contribution of global groundwater depletion since 1900 to sea-level rise. Geophysical Research Letters, V. 38, L17401, doi:10.1029/2011GL048604

225. Konikow, L.F., and C.E. Neuzil, 2007, A method to estimate groundwater depletion from confining layers. Water Resource Research, V. 43, W07417. doi:10.1029/2006WR005597

226. Korten, D.C., 2007, The Great Turning: From Empire to Earth Community. Berrett-Koehler Publishers, San Francisco, CA, 402 p.

227. Kreamer, D.K., et al., 2012, Water and international security. Journal of Contemporary Water Research and Education, Issue 149. ucowr.org/journal/item/315-issue-149-water-and-international-security.

228. Kresic, Neven, 2008, Groundwater Resources: Sustainability, Management, and Restoration. McGraw-Hill, New York, NY, 852 p.

229. Kresic, Neven, 2013, Water in Karst: Management, Vulnerability, and Restoration. McGraw-Hill, New York, NY, 708 p.

230. Kromm, D.E., and White, S.E. (Eds), 1992, Groundwater Exploitation in the High Plains. University Press of Kansas, Lawrence, KS, 240 p.

231. Kubato, S.T., and C.L. Lant, 2013, Agricultural virtual water trade and water footprint of U.S. states. Annals of the Association of American Geographers, V. 103, Issue 2, p. 385-396.

232. Kuss, Amber, et al., 2012, Groundwater storage estimates in the Central Valley aquifer using GRACE data. www.earthzine.org/2012/01/01/

233. Larson, Christina, 2011, An unsung carbon sink. Science, V. 334, p. 886-887.

234. Larson, Christina, 2013, Losing arable land, China faces stark choice: adapt or go hungry. Science, V. 339, p. 644-645.

235. Lee, C.H., 1915, The determination of safe yield of underground reservoirs of the closed basin type. Transactions of the American Society of Civil Engineers, V. 78, p. 148-151.

236. Lee, K., Fetter, C.W., and J.E. McCray, 2003, Hydrogeology Laboratory Manual. Pearson Education, Upper Saddle River, NJ, 150 p.

237. Lee, Sukyoung, and S.B. Feldstein, 2013, Detecting ozone- and greenhouse gas-driven wind trends with observational data. Science, V. 339, p. 563-567.

238. LeGrand, H.E., 1988, Region 21, Piedmont and Blue Ridge *in* Back, William, et al. (Eds), Hydrogeology. Geological Society of America, Boulder, CO, p. 201-208.

239. Lenzer, Anna, 2009, Spin the bottle. Mother Jones, V. 34, No. 5, p.34-39, 81-82.

240. Leonard Rice Engineers, Inc., Meurer and Associates, and Ryley, Carlock, and Applewhite, January 2007, Holistic Approach to Sustainable Water Management in northwest Douglas County, Colorado.

241. Leopold, L.B., 1997, Water, Rivers and Creeks. University Science Books, Sausalito, CA, 185 p.

242. LePage, Michael, 2012, Global Warning. New Scientist, 17 November 2012, p.34-39.

243. Leslie, Jacques, 2005, Deep Water: The Epic Struggle Over Dams, Displaced People, and the Environment. Farrar, Straus and Giroux, New York, NY, 352 p.

244. Lindsey, B.D., et al., 2009, Factors affecting water quality in selected carbonate aquifers in the United States, 1993-2005. US Geological Survey Scientific Investigations Report 2008-5240, 117 p.

245. Liu, Jianguo, and Wu Yang, 2012, Water sustainability for China and beyond. Science, V. 337, p. 649-650.

246. Liu, Yingling, 2006, Groundwater overdraft problem persists *in* Starke, Linda (Ed), Vital Signs 2006-2007. Worldwatch Institute, W.W. Norton, New York, p. 104-105.

247. Lovelock, James, 2009, The Vanishing Face of Gaia: A Final Warning. Basic Books, New York, NY, 278 p.

248. MacDonald, A.M., et al., 2012, Quantitative maps of groundwater resources in Africa. Environmental Research Letters, V. 7, No.2. doi:10.1088/1748-9326/7/2/024009

249. Malakoff, David, 2011, Are more people necessarily a problem? Science V. 333, p. 544-546.

250. Manahan, S.E., 1993, Fundamentals of Environmental Chemistry. CRC Press, Boca Raton, FL, 855 p.

251. Manahan, S.E., 1997, Environmental Science and Technology. Lewis Publishers, Boca Raton, FL, 641 p.

252. Mason, M., 2009, World's highest drug level in Indian stream. Associated Press, 23 January 2009.

253. Mastny, Lisa, and R. P. Cincotta, 2005, Examining the connections between population and security *in* Starke, Linda (Ed), State of the World 2005, W.W. Norton, New York, NY, p.22-39.

254. Maxwell, Steve, 2011, Water Market Review. TechKNOWLEDGEy Strategic Group, Boulder, CO. www.tech-strategy.com

255. Maxwell, Steve, and Scott Yates, 2011, The Future of Water. American Water Works Association, Denver, CO, 256 p.

256. Mays, L.W. (Ed), 1996, Water Resources Handbook: McGraw Hill, New York, NY, 1568 p.

257. McCaffrey, Steven, 2007, The Law of International Watercourses. Oxford University Press, Oxford, UK 550 p.

258. McDonald, Bernadette, and Douglas Jehl (Eds), 2003, Whose Water Is It? National Geographic Society, Washington, DC, 232 p.

259. McDonald, M.G. and A.W. Harbaugh, 1988, A modular three-dimensional finite-difference ground-water flow model. US Geological Survey, Techniques of Water-Resources Investigations 06-A1, 576 p.

260. McElroy, Michael, and D.J. Baker, 2012, Climate Extremes: Recent Trends with Implications for National Security. Harvard Workshop Report, 138 p. http://environment.harvard.edu/climate-extremes.

261. McGuire, V.L., 2013, Water-level and storage changes in the High Plains aquifer, predevelopment to 2011 and 2009-11. US Geological Survey Scientific Investigations Report 2012-5291, 15 p.

262. McGuire, V.L., et al., 2003, Water storage and approaches to groundwater management, High Plains aquifer, 2000. US Geological Survey, Circular 1243, 56 p.

263. Meinshausen, Malte, et al., 2009, Greenhouse-gas emission targets for limiting global warming to 2°C. Nature V. 458, p. 1158-1162.

264. Meinzer, O.E., 1923, The occurrence of ground water in the United States, with discussion on principles. US Geological Survey Water Supply Paper 489, 321 p.

265. Meinzer, O.E., 1927, Plants as indicators of groundwater. US Geological Society Water Supply Paper 577, 95 p.

266. Meinzer, O.E., 1928, Compressibility and elasticity of artesian aquifers. Economic Geology 23, p. 263-291.

267. Meinzer, O.E. (Ed), 1942, Hydrology. McGraw-Hill, New York, NY, 712 p.

268. Merritts, Dorothy, Andrew De Wet , and Kirsten Menking, 1998, Environmental Geology: An Earth System Science Approach. W.H. Freeman, San Francisco, CA, 550 p.

269. Micale, Giorgio, Andrea Cipollina, and Lucio Rizzuti, 2009, Seawater Desalination for Freshwater Production *in* Cipollina, Andrea, et al., Seawater Desalination: Green Energy and Technology 2009, p. 1-15. Springer-Verlag, Berlin, Germany. DOI10.1007/978-3-642-01150-4_1

270. Midkiff, Kenneth, 2007, Not a Drop to Drink: the American Water Crisis and What You Can Do. New World Library, Novato, CA, 212 p.

271. Miller, J.A., 1988, Coastal Plain deposits *in* Back, William, et al. (Eds), 1988, Hydrogeology. Geological Society of America, Boulder, CO, p. 315-322.

272. Miller, Lisa, 2007, Bless this bottled water. Newsweek, 17 December 2007, p. 16.

273. Moore, J.E., 2011, Field Hydrogeology: A Guide for Site Investigations and Report Preparation, 2nd Edition. CRC Press, Boca Raton, FL, 190 p.

274. Moore, K.D., and M.P. Nelson, 2011, Moral Ground: Ethical Action for a Planet in Peril. Trinity University Press, San Antonio, TX, 524p.

275. Musgrave, G.W., and H.N. Holtan, 1964, Section 12: Infiltration *in* Chow, Vente (Ed), Handbook of Applied Hydrology, McGraw-Hill, New York, NY.

276. Naftz, David, et al. (Editors), 2002, Handbook of Groundwater Remediation using Permeable Reactive Barriers: Applications to Radionuclides, Trace Metals, and Nutrients. Academic Press, Waltham, MA, 544 p.

277. Narasimhan, T.N., 2009A, Groundwater: from mystery to management. Environmental Research Letters, V. 4, p. 1–11. iopscience.iop.org/1748-9326/4/3/035001

278. Narasimhan, T.N., 2009B, Groundwater Mining: American Experience. The Hindu, 28 December 2009. www.hindu.com/2009/12/28/stories

279. National Academy of Science, 2012A, Alternatives for managing the nation's complex contaminated groundwater sites. National Academies Press, Washington, DC, 320 p. http://www.nap.edu

280. National Academy of Science, 2012B, Himalayan Glaciers: Climate Change, Water Resources, and Water Security. National Academies Press, Washington, DC, 143 p. http://dels.nas.edu/Report/Himalayan-Glaciers-Climate-Change-Water-Resources/13449

281. National Academy of Science, 2012C, Sustainable Water and Environmental Management in the California Bay-Delta. http://dels.nas.edu/Report/Sustainable-Water-Environment/13394

282. National Ground Water Association, 2005, Ground Water Sustainability: A White Paper. National Ground Water Association, Westerville, OH, 13 p.

283. National Intelligence Council, 2012, Global Water Security. ICA 2012-08, 2 February 2012.
http://www.dni.gov/files/documents/Special%20Report_ICA%20Global%20Water%20Security.pdf

284. Nelson, D.M., 1991, Practical Handbook of Groundwater Monitoring. Lewis Publishers, Boca Raton, FL, 728 p.

285. Newton, David E. 2003, Encyclopedia of Water. Greenwood Press, Westport, CT, 424 p.

286. Ney, Jr., R.E., 1990, Where Did That Chemical Go? A Practical Guide to Chemical Fate and Transport in the Environment. Van Nostrand Reinhold, New York, NY, 192 p.

287. Nghiem, et al., 2012, The extreme melt across the Greenland ice sheet in 2012. Geophysical Research Letters, V. 39, Issue 20. onlinelibrary.wiley.com/doi/10.1029/2012GL053611.

288. Nielsen, D.M. (Ed), 2005, Practical Handbook of Environmental Site Characterization and Groundwater Monitoring, 2nd Edition. CRC Press, 1328 p.

289. Nielsen, D.M. and Gillian, 2007, The Essential Handbook of Ground-water Sampling. CRC Press, Boca Raton, FL, 328 p.

290. Nierenberg, Danielle, and Brian Halweil, 2005, Cultivating food security *in* Starke, Linda (Ed), State of the World 2005, Norton & Co., New York, p. 62-77.

291. Novikov, A.P., et al., 2006, Colloid transport of plutonium in the far-field of the Mayak Production Association, Russia. Science, V. 314, p. 638-641.

292. Nyer, E.K., et al., 1996, *In Situ* Treatment Technology. Lewis Publishers, Boca Raton, FL, 329 p.

293. Organization for Economic Cooperation and Development, 2008, OECD Environmental Outlook to 2030. OECD Publishing, Paris, France, 519 p. www.oecd.org/dataoecd/29/33/40200582.pdf

294. Office of Technology Assessment, 1984, Protecting the Nation's Groundwater from Contamination. Office of Technology Assessment, OTA-0-233. OTA, Washington, D.C., 244 p.

295. Oki, Taikan, and Shinjiro Kanae, 2006, Global hydrological cycles and world water resources. Science, V. 313, p. 1068-1072.

296. Onda, K., J. LoBuglio, and J. Bartram, 2012, Global access to safe water: Accounting for water quality and the resulting impact on MDG progress. International Journal of Environmental Research and Public Health, V. 9, p. 880-894.

297. Outwater, Alice, 1997, Water: A Natural History. Basic Books, New York, NY, 224 p.

298. Pacala and Robert Socolow, 2004, Stabilization wedges: solving the climate problem for the next 50 years with current technologies. Science V. 305, p. 968-972.

299. Palaniappan, Meena, et al., 2012, Water Quality *in* Gleick, P.H., The World's Water Volume 7. Island Press, Washington, DC, p. 45-72.

300. Palmer, A.N., 1990, Groundwater processes in karst terranes, *in* Higgins, C.G., and Coates, D.R. (Eds), Groundwater Geomorphology: The Role of Subsurface Water in Earth-Surface Processes and Landforms. Boulder, Colorado, Geological Society of America Special Paper 252, p. 177-209.

301. Park, W.S., and Carmichael, J.S., 1990, Geology and ground-water resources of the Memphis Sand in western Tennessee. UW Geological Survey Water Resources Investigation Report 89-4131. pubs.usgs.gov/wri/wrir88-4182/pdf/wrir_88-4182_a.pdf

302. Pearce, Fred, 2004, Asian farmers sucking the continent dry. New Scientist. www.newscientist.com/articles/dn6321-asian-farmers-sucking-the-continent-dry.html

303. Pearce, Fred, 2006, When the Rivers Run Dry: Water - the Defining Crisis of the 21st Century. Beacon Press, Boston, MA, 324 p.

304. Pearce, Fred, 2012, The Land Grabbers: The New Fight Over Who Owns the Earth. Beacon Press, Boston, MA, 301 p.

305. Pederson, N., et al., 2012, A long-term perspective on a modern drought in the American Southeast. Environmental Research Letters, V. 7.014034. doi:10.1088/1748-9326/7/1/014034

306. Perry, Alex, 2012, Africa Rising. Time, V. 180, No. 23, p. 48-52.

307. Perry, Michael, 2008, Ancient Water Source for Australia. Reuters, 23 December 2008.

308. Petley, D.N. and Petley, D.J. 2006, On the initiation of large rockslides: perspectives from a new analysis of the Vaiont movement record *in* Evans, S.G., et al. (Eds), Massive Rock Slope Failure. Kluwer, Rotterdam (NATO Science Series, Earth and Environmental Sciences 49), p. 77-84.

309. Pittman, Craig, 2012, Florida's vanishing springs. Tampa Bay Times. http://www.tampabay.com/news/environment/water/floridas-vanishing-springs/1262988

310. Pitzke, Marc, 2011, Hanford nuclear waste still poses serious risks. www.spiegel.de/international/world/0,1518,752944,00.html

311. Poehls, D.J., and G.J. Smith (Editors), 2009, Encyclopedic Dictionary of Hydrogeology. Academic Press, Waltham, MA, 517 p.

312. Porgans, Patrick, and Carter, L.G., 2011, Budgets, billionaires, bonds, big profits and the Brown family, Parts One and Two. 4 August 2011 and 8 August 2011. www.lloydgcarter.com/files_lgc/

313. Postel, S.L., 1999, The Pillar of Sand: Can the Irrigation Miracle Last? The Worldwatch Institute, W.W. Norton, New York, NY, 313 p.

314. Postel, S.L, 2010, Will there be enough? Yes! Magazine, Summer, 2010, Issue 54, p.18-23.

315. Postel, S.L, 2011, Getting more crop per drop *in* Starke, Linda (Ed), State of the World 2011. The Worldwatch Institute, W.W. Norton, New York, NY, p. 39-48.

316. Postel, S.L. and Amy Vickers, 2004, Boosting water productivity, *in* Starke, Linda (Ed), State of the World 2004. The Worldwatch Institute, W.W. Norton, New York, NY, p. 46-65.

317. Powell, J.L., 2008, Dead Pool: Lake Powell, Global Warming, and the Future of Water in the West. University of California Press, Berkeley, CA, 284 p.

318. Powell, J.W., 1878, Report on the lands of the arid region of the United States, 2nd ed. US Government Printing Office, Washington, DC, 203 p. pubs.er.usgs.gov/publication/70039240

319. Pratka, Ruby, 2012, Water and sanitation in Africa. World Press, 26 March 1012. http://worldpress.org/Africa/3897.cfm

320. Prudhomme, Alex, 2011, The Ripple Effect: The Fate of Freshwater in the Twenty-First Century. Scribner, New York, NY, 435 p.

321. Qiu, Jane, 2011, China to spend billions cleaning up groundwater. Science, V. 334, p. 745.

322. Qiu, Jane, 2012, Winds of change. Science, V. 338, p. 879-881.

323. Radford, Benjamin, 2011, Dowsing: dubious, discredited, and dangerous. Skeptical Inquirer, V. 35, Issue 5, p. 36-37.

324. Rawe, Kathryn, et al., 2012, A Life Free from Hunger: Tackling Child Malnutrition. Nutrition Report 2012. Save the Children, London, UK. www.savethechildren.org

325. Reij, Chris, 2011, Investing in trees to mitigate climate change *in* Starke, Linda (Ed), State of the World 2011. The Worldwatch Institute, W.W. Norton, New York, NY, p. 86-93.

326. Reisner, Marc, 1986, Cadillac Desert: The American West and its Disappearing Water. Viking Penguin Books, New York, NY, 582 p.

327. Rignot, E., et al., 2011, Acceleration of the contribution of the Greenland and Antarctic ice sheets to sea level rise. Geophysical Research Letters, V. 38, LO5503, doi:10.1029/2011GLO46583.

328. Robb, J.M., 1990, Groundwater processes in the submarine environment, *in* Higgins, C.G., and Coates, D.R. (Eds), Groundwater Geomorphology; The Role of Subsurface Water in Earth-Surface Processes and Landforms: Boulder, Colorado, Geological Society of America Special Paper 252, p. 267-281.

329. Rodell, Matthew, Isabella Velicogna, and J.S. Famiglietti, 2009, Satellite-based estimates of groundwater depletion in India. Nature, V. 460. doi:10.1038/nature08238

330. Rosenshein, J.S., and J.E. Moore, 2012, History of the Development of Hydrogeology in the United States. National Ground Water Association Press, Columbus, OH, 200 p.

331. Rozema, Jelte, and Timothy Flowers, 2008, Crops for a salinized world. Science V. 322, p. 1478-1480.

332. Rulli, M.C., Antonio Saviori, and Paolo D'Odorico, 2013, Global land and water grabbing. Proceedings of the National Academy of Science, V. 110, No. 3, p. 892-897. www.pnas.org/content/early/2013/01/02/1213163110.abstract

333. Rural Water Supply Network, 2009, Myths of the rural water supply sector. Perspectives No. 4, RWSN, St. Gallen, Switzerland, 7 p.

334. Saatchi, Sassan, et al., 2013, Persistent effects of a severe drought on Amazonian forest canopy. Proceedings of the National Academy of Science, V. 110, No. 2, p. 565-570. www.pnas.org/content/110/2/

335. Sabo, J.L., et al., 2010, Reclaiming freshwater sustainability in the Cadillac Desert. Proceedings of the National Academy of Science, V. 197, No. 50. www.pnas.org/cgi/doi/10.1073/pnas.1009734108)

336. Sahagian, D.L., F.W. Schwartz, and D.K. Jacobs, 1944, Direct anthropogenic contributions to sea level rise in the twentieth century. Nature, V. 367, p. 54-57.

337. Salinas, Irena (Ed), 2010, Written in water: Messages of hope for Earth's most precious resource. National Geographic, Washington, DC, 304 p.

338. Sampat, Payal, 2000, Deep trouble: The hidden threat of groundwater pollution. Worldwatch Paper 154, Worldwatch Institute, Washington, DC, 55 p.

339. Sanders, K.T., and M.E. Webber, 2012, Evaluating the energy consumed for water use in the United States. *Environmental Research Letters* V. 7, No. 3 http://iopscience.iop.org/1748-9326/7/3/034034.

340. Sanders, Laura L., 1998, A Manual of Field Hydrology: Prentice Hall, Upper Saddle River, NJ, 381 p.

341. Sandia National Laboratories, 2005, The Electricity/Water Nexus: U.S. Energy Sustainability, The Missing Piece. www.sandia.gov/energy-water/nexus_overview.htm

342. Sarni, Will, 2011, Corporate Water Strategies. Routledge, London, UK, 224 p.

343. Scherr, Sara J., Jeffrey Milder, and Louise Buck, 2012, Landscapes for people, food and nature: the vision, the evidence and next steps. EcoAgriculture Partners for the Landscapes for People, Food and Nature Initiative, 26 p. http://www.conservation.org/Documents/LPFN-ReportLandscapes-for-People-Food-and-Nature_Eco-agriculture_2012.pdf

344. Schiffries, C.M., 2004, Closing the gap between water sciences and water policy. Geotimes, May 2004, p. 17. agiweb.org/geotimes/may04/comment.html

345. Schneider, S.J., 2011, Water supply well guidelines for use in developing countries. Stephen J. Schneider, 46 p. http://aquadoc.typepad.com/files/water-supply-well-guidelines—first-edition-printii.pdf

346. Schröter, Dagmar, et al., 2005, Ecosystem service supply and vulnerability to global change in Europe. Science, V. 310, p. 1333-1337.

347. Schwartz, F.W., 1975, On radioactive waste management: An analysis of the parameters controlling subsurface contaminant transfer. Journal of Hydrology, V. 27, p. 51-71.

348. Schwartz, F.W., and Hubar Zhang, 2002, Fundamentals of Ground Water. John Wiley, New York, NY, 592 p.

349. Schwarzenbach, et al., 2006, The challenge of micropollutants in aquatic systems. Science, V. 313, p. 1072-1077.

350. Seed Magazine, 2009, The truth about water wars. 14 May 2009. SeedMagazine.com/content/article/the_truth_about_water_wars/

351. Selby, Jan, 2013, Cooperation, domination and colonization: The Israeli-Palestinian Joint Water Committee. Water alternatives, V. 6 No. 1, p. 1-24. www.water-alternatives.org/

352. Serrano, S.E., 2010, Hydrology for Engineers, Geologists, and Environmental Professionals, Second Edition: An Integrated Treatment. HydroScience Inc., Lexington, KY, 590 p.

353. Service, R.F., 2006, Desalination freshens up. Science, V. 313, p. 1088-1090.

354. Service, R.F., 2009, California's water crisis: worse to come? Science, V.323, p. 1665.

355. Sever, Megan, 2004, News notes: Volcanic avalanches. Geotimes, July 2004, p. 12-13.

356. Sever, Megan, 2006, Global water supply takes some heat. Geotimes, March 2006. www.geotimes.org/mar06/trends.html

357. Shankun, Jeremy, et al., 2012, Global warming preceded by increasing carbon dioxide concentration during the last deglaciation. Nature, V. 484, p. 49-54.

358. Sharp, Jr., J.M., 1988, Alluvial aquifers along major rivers *in* Back, William, et al. (Eds), Hydrogeology. Geological Society of America, Boulder, CO, p. 273-282.

359. Shepherd, Andrew, et al., 2012, A reconciled estimate of ice-sheet mass balance. Science V. 338, 1183-1189.

360. Shiklomanov, I.A., 1993, World fresh water resources *in* Gleick, P.H. (Ed), Water in Crisis, Oxford University Press, New York, NY, p. 13-24.

361. Shiklomanov, I.A, 1997, Comprehensive Assessment of the Freshwater Resources of the World. World Meteorological Organization, Geneva, Switzerland, 88 p.

362. Shiklomanov, I.A., 1998, World water resources: A new appraisal for the 21st century. IHP Rep. UNESCO, Paris, France.

363. Shiklomanov, I.A., 2000, Appraisal and assessment of world water resources. Water International V. 25, No. 1, p. 11-32.

364. Shiklomanov, I.A., and J.C. Rodda, 2003, World Water Resources at the Beginning of the 21st Century. Cambridge University Press, Cambridge, UK, 452 p.

365. Shiva, Vandana, 2002, Water Wars: Privatization, Pollution and Profit. South End Press, Cambridge, MA, 158 p.

366. Slater, Dashka, 2012, The frog of war. Mother Jones, V. 37, No. 1, p. 44-49, 67.

367. Sloan, C.E., and van Everdingen, R.O., 1988, Region 28, Permafrost region *in* Back, William, et al. (Eds), Hydrogeology. Geological Society of America, Boulder, CO, p. 263-270.

368. Smith, Michael, 2013, South Americans face upheaval in deadly water battles. Bloomberg Markets Magazine. http://www.bloomberg.com/news/2013-02-13/

369. Soliman, M.M., et al.,1998, Environmental Hydrogeology. CRC Press LLC, Boca Raton, FL, 386 p.

370. Solomon, Steven, 2011, Water: The Epic Struggle for Wealth, Power, and Civilization. Harper Collins, New York, NY, 624 p.

371. Speth, J.G., 2004, Red Sky at Morning. Yale University Press, New Haven, CT, 301 p.

372. Speth, J.G., 2008, The Bridge at the Edge of the World: Capitalism, the Environment, and Crossing from Crisis to Sustainability. Yale University Press, New Haven, CT, 320 p.

373. Starke, Linda (Ed), 2007, State of the World 2007: Our Urban Future. Norton, New York, NY, 250 p.

374. Starke, Linda (Ed), 2011, State of the World 2011: Innovations that Nourish the Planet. Norton, New York, NY, 237 p.

375. Stein, R.J. (Ed), 2008, Water Supply (Reference Shelf). H.W. Wilson Company, The Bronx, NY, 195 p.

376. Steltzer, Heidi, et al., 2009, Biological consequences of earlier snowmelt from desert dust deposition in alpine landscapes. Proceedings of the National Academy of Science, V. 106, No. 28, 11629-11634.

377. Stephenson, D.A., Fleming, A.H., and Mickelson, D.M., 1988, Glacial Deposits *in* Back, William, et al. (Eds), 1988, Hydrogeology. Geological Society of America, Boulder, CO, 301-314.

378. Stone, W.J., 1999, Hydrogeology in Practice. Prentice-Hall, Upper Saddle River, NJ, 248 p.

379. Sultana, Farhana, and Alex Loftus, eds, 2011, The Right to Water: Politics, Governance and Social Struggles. Routledge, Abington, Oxford, UK, 288 p.

380. Swihart, Thomas, 2008, Florida's Water: A Fragile Resource in a Vulnerable State. H.W. Wilson Company, The Bronx, NY, 195 p.

381. Teibel, Amy, 2007, US aid sanctions turn taps off critical Palestinian water, wastewater projects. Associated Press, 5 March 2007.

382. Tennesen, Michael, 2008, When juniper and woody plants invade, water may retreat. Science, V. 322, p. 1630-1631.

383. Terzaghi, K., and Peck, R.B., 1967, Soil Mechanics in engineering Practice. John Wiley, New York, NY, 729 p.

384. Testa, L.M., 2004, Highlights: Hydrogeology. Geotimes, July 2004. V. 49, No. 7. www.geotimes.org/july04/printTOC.html.

385. Theis, C.V., 1935, The relation between the lowering of the piezometric surface and the rate of discharge of a well using ground water storage. Transactions of the American Geophysical Union V. 16, p. 519-524.

386. Theis, C.V., 1940, The source of water derived from wells – essential factors controlling the response of an aquifer to development. Civil Engineering, American Society of Civil Engineers, p. 277-280.

387. Thornthwaite, C.W., and Mather, J.R., 1957, Instructions and tables for computing potential evapotranspiration and the water balance. Publication 10, Laboratory of Climatology, Centerton, NJ, p. 185-311.

388. Tindall, J.A., and J.R. Kunkel, 1999, Unsaturated Zone Hydrology for Scientists and Engineers. Pearson Education, Upper Saddle River, NJ, 624 p.

389. Todd, D.K., 1980, Groundwater Hydrology, 2nd Edition. John Wiley, New York, NY, 535 p.

390. Todd, D.K., and Mays, L.W., 2005, Groundwater Hydrology, 3rd Edition. John Wiley, New York, NY, 636 p.

391. Tolman, C.F., 1937, Ground Water. McGraw-Hill, New York, NY, 593 p.

392. Toth, J., 1963, A theoretical analysis of groundwater flow in small drainage basins. Journal of Geophysical Research, V. 68, p. 4795-4812.

393. Trainer, F.W., 1988, Plutonic and metamorphic rocks, *in* Back, William (Eds), 1988, Hydrogeology. Geological. Society of America, Boulder, CO, p. 367-380.

394. Treidel, Holger, J.L. Martin-Bordes, and J.J. Gurdak (Eds), 2011, Climate Change Effects on Groundwater Resources: A Global Synthesis of Findings and Recommendations. CRC Press, Zug, Switzerland, 414 p.

395. Turner, John, et al. (Eds), 2012, Antarctic Climate Change and the. Environment. British Antarctic Survey. www.scar.org/publications/occasionals/acce.html.

396. United Nations, 2009, The United Nations World Water Development Report 3: Water in a Changing World (Two Vols.). Routledge, London, UK, 432 p. www.unesco.org/water/wwap/wwdr/wwdr3/

397. United Nations Environment Programme, 2008, Vital Water graphics, 2nd edition. www.unep.org/dewa/vitalwater

398. United Nations Environment Programme, 2009, The Greening of Water Law: Managing Freshwater Resources for People and the Environment. www.unep.org/delc/PDF/UNEP_Greening_water_law.pdf

399. United Nations Environment Programme, 2012, Policy Implications of Warming Permafrost. http://is.gd/LBEOzg

400. United Nations Children's Fund and World Health Organization, 2012, Progress on Drinking Water and Sanitation: 2012 Update. www.unicef.org/media/files/JMPreport2012.pdf

401. United Nations Secretary-General's High-Level Panel on Global Sustainability, 2012, Resilient People, Resilient Planet – A Future worth Choosing. 30 January 2012. www.un.org/gsp/

402. United States Department of the Interior, Bureau of Reclamation, 1995, Ground Water Manual: A Water Resources Technical Publication, 2nd Edition. US Government Printing Office, Denver, CO, 661 p.

403. United States Environmental Protection Agency, 1987, Guidelines for Delineation of Wellhead Protection Areas. EPA 440/6-87-010, 215 p. http://nepis.epa.gov/Exe/ZyPURL.cgi?Dockey=2000LO01.txt

404. United States Environmental Protection Agency, 2001, Federal Remediation Technologies Roundtable Guide. www.frtr.gov/pubs.htm

405. United States Environmental Protection Agency, 2012, Contaminant MCLs. http://water.epa.gov/drink/contaminants/index.cfm.

406. United States Geological Survey, 2000, Ground Water Atlas of the United States. HA 730, USGS, Denver, CO, 300 p. pubs.usgs.gov/ha/ha730/.

407. United States Intelligence Community Assessment, 2012, Global Water Security. www.dni.gov/nic/ICA_Global Water security.pdf

408. Vajpeyi, D.K. (Ed), 1998, Water Resource Management. Praeger Publishers, Westport, CT, 192 p.

409. van der Gun, Jac, 2012, Groundwater and Global Change. UNESCO, Paris, France. http://is.gd/8QJ2gF

410. van Steenbergen, Frank, 2012, The Qinxu Groundwater Management System (video). www.thewaterchannel.tv/en/videos/categories/viewvideo/1577/groundwater/the-qinxu-groundwater-management-system

411. Vartabedian, Ralph, 2009, Nevada's hidden ocean of radiation. Los Angeles Times, 11/13/09.

412. Vaux, H.J., Jr., et al., 2011, A review of the use of science and adaptive management in California's draft Bay Delta Conservation Plan. National Academy of Sciences, Washington, DC. http://dels.nas.edu/Report/Review/13148.

413. Vengosh, Avner, 2004, Natural Boron Contamination in Mediterranean Groundwater. Geotimes, May 2004. http://www.geotimes.org/may04/feature_boron.html

414. Vengosh, Avner, et al., 2012, An Overview on the potential of groundwater contamination from shale gas development and hydro-fracturing. IAH 39thCongress, 9/18/12 sessions.

415. Verner, Dorte, 2012, Adaptation to a changing climate in the Arab countries : overview and technical summary. The World Bank MENA development report, Washington D.C. http://documents.worldbank.org/curated/en/2012/07/16919186/adaptation-changing-climate-arab-countries-overview-technical-summary

416. Vess, C.I., Editor, 2005, The future of hydrogeology. Ground Water, V. 13, No. 1, p. 1-349.

417. Vestra, S., L.V. Alexander, and F.W. Zwiers, 2012, Global increasing trends in annual maximum daily precipitation. Journal of Climate. doi:10.1175/JCLI-D-12-00502.1.

418. Vineis, Paolo, and Aneire Khan, 2012, Climate Change-Induced Salinity Threatens Health. Science, V. 338, 1028-1029.

419. Vorosmarty, C.J., et al., 2010, Global threats to human water security and river biodiversity. Nature, V. 467, p. 555–561. www.nature.com/nature/journal/v467/n7315/full/nature09440.html.

420. Voss, K. A., et al., 2013, Groundwater depletion in the Middle East from GRACE with implications for transboundary water management in the Tigris-Euphrates-Western Iran region. Water Resources Research, V. 49. http://onlinelibrary.wiley.com/doi/10.1002/wrcr.2007

421. Wada, Y., et al., 2010, Global depletion of groundwater resources. Geophysical Research Letters, V. 37, L20402, doi:10:1029/2010GL044571.

422. Ward, A.D., and Elliot, W.J., 1995, Environmental Hydrology. CRC Press, Inc. Boca Raton, FL, 462 p.

423. Watson, Ian, and A.D. Burnett, 1995, Hydrology: An Environmental Approach. CRC Press LLC, Boca Raton, FL, 702 p.

424. Waugh, D.W., et al., 2013, Recent changes in the ventilation of the southern oceans. Science, V. 339, p. 569-570.

425. Wells, J.D., et al., 2010, A Forest of Blue - Canada's Boreal Forest: The World's Waterkeeper. International Boreal Conservation Campaign, Seattle, WA, 74 p.

426. Wendland, Edson, 2009, Guarani Aquifer System: Groundwater for South America. German-Brazilian Workshop on Research for Sustainability, Sao Paulo, Brazil, March 13, 2009. www.dialogue4s.de/en/147.php.

427. Western Governors' Association, 2012, Water Transfers in the West. www.westgov.org/policies/doc_download/1657-water-transf...

428. White, W.B., 1988, Geomorphology and Hydrology of Karst Terrains. Oxford University Press, New York, NY, 464 p.

429. White, W.B., 1990, Surface and near-surface karst landforms, *in* Back, William, et al. (Eds), Hydrogeology. Geological Society of America, Boulder, CO, p. 157-175.

430. WHYMAP, and J. Margat, 2008, Groundwater Resources of the World. http://www.whymap.org/whymap/EN/downloads/Global_maps; http://is.gd/V1jA5z

431. Wijnen, Marcus, et al., 2012, Managing the Invisible: Understanding and Improving Groundwater Governance. World Bank Water Paper, June 2012. http://www.worldbank.org/water.

432. Wilkinson, C.F., 1992, Crossing the Next Meridian: Land, Water, and the Future of the West. Island Press, Washington, DC, 400 p.

433. Williams, Ted, 2009, Watered Down. Audubon, V. 111, No. 2, p. 45-51.

434. Williams, Ted, 2011, Tarred and Feathered. Audubon, V. 113, No. 4, p. 24-34.

435. Williams, Ted, 2012, Breaching a Boondoggle. Audubon, V. 114, No. 4, p. 26-33.

436. Wolf, A.T., et al., 2005, Managing water conflict and cooperation *in* Starke, Linda (Ed), State of the World 2005. Worldwatch Institute, Norton, New York, NY, p. 80-95.

437. Wolff, E.W., 2012, Climate change: a tale of two hemispheres. Nature, Vol. 484, p. 41-42.

438. Wood, W.W., and L. A. Fernandez, 1988, Volcanic rocks, *in* Back, William, et al. (Eds), 1988, Hydrogeology. Geological Society of America, Boulder, CO, p. 351-365.

439. World Bank, 2010, The Economic Impacts of Inadequate Sanitation in India. World Bank, Washington, DC. http://water.worldbank.org/water/publications/inadequate-sanitation-costs-india-equivalant-64-percent-gdp

440. World Bank, 2012A, Renewable Energy Desalination: An Emerging Solution to Close the Water Gap in the Middle East and North Africa. World Bank, Washington, DC. http://siteresources.worldbank.org/INTMNAREGTOPWATRES/Resources/Desal_An_Emerging_Solution_to_Close_MENAs_Water_Gap.pdf

441. World Bank, 2012B, Red Sea – Dead Sea Water Conveyance Study Program Draft Final Feasibility Study Report. World Bank, Washington, DC. http://web.worldbank.org/WBSITE/EXTERNAL/COUNTRIES/MENAEXT/EXTREDSEADEADSEA/0

442. World Water Council, 2009, Water at a crossroads: Dialogue and debate at the Fifth World Forum report. World Water Council, Marseilles, 70 p.

443. Yudelson, Jerry, 2010, Dry Run: Preventing the Next Urban Water Crisis. New Society Publishers, Gabriola Island, British Columbia, Canada, 304 p.

444. Zachara, J.M., et al., 2007, Geochemical processes controlling migration of tank wastes in Hanford's vadose zone. Vadose Zone Journal V. 6, No. 4, p. 985-1003.

445. Zetland, David, 2011, The End of Abundance: Economic Solutions to Water Scarcity. Aquanomics Press, Amsterdam, Netherlands, 294 p.

446. Zuin, Valentina, et al., 2011, Water supply services for Africa's urban poor: the role of resale. Journal of Water and Health, V. 9, No. 4, p. 773-784.

447. Zweynert, Astrid, 2012, "Whole landscape" approach challenges conventional wisdom in solving resource problems. 15 June 2012, www.trust.org/alertnet.

II Miscellaneous (Websites, Organizations, Blogs)

This list has been selected from the thousands of agencies, organizations, websites, and other sources of information about water. The name of the source is followed by its Internet URL (web address) and a brief description. Visit the websites for additional information including news, publications, conferences, and other activities.

Included here are major sources for information on water along with general references cited in this book. If I had to choose one source that I found most useful, it would be Water Wired, a blog by Dr. Michael Campana of Oregon State University; the blog provides an abundance of current water-related news and links to other sources.

448. **Advisory Committee on Water Information (ACWI),** www.acwi.gov/. US government organization created to identify water information needs, evaluate their effectiveness of water information programs and recommend improvements.

449. **AlertNet,** www.trust.org/alertnet. "The world's humanitarian news site."

450. **Alliance for Water Efficiency,** www.allianceforwaterefficiency.org/. Non-profit organization dedicated to the efficient and sustainable use of water.

451. **American Association for the Advancement of Science (AAAS),** www.aaas.org/. Largest general scientific organization in the US; publishes Science magazine.

452. **American Geophysical Union (AGU),** sites.agu.org/. Worldwide scientific community.

453. **American Ground Water Trust** www.agwt.org. Non-profit educational organization.

454. **American Institute of Hydrology (AIH),** www.aihydrology.org/. Organization founded in1981 to promote hydrology; certifies the competence and ethical conduct of professionals in all fields of hydrology.

455. **American Rainwater Catchment Systems Association,** www.arcsa.org/. Promotes sustainable rainwater harvesting practices.

456. **American Society for Testing and Materials (ASTM),** www.astm.org/. Develops international standards for materials, products, systems and services used in construction, manufacturing and transportation.

457. **American Society of Civil Engineers (ASCE),** www.asce.org/. Founded in 1852 to advance civil engineering, and serve its members and the public good.

458. **American Water Resources Association (AWRA),** www.awra.org/. Multidisciplinary organization founded in 1964. Publishes two peer-reviewed journals, JAWRA & IMPACT; sponsors numerous excellent conferences.

459. **American Water Works Association,** www.awwa.org/. Focuses on safe and sustainable water delivery of water to the public.

460. **Aquafed,** www.aquafed.org/. International Federation of Private Water Operators, created to connect all private sector providers of water and sanitation services.

461. **Aquanomics,** http://www.aguanomics.com/. Excellent, feisty blog by David Zetland, an economist specializing in water issues.

462. **The Arctic Monitoring and Assessment Programme (AMAP)**, www.amap.no/. Focuses on environmental protection in the Arctic.

463. **Chance of Rain**, chanceofrain.com/. Very good blog started by Emily Green; focused on water issues in the western US.

464. **The Chronicles Group**, http://www.chroniclesgroup.org/. A nonprofit based in California, launched by Jim Thebaut and others, and focused on raising awareness of water issues, especially by producing documentary films such as the "Running Dry Project."

465. **Coalition Eau**, www.coalition-eau.org/. A French coalition of NGOs devoted to improving access to water in developing countries.

466. **Columbia Water Center**, http://water.columbia.edu. Associated with the Earth Institute at Columbia University. Its mission is to creatively tackle issues of global water scarcity.

467. **Consultative Group on International Agricultural Research (CGIAR)**, www.cgiar.org/. Supports a network of various international agricultural research centers; associated with the International Water Management Institute.

468. **Development Bank of South Africa**, www.afdb.org/en/countries/southern-africa/south-africa/. Owned by the South African government, the bank encourages and funds economic growth, human resource development, and related projects in southern Africa.

469. **Earth Policy Institute**, www.earth-policy.org. Research organization founded by Lester R. Brown and dedicated to planning a sustainable future through its focus on global environmental and economic trends and solutions.

470. **European Environmental Agency (EEA)**, www.eea.europa.eu/. Major information source on water and other environmental topics in Europe; established by the European Economic Community in 1994.

471. **Food and Agricultural Organization (FAO)**, www.fao.org/nr/water/aquastat/. UN agency focused on eliminating hunger. Provides an abundance of global water data; includes the AQUASTAT and FAOSTAT databases.

472. **Food and Water Watch (FWW)**, www.foodandwaterwatch.org/. NGO and consumer advocacy group focusing on agriculture, food safety, and water quality.

473. **Geological Society of America (GSA)**, www.geosociety.org/. Devoted to advancing the geosciences; many publications, meetings.

474. **Geological Society of Canada**, www.gac.ca/. Promotes and develops the geological sciences in Canada.

475. **Global Environment and Technology Foundation,** www.getf.org/. Non-profit organization that promotes sustainable development through partnerships and targeted action.

476. **Global Water Forum,** www.globalwaterforum.org. UNESCO initiative intended to present knowledge and insight from leading water researchers and practitioners.

477. **The Groundwater Foundation**, www.groundwater.org. Nonprofit organization to educate and motivate people, including children, about groundwater.

478. **Global Water Partnership (GWP),** www.gwp.org/. International organization to support the sustainable development and management of water resources.

479. **Hydrogeologists Without Borders (HWB),** www.hwbwater.org. New organization; its goal is to provide hydrogeological expertise to the developing world.

480. **Hydro-Logic,** hydro-logic.blogspot.com. Matthew Garcia's excellent blog provides lists and summaries of recent reports on hydrology and water resources.

481. **International Association of Hydrogeologists (IAH),** www.iah.org. Membership organization headquartered in the UK; promotes groundwater research, education, conferences, et al.

482. **International Benchmarking Network for Water and Sanitation (IBNET),** www.ib-net.org/. Home of the world's largest database for water and sanitation.

483. **International Center for Technology Assessment (ICTA),** www.icta.org/. Provides information to the public on impacts of technology on society.

484. **International Energy Agency (IEA),** www.iea.org/. Implements an international program of energy cooperation.

485. **International Groundwater Resource Assessment Center,** www.un-igrac.org/. Assesses global groundwater resources; developing a Global Groundwater Information System.

486. **International Water Association,** www.iwahq.org/. Global network of 10,000 water professionals: publications, conferences, water data.

487. **International Water Law,** http://internationalwaterlaw.org/. Clearinghouse for international water law rights and related information.

488. **International Water Management Institute,** www.iwmi.cgiar.org/. Focuses on research on water management in agriculture, irrigation, and related topics.

489. **International Water Resources Association,** www.iwra.org/. International network of multidisciplinary experts on water resources; hosts the World Water Congresses and related conferences.

490. **The Land Institute,** http://www.landinstitute.org. Major focus is development of an ecologically stable agricultural system.

491. **National Academy of Science (NAS),** www.nas.edu/. Serves as the major adviser to the US on science, engineering, and medicine. Publishing activities include the Proceedings of the NAS and the National Academies Press.

492. **National Association of Clean Water Agencies (NACWA),** www.nacwa.org. Represents the interests of publicly owned wastewater treatment facilities, collection systems, and stormwater management agencies.

493. **National Ground Water Association (NGWA),** www.ngwa.org. Major US organization for groundwater professionals. Numerous publications, conferences.

494. **National Oceanic and Atmospheric Administration (NOAA),** http://noaa.gov. US government organization; primary source of climatic data for US.

495. **Natural Resources Defense Council (NRDC),** www.nrdc.org/. One of the most effective and informative environmental action groups.

496. **National Water Monitoring Council**, acwi.gov/monitoring/. US government organization created to provide a forum to improve the Nation's water quality.

497. **National Water Quality Monitoring Council (NWQMC)**, www.waterqualitydata.us/. US government source for water quality information; associated with the USGS and EPA.

498. **National Water Research Institute**, www.nwri-usa.org/. California-based nonprofit; sponsors projects and programs focused on ensuring safe, reliable sources of water.

499. **Office of Ground Water and Drinking Water**, http://water.epa.gov/type/ groundwater/. Part of the US EPA that focuses on groundwater protection.

500. **Organization for Economic Cooperation and Development (OECD)**, www.oecd.org/. International organization; primary function is to provide assistance on the economic, social and governance challenges of a globalized economy for its 34 member countries.

501. **Pacific Institute**, www.pacinst.org. Focuses on real-world solutions to problems like water shortages, habitat destruction, global warming, and environmental injustice.

502. **Raincatcher**, http://www.raincatcher.org. Non-profit organization committed to providing clean drinking water solutions to impoverished regions around the world.

503. **The Resilience Alliance**, www.resalliance.org/. Research organization of practitioners from many disciplines who collaborate to explore the dynamics of social-ecological systems; examines sustainability, adaptation, collapse, renewal.

504. **Rural Water Supply Network (RWSN)**, www.rwsn.ch. Global organization promoting sound practices in rural water supply.

505. **Save the Children**, www.savethechildren.org/. Internationally active NGO serving children in need in the United States and around the world.

506. **Soil Science Society of America**, https://www.soils.org/. International scientific society that fosters the transfer of knowledge and practices to sustain global soils.

507. **Stephens, Daniel B., & Associates**, www.dbstephens.com. Engineering and geoscience firm headquartered in Albuquerque, New Mexico.

508. **Stockholm International Water Institute**, www.siwi.org/. Organized to combat the global water crisis through research and administration of awards; sponsors **World Water Week**, an annual international conference.

509. **TechKNOWLEDGEy Strategic Group**, www.tech-strategy.com/. Colorado-based banking and management consulting firm focused on commercial water and environmental services industries.

510. **United Nations (UN)**, www.un.org/en/. World's largest, most prominent international organization.

511. **UN Children's Fund (UNICEF)**, www.unicef.org/. Focuses on children's rights, protection, and development, including water and sanitation needs.

512. **UN Educational, Scientific, and Cultural Organization (UNESCO)**, www.unesco.org/. Promotes collaboration among nations, conducts studies, facilitates knowledge and sustainable development.

513. **UN Environment Program (UNEP)**, www.unep.org/. Provides leadership in environmental issues within the UN system.

514. **UN International Water Law Commission**, http://internationalwaterlaw.org. Promotes the progressive development of international law as it pertains to waters that cross international boundaries.

515. **US Agency for International Development (USAID)**, www.usaid.gov/. Responsible for administering civilian foreign aid in support of foreign policy goals.

516. **US Department of Energy, Hanford**, www.hanford.gov/. Branch of the DOE which oversees operations at the Hanford Nuclear Reservation in Washington state.

517. **US Environmental Protection Agency (EPA)**, http://epa.gov. Government agency created to protect human health and the environment; includes an Office of Ground Water and Drinking Water: www.epa.gov/OGWDW/.

518. **US Federal Remediation Technologies Roundtable**, www.frtr.gov/. Provides information on hazardous waste treatment methods; no longer updated by EPA.

519. **US Geological Survey (USGS)**, www.usgs.gov. A major federal source for information about Earth, its natural and living resources, natural hazards, and the environment.

520. **US Water Alliance,** www.uswateralliance.org/. An educational organization founded, as the Clean Water America Alliance, in 2008 by water utilities and private corporations.

521. **US Water Partnership**, www.uswaterpartnership.org. Created in 2012; intended to generate opportunities for international cooperation and information sharing on water issues.

522. **WaterCan**, www.watercan.com/. Canadian NGO focusing on water and sanitation needs of the world's poorest people, especially in East Africa.

523. **Water Citizen News**, www.watercitizennews.com/. Provides both "hard" and "soft" water news for average citizens.

524. **Water-Culture Institute**, www.waterculture.org/. Charity promoting sustainable management of rivers, lakes, springs, and groundwater.

525. **Water Data Hub**, www.waterdatahub.org/. A centralized index of water data sources launched in 2012 by David Zetland and Ian Wren.

526. **Water 50/50**, blog.ucchm.org/. Prof. Jay Famiglietti's blog about the changing water cycle, groundwater depletion, and the future of freshwater availability.

527. **Water Footprint Network**, www.waterfootprint.org. Maintains a global database on the water footprint of products.

528. **Water for the Ages**, www.waterfortheages.org/. Abby Brown's blog on water and sanitation; focuses on need for toilets and related important, but often-avoided, topics.

529. **Watery Foundations**, http://www.wateryfoundation.com/. Tom Swihart's blog focusing on water management in Florida.

530. **Water Integrity Network (WIN),** www.waterintegritynetwork.net/. Promotes anti-corruption solutions in water, sanitation, and water resources management worldwide.

531. **Waterkeeper Alliance,** www.waterkeeper.org/. Advocacy organization dedicated to preserving and protecting water from polluters.

532. **Water Research Foundation,** www.waterrf.org/. Colorado-based research organization devoted to drinking water research.

533. **WaTER Technologies for Emerging Regions,** water.ou.edu/. The WaTER Center at the University of Oklahoma focuses on sustainable water and sanitation solutions for impoverished regions; conferences and outreach programs.

534. **Water Wired,** aquadoc.typepad.com/waterwired/. Michael Campana's excellent blog about "all things fresh water."

535. **World Bank,** www.worldbank.org. A major source of loans to the developing world; numerous publications related to water and sanitation.

536. **World Health Organization,** www.who.int/. UN agency concerned with international public health; many databases, publications, and related information sources.

537. **World Meteorological Organization,** www.wmo.int/. Geneva-based organization providing scientific information on Earth's atmosphere and climate.

538. **World Resources Institute,** www.wri.org/. Non-profit organization committed to change for a sustainable world.

539. **World Watch Institute,** www.worldwatch.org/. Analyzes and publishes interdisciplinary environmental data from around the world; emphasizes sustainability.

540. **World Water Council,** www.worldwatercouncil.org/. Independent international organization focused on cooperation among various water interests; sponsors the **World Water Forum** every three years.

541. **World-wide Hydrological Mapping and Assessment Program (WHYMAP),** www.whymap.org/. Program initiated in 2000 to provide data about the major groundwater resources of the world.

542. **World Wildlife Fund (WWF),** www.worldwildlife.org/. A leading organization for the conservation of wildlife and endangered species.

III Addendum

These sources were added as information became available while the manuscript was being finalized.

543. Aquafornia, www.aquafornia.com/. Blog focused on California water issues.

544. Barber, N.L., 2009, Water use in the United States. US Geological Survey Fact Sheet 2009-3098.

545. Calloway, Devin, David R. Jones, and S. E. Ingebritsen (Eds), 1999. Land Subsidence in the United States. U. S. Geological Survey Circular 1182.

546. De Grey, Laura, and Paul Link, nd, "Snake River Plain Aquifer," http:// geology.isu.edu/Digital _Geology_Idaho/Module15/mod15.htm.

547. Finkel, Elizabeth, 2009, Making every drop count in the buildup to a blue revolution. Science, V. 323, p. 1004-1005.

548. General Electric, 1997-2012, Handbook of Industrial Water Treatment. http://www.gewater.com/handbook

549. Gleick, P.H., and Heather Cooley, 2009, Energy implications of bottled water. Environmental Research Letters 4. doi: 10.1088/1748-9326/4/1/014009

550. Gleick, P.H., and Heather Cooley, 2012, Bottled water and energy, in The World's Water, Volume 7. Island Press, Washington, DC, p.157-164.

551. Gupta, R.S., 1997, Environmental Engineering and Science: An Introduction. Government Institutes, Rockville, MD, 498 p.

552. Heath, R.C., 1984. Ground-Water Regions of the United States. US Geological Survey Water-Supply Paper 2242.

553. International Alert, Peacebuilding organization. http://www.international-alert.org

554. Kohler, M.A., T. Nordenson, and D. Baker, 1959. Evaporation Maps for the United States, US Weather Bureau Technical Paper 37.

555. Leopold, L.B., M.G. Wolman, and M.P. Miller, Fluvial Processes in Geomorphology. W.H. Freeman, San Francisco, CA, 522 p.

556. Love, J.D., and J.C. Reed, Jr, 1968, Creation of the Teton Landscape. Grand Teton Natural History Association, 120 p.

557. Margat, Jean, and Jac van der Gun, 2013, Groundwater Around the World. CRC Press, Boca Raton, FL, 376 p.

558. Nader, Ralph, 2012, The Seventeen Solutions. Harper Collins, New York, NY, 357 p.

559. National Geographic Society, 1999. The National Geographic Desk Reference. Stonesong Press, New York, NY.

560. National Intelligence Council, 2008, Global Trends 2025: A Transformed World. Washington, DC: US Government Printing Office.

561. Pidwirny, M., 2006, Fundamentals of Physical Geography, 2nd Edition. www.physicalgeography.net/fundamentals/

562. Plummer, C.C., D.H. Carlson, and Lisa Hammersley, 2013, Physical Geology, 14th Edition. McGraw-Hill, New York, NY, 677 p.

563. Qui, Jane, 2013, Pollutants capture the high ground in the Himalalyas. Science, V. 339, p. 1030-1031.

564. Thomas, H.E., 1952, Ground-water regions of the United States; Their storage facilities, in The Physical and Economic Foundations of Natural Resources. U.S. 83rd Congress, House committee on Interior and Insular Affairs, V. 3, p. 3-78.

565. Thornthwaite, C.W., 1948, An approach toward a rational classification of climate. Geographical Review, V 38, p. 55-94.

566. Transparency International, www.transparency.org/.

5678. US Department of Agriculture, www.usda.gov/.

569. World Economic Forum, www.weforum.org/. Provides annual Global Risks 2013 reports.

IV Selected Periodicals

The periodicals listed here are important sources of information about groundwater. Many other periodicals can be found on the websites of the organizations listed above.

Advances in Water Resources, www.journals.elsevier.com/advances-in-water-re-sources/.

Canadian Water Resources Journal, www.cwra.org/Publications/Journal/.

Congress Memoirs - International Association of Hydrogeologists, www.iah.org/publications_congressmemoirs.asp.

Environmental Earth Sciences, http://link.springer.com/journal/254.

Environmental Science and Technology, pubs.acs.org/journal/esthag.

Geophysical Research Letters, http://onlinelibrary.wiley.com/journal/10.1002/%28ISSN%291944-8007.

Ground Water, onlinelibrary.wiley.com/journal/10.1111/(ISSN)1745-6584.

Ground Water Monitoring and Remediation, onlinelibrary.wiley.com/journal/10.1111/(ISSN)1745-6592.

Hydrogeology Journal, http://link.springer.com/journal/10040.

IMPACT, www.awra.org/impact/.

International Journal of Water (IJW), www.inderscience.com/jhome.php?jcode=IJW.

Journal of Contaminant Hydrology, www.journals.elsevier.com/journal-of-contami-nant-hydrol...

Journal of Geophysical Research, http://onlinelibrary.wiley.com/journal/10.1002/%28ISSN%292156-2202.

Journal of Hydrology, www.journals.elsevier.com/journal-of-hydrology/.

Journal of the American Water Works Association (JAWRA), www.awra.org/jawra/

Journal of Water and Health, www.iwaponline.com/jwh/.

Journal of Water Resources Planning and Management, ascelibrary.org/journal/jwrmd5.

Nature, www.nature.com/nature/.

Proceedings of the National Academy of Science, www.pnas.org/.

Quarterly Journal of Engineering Geology and Hydrogeology. www.geolsoc.org.uk/qjegh.

Science, www.sciencemag.org.

Stygoscope, www.ngwa.org/sig/transboundary.

Vadose Zone Journal, www.soils.org/publications/vzj.

Water, http://www.mdpi.com.

Water Alternatives, www.water-alternatives.org/.

The Water Channel, www.thewaterchannel.tv.

Water Research, www.journals.elsevier.com/water-research/.

Water Resources Research, onlinelibrary.wiley.com/journal/10.1002/(ISSN)1944-7973.

wH2O, http://wh2ojournal.com.

Index

Pages in **boldface** contain definitions or explanations of the term. The letter P indicates a color Plate. Subentries are listed by page number.

absolute humidity **86**
acid **30-31**, 33, 336, 339-340, 370
acid-base reaction **339**-340
acid fallout **342**, 370, 382
acidification 370-371, 557
acidity **31**, 277, 333, 339, 343, 370-371, 389, 499, 557
acid mine drainage 342, **370**, P15
acid precipitation (*see also* acid fallout) 32, **370**-371
acid rain **32**, 370
active layer (permafrost) 320-321
acute health impacts **356**, 385
adhesion **26**, 331, 345
adsorbent **345**, 423
adsorption **345**-346, 393-394, 420, 424, 429, 437
advection **370**, 390-391, 393, 395, 400
aeolian processes **62-63**
Africa 554-556
agriculture 460, 504-508
air sparging 424, **429**-431
air stripping 242, **426**-427, 431
Alapaha Rise 142
Albian sands 6-7
aliphatic hydrocarbons **379**-380
alkalinity **31**, 371
All-American Canal 539, P16
alluvial aprons/fans **296**
alluvial basins and aquifers 266, **295**-304, 319-320, 330
alluvial plains and aquifers **292**-295

alluvial valleys and aquifers 266, **288**-292
alluvium **62-64**, 288-290, 291, 293, 298, 398
alpine areas 96, 311-314, 495-497, 549, 559
alternative water supplies 425, 537-542
American Society for Testing and Materials (ASTM) 224
ammonia 382, 389
Andes Mountains 559
anion **14**, 32-33, 346
anisotropic **185**, 190, 194, 200-201
annual hydrograph **124-125**
annulus **218**-219, 222, 228
antecedent moisture **105**, 263
anticline **73-75**, 77
Antarctic 43-44, 322
applied hydrogeology 11-13, 405-443
aquaculture 461
aqueducts 4, 299-304
aquiclude **248**, 250, 253, 330
aquifer **68**, 245-330; definitions and properties of aquifers 245-248; major aquifers of the world 246-247; types of aquifers 249-254; surficial processes and groundwater 254-263; weathering and groundwater 255-258; erosion by groundwater 259-262; mass wasting and groundwater 262-263; hydrogeologic

(aquifer, continued)
   regions 263-266; sedimentary rock
   266-281; horizontal sedimentary
   rocks 268-269; homoclinal sedimentary rocks 269-272; in coastal
   plains 271-272; folded sedimentary
   rocks 272; carbonate rocks and karst
   272-281; aquifers and plutonic and
   metamorphic rock 281-283; aquifers and volcanic rock 283-287; lava
   rock 283-286; pyroclastic rock 286-
   287; aquifers and unconsolidated
   sediment 287-306; alluvial valleys
   288-292; in alluvial plains 292-295;
   in alluvial basins 295-304; in glacial deposits 304-306; aquifers and
   coastal environments 306-311; relations between fresh and salt water 306-309; human impacts 310-
   311; in mountainous terrain 311-
   314; in arid environments 315-320;
   in cold environments 320-322; in
   geothermal areas 322-327; in deep,
   high-pressure environments 327-330
aquifer pumping tests **237**-243
aquifer recharge 101, 285, 508, 514
aquitard **248**, 265, 267
Arayo, Francois 6-7
Arctic 320-322, 492-494
area (zone) of influence **211**-213
Arica, Chile P10
arid environments 107-**108**, 315-320,
   497
aromatic hydrocarbons 379-**380**
arsenic poisoning **384**-386, 422, 550
artesian aquifer **250**, 27-272
artesian springs 135, **138**-139, 250-
   252, 301
artesian water **157**
artesian well 211, **250**, 267-268, 293-
   295, 448
asbestos 357, 389
Asia 546-554
asthenosphere **46**
Atacama Desert P1

Atlantic Coastal Plain 269, 271-272,
   346-347
atmosphere **45**, 81
atmospheric pressure **155**
atmospheric water **42**, 81
Atomic Energy Commission (US) 387
atomic mass **18**
atomic number **15**
atoms **13**-18
attenuation 213-214, 345, **393**-395
attitude 409, 450, 503, 517-518, 562-
   563
augur **226**-228, 230, 233-235
Australia 267-268, 373, 479, 560

badlands 53, **63**, 258, 262
bailers **219-220**, 226, 413-415
Bakken Shale 366
Bandai volcano, Japan 326-327
Bangladesh 385-386, 550
Barnett, Cynthia 459, 508-509, 565
basal water **306**, 307
basalt **54**
base (chemical) **30-31**, 370-371
base flow **121**
base flow recession curve 121-122
base level **63**, 160
basin (structural) **73**
Basin and Range Province 296-299,
   316, 319
Bay Delta Conservation Plan 303
bedding planes **70**, 72-73, 138, 170,
   174, 201, 269, 273, 278-279
Big Bend National Park P6
biological pollutant **355**
bioremediation 423-425, **428**
biosphere **45**, 488, 562
boiler-plate outline **441**
boiling point **22**-24, 39, 323-324, 326
Bolivia 314, P10, P16
bonds **14**, 19, 34, 379
Bonnechere River P4
bottled water 5, 136, 461, 528-529
Boundary Waters Treaty 479
brackish water **41**, 330

braided stream **288**
brine **41**, 277, 327, 347
brittle (deformation) **45**-46, 56, 57, 73
BTEX **379**, 429, 567
bucket auger **225**
buffer **31**, 132, 213
Bureau of Land Management 319-320

cable tool (percussion, spudder) method **226**
caliche 255, 256, **339**
California 58, 71, 95, 134-135, 207, 297-304, 317-316, 327, 360, 462, 470, 473, 475, 504-505, 516, 539, 540, 541-542, 557-558, P11, P15, P16
Canada 132, 557
canopy interception **94**
CAP **418**-419, 567
capillary action **26**, 97-98
capillary fringe 43, 109, 112-113, 115, 147, 149, **152**-153, 161, 376
capillary water 148-**149**
Capitol Reef National Park P7
capture zone **213**-215
carbonate rock **49**, 272-281
carbon dioxide 32, 35, 40, 132, 274, 334, 336, 337, 339, 343, 353, 366, 389, 394, 470, 487, 489, 493
carcinogenic **387**
Carlsbad Caverns 278
casing (well) **217**-219, 328, 330, 363-368
catalyst **343**
cation **14**, 32, 346
cation-exchange capacity **346**
cave 6, 12, 47, 55, 73, 170, 185, 256, **274**-279, 397
Central Valley of California 297-304, 558
CERCLA 352, **432**, 567
chain-of-custody **416**
channel flow **110**, 113-117
chelating agents **345**
chelation **345**, 394

chemical equation **20**, 340
chemical formula **17**
chemical pollutants **355**-357, 363, 389, 394, 575-581 (*see also* ground-water contaminants)
chemical precipitates 49, 50, 54
chemical reactions **14**, 20, 30, 336-349, 386, 393-394, 401
chemical sedimentary rocks **49**
chemical weathering **59**
Cherrapunji, India 8
Chile P1, P10, P16
China 472, 521, 546-548, 555
chlorinated hydrocarbons **379**, 557
chlorine 371, 379, 424, 461
chlorofluorocarbons 494-495
chronic health impacts **356**, 380, 385, 463
cistern 4, **205**, 510
clastic rocks **49**, 50, 53, 54-55, 68, 78-79, 272
climate **107**-108, 165-166, 296-297, 486-499
climate change 486-499
closed basins **296**
coal ash 362
coastal aquifers/environments 271-272, 306-313, 346-347, 497-498
Coastal aquifer (Israel) 551-552
coefficient of permeability (hydraulic conductivity) 173-**174**
cohesion **26**, 261-262
cold environments 320-322
collector well **231**, 233
colloid **26**
colluvium **59**, 62, 287-288
Colorado 52-53, 88, 257, 264, 266, 368, 480, 495, P12
Colorado Plateau 317
Colorado River 87, 117, 297, 299-304, 317-318, 387, 466, 480, 539
Columbia River 403
columnar jointing 71-72
Commoner, Barry 330
communication skills 409

complex **344**

complexation reaction **344**-345, 402-403

composite cone of depression **201**

compound **16**

Comprehensive Environmental Response, Compensation, and Liability Act of 1980 (CERCLA) 352, 432, 567

computer modeling 433-438

concentration **28-29**

condensation **22**, 92-93

conductivity **28**, 151, 338, 415, 533

cone of depression 208-211, **209**, 212, 216, 234, 237, 240-241, 280, 292, 310-311, 399-400, 426, 467 (*see also* area of influence)

confined aquifer **250**-253

confined water **157**, 203, 250-252

confining bed 157, **248**, 290

conflict 483-486

connate water **157**, 372

conservation 502-519

conservative solute **393**

constant-displacement pump **207**

consulting activities 407-443

consumption vs. use 455-457

contact springs 134, **137**-138

contamination (*see* groundwater contaminants)

contaminant plume 395-403

contaminant transport and fate 389-403

contaminated water **42**, 354

continental climate **108**

continental crust 56, 57

continuous source loading (pollution) **360**

contour lines 101, 189, 398

convergent boundary **57**-58

corrective action plan (CAP) **418**-419, 567

covalent bond **19**

creep **59**

crops 460, 462-463, 505-507

crust **45-46**, 55-57, 72-73, 76, 322-324

crystalline solid 38, **48-49**, 174, 281

crystalline texture **51**, 170

cutoff wall **419**-421

cyanide 389

Dakota aquifer 269

darcies (units) **176**

Darcy, Henry 7, 179, 180

Darcy's Law **179-185**

Dark Ages 351

de Pitot, Henri 6

Dead Sea 474, 550-553

Death Valley 295-296, P11

dedicated bailer **414**

deep-well injection 367-368

Deepwater Horizon 364

deltas **64**, 308-309

denudation **66**-67, 279

Denver, Colorado 368

depletion (*see* groundwater depletion)

deposition 62, **63**-65, 259-262

depression springs **137**-138

depression storage **110**

desalination 376, **538**-539, 547, 551, 554

deserts **108**, 315-320, 467, 497, 554-556, P1, P16 (*see also* arid environments)

desertification **316**-320, 496-497

desorption **345**-346

detrital sediment **54**

dew point **91-93**

diffusion 277, 347, **391**-393

Dijon, France 179-182

Dinaric karst aquifer system 280-281

dioxins **381**

dipolar molecule 34-38

directional drilling **233**

discharge area (*see* groundwater discharge; stream discharge)

discharge lake **126**-128

disintegration 59, 255

dispersion **390**, 391-393, 394, 397, 400, 433

dissociation of water molecule 30-31, 33
dissolution **27**, 274-275, 277-279, 336-339
distribution coefficient **393**
distribution of water 8-9, 43-44, 447-449
divergent boundary **56**
DNAPLs (denser nonaqueous phase liquids) **376**-377, 379
dome **73**
dowsing **537**
drainage basin **117**-118, 164, 263-264
drainage divide **117**-118, 158, 164, 197, 213, 435
drawdown **209**-210, 221, 234, 236-239, 242, 433
drill bit **226**-227
drip irrigation **507**
dry climate **107**-108, 497
due diligence **433**
Dupuit 240
duricrust **339**
dynamic equilibrium **83**, 113

earthquakes **47**, 58, 76, 236, 263, 326-327, 329-330, 347, 368
Edwards aquifer 280, 508-509
Edwards Plateau 508-509
effective porosity **170**, 183, 245, 391, 420
effective stress **156**
efficiency 238-239, 410, 504
effluent stream 115, 399, 466
Egypt 4, 555-556
electrical conductance **27**-28, 338
electrical resistivity **151**, 533, 534
electrolyte **28**
electromagnetic induction **533**, 534
electron **13**-15, 19-20, 34-35, 37, 340-343, 387, 518
electron acceptor **340**
electron donor **340**
electronegativity **15**-16
electron shell **14**-15, 34

elements **15**-18
elemental pollutants **383**-386
elevation head **186**-187
energy **21**-22
energy and water 460, 462-464
English system (of measurement) 22-23, 571-572
enhanced recovery **233**
ephemeral stream **115**, 117, 254-255
epigenic cave **278**
epochs **47**, 48, 291, 293, 544
equipotential lines **189**-190, 192-195, 198, 203
equilibrium conditions 335-336
eras **47**
erosion **63**-65; by groundwater 259-262
escarpments **75**, 258
Euler, Leonard 6
Europe/European Union 352, 556-557
eutrophication **383**
evaporation **22**, 84-87
evaporation pan **85-86**
evapotranspiration **88**-90
Everglades 131, P8
exfoliation dome **72**, 282
exotic stream **117**
exploration for groundwater 532-537
exsolution **27**, 338-339
extraction well **206**, 363-367, 426, 429-431
extrusive rock **49**-50
exudation **255**
fault **46**, 75-77
fault gouge **76**
faulting **46**, 73-77
feldspars 30, **49**, 59, 339
felsic **49**-52, 56, 283
field blanks **416**
field capacity **149**, 151-152
Fiji Water 528-529
Floridan aquifer 272, 280
Florida 142, 272-273, 276, P8, P9
filter pack **218**-219, 222
flash flooding **111**, 122

flood crest **120**-123
flood irrigation **506**
flood wave **120**-122, 125
floodplain **63**, 288-290
Florida 142, 271-273, P8, P9
Floridan aquifer 272, 280
flow lines **186**, 190-204
flow net **190**-196
flow net analysis **195**
flowing artesian spring or well 211, **250**-251, 293, 301, 448
fluid injection wells **368**
fluid pressure 130, 148, **156**, 327, 330
fluorine **371**
fluorosis **371**
fluvial processes **63**, 113, 259
fog precipitation **95**
folding **46**, 73-77, 272
foliation 53, **55**, 185
food 453-455, 460, 462-465, 505, 518
fossil water **105**, 157, 296-297, 317, 541
"fracking" (see hydrofracking)
fracture springs **138**
free product 348, **376**-377, 418, 424
fresh water **41**-44, 82, 109, 270, 297, 306-313, 445-446, 452, 514-515
friction **113**
frost action **25**, 258
frost blisters **321**
fumaroles 323, 324, **326**

gaging stations **119**, 121
Ganges River 3-4, 246-247, 498, 550
Gangotri, India 3-4
gas **21**
Gaza aquifer 550-553
Geldof, Bob 555
geographic information system (GIS) **438**, 567
geohydrology **10**, 12
geologic time **47**-48
geology **10,** 45-79
geomorphology **10**, 12
geophysical techniques 532-536

geosphere **45**-46, 562
geothermal area **322**-327, P14
geothermal energy 326-327
geothermal gradient **136**-137, 322
geyser **324**-327
Ghyben-Herzberg ratio **306**, 310
GIS **438**
glacial deposits and aquifers 304-306
glacials **47**-48
glacier **43-44**, 63
global warming 486-499; and water 489-499
GRACE Satellites 294, 536
Grace, Stephen 318
grading 54-**55**
granite **50**-52
gravity techniques 534-536
gravity **13**
gravity flow **97**-98
gravity springs **137**-138
gravity water 99, 148-**149**, 201, 230
Gravity Recovery and Climate Experiment (GRACE) 294, **536**
Great Artesian Basin, Australia 267-268
Great Basin 264, **319**-320 (*see also* Basin and Range Province)
Great Basin aquifer 319-320
Great Man-Made River Project **556**
"Great Las Vegas Water Grab, The" 320
Great Plains 96, 198-200, 246-247, 250, 268, 269, 280-281, 293-295, 338-339
greenhouse gas **42**, 486-489
Greenland 43, 322, 494
Grenelle, France 6
grid **435**
ground penetrating radar 534-**535**
groundwater **10**, 42, 43; age 107; mining 105
groundwater augmentation 512-516
groundwater banking **515**
groundwater basin 158-**159**, 281, 435, 531

groundwater budget **104**, 106, 239-240, 489

groundwater chemistry 331-349; isotopes of hydrogen and oxygen 331-332; natural impurities in groundwater 332-336; gases and organic matter 332-334; major and minor chemical constituents 334-335; conditions of equilibrium and inequilibrium 335-336; important chemical reactions and processes 336-349; dissolution and exsolution 337-339; influences on solubility 337-338; electrical conductance and TDS 338; exsolution 338-339; acid-base reactions 339-340; reduction/oxidation 340-344; hydrolysis and hydration 344; complexation reactions 344-345; adsorption and desorption 345; ion exchange 346-347; mixing 347-348; particle transport 348; volatization 348; isotopic processes 348-349

groundwater conservation 502-519; pollution control 503-504; improved efficiency of use 504; improved use of agricultural water 504-506; change of crops 506; improving irrigation methods 506-507; improving land cover 508-509; modifying urban systems 509-512; practicing groundwater augmentation 512-516; modifying infrastructure 516-517; changing consumer habits 517-519

groundwater depletion 466-476; impacts 466-476

groundwater discharge **101**-102, 106, 160-164, 192-194, 196-198, 272; in geothermal areas 322-327

groundwater divide **158**-159

groundwater flow systems **196-198**; influence of topography 198-200; influence of geology and structure 200-201; influence of infiltrating water and refraction 201; influence of permeability 203-204

groundwater footprint **455**

groundwater geology **10**

groundwater hydrology **10**

groundwater contaminants (impurities, pollutants) 332-336, 351-403; historical perspectives 351-354; pollution, pollutants, and contaminants 354-359; sources of pollution 359-368; sources and loading rates 360; storage tanks 360-361; landfills 361; septic systems 361-362; storage ponds and land applications 362-363; wells 363-368; mining operations 368-369; common groundwater pollutants 369-389; acids, bases, and salts 370-376; non-aqueous-phase liquids 376-377; organic compounds 377-380; pesticides 381; pathogens 381-382; nutrients 382-383; elemental pollutants 383-386; particulates 386; heat/thermal pollution 386; radioactive materials 386-388; medicines and related substances 388-389; contaminant transport and fate 389-403; MCLs/sources/health impacts 573-582

groundwater recession curve **161**, 162

groundwater recharge 48, **101**, 102, 105, 109, 122-126, 201, 206, 213-215

groundwater remediation 420-432

groundwater pollution (*see* groundwater contaminants)

groundwater science (origin) 6-8

groundwater storage 515-516

grout **218**, 219, 222

grout curtain **420**, 423

Guarani aquifer 246, 269, 559-560

Gulf Coastal Plain 271-272, 329

Haihe River wetlands 132-133

half-life **18**, 332, 387

Hall, William B. xiii, 76

halogens **15**, 371, 380
Hanford Nuclear Facility 402-403
Hanson, James 492
hardness (of water) 334, 339-**340**
head 176-177, **181**-189, 193-198,208, 240-242, 248-253
headwall sapping **259**-261
health and sanitation 458-459
heat capacity **23**
heat flow **322**
heat of fusion **25**, 39
heat of vaporization **24**, 25, 39
Heath, Ralph C. 265
heavy metals 344-345, **384**
High Plains (Ogallala) aquifer 254, 293-295, 558
Himalayan Mountains 3-4, 57, 314, 385-386, 485, 495-496, 514, 549
historical perspectives 3-8
Hoekstra, Arjen 453
holistic approach 520, **531**, 562, 564
hollow-stem auguring **227**, 230, 233
homocline **269**
horizons (soil) **66**, 138, 255, 339
horizontal pipes/wells **229**-233
Horton, Robert E. 110
hot springs 134, **136**-137, P14
humidity **86**-87
hydration **344**
hydraulic conductivity **173**-**179**
hydraulic damming **119**
hydraulic gradient 176, 178, **181**-182, 184, 188-189, 209-210, 374, 426, 567
hydraulic head **181**, 186-188, 193-194, 270, 567
hydrocarbons **378**-379
hydrofracking (hydraulic fracturing) **233**, 364-367
hydrogen bond **34**-38
hydrogen ions **30**
hydrogen isotopes **331**-332
hydrogen sulfide 389
hydrogeological cross-sections **192**-193, 312

hydrogeology: history of 6-8; terminology **10**-**11**; careers 11-13; 405-443; prerequisites 407-410; consulting activities 410-439
hydrograph **119**-125
hydrologic budgets 102-107, **103**
hydrologic cycle **81**-108; volume of water moving 81-83; residence time 84, 107; evaporation 84-87; transpiration 87-90; evapotranspiration 88-90; precipitation 90-94; interception 94-95; snow hydrology 95-96; infiltration 96-98; subsurface water 99-102; subsurface water pressure 100-102; hydrologic budget 102-104; groundwater budget 104-107; weather and climate 107-108
hydrology **10**
hydrolysis **344**
hydronium ion **30**, 36
hydropedology **143**
hydrophilanthropy **542**
hydrophobic **345**
hydrosphere **45**
hydrostatic pressure **101**, 155-156, 173
hydrostratigraphic unit **248**
hydrothermal water 134, 136-137, **322**-323, 327, P14
hydroxide ions **30**-31, 339, 343-344
hygroscopic water **148**-149
hypogenic cave 278
hypothesis **1**

ice lenses **321**
icebergs 540
Idaho 52-53, 60, 64-65, 74, 115, 134-135, 260, 285-286, 296-297, P12, P15
Idaho National Engineering Laboratory 285-286, 287
igneous rocks **49**-54; as aquifers 79
immiscible liquids **348**, 376
Imperial Valley 539
impermeable cap **419**, 421
impurities in groundwater 332-336

India 548-550
in situ remediation **428**-432
inert **15**
infiltration **96**-100; from streams and lakes 115-117, 126, 165
infiltration capacity/rate **96**-98, 111, 120, 124, 143-146, 200, 279, 311, 421, 451, 513
infiltration gallery **230**-231
infiltration ring **146**
influent stream **115**-117
infrastructure 516-517
injection well **206**, 286, 330, 347, 359, 363, 364, 367-368, 374, 375, 392, 429, 431, 514-515
inner core **46**
inorganic compounds **19**
inorganic pollutants 382-389, 394
integrated water resources management **520**
interbeds (in lava rock) 79, 134, **284**, 287
interception **94**-95, 110
interflow **99-100**, 112-113, 120, 121, 123, 161
interglacial **47**-48, 289, 297, 487
Interlinking of the Rivers Project **549**
intermediate belt (vadose zone) 150, **152**
intermediate flow system **197**
intermittent stream **113**, 115-117
International Hydrologic Decade 7-8, 352-354
intrusive rock **49**-52, 72; as aquifers 78, 281, 283
inverse pricing **525**
ion **14**-15
ion exchange 335, **346**-347, 371, 394, 403
ionic bond **14**, 15, 17, 33
ionization potential **14**-15
ionizing radiation **387**
Iran 550, 554
irrigation 372-373, 460, 504-507, 548, 550, 553

island arc **58**
isotope **18**, 33, 331-332
isotopic processes 348-349
isotropic **185**, 190, 192, 194, 195
Israel 474, 550-553

Jackson Hole, Wyoming 75-76, P6
joints and jointing **71**-73
Jordan 474
Jordan River 550-552

karst 53, **55**, 73, 135, 159, 259, 262, 272-281, 320, 397, 400, 472
karst aquifer **272**, 280-284, 508-509
Kern Water Bank **516**
kinetic energy **21**, 24, 36, 87, 207

La Paz, Bolivia 314, P10
lag time **122**, 123, 415
lakes **125**-130, 296-298, 321
Lake Chernika 277
lake deposits 63, 140, 293, 296, 304, 305
Lake Mead 87, 318
Lake Powell 318
laminar flow **185**, 186, 241
landfills 361, 400-401
landscaping 459-460, 512, 519
land use 145, 508-509
Laramie Range 52-53, P5
Las Vegas, Nevada 319-320
lateral planation **63**
Latin America 558-560
lava/lava rock 40, 47, **49**, 51, 52, 53, 54, 71, 72, 79, 134, 138, 170, 266, 283-286, 559
law (legislative) 352-353, 432-433, 467, 478-483
law (scientific) **1**, 179-185, 195, 240, 279, 354, 391, 434
LD50 (lethal dose 50) **355**, 381, 568
leachate **30**, 347, 361, 374, 391, 399, 400, 419
leaching **30**, 360, 460
leaky confined aquifer **252**

Libya 555-556
liquid **21**
lithify **54**
lithosphere **45**, 46, 47, 56-57
litter interception **94**
LNAPLs **376**, 377, 568
load (sediment) **63**, 64, 296
loading rate (pollution) **360**
local base level **160**, 474
local flow system **196-197**, 200
loess 62, **63**, 145, 172, 304, 305
log: borehole **233**, 234, 235; field record 439
longitudinal dispersion **392**
Lovelock, James 562
Lusi (volcano) **328**-329
lysimeter **88**

macropollutant **369**
mafic **49**, 50, 52, 54, 56, 281, 283
magma **49**, 51, 57, 72, 137, 322-324, 327
major constituents **334**
Mamani, Abel 477
management 519-529
mantle **46**, 56-57
Marcellus Shale 366
mass **13**
mass wasting **59**, 61, 130, 167, 262-263, P3
matter 5, **13**, 21-22, 28, 40
maximum contaminant levels **358-**359, 573-582
MCLs 358-359
meandering stream **288**-290
mechanical weathering **59**, 289
medicines (as pollutants) 388
Mediterranean Sea 308-309, 384, 550-553, 557
megascale problems 561-563
megawatersheds **541**
Meinzer, Oscar E. 7, 265
meinzers (units) **176**
melting point **22**-24
Memphis Sand (Sparta) aquifer 291-

292, 319, 485
Mesopotamia 4, 225, 230-231
metalloid 333, **384**-386
metamorphic rocks **49**-53, 55; as aquifers 78, 185, 249, 281-283, 284
meteoric water **81**, 143, 260, 288, 322, 323, 324, 328, 329, 332, 372, 394, 419
metric system (of measurement) **22-**23, 176, 454, 568, 571-572
Mexico 296-297, 317-318, 473-474, 475, 477-478, 479, 510, 539, 545, 558-559, P6
Mexico City 473-475, 510
microirrigation **506**
micropollutant 369
Middle East 550-554
mid-ocean ridge **56**
millennium development goals 459, **522**
mineral **48**-49
mining operations 342, 368-369
mining of groundwater **105**
minor constituents **334**
Mississippi River 264, 266, 290, 291-292, 308, 318, 322, 540
Mississippi River Valley aquifer 291-292
mitigation methods 420-432
mixing **347**-348, 391
model **434**
modeling 407, 433-438, 443, 464, 465, 468, 489-490, 497, 502, 560, 562
MODFLOW **435**-436
mole **20**
molecule **19**-21, 34-38, 338, 340, 341
monitoring (observation) well **206,** 218, 220, 221-225, 234-237, 240-241, 398-401, 411-416, 432
Montana 61, 76, 140, 366-367, 495, P13
moraine **64**-65
Morocco 232, 315, 554-555, P10
Mountain aquifer (Israel) 550-552
mountains (as a water source) 96, 311-

314, 495-497, 549, 559
MTBE **379**, 568
mud volcano **326**, 328-329
Mulvaney 7
Murray-Darling River 373, 560
mutagenic impacts **387**
mycoremediation **428**

NAPLs **376**-381, 535, 567, 568
National Water Use Information Program (USGS) 2
Netherlands, The 470-471, P15
neutron **13**, 18, 151, 152
neutron probe **151**
New Mexico 330
New York 261, 276, 360-361, 364-367, 497-498, P7
Nevada 295-298, 319-320, 386-387
Nile Delta 308-309
Nile River 4, 87, 117, 133, 167, 308-309, 456, 466, 485, 498
nitrate pollution 280, 369, **382**-383
nonaqueous-phase liquids (NAPLs) **376**-381, 535, 567, 568
non-elastic deformation **253**
nonequilibrium conditions **241**-242
nongravity springs **136**-137
nonpoint source (pollution) **360**
normal **201**, 204
North America 557-558
North China Plain 246, 547
North Dakota 52-53, 110, 258, 261, 366-367, P3, P11
Nubian Sandstone aquifer 269, **555**-556
nucleus **13**, 14, 18, 34
nutrients 28, **333**, 369-371, 382-383, 384, 415, 424, 428, 430, 463, 511, 538

oceanic crust **56**-57
oceanic trench **57**
oceans 43-44, 82-85, 499
offshore aquifers **541**
Ogallala Formation 246, 293-295

Oklahoma 368
organic compounds **18**-19, 28, 333, 334, 341, 377-380, 381, 394, 403, 415, 426, 577-581
orogeny **58**, 269
orographic effect **92-94**
Ouarzazate, Morocco 232
outer core **46**
outgassing **40**
outwash 62, **63**, 140, 289, 304, 305-306
outwash plain **305**
overland flow **63**, 110-115, 120-124
Owens Valley, California 299
oxidant **340**
oxidation 132, 335, 336, **340**-344, 346, 368, 383, 393, 424, 429, 470
oxidizing agent **341**, 343, 425
oxidizing environment **342**-343
oxygen isotopes **331**-332
ozone layer **494**-495

PAHs **380**, 563
Pakistan 549-550
Palestine 550-553
Palissy, Bernard 6
particle transport **348**
particulates **386**
partitioning **345**
pathogen 333, 335, 363, **381**-382, 416, 511
PCBs 357, 379-**380**, 568
pE **342**-343
peat 62, **132**, 169, 172, 270, 470
pediment **63**, 258
Pennsylvania 226, 364-367, P5, P8
perched aquifer **250**
perched (ground)water **99**, 137, 152, 157, 200-201, 256, 261, 284, 320
perched water table **99**, 132, 157, 223, 275, 302
perennial (permanent) stream **113**, 117, 126, 147, 148, 159, 225, 281, 505
periglacial geology **59**, 258

period (geological) **47**, 48, 105, 296, 315, 541

Periodic Table of Elements 15-17, 341, 384

permafrost 44, 132, 311, **320**-321, 492-493

permeability **68**-73, 76, 78-79, 99, 105, 129, 137, 138, 170, 173-179, 180, 182, 184, 185, 190; influence on groundwater flow direction 194-195, 200-204

permeameter **176**-177, 180, 184

pesticides **381**

petroleum 7, 54, 105, 205, 207, 224, 226, 278, 294, 328, 348, 352, 359, 360, 364-366, 368, 376, 377, **379**, 380, 399, 419, 424, 487, 548, 568

pH **31-32**, 333, 339-340, 342, 395, 415, 429, 537

phosphorous **383**

phreatic water **43**, 147, 155-204, 205-213, 229, 250, 279; types of phreatic water 156-157; water table 158-168; porosity 169-173; permeability and hydraulic conductivity 173-179; piezometric pressure and groundwater migration 185-196; groundwater flow systems 196-198; additional influences on groundwater flow 198-204

phreatic zone **43**, 155-204

phreatophyte **89**-90, 106, 468

physical (or mechanical) mixing 390, **391**

Piedmont Province 281

piezometer **181**, 185-196

piezometric gradient **189**

piezometric pressure 185-196, **188**

piezometric (or potentiometric) surface **189**-192, 210, 211, 215, 216, 241, 251, 252, 395

piezometric surface map **189**

pingo **321**

pipes (geological) **260**-262, 275

piping **260**-262, 279

plastic deformation **45**, 46, 56

plate tectonics 46-47, 55-58, **56**

playa 255, 295, **296**, P11

plume (of contamination) **30**, 395-403

point source (pollution) 225, **360**, 363, 392, 395

Poland, Joseph 475

polar regions 92, **108**, 132, 492-495

polluted water **42**, 372, 429, 458, 542

pollution of groundwater, sources of: storage tanks 360-361; landfills 361; septic systems 361-362; storage ponds and land applications 362-363; deep extraction wells 363-367; hydrofracking 364-367; deep-well injection 367-368; well abandonment 368; mining operations 368-369

pollution of groundwater, types of pollutants: acid mine drainage 370; acid precipitation 370-371; fluorine and chlorine 371; sodium chloride 371-376; nonaqueous-phase liquids (NAPLs) 376-377; organic compounds 377-380; pesticides 381; pathogens 381-382; nutrients 382-383; elemental pollutants 383-386; heavy metals 384; metalloids 384-386; particulates 386; heat/thermal pollution 386; radioactive materials 386-388; medicines and related substances 388; miscellaneous inorganics 389

pollution prevention/control 374-376, 417-420, 432-433, 503-504, 531

pollution (water) 351-403, 419-432, 458-459, 503-504, 515, 546-547, 551

polychlorinated biphenyls (PCBs) 357, 379-**380**, 568

polycyclic aromatic hydrocarbons (PAHs) **380**, 563

population (human) 543-546, 548, 554

pore-water pressure 156, **262**

porosity **67**-69, 73, 78, 79, 169-173,

176, 245, 253, 267, 273, 274, 281, 282, 283-286, 301, 391, 420
potable water 3, 4, **41**, 364, 420, 448, 449, 459, 461, 469, 541
potential energy **21**, 24
potential evapotranspiration **90**, 108
Powell, John Wesley 318
Powell, Laurence 318
precipitates (chemical) **27**, 28, 138-141, 323, 335-340
precipitation (meteoric) 81-83, **90-94**, 110, 314, 489, 513-514
pressure head **186**-187, 253
pricing 525-529
primary permeability **68**, 69, 267, 273, 281, 283, 285, 287
primary porosity **67**, 68, 273, 281, 283, 285
primary properties (geological) **67**, 170
priority pollutants 356-357
privatization **526**-529
probe 224, 234, 430, **533**
product (chemical) **20**, 348
proton **13**-15, 18, 30, 31, 34, 339, 342
pseudokarst **262**
Puerto Rico 266, P1
pulse loading (pollution) **360**
pump 167, **207**-208, 210, 219, 220, 234, 237-243, 432; pump installation 219; pumping tests 237-243
pump-and-treat 424, **426**-428, 429, 431
pumping tests 11, 215, 234, **237**-243, 432
public water supplies **461**
purging (wells) **413**-415
pyroclastic rock 50, **54**, 170, 286-287

qanat **230**-232, P10
quartz **49**, 51, 54, 55, 68, 219, 344
Quaternary Period **47**, 48, 105, 296, 315, 541
Qinxu Groundwater Management System **521**

radioisotopes **18**, 204, 332, 386-388
radon 349, 358, 384, **387**-388
radon springs 387
rainfall characteristics 144
rainwater harvesting 504, 508, 510, **513**-515, 555
reactant **20**, 340, 344, 423, 425
reactive solute **393**
recession curve **120**
recharge areas (*see* groundwater recharge)
recharge basins/pits **513**-514
recharge lake **126**, 129
recharge well **206**, 514-515
recharge zone **508**-509
recirculation well 425, **431**
recycling of water 541-542
redox reactions **341**, 343
reducing agent **341**
reducing environment **342**-343, 389, 394
reduction (chemical) 340-344, **341**
refraction (of groundwater flow) **201**-204
regional flow systems **197**-198
regional perspectives 544-560
regolith 62, **66**, 281-282, 287-306, 429
regression (of sea) **270**
Reisner, Marc, 318
relative humidity **86**, 90
relief (topographic) **101**, 132, 196-200, 270, 297, 305, 306, 312, 313
remediation 420-432
remote sensing **535**-537
report writing 438-439
reservoirs **130**-131, 237
residence time 84, 107, 198, 304, 321, 335-336
retardation factor **393**
reverse aquifer pumping test **238**
reverse osmosis **538**
rift zone **56**, 474
rill wash 110, **111**, 112
Rio Grande 117, 264, P6
riser (pipe) **218**, 220, 228, 239

risk-based analysis **418**
rock **48**, 49-55, 78-79
rocks and minerals 48-55; classification 48-51; origins and properties 51-55
Rocky Mountain Arsenal 368
Rocky Mountains 269, 285-286, 293-295, 314, 317-318, 495-497
rooftop harvesting **514**
rotary method **226**
runoff **63**, 82, 96-97, 110-117, 146, 510-514

Sacramento River 299-304
Safe Drinking Water Act (US) 32, 352, 358, 363
safe yield **239**-240; myth 464-465
safety procedures 408
Sahara Desert 315, 554-556
saline water **41**, 44, 306-313, 363, 371-375, 506, 538-539, 555-556
salinization **255**, 315-316, 339, 372-373, 506
salt (chemical) 15, 23, **32**-33, 41, 50, 62, 255-258, 270, 296, 302, 333, 359, 365, 367, 369, 370-376, 469, 506
salt-tolerant crops 506
salt water (*see* saline water)
salt-water encroachment 307-311
sampling procedures 412-417
San Antonio 508-509
sanitation 458-459, 476-478, 511-512
San Joaquin River/Valley 299-303, 308, 473, 516
San Pedro River 467-468
saprolite **59**, 60, 62, 68, 78, 281-282, 288
satellite imagery 536-537
saturated solutions **28**, 29, 43
saturation overland flow **113**, 115, 123
saturation vapor pressure **87**
Saudi Arabia 553
scarp **75**, 76, 255, 256, 258
scarp retreat **259**

scientific method **1**
screen (well) **218**, 219, 220, 222, 228, 239, 240, 242, 243, 401
secondary permeability **69**, 79, 272, 273
secondary porosity **67**-68, 79
secondary properties **67**
sediment **54**, 69, 78-79, 168-179, 287-306, 469-474
sedimentary rocks **49**-55, 67, 70; as aquifers 78-79, 266-281
sedimentation **63**, 277
seepage area 106, **133**, 256, P11
seepage erosion **259**-260
seepage lake **126**, 129, 352
seepage meter **104**
seepage pressure **106**, 259, 263
seepage run **104**
seismic methods **533**, 535
semiarid **108**
septic systems **361**-362, 379, 382-383
Shanghai, China 472
sheeting **72**, 282
sheetwash **110**-111, 115
Shelby tube **227**
Shiklomanov, I. A. 2, 103
Shoshone River 52-53, P4
SI (Système International d'Unités; System Internationalle) **22**, 176, 568
sinkhole **55**, 142, 262, 275, 276, 277, 279, 508
site characterization **11**, 417-418
site remediation **11**, 409
site selection 410
slope 66, 111, 113, **159**, 176, 189
slug test **242**-243
slurry wall **420**, 423
Snake River 52-53, 75, 260, 285-286, 287
Snake River Plain 285-286, 287, 297
Snake River Plain aquifer 285-286, 287
snow hydrology **95**-96
snowmelt **96**, 105, 121, 158, 160, 163, 201, 260, 277

snowpack 96, 314, 496, 497, 514
sodium chloride (salt pollution) 371-376
soil **66**, 143-144
soil moisture belt 43, 44, 84, 88, 96, 144, **149**-152
soil moisture cycle **150**-152
soil-vapor extraction 424, **429**-431
solid **21**
solubility **28**, 337-338
solute **27**, 28, 29
solution **27**
solutions (to water crises) 501-542, 564-566
solvent **27**-30
sorption **345**, 394
sorting **54**, 55, 144
source control (contaminant) 419-420
South America 559-560
South Asia 548-554
Southern Nevada Water Authority 319
Sparta (Memphis Sand) aquifer **291**-292, 319, 485
specific capacity **239**-240
specific electrical conductance (conductivity) **28**, 338
specific heat **23**, 39
specific (intrinsic) permeability **173**
specific retention **170**-171
specific storage **253**
specific yield **171**-173, 245, 249, 250
spectrochemical analyses **29**
spiked samples **416**
split samples **416**
split-spoon sampler **227**, 229
springs **133**-142; types of springs 136-142; degradation of springs 140, 142
sprinkler irrigation **506**-507
Sri Lanka 373
states of matter **21**-22
static water level **208**-209, 212, 238, 242
stemflow **94**
step drawdown test **238**
step well **4**-5

stomata **87**
storage capacity **122**, 521
storage coefficient **171**, 250
storage ponds 362
storage tanks 360-361
storativity **171**-173, **248**-249, 253, 568
strain **56**, 71-72
strata 53, **54**, 67, 70, 200, 252, 267-272
stratification 53, **54**
stream discharge **118**-119
streamflow **63**, 113, 115, 117, 119-121, 262
stream gaging **119**
streams **113**-125
stream types 113-117
stress **56**
subatomic particles **13**
subduction **57**, 329-330
sublimation **25**, 82, 84
subsidence **47**, 469-475
subsurface barriers 374, **419**-420, 423
subsurface water **42**-43, 150
subsurface water pressure 100-102
subtropical climate **108**
Sumerians 4
supercooled fluid **37**
supersaturated solution **28**, 92
supply wells **205**, 215-221, 283, 369, 521
surface detention **111**
surface tension **26**, 27
surface water: **42**, 109-142; runoff 110-117; overland flow 110-113; channel flow 113-117; drainage basins 117-118; discharge 118-119; hydrographs 119-125; lakes 125-130; wetlands 130-133; springs 133-142
surficial processes 58-67; and groundwater 254-263
syncline **73**, 75, 77

talik 320-321
tectonic processes 46-47, 70, 75

tectonic plates **56**, 58
temperate regions 499
temperature **21**-22
Tennessee 362
tensiometer **148**
teratogenic impacts **387**
Teton Dam 262
Teton Range 64-65, 75, P2, P6
Theis method 171, **242**
Theis, Charles 7, 171, 184, 242, 465
Theim equation **240**-241
theoretical hydrogeology **405**
theory **1**
thermal/geothermal areas **322**-327
thermal distillation **538**
thermal pollution **386**
thermal springs134, **136**-137, 323-324
thermobaric water **328**-329
Thermopolis, Wyoming P14
Thousand Springs 285-286, P12
Three Gorges Dam 263
throughfall **94**
through-flow (or flow-through) lake
    126-128
Tigris-Euphrates River 4, 485, 550
till 62, **63**, 68, 132, 248, 261, 305-306
toilets 511-512
topographic relief **101**, 270
topography **145**, 198-200
total alkalinity **334**
total dissolved solids (TDS) 198, 203,
    283, 284, 290, 293, 333, **338**, 568
trace constituents/elements **334**-335,
    358, 383-386
transboundary water issues 478-479,
    483-486
transform boundary **58**
transform fault **58**
transgression **270**
transient flow **241**-242
transient groundwater **103**
transmissivity **178**-179
transparency of water 33
transpiration **87**-90
transverse horizontal dispersion **392**

transverse vertical dispersion **392**
travertine 62, **140**, 141, 274
tremie pipe **219**
tritium **18**, 107, 286, 331-332
tropical environments **107**, 498-499,
    P1
true infiltration capacity **145**-146
tsunami 373
tubular springs 135, **138**-139, 142
tufa 62, **140**, 141
tunnel scour **260**
turbulent flow **185**-186, 238, 306

ultimate base level **160**
unconfined aquifer 214-216, **250**
unconfined water 156-**157**
unconformity **70**-71
underground storage tanks (USTs)
    360-361
United Nations (UN) 7, 281, 352-353,
    447, 453, 459, 476-477, 482, 486,
    492, 505, 509, 517, 522-523, 554,
    561, 568
United States 557-558 (*see also* indi-
    vidual states, localities)
unloading **72**-73, 282
urban environments/conservation 509-
    512, 544
USGS (United States Geological Sur-
    vey) 2, 459
Utah 52-53, 257, 297, 316, 319-320,
    368-369, P7

vadose water **43**, 143-153; and infil-
    tration rates 143-145; and soils 143-
    144; and rainfall 144; and vegeta-
    tion 144-145; and land use 145; and
    topography 145; infiltration capac-
    ity 145-146; characteristics 148-
    149; zones 149-153; soil moisture
    belt 149-152; intermediate belt 152;
    capillary fringe 152-153
vadose zone **43**, 143-153
vadose zone contamination 402-403
valence **20**

valley and ridge terrain 73-75, 272
valley train **305**
vapor phase 376-379, 424, 429-431
vapor pressure **86**-87
variable-displacement pump **208**
vernal pool **129**-130
vesicles 50, **170**, 284
Viaont Dam 263
Virginia 52-53, 74, 136, 141, 228, 251, 276, 323-325, 366, P13
virtual water **453**-455,
viscosity **33**
volatile organic chemicals/compounds (VOCs) **378**-379, 426, 429, 568
volatiles **40**, 170, 429
volatization **348**
volcanic processes 46-**47**
volcanic rock 49-54; aquifers 283-287
volcano **47**, 52, 54, 57, 58, 284, 286-287
vug **170**

warm springs **136**, 323-325
Washington (state) 52-53, 61, 115, 256, 402-403, P2
water, and humans: historical perspectives 3-8, 445-447; correlation of distribution 8-9, 448-449; utilization 9, 457-465; depletion of resource 9, 448, 466; and the groundwater budget 106; impacts on the water table 163-168; diversion/transfers 318. 539-540; stress 445-447; competition for the resource 449; inequitable access 449; waste 449; contemporary use by humans 451-465; depletion 466-476; ethical and legal issues 476-483; conflict 483-486; global warming impacts 489-499; facing the challenge 501-542; future perspectives 543-566
water, the resource: importance 3; science 6-8, 9-13; as limiting resource 9; occurrence on Earth 40-41; distribution 43-44; scarcity 445-450; and environmental change 450, 486-499; use 451-465; conservation 502-519; management 519-532
water: states of (phases of) 21-23; specific heat 23; heat of vaporization 24; heat of fusion 25; expansion during freezing 25; wetting ability 26; surface tension 26; capillary action 26; universal solvent 27-30; electrical conductance 27-28; impurities 29-30; stability and neutrality 30-33; ions 30; acidity 30-31; alkalinity 30-31; pH 31-32; transparency 33; viscosity and mass 33; origin 38-41 ; physical properties of 39; occurrence on Earth 40-41, 156; types 41-43; distribution 43-44; surface/subsurface relationships 42-43, 109-204; age of 107
"water bank" 515-516
water contaminants (impurities, pollutants) (*see* groundwater contaminants)
water-food-energy nexus 462-464
water footprint, the **453**-455
water law 478-483
water molecule 34-38, **35**; hydrogen bond 34-38
water pressure: subsurface 100-102; hydrostatic pressure 101, 155-156; seepage pressure 106; negative pressure of vadose water 148
water sampling 412-417
water scarcity 9, 445-450, **447**
watershed **117**-118
water stressed (definition) **447**
water supply wells 5, **205**, 215-221, 410-417
water table **42**, 66, 89-90, 99, 100, 101, 105, 116, 126, 128, 155; characteristics 146-148, 158-163; human impacts on 163-168; 196, 199, 237, 239, 250, 263, 290, 299, 376, 468, 472-474, 547, 569
water table map **189**-190

water transfers 539-540
water vapor 21-22, 24-25, 39, 42, 81, 86-87, 90, 149
water witching **537**
weather **107**
weathering **59**, 60, 62; and groundwater 255-258, 281-282
well **205**-243; well functions 205-206; pumps 207-208; cone of depression 208-211; areas of influence and contribution 211-213; wellhead protection 213-215; water supply wells 5, 215-221; general well protocols 215-217; well construction and design 217-219; pump installation 219; well development 219-221; monitoring wells 221-225; purpose of monitoring wells 221; construction of monitoring wells 221-224; surveying for placement 224; placement of the well 224-225; installation methods 225-234; dug wells 5, 206, 225; drilled wells 226; bored wells 226-228; driven wells 228; jetted wells 229; horizontal wells 229-233; special techniques 233; borehole logs 233-234; Influences on water levels in wells 234-237; pumping tests 237-243; installation 411-412; purging 413-415
well(s), types: by function 205-206; dug wells 5, 206, 225; drilled wells 226; bored wells 226-228; driven wells 228; jetted wells 229; horizontal wells 229-233

well abandonment 368
well construction and design 217-219
well efficiency **238**
well development **219**-221, 411-412
well functions **205-206**
well installation 225-234, 411-412
well loss **238**
well losses **239**
well protocols 215-217
wellhead protection area **213**-215
wetlands 44, 85, **130**-133, 163, 167, 310, 313, 470-471, 476
wetting ability **26**
wetting front **98**, 99, 112-113, 115
wilting point **149**-150, 151
windmill 207, 470, 471
work **21**
World Bank 477, 492, 521, 523, 526
World Health Organization (WHO) 32
World Water Forum (WWF) 477, 523, 568
Wyoming 52-53, 64-65, 75, 134, 262, 266, 270, 323, P2-P6, P9, P14

Yellowstone National Park 76, 134, 323, 325, P14
Yemen 554

zone of aeration **42**-43, 99, 104, 138, 146-148, 156, 209, 250, 402
zone of contribution **213**
zone of influence **211**-215
zone of saturation **42**-43, 99, 101, 146-148, 157, 250